96 Common Challenges in Power Query

Practical Solutions for Mastering Data Transformation in Excel and Power BI

Omid Motamedisedeh

Apress®

96 Common Challenges in Power Query: Practical Solutions for Mastering Data Transformation in Excel and Power BI

Omid Motamedisedeh
Coorparoo, QLD, Australia

ISBN-13 (pbk): 979-8-8688-1287-3 ISBN-13 (electronic): 979-8-8688-1288-0
https://doi.org/10.1007/979-8-8688-1288-0

Copyright © 2025 by Omid Motamedisedeh

This work is subject to copyright. All rights are reserved by the Publisher, whether the whole or part of the material is concerned, specifically the rights of translation, reprinting, reuse of illustrations, recitation, broadcasting, reproduction on microfilms or in any other physical way, and transmission or information storage and retrieval, electronic adaptation, computer software, or by similar or dissimilar methodology now known or hereafter developed.

Trademarked names, logos, and images may appear in this book. Rather than use a trademark symbol with every occurrence of a trademarked name, logo, or image we use the names, logos, and images only in an editorial fashion and to the benefit of the trademark owner, with no intention of infringement of the trademark.

The use in this publication of trade names, trademarks, service marks, and similar terms, even if they are not identified as such, is not to be taken as an expression of opinion as to whether or not they are subject to proprietary rights.

While the advice and information in this book are believed to be true and accurate at the date of publication, neither the authors nor the editors nor the publisher can accept any legal responsibility for any errors or omissions that may be made. The publisher makes no warranty, express or implied, with respect to the material contained herein.

>Managing Director, Apress Media LLC: Welmoed Spahr
>Acquisitions Editor: Shaul Elson
>Development Editor: Laura Berendson
>Coordinating Editor: Gryffin Winkler
>Copy Editor: Kezia Endsley

Cover designed by eStudioCalamar

Cover Photo by Job Savelsberg on Unsplash

Distributed to the book trade worldwide by Springer Science+Business Media New York, 1 New York Plaza, New York, NY 10004. Phone 1-800-SPRINGER, fax (201) 348-4505, e-mail orders-ny@springer-sbm.com, or visit www.springeronline.com. Apress Media, LLC is a Delaware LLC and the sole member (owner) is Springer Science + Business Media Finance Inc (SSBM Finance Inc). SSBM Finance Inc is a **Delaware** corporation.

For information on translations, please e-mail booktranslations@springernature.com; for reprint, paperback, or audio rights, please e-mail bookpermissions@springernature.com.

Apress titles may be purchased in bulk for academic, corporate, or promotional use. eBook versions and licenses are also available for most titles. For more information, reference our Print and eBook Bulk Sales web page at http://www.apress.com/bulk-sales.

Any source code or other supplementary material referenced by the author in this book is available to readers on GitHub (https://github.com/Apress). For more detailed information, please visit https://www.apress.com/gp/services/source-code.

If disposing of this product, please recycle the paper

May your life's queries always fetch the most favorable outcomes!

Table of Contents

About the Author .... **xiii**

About the Technical Reviewers ....**xv**

Acknowledgments ....**xvii**

Introduction ....**xix**

Chapter 1: Data Extraction from Sources **1**

    Combining Data from Excel Files with Consistent Column Names 3

    Combining Data from Excel Files with Different Column Names: Case Sensitivity 11

    Combining Data from Excel Files with Different Column Names: Comprehensive Solution 19

        Scenario 1: Different Column Headers but the Same Number and Order of Columns Across All Files 21

        Scenario 2: The Number and Order of Columns Varies Across Different Files 23

    Extracting Values Outside of Tables 31

    Handling Multi-Row Headers in Excel Tables 38

    Loading Data from a Webpage 47

    Loading Data from a Webpage, Part 2 51

    Loading Tables from an Excel File 58

    Manually Adding Columns to the Query 62

    Using a Data Load Tracker (Log) 67

    Creating a Date Table 74

    Summary 80

Chapter 2: Referencing **81**

    Referencing Cells in Power Query 88

    Referencing the Previous Row 92

TABLE OF CONTENTS

    Solution 1: Based on Filtering the Rows 93

    Solution 2: Based on Merging 97

    Solution 3: Based on the Fill Down Function 101

    Solution 4: Based on the List of Functions 103

Referencing Multiple Previous Rows 110

Adding Multiple Columns at Once 113

Using VLOOKUP with Approximate Match in Power Query 117

Extracting Data from the Price List Table 125

Summary 131

Chapter 3: Sorting and Filtering 133

Filtering Across Multiple Columns, Part 1 138

Filtering Across Multiple Columns, Part 2 140

Filtering Across Multiple Columns, Part 3 143

    Solution 1: Initial Filtering 144

    Solution 2: Unpivoting and Using Group By 146

Extracting a First Purchasing Date 149

    Solution 1: Based on Sorting 149

    Solution 2: Grouping 154

Filtering Based on a List of Values 155

Filtering Based on Sequence 162

Using Random Selection 167

    Solution 1: Reordering Rows and Removing Duplicates 168

    Solution 2: Shuffle the Table Rows 170

Using Advanced Filtering Criteria 172

Summary 177

Chapter 4: Column Splitting and Merging 179

Dynamic Splitting by Delimiter 184

Splitting Text by Multiple Delimiters 188

Splitting Text by Position 193

Extracting Text Between Parentheses 201

Solution 1: Splitter-Based	202
Solution 2: Text Functions	208
Solution 3: Using Text.Split	210
Extracting Email Addresses	212
Using a Multiline Splitter	217
Solution 1	218
Solution 2	221
Splitting Text by Changing Character Type, Part 1	223
Splitting Text by Changing Character Type, Part 2	228
Merging with a Custom Operation	233
Merging Instead of Adding a Column	237
Merging Date Information	242
Summary	245

Chapter 5: Pivoting and Unpivoting Tables 247

Managing Product IDs	251
Solution 1: Using Unpivoting	252
Solution 2: Using M Functions	254
Value Repeated in Several Columns	257
Removing Blank Columns	265
Transforming Columns, Part 1	267
Transforming Columns, Part 2	274
Transforming Columns, Part 3	277
Merging Rows	281
Merging Several Tables at Once	284
Transformations, Part 4	290
Summary	295

Chapter 6: Grouping Rows with Table.Group() 297

Introducing Table.Group()	297
Modifying the Third Input in Table.Group()	303

vii

TABLE OF CONTENTS

Matching Items in Groups 309
Identifying All-Season Products 314
Grouping Based on the Date 318
Using the Fourth Input in Table.Group() 323
Ignoring Case Sensitivity in Grouping 326
    Solution 1: Based on UI 327
    Solution 2: Using the Fifth Argument of Table.Group() 329
Using Value.Comparer for Grouping 332
    Solution 1: Using a Custom Column 334
    Solution 2: Using the Fifth Argument in the Table.Group() 336
Using the Fifth Input in Table.Group() Based on One Value 340
    Solution 1: Using Fill Down Followed by Table.Group() 341
    Solution 2: Using Table.Group() Directly 342
Transforming Tables 346
Transforming Tables Within Table.Group() 350
Grouping Consecutive Dates 355
    Solution 1: Using a Helper Column 357
    Solution 2: Using the Fifth Argument 359
Using the Fifth Input in Table.Group Based on Two Values 366
Using the Fifth Input in Table.Group Based on All the Group items 369
Summary 385

Chapter 7: Merging and Appending Tables 387

Combining Tables 397
Calculating Weighted Averages 399
Reconciliation, Part 1 406
Reconciliation, Part 2 412
Fuzzy Merging 419
Conditional Merging 424
Self-Merging 431

Solution 1: Based on Merging Logic 433
Solution 2: Using the List.Generate() Function 445
Summary 450

Chapter 8: Handling Missing Values 451

Filling Nulls with Previous Values 452
Handling Missing Rows 455
Solution 1: Using the Merge Command 459
Solution 2: Based on Appending the Queries 462
Extracting Missing Values 464
Solution 1: Based on Appending/Merging 464
Solution 2: Using Merging 465
Solution 3: Based on Grouping the Rows 466
Linear Interpolation for Missing Data 470
K-Nearest Neighbors (K-NN) for Imputation 477
Summary 488

Chapter 9: Looping in Power Query 489

The For-Each Loop 489
The For-Next Loop 489
The Do-While Loop 490
Looping in Power Query 490
List.Transform() 490
List.TransformMany() 498
List.Accumulate() 505
List.Generate() 510
Running Totals by List.Accumulate() 516
Solution 1: Based on the For-Each Loop 516
Solution 2: Based on the For-Next Loop 518
Running Totals by List.Generate() 520

TABLE OF CONTENTS

Solution 1: Basic Option 520
Solution 2: Efficient Option 521
Calculating the Running Total by List.Transform() 524
Generating the Fibonacci Sequence by List.Accumulate() 524
Generating the Fibonacci Sequence with List.Generate 526
Implementing Sumproduct 528
Solution 1: Using List.Transform() 528
Solution 2: Using List.Accumulate() 529
Applying Transformation Over the Columns 530
Solution 1: Using List.Accumulate() 533
Solution 2: Using List.Transform() 534
Adding Multiple Columns Simultaneously 537
Solution 1: Using List.Transform() 538
Solution 2: Using List.Accumulate(), Variation 1 540
Solution 3: Using List.Accumulate(), Variation 2 540
Handling the Sequences 543
Solution 1: Using List.Transform() 546
Solution 2: Using List.Accumulate(), Variation 1 550
Solution 3: Using List.Accumulate(), Variation 2 551
Implementing Stepped Tax Calculations 556
Solution 1: Using a Nested if 558
Solution 2: Using List.Transform() 559
Solution 3: Using List.Accumulate() 562
Changing Data Granularity 563
Solution 1: Column Name-Based Approach 565
Solution 2: Using the Unpivoting Column 568
Solution 3: Using List.Transform() 572
Solution 4: Using List.Accumulate() 578
Product Combinations 582
Working with Set Combinations (Cartesian Product) 584

Solution 1: Merging the Table Columns 585

Solution 2: Based on List.Accumulate() 589

Solution 3: Combining List.Accumulate() and List.TransformMany() 590

Summary 594

Chapter 10: Leveraging Scripting and External Integrations in Power Query 595

Using a Regex Function Based on JavaScript in Power Query 595

Integrating Python with Power Query 602

Integrating R with Power Query 606

Translating Text Using the Google Translate API 610

Automating Query Export to CSV Files 616

Summary 618

Chapter 11: Error-Handling Strategies 619

Removing Rows with Errors 625

Extracting the Causes of Errors 627

Summary 631

Chapter 12: Custom Functions 633

Implementing Sumproduct as a Custom Function 642

Documenting Custom Functions 645

Sharing Custom Functions Across Files 652

Creating Recursive Functions 658

Using Optional Input Parameters 660

Summary 661

Appendix A 663

Index 669

About the Author

Dr. Omid Motamedisedeh is a data analyst, author, and educator specializing in Power BI, Power Query, and Excel. A Microsoft Super User with a Ph.D. in industrial engineering, he shares his expertise through books, blog articles (Omid BI), and his YouTube channel, OmidBI, where he provides in-depth insights on data transformation and analytics.

Passionate about knowledge sharing, Omid has authored several books on Microsoft technologies. He is a speaker at various data-related boot camps, communities, and user group meetings. Through his blog and YouTube channel, he provides in-depth tutorials, problem-solving techniques, and practical applications of Power Query and Power BI, helping users at all levels master data transformation efficiently.

Connect with Omid on LinkedIn: `linkedin.com/in/omidmot`

About the Technical Reviewers

Zoran Milokanović is a Power BI trainer and consultant at BitanBit. Drawing on his background in data warehousing and business intelligence, he helps organizations streamline their data workflows and make more informed decisions. As a Microsoft Certified Trainer and Power BI Data Analyst, Zoran actively shares his expertise with the data community by solving practical challenges—an effort that has earned him recognition among fellow professionals and authors.

Pavel Adam, Ph.D., is a seasoned Power BI consultant, educator, and founding member of the Power BI Center of Excellence at Škoda Auto a.s. He has extensive experience delivering company-specific training programs, workshops, and tailored Power BI solutions. His core expertise lies in backend development, with a focus on advanced functionalities in Power Query and DAX, as well as the integration of custom visuals—particularly those based on SVG and DENEB—and Power Apps within the Power BI ecosystem.

Acknowledgments

I would like to express my heartfelt gratitude to my family, and everyone who has played an invaluable role in supporting me throughout the journey of writing this book. My appreciation extends to those within my professional circle and those who have personally impacted my life.

A special thank you to Pavel Adam and Zoran Milokanović, the esteemed technical reviewers, whose insightful feedback and encouragement have greatly enriched the quality of this work. Your expertise and meticulous attention to detail have been instrumental in refining the content.

I am also deeply grateful to Vahid Doustimajd, for his unwavering support and inspiration. Your encouragement has meant a great deal to me, and I truly appreciate your role in this journey.

Furthermore, I extend my sincere thanks to the Apress team, especially Shaul Elson (Acquisitions Editor), Nirmal Selvaraj (Production Editor), and Gryffin Winkler (Coordinating Editor), for their professionalism and collaborative approach. Their dedication and expertise have made working with Apress a truly rewarding experience.

Lastly, I want to acknowledge the incredible LinkedIn community. Over time, I have posted challenges on my LinkedIn page —many of which are included in this book— where numerous professionals have actively participated by sharing their solutions. Their diverse approaches and creative insights have inspired me to view problems from different perspectives. My profound appreciation goes to all those who have contributed their solutions and engaged in these discussions. This includes but is not limited to:

Brian Julius, Abdallah Ally, Aditya Kumar, Alejandro Simón, Alex Popoff, Alexis Olson, Amit Ahuja, Amit Patel, An Nguyen, Andy Heybruch, Anil Kumar Goyal, Ankur Sharma, Arden Nguyen, Asheesh Pahwa, Ashutosh Sharma, Bhavya Gupta, Bilal Mahmoud, Bilal Mahmoud Kh, Bo Rydobon, Burhan Cesur Dinesh, Ca Raghunath Gundi, Ca Raghunath Gundi, Charles Roldan, Cindy C, Craig Hatmaker, Crispo Mwangi, Cristobal Salcedo Beltran, Daniel Madhadha, Darak IN, Diarmuid Early, Eric Laforce, Ernesto Vega Castillo, Ferhat Ck, Gabriel Raigosa, Gerson Pineda, Glyn Willis, Gowthaman V, Harsha Vijayantha, Henk-Jan Van Well, Hussein Satour Leonard Ochea, Ibrahim Sadiq, Iván Cortinas Rodríguez, Jan Willem Van Holst, John Jairo, Josh Brodrick,

ACKNOWLEDGMENTS

Julian Poeltl, Konrad Gryczan, Kris Jaganah, Krzysztof Nowak, Kumar Bhatia, Luan Rodrigues, Luis Florentino Couto Cortegoso, Mahmood Shaban, Mahmoud Bani Asadi, Masoto Lazarus Kanyane, Masoud Karami, Md Ismail Hosen, Md. Zohurul Islam, Murat Bayraktar, Navid Esmaeilzadeh, Ned Navarrete, Nelson Mwangi, Nicolas Micot, Oscar Javier, Oscar Mendez, Owen Price, Pankaj Sharma, Peter Compton, Peter Krkos, Peter Tholstrup, Pieter De B, Pieter De Bruijn, Rahim Zulfiqar Ali, Ramiro Ayala Chávez, Raphael Okoye, Rayan Saud, Rick Rothstein, Roca Farell, Rosero Jiménez, Saikrishnaa R, Seema Dabas, Sunny Baggu, Surendra Reddy, Taeyong Shin, Talha Parkar, Tamer Salem, Thang Van, Theerapun Maneethap, Tyler Cameron, Vergara Domínguez, and Ziad Ahmed.

Introduction

The Story Behind This Book and How to Use It

The idea for this book was born on February 3, 2024, when I posted my first Power Query challenge on LinkedIn. That initial challenge sparked a wave of engagement, with experts providing solutions using Excel, Python, R, Power Query, DAX, and more. Encouraged by the response, I continued posting new challenges every other day. Over time, participation grew significantly. By the time I posted Challenge #52, more than 100 comments flooded in within just 10 hours.

Since that day, I have continued sharing challenges regularly, and as of today, the 224th challenge has been posted. Seeing the enthusiasm of professionals eager to tackle these problems, propose their own solutions, and learn from others, I realized the impact of a book built around a challenge-based structure. So, I started to write this book. This book is designed not only to teach Power Query but also to sharpen your problem-solving skills by exposing you to a variety of real-world scenarios and solutions.

How This Book Is Structured

In this book, each chapter begins with an introduction to key concepts, followed by a series of carefully selected challenges related to the chapter's topic. For each challenge, I provide step-by-step solutions, along with tips, tricks, and best practices to help you better understand Power Query's functionality.

Whenever multiple logics are possible, I compare them, evaluating performance for larger datasets so that you can choose the most efficient approach for your own use case. Most solutions begin with the Power Query UI, after which you'll manually modify the generated formula to tailor it for specific needs and uncover hidden features of Power Query's M language.

While basic familiarity with M will make it easier to follow this book, I have carefully explained each modification, making it accessible even to those who are not fully comfortable with M yet. However, if you are completely new to Power Query, I recommend starting with an introductory book before diving into this one.

INTRODUCTION

How to Get the Most Out of This Book

This book is organized into 12 chapters, and I recommend reading them in order. However, if you struggle with Chapters 2 and 3, particularly when working with custom functions, I suggest jumping to Chapter 12, reading its introduction, and then returning to continue. This will help make the logic clearer.

When reading each chapter, I highly recommend taking a moment to think through each challenge before looking at the solution. Try to solve it yourself first, then compare your approach with the provided solutions. This will sharpen your problem-solving mindset and prepare you for real-world challenges you might encounter in your work.

Chapter Overview

1. **Data Extraction from Sources**: Learn how to load data from various sources, handle unstructured data (e.g., Excel, CSV), and deal with challenges like inconsistent column names, multi-row headers, and Merging cells. You'll also learn how to import data from the web and combine Power Query results with Excel tables while maintaining order after refresh.

2. **Referencing**: Understand how to reference specific columns, rows, or cells inside a Power Query table. Explore techniques such as searching rows dynamically, referencing previous rows, and performing approximate lookups similar to VLOOKUP.

3. **Sorting and Filtering**: Master Power Query's filtering and sorting capabilities, including dynamic filtering across multiple columns. Learn how to overcome Power Query's unexpected sorting behaviors by using `Table.Buffer` for stability.

4. **Column Splitting and Merging:** Learn how to dynamically split columns using multiple delimiters or custom criteria. Explore advanced techniques for merging columns using different operators.

5. **Pivoting and Unpivoting Tables:** Understand how to transform messy data into an analysis-ready structure by pivoting and unpivoting tables.

6. **Grouping Rows with Table.Group:** Discover advanced grouping techniques using `Table.Group()`, including custom grouping logic, modifying aggregation behavior, and optimizing performance.

7. **Merging and Appending Tables:** Learn how to combine multiple datasets, whether by appending (stacking) tables or merging (joining) them side by side. This chapter also covers fuzzy merging and recursive self-merging techniques.

8. **Handling Missing Values:** Explore methods for identifying and replacing missing values, including linear interpolation and machine learning approaches like KNN.

9. **Looping in Power Query:** Master four key functions that enable looping in Power Query:

    - `List.Transform()`
    - `List.TransformMany()`
    - `List.Accumulate()`
    - `List.Generate()`

    You learn how to use them for complex scenarios and repetitive tasks across different tables and columns.

10. **Leveraging Scripting and External Integrations in Power Query:** Discover how to integrate Power Query with JavaScript, R, and Python for enhanced functionality. Learn how to export CSV files mid-query and use regular expressions (Regex) in Power Query.

11. **Error-Handling Strategies:** Understand Power Query's different error types and learn best practices for creating robust, error-resistant queries.

12. **Custom Functions:** Learn how to build custom functions in Power Query and share them across multiple workbooks. This chapter also covers adding documentation to your functions. If you find Chapter 2 challenging, reading Chapter 12's introduction first will help clarify key concepts.

13. **The Appendix: A Challenge Hub:** Unlike most books, your learning doesn't stop after Chapter 12. The appendix includes an index of challenges related to each chapter from my LinkedIn page, where you can test what you've learned by solving real-world problems. These challenges provide a great opportunity to reinforce your knowledge while also seeing alternative solutions from other experts.

A Note on Efficiency and Performance

Throughout this book, I have included efficiency tips to help you optimize Power Query performance. When comparing solution runtimes, keep in mind that execution speed depends on multiple factors, including your dataset size and system specifications. While your results may vary, these comparisons will help you understand performance tradeoffs and choose the best solution for your case.

Additionally, all examples (files are available at `www.OmidBI.com`) assume that data is imported from Excel into the Excel version of Power Query using the From Table command. In many cases, I have removed the Changed Type step to better demonstrate function behavior. However, in real-world scenarios, defining correct column types is highly recommended, as it affects both performance and accuracy.

Final Thoughts

Like any book, this one isn't flawless—and I truly welcome your feedback! If you find any mistakes, no matter how small, please let me know. You can easily reach me on LinkedIn or by sending me an email at `Omid_Motamedi@Outlook.com`. I would love to hear from you.

Now, let's dive in and start solving some Power Query challenges!

CHAPTER 1

Data Extraction from Sources

The Power Query journey, as a powerful ETL (Extract, Transform, Load) tool, begins with its primary function of extracting data from various sources. It allows users to load data from a wide range of sources, ranging from simple file formats like CSV, TXT, Excel, and PDF, to more complex sources such as entire folders of files or databases like SQL Server. Additionally, Power Query supports data extraction from online sources, including websites, APIs, and cloud-based services, making it a versatile solution for handling both structured and unstructured data.

Data extraction in Power Query refers to the process of connecting to a data source and retrieving the necessary data. The main functions for extracting data from different sources are shown in Table 1-1.

Table 1-1. *Functions for Extracting Data*

Function	Description
Csv.Document()	Reads data from a CSV file.
Excel.Workbook()	Loads data from an Excel workbook, allowing you to select specific sheets or tables.
Text.Csv()	Loads data from a text source.
Pdf.Tables()	Extracts tables from a PDF file.
Folder.Files()	Returns a table of all the files in a specified folder.
Web.Contents()	Retrieves data from a web URL, useful for loading data from websites or APIs.

(continued)

CHAPTER 1   DATA EXTRACTION FROM SOURCES

Table 1-1. *(continued)*

Function	Description
Odbc.DataSource()	Connects to ODBC-compatible databases.
OData.Feed()	Connects to an OData feed, typically used for accessing web services.
Sql.Database()	Connects to an SQL Server database to extract data.
Access.Database()	Extracts data from a Microsoft Access database.
SharePoint.Files()	Loads files from a SharePoint site.
Json.Document()	Extracts data from a JSON document, typically used for APIs or web services.
Xml.Tables()	Retrieves data from XML files, often used in web services or data exchanges.
BinaryFile.Contents()	Loads data from binary files, often used for non-standard file formats.
Exchange.Contents()	Connects to Microsoft Exchange to retrieve data such as emails, contacts, and calendar entries.
ActiveDirectory.Domains()	Retrieves data from Active Directory domains, useful for organizational data.
Salesforce.Data()	Extracts data from Salesforce, commonly used in customer relationship management.

In most cases, the journey of using Power Query begins with one of the functions listed in Table 1-1. Despite the importance of these functions, they are less known since the extraction process in Power Query is typically managed through the user-friendly interface of this tool, rather than direct use of functions. However, there are scenarios where modifying these functions becomes necessary to achieve more advanced or customized transformations.

CHAPTER 1   DATA EXTRACTION FROM SOURCES

This chapter presents the process of loading data using the Power Query user interface (UI), providing a step-by-step guide for connecting to and importing data with ease. Following this, the chapter delves into the hidden features of some of the functions in Power Query. These functions, though often managed behind the scenes by the UI, hold powerful capabilities that can significantly enhance data extraction and transformation when utilized directly. This combination of UI-based guidance and advanced function insights equips users with a comprehensive understanding of both basic and advanced Power Query workflows.

Combining Data from Excel Files with Consistent Column Names

Historical yearly sales data from different stores is stored in several Excel files in a folder. Consider the case that the column names are identical across all files, as shown in Figure 1-1. Combine all the data into a single table, ensuring that store numbers are included (store numbers should be extracted from the filenames).

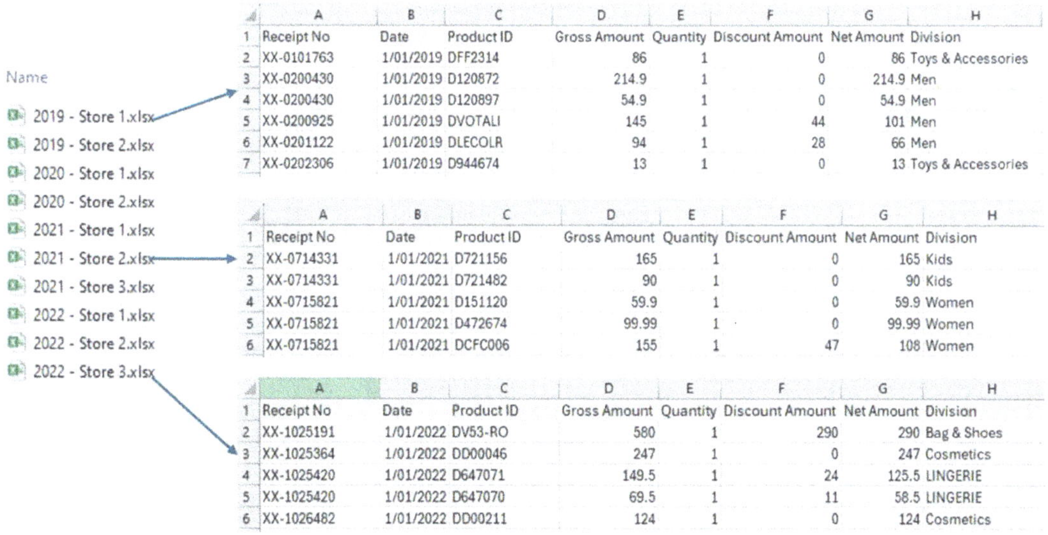

Figure 1-1. Excel files

Note   The Excel files used in this example are provided in the folder titled 01.

3

CHAPTER 1 DATA EXTRACTION FROM SOURCES

To solve this problem using Excel (or Power BI), open a new Excel (Power BI) file, from the Data (Home) tab, use the Get Data command, then select From File, and among the options, choose From Folder. Provide the folder path containing the Excel files and then click OK. You'll access the new window shown in Figure 1-2.

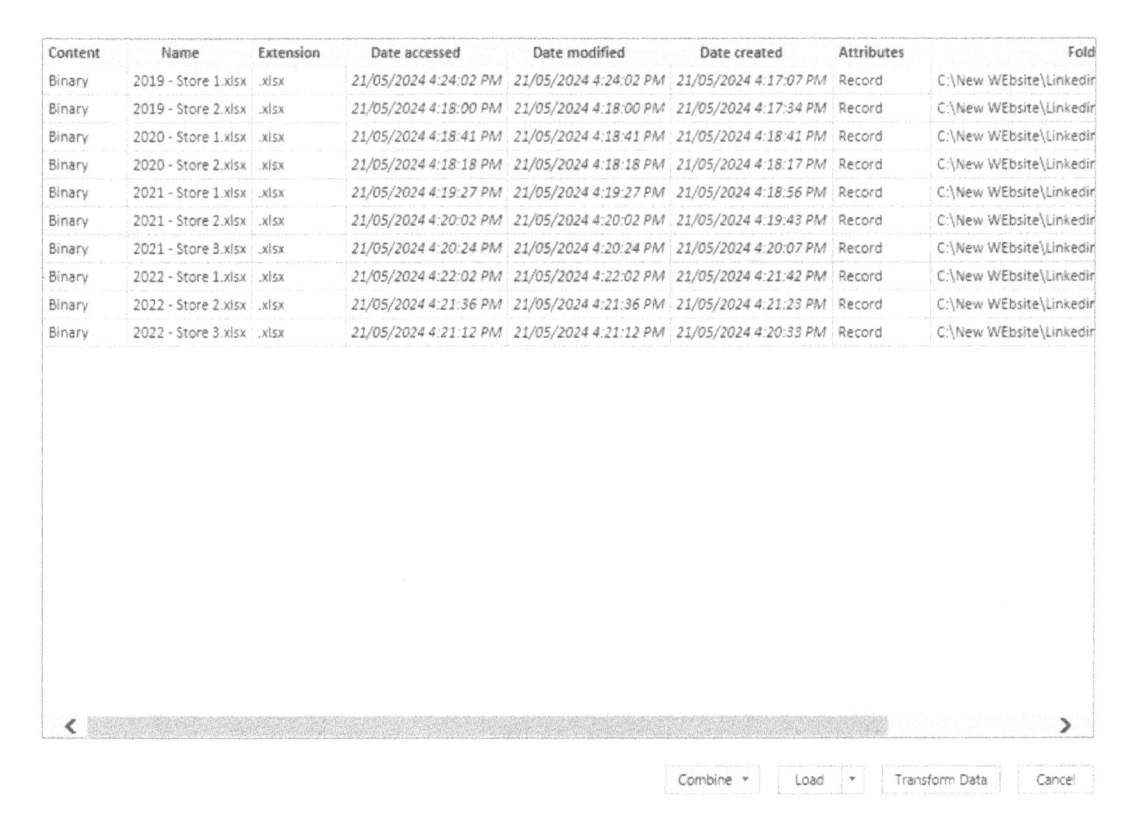

Content	Name	Extension	Date accessed	Date modified	Date created	Attributes	Fold
Binary	2019 - Store 1.xlsx	.xlsx	21/05/2024 4:24:02 PM	21/05/2024 4:24:02 PM	21/05/2024 4:17:07 PM	Record	C:\New WEbsite\Linkedir
Binary	2019 - Store 2.xlsx	.xlsx	21/05/2024 4:18:00 PM	21/05/2024 4:18:00 PM	21/05/2024 4:17:34 PM	Record	C:\New WEbsite\Linkedir
Binary	2020 - Store 1.xlsx	.xlsx	21/05/2024 4:18:41 PM	21/05/2024 4:18:41 PM	21/05/2024 4:18:41 PM	Record	C:\New WEbsite\Linkedir
Binary	2020 - Store 2.xlsx	.xlsx	21/05/2024 4:18:18 PM	21/05/2024 4:18:18 PM	21/05/2024 4:18:17 PM	Record	C:\New WEbsite\Linkedir
Binary	2021 - Store 1.xlsx	.xlsx	21/05/2024 4:19:27 PM	21/05/2024 4:19:27 PM	21/05/2024 4:18:56 PM	Record	C:\New WEbsite\Linkedir
Binary	2021 - Store 2.xlsx	.xlsx	21/05/2024 4:20:02 PM	21/05/2024 4:20:02 PM	21/05/2024 4:19:43 PM	Record	C:\New WEbsite\Linkedir
Binary	2021 - Store 3.xlsx	.xlsx	21/05/2024 4:20:24 PM	21/05/2024 4:20:24 PM	21/05/2024 4:20:07 PM	Record	C:\New WEbsite\Linkedir
Binary	2022 - Store 1.xlsx	.xlsx	21/05/2024 4:22:02 PM	21/05/2024 4:22:02 PM	21/05/2024 4:21:42 PM	Record	C:\New WEbsite\Linkedir
Binary	2022 - Store 2.xlsx	.xlsx	21/05/2024 4:21:36 PM	21/05/2024 4:21:36 PM	21/05/2024 4:21:23 PM	Record	C:\New WEbsite\Linkedir
Binary	2022 - Store 3.xlsx	.xlsx	21/05/2024 4:21:12 PM	21/05/2024 4:21:12 PM	21/05/2024 4:20:33 PM	Record	C:\New WEbsite\Linkedir

Figure 1-2. *Choosing From Folder*

If you select Combine and Load, the Combine Files window will appear as shown in Figure 1-3.

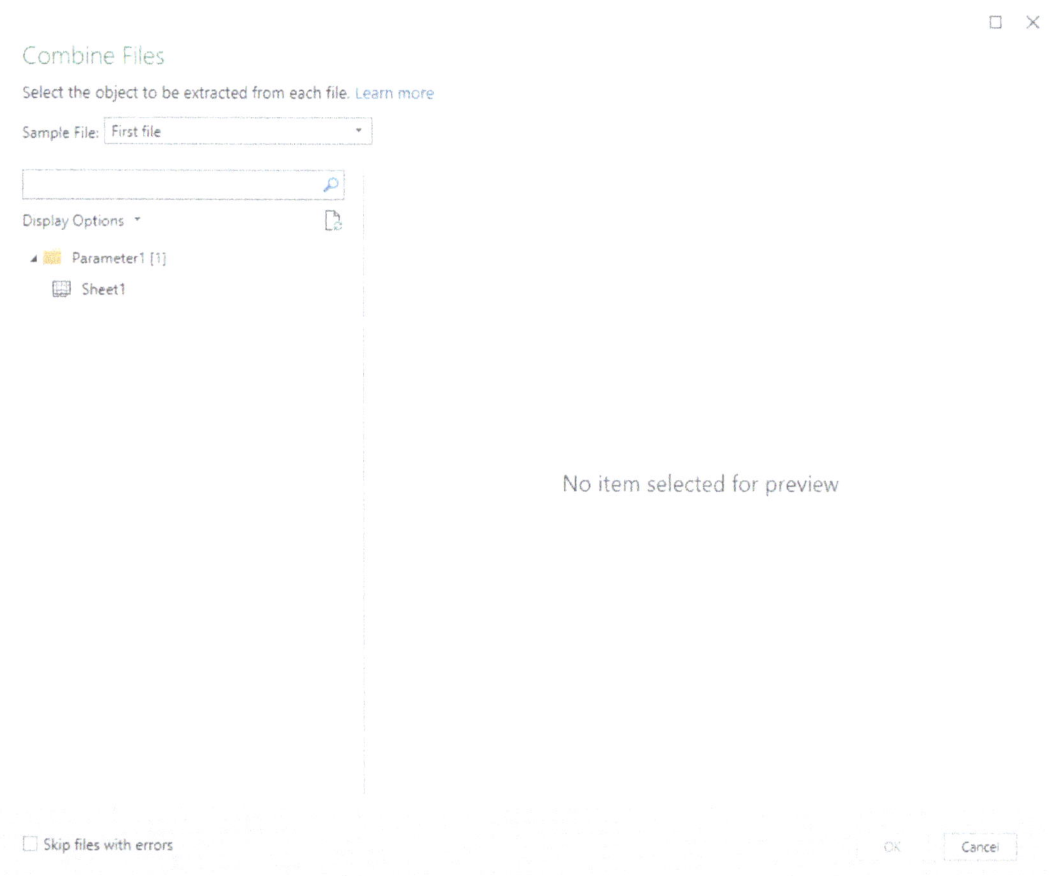

Figure 1-3. Combining files

Adjust the settings, as shown in Figure 1-4, by selecting 2019 Store 1.xlsx as the sample file and choosing Sheet 1 as the sample sheet (as long as the data structure in all files is the same, no matter which workbook and sheet is selected). By clicking OK, the combined table will be generated as shown in Figure 1-5.

CHAPTER 1 DATA EXTRACTION FROM SOURCES

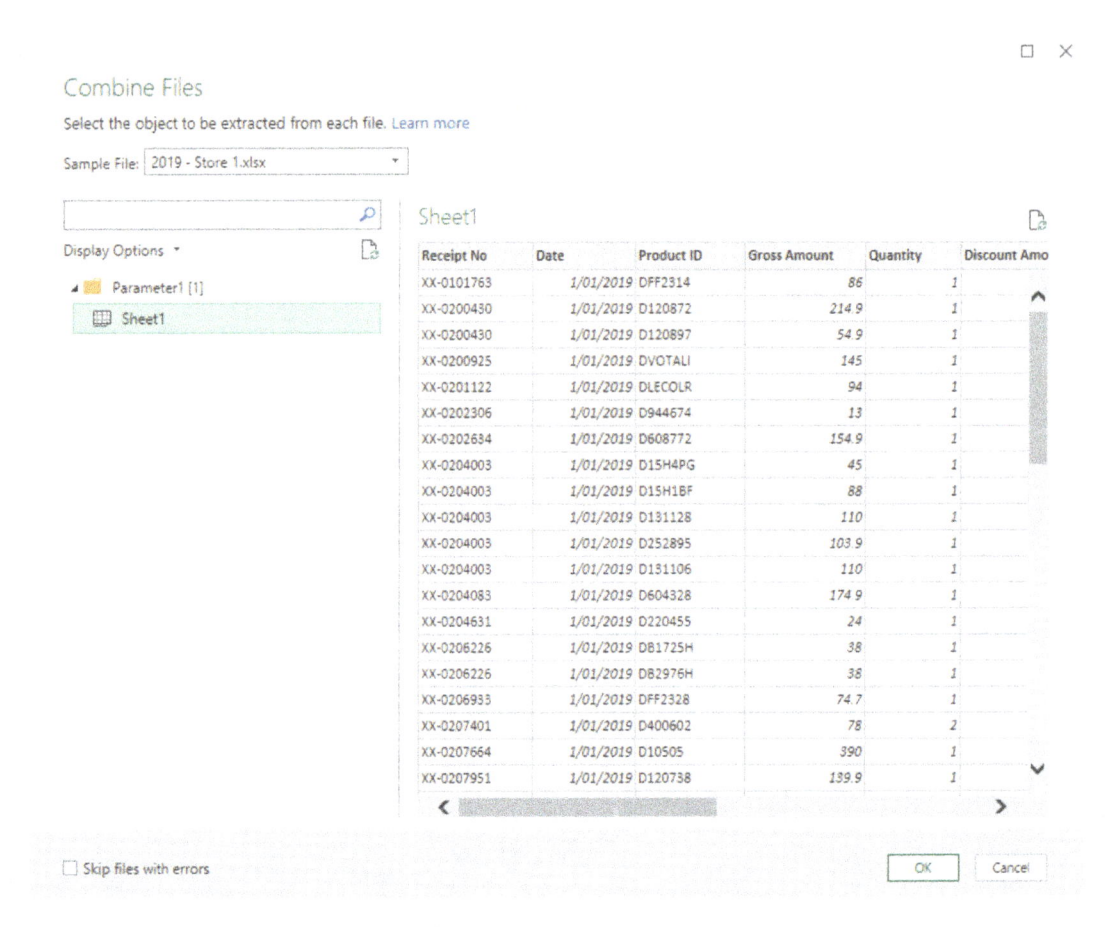

Figure 1-4. Selecting a sample file

Figure 1-5. Combined table

CHAPTER 1 DATA EXTRACTION FROM SOURCES

Note Data sources such as Excel, CSV, and Text are considered unstructured data sources. Power Query provides a setting to automatically detect headers and column types before loading the data. This setting is defined in the Power Query Editor. To access it, in the Power Query Editor, go to the File tab, then select Options and Settings, and choose Query Options. In the window that opens, navigate to the Data Load section, to see the setting, as shown in Figure 1-6 in the Type Detection part.

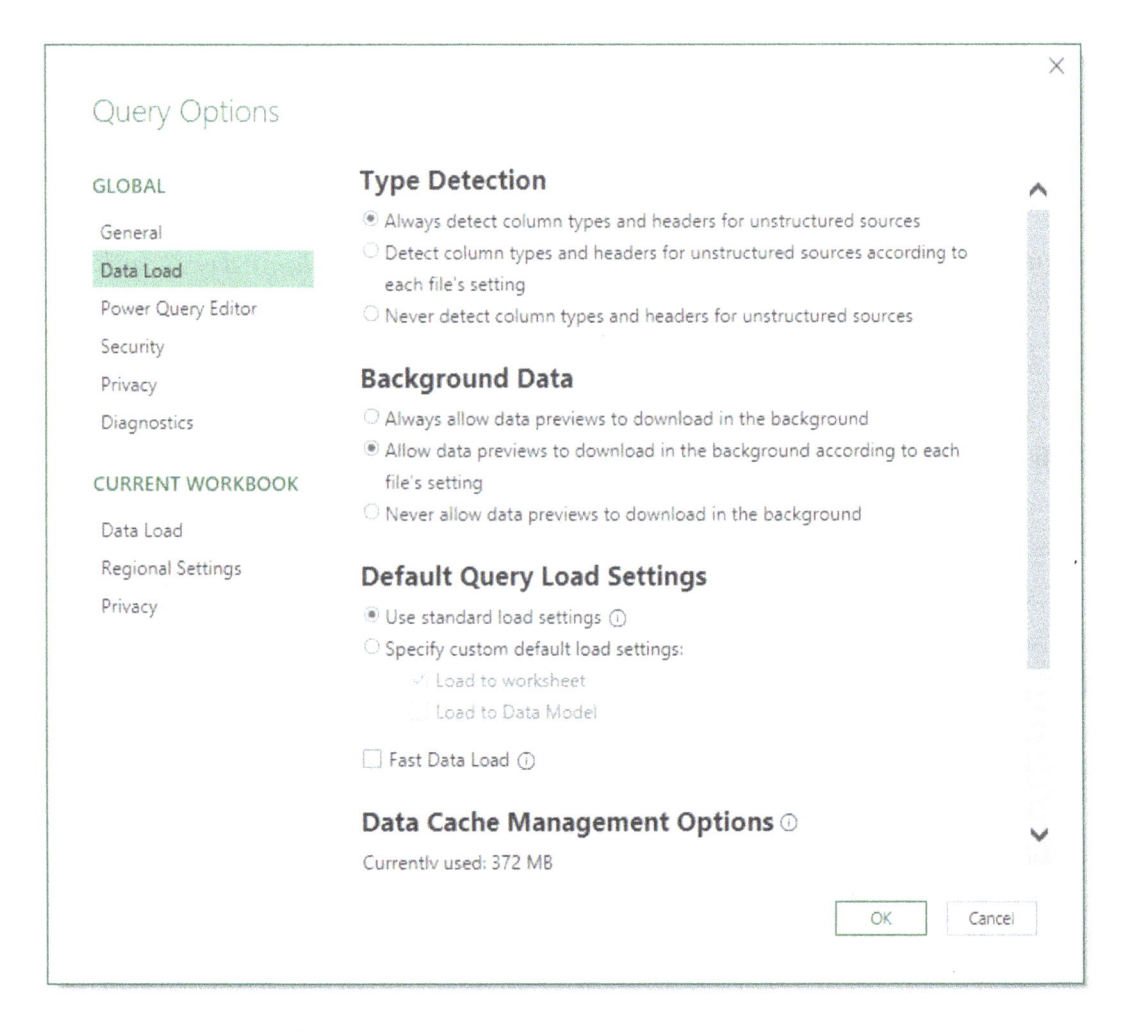

Figure 1-6. Setting for type detection

CHAPTER 1   DATA EXTRACTION FROM SOURCES

The predefined setting has the "Always Detect Column Types and Headers for Unstructured Data" option selected by default, but you can change it to another setting. If you choose the "Never Detect Column Types and Headers for Unstructured Sources" option and then do the process shown in this section, the result of the previous step would be different, as shown in Figure 1-7.

Source.Name	Column1	Column2	Column3	Column4	Column5	Column6	Column7
	Receipt No	Date	Product ID	Gross Amount	Quantity	Discount Amount	Net Amount
2019 - Store 1.xlsx	XX-0101763		D##F2314	86	1	0	
2019 - Store 1.xlsx	XX-0200430	1/01/2019	D120872	214.9	1	0	
2019 - Store 1.xlsx	XX-0200430	1/01/2019	D120897	54.9	1	0	
2019 - Store 1.xlsx	XX-0200925	1/01/2019	DVOTALI	145	1	44	
2019 - Store 1.xlsx	XX-0201122	1/01/2019	DLECOLR	94	1	29	
2019 - Store 1.xlsx	XX-0202306	1/01/2019	D944674	15	1	0	
2019 - Store 1.xlsx	XX-0202654	1/01/2019	D608772	154.9	1	0	
2019 - Store 1.xlsx	XX-0204003	1/01/2019	D15H4PG	45	1	0	
2019 - Store 1.xlsx	XX-0204003	1/01/2019	D15H18F	88	1	0	
2019 - Store 1.xlsx	XX-0204003	1/01/2019	D131128	110	1	33	
2019 - Store 1.xlsx	XX-0204003	1/01/2019	D252895	105.9	1	0	
2019 - Store 1.xlsx	XX-0204003	1/01/2019	D131106	110	1	33	
2019 - Store 1.xlsx	XX-0204083	1/01/2019	D604328	174.9	1	0	

Figure 1-7. *The result of the query using the Never Detect Column Types option*

As shown, in the new result, instead of using the data headers as column names in the new combined table, the columns are labeled Column 1, Column 2, and so on, and the headers of each file are considered rows of data.

The resultant table includes all the historical data, as well as the whole name of the source files (first column). To extract the store number from the Source.Name column, right-click the query named 01 (this is the same name as the folder containing the Excel files) and select Edit to open the Power Query Editor. (If you cannot find the queries in Excel, activate the Queries & Connections toggle button located in the Data tab. This will display the list of queries on the right side of the worksheet.)

The store numbers are listed in the Source.Name column, located between the text "Store" and the period (.). In Power Query, the Text.BetweenDelimiters() function can be used to extract values located between two specified text delimiters, as in this case. The function takes the text as its first input, followed by the delimiters as the second and third inputs.

CHAPTER 1   DATA EXTRACTION FROM SOURCES

So, to extract the store numbers into a new column, select the Custom Column command from the Add Column tab. As shown in Figure 1-8, enter **Store Number** as the name of the new column and use Text.BetweenDelimiters() as the following formula in the Custom Column window. This extracts the values between "Store" and the period as the delimiters, resulting in Figure 1-9.

= Text.BetweenDelimiters([Source.Name],"Store",".")

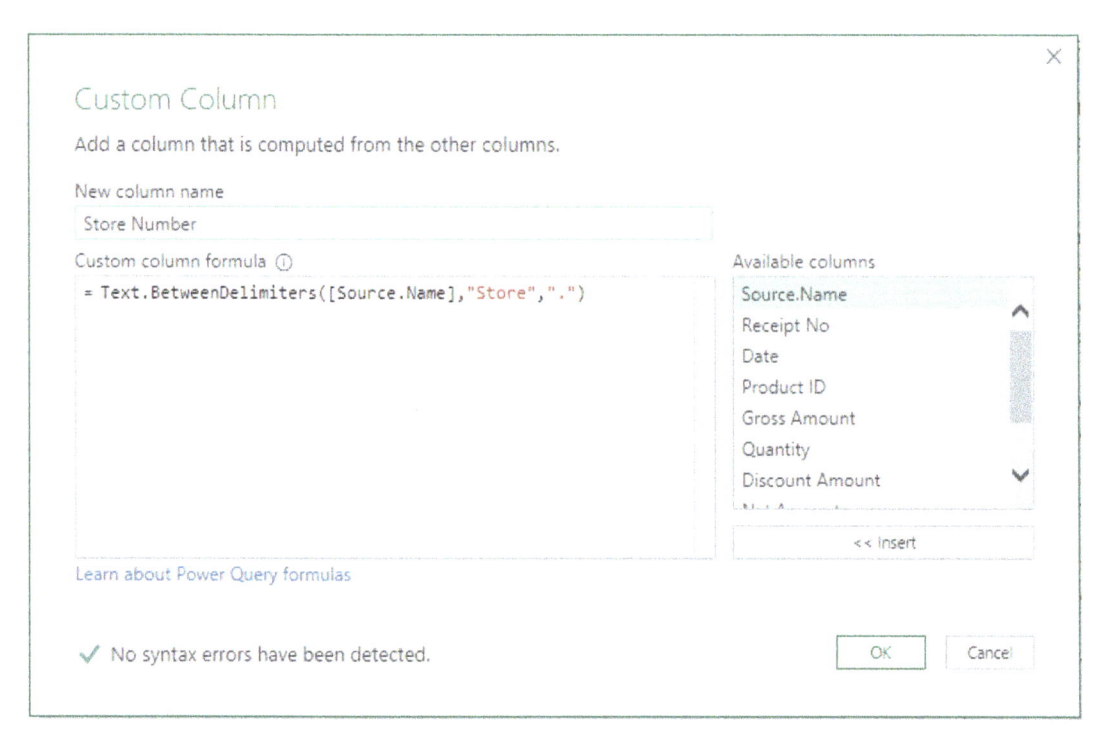

Figure 1-8. Adding a custom column to extract the store numbers

CHAPTER 1 DATA EXTRACTION FROM SOURCES

1.2 Gross Amount	1²₃ Quantity	1²₃ Discount Amount	1.2 Net Amount	A⁵c Division	A⁵c Item Description	ABC Store Number
86	1	0	86	Toys & Accessories	puzzle	1
214.9	1	0	214.9	Men	JJJAMES JJEARL AKM DARK NAVY NOOS	1
54.9	1	0	54.9	Men	bjorDOW SL TANK TOP	1
145	1	44	101	Men	slack slim stretch	1
94	1	28	66	Men	Pique stripe polo collar & sleeves	1
13	1	0	13	Toys & Accessories	SIMBA - MONSTERS UNIVERSITY PENCIL TOPPE	1
154.9	1	0	154.9	Men	DRIVE PCM fj coton uni	1
45	1	0	45	Kids	SCARF	1
88	1	0	88	Kids	PANTS	1
110	1	33	77	Kids	JEANS MALE WOV CO100	1
103.9	1	0	103.9	Kids	PZ girls sweatshirts from cotton, knitted	1
110	1	33	77	Kids	SKIRT FEM WOV CO98/EA2	1
174.9	1	0	174.9	Men	AWASH Pantsep PES/VI Slim	1
24	1	7	17	Toys & Accessories	Thank you	1
38	1	0	38	Toys & Accessories	TRA RID LEGION AST 0065	1
38	1	0	38	Toys & Accessories	TRA RID LEGION AST 0065	1
74.7	1	0	74.7	Toys & Accessories	block puzzles	1
78	2	0	78	Toys & Accessories	Think Big / XXXL Eraser, white, ca. 18,5	1
390	1	0	390	Toys & Accessories	Play House	1
139.9	1	70	69.9	Men	MARVIN SHIRT S/S 1-2-3 2014 NOOS PRM	1
-185	-1	0	-185	Men	FESMOOTH V PCV fi uni	1

Figure 1-9. *Resultant table*

Note Power Query is case-sensitive in all cases. So, in the previous example, if the file is named 2019 - store 1.xlsx, the previous formula will return nothing for this file. To address this, it is recommended to use the following formula, which is not case-sensitive. This formula first converts all the text to lowercase before attempting to extract the store number.=Text.BetweenDelimiters(Text.Lower([Source.Name]),"store",".")

In the next step, finalize the solution by right-clicking the Source.Name column and selecting the Remove command. This will delete this column.

Performance Tips The speed of loading data from sources depends on several factors, including the system being used, the type of file, and the number of sheets in an Excel workbook. However, in general, the process of loading data from an Excel file is relatively fast. For a case with 100 Excel files in a folder, each containing approximately 16,000 rows, it takes 27 seconds to load and combine them. Loading data from CSV files follows a similar process, but is significantly faster. For the same case of 100 files with around 16,000 rows each, it takes 3 seconds to load and combine them.

CHAPTER 1   DATA EXTRACTION FROM SOURCES

Combining Data from Excel Files with Different Column Names: Case Sensitivity

Consider the previous example, but the column names in some of the files are uppercase, and in others, they are lowercase, as shown in Figure 1-10. Combine all the data and provide a unique table.

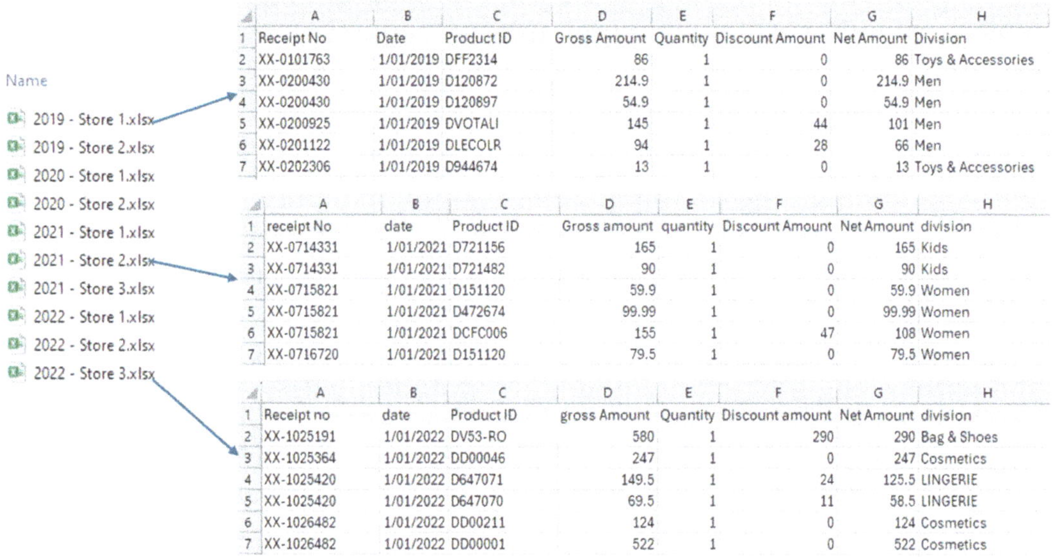

Figure 1-10. Source tables with different column names

Note   The Excel files used in this example are provided in the folder titled 02.

To solve this problem, follow the process shown in the previous example, which is leading the result. This is shown in Figure 1-11, where blank values are provided for columns with names that differ by case across the files.

11

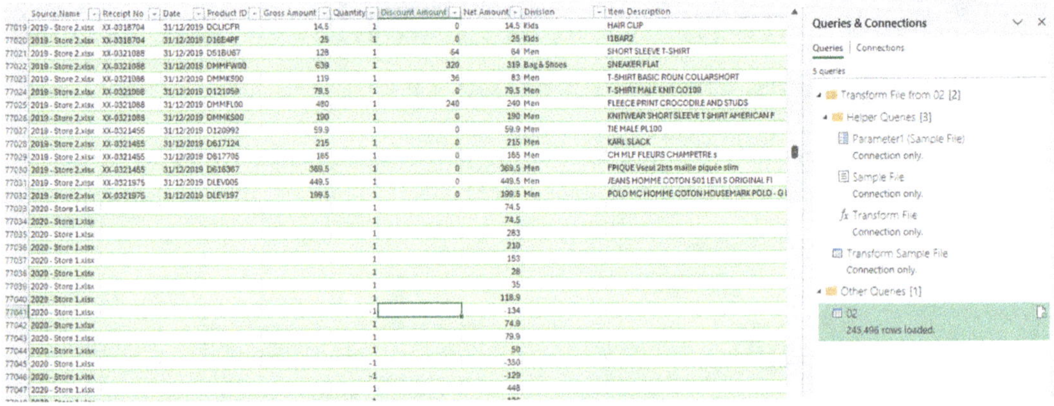

CHAPTER 1 DATA EXTRACTION FROM SOURCES

Figure 1-11. Result of combined tables

As shown in the resultant table, the column names of the combined table match those in the selected sample file (`2019 Store 1.xlsx`). For other files, if the column title differs (Power Query is a case-sensitive language, so Division is different from division), a null value is provided. To address this issue, let's take a closer look at the generated queries (shown on the right side of the Excel window), which are named Parameter1 (Sample File), Sample File, Transform File, Transform Sample File, and 02. Right-click any of these queries and select Edit to view the queries in the Power Query Editor, as shown in Figure 1-12.

CHAPTER 1 DATA EXTRACTION FROM SOURCES

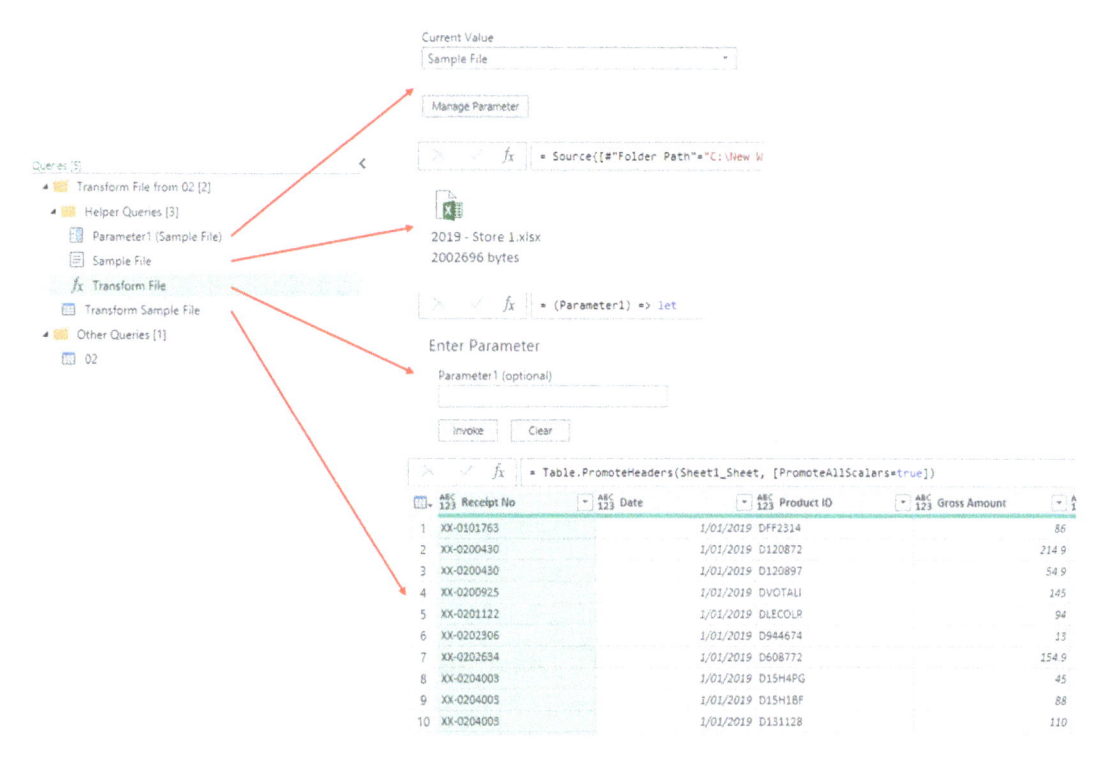

Figure 1-12. *Automatically generated queries*

Note As shown in Figure 1-13, the Power Query Editor includes eight sections:

1. **Ribbon:** The Ribbon contains all the commands you need to manipulate data, transform columns, apply filters, and work with queries. It is similar to the Ribbon in Excel, with tabs like Home, Transform, Add Column, View, and so on.

2. **Query Pane (Left Section):** This pane shows the list of all the queries currently in your workbook. You can manage queries here by right-clicking them to edit, delete, rename, or refresh them. You can also reorder the queries or create new queries, or group them.

3. **Applied Steps (Right Section):** The Applied Steps pane lists all the transformations applied to the data, step-by-step. Each time you perform an action (like changing a column's data type or removing

rows), a new step is added here. You can delete, reorder, and edit steps by clicking the gear icon next to each step. This section allows you to track your transformations and undo any steps if necessary.

4. **Data Preview (Middle Section):** This is where you can see a preview of your data in tabular form as you apply transformations. The data preview is updated as you apply each step in the Applied Steps pane. You can scroll through the data, select rows, and observe how your transformations affect the dataset. You can also filter or search the data directly in this section.

5. **Formula Bar (Top of the Data Preview Section):** The formula bar displays the formula for the current step, providing a detailed view of the applied M code. If the formula bar is not visible, you can enable it from the View tab in the Ribbon. The formula bar is especially useful for writing custom M code or adjusting existing transformations manually.

6. **Query Settings (Right Section):** Under the Query Settings pane, you can see the properties of the query, such as its name and data source information. You can rename the query, and access additional settings related to the query's behavior.

7. This section provides a detailed preview of the selected row or cell when you click a specific value in the data preview table. It is helpful for inspecting individual cell contents or rows, especially when working with complex data transformations or large datasets.

8. This section shows a summary of the dataset that's currently loaded into the Power Query Editor. It includes key information such as the total number of rows (how many rows are currently loaded in the dataset) or total number of columns (the total number of columns in the dataset). This is a quick reference for understanding the size and structure of your data.

CHAPTER 1   DATA EXTRACTION FROM SOURCES

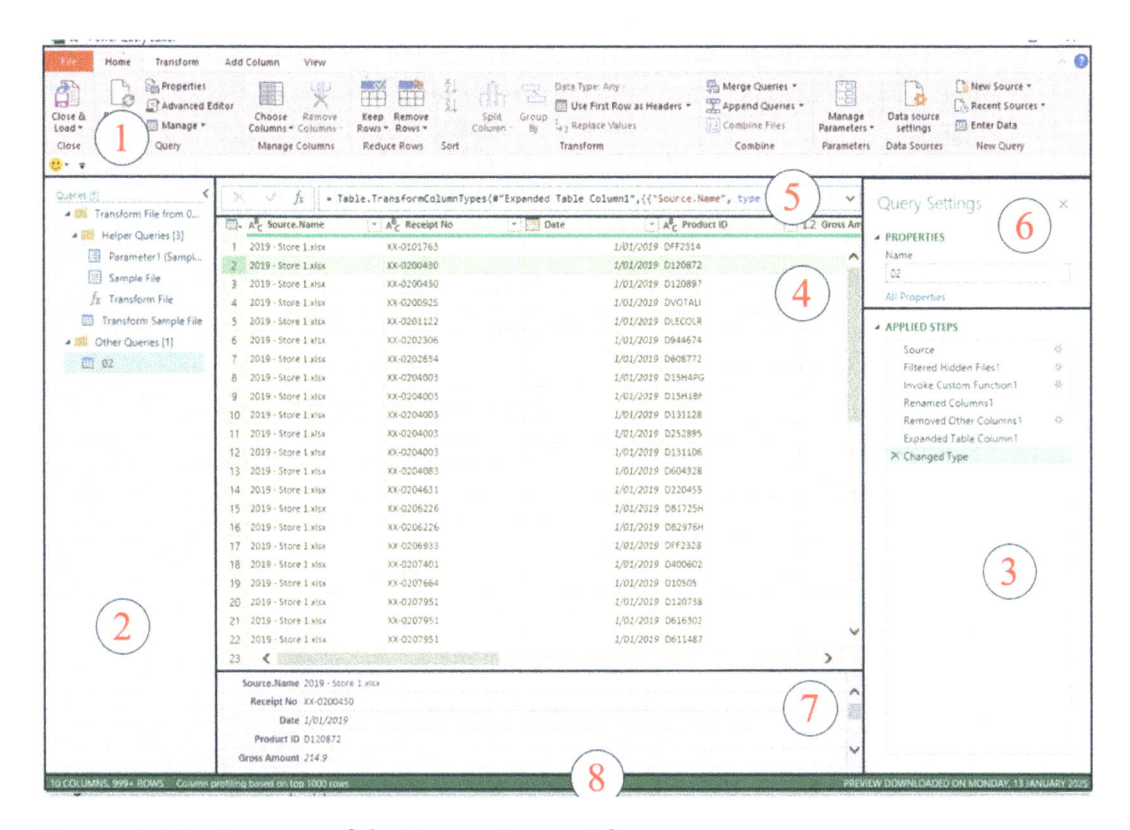

Figure 1-13. Sections of the Power Query Editor

When you load data from a folder using Power Query, it automatically generates these queries to handle the files within that folder. These queries are:

> **Parameter1 (Sample File)**: This query likely represents a sample file chosen from the folder. Power Query uses a sample file to infer the structure of the data and the transformations needed. It may act as a placeholder or template for applying transformations to the other files in the folder.
>
> **Sample File**: This query is based on the sample file selected in the process of loading data. It could be the initial query that loads and previews the data from the sample file.
>
> **Transform File**: This function is created based on the Transform Sample File query and plays a key role in fetching data from the files. It converts all the steps of the Transform Sample File query into a reusable function. During the process of combining data

15

from the files, this function is first applied to each file individually, and then the results from all the files are combined into a single dataset.

If you select this query and, from the Home tab, choose the Advanced Editor command, the message displayed in Figure 1-14 will show that this query is connected to Transform Sample File. Therefore, any changes made to the Transform Sample File query also affect this function, and the same change will be added as a step of this function. As a result, any updates to the Transform Sample File query will automatically be applied to the data-loading process for all files in the folder.

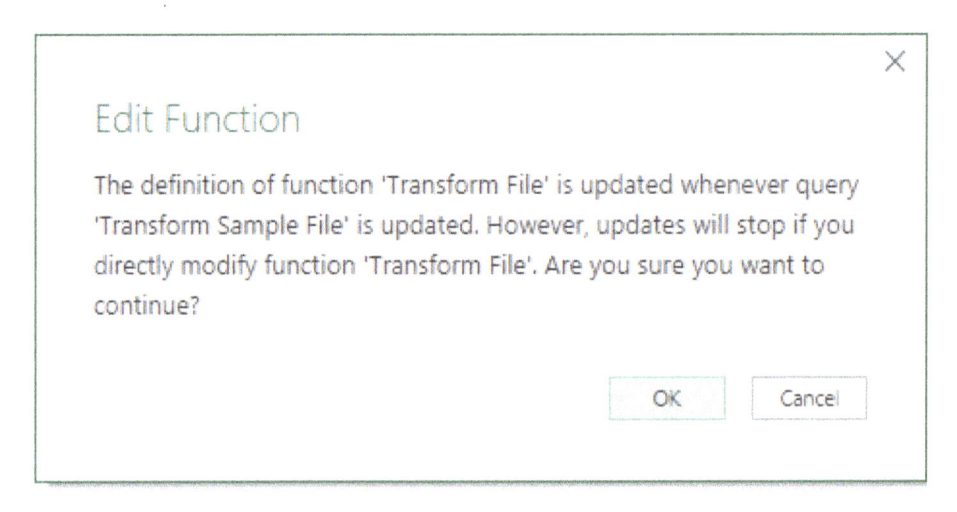

> Edit Function
>
> The definition of function 'Transform File' is updated whenever query 'Transform Sample File' is updated. However, updates will stop if you directly modify function 'Transform File'. Are you sure you want to continue?
>
> OK   Cancel

Figure 1-14. *Edit Function massage*

Transform Sample File: In the process of combining data from files using the UI, this query plays a crucial role. This query serves as a sample and allows you to modify the cleaning process. Any changes made to this query will impact the loaded data from other files in the selected folder. For example, if you select this query, go to the Home tab, and in the Reduce Rows section, choose Keep Rows and then Keep Top Rows, entering 5 in the dialog box, it will keep only the top five rows of the table. This results in Figure 1-15, but its impact is not limited to this query, as this change will also add to the Transform File query automatically and will apply it

CHAPTER 1   DATA EXTRACTION FROM SOURCES

to all the files on the selected folder. This means that during the data-loading process from the files in the selected folder, only the top five rows of each file are loaded. If you select the 02 query, its result will be updated to Figure 1-16.

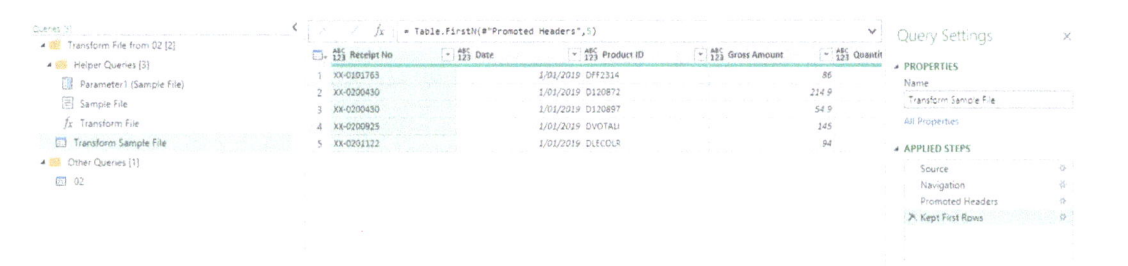

Figure 1-15. Keep the top five rows of the Transform Sample File

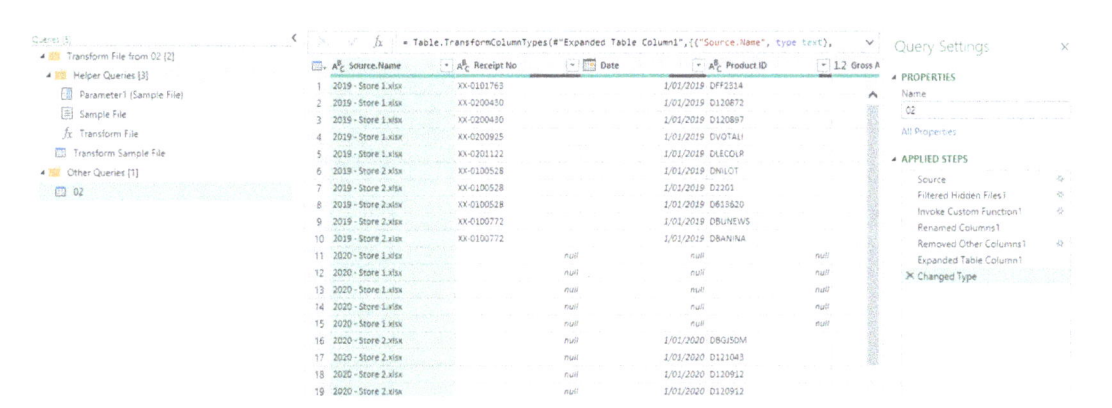

Figure 1-16. Impact of the Transform Sample File over the general result

02: Among all the automatically generated queries, this is what you see as the final result, including the combination of files, and its name is generated based on the folder from which the data was loaded.

Based on this explanation, to solve this problem and combine the data from all the files in the correct format, you can modify the Transform Sample File query. Any changes made to this query will automatically be applied to all files in the folder, in the process of data loading. For instance, if you convert all column headers in this query to

17

CHAPTER 1 DATA EXTRACTION FROM SOURCES

lowercase (or uppercase), during the data-loading process from the selected folder, the column headers in each file will first be converted to lowercase (or uppercase) before the data is combined. So, all the column names become the same over the files.

To ensure consistent column headers, select this query and convert all column names to lowercase. However, renaming column headers manually does not work, as it generates hard-coded names in the formula bar as presented in follow. For example, if in Transform Sample File query you rename the Date column to date, it produces a hard-coded formula, which only works for files where the column name is exactly Date. If another file uses the DATE column name, this change will not apply for that column.

```
= Table.RenameColumns(#"Promoted Headers",{{"Date", "date"}})
```

To handle this issue dynamically, you should use a formula that converts all column headers dynamically. The `Table.TransformColumnNames()` function is an excellent tool for handling such situations. It takes two arguments: the table name as the first argument and the transformation function to be applied as the second argument.

To proceed, select the Transform Sample File query and click the fx button next to the formula bar. This will create a new step, with the formula = `#"Promoted Headers"` (referring to the previous step) displayed in the formula bar. Replace this formula with the following one in the formula bar, which converts all the column headers of `#"Promoted Headers"` to lowercase. The result is shown in Figure 1-17.

```
= Table.TransformColumnNames(#"Promoted Headers",Text.Lower)
```

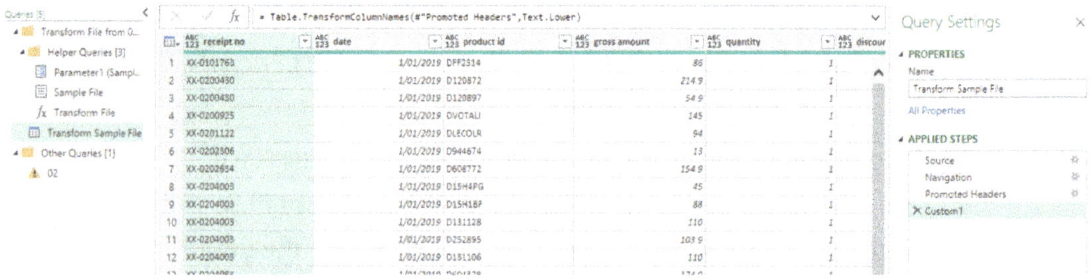

Figure 1-17. Converting the column names to the lowercase

As shown in Figure 1-18, this change causes the 02 query to return an error, stating that the Receipt No column does not exist. This issue occurs because the last step of the query, Changed Type, relies on the previous column names, which have now been modified. To resolve this issue, simply remove the Changed Type step, which will eliminate the error and produce the correct result, shown in Figure 1-19.

CHAPTER 1   DATA EXTRACTION FROM SOURCES

Figure 1-18. Result of query 02

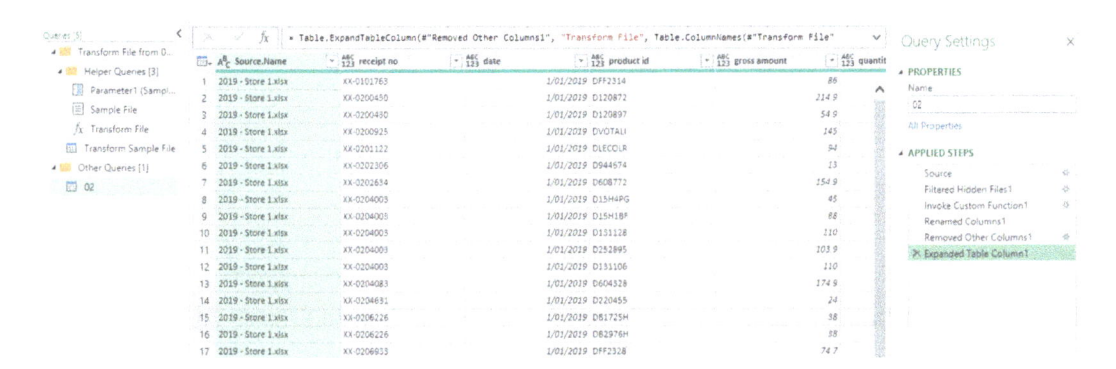

Figure 1-19. Final table

Combining Data from Excel Files with Different Column Names: Comprehensive Solution

Consider the previous example, but in this case, the column names in some files are completely different, as shown in Figure 1-20. For example, a column might be called Quantity in some files and QTY in others. Combine all the data and provide a unique table.

19

CHAPTER 1   DATA EXTRACTION FROM SOURCES

Figure 1-20. Source files

Note   The Excel files used in this example are provided in the folder titled 03.

To solve this problem, as in the previous example, you use the From Folder command, navigate to the folder, and then choose Combine & Transform Data, by selecting any sample file. You'll get the result shown in Figure 1-21.

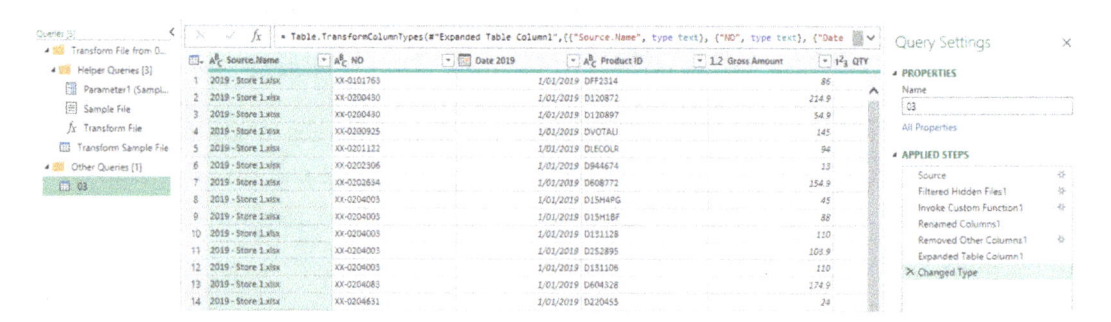

Figure 1-21. Combining and loading data into the Power Query Editor

In this example, you will see how to solve this problem using two different scenarios.

CHAPTER 1　DATA EXTRACTION FROM SOURCES

Scenario 1: Different Column Headers but the Same Number and Order of Columns Across All Files

If the column headers differ between files but the number and order of columns are the same, you can standardize the process by using generic headers like Column1, Column2, and so on, instead of relying on the headers from the files themselves.

So, select the Transform Sample File query in the Power Query Editor, locate the last step in the Applied Steps pane, which is named Promoted Headers, and remove this step to revert to the default headers (Column1, Column2, etc.). See Figure 1-22.

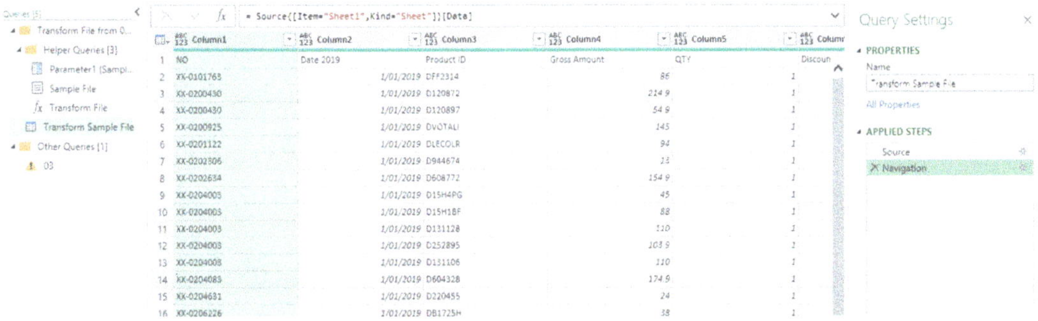

Figure 1-22. Result of removing the Promote Header step

Now, go to the 03 query, which currently results in an error. The error occurs because the column names from the files do not match. To fix this, remove the last step, Changed Type, from the Applied Steps pane. Now you'll see the result shown in Figure 1-23.

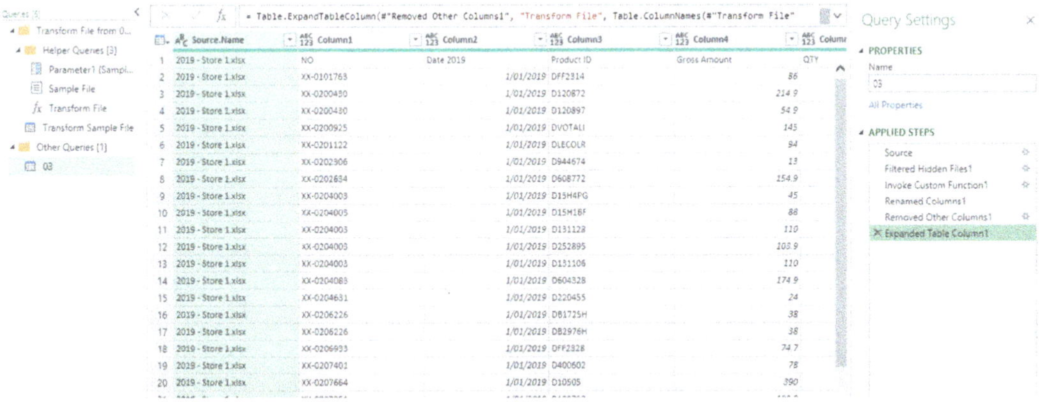

Figure 1-23. Result of removing the Changed Type step

21

CHAPTER 1 DATA EXTRACTION FROM SOURCES

As shown, the column headers of the tables in the loaded files have been neglected. You need to promote the first row to be used as the column headers and remove any rows that are not relevant (rows related to the header of files in the selected folder). So, from the Transform tab, click Use First Row as Headers to promote the first row to column headers; see Figure 1-24.

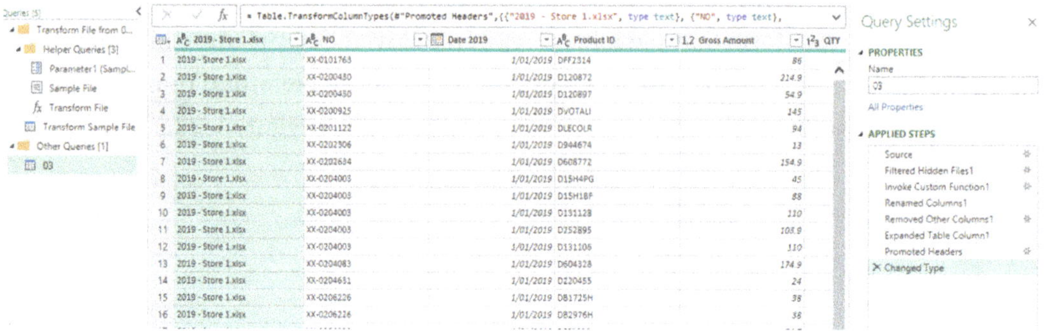

Figure 1-24. Result of promoting the headers

After making this change, two steps—Promoted Headers and Changed Type—will be added to the list of applied steps. To proceed, remove the Changed Type step from the Applied Steps pane, and, for a column that contains numeric values, such as QTY, click the filter icon next to the column name. Then select Load More to view all the values in that column, as shown in Figure 1-25. Deselect the values that are related to the titles of other files and click OK.

CHAPTER 1   DATA EXTRACTION FROM SOURCES

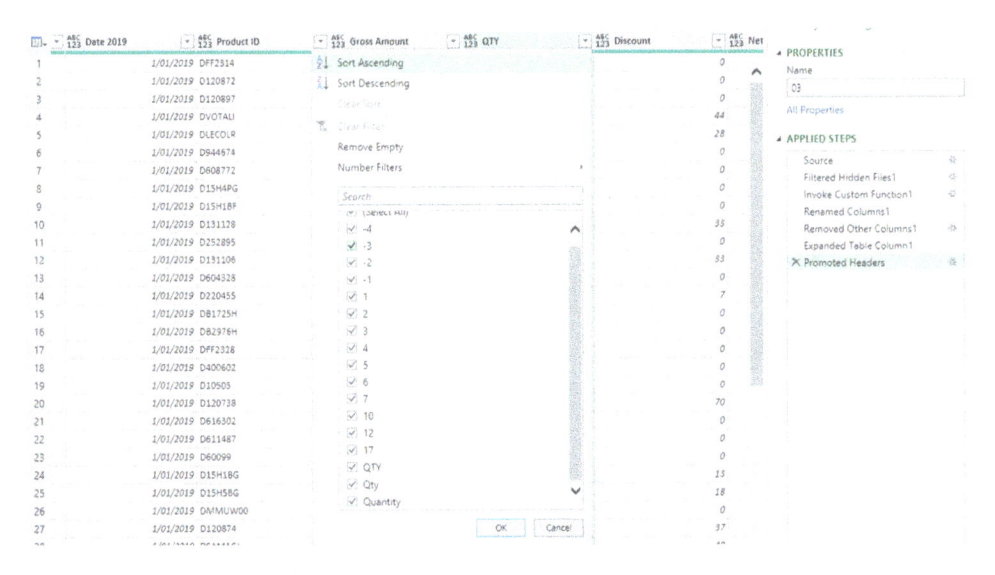

Figure 1-25. *Setting for filtering*

This will resolve the issue and ensure that only the relevant data is included in the query.

Scenario 2: The Number and Order of Columns Varies Across Different Files

In this scenario, since the order of columns varies across different files, you need to extract all the column name variations and define a generic name for each similar column. Then, you will replace the original column names with the new generic names across the tables in the files.

To address this issue, first assume that you know all the variations of column names. (At the end of this chapter, I explain how to extract the column names.) From the Home tab in the Power Query Editor, go to the New Query section and select Enter Data. As shown in Figure 1-26, create a table called Names with two columns: one for the old names and another for the new generic names. (Alternatively, if you're using Excel, you can create this table directly in Excel and then load it into the Power Query Editor.)

CHAPTER 1 DATA EXTRACTION FROM SOURCES

Figure 1-26. Creating a new query

In this case, you need to replace the old column names with new generic names across all the files using the Transform Sample File query. To understand the process for changing column names in Power Query, let's first explore the logic. So, select the Transform Sample File query and manually rename the NO column to Receipt No. This will generate the following formula in the formula bar:

= Table.RenameColumns(#"Promoted Headers",{{"NO", "Receipt No"}})

If you also change the column name from Date 2019 to Date, the formula will be updated to:

= Table.RenameColumns(#"Promoted Headers",{{"NO", "Receipt No"}, {"Date 2019", "Date"}})

CHAPTER 1 DATA EXTRACTION FROM SOURCES

From these examples, it becomes clear that, in order to change column names in a table (like #"Promoted Headers"), you need to input the table name as the first argument of the Table.RenameColumns() function. The second argument is a list of sub-lists, each containing the old and new column names.

Now, to apply this logic to all files, you need to change the format of the Names query from a table to a list. So, select the Names query and, next to the formula bar, click fx next to the formula bar, which generates = #"Changed Type" (where #"Changed Type" is the name of the previous step) in the formula bar.

Replace this formula with the following one to convert the table into a list. See Figure 1-27 (the Table.ToRows() function converts a table into a list, with each row represented as a sublist).

= Table.ToRows(#"Changed Type")

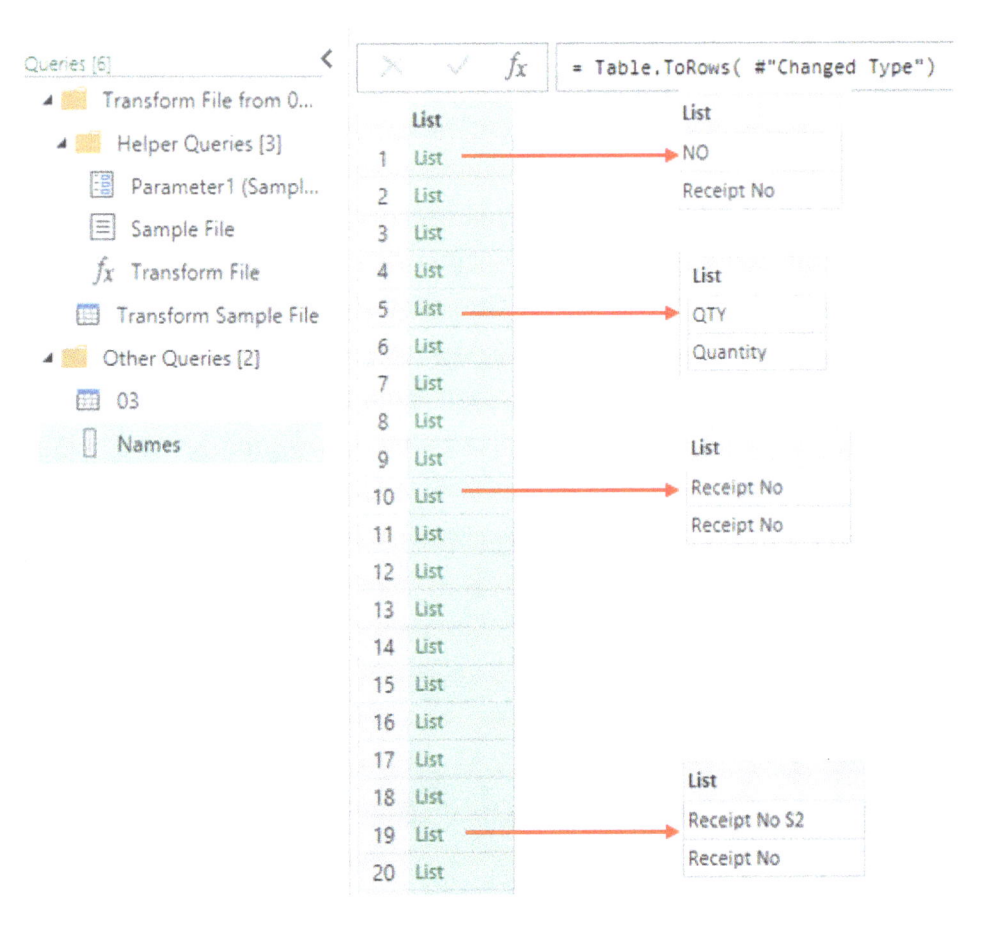

Figure 1-27. Result of using Table.ToRows()

CHAPTER 1　DATA EXTRACTION FROM SOURCES

Note In Power Query, a list is a simple, ordered collection of values. It is a fundamental data type used to represent a sequence of items, similar to an array in programming. Lists are versatile and play an essential role in many Power Query operations, such as filtering, aggregating, and performing iterative calculations. A list maintains the order of its items, like ={1,2,3,4}, as shown in Figure 1-28.

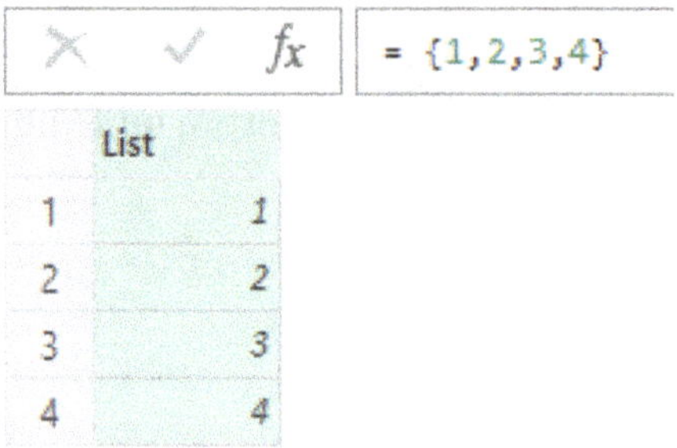

Figure 1-28. Defining a list in Power Query

Additionally, a record is a data type that represents a single structured entity, similar to a row in a table or a key-value pair in a dictionary. A record consists of one or more fields, each of which has a field name (key) and an associated value. Records are often used to store and process structured data with a fixed set of attributes. Each field in a record has a unique name (the key) and a corresponding value. For example, a record might look like [Name = "John", Age = 30, Country = "Australia"], as shown in Figure 1-29.

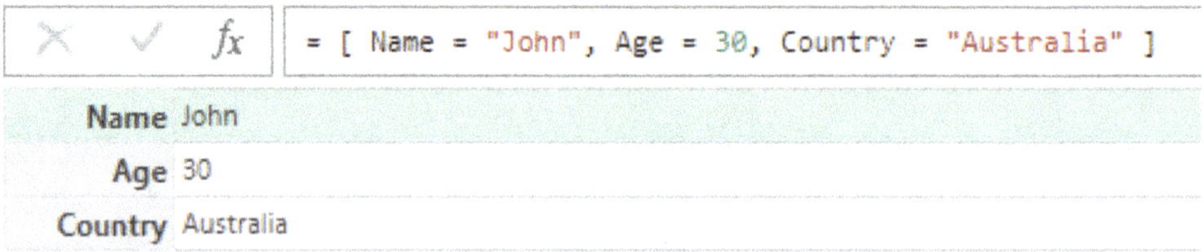

Figure 1-29. Defining a record in Power Query

CHAPTER 1 DATA EXTRACTION FROM SOURCES

Now that the result of the Names query is ready, you can use it in the second argument of the Table.RenameColumns() function. To proceed, go to the Transform Sample File query and click *fx* next to the formula bar, which will display = #"Promoted Headers" in the formula bar. Replace this formula with the following:

= Table.RenameColumns(#"Promoted Headers",Names)

However, this will result in an error for query 03, as shown in Figure 1-30, because some of the old column names listed in the Names query do not exist in the table. This error occurs because Power Query is unable to find certain column names that are specified in the Names query within the current table.

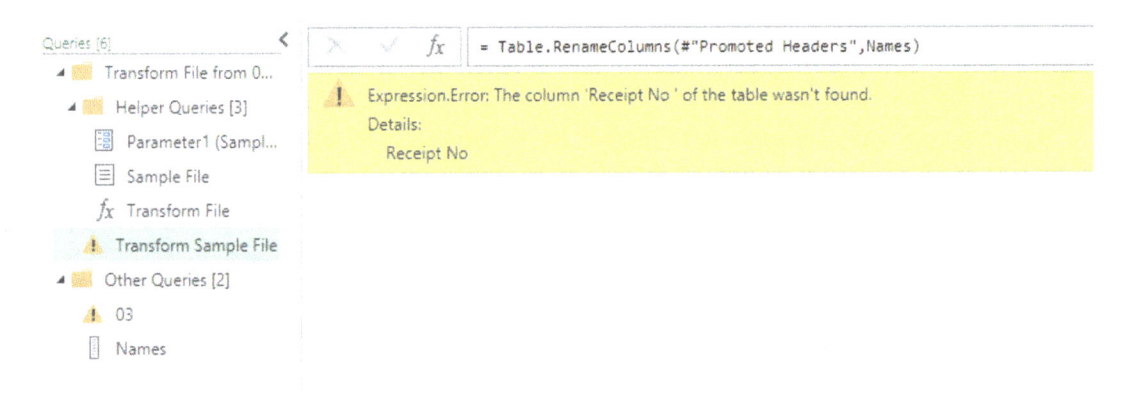

Figure 1-30. Result of renaming the column headers

To address this issue and ignore nonexistent columns in the renaming process, rewrite the formula as shown here. Adding MissingField.Ignore (or 1) as the third argument in the Table.RenameColumns() will cause nonexistent column headers to be ignored, thus preventing errors. The updated formula will result in the table shown in Figure 1-31.

Table.RenameColumns([Custom.Data],Names,MissingField.Ignore)

CHAPTER 1   DATA EXTRACTION FROM SOURCES

Figure 1-31. Solving the problem by adding MissingField.Ignore

As in the previous scenario, to complete the solution, go to query 03 and remove the last step (related to changing the type) to solve the problem.

Note To solve the problem in the second scenario, it is assumed that you already know all the variations of column names across the files in a folder. This note explains how to extract this data.

To extract the column names from the files in a folder, open an Excel file. Then use the From Folder command to navigate to the folder containing the files, select Combine & Transform Data, and choose any sample file to proceed. This will lead to the result shown in Figure 1-32.

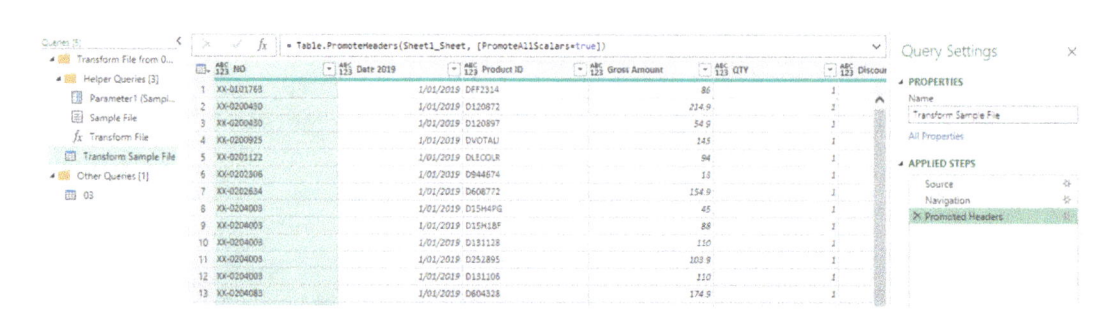

Figure 1-32. Result of loading the data

28

CHAPTER 1   DATA EXTRACTION FROM SOURCES

Then, go to the Transform Sample File query, click fx to add a new step, and replace the generated formula with the following:

= Table.ColumnNames(#"Promoted Headers")

This will result in a list that includes all the column names from the selected sample file, as shown in Figure 1-33.

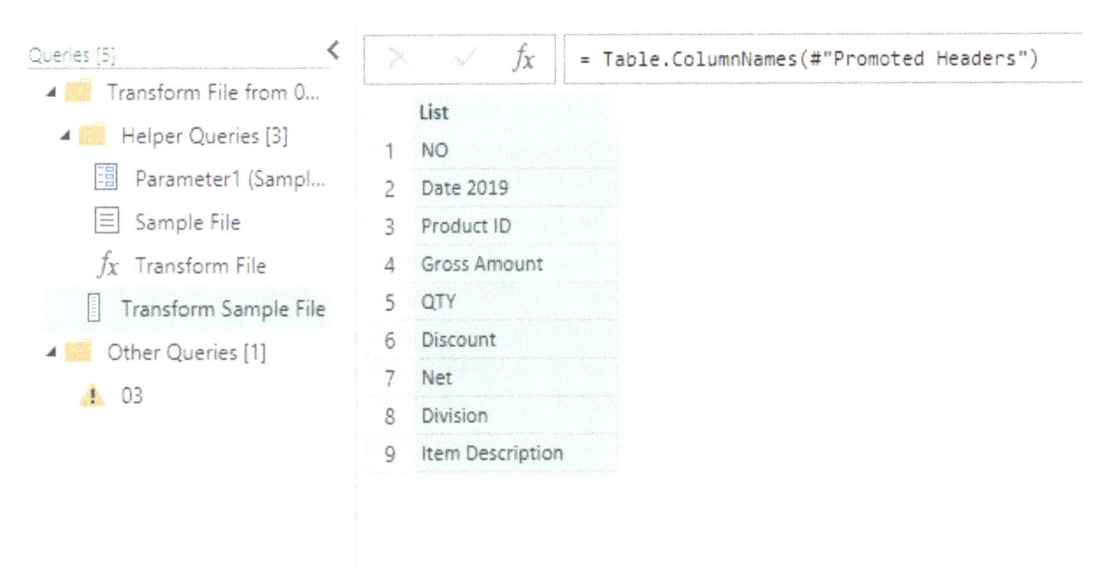

Figure 1-33. Result of using the Table.ColumnNames() function

By doing this, the result of query 03 will change to an error. To fix this, remove the last two steps of this query (Changed Type and Expanded Table Column1), and you'll reach the result shown in the Figure 1-34. Next, use the Expand icon next to the column Transform File to expand its values. You'll see the result in Figure 1-35.

CHAPTER 1   DATA EXTRACTION FROM SOURCES

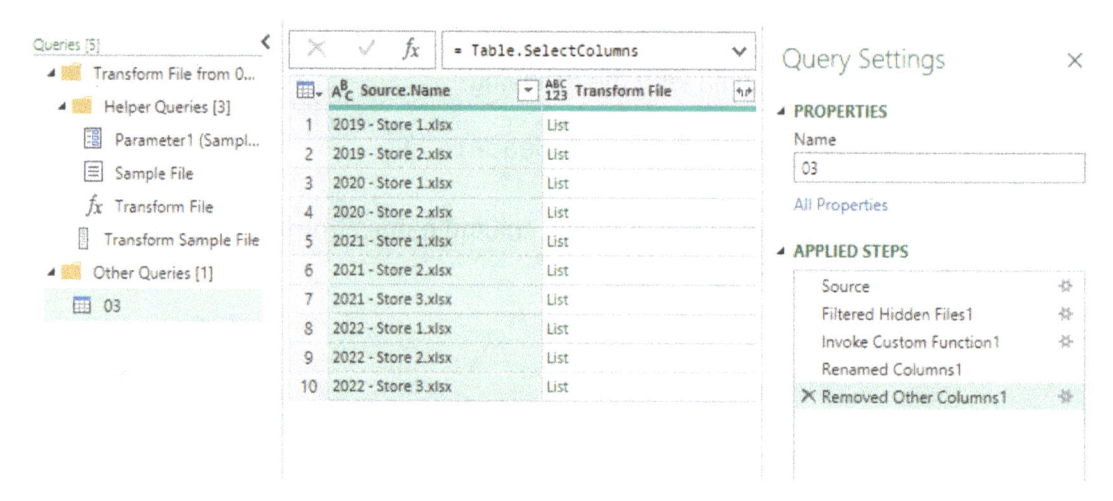

Figure 1-34. Result of removing the steps

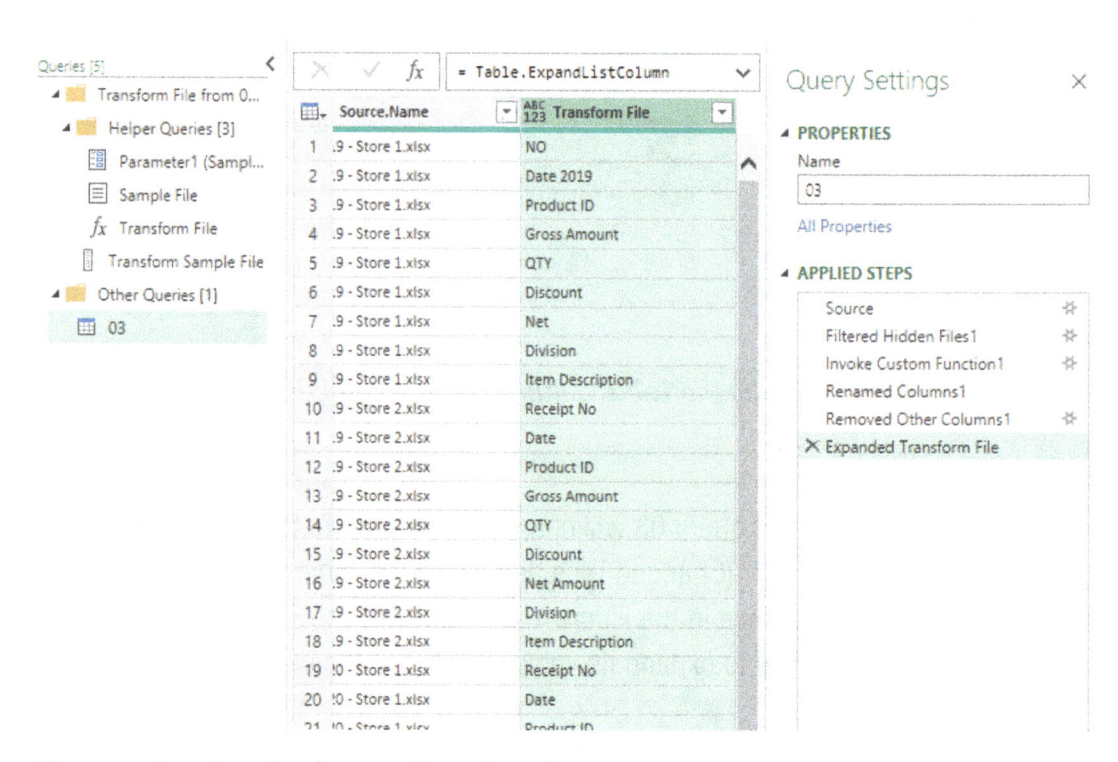

Figure 1-35. Result of expanding the column

CHAPTER 1 DATA EXTRACTION FROM SOURCES

Now, all the column names from the different files, along with their source files, will be displayed. As you do not need the Source.Name column, remove it. Then right-click the Transform File column and select the Remove Duplicates command to get a unique list of column header variations across all the files.

Extracting Values Outside of Tables

Consider Example 1 in this chapter, but in this case, the store numbers are not mentioned in the names of the files and are instead provided in a cell above the table; see Figure 1-36. Combine the files by keeping the values of the store name.

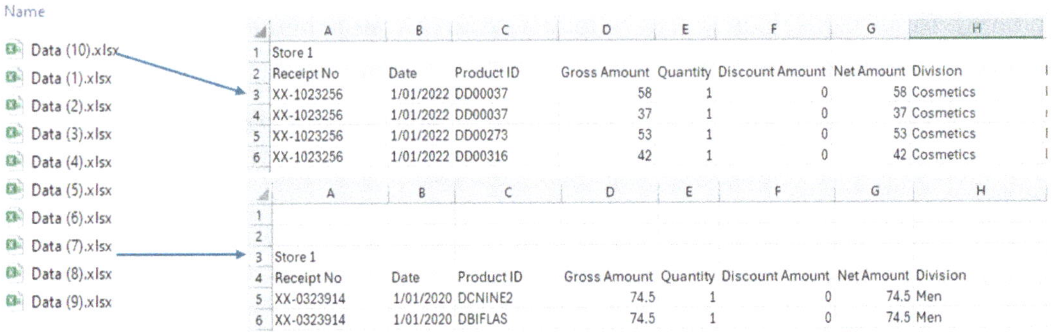

Figure 1-36. Source files

Note The Excel files used in this example are provided in the folder titled 04.

To solve this problem, as in the previous example, use the From Folder command, navigate to the folder, and then choose Combine & Transform Data, by selecting any sample file. You'll see the result in Figure 1-21.

31

CHAPTER 1   DATA EXTRACTION FROM SOURCES

Figure 1-37. Combining and loading data into the Power Query Editor

As shown in this example, the store name is shown one row above the main table, causing the rows to be treated as header rows (as seen in the name of the second column). To solve this issue, you need to first extract the store name and then promote the first row as the header. To do this, select the Transform Sample File query and remove its last step (Promoted Headers) to access the previous steps; see Figure 1-38.

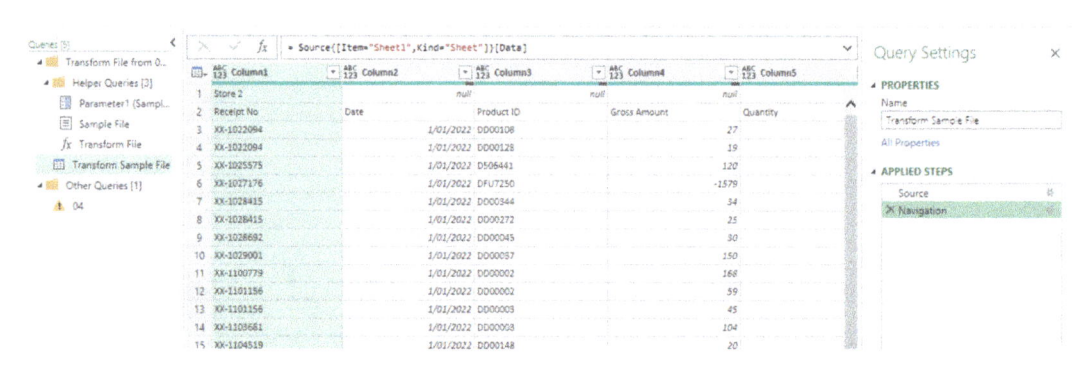

Figure 1-38. Removing the promote headers

Then, right-click the first cell in Column1 (where Store 2 is located) and select Drill Down to access the store name; see Figure 1-39.

CHAPTER 1 DATA EXTRACTION FROM SOURCES

Figure 1-39. Result of drilling down

Before continuing with the rest of the solution, there is a strange behavior after performing the Drill Down action in the previous step that you need to investigate. The program does not add a new step in the Applied Steps section, and in the formula bar, the name of the previous step is shown as Sheet1_Sheet, which does not appear in the list of steps in the Applied Steps section. To investigate the issue, go to the Home tab and click the Advanced Editor. In the window that opens, shown in Figure 1-40, you'll see three steps, whereas in the Applied Steps section, only two steps are shown—Sheet1_Sheet and Column1—both listed under the Navigation step.

```
1  let
2      Source = Excel.Workbook(Parameter1, null, true),
3      Sheet1_Sheet = Source{[Item="Sheet1",Kind="Sheet"]}[Data],
4      Column1 = Sheet1_Sheet{0}[Column1]
5  in
6      Column1
```

Figure 1-40. Advanced Editor

33

CHAPTER 1   DATA EXTRACTION FROM SOURCES

Note The Advanced Editor in Power Query allows you to view and edit the M code behind your queries. While the Power Query Editor provides a user-friendly interface with options like transformations, filters, and other data manipulation features, the Advanced Editor provides a deeper level of control by exposing the underlying code that defines the sequence of operations applied to your data.

In the Advanced Editor, as shown in Figure 1-41, all the steps are defined between the `let` and `in` keywords. Each step begins with a step name (except for the navigation task, which is exactly as shown in the Applied Steps window) and ends with a comma (,). The only exception is the last step, which does not require a comma.

If a step name contains spaces, it should be enclosed in #" and ". For example, if the step name is Promoted Headers, it should be written as #"Promoted Headers". This ensures that Power Query correctly recognizes the step name.

The `in` keyword is used to define the result of the query. It usually refers to the final expression or the last step to be executed, which will return the result of the entire query.

```
Transform Sample File

1  let
2      Source = Excel.Workbook(Parameter1, null, true),
3      Sheet1_Sheet = Source{[Item="Sheet1",Kind="Sheet"]}[Data],
4      Column1 = Sheet1_Sheet{0}[Column1]
5  in
6      Column1
```

Figure 1-41. View of the Advanced Editor

CHAPTER 1   DATA EXTRACTION FROM SOURCES

This behavior occurs due to Power Query's logic of grouping steps related to navigation across tables, columns, and rows under the name Navigation. However, be cautious, as you cannot refer to Navigation directly in the formula; instead, you should use the names shown in the Advanced Editor.

So based on this explanation, to refer to the table before the Drill Down, use the name Sheet1_Sheet, and to refer to the store name that was extracted, use the step named Column1.

For the rest of the solution, click the *fx* next to the formula bar, and in the formula bar, enter =Sheet1_Sheet to access the table before the Drill Down, as shown in Figure 1-42.

Figure 1-42. Referring to the previous step

In this table, since the store number has been extracted, you no longer need the first row. To remove it, go to the Home tab, and under the Reduce Rows section, select Remove Rows, then choose Remove Top Rows. In the dialog that appears, enter 1 to remove the first row. Next, go to the Transform tab and choose the Use First Row as Headers command to reach the result shown in Figure 1-43.

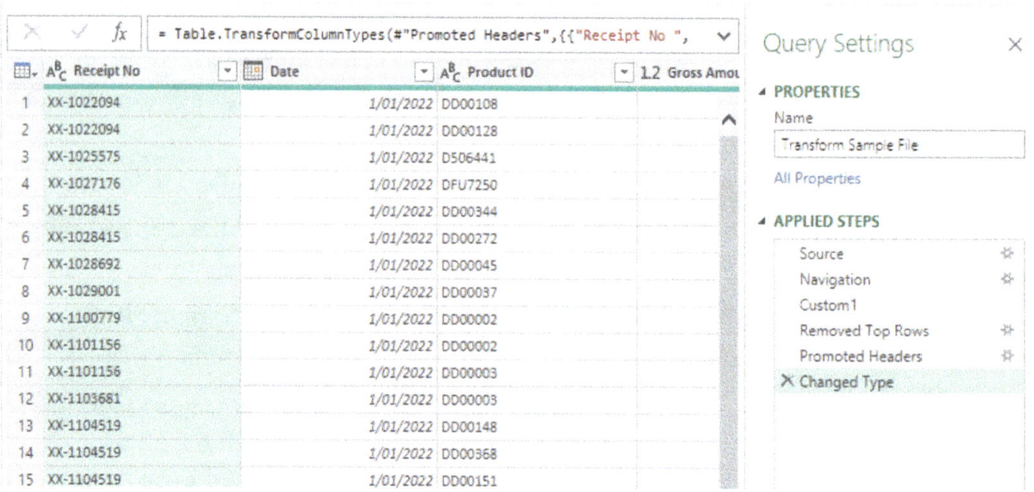

CHAPTER 1   DATA EXTRACTION FROM SOURCES

Figure 1-43. Result of promoting the headers

In the next step, go to the Add Column tab and click the Custom Column command. In the open window, shown in Figure 1-44, name the column Store and enter the =Column1 formula (which extracts the store name from the two steps previously). This will result in the table shown in Figure 1-45, creating a new column that includes the store number for all the rows.

CHAPTER 1 DATA EXTRACTION FROM SOURCES

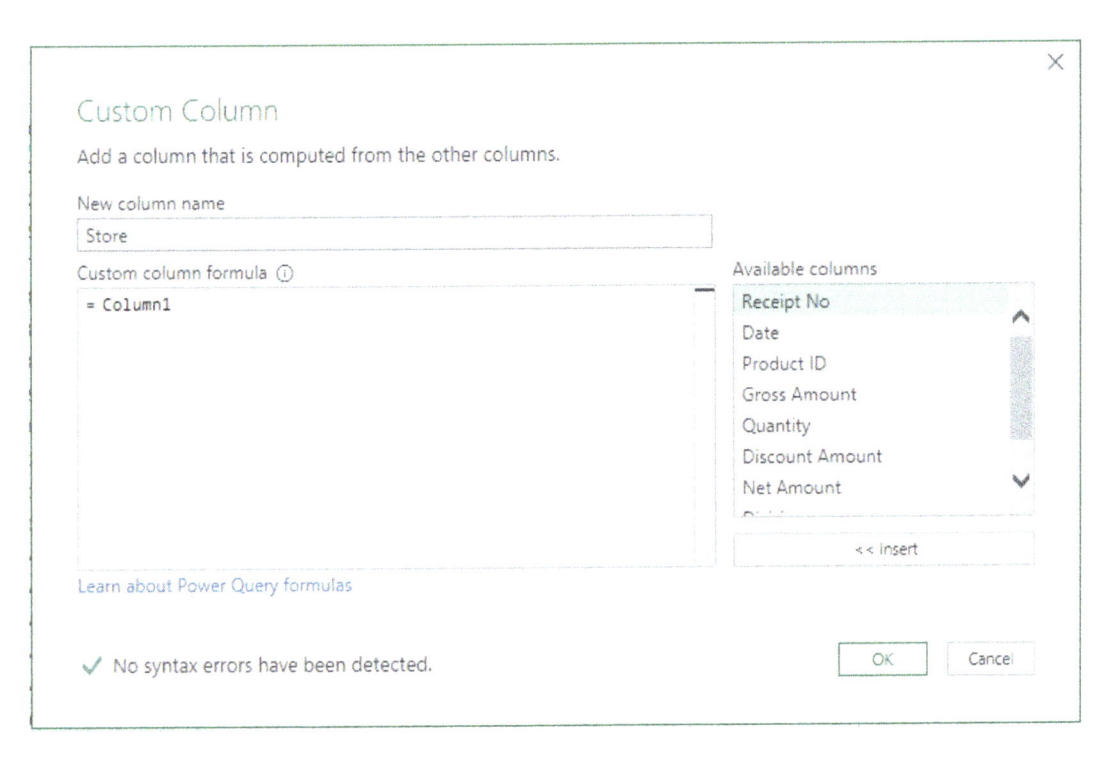

Figure 1-44. Custom column window

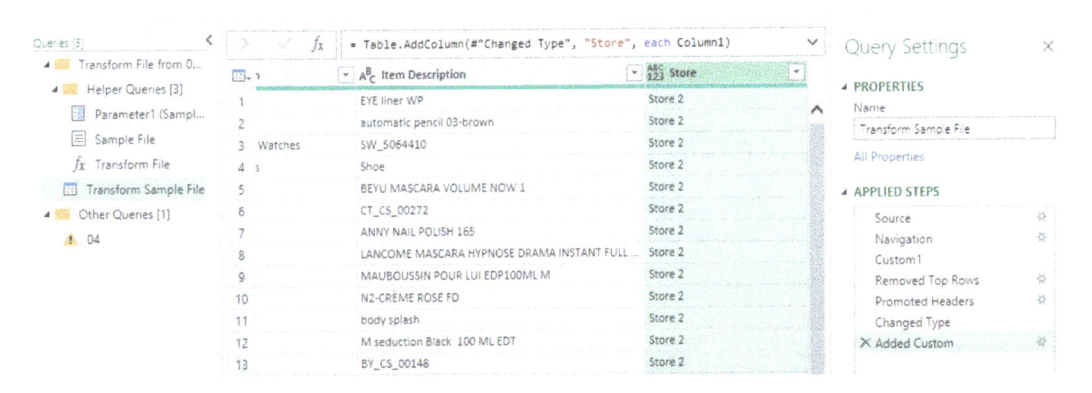

Figure 1-45. Adding a custom column

By following these steps, the result of Query 04 will return an error. To finalize the solution, go to this query and simply remove the last step (Change Type).

CHAPTER 1   DATA EXTRACTION FROM SOURCES

Handling Multi-Row Headers in Excel Tables

The budget/cost data for two different stores of a company over different years is saved in Excel file as the Source table (see Table 1-2). Since you cannot use merged cells in Power Query, combine the first two rows and treat their combination as headers, such as Budget:2019, Budget:2020, Budget:2021, and so on.

Table 1-2. Source Table

Store	Dept	Budget					Actual				
		2019	2020	2021	2022	2023	2019	2020	2021	2022	2023
1	HR	760	387	807	467	193	914	298	1065	505	254
	Sales	156	885	867	949	323	151	1191	1188	1153	270
	Strategic	241	552	130	985	190	296	516	99	1141	177
	Finance	783	168	623	740	815	823	178	519	718	726
	CRM	835	884	355	840	989	686	602	249	738	874
	Marketing	456	611	636	745	871	449	767	534	854	638
2	HR	121	337	273	771	928	89	341	285	494	1031
	Sales	915	630	467	529	277	1361	480	498	511	363
	Strategic	847	865	748	336	786	747	614	769	323	811
	Finance	261	786	979	816	593	313	945	986	453	586
	CRM	647	667	823	310	530	845	525	754	260	667
	Marketing	365	299	601	557	911	314	401	460	699	796

Note   The data in this example is provided in an Excel file titled Budget.xlsx.

To solve this problem, open a blank Excel file, and from the Data tab, in the Get Data section, select From File, then From Excel Workbook (see Figure 1-46). In the open window, navigate to the Excel file (Budget.xlsx), and in the Navigator window, select Sheet 1. Then, click the Transform Data button to load the data into the Power Query Editor, as shown in Figure 1-47.

CHAPTER 1 DATA EXTRACTION FROM SOURCES

Figure 1-46. Navigation Excel file

Figure 1-47. The Power Query Editor

39

CHAPTER 1   DATA EXTRACTION FROM SOURCES

If you follow this process, a query named Sheet1 with four steps—Source, Navigation, Promoted Headers, and Changed Type—will be generated. Remove the last two steps (Promoted Headers and Changed Type) to reach Figure 1-48, where null values are provided for any merged cell. (As in the source table, cells C1:C8 are merged, and the word "Budget" is written in them. If you unmerge the cells, the text "Budget" will remain in cell C1, while the other cells will become blank.)

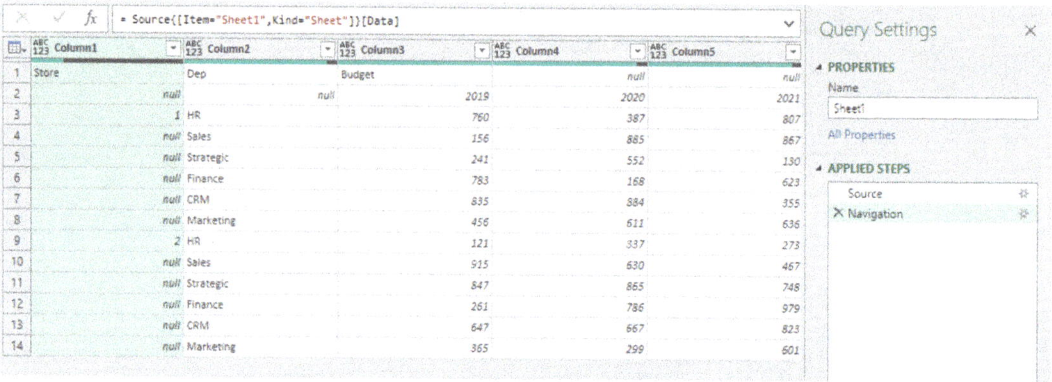

Figure 1-48. Navigation step

To solve the rest of this problem, you need to extract the first two rows and merge them to create the correct column names, which you will then use as the header. While this can be done within the same query, to make the process clearer, you can perform these steps in a separate query. From the query pane, right-click the query name and choose the Duplicate command to copy the query. Rename one of the queries Data and another one Headers. See Figure 1-49.

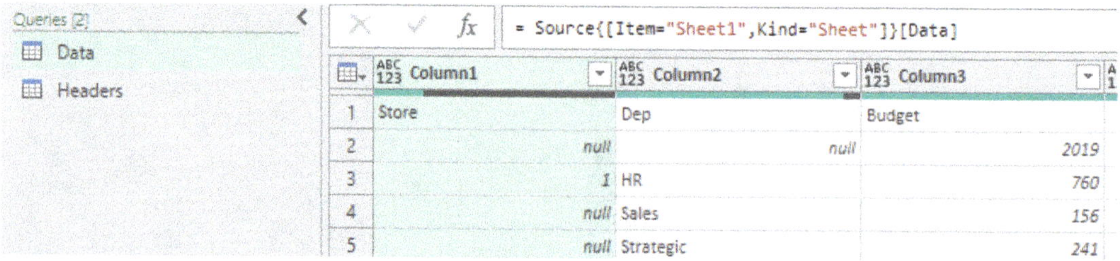

Figure 1-49. Duplicating a query

40

CHAPTER 1 DATA EXTRACTION FROM SOURCES

On the Data query, from the Home tab, in the Reduce Rows section, select the Remove Rows command, then choose the Remove Top Rows option. Then enter 2 in the open window, as shown in Figure 1-50. Click OK to remove the top rows; see Figure 1-51.

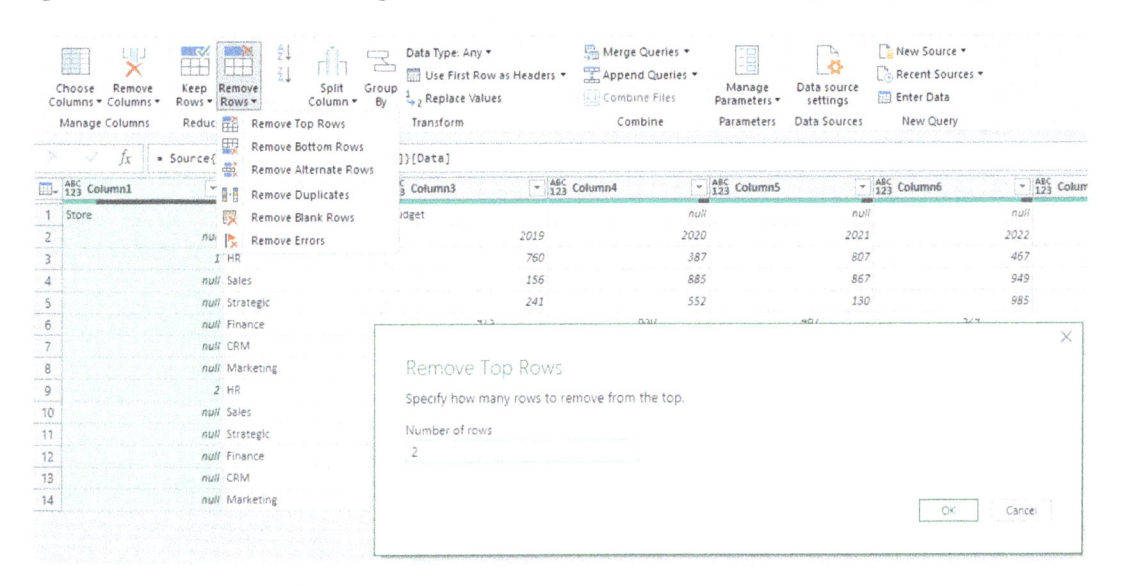

Figure 1-50. Remove top rows

Figure 1-51. The result of removing the top rows

In the Headers query, from the Home tab, in the Reduce Rows section, select Keep Rows and then Keep Top Rows. Enter 2 in the open window, as shown in Figure 1-52. This process results in Figure 1-53.

41

CHAPTER 1   DATA EXTRACTION FROM SOURCES

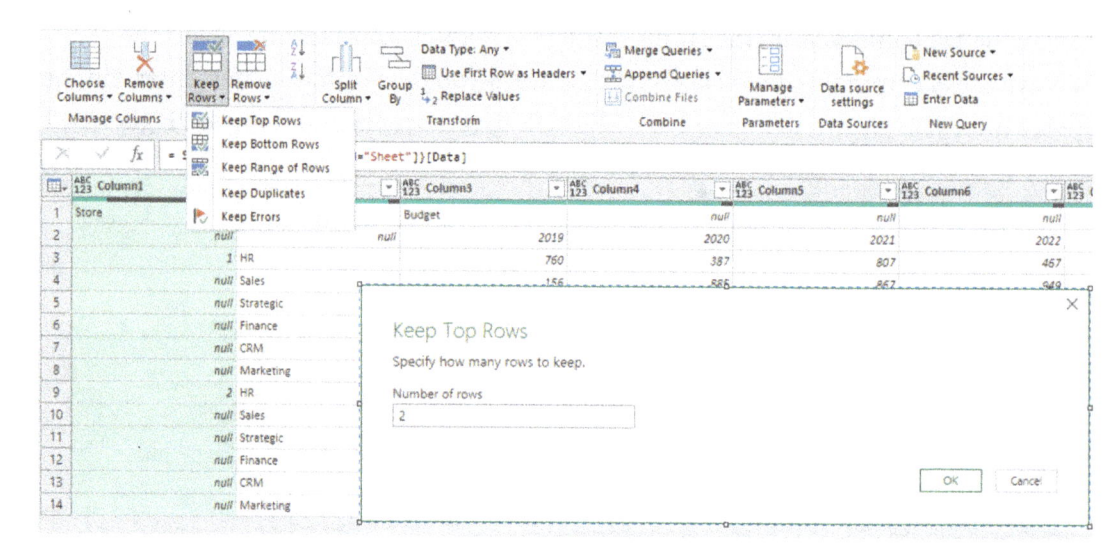

Figure 1-52. Keep the top rows

Figure 1-53. The result of keeping the top rows

Then, in the Headers query, from the Transform tab, select Transpose to achieve the transpose version of the data, as shown in Figure 1-54.

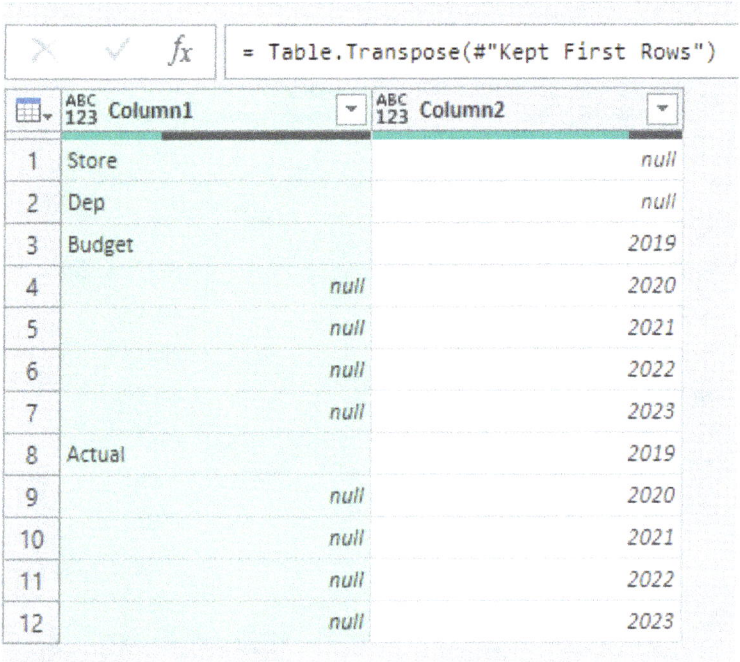

CHAPTER 1   DATA EXTRACTION FROM SOURCES

Figure 1-54. *Transposing the table*

At this step, you need to replace any null values in Column1 with the previous non-null value in this column. Select the Column1 column, and from the Transform tab, choose Fill Down to replace the null cells with the value from the upper cells, resulting in Figure 1-55.

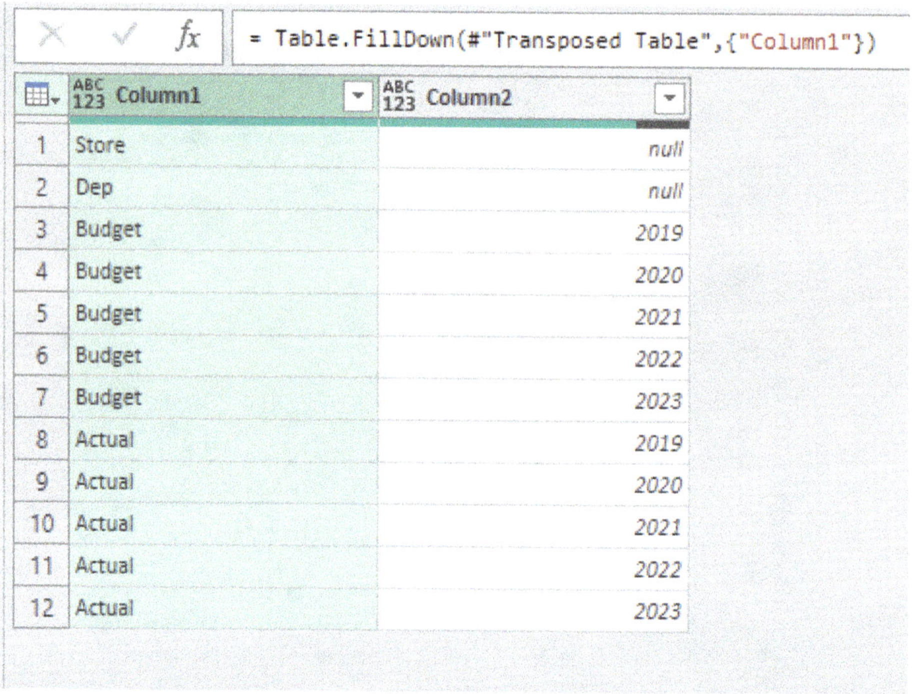

CHAPTER 1   DATA EXTRACTION FROM SOURCES

= Table.FillDown(#"Transposed Table",{"Column1"})

#	Column1	Column2
1	Store	null
2	Dep	null
3	Budget	2019
4	Budget	2020
5	Budget	2021
6	Budget	2022
7	Budget	2023
8	Actual	2019
9	Actual	2020
10	Actual	2021
11	Actual	2022
12	Actual	2023

Figure 1-55. Using Fill Down

Next, select the Column1 column, hold Ctrl, and then select the Column2 column. Right-click one of them, choose Merge Columns, and select Colon as the separator in the open window. Figure 1-56 shows the right column names.

CHAPTER 1   DATA EXTRACTION FROM SOURCES

	Merged
1	Store:
2	Dep:
3	Budget:2019
4	Budget:2020
5	Budget:2021
6	Budget:2022
7	Budget:2023
8	Actual:2019
9	Actual:2020
10	Actual:2021
11	Actual:2022
12	Actual:2023

Figure 1-56. Merging columns

To use this column name, from the Transform tab, select the Transpose command to achieve Figure 1-57.

Figure 1-57. Transposing

By following these steps, two queries—Headers and Data—are created, as shown in Figure 1-58. In the next step, you simply need to combine these two queries by placing one under the other, a process referred to as *appending* in Power Query.

Figure 1-58. The two results tables

45

CHAPTER 1   DATA EXTRACTION FROM SOURCES

In the next step, while the Header query is still selected, from the Home tab, select the Append Queries command. In the open window, choose the Data query as the table to append (see Figure 1-59). Click OK, which results in Figure 1-60.

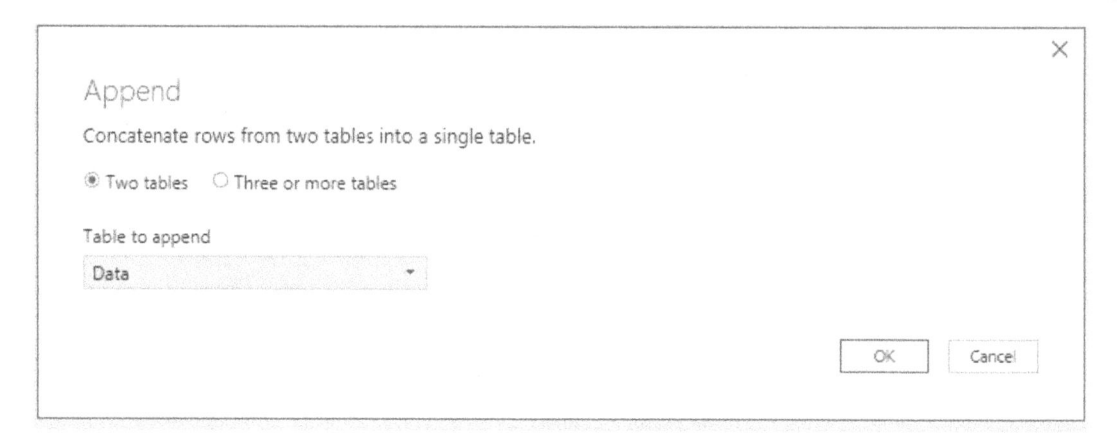

Figure 1-59. Appending queries

Figure 1-60. The result of appending queries

In the final step, from the Transform tab, select the Use First Row as Headers command; see Figure 1-61.

Figure 1-61. The result of using the first row as headers

46

Now that the problem is almost resolved, rename the first two columns, removing the **:** (colon) from the end of their names. Additionally, use the Fill Down command for the Store column to replace null cells with the values from the upper cells.

Note To solve this problem, you initially duplicated the query, extracted the first two rows as headers, and applied several steps to format the column headers appropriately. While it would have been possible to apply all these steps (transposing, filling down, and merging the column) directly to the main query, there isn't a significant difference between the solutions in this example. However, when dealing with large datasets, applying these transformations to the entire dataset is confusing. Therefore, it is better to follow the approach presented here, by separating the first two rows and applying the transformations on them, rather than applying all the steps to the entire dataset.

Loading Data from a Webpage

This example explores how to load data from a webpage. Consider the following URL, which contains information about 10,072 companies, sorted based on their market cap, as shown in Figure 1-62. Each page provides information on 100 companies. Try to load the data for the first 100 largest companies, shown in the first page.

https://companiesmarketcap.com/aud/

CHAPTER 1   DATA EXTRACTION FROM SOURCES

Figure 1-62. Appearance of website

On the first page, information about the first 100 companies is provided, so you only need to load the data from this page. In Excel, go to the Data tab, and in the Get & Transform section, select From Web. Then, paste the URL in the open window, as shown in Figure 1-63.

Figure 1-63. Choosing From Web

Clicking OK will open a new window related to Access Web Content, as shown in Figure 1-64. In this window, click Connect to reach the Navigation window.

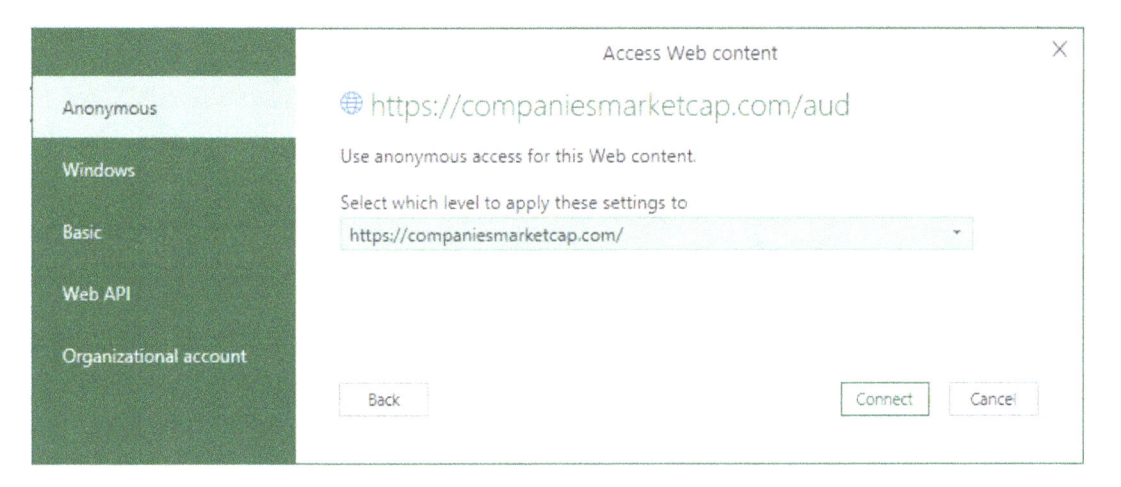

Figure 1-64. *Accessing web content*

Note When loading data from the web, be aware of company-specific limitations on accessing data sources in Anonymous mode. Ensure compliance with data security policies and verify whether authentication is required for the intended source.

Next, in the Navigator window, select your desired table, as shown in Figure 1-65. In this example, it appears that the information shown in Table 5 is appropriate. Select this table and click Load to import the data into Excel.

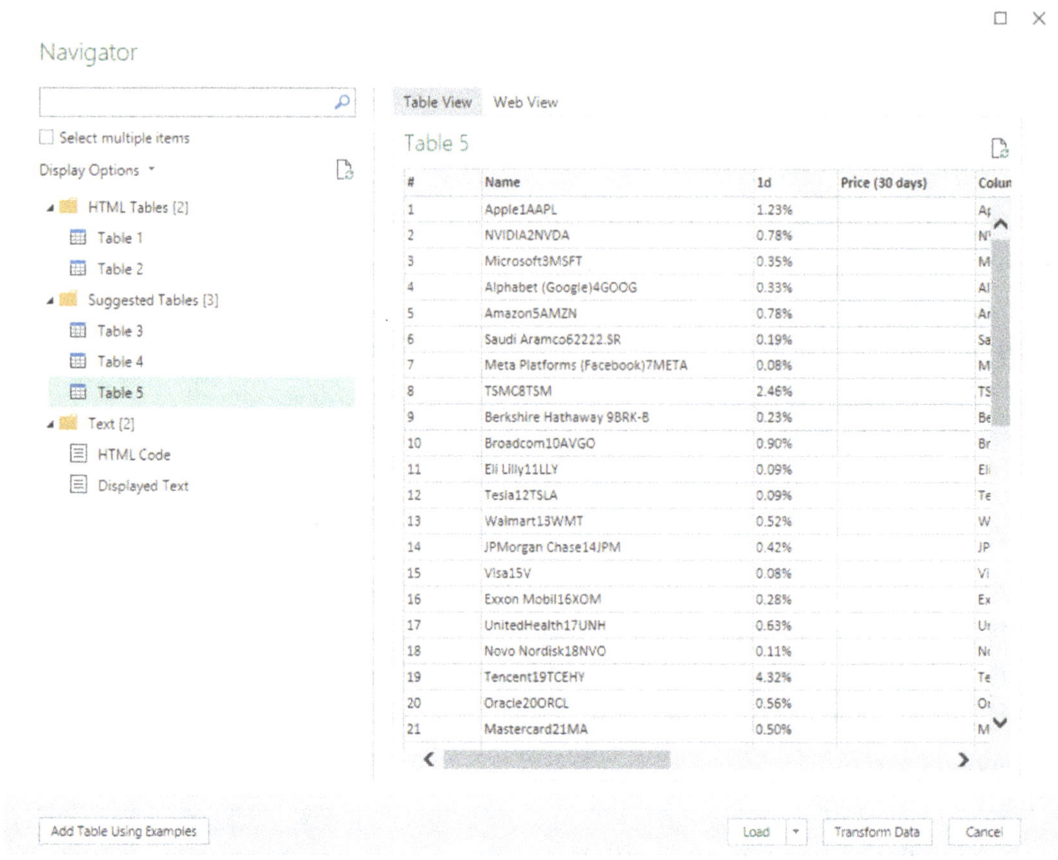

CHAPTER 1   DATA EXTRACTION FROM SOURCES

Figure 1-65. Navigator pane

After loading the data into Excel, it indicates that 101 rows have been loaded, as shown in Figure 1-66. This is due to the last row, which is not required, presenting some different information. To remove this row, right-click the query and select Edit. In the Power Query Editor, go to the Home tab, and in the Reduce Rows section, select Remove Bottom Rows. Enter 1 to remove the last row.

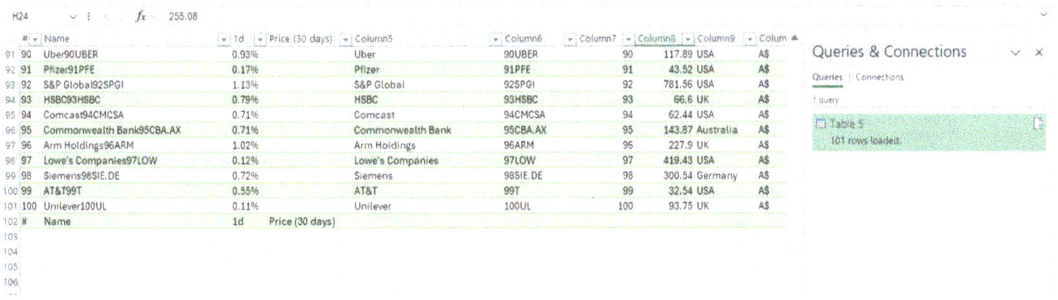

CHAPTER 1 DATA EXTRACTION FROM SOURCES

Figure 1-66. Resultant table

Loading Data from a Webpage, Part 2

Consider the previous example and try to load the information for all the companies listed on the webpage.

Before attempting to load data from all the pages in the provided link, let's first review the code used in the previous example, for loading the information on the first page. To do this, open the final file related to the previous example, go to the Power Query Editor, and from the Home tab, click Advanced Editor to view the complete steps for solving the problem, as shown in Figure 1-67.

```
let
    Source = Web.BrowserContents("https://companiesmarketcap.com/aud/"),
    #"Extracted Table From Html" = Html.Table(Source, {{"Column1", ".d-none"}, {"Column2", ".d-none + *"}, {"Column3",
        ".rh-sm"}, {"Column4", ".rh-sm + *"}, {"Column5", ".company-name"}, {"Column6", ".company-code"}, {"Column7",
        ".rank"}, {"Column8", ".td-right:nth-child(5)"}, {"Column9", ".p-0 + *"}, {"Column10",
        ".currency-symbol-left"}}, [RowSelector=".d-none"]),
    #"Promoted Headers" = Table.PromoteHeaders(#"Extracted Table From Html", [PromoteAllScalars=true]),
    #"Changed Type" = Table.TransformColumnTypes(#"Promoted Headers",{{"#", type text}, {"Name", type text}, {"1d",
        type text}, {"Price (30 days)", type text}, {"Column5", type text}, {"Column6", type text}, {"Column7",
        Int64.Type}, {"Column8", Currency.Type}, {"Column9", type text}, {"Column10", type text}}),
    #"Removed Bottom Rows" = Table.RemoveLastN(#"Changed Type",1)
in
    #"Removed Bottom Rows"
```

Figure 1-67. The Advanced Editor

As presented, the data is extracted in five steps—Source, #"Extracted Table From Html", #"Promoted Headers", #"Changed Type", and #"Removed Bottom Rows". The URL for loading data is defined in the first step. If you change this URL and replace it with the URL of the second page, you can retrieve the data from the second page.

51

CHAPTER 1 DATA EXTRACTION FROM SOURCES

As shown in Figure 1-68, go to your browser, scroll to the end of the table, and click Next 100. The URL will be displayed, as shown in Figure 1-69.

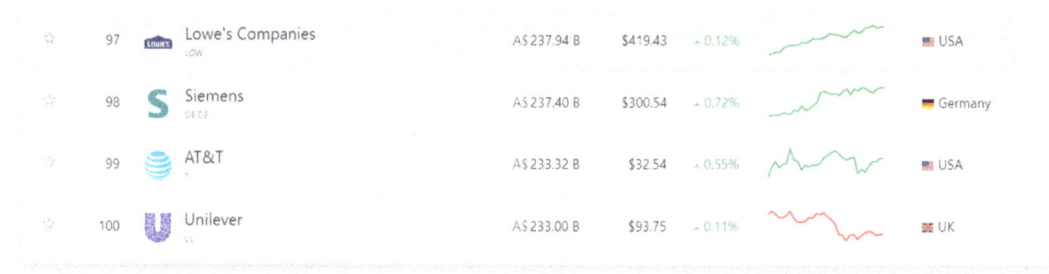

	97	Lowe's Companies LOW	A$ 237.94 B	$419.43	▲ 0.12%		USA
	98	Siemens SIE.DE	A$ 237.40 B	$300.54	▲ 0.72%		Germany
	99	AT&T	A$ 233.32 B	$32.54	▲ 0.55%		USA
	100	Unilever UL	A$ 233.00 B	$93.75	▲ 0.11%		UK

This is the list of the world's biggest companies by market capitalization. It ranks the most valuable public companies. Private companies are not included in our lists as it is difficult to calculate their market value and know their financials.

Next 100 >

Figure 1-68. *Going to the next page*

companiesmarketcap.com/aud/page/2/

Figure 1-69. *The URL for the second page*

Copy this URL and use it instead of the previous URL in Advance Editor, This will update the result of the query and will show the information related to the next page. So, in the advanced editor by replacing the URL with the URL of any page, you can retrieve the data from that specific page. Based on this, you can convert the query into a function that accepts an URL for a page of the website. The function will apply all five steps—Source, #"Extracted Table From Html", #"Promoted Headers", #"Changed Type", and #"Removed Bottom Rows"—to extract and return the company information from that page.

Converting this query into a function is an easy step. Simply go to the Advanced Editor, add (URL) => at the beginning of the query, and replace the used URL with the variable URL, as shown in Figure 1-70. Then, click OK to create the function. Rename this query `LoadTopCompanies`. The result is shown in Figure 1-71.

CHAPTER 1   DATA EXTRACTION FROM SOURCES

```
1   (URL)=>
2
3   let
4       Source = Web.BrowserContents(URL),
5       #"Extracted Table From Html" = Html.Table(Source, {{"Column1", ".d-none"}, {"Column2", ".d-none + *"},
            {"Column3", ".rh-sm"}, {"Column4", ".rh-sm + *"}, {"Column5", ".company-name"}, {"Column6",
            ".company-code"}, {"Column7", ".rank"}, {"Column8", ".td-right:nth-child(5)"}, {"Column9", ".p-0 + *"},
            {"Column10", ".currency-symbol-left"}}, [RowSelector=".d-none"]),
6       #"Promoted Headers" = Table.PromoteHeaders(#"Extracted Table From Html", [PromoteAllScalars=true]),
7       #"Changed Type" = Table.TransformColumnTypes(#"Promoted Headers",{{"#", type text}, {"Name", type text},
            {"1d", type text}, {"Price (30 days)", type text}, {"Column5", type text}, {"Column6", type text},
            {"Column7", Int64.Type}, {"Column8", Currency.Type}, {"Column9", type text}, {"Column10", type text}}),
8       #"Removed Bottom Rows" = Table.RemoveLastN(#"Changed Type",1)
9   in
10      #"Removed Bottom Rows"
```

✓ No syntax errors have been detected.

Figure 1-70. Converting the query to a function

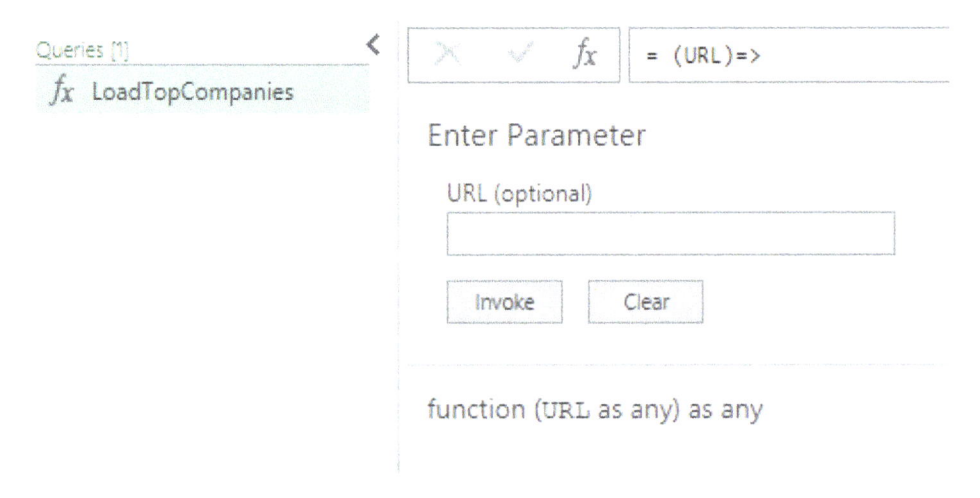

Figure 1-71. Result of the function

In this function, if you put the URL of any page as its input and click Invoke, the information of that page will be extracted. Based on this, you need to create the list of URLs and then use this function for any URL.

As presented, the URLs (even for the first page) are in the `https://companies marketcap.com/aud/page/2/` format, where the page number is specified at the end.

53

CHAPTER 1   DATA EXTRACTION FROM SOURCES

To start, let's assume the number of pages is known and predefined as 10. So, the List.Transform() function can used to create the URL for the first ten pages using the following formula, which generates the links for the first ten pages, as shown in Figure 1-72.

```
= List.Transform({1..10}, each "https://companiesmarketcap.com/aud/page/" & 
Text.From(_)&"/")
```

	List
1	https://companiesmarketcap.com/aud/page/1/
2	https://companiesmarketcap.com/aud/page/2/
3	https://companiesmarketcap.com/aud/page/3/
4	https://companiesmarketcap.com/aud/page/4/
5	https://companiesmarketcap.com/aud/page/5/
6	https://companiesmarketcap.com/aud/page/6/
7	https://companiesmarketcap.com/aud/page/7/
8	https://companiesmarketcap.com/aud/page/8/
9	https://companiesmarketcap.com/aud/page/9/
10	https://companiesmarketcap.com/aud/page/10/

Figure 1-72. *Result of List.Transform*

Note   List.Transform() is a powerful function in Power Query that takes two inputs: the first is a list, and the second is the transformation function.

For example, the =List.Transform({1,2}, each _ * 10) formula means that for each item in the main list {1, 2}, represented by _, it multiplies the item by 10. So, the result will be {10, 20}.

Additionally, the =List.Transform({1,2}, each "X" & Text.From(_)) formula works as follows: for each item in the list {1, 2}, it first converts the item into text using Text.From(_), then concatenates "X" to the item. The result is {"X1", "X2"}.

CHAPTER 1　DATA EXTRACTION FROM SOURCES

Simultaneously, you can apply the LoadTopCompanies() function over the generated URLs, by rewriting the previous formula as shown here (this results in the table in Figure 1-73):

```
= List.Transform({1..10}, each LoadTopCompanies("https://
companiesmarketcap.com/aud/page/" & Text.From(_)&"/"))
```

	Name	Id	Price (30 days)	Column5	Column6	Column7	Column8	Column9	Column10
501	Nordea Bank501NDA-FI.HE	0.32%		Nordea Bank	501NDA-FI.HE	501	17.92	Finland	AS
502	Vertiv Holdings 502VRT	1.78%		Vertiv Holdings	502VRT	502	167.05	USA	AS
503	Emirates Telecom (Etisalat Group)503EAND.AE	0.91%		Emirates Telecom (Etisalat Group)	503EAND.AE	503	7.16	UAE	AS
504	ENGIE504ENGI.PA	0.59%		ENGIE	504ENGI.PA	504	25.77	France	AS
505	GE HealthCare Technologies505GEHC	0.61%		GE HealthCare Technologies	505GEHC	505	135.93	USA	AS
506	Kenvue506KVUE	1.26%		Kenvue	506KVUE	506	32.32	USA	AS
507	UOB507U11.SI	0.12%		UOB	507U11.SI	507	37.00	Singapore	AS

Figure 1-73. *Using a custom function in List.Transform*

Now, to finalize, go to the Transform tab, select the To Table command, and then click the Expand icon next to the column to extract the information from the first 10 pages into a table, as shown in Figure 1-74.

CHAPTER 1   DATA EXTRACTION FROM SOURCES

#	Name	Id	Price (30 days)	Column5	Column6	Column7
1	Apple1AAPL	1.23%		Apple	1AAPL	1
2	NVIDIA2NVDA	0.78%		NVIDIA	2NVDA	2
3	Microsoft3MSFT	0.35%		Microsoft	3MSFT	3
4	Alphabet (Google)4GOOG	0.33%		Alphabet (Google)	4GOOG	4
5	Amazon5AMZN	0.78%		Amazon	5AMZN	5
6	Saudi Aramco62222.SR	0.19%		Saudi Aramco	62222.SR	6
7	Meta Platforms (Facebook)7META	0.08%		Meta Platforms (Facebook)	7META	7
8	TSMC8TSM	2.46%		TSMC	8TSM	8
9	Berkshire Hathaway 9BRK-B	0.23%		Berkshire Hathaway	9BRK-B	9
10	Broadcom10AVGO	0.90%		Broadcom	10AVGO	10
11	Eli Lilly11LLY	0.09%		Eli Lilly	11LLY	11
12	Tesla12TSLA	0.09%		Tesla	12TSLA	12
13	Walmart13WMT	0.52%		Walmart	13WMT	13
14	JPMorgan Chase14JPM	0.42%		JPMorgan Chase	14JPM	14
15	Visa15V	0.08%		Visa	15V	15
16	Exxon Mobil16XOM	0.28%		Exxon Mobil	16XOM	16
17	UnitedHealth17UNH	0.63%		UnitedHealth	17UNH	17
18	Novo Nordisk18NVO	0.11%		Novo Nordisk	18NVO	18
19	Tencent19TCEHY	4.32%		Tencent	19TCEHY	19
20	Oracle20ORCL	0.56%		Oracle	20ORCL	20
21	Mastercard21MA	0.50%		Mastercard	21MA	21
22	Home Depot22HD	0.14%		Home Depot	22HD	22
23	Procter & Gamble23PG	0.00%		Procter & Gamble	23PG	23
24	Johnson & Johnson24JNJ	0.40%		Johnson & Johnson	24JNJ	24

Figure 1-74. Resultand table

The previous step was enough to extract the info from the pages if the number of pages are predefined. But if you do not know the total number of pages in the URL, it's better to start from the first page, and then continue the process of loading data page by page until you reach the last page (a page without a table). To accomplish this, you can use the List.Generate() function as follows.

```
= List.Generate(
    ()=>[page=1, t=LoadTopCompanies("https://companiesmarketcap.com/aud/
    page/" & Text.From(page)&"/")],
    each not Table.IsEmpty([t]) ,
    each [page=_[page]+1, t=LoadTopCompanies("https://companiesmarketcap.
    com/aud/page/" & Text.From(page)&"/")] ,
    each _[t])
```

Note   The List.Generate function is an advanced function and is covered in Chapter 9. If you find this formula challenging, feel free to skip it for now. After reading Chapter 9, come back and review it.

CHAPTER 1   DATA EXTRACTION FROM SOURCES

In this formula, a loop is created by the List.Generate() function. In each iteration of List.Generate(), a record containing the fields page, which represents the page numbers in the URL, and t, which contains the information about the companies on that page, will be created. Initially, the page is set to 1, and t includes the information from the first page (https://companiesmarketcap.com/aud/page/1/).

As the process continues, the page value is updated to 2, and t reflects the information from the second page. This continues until the condition in the second argument of List.Generate() evaluates to false, indicating that you have encountered an empty table. In other words, the process continues until t becomes a blank table.

The result of this formula is a list containing 101 items, with each item representing a table that includes the company information for a specific page of the website, as shown in Figure 1-75.

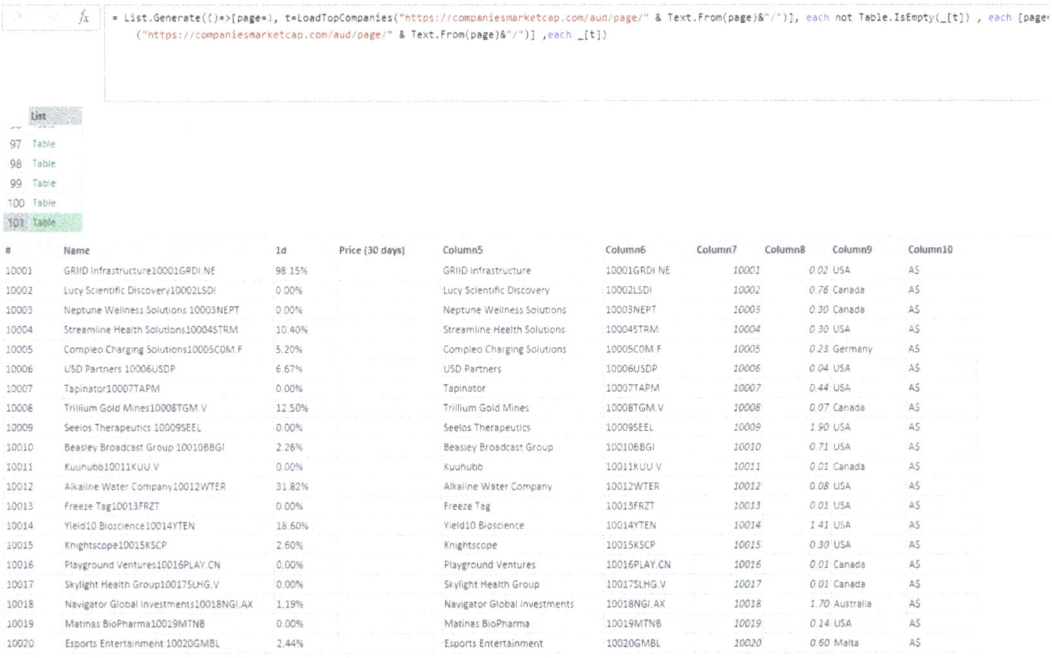

Figure 1-75. Result of List.Generate

To combine the tables in the resulting list, go to the Transform tab, select the To Table command, and then click the Expand icon next to the column to extract the information from all the pages into a table, as shown in Figure 1-76.

57

CHAPTER 1   DATA EXTRACTION FROM SOURCES

Figure 1-76. Result of all the companies

Loading Tables from an Excel File

Consider an Excel file that contains three tables (with the potential for additional tables in the future), each in one sheet, as shown in Figure 1-77, and each containing sales information for different years. Load all these tables into Power Query and stack them vertically.

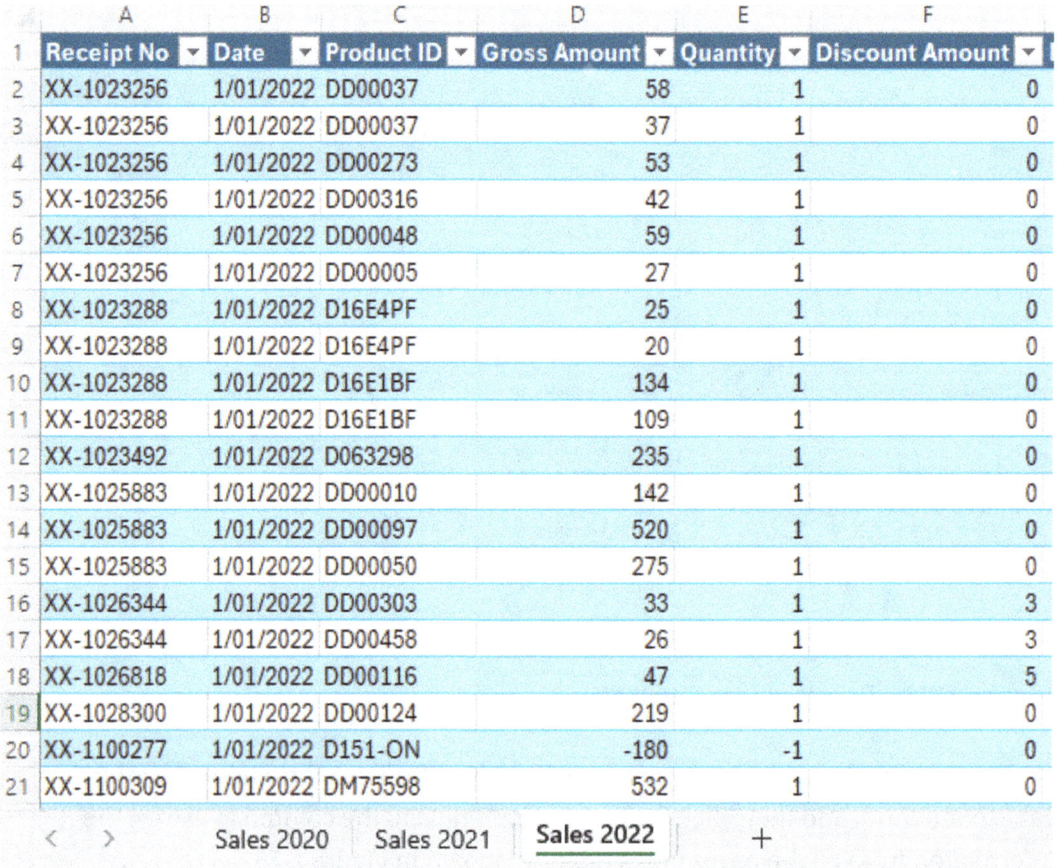

Receipt No	Date	Product ID	Gross Amount	Quantity	Discount Amount
XX-1023256	1/01/2022	DD00037	58	1	0
XX-1023256	1/01/2022	DD00037	37	1	0
XX-1023256	1/01/2022	DD00273	53	1	0
XX-1023256	1/01/2022	DD00316	42	1	0
XX-1023256	1/01/2022	DD00048	59	1	0
XX-1023256	1/01/2022	DD00005	27	1	0
XX-1023288	1/01/2022	D16E4PF	25	1	0
XX-1023288	1/01/2022	D16E4PF	20	1	0
XX-1023288	1/01/2022	D16E1BF	134	1	0
XX-1023288	1/01/2022	D16E1BF	109	1	0
XX-1023492	1/01/2022	D063298	235	1	0
XX-1025883	1/01/2022	DD00010	142	1	0
XX-1025883	1/01/2022	DD00097	520	1	0
XX-1025883	1/01/2022	DD00050	275	1	0
XX-1026344	1/01/2022	DD00303	33	1	3
XX-1026344	1/01/2022	DD00458	26	1	3
XX-1026818	1/01/2022	DD00116	47	1	5
XX-1028300	1/01/2022	DD00124	219	1	0
XX-1100277	1/01/2022	D151-ON	-180	-1	0
XX-1100309	1/01/2022	DM75598	532	1	0

Sales 2020   Sales 2021   **Sales 2022**

Figure 1-77. An Excel file including three sheets

58

CHAPTER 1   DATA EXTRACTION FROM SOURCES

Note   The data in this example is provided in an Excel file titled `08 Excel.CurrentWorkbook.Xlsx`.

A useful function in the Excel version of Power Query is the `Excel.CurrentWorkbook()` function, which can help load all the tables in a workbook. The syntax of this function is as follows (this function comes with no argument):

`Excel.CurrentWorkbook() as table`

To solve this problem, go to the Power Query Editor by pressing Alt+F12 and create a blank query (it is named Query1). Click fx next to the formula bar to add a new step and enter the =Excel.CurrentWorkbook() formula in the formula bar. This will load all tables and named ranges from the Excel file into the Power Query Editor, as shown in Figure 1-78.

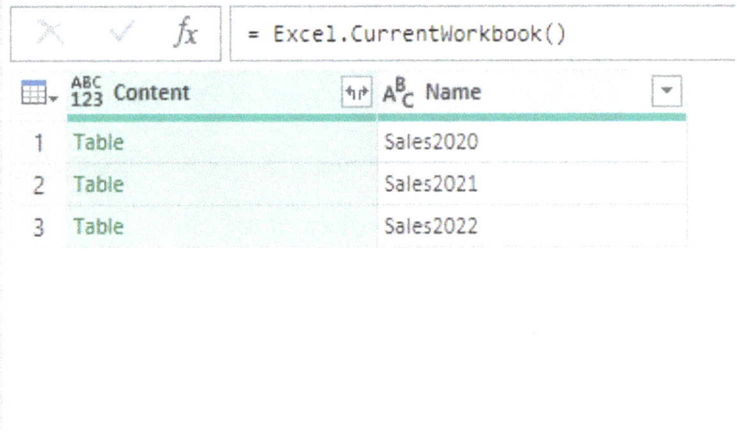

	Content	Name
1	Table	Sales2020
2	Table	Sales2021
3	Table	Sales2022

Figure 1-78. *Result of Excel.CurrentWorkbook()*

By expanding the Content column, you can combine all the tables. After this step, use Close & Load to load the resulting table into Excel, as shown in Figure 1-79, which includes 66121 rows.

CHAPTER 1   DATA EXTRACTION FROM SOURCES

Figure 1-79. Loading the result in Excel

While it may seem like the problem is resolved at this point, right-clicking the resulting table and selecting Refresh will reveal that new rows are added to the result table, and with the next refresh, the number of rows will increase to 132241 rows, as shown in Figure 1-80.

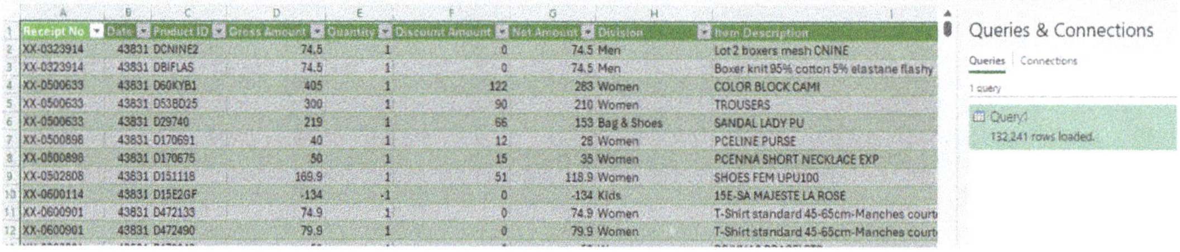

Figure 1-80. Increasing the row number by each refresh

To investigate the cause of this issue, let's edit the query and check the first step. You do this by right-clicking the query name and selecting Edit Query. If you select the first step in the Applied Step section, shown in Figure 1-81, you'll see that four tables are now loaded into the query, while at the time of creating the query, it initially included only three tables. It appears that the result of the query is also included in the list of tables and considered as the input of itself. Consequently, each Refresh adds all the data from the result query to the rows of the other tables, causing the problem.

CHAPTER 1   DATA EXTRACTION FROM SOURCES

	Content	Name
1	Table	Sales2020
2	Table	Sales2021
3	Table	Query1
4	Table	Sales2022

Figure 1-81. Four tables in the query

To resolve this issue and solve the problem, simply filter the table names to exclude the table associated with the query, as shown in Figure 1-82. In the filtering step, you can also exclude other tables that you do not want to include in the result table.

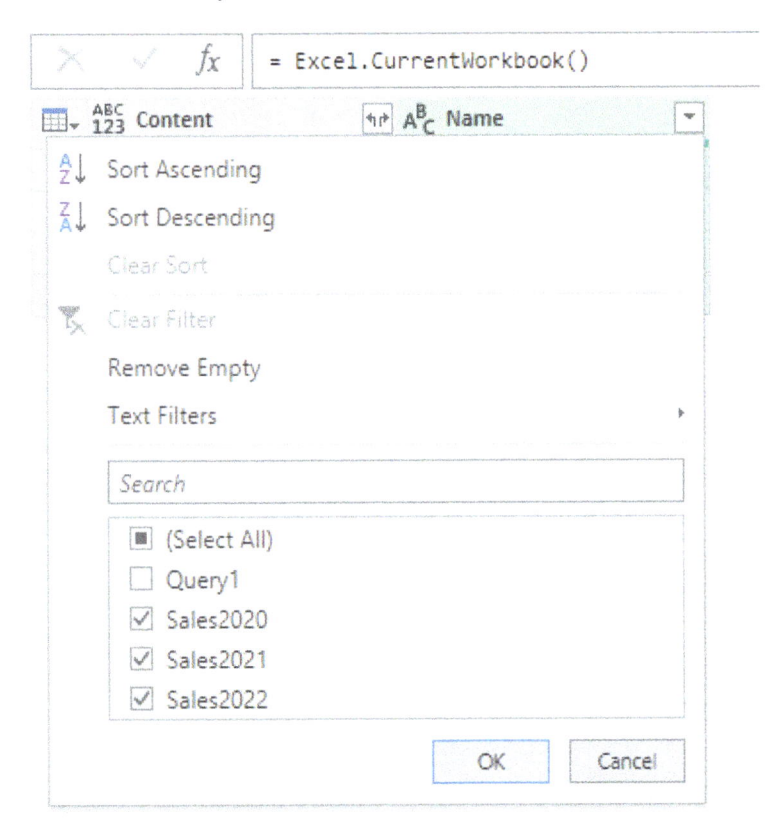

Figure 1-82. Filtering the query result table

61

CHAPTER 1 DATA EXTRACTION FROM SOURCES

Manually Adding Columns to the Query

Consider the task assignments table shown in Figure 1-83, which is imported from a CSV file into an Excel file using the Load From CSV query. In the Excel worksheet, an additional column is manually added (highlighted in yellow) to write comments about the tasks. However, when the query is refreshed, the order of the task rows in Power Query may change, causing a mismatch between the tasks and the comments. How can this issue be resolved?

Task Name	Assigned To	Deadline	Priority	Comment
Task 1	John Doe	1/10/2025	High	
Task 2	Jane Smith	1/10/2030	Medium	Out of Budget
Task 3	Alice Johnson	1/11/2005	Low	
Task 4	Mark Wilson	1/11/2010	High	
Task 5	Emily Davis	1/11/2015	Medium	

Figure 1-83. *Combination of Query and Excel column*

Note The data in this example is provided in an Excel file titled `09 Manually adding column into the Query.CSV`.

In this example, if a new task is added to the top of the CSV file and the query is refreshed, the row order in the Power Query will change, as shown in Figure 1-84. However, the order of the comments remains unchanged, as this column is not linked to the query columns. As a result, the comments no longer correspond to the original tasks.

Task Name	Assigned To	Deadline	Priority	Comment
Task 6	Omid	1/10/2026	High	
Task 1	John Doe	1/10/2025	High	Out of Budget
Task 2	Jane Smith	1/10/2030	Medium	
Task 3	Alice Johnson	1/11/2005	Low	
Task 4	Mark Wilson	1/11/2010	High	
Task 5	Emily Davis	1/11/2015	Medium	

Figure 1-84. *Result of adding a new task in the CSV file*

CHAPTER 1　DATA EXTRACTION FROM SOURCES

Before starting to solve this problem, it is worth mentioning that, since the result of the query is saved as a table in Excel when a comment column is added, it becomes part of that table. So you have a table with some columns that came from the query and others that came from Excel.

To solve this problem, you need to link each comment to its corresponding task. This requires loading the latest version of the Excel table with comments into Power Query, as well as the most recent list of tasks from the CSV files. Then, you will transfer the comments from the first query to the second query based on the Task Name.

In Excel, select the entire table (including both the query result and the comment column) and load it into Power Query by going to the Data tab and choosing From Table/Range in the Get & Transform Data section. Name this query `QueryPlusComment`. At this point, as shown in Figure 1-85, the Power Query Editor contains two queries, one for loading tasks from the CSV file (Load From CSV) and one for loading the table from Excel, including the result of the previous query and the Comment column.

Queries	#	Task Name	Assigned To	Deadline	Priority
Load From CSV	1	Task 1	John Doe	1/10/2025	High
QueryPlusComment	2	Task 2	Jane Smith	1/10/2030	Medium
	3	Task 3	Alice Johnson	1/11/2005	Low
	4	Task 4	Mark Wilson	1/11/2010	High
	5	Task 5	Emily Davis	1/11/2015	Medium

Figure 1-85. *Loading data in Power Query*

After loading both queries, you need to combine them. Select the Load From CSV query, and from the Home tab, select the Merge Queries command (this command is fully explained in Chapter 7). Make the setting provided in Figure 1-86. (In the Merge settings, choose the Task Name column from both queries and set the join kind to Inner Join.)

CHAPTER 1   DATA EXTRACTION FROM SOURCES

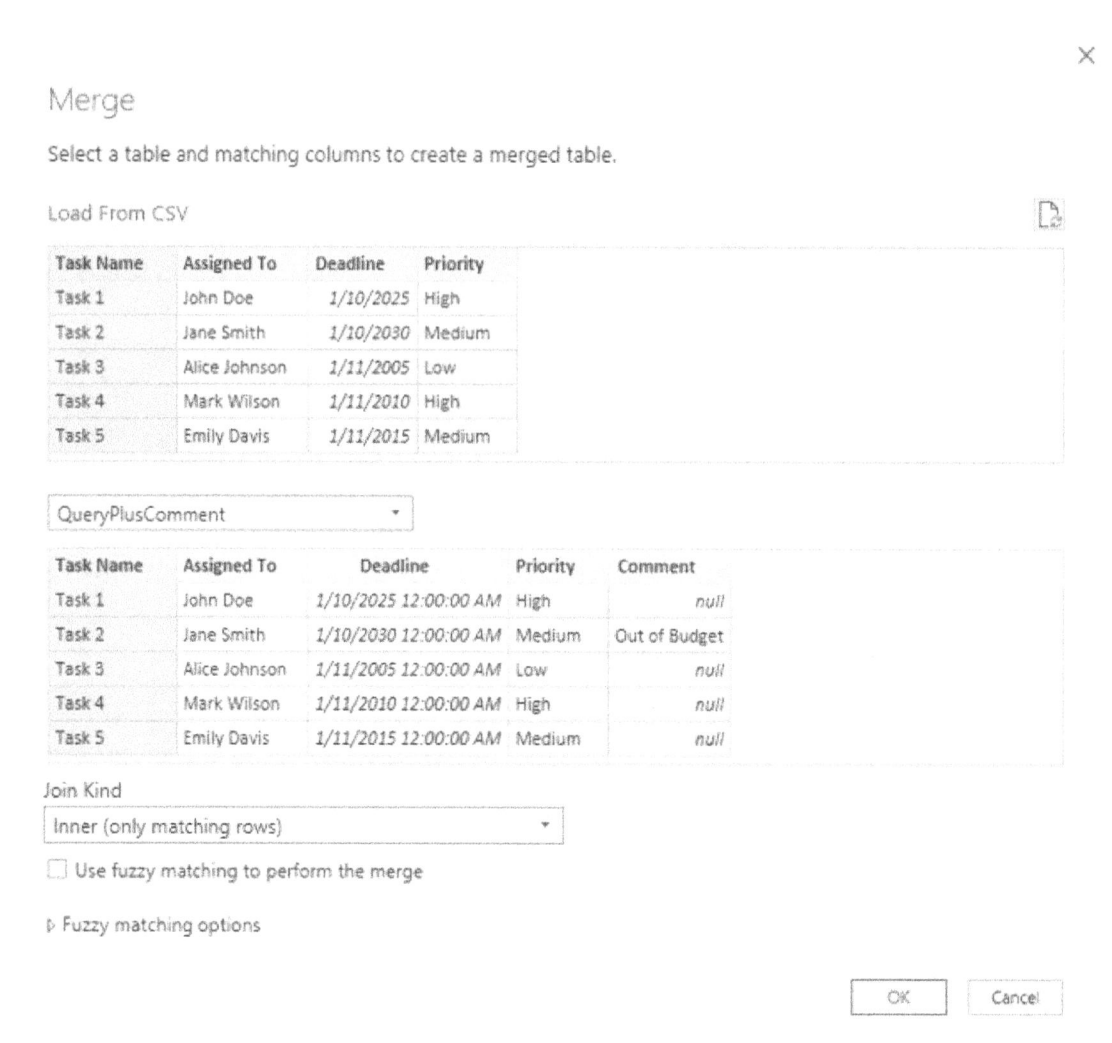

Figure 1-86.   Merging tables

Note   In the previous step, Task Name was selected as the common column between the tables. In this case, this column must contain unique values, without any duplicates.

After the previous step, you may encounter a Privacy Level message. If this happens, simply confirm it. Next, expand the newly added column, as shown in Figure 1-87, and click OK to proceed to Figure 1-88.

CHAPTER 1   DATA EXTRACTION FROM SOURCES

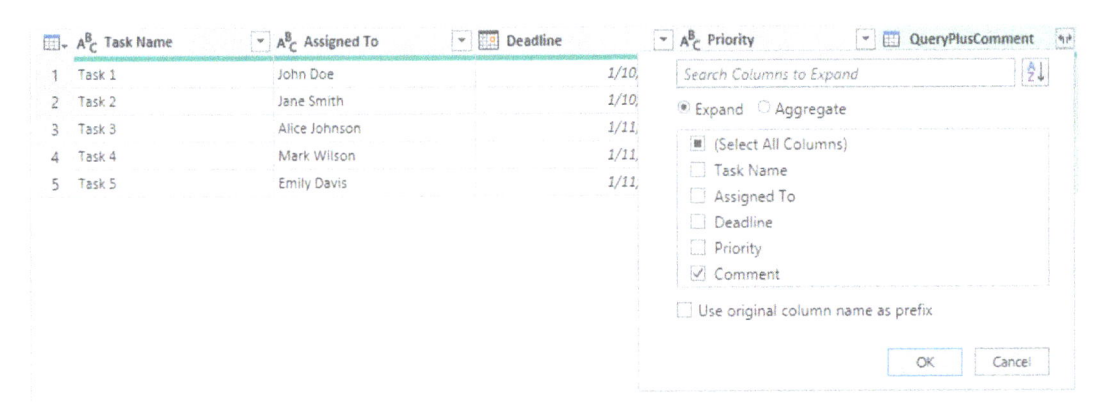

Figure 1-87. *Setting for expanding the comment column*

Figure 1-88. *Expanding the comment column*

At this step, from the Close & Load dropdown, select Close & Load To. In the open window, choose Only Create Connection, as shown in Figure 1-89.

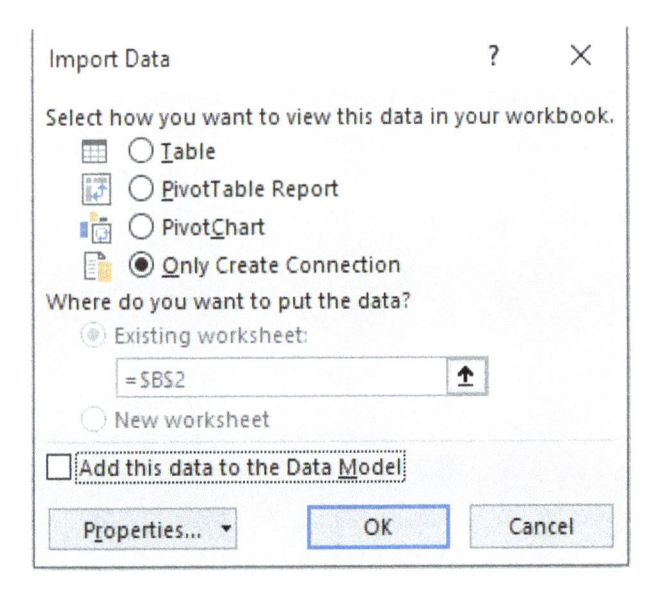

Figure 1-89. *Loading as a connected table*

65

CHAPTER 1 DATA EXTRACTION FROM SOURCES

After you do this, the table in Figure 1-90 will appear with the Comment column, which is integrated as part of the query, and another column called Comment2 (showing the columns that were added manually).

Task Name	Assigned To	Deadline	Priority	Comment	Comment2
Task 1	John Doe	1/10/2025	High		
Task 2	Jane Smith	1/10/2030	Medium	Out of Budget	Out of Budget
Task 3	Alice Johnson	1/11/2005	Low		
Task 4	Mark Wilson	1/11/2010	High		
Task 5	Emily Davis	1/11/2015	Medium		

Figure 1-90. Result of the loaded table

The problem is solved. You can now remove the Comment2 column and add your comments in the Comment column, as shown in Figure 1-91.

Task Name	Assigned To	Deadline	Priority	Comment
Task 1	John Doe	1/10/2025	High	
Task 2	Jane Smith	1/10/2030	Medium	Out of Budget
Task 3	Alice Johnson	1/11/2005	Low	In Progress
Task 4	Mark Wilson	1/11/2010	High	
Task 5	Emily Davis	1/11/2015	Medium	Behind the Schedule

Figure 1-91. Adding new comments

By adding new tasks to the CSV file, rearranging the previous tasks, and refreshing the query, you will see that the comments are correctly aligned with their respective tasks; see Figure 1-92.

CHAPTER 1　DATA EXTRACTION FROM SOURCES

Load From CSV

Task Name	Assigned To	Deadline	Priority	Comment
Task 6	Omid	1/10/2026	High	
Task 1	John Doe	1/10/2025	High	
Task 4	Mark Wilson	1/11/2010	High	
Task 3	Alice Johnson	1/11/2005	Low	In Progress
Task 7	Omid	1/10/2026	Low	
Task 8	Omid	1/10/2026	Medium	
Task 2	Jane Smith	1/10/2030	Medium	Out of Budget
Task 5	Emily Davis	1/11/2015	Medium	Behind the Schedule

Figure 1-92. Result of refreshing the query after adding some tasks

Using a Data Load Tracker (Log)

Extract the price of gold from the GoldPrice.org website. Ensure that each time the data is refreshed, the historical data is preserved.

Note The idea of this solution came from the TheBICCOUNTANT website, written by Microsoft MVP Imke Feldmann: https://www.thebiccountant.com/2016/02/09/how-to-create-a-load-history-or-load-log-in-power-query-or-power-bi/.

To extract the price of gold from the GoldPrice.org website, in Excel, go to the Data tab and select Get Data. Then, choose From Other Sources and From Web. Then, enter the URL of the gold price page in the URL box, as shown in Figure 1-93. Click OK to access the data shown in Figure 1-94.

CHAPTER 1   DATA EXTRACTION FROM SOURCES

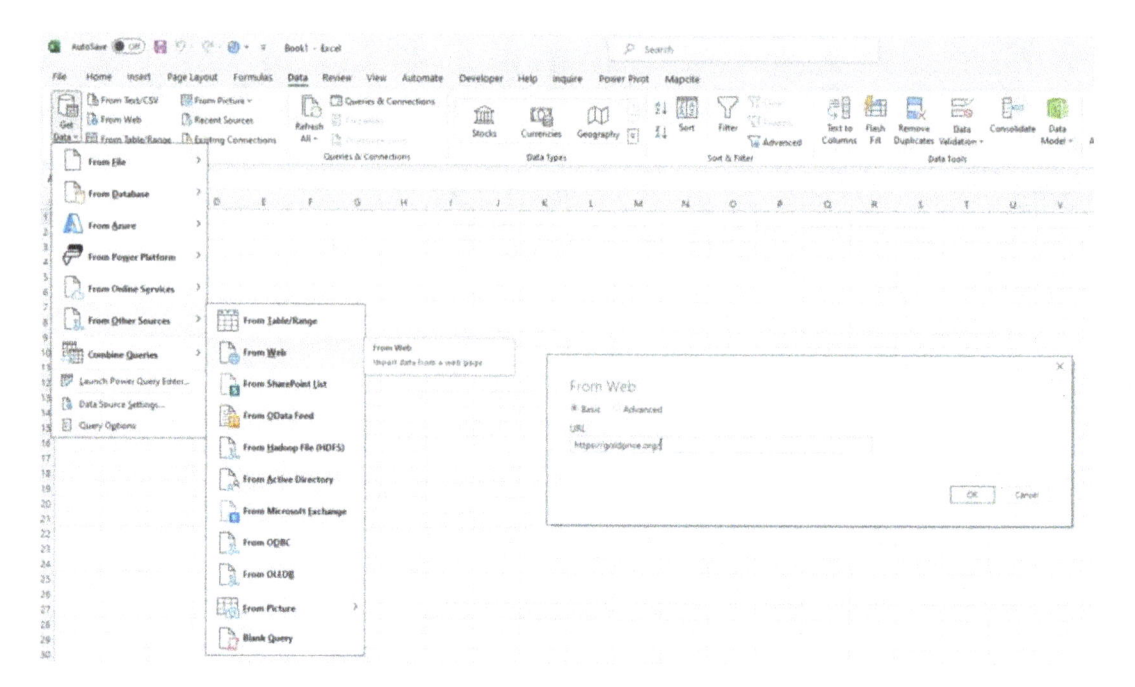

Figure 1-93. Using From Web

CHAPTER 1 DATA EXTRACTION FROM SOURCES

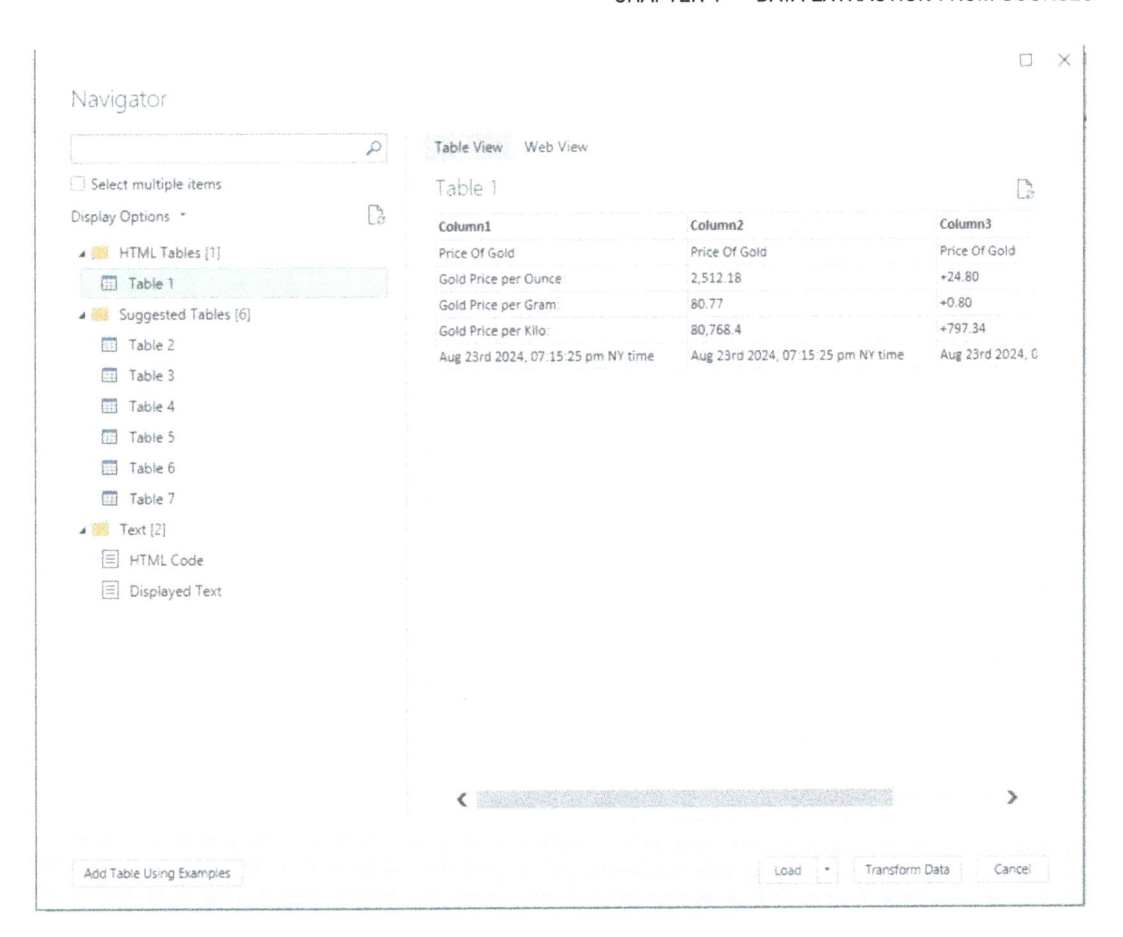

Figure 1-94. The Navigator pane

In the Navigator pane, select Table 1 (which includes the desired info) and click Transform Data to load the data into the Power Query Editor. This will initiate the steps: Source, Extracted Table From HTML, and Change Type.

Out of all the provided data, you are searching for the values of Gold Price per Ounce, Gold Price per Gram, and Gold Price per Kilo in different columns, as well as the date and time of collecting the data. To extract the desired info, in the Power Query Editor, go to the Transform tab and select Transpose. This rearranges the table, as shown in Figure 1-95.

CHAPTER 1 DATA EXTRACTION FROM SOURCES

	Column1	Column2	Column3	Column4	Column5
1	Price Of Gold	Gold Price per Ounce:	Gold Price per Gram:	Gold Price per Kilo:	Aug 23rd 2024, 07:15:25 pm NY time
2	Price Of Gold	2,512.18	80.77	80,768.4	Aug 23rd 2024, 07:15:25 pm NY time
3	Price Of Gold	+24.80	+0.80	+797.34	Aug 23rd 2024, 07:15:25 pm NY time

Figure 1-95. Transposed table

Remove Column1 and Column5, and from the Transform tab, choose the Use First Row as Headers command to set the first row as the headers, resulting in Figure 1-96.

1.2 Gold Price per Ounce:	1.2 Gold Price per Gram:	1.2 Gold Price per Kilo:
1	2512.18	80.77	80768.4
2	24.8	0.8	797.34

Figure 1-96. The result of promoting the headers

To remove the unnecessary second row, go to the Home tab, select Keep Rows, then Keep Top Rows, and enter 1 in the empty box. This will result in Figure 1-97.

`= Table.FirstN(#"Changed Type1",1)`

1.2 Gold Price per Ounce:	1.2 Gold Price per Gram:	1.2 Gold Price per Kilo:
1	2512.18	80.77	80768.4

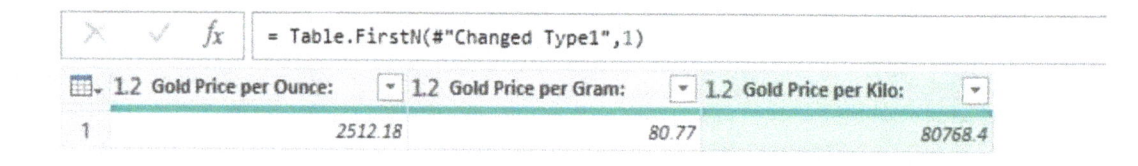

Figure 1-97. The result of removing extra columns

To record the refreshing time and date, add a new column named Date with the following formula in the Custom Column window, resulting in Figure 1-98:

`=DateTime.LocalNow()`

`= Table.AddColumn(#"Kept First Rows", "Date", each DateTime.LocalNow())`

1.2 Gold Price per Ounce:	1.2 Gold Price per Gram:	1.2 Gold Price per Kilo:	Date
1	2512.18	80.77	80768.4	24/08/2024 9:35:42 AM

Figure 1-98. Adding a date column

CHAPTER 1   DATA EXTRACTION FROM SOURCES

Using the previous steps, the last price of the gold is extracted, but in each refresh, it just includes the last price. To create a load tracker and preserve the historically loaded prices after each refresh, you need two queries: one to load the latest price and another to retain the previously loaded prices. Finally, you'll append these two queries together.

So, in the Query Pane, right-click the query name and select Duplicate to create a copy of the query. Rename one query `Call_From_Web` and the other `Result`. Then, click Close & Load to load both queries into Excel and achieve the result shown in Figure 1-99.

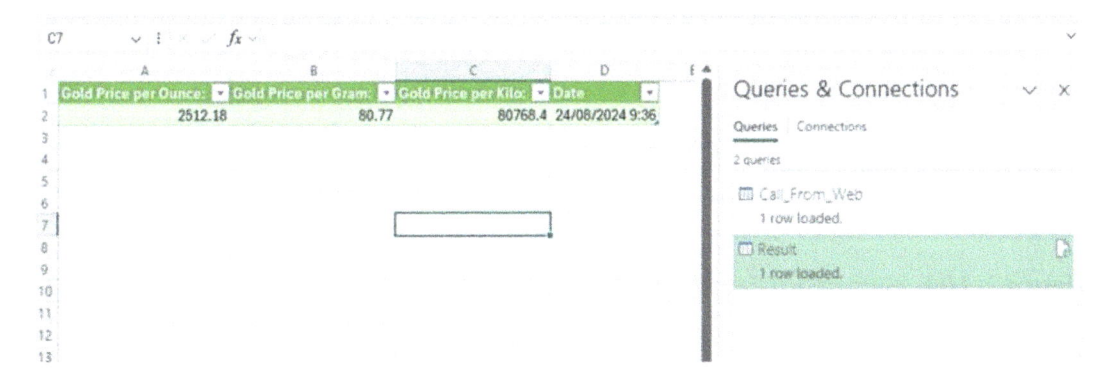

Figure 1-99. Queries and connection

The task of the `Call_From_Web` query is to load the latest price, which will later be appended to the historically loaded prices in the `Result` query. Since you don't need to display it as a table, right-click it in the Queries & Connections section, and as shown in Figure 1-100, select Only Create Connection.

CHAPTER 1   DATA EXTRACTION FROM SOURCES

Figure 1-100. Setting for Load To

Then, right-click the query named Result and select Edit. In the Power Query Editor, as shown in Figure 1-101, remove all the steps except for the Source step.

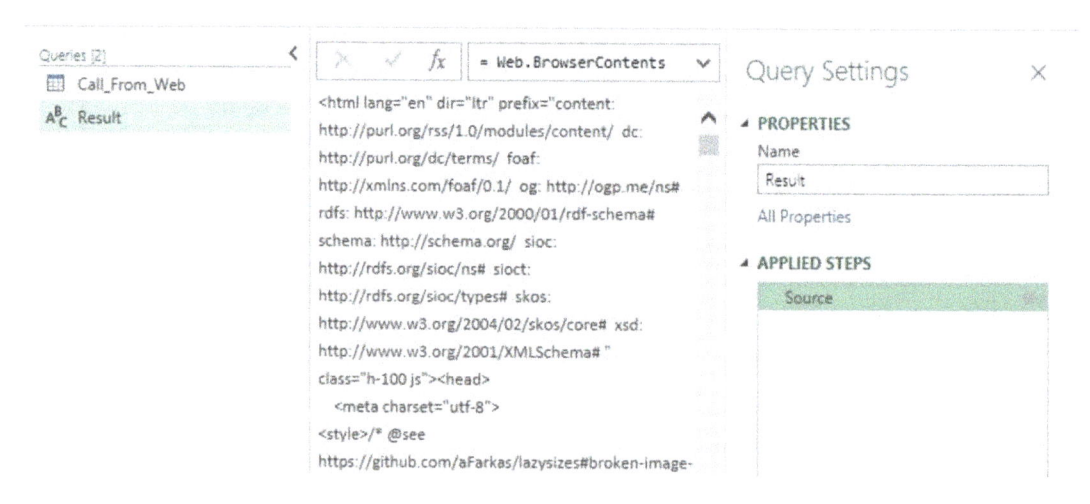

Figure 1-101. The Power Query Editor

Replace the formula for the Source step with the following formula:

= Excel.CurrentWorkbook(){[Name= "Result"]}[Content]

CHAPTER 1 DATA EXTRACTION FROM SOURCES

This will refer to the Result table, which includes historical values, as shown in Figure 1-102.

Gold Price per Ounce:	Gold Price per Gram:	Gold Price per Kilo:	Date
2512.18	80.77	80768.4	24/08/2024 9:36:01 AM

`= Excel.CurrentWorkbook(){[Name="Result"]}[Content]`

***Figure 1-102.** Historical values are shown*

This step is crucial for maintaining historical data. This query results were loaded into an Excel table, also named Result. The first step of this query refers to this table, ensuring that historical values are initially loaded into the query. Subsequently, the new gold price extracted by the Call_From_Web query will be appended to the bottom of this historical data and then the appended table (including the historical and new prices) will be loaded into the Result table.

So, select the Result query and, from the Home tab, choose the Append Queries command. Configure the settings as shown in Figure 1-103, then click OK to add the new price to the bottom of historically loaded price, as shown in Figure 1-104.

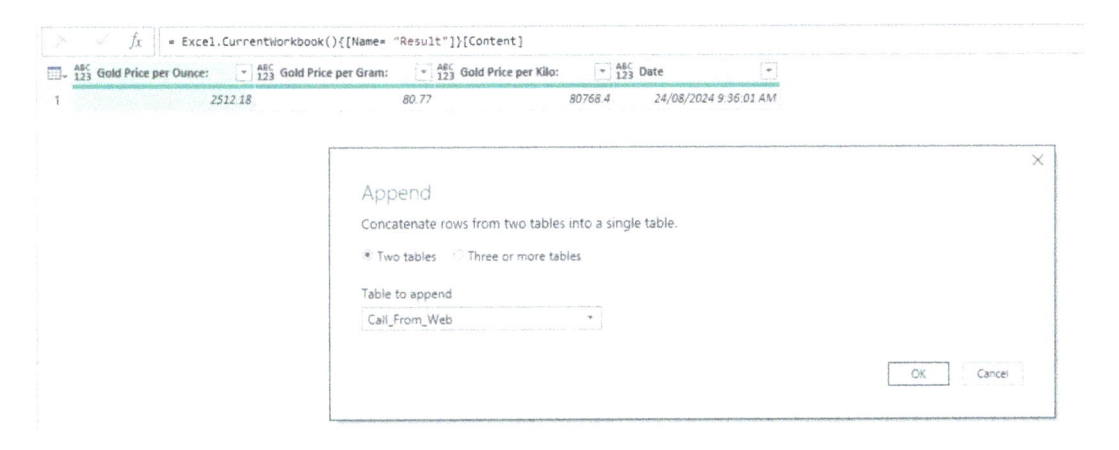

***Figure 1-103.** Setting for Append*

73

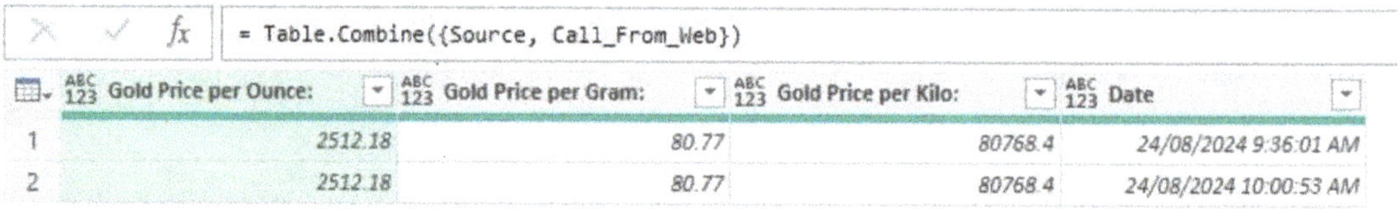

CHAPTER 1   DATA EXTRACTION FROM SOURCES

Gold Price per Ounce:	Gold Price per Gram:	Gold Price per Kilo:	Date
2512.18	80.77	80768.4	24/08/2024 9:36:01 AM
2512.18	80.77	80768.4	24/08/2024 10:00:53 AM

Formula: `= Table.Combine({Source, Call_From_Web})`

***Figure 1-104.** Result of Append*

After the last step, the new gold price will be added as a new row to the end of the existing historical data. Click Close & Load from the Home tab to update the Excel table. With each refresh, new values will be appended to the historical data, as depicted in Figure 1-105.

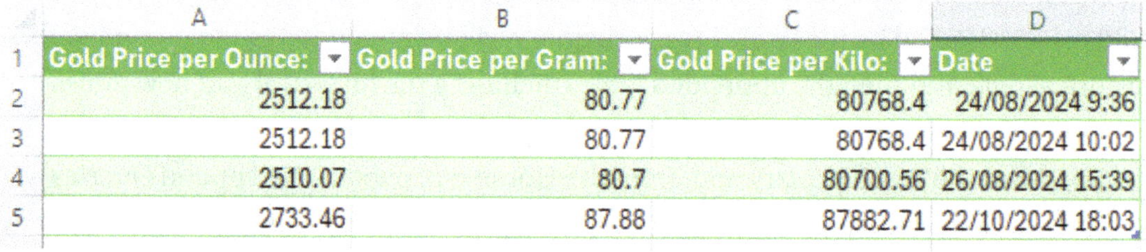

	A	B	C	D
1	Gold Price per Ounce:	Gold Price per Gram:	Gold Price per Kilo:	Date
2	2512.18	80.77	80768.4	24/08/2024 9:36
3	2512.18	80.77	80768.4	24/08/2024 10:02
4	2510.07	80.7	80700.56	26/08/2024 15:39
5	2733.46	87.88	87882.71	22/10/2024 18:03

***Figure 1-105.** Adding new value to the historical values*

Creating a Date Table

Create a data table including all the dates in 2023 and 2024 and the following columns:

– Data in the format of d/m/yyyy

– Year

– Month as a number and as text

– Day (as a number)

– Weekday as a number and as text

– Week of month and week of the year

– Quarter as a number and as text

– Starting and ending date of that month

CHAPTER 1   DATA EXTRACTION FROM SOURCES

This problem can be solved in several ways, but thanks to the Table.FromList() function, it can be solved easily. Let's check this function first and then try to solve this problem. The syntax of Table.FromList() is as follows:

```
Table.FromList(
    list as list,
    optional splitter as nullable function,
    optional columns as any,
    optional default as any,
    optional extraValues as nullable number) as table
```

It includes five arguments, the first being mandatory and the others being optional. As the name suggests, it converts the list in its first argument into a table. For example, the result of =Table.FromList({"a".."n"}) is the table displayed in Figure 1-106.

	Column1
1	a
2	b
3	c
4	d
5	e
6	f
7	g
8	h
9	i
10	j
11	k
12	l
13	m
14	n

Figure 1-106. *The result of Table.FromList*

Using the second argument, new columns can be added to the created table by defining a transformation function based on the generated list. For example, the result of =Table.FromList({"a".."n"}, each {_}) is the same as the previous formula.

75

CHAPTER 1   DATA EXTRACTION FROM SOURCES

However, the result of =Table.FromList({"a".."n"}, each {_, Text.Upper(_)}) produces a table with two columns: the first containing lowercase letters and the second containing the corresponding uppercase letters. See Figure 1-107.

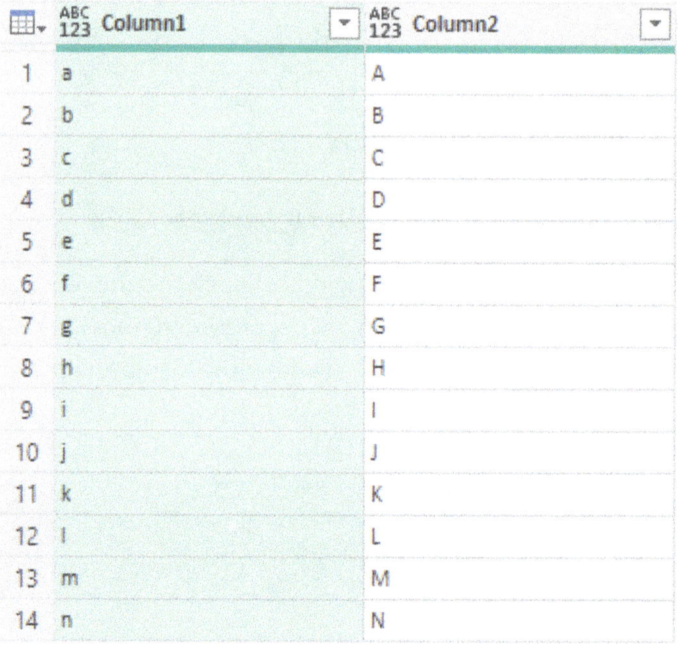

	Column1	Column2
1	a	A
2	b	B
3	c	C
4	d	D
5	e	E
6	f	F
7	g	G
8	h	H
9	i	I
10	j	J
11	k	K
12	l	L
13	m	M
14	n	N

Figure 1-107. *Using the second argument of Table.FromList*

The column names can be modified using the third argument. For example, rewriting the previous formula as =Table.FromList({"a".."n"}, each {_, Text.Upper(_)}, {"Lowercase", "Uppercase"}) will result in Figure 1-108.

CHAPTER 1   DATA EXTRACTION FROM SOURCES

	ABC 123 Lower case	ABC 123 Upper Case
1	a	A
2	b	B
3	c	C
4	d	D
5	e	E
6	f	F
7	g	G
8	h	H
9	i	I
10	j	J
11	k	K
12	l	L
13	m	M
14	n	N

Figure 1-108. Using the third argument of Table.FromList

Based on the explanation, try creating a Date table. To do this, you need a list containing all the dates from 2023 and 2024, which can be achieved using the following formula:

=List.Dates(Date.From("1/1/2023"), 2*365, #duration(1,0,0,0)).

To convert this list into a table, use Table.FromList() as shown here, which results in Figure 1-109:

= Table.FromList(List.Dates(Date.From("1/1/2023"),2*365,#duration(1,0,0,0)),
each {_},{"Date"})

CHAPTER 1   DATA EXTRACTION FROM SOURCES

	Date
1	1/01/2023
2	2/01/2023
3	3/01/2023
4	4/01/2023
5	5/01/2023
6	6/01/2023
7	7/01/2023
8	8/01/2023
9	9/01/2023
10	10/01/2023
11	11/01/2023
12	12/01/2023
13	13/01/2023
14	14/01/2023
15	15/01/2023
16	16/01/2023
17	17/01/2023
18	18/01/2023

Figure 1-109. *The result of Table.FromList*

To add columns for the year, month (both as a number and as text), and day, rewrite the formula as follows, which results in Figure 1-110:

```
Table.FromList(
  =List.Dates(Date.From("1/1/2023"), 2 * 365, #duration(1, 0, 0, 0)),
    each {_, Date.Year(_), Date.Month(_), Date.MonthName(_), Date.
    Day(_)},
    {"Date", "Year", "Month-Number", "Month-Text", "Day"})
```

CHAPTER 1   DATA EXTRACTION FROM SOURCES

	Date	Year	Month-Number	Month-Text	Day
1	1/01/2023	2023	1	January	1
2	2/01/2023	2023	1	January	2
3	3/01/2023	2023	1	January	3
4	4/01/2023	2023	1	January	4
5	5/01/2023	2023	1	January	5
6	6/01/2023	2023	1	January	6
7	7/01/2023	2023	1	January	7
8	8/01/2023	2023	1	January	8
9	9/01/2023	2023	1	January	9
10	10/01/2023	2023	1	January	10
11	11/01/2023	2023	1	January	11
12	12/01/2023	2023	1	January	12
13	13/01/2023	2023	1	January	13
14	14/01/2023	2023	1	January	14
15	15/01/2023	2023	1	January	15
16	16/01/2023	2023	1	January	16
17	17/01/2023	2023	1	January	17
18	18/01/2023	2023	1	January	18

Figure 1-110. Using the second and third arguments in Table.FromList

The complete solution is provided by the following formula:

```
=Table.FromList(
    List.Dates(Date.From("1/1/2023"), 2 * 365, #duration(1, 0, 0, 0)),
    each {
        _,
        Date.Year(_),
        Date.Month(_),
        Date.MonthName(_),
        Date.Day(_),
        Date.DayOfWeek(_),
        Date.DayOfWeekName(_),
        Date.WeekOfMonth(_),
        Date.WeekOfYear(_),
        Date.QuarterOfYear(_),
        Date.StartOfMonth(_),
        Date.EndOfMonth(_)
    },
    {
        "Date",
        "Year",
```

```
            "Month-Number",
            "Month-Text",
            "Day",
            "WeekDay-Number",
            "WeekDay-Text",
            "WeekMonth",
            "WeekYear",
            "Quarter",
            "Start Date of Month",
            "End Date of Month"
        }
)
```

Summary

The journey into Power Query as an ETL (Extract, Transform, Load) tool begins with data extraction from multiple sources. This chapter explored techniques for loading data with varying structures, discussed ways to handle and combine tables with inconsistent column names, manage complex multi-row headers, and extract information outside the table boundaries. It also covered creating a loading log in Excel to monitor data processing and merging query results, with manually entered data for added flexibility. The chapter also included a solid foundation in establishing data connectivity and overcoming structural challenges, setting the stage for advanced transformations presented in this chapter.

In the next chapter, you continue this journey by learning the functions and operators used to refer to a specific item inside tables, lists, and records.

CHAPTER 2

Referencing

In various real-world scenarios, you may need to extract values of a specific column, row, or even a cell in a table or search for a specific field in a record or item in a list. There are several methods and different functions to reference specific values in a table, list, or record. This chapter explores various Power Query functions for referencing data, including extracting the first or last N items or rows, retrieving middle items or rows, and extracting values based on specific conditions in real-word problems. Before starting the problems in this section, let's review some tips for referencing.

Consider the table named Source, shown in Table 2-1. It shows the distances between cities.

Table 2-1. *Source: Distances Between Cities*

FromTo	A	B	C	D
A	0	73	85	13
B	73	0	91	41
C	85	91	0	31
D	13	41	31	0
C	85	91	0	31

To reference one or multiple columns in this table, you can use the Table.SelectColumns() function by entering two inputs for it—the first parameter is the name of the table, and the second is a list of column names to be selected. The following formula results in a table with only the specified columns, whose names are mentioned

CHAPTER 2 REFERENCING

in the second argument. The result is shown in Figure 2-1. (If you select both the columns—FromTo and A—right-click one of them, and then choose the Remove Other Columns command, the same formula will generated in the formula bar.)

= Table.SelectColumns(Source,{"FromTo","A"})

	FromTo	A
1	A	0
2	B	73
3	C	85
4	D	13
5	C	85

Figure 2-1. *Using Table.SelectColumns*

Alternatively, you can achieve the same result using the following formula, where the column names are listed in the [ ]:

= Source[[FromTo],[A]]

The same result can be achieved by removing unwanted columns using the Table.RemoveColumns() function, as shown in the following formula. In this formula, the name of the columns that you want to remove should be provided in the second argument. (The same formula will be generated if you select the B, C, and D columns, right-click one of them, and choose the Remove Columns command.)

= Table.RemoveColumns(Distance,{"B", "C", "D"})

In another case, to address a specific column (just one column) in a table, you can use the Table.Column() function. The following formula returns the values of the specified column in the second argument as a list (not a table), as shown in Figure 2-2.

= Table.Column(Source,"A")

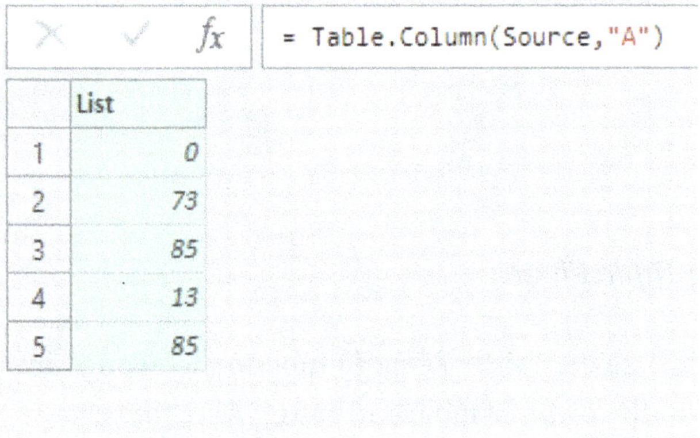

CHAPTER 2 REFERENCING

	List
1	0
2	73
3	85
4	13
5	85

fx = Table.Column(Source,"A")

Figure 2-2. Using Table.Column

The =Source[A] formula also returns a list, like the previous formula. (However, be careful with the syntax used for referencing. The result of Source[A] and Table.Column(Source,"A") is a list, whereas Source[[A]] and =Table.SelectColumns(Source,{"A"}) returns a table with just one column.)

Just as you can select specific columns in a table, there are functions available in Power Query to select the desired rows. To extract specific rows from a table based on its value on a specific column, you can use the Table.SelectRows() function. (This function is explained in depth in Chapter 3.) To use this function by UI, select the filter icon next to the FromTo column name and choose the desired city, like A, from the list. It results in the table shown in Figure 2-3 based on the following formula, which is shown in the formula bar.

= Table.SelectRows(Source, each ([FromTo] = "A"))

fx = Table.SelectRows(Source, each ([FromTo] = "A"))

FromTo	A	B	C	D
1 A	0	73	85	13

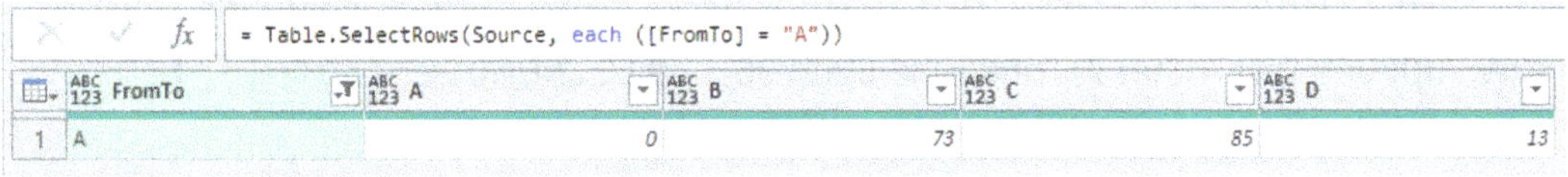

Figure 2-3. Using Table.SelectRows

To select the top or bottom *N* rows of a table, use the Table.FirstN() and Table.LastN() functions. To remove the top or bottom *N* rows of a table, use the Table.RemoveFirstN() and Table.RemoveLastN() functions. You can specify *N* as a number or a condition in the second argument. For example, the following formula shows the first three rows in the Source table, as shown in Figure 2-4.

CHAPTER 2   REFERENCING

= Table.FirstN(Source,3)

FromTo	A	B	C	D	
1 A		0	73	85	13
2 B		73	0	91	41
3 C		85	91	0	31

Figure 2-4. Using Table.FirstN

Similarly, you can use the Table.Range() function to extract rows based on their position from the middle rows of a table and Table.AlternateRows() to remove the table rows based on a specific pattern. For example, the following formula returns three rows from the source table, starting from the second row (as indexing in Power Query starts from 0) of the table shown in Figure 2-5.

= Table.Range(Source,1,3)

FromTo	A	B	C	D	
1 B		73	0	91	41
2 C		85	91	0	31
3 D		13	41	31	0

Figure 2-5. Using Table.Range

Note   To select or remove the top or bottom rows in Power Query using the UI, navigate to the Home tab and choose the desired command from the Reduce Rows section. Using the Keep Rows options will generate functions like Table.FirstN(), Table.LastN(), or Table.Range(). In contrast, using the Remove Rows options will result in functions such as Table.RemoveFirstN(), Table.RemoveLastN(), or Table.AlternateRows().

In addition to using the previously mentioned functions, you can also extract a row of a table by using the indexing sign after the table name. Since indexing starts at 0 in Power Query, the following formula refers to the first row of the Source table, as shown in Figure 2-6.

= Source{0}

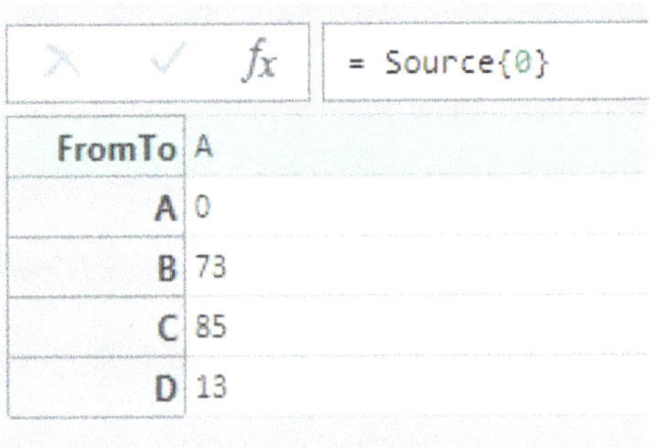

CHAPTER 2   REFERENCING

```
×  ✓  fx    = Source{0}

FromTo  A
     A  0
     B  73
     C  85
     D  13
```

Figure 2-6. Using Source{0}

Note Using the list sign to reference a row returns a record, whereas Table. SelectRows() always returns a table. To extract the first row of a table not using Source{0}, you can use Table.First(Source) to reach the same result as the record. Similarly, you can use Table.Last() to reach the last row of a table, which will also return the result in a record type.

Besides referencing a row by mentioning the row number in the index sign, you can use the index sign to apply the filter on a table, based on the cell values like the following formula:

=Source{[FromTo="A"]}

The previous formula will result in a record as long as the A value is just entered once in the FromTo column. Otherwise, it results in an error. The result of the following formula is the error shown in Figure 2-7.

= Source{[FromTo="C"]}

85

CHAPTER 2 REFERENCING

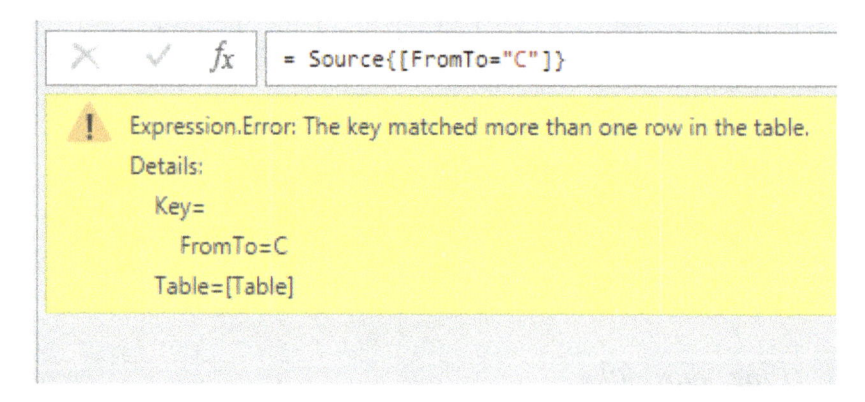

```
×  ✓  fx   = Source{[FromTo="C"]}

⚠  Expression.Error: The key matched more than one row in the table.
   Details:
      Key=
         FromTo=C
      Table=[Table]
```

Figure 2-7. Using Source {[FromTo="C"]}

In addition to tables, records and lists are other commonly used data types in Power Query. When working with records, the field values can be extracted by using the Record.Field() function or by using the field name directly after the record sign. For example, if the source record is represented as [A=13, B=41, C=31, D=0], both Record.Field(Source, "A") and Source[A] will return the same result, which is 13.

In the case of lists, you can extract the value at a specific index by placing the desired index in curly braces {} after the list name. For instance, if the source list is {1, 2, 4, 6, 8}, then Source{2} will return 4 (since indexing starts at 0).

In addition to the methods for extracting specific values from a table, record, or list, there are other functions, summarized in Table 2-2. These functions are explained further with examples in this chapter.

Table 2-2. Referencing and Removing Functions

Function	Description
List.FirstN()	Returns the first *N* items from a list.
List.LastN()	Returns the last *N* items from a list.
List.Range()	Extracts a range of items from a list based on their positions.
List.RemoveFirstN()	Removes the first *N* items from a list.
List.RemoveItems()	Removes specified items from a list.
List.RemoveLastN()	Removes the last *N* items from a list.
List.RemoveNull()	Removes null values from a list.

(continued)

Table 2-2. (*continued*)

Function	Description
List.RemoveRange()	Removes a range of items from a list based on their positions.
List.Select()	Selects items from a list based on a specified condition.
Record.Field()	Retrieves the value of a specified field from a record.
Record.FieldOrDefault()	Retrieves the value of a specified field from a record or returns a default value if the field does not exist.
Record.RemoveFields()	Removes specified fields from a record.
Record.SelectFields()	Selects specified fields from a record.
Table.AlternateRows()	Selects alternate rows from a table.
Table.FirstN()	Returns the first N rows from a table. N can be a specific number or a condition.
Table.FirstValue()	Retrieves the first value from a specified column in a table.
Table.LastN()	Returns the last N rows from a table. N can be a specific number or a condition.
Table.Max()	Returns the maximum value from a specified column in a table.
Table.MaxN()	Returns the maximum N rows from a specified column in a table.
Table.Min()	Returns the minimum value from a specified column in a table.
Table.MinN()	Returns the minimum N rows from a specified column in a table.
Table.Range()	Extracts a range of rows from a table based on their positions.
Table.RemoveBottomRows()	Removes a specified number of rows from the bottom of a table.
Table.RemoveFirstN()	Removes the first N rows from a table.
Table.RemoveLastN()	Removes the last N rows from a table.
Table.RemoveMatchingRows()	Removes rows from a table that match specified criteria.
Table.RemoveRows()	Removes specified rows from a table based on their position or condition.

(*continued*)

CHAPTER 2   REFERENCING

Table 2-2. *(continued)*

Function	Description
Table.RemoveRowsWithErrors()	Removes rows that contain errors from a table.
Table.RemoveTopRows()	Removes a specified number of rows from the top of a table.
Table.SelectRows()	Selects rows from a table based on a condition or criteria.
Table.SelectRowsWithErrors()	Selects rows that contain errors from a table.
Table.Skip()	Skips the first *N* rows of a table and returns the remaining rows.

Referencing Cells in Power Query

Consider the Distance table shown in Table 2-3, which presents the distances between cities, and consider the Source table shown in Table 2-4. Both tables are loaded into Power Query as separate queries with the names Distance and Source.

Table 2-3. *Distance: Distances Between Cities*

FromTo	A	B	C	D
A	0	73	85	13
B	73	0	91	41
C	85	91	0	31
D	13	41	31	0

Table 2-4. *Source Table*

From	To
A	B
A	A
B	D
A	D

CHAPTER 2　REFERENCING

Add a new column to the Source table that calculates the distance between the cities specified in the From and To columns.

To solve this problem, initially try to calculate the distance from city B to city C on the Distance table, then modify the formula for all the cases. To calculate the distance from B to C, right-click the value 91 (the distance from B to C) in the Distance table and select the Drill Down command. This action will generate the following formula in the formula bar:

= Distance{1}[C]

In the formula generated from the Drill Down operation, Distance{1} returns a record containing five fields—FromTo, A, B, C, and D—each with different values (see Figure 2-8). By using [C] after this record, the value for the C field, which is 91, is extracted.

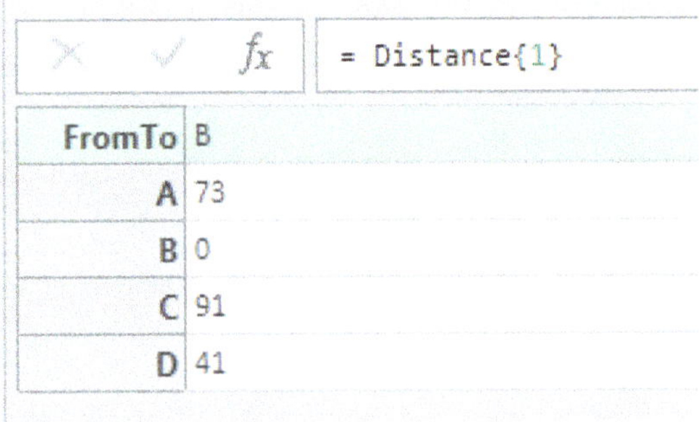

FromTo	B
A	73
B	0
C	91
D	41

fx = Distance{1}

Figure 2-8. *Using Distance {[FromTo="C"]}*

The previous formula works correctly for the distance from B to C. To make the previous formula dynamic, it can be rewritten as follows (instead of using 1 as hard code):

= Distance {[FromTo="B"]}[C]

In the formula, B (the source city) is still hardcoded but can be replaced with a variable like x as it is in type text. However, C (the destination city) cannot be replaced directly by a variable as it is not in type text and the whole [C] comes together as the record operator. To make the formula more flexible, instead of extracting the field value for the city C using [C], you can use the Record.Field() function, thus allowing both cities' names to be dynamic. So, the revised formula is:

= Record.Field(Distance {[FromTo="B"]},"C")

CHAPTER 2 REFERENCING

This approach enables both cities (B and C) in type text, which can be replaced with variables or values from other columns. Using this formula, let's back to the question and try to solve the problem.

To add a distance column to the Source table, select the Source table, go to the Add Column tab, and choose Custom Column. Using the following formula in the Custom Column window will result in the distance from B to C for all the rows:

= Record.Field(Distance {[FromTo="B"]},"C")

To use the formula to calculate the distance of cities in each row, rewrite the previous formula by replacing B with [From] (the values of the From column in the Source table) and C with [To] (equal to values of the To column in the Source table), as shown in Figure 2-9.

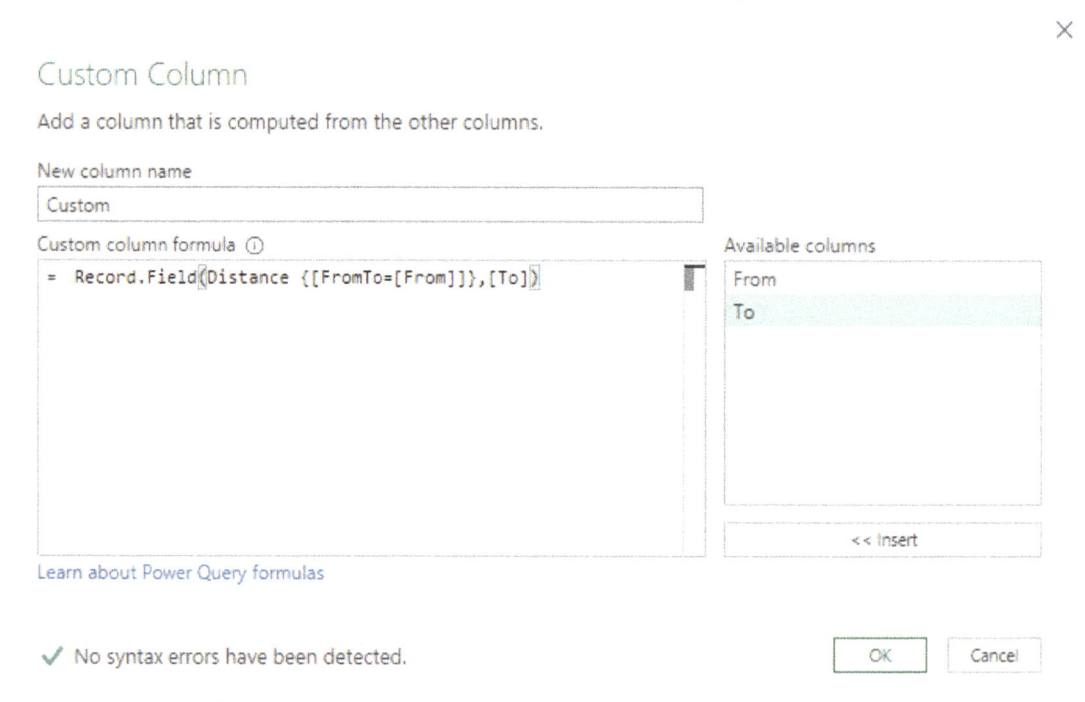

Figure 2-9. Adding a new column

= Record.Field(Distance {[FromTo=[From]]}, [To])

The result of the previous formula is shown in Figure 2-10.

CHAPTER 2 REFERENCING

	A^B_C From		A^B_C To		ABC 123 Custom	
1	A		B			73
2	A		A			0
3	B		D			41
4	A		D			13

Figure 2-10. Result of adding a column

By following the previous steps, you can resolve the problem. To view the entire set of query steps, select the Source query and click the Advanced Editor command in the Home tab. The whole code for solving this problem is as follows:

```
let
    Source = Excel.CurrentWorkbook(){[Name="Table4"]}[Content],
    #"Added Custom" = Table.AddColumn(Source, "Custom", each Record.Field
    (Distance{[FromTo=[From]]},[To]))
in
    #"Added Custom"
```

Efficiency Tips Let's examine the execution time of this problem in two scenarios: a small distance table with ten rows and columns, and a larger distance table with 1,000 rows and columns (though this scenario is uncommon in practice).

In the small distance table scenario, with a source table of 1,000 rows, the execution time without buffering the distance table is 1.16 seconds, and with buffering, it is reduced to 0.08 seconds. For a source table with 1 million rows, the execution time is 50 seconds (for more information about buffering, read this post https://learn.microsoft.com/en-us/powerquery-m/table-buffer).

In the large distance table scenario, if the source table has nine rows, the execution time is about four to six seconds. However, with 1,000 rows in the source table, the execution time increases to around 500 seconds without Table.Buffer. Even using Table.Buffer, the execution time only reduces to

CHAPTER 2　REFERENCING

350 seconds. By replacing the X{[FromTo=[From]]} part of the formula with Table.SelectRows(X, (x) => x[FromTo] = _[From]){0}, the execution time decreases to 140 seconds, though this is still quite high.

In this example, you are searching for values in the From column of the source table over the FromTo column of the Distance table, but all 999 other columns are also being considered. To improve execution time, it is better to separate the FromTo column from the Distance table and use it in a different variable for buffering. Then, you can find the position the value in the From column over this list.

The revised formula, which solves the problem in 0.87 seconds, is provided here. In the small distance table scenario, with a source table of 1 million rows, the execution time using this revised formula is eight seconds.

```
let
    Source = Excel.CurrentWorkbook(){[Name="Table4"]}
    [Content],
    X=Table.Buffer(Distance),
    Y=List.Buffer(Table.Column(X,"FromTo")),
    #"Added Custom" = Table.AddColumn(Source, "Custom", each 
    Record.Field(Table.Range(X, List.PositionOf(Y,[From]),1)
    {0},[To]))
in
    #"Added Custom"
```

Referencing the Previous Row

In the Source table, as shown in Table 2-5, the monthly sales data is provided (the table is sorted based on month). Calculate the growth rate for each month compared to the previous month.

Table 2-5. Source: Monthly Sales

Month	Sales
1	69
2	81
3	39
4	15
5	68
6	77
7	75
8	29
9	81
10	52
11	97
12	80

Four different solutions are provided to solve this problem. In all the solutions, to extract the information from the previous row in Power Query, an index column with consecutive values (numbers or dates) is helpful. If no such column exists, you can add one by selecting the Add Index Column command under the Add Column tab. However, in this example, the Month column can serve as the index column. So, don't bother to add an index column for this problem.

Solution 1: Based on Filtering the Rows

To solve this problem, from the Add Column tab, choose Custom Column. This adds a new column to the table. Name this new column Monthly Growth Rate and enter the following formula into the Custom Column window (Source is the name of the previous step). Click OK.

```
=Source
```

CHAPTER 2 REFERENCING

Using this formula will result in the same values being repeated for all rows, with every cell in this column containing all the rows and columns of the Source table. To calculate the monthly growth rate, only the values in the Sales column are needed. Replace the previous formula with the following one to generate a list of all the sales values for every row:

=Source[Sales]

To calculate the growth rate, you need the sales value from the previous month for each row. For example, out of all the values in this list, for Month = 2, you need to extract the value for Month=1, which is presented as the first item in the list. As Power Query indexing starts from 0, for this month, the value with index 0 should be extracted. Similarly, for Month=3, the item in index 1 should be extracted. So, for each month, the value in index [Month]-2 should be extracted. To reach the values of the previous month, the previous formula should be replaced with the following formula, which results in Figure 2-11.

=(Source[Sales]){[Month]-2}

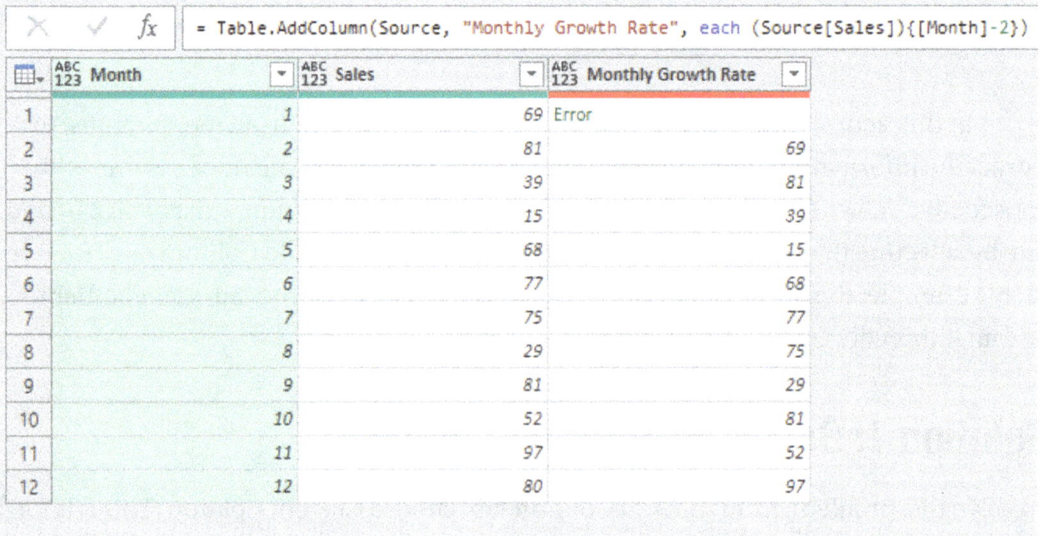

Month	Sales	Monthly Growth Rate
1	1	69 Error
2	2	81	69
3	3	39	81
4	4	15	39
5	5	68	15
6	6	77	68
7	7	75	77
8	8	29	75
9	9	81	29
10	10	52	81
11	11	97	52
12	12	80	97

formula bar: = Table.AddColumn(Source, "Monthly Growth Rate", each (Source[Sales]){[Month]-2})

Figure 2-11. *Referring to the previous value in the same column*

The previous formula results in the sales value of the previous month. To calculate the growth rate, the formula can be rewritten as follows, resulting in Figure 2-12:

=[Sales]/(Source[Sales]){[Month]-2}

CHAPTER 2 REFERENCING

fx = Table.AddColumn(Source, "Monthly Growth Rate", each [Sales]/(Source[Sales]){[Month]-2})

Month	Sales	Monthly Growth Rate
1	1	69 Error
2	2	81 1.173913043
3	3	39 0.481481481
4	4	15 0.384615385
5	5	68 4.533333333
6	6	77 1.132352941
7	7	75 0.974025974
8	8	29 0.386666667
9	9	81 2.793103448
10	10	52 0.641975309
11	11	97 1.865384615
12	12	80 0.824742268

Figure 2-12. *Result of growth rate*

To handle potential error values in the first row, you can use the try-otherwise expression by replacing the previous formula with the following formula. This new formula calculates [Sales]/(Source[Sales]){[Month]-2} for all the rows. If it results in an error, it replaces the error with the value presented after otherwise, which is "-" in this example.

=try [Sales]/(Source[Sales]){[Month]-2} otherwise "-"

Applying the previous steps results in the following formula using the Table.AddColumn() function in the formula bar:

```
= Table.AddColumn(
      Source,
      "Monthly Growth Rate",
      each try [Sales]/(Source[Sales]){[Month]-2} otherwise "-")
```

To improve the readability of results and convert the values in this column into percentages, you can use the fourth argument of this function, shown here:

```
= Table.AddColumn(
      Source,
      "Monthly Growth Rate",
      each try [Sales]/(Source[Sales]){[Month]-2} otherwise "-",
      Percentage.Type)
```

CHAPTER 2 REFERENCING

This results in Figure 2-13.

	Month	Sales	% Monthly Growth Rate
1	1	69	-
2	2	81	117.39%
3	3	39	48.15%
4	4	15	38.46%
5	5	68	453.33%
6	6	77	113.24%
7	7	75	97.40%
8	8	29	38.67%
9	9	81	279.31%
10	10	52	64.20%
11	11	97	186.54%
12	12	80	82.47%

Figure 2-13. *Changing the value type*

Using the previous steps, the problem is solved. In the proposed solution, the (Source[Sales]){[Month]-2} formula is used. This formula first extracts the values of the Sales column as a list and, from that list, it retrieves the value with an index equal to [Month]-2. However, this logic can be revised by extracting the ([Month]-2)th row of the table first, which is in type of record, and then retrieving the value of the Sales field using the following formula:

=Source{[Month]-2}[Sales]

Similarly, the previous formula can be replaced by any of the following formulas with the same result, and each is equal to the value in the Sales column for the previous row (the last two formulas are useable even if the rows are not sorted based on the month).

=Record.Field(Source{[Month]-2},"Sales")

=Source{[Month=[Month]-1]}[Sales]

=Table.SelectRows(Source, (x)=> x[Month]=[Month]-1)[Sales]{0}

Solution 2: Based on Merging

Consider the Source table. Go to the Add Column tab and select Custom Column. Name the new column Month +1 and enter the following formula:

=[Month]+1

This formula adds one to the values in the Month column, resulting in the Figure 2-14.

Month	Sales	Month+1
1	69	2
2	81	3
3	39	4
4	15	5
5	68	6
6	77	7
7	75	8
8	29	9
9	81	10
10	52	11
11	97	12
12	80	13

Figure 2-14. *Result of [Month]+1*

In the next step, to solve this problem, as shown in Figure 2-15, you just need to search for the values in the Month column in the Month+1 column and select that row. The selected row presents the values related to the previous month.

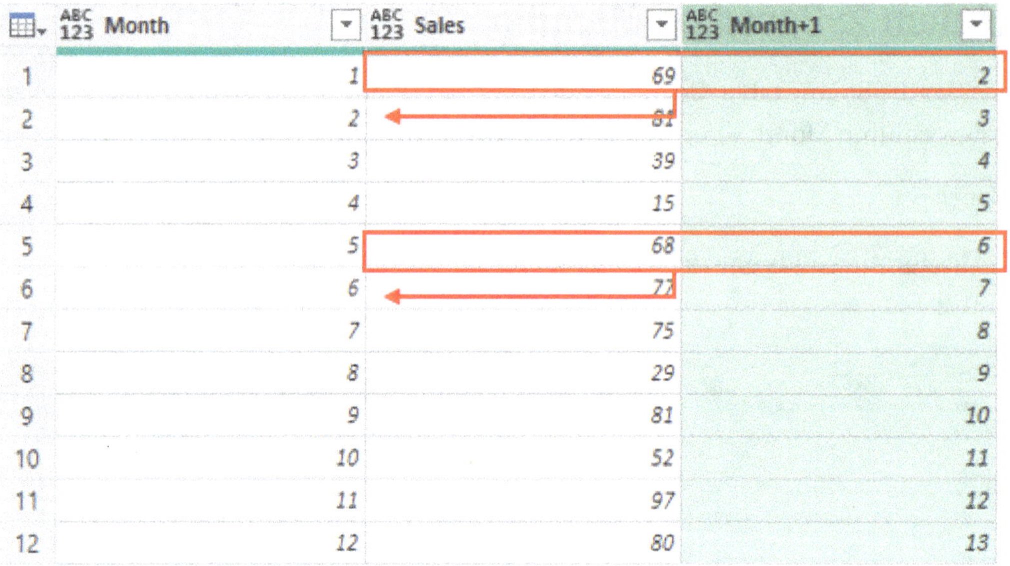

CHAPTER 2 REFERENCING

Month	Sales	Month+1
1	69	2
2	61	3
3	39	4
4	15	5
5	68	6
6	77	7
7	75	8
8	29	9
9	81	10
10	52	11
11	97	12
12	80	13

Figure 2-15. *Value of the next month*

From the Home tab, select the Merge Queries command (explained in detail in Chapter 7). Then, as shown in Figure 2-16, select the Source table for both parts of the Merge window. Choose the Month column in the top table and the Month +1 column in the bottom table as the common columns.

CHAPTER 2 REFERENCING

Merge

Select a table and matching columns to create a merged table.

Source

Month	Sales	Month+1
1	69	2
2	81	3
3	39	4
4	15	5
5	68	6

Source (Current) ▼

Month	Sales	**Month+1**
1	69	2
2	81	3
3	39	4
4	15	5
5	68	6

Join Kind

Left Outer (all from first, matching from second) ▼

☐ Use fuzzy matching to perform the merge

▷ Fuzzy matching options

✓ The selection matches 11 of 12 rows from the first table.   OK   Cancel

***

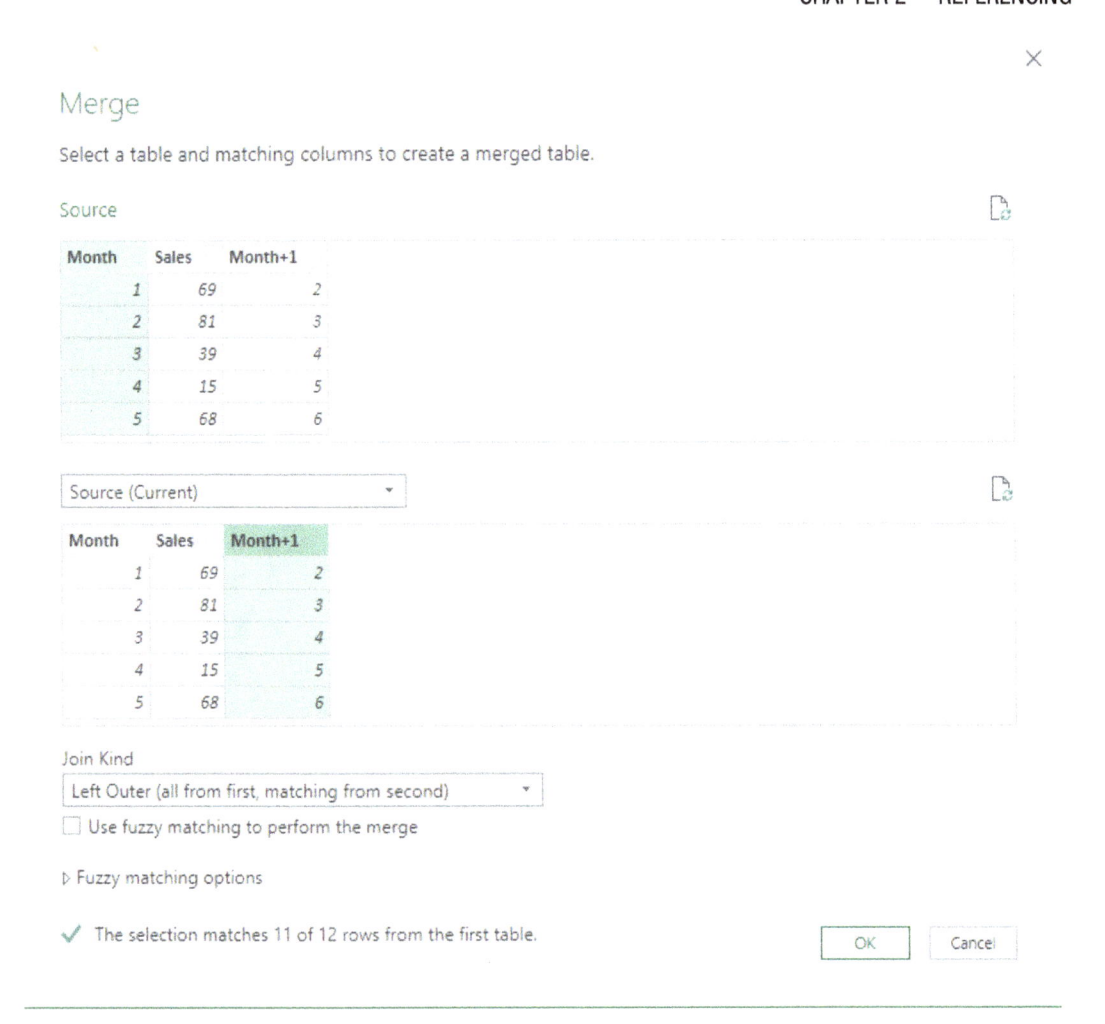

Figure 2-16. Setting for merging

Clicking OK will create a new column named Added Custom, as shown in Figure 2-17. It contains values in the form of a table that correspond to the previous month.

CHAPTER 2   REFERENCING

Month	Sales	Month+1	Added Custom
1	1	69	2 Table
2	2	81	3 Table
3	3	39	4 Table
4	4	15	5 Table
5	5	68	6 Table
6	6	77	7 Table
7	7	75	8 Table
8	8	29	9 Table
9	9	81	10 Table
10	10	52	11 Table
11	11	97	12 Table
12	12	80	13 Table

Month	Sales	Month+1
1	69	2

***Figure 2-17.** Result of merging*

To extract the sales values for the previous month, click the expand icon ( ) next to the Added Custom column. From the available options, select Sales and click OK to get the result, as shown in Figure 2-18.

Month	Sales	Month+1	Added Custom.Sales
1	2	81	3	69
2	3	39	4	81
3	4	15	5	39
4	5	68	6	15
5	6	77	7	68
6	7	75	8	77
7	8	29	9	75
8	9	81	10	29
9	10	52	11	81
10	11	97	12	52
11	12	80	13	97
12	1	69	2	null

***Figure 2-18.** Result of expanding*

CHAPTER 2 REFERENCING

Following the previous steps, you can extract the sales values for the previous month. To calculate the growth rate, simply add another Custom Column named Growth Rate and use the following formula in this column:

```
=[Sales]/[Added Custom.Sales]
```

Solution 3: Based on the Fill Down Function

Consider the Source table. In the first step, you will add two new columns, named Odd and Even, using the following formulas (enter the formulas separately in the Custom Column window), which will result in Figure 2-19.

```
=if Number.IsOdd([Month]) then [Sales] else null
=if Number.IsEven([Month]) then [Sales] else null
```

Month	Sales	Odd	Even
1	1	69	69	null
2	2	81	null	81
3	3	39	39	null
4	4	15	null	15
5	5	68	68	null
6	6	77	null	77
7	7	75	75	null
8	8	29	null	29
9	9	81	81	null
10	10	52	null	52
11	11	97	97	null
12	12	80	null	80

Figure 2-19. Adding new columns

Using the Fill Down feature for both columns will result in Figure 2-20. As shown in the resultant table, for rows with months like 2, 4, 6, and 8, the values from the previous month are filled in the Odd column in the same row. Similarly, for rows with months like 3, 5, and 7, the sales from their previous month are provided in the Even column in the same row.

CHAPTER 2 REFERENCING

Month	Sales	Odd	Even
1	1	69	69	null
2	2	81	69	81
3	3	39	39	81
4	4	15	39	15
5	5	68	68	15
6	6	77	68	77
7	7	75	75	77
8	8	29	75	29
9	9	81	81	29
10	10	52	81	52
11	11	97	97	52
12	12	80	97	80

Figure 2-20. *Using Fill Down*

Adding another custom column and using the following formula for it results in the value from the previous month, as shown in Figure 2-21.

```
=if Number.IsOdd([Month]) then [Even] else [Odd]
```

Month	Sales	Odd	Even	Monthly Growth Rate
1	1	69	69	null	null
2	2	81	69	81	69
3	3	39	39	81	81
4	4	15	39	15	39
5	5	68	68	15	15
6	6	77	68	77	68
7	7	75	75	77	77
8	8	29	75	29	75
9	9	81	81	29	29
10	10	52	81	52	81
11	11	97	97	52	52
12	12	80	97	80	97

Figure 2-21. *Extracting the value of the previous month*

Revising the previous formula and rewriting it as follows provides the growth rate:

```
try [Sales]/(if Number.IsOdd([Month]) then [Even] else [Odd])
otherwise "-"
```

This formula solves the problem, but when using this method, you must sort the source table by month.

Solution 4: Based on the List of Functions

Consider the Source table. At first glance, it may seem like a good idea to separate the Sales column, add a new row at the top with a null value, shift all the existing values down by one row, and then reconnect it to the table. This would allow you to create a new column containing the values from the previous row. Unfortunately, this operation cannot be performed directly on a table. However, it is possible to achieve this by working with the values as a list.

In this solution, you will:

1. Convert the table into a list of column values.
2. Shift the Sales values down by one row (pushing the values down with a null at the top).
3. Reconnect the shifted list to the origin list.
4. Convert the list back into a table.

To begin, select the Source table and click the *fx* button on the left side of the formula bar to add a new step named Custom1. Enter the following formula in the formula bar:

= Table.ToColumns(Source)

As shown in Figure 2-22, this formula will convert the Source table into a list, including one sublist for any column in the Source table.

CHAPTER 2 REFERENCING

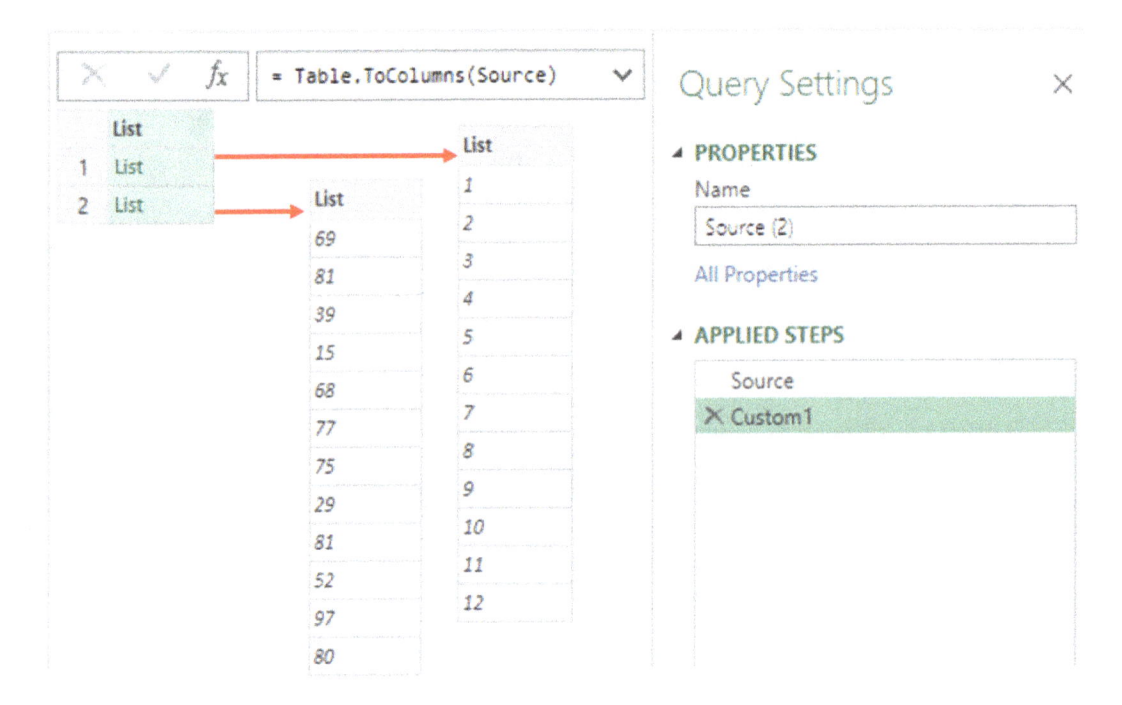

Figure 2-22. The result of using Table.ToColumns()

As shown on the right side of the window, the name of this list is Custom1. In this list, you need to extract the second sublist and shift its values down by one row, then reconnect the result to the list.

To do this, click the *fx* button to add another step named Custom2. Then enter the following formula in the formula bar, which results in Figure 2-23:

=Custom1{1}

Since indexing in Power Query starts from 0, this formula will return the second sublist from the Custom1 list.

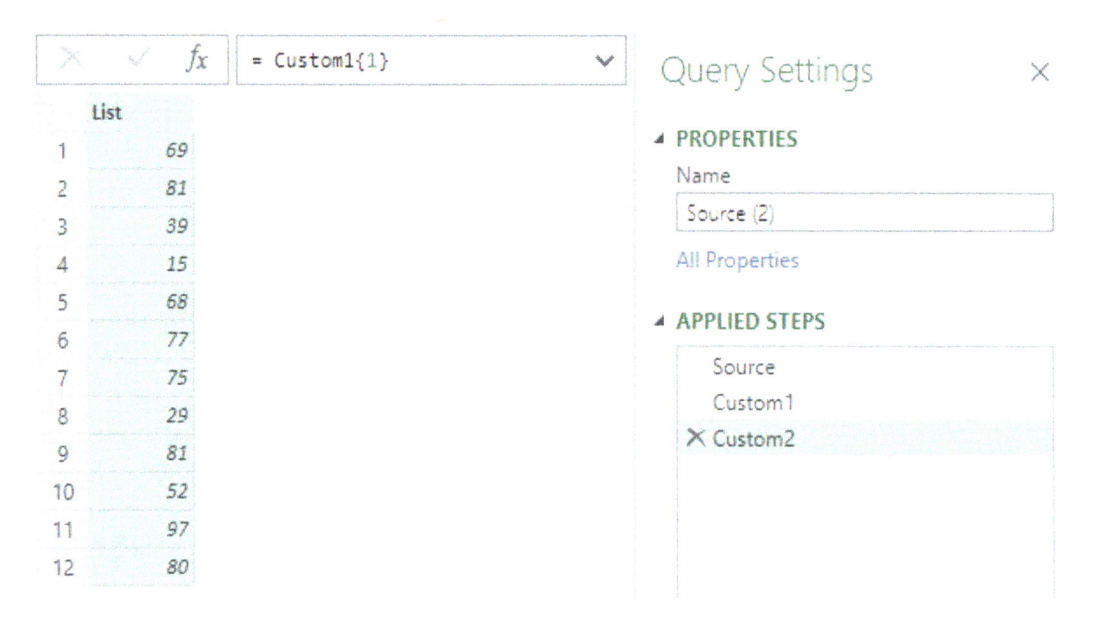

Figure 2-23. The result of Custom1{1}

To shift the values in the list down by one row and add a null value at the beginning, rewrite the previous formula as follows:

= {null}&Custom1{1}

This formula inserts a null value at the beginning of the second sublist (Custom1{1}), shifting all existing values down by one row, as shown in Figure 2-24.

CHAPTER 2 REFERENCING

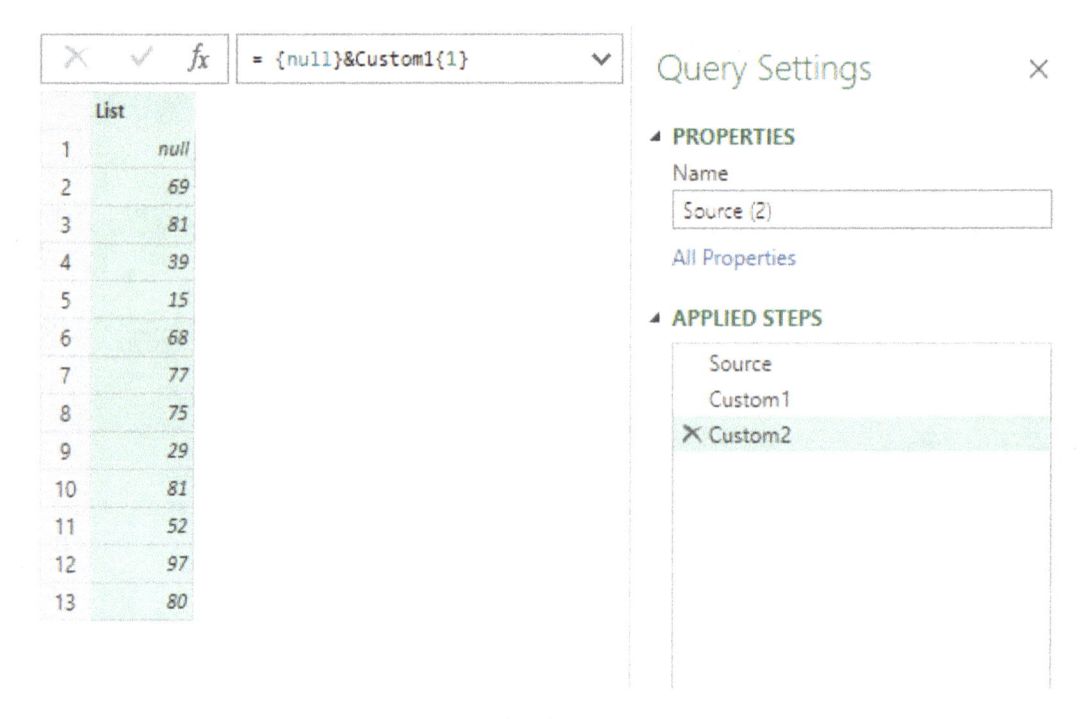

Figure 2-24. Adding a null

By adding a null to the beginning of this list, the length of this list increases by one compared to the other sublists in Custom1. To correct this, you need to remove the last item from this list. To do this, rewrite the previous formula as follows:

= List.RemoveLastN({null}&Custom1{1},1)

This formula first inserts the null value at the beginning of the second sublist (Custom1{1}), then removes the last item from the list, resulting in Figure 2-25.

CHAPTER 2 REFERENCING

```
fx  = List.RemoveLastN({null}&Custom1{1},1)
```

	List
1	null
2	69
3	81
4	39
5	15
6	68
7	77
8	75
9	29
10	81
11	52
12	97

Query Settings

▲ PROPERTIES
Name
Source (2)
All Properties

▲ APPLIED STEPS
Source
Custom1
✕ Custom2

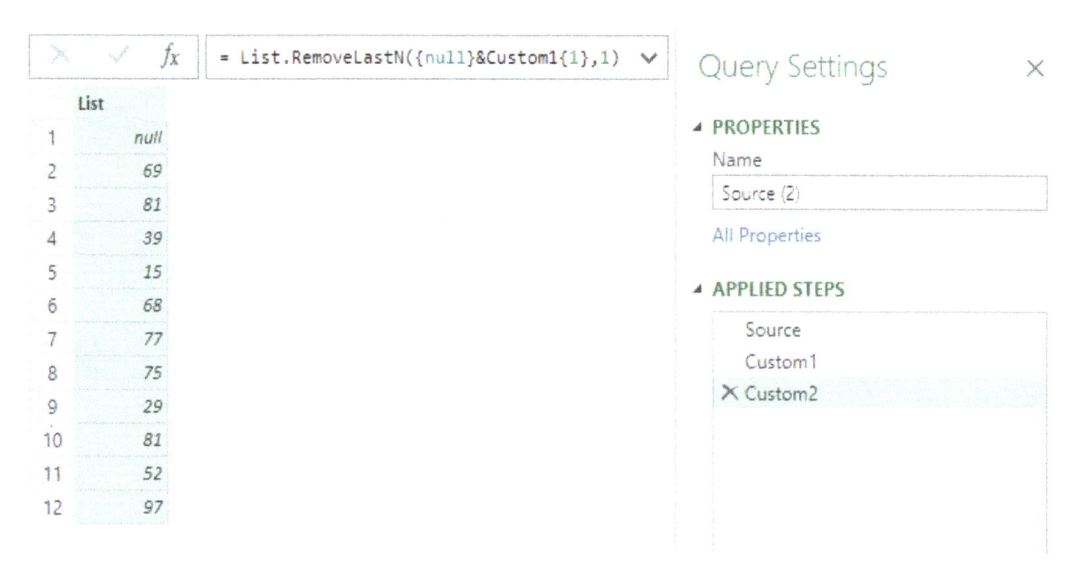

Figure 2-25. Removing the last item

To add this modified list (with the null at the beginning and the last item removed) to the other sublists in the Custom1 list, revise the formula as follows:

= Custom1& {List.RemoveLastN({null}&Custom1{1},1)}

This formula inserts the modified list (with the null added and the last item removed) back into the Custom1 list at the third position (index 2), resulting in Figure 2-26.

107

CHAPTER 2 REFERENCING

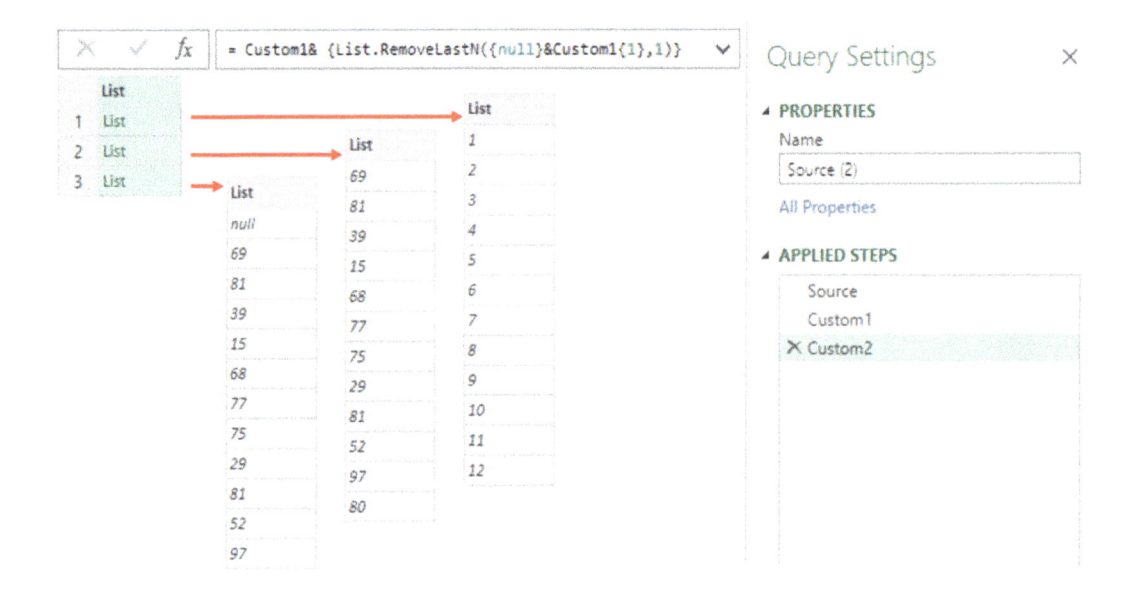

Figure 2-26. Combining the lists

To convert the result into a table, rewrite the previous formula as follows:

=Table.FromColumns(Custom1& {List.RemoveLastN({null}&Custom1{1},1)})

This formula converts the result into a table, with the list modified as described, resulting in Figure 2-27.

Figure 2-27. Converting the list into a table

108

CHAPTER 2 REFERENCING

In this case, because there are two columns, you can manually rename them. However, in real-world scenarios, where you may face numerous columns, you can use the second argument of the Table.FromColumns() function to rename all columns at once.

To achieve this, rewrite the formula as follows:

```
= Table.FromColumns( Custom1& {List.RemoveLastN({null}&Custom1{1},1)},
Table.ColumnNames(Source)&{"sales in Previous month"})
```

This formula renames all columns based on the column names in the Source table, resulting in Figure 2-28.

	Month	Sales	sales in Previous month
1		1	69	null
2		2	81	69
3		3	39	81
4		4	15	39
5		5	68	15
6		6	77	68
7		7	75	77
8		8	29	75
9		9	81	29
10		10	52	81
11		11	97	52
12		12	80	97

Figure 2-28. Final result

In the next step, add another column named Growth Rate using the following formula in the Custom Column window to solve the problem:

```
=[Sales]/[sales in Previous month]
```

109

CHAPTER 2 REFERENCING

Efficiency Tips   This example presents four different types of solutions. Among them, the first solution is the least efficient in terms of execution time, taking over 30 seconds even for a small table containing just 10,000 rows. Additionally, applying the `Table.Buffer()` or `List.Buffer()` functions does not significantly improve its efficiency compared to the other solutions.

The remaining three solutions perform well, even with larger datasets. These solutions were tested across four different scenarios, with table sizes of 1,000, 10,000, 100,000, and 500,000 rows. Based on the results, the solution using the Fill Down logic demonstrates the highest efficiency.

Number of Rows	Solution 2: Merge	Solution 3: Fill Down	Solution 4: Convert to List
1000	0.031337	0.046659	0.08671
10000	0.097672	0.079737	0.123611
100000	0.786016	0.266608	0.928861
500000	4.335289	0.941159	5.201284

Referencing Multiple Previous Rows

Consider the table provided in the previous question and calculate the sales growth rate for each month in comparison to the average sales values of all the preceding months.

In the previous example, the `=(Source[Sales]){[Month]-2}` formula was used to reference the value in the Sales column in the previous row. However, in this example, for month N, it must calculate the average of the sales values in the previous $N-1$ months.

To extract the first N values from a list, you can use the `List.FirstN()` function. Therefore, you can use the following formula for a new custom column to extract the sales values of the previous $N-1$ months for the row with the month equal to N, which results in Figure 2-29:

```
=List.FirstN(Source[Sales],[Month]-1)
```

CHAPTER 2 REFERENCING

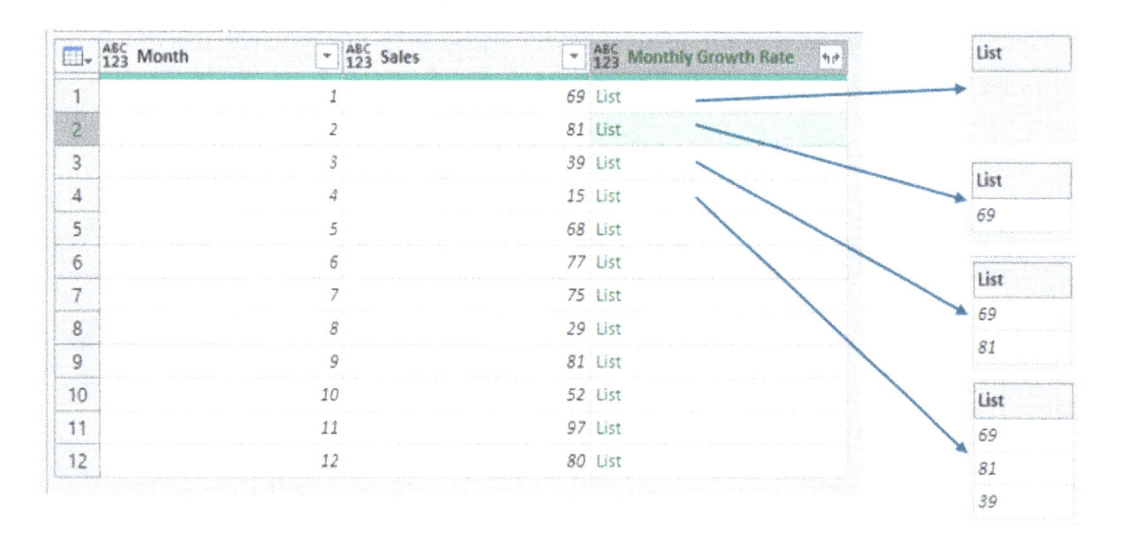

Figure 2-29. Changing the value type

Since the result of the previous formula is a list, you can use the List.Average() function to calculate the average of its items. You can update the formula as follows, which results in the average of sales values in the previous months for each row, as shown in Figure 2-30:

```
=List.Average(List.FirstN(Source[Sales],[Month]-1))
```

	Month	Sales	Monthly Growth Rate
1		1	null
2		2	69
3		3	75
4		4	63
5		5	51
6		6	54.4
7		7	58.16666667
8		8	60.57142857
9		9	56.625
10		10	59.33333333
11		11	58.6
12		12	62.09090909

Figure 2-30. Result of List.Average

111

CHAPTER 2   REFERENCING

Similar to the previous example, to calculate the growth rate, you can use the following formula, which results in Figure 2-31.

```
=[Sales]/List.Average(List.FirstN(Source[Sales],[Month]-1))
```

Month	Sales	Monthly Growth Rate
1	69	null
2	81	1.173913043
3	39	0.52
4	15	0.238095238
5	68	1.333333333
6	77	1.415441176
7	75	1.289398281
8	29	0.478773585
9	81	1.430463576
10	52	0.876404494
11	97	1.655290102
12	80	1.288433382

***Figure 2-31.** Result of List.Average*

To handle null results and replace them with a dash ("-") for the first row, modify the formula by adding ?? to the end of the formula:

```
=[Sales]/List.Average(List.FirstN(Source[Sales],[Month]-1)) ??"-"
```

Note To explain further, you can use the ? operator to handle null values. Suppose x and y are two different formulas. The expression x? checks the result of x and compares it to a null value. It evaluates to true if the result of x is null and false if the result of x is anything other than null. Additionally, the ?? operator can replace null values with an alternative. For example, x??y means: evaluate x and use its result unless the result of x is null; then evaluate y and use it as the result instead.

CHAPTER 2 REFERENCING

By using the previous formula, you can solve the problem. In this solution, `List.FirstN(Source[Sales], [Month]-1)` initially selects the sales values from the Source table and then filters the first *N* values. However, this can be replaced with `Table.FirstN(Source, [Month]-1)[Sales]`, which filters the first *N* rows of the table and then extracts the sales values as a list.

Similarly, all the following formulas will yield the same results:

```
=List.FirstN(Source[Sales],[Month]-1)

=Table.FirstN(Source,[Month]-1) [Sales]

=Table.Column(Table.FirstN(Source,[Month]-1) ,"Sales")

=List.Range(Source[Sales],0,[Month]-1))

=Table.Range(Source,0,[Month]-1) [Sales]
```

Adding Multiple Columns at Once

Consider the Source table as Table 2-6, which provides coding information in a hierarchical format. All codes for products' names (third level) are three characters long. The products' families (level 1) are determined by the left-most character of the code, and the group (level 2) is determined by the first two characters.

For example, the product with code 111 is Compact Powder. Its family (first level) is Cosmetic (code=1), and its group (second level) is Face (code =11).

Instead of displaying all the codes in two columns, separate them into three distinct levels—family, group, and product.

CHAPTER 2   REFERENCING

Table 2-6. Source: Coding

Code	Description
1	Cosmetics
11	Face
111	Compact Powder
12	Lip
121	Lipstick
122	Lip Gloss
2	Men
21	Accessories
211	Belt
212	Hat
213	Sunglasses
22	Shirt
221	Shirt Casual
3	Toys & Accessories
31	Construction Toys
311	Legos

This problem can be addressed in several ways, including merging or using advanced functions, but, in this section, you'll see how to use this table and solve the problem by adding new columns, one for the product's group, another for the products' family, and then filter the desired rows. Consider the product code equal to 211. To extract the product family and group for this code, you can use the following formulas separately in the formula bar (since all values in the Code column are unique).

=Source{[Code=2]}[Description]

=Source{[Code=21]}[Description]

CHAPTER 2   REFERENCING

Writing these two formulas in the custom column window will return the product family and product group for the product with code 211 across all rows. Instead of using the value of 2, and 21 for all the cases, you can use the `Number.IntegerDivide()` function as `Number.IntegerDivide(211, 100)` and `Number.IntegerDivide(211, 10)`. Replacing the value of 211 in these two formulas will make the formula dynamic for all the rows. Add a Custom column to the Source table and use the following formula in the Custom column, resulting in Figure 2-32.

= Source{[Code=Number.IntegerDivide([Code],100)]}[Description]

	Code	Description	Custom
1		1 Cosmetics	Error
2		11 Face	Error
3		111 Compact Powder	Cosmetics
4		12 Lip	Error
5		121 Lip stick	Cosmetics
6		122 Lip Gloss	Cosmetics
7		2 Men	Error
8		21 Accessories	Error
9		211 Belt	Men
10		212 Hat	Men
11		213 Sunglasses	Men
12		22 Shirt	Error
13		221 Shirt Casual	Men
14		3 Toys & Accessories	Error
15		31 Construction Toys	Error
16		311 Lego	Toys & Accessories

Figure 2-32. Adding product families

To extract the product group, add another Custom column using a similar formula:

= Source{[Code=Number.IntegerDivide([Code],10)]}[Description]

After adding these two columns, the problem will be solved by filtering the rows with code greater than 100 or removing the rows including errors on the newly added columns.

115

CHAPTER 2 REFERENCING

As shown, two new columns are added to the Source table, in two different steps, to solve this problem. What if you have to add more columns in a real-world case? Instead of adding the columns separately, all the columns can be added at once by using the characteristic of records in Power Query.

For example, using the Source table, from the Add Column tab, choose the Custom Column command, then use the following formula in the Custom column window:

```
=[
    Family=Source{[Code=Number.IntegerDivide([Code],100)]}[Description],
    Group=Source{[Code=Number.IntegerDivide([Code],10)]}[Description]
]
```

This formula results in Figure 2-33, including the value for both the columns of product's family and group, in the type of record.

#	Code	Description	Custom
1	1	Cosmetics	Record
2	11	Face	Record
3	111	Compact Powder	Record
4	12	Lip	Record
5	121	Lip stick	Record
6	122	Lip Gloss	Record
7	2	Men	Record
8	21	Accessories	Record
9	211	Belt	Record
10	212	Hat	Record
11	213	Sunglasses	Record
12	22	Shirt	Record
13	221	Shirt Casual	Record
14	3	Toys & Accessories	Record
15	31	Construction Toys	Record
16	311	Lego	Record

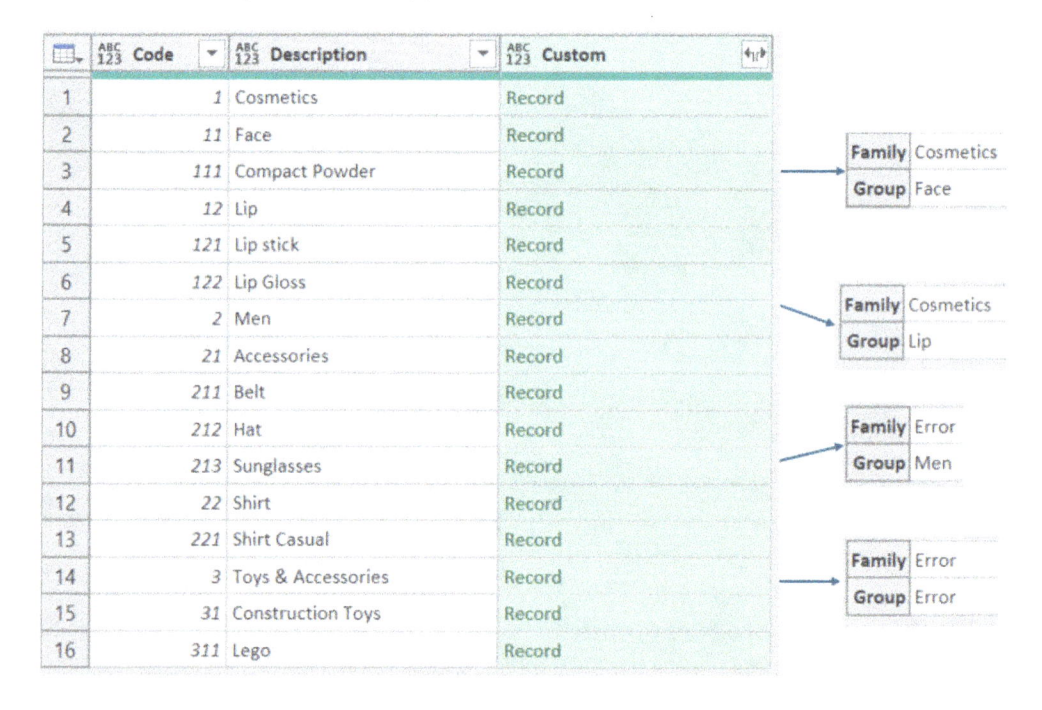

Callouts:
- Family: Cosmetics, Group: Face
- Family: Cosmetics, Group: Lip
- Family: Error, Group: Men
- Family: Error, Group: Error

Figure 2-33. Using a record to add columns once

Next, by expanding this new column, you will get Figure 2-34, in which both the columns are added once. (Even if you define additional fields for the record in the previous step, all of them will be added here.) Select the Remove Errors command from the Remove Rows section in the Home tab. The result is shown in Figure 2-35.

CHAPTER 2   REFERENCING

Code	Description	Family	Group
1	Cosmetics	Error	Error
11	Face	Error	Cosmetics
111	Compact Powder	Cosmetics	Face
12	Lip	Error	Cosmetics
121	Lip stick	Cosmetics	Lip
122	Lip Gloss	Cosmetics	Lip
2	Men	Error	Error
21	Accessories	Error	Men
211	Belt	Men	Accessories
212	Hat	Men	Accessories
213	Sunglasses	Men	Accessories
22	Shirt	Error	Men
221	Shirt Casual	Men	Shirt
3	Toys & Accessories	Error	Error
31	Construction Toys	Error	Toys & Accessories
311	Lego	Toys & Accessories	Construction Toys

Figure 2-34.   Result of expanding a column

Code	Description	Family	Group
111	Compact Powder	Cosmetics	Face
121	Lip stick	Cosmetics	Lip
122	Lip Gloss	Cosmetics	Lip
211	Belt	Men	Accessories
212	Hat	Men	Accessories
213	Sunglasses	Men	Accessories
221	Shirt Casual	Men	Shirt
311	Lego	Toys & Accessories	Construction Toys

Figure 2-35.   Result of removing errors

Using VLOOKUP with Approximate Match in Power Query

Based on the tax rates provided in the TaxRates table in Table 2-7 and the income data in the People_Income table in Table 2-8, add a new column to the People_Income table to calculate each person's tax. (Both tables are loaded into Power Query, called TaxRates and People_Income.)

117

CHAPTER 2 REFERENCING

Table 2-7. TaxRates Table

From	To	Tax Rate
$0	$18,200	0%
$18,201	$45,000	19%
$45,001	$120,000	33%
$120,001	$180,000	37%
$180,001	Over	45%

Table 2-8. People_Income table

Person ID	Income
A	199,920
B	26,068
C	106,439
D	28,521
E	142,566

To compute the tax, use the following logic: For each income value, find its related row in the TaxRates table where income falls between the numbers in the From and To columns, retrieve the tax rate on that row, and multiply it by the income.

This problem can be easily solved in Excel using the VLOOKUP or XLOOKUP function with an approximate match. However, in Power Query, the VLOOKUP function is not available, so you need to combine several functions to achieve the same result.

Before solving this problem for all the people, let's solve it just for the Person ID = "E" with an income of 142,566. By examining the TaxRates table, you can see that this income falls within the range specified in the fourth row of the table, where the tax rate is 37 percent, so the tax value is 0.37*142566.

If you solve this problem using Excel's VLOOKUP, it searches for the value 142566 in the From column, identifies the row with the largest value that is less than or equal to 142566, and returns the tax rate from that row as the result.

118

CHAPTER 2 REFERENCING

In Power Query, you apply a similar logic. First, you filter the rows in the Tax_Rate table where the value in the From column is less than or equal to 142566. Then, you extract the row with the highest value in the From column (i.e., the last row) and use the tax rate from that row for the calculation.

To solve the problem for this person, Go to the TaxRates query, then filter the table based on the values in the From column, and filter all the values less than 142566, as shown in Figure 2-36, to get the result in Figure 2-37.

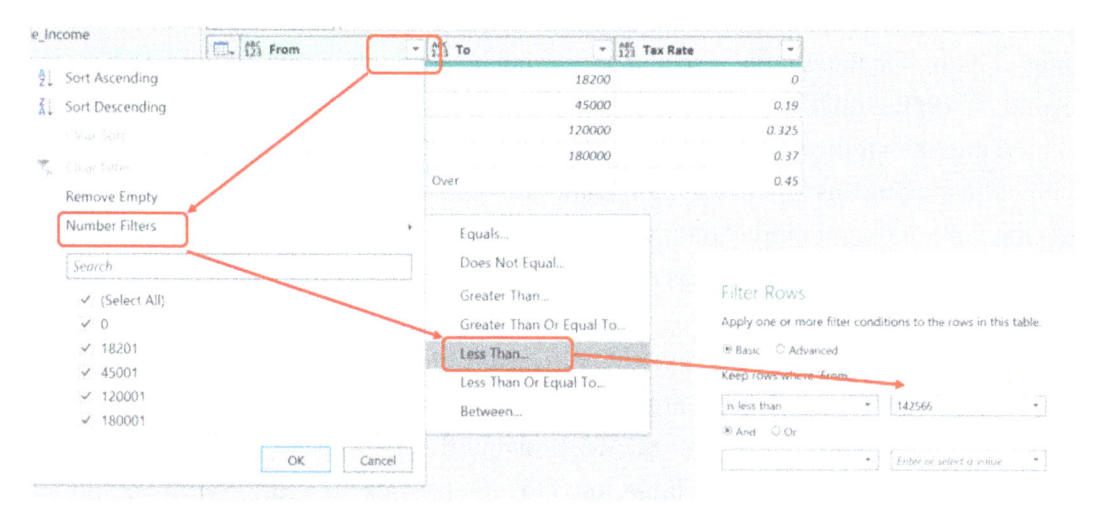

Figure 2-36. Filtering the table

	From	To	Tax Rate
1		0	18200	0
2		18201	45000	0.19
3		45001	120000	0.325
4		120001	180000	0.37

Figure 2-37. The result of filtering

The filtering step will lead to the following formula in the formula bar. (Source is the first step in the Tax_Rates query.)

= Table.SelectRows(Source, each [From] < 142566)

119

In the result table, the last value in the Tax Rate column represents the tax rate for this person. So, to reach tax rates, add [Tax Rate] to the end of the previous formula. It results in a list of tax rates from the filtered table, equal to {0, 0.19, 0.325, 0.37}. To extract the last value from this list, use the List.Last() function. To reach the tax rate for this person, the previous formula can be rewritten as follows:

= List.Last(Table.SelectRows(Source, each [From] < 142566)[Tax Rate])

The previous formula works like VLOOKUP with approximate match logic in Power Query. (If the Tax_Rates table is sorted ascending based on the From column.) This formula filters the rows in the TaxRates table where the From column values are less than 142,566 and then returns the last value on the Tax Rate column in the filtered table.

Before making this formula dynamic and using it as a custom column in the People_Income table, let's first modify the part related to the Table.SelectRows() function. (The reason for this modification is explained at the end of this question and in the next chapter.)

Currently, the formula is written as Table.SelectRows(Source, each [From] < 142566). In this formula, the first argument, Source, specifies the table to filter, and the second argument, each [From] < 142566, provides the filtering condition. The each keyword refers to each row in the table, and [From] accesses the From column of the current row.

Although each usually appears with the underscore character "_" in Power Query, like the form of "each _[From]", the result is the same even if "_" is omitted. In other words, the full version of the formula is Table.SelectRows(Source, each _[From] < 142566).

Here, each _ explicitly refers to every row in the Source table. In this case, since only one table (Source) is being used, the underscore can be skipped without affecting the outcome. However, when working with more complex formulas involving nested functions, it's a good idea to include the underscore to clearly indicate the reference to the row. So, let's consider the full version of the formula as: Table.SelectRows(Source, each _[From] < 142566) and make another change to it.

In Power Query, the each _ expression is equivalent to writing "(x)=> x", " (y)=>y", or any placeholder name like (variable_name) => variable_name. (There is a small difference between each _ and the general definition of (variable_name) => variable_name, which I explain in depth in Chapter 12.) Based on this understanding,

CHAPTER 2 REFERENCING

the following two formulas are identical in functionality and produce the exact same result, differing only in their notation:

```
Table.SelectRows(Source, each _[From] < 142566)
Table.SelectRows(Source, (x)=>x[From] < 142566)
```

Based on this alteration of the Table.SelectRows() part, the formula for extracting the tax rate for person D can be rewritten as follows without changing the result.

```
= List.Last(Table.SelectRows(Source, (x)=> x[From] < 142566)[Tax Rate])
```

This formula can be applied to any person by substituting 142,566 with the income of that person. To apply this logic to the original problem, go back to the problem and consider the queries unchanged. Then, select the People_Income table, go to the Add Column tab, and select Custom Column. Then, use the following formula in the Custom column window to create a new column named Tax Rate:

```
= List.Last(Table.SelectRows(Tax_Rates, (x)=> x[From] < [Income])
[Tax Rate])
```

This is exactly like the previous formula, in which 142566 is replaced with values on the Income column and the Source query is changed to the TaxRates query, as Source is the name of a step in the TaxRates query and, from the People_Income query, you can't directly refer to the name of middle steps of another query.)

Clicking OK results in the tax rate, as shown in Figure 2-38.

#	Person ID	Income	Tax Rate
1	A	199920	0.45
2	B	26068	0.19
3	C	106439	0.325
4	D	28521	0.19
5	E	142566	0.37

Figure 2-38. The tax rate

To calculate the tax, you just need to add another Custom column and multiply the values on the Income and Tax Rate columns using the following formula in the custom column window.

CHAPTER 2   REFERENCING

Note As shown in the steps, to solve this problem, each `[From]` is changed to `(x)=>x` and then used in the custom column for the `People_Info` query. Let's see the reason for this change.

So, considering the unchanged queries, go to the `People_Info` query, then select the Custom Column command. In the open window, write the original formula as follows:

= List.Last(Table.SelectRows(Tax_Rates, each [From] < [Income])[Tax Rate])

Clicking OK will result in an error for the values of the newly added column, as shown in Figure 2-39.

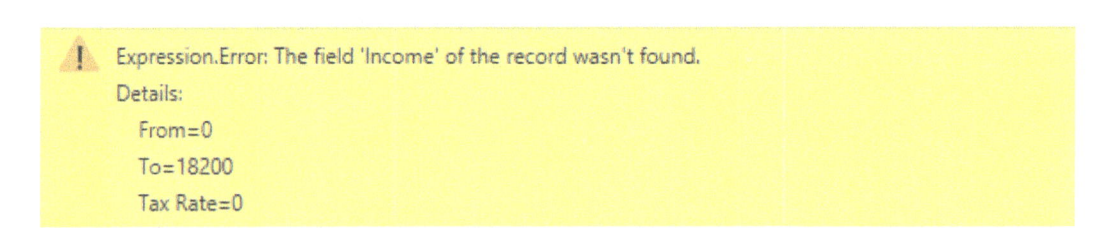

	Person ID	Income	Tax Rate
1	A	199920	Error
2	B	26068	Error
3	C	106439	Error
4	D	28521	Error
5	E	142566	Error

Expression.Error: The field 'Income' of the record wasn't found.
Details:
   From=0
   To=18200
   Tax Rate=0

Figure 2-39. *The result is an error*

To extract the source of error, look at the entire formula in the formula bar, as follows:

```
= Table.AddColumn(
      Source,
      "Tax",
      each List.Last(
                  Table.SelectRows(
                        Tax_Rates,
                              each [From] < [Income]
                                          )[Tax Rate]
      ))
```

As shown, after clicking OK in the Custom Column window, the formula entered is included as part of the third argument in the Table.AddColumn() function. In other words, to add a new column to a table, you use the Table.AddColumn() function. This function typically takes three arguments: the name of the table to which the new column will be added, the name of the new column, and the formula used to calculate the values for the new column.

The formula uses two tables: Source (referring to the last step of People_Income query) and Tax_Rates. In the third argument of Table.AddColumn(), the each _ logic is used twice—once to refer to the rows in the Source table and another time to refer to the rows in the People_Info table. However, it is not clear to Power Query that each _ refer to rows in which table.

In Figure 2-28, the underscores are added before the name of columns. This determines which "_" is related to which each, and which each is related to which "table". This is clear to humans, but due to using each _ to refer to the rows of both tables, it leads to the error in Power Query.

CHAPTER 2 REFERENCING

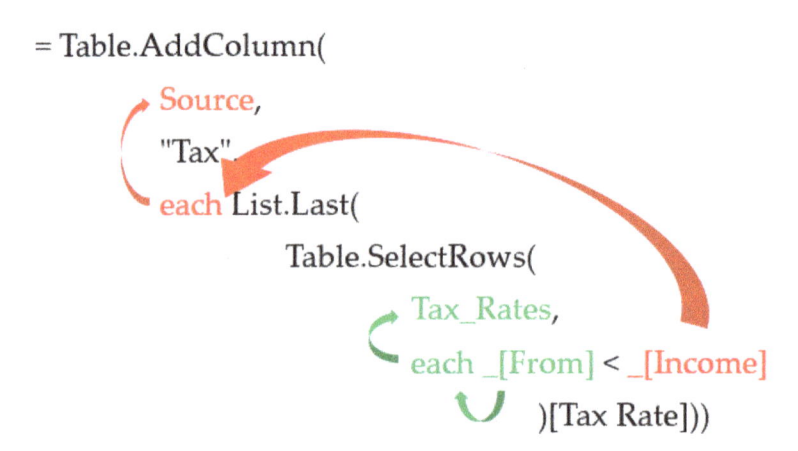

```
= Table.AddColumn(
        Source,
        "Tax",
        each List.Last(
                Table.SelectRows(
                        Tax_Rates,
                        each _[From] < _[Income]
                )[Tax Rate]))
```

Figure 2-40. Dependency of each and tables

To resolve this issue and clarify the reference table for each _, replace the each _ logic with function definition syntax, such as (x) =>, in at least one of the functions. This adjustment ensures that the formula explicitly identifies the reference of each.

The formula can then be rewritten in one of the following forms:

```
= Table.AddColumn(
    Source,
    "Tax",
    (x)=> List.Last(
                Table.SelectRows(
                        Tax_Rates,
                        (y)=> y[From] < x[Income]
                                )[Tax Rate]
    ))
= Table.AddColumn(
    Source,
    "Tax",
    (x)=> List.Last(
                Table.SelectRows(
                        Tax_Rates,
```

```
                              each [From] < x[Income]
                                            )[Tax Rate]
    ))
= Table.AddColumn(
    Source,
    "Tax",
    each List.Last(
            Table.SelectRows(
                Tax_Rates,
                    (y)=> y[From] < [Income]
                                    )[Tax Rate]
    ))
```

Considering the first variation of the formula, it is now clear that x refers to the Source table (the first step of the People_Income query) and y refers to the Tax_Rates table. Therefore, using y[From] < x[Income] clarifies that the From column comes from the Tax_Rates table and the Income column comes from the People_Income table.

Extracting Data from the Price List Table

The price list for the two products is shown in Table 2-9, and historical sales data is shown in Table 2-10. Both tables are loaded into Power Query as separate queries, named PriceList and Historical_Data. Add a new column called Price to the Historical_Data table equal to the last recorded price on the PriceList table with the date before the transaction date. (For example, for the transaction on 22/04/2023, as the last recorded price before this date on the PriceList table is related to 17/04/2023, the price for A and B on this date are, respectively, 15 and 18.)

Table 2-9. *The PriceList Table*

From Date	Product	Price
1/01/2023	A	10
1/01/2023	B	12
17/04/2023	A	15
17/04/2023	B	18
26/07/2023	A	18
3/11/2023	A	21
3/11/2023	B	20

Table 2-10. *The Historical_Data: Historical Sales Values*

Date	Product	Quantity
21/02/2023	B	41
1/03/2023	A	10
10/03/2023	B	10
22/04/2023	B	9
26/04/2023	B	6
2/05/2023	A	39
2/05/2023	B	42
1/06/2023	A	12
19/08/2023	A	18
21/09/2023	B	13
24/10/2023	B	49
27/11/2023	A	32
5/12/2023	B	31

CHAPTER 2　REFERENCING

Before solving the problem for all rows in the Historical_Data table, let's test it by addressing it for the sixth row and extracting the price of product A on 2/05/2023. To do this, select the PriceList query and from the drop-down list next to the Product column, select A, as shown in Figure 2-41. Click OK, which will result in the following formula in the formula bar and lead to Figure 2-42 (Source is the name of first step in the PriceList query).

= Table.SelectRows(Source, each ([Product] = "A"))

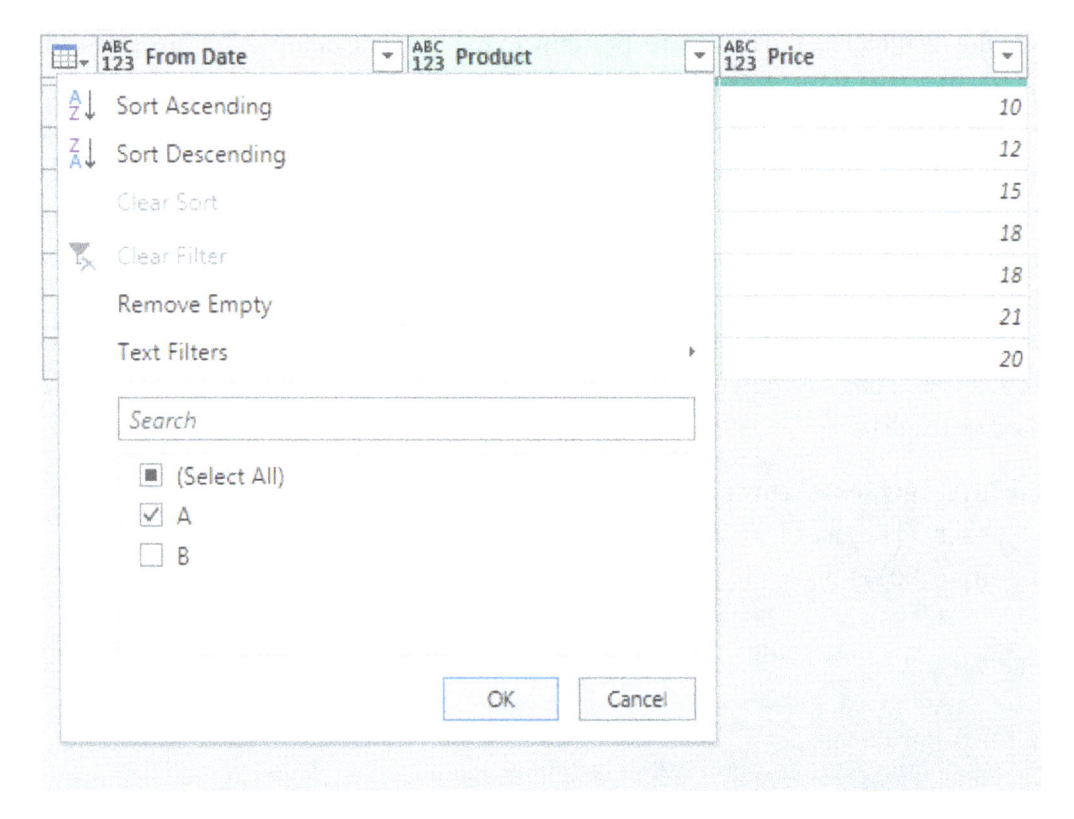

Figure 2-41. Filtering product A

CHAPTER 2   REFERENCING

	From Date	Product	Price
1	1/01/2023 12:00:00 AM	A	10
2	17/04/2023 12:00:00 AM	A	15
3	26/07/2023 12:00:00 AM	A	18
4	3/11/2023 12:00:00 AM	A	21

Figure 2-42. *Result of filtering product A*

In the result table, the row corresponding to the last date before 2/05/2023 should be extracted. Therefore, the From Date column should also be filtered. You can do this filter using UI, like in the previous step, or apply it by modifying the formula in the formula bar. To modify the previous formula, the new criteria for filtering can be added to the second argument of the Table.SelectRows() function by providing the filtering criteria. The formula can be rewritten as the next to apply filters on both columns once, which results in Figure 2-43. In this example, the values in the From Date column are in type DateTime, so <=#datetime(2023, 5, 2, 0, 0, 0) filters any rows with values less than 2023/05/2 00:00 on this column. If the values are in type date, #date(2023, 5, 2) should be used:

```
= Table.SelectRows(Source,
    each ([Product] = "A") and ([From Date] <= #datetime(2023, 5, 2,
    0, 0, 0)))
```

	From Date	Product	Price
1	1/01/2023 12:00:00 AM	A	10
2	17/04/2023 12:00:00 AM	A	15

Figure 2-43. *Result of filtering on Product and Date From*

In the resulting table, the value in the Price column for the last row represents the value that you are searching for (as the rows are sorted ascending based on the dates). This can be extracted by first obtaining the values from the Price column, by adding

CHAPTER 2 REFERENCING

[Price] to the end of the formula, which results in a list including all price list as {10,15}, and then applying the List.Last() formula on the resulted list to reach the value 15. So the previous formula can be rewritten as follows.

= List.Last(Table.SelectRows(Source, each ([Product] = "A") and ([From Date] <= #datetime(2023, 5, 2, 0, 0, 0)))[Price])

Alternatively, the following formula can also be used to extract the values from the last row of the table first by using the Table.Last() function. This function will result in a record including all the values of the last row. Then, to extract the value of the field price, [Price] is written at the end of the formula.

= Table.Last(Table.SelectRows(Source, each ([Product] = "A") and ([From Date] <= #datetime(2023, 5, 2, 0, 0, 0))))[Price]

This formula results in the price for product A on the date 2023/05/02. You can now apply this formula to all rows in the Historical_Data table by replacing A and #datetime(2023, 5, 2, 0, 0, 0) with values from the Product and Date columns, respectively. However, to avoid the errors associated with using two each _ expressions (the condition mentioned in "2.5. Using VLOOKUP with Approximate Match in Power Query"), the formula should be modified first by replacing each _ logic with (x) =>x logic, as follows:

= Table.Last(Table.SelectRows(Source, (x)=> (x[Product] = "A") and (x[From Date] <= #datetime(2023, 5, 2, 0, 0, 0))))[Price]

So, back to the question, considering both the queries unchanged. You select the Historical_Data query and add a new custom column named Price. Then use the following formula in it:

= Table.Last(Table.SelectRows(PriceList, (x)=> (x[Product] = "A") and (x[From Date] <= #datetime(2023, 5, 2, 0, 0, 0))))[Price]

(This is the same as the previous formula, but the step name Source in the PriceList query is replaced with the query name, as you cannot refer to a step in another query directly.) Using this formula will result in Figure 2-44, where the value 15 is repeated for all rows.

CHAPTER 2   REFERENCING

	Date	Product	Quantity	price
1	21/02/2023 12:00:00 AM	B	41	15
2	1/03/2023 12:00:00 AM	A	10	15
3	10/03/2023 12:00:00 AM	B	10	15
4	22/04/2023 12:00:00 AM	B	9	15
5	26/04/2023 12:00:00 AM	B	6	15
6	2/05/2023 12:00:00 AM	A	39	15
7	2/05/2023 12:00:00 AM	B	42	15
8	1/06/2023 12:00:00 AM	A	12	15
9	19/08/2023 12:00:00 AM	A	18	15
10	21/09/2023 12:00:00 AM	B	13	15
11	24/10/2023 12:00:00 AM	B	49	15
12	27/11/2023 12:00:00 AM	A	32	15
13	5/12/2023 12:00:00 AM	B	31	15

Figure 2-44. *Adding a new column*

To make the formula dynamic for all rows, modify the formula in the Custom column window and replace A and #datetime(2023, 5, 2, 0, 0, 0) in the formula with [Product] and [Date], respectively, as provided in the following formula. This modification will produce the updated formula shown in Figure 2-45.

= Table.Last(Table.SelectRows(PriceList, (x)=> (x[Product] = [Product]) and (x[From Date] <= [Date])))[Price]

	Date	Product	Quantity	price
1	21/02/2023 12:00:00 AM	B	41	12
2	1/03/2023 12:00:00 AM	A	10	10
3	10/03/2023 12:00:00 AM	B	10	12
4	22/04/2023 12:00:00 AM	B	9	18
5	26/04/2023 12:00:00 AM	B	6	18
6	2/05/2023 12:00:00 AM	A	39	15
7	2/05/2023 12:00:00 AM	B	42	18
8	1/06/2023 12:00:00 AM	A	12	15
9	19/08/2023 12:00:00 AM	A	18	18
10	21/09/2023 12:00:00 AM	B	13	18
11	24/10/2023 12:00:00 AM	B	49	18
12	27/11/2023 12:00:00 AM	A	32	21
13	5/12/2023 12:00:00 AM	B	31	20

Figure 2-45. *Making the formula dynamic*

So, by adding this column, the formula in the formula bar will be as follows:

```
= Table.AddColumn(
    Source,
    "price",
    each Table.Last(
              Table.SelectRows(
                    PriceList,
                    (x)=> (x[Product] = [Product]) and
                    (x[From Date] <= [Date])
                                          )
                    )[Price]
              )
```

Summary

In real-world scenarios, there are many instances where you need to search for specific values or sets of values across different tables. In this chapter, you learned how to utilize functions and operators to extract these specific values from tables, records, and lists.

While the effectiveness of these techniques can vary based on the cases, most of the time, using functions like Table.SelectRows() is more efficient in terms of time than using operators. Additionally, in a lengthy table, employing the Table.Buffer() and List.Buffer() functions can further optimize the performance of referencing.

The next chapter provides additional tips regarding the Table.Sort() and the Table.SelectRows() functions.

CHAPTER 3

Sorting and Filtering

Sort and Filter are essential commands for cleaning datasets and extracting the desired rows in the desired order. This chapter covers these two important tasks. But before diving into the main problems, you should be familiar with the basics of these two functions.

In Power Query, sorting and filtering rows is straightforward. Consider the Source table shown in Table 3-1.

Table 3-1. Source: Sales Data

Date	Product	Quantity
12/05/2024	b	11
15/05/2024	B	52
14/05/2024	C	29
15/05/2024	B	42
17/05/2024	a	63
15/05/2024	A	47
17/05/2024	A	39

To sort data in ascending order based on the values in the Date column, simply click the down arrow next to the column name and choose Sort Ascending, as shown in Figure 3-1. This will generate the following formula in the formula bar:

```
= Table.Sort(Source,{{"Date", Order.Ascending}})
```

CHAPTER 3 SORTING AND FILTERING

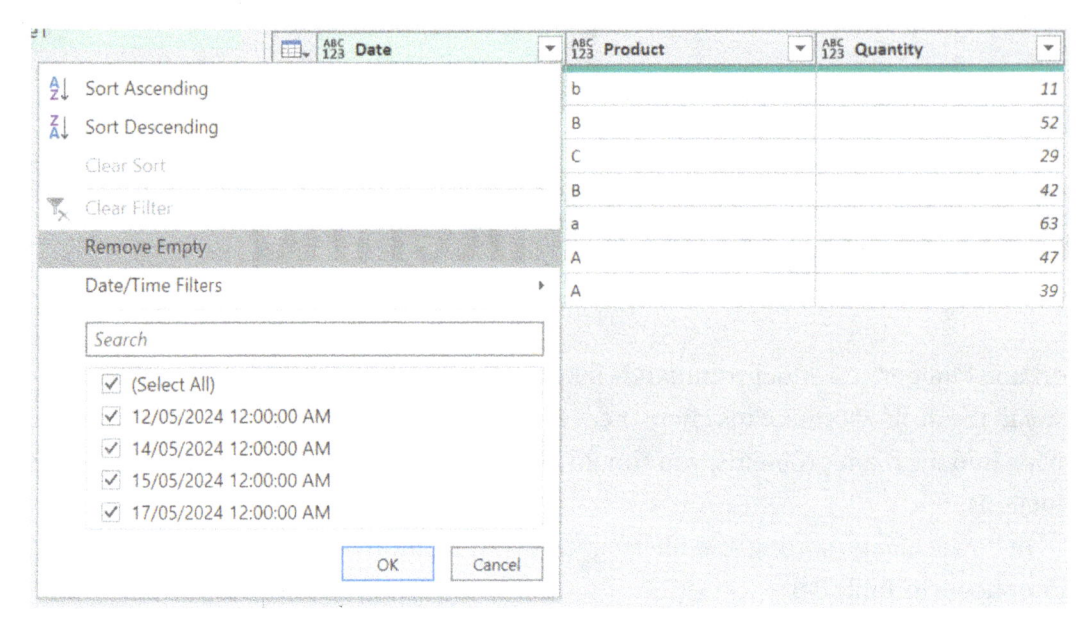

Figure 3-1. The Sort Ascending option

In the resulting table, rows are sorted in ascending order based on the Date column. Since 15/05/2024 12:00:00 AM appears three times in this column, you can add another sorting criterion to sort these rows. To sort rows with the same date in descending order based on the Quantity column, just click the down arrow next to this column and select Sort Descending (see Figure 3-2). Here is the formula in the formula bar:

= Table.Sort(Source,{{"Date", Order.Ascending}, {"Quantity", Order.Descending}})

#	Date	Product	Quantity
1	12/05/2024 12:00:00 AM	b	11
2	14/05/2024 12:00:00 AM	C	29
3	15/05/2024 12:00:00 AM	B	52
4	15/05/2024 12:00:00 AM	A	47
5	15/05/2024 12:00:00 AM	B	42
6	17/05/2024 12:00:00 AM	a	63
7	17/05/2024 12:00:00 AM	A	39

Figure 3-2. Two column sort

CHAPTER 3 SORTING AND FILTERING

In the previous formulas, Order.Descending and Order.Ascending are enumerations that determine the sorting directions, and instead of using them, you can use the values that represent them. The value for Order.Descending is 1, and the value for Order.Ascending is 0. Therefore, without altering the result, the previous formula can be rewritten as shown here:

= Table.Sort(Source,{{"Date", 0}, {"Quantity", 1}})

Like other functions in Power Query, sorting is also case-sensitive. So, sorting the Source table in ascending order based on the Product column results in Figure 3-3. (Later in this chapter, custom logic for sorting is defined.)

	Date	Product	Quantity
1	15/05/2024 12:00:00 AM	A	47
2	17/05/2024 12:00:00 AM	A	39
3	15/05/2024 12:00:00 AM	B	52
4	15/05/2024 12:00:00 AM	B	42
5	14/05/2024 12:00:00 AM	C	29
6	17/05/2024 12:00:00 AM	a	63
7	12/05/2024 12:00:00 AM	b	11

Figure 3-3. Sort based on the Product column

Similar to the sorting process, the filtering process is straightforward in Power Query. To filter rows where the Date is equal to 15/05/2024, as in Figure 3-4, click the down arrow next to the column name and select this date among all the available dates. This results in Figure 3-5, which is generated by the following formula:

= Table.SelectRows(Source, each ([Date] = #datetime(2024, 5, 15, 0, 0, 0)))

135

CHAPTER 3 SORTING AND FILTERING

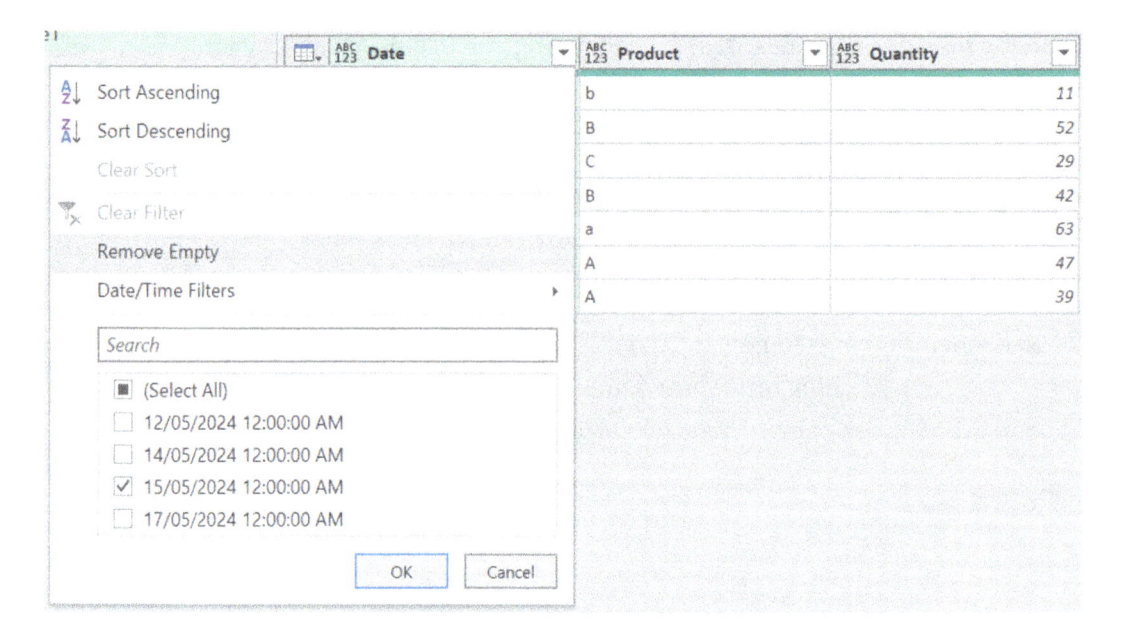

Figure 3-4. Filter date equal to 15/05/2024

Date	Product	Quantity
15/05/2024 12:00:00 AM	B	52
15/05/2024 12:00:00 AM	B	42
15/05/2024 12:00:00 AM	A	47

Figure 3-5. Result of the filter

If you add a filter to the Quantity column and select 52, for example, the formula changes to the following:

= Table.SelectRows(Source, each ([Date] = #datetime(2024, 5, 15, 0, 0, 0)) and ([Quantity] = 52))

The result of the previous formula is exactly the same as the following formula, with the only difference being that the "_" was removed. Since all the column names, in this example, came from the same table, the "_", which represents the table name for each column, can be removed.

CHAPTER 3 SORTING AND FILTERING

```
= Table.SelectRows(Source, each (_[Date] = #datetime(2024, 5, 15, 0, 0, 0))
and (_[Quantity] = 52))
```

In this formula, the condition will be evaluated for each row of the table. If the condition is true for a row, that row will be displayed in the result table. As shown, the function includes two arguments: the name of the table (in the type of table) and the selection criteria (in the type of function). The second argument usually starts with the word each, which is used in Power Query to define a custom function.

As a general rule in Power Query, when you're using each to create a custom function, its optional input variable is represented by an underscore ("_"). For example, when using each _ in the second argument of Table.SelectRows(), for each row of the table, "_" represents a record containing the values of that row, with the field names corresponding to the column headers. For example, for the first row, each _ is equal to [Date="12/05/2024", Product="b", Quantity= 11]. So _[Date] refers to the value in the Date field for that particular record, which is the same as the value in the Date column for that row.

Instead of using the each expression to define a custom function with the variable name of "_", you can use the general custom function definition with any variable (or variables) like x, as in (x) =>. In this case, the ()=> syntax is used to define a function, and the variable name is enclosed in parentheses. So, in the previous formula, each can be replaced with (x)=>, and then "_" should be replaced with x. The previous formula can be rewritten as the following with the same result:

```
= Table.SelectRows(Source, (x)=> (x[Date] = #datetime(2024, 5, 15, 0, 0, 0)) and (x[Quantity] = 52))
```

(If you're wondering why you need to replace the each _ logic with (x) => logic, just wait for Example 3-8 in this chapter.)

Efficiency Tips Filtering rows in Power Query is an important task for improving query execution time, and it is generally recommended to filter out unwanted rows in the early steps. But there is also another rule related to applying filtering commands over the rows.

A key factor in optimizing the consumption time of a filtering action is to simplify the condition as much as possible. For example, consider a table, called Source,

CHAPTER 3 SORTING AND FILTERING

with 10,000 rows including four columns, with the first row shown in Table 3-2. If you want to filter all the rows in this table, and include at least one value in the Objective columns that is greater than the value of the corresponding objective in the first row of the table, you can use the following formula, which takes 29 seconds to execute.

Table 3-2. The First Row

Solution ID	Objective 1	Objective 2	Objective 3
1	32	5	32

```
=Table.SelectRows(Source, each ([Objective 1] >= 
Source[Objective 1]{0} or [Objective 2] >= Source[Objective 
2]{0} or [Objective 3] >= Source[Objective 3]{0}))
```

However, directly referencing the values of the first row in the filter condition, as shown here, reduces the time to just 0.02 seconds:

```
= Table.SelectRows(Source, each ([Objective 1] >= 32 or 
[Objective 2] >= 5 or [Objective 3] >= 32)
```

Based on the basic information provided at the beginning of this chapter, in the rest of this chapter, sort and filter tips are presented using several examples.

Filtering Across Multiple Columns, Part 1

Consider the sales data provided in the Source table shown in Table 3-3 and filter the rows that include the character "*" in at least one column.

CHAPTER 3 SORTING AND FILTERING

Table 3-3. Source: Historical Sales

Date	Product_ID	Customer_ID	Quantity
18/01/2024	P-5	C-03	9
19/01/2024	P-4	C-02	5
20/01/2024	*	C-02	1
*	P-2	C-02	*
23/01/2024	P-3	C-03	7
24/01/2024	P-2	*	8
*	P-5	C-03	6
30/01/2024	P-1	C-03	2
31/01/2024	P-3	C-02	7

Note The data in this example is provided in an Excel file titled `01 Filtering Across Multiple Columns Part 1.xlsx`.

To solve this problem, filter "*" in the Product_ID column. This leads to Figure 3-6 and generates the following formula in the formula bar:

```
= Table.SelectRows(Source, each ([Product_ID] = "*"))
```

Date	Product_ID	Customer_ID	Quantity
20/01/2024 12:00:00 AM	*	C-02	1

Figure 3-6. Result of filtering "" on the Product_ID column*

The previous formula checks for the availability of "*" in the Product_ID column. Similarly, the condition for checking the availability of "*" in other columns can be added by using or between the conditions. The formula can be rewritten as follows:

```
= Table.SelectRows(
      Source, each ([Product_ID] = "*" or [Quantity]="*" or [Date]="*" or
      [Customer_ID]="*"))
```

CHAPTER 3 SORTING AND FILTERING

The problem will be solved efficiently using the previous formula, but in cases where you have more columns, instead of using the previous formula, you can also use the following formula, which results in Figure 3-7.

```
= Table.SelectRows(Source, each List.Contains(Record.ToList(_), "*"))
```

Date	Product_ID	Customer_ID	Quantity
20/01/2024 12:00:00 AM	*	C-02	1
*	P-2	C-02	*
24/01/2024 12:00:00 AM	P-2	*	8
*	P-5	C-03	6

Figure 3-7. *The result of filtering on all the columns*

In this example, as presented in the beginning of this chapter, "_" refers to the values of each row of the Source table, and it is in the type of Record. So, using Record.ToList(_) will convert the record to the list including the values of each row. Using the List.Contains() function, it checks if the list presented in its first argument contains "*".

This formula filters rows across many columns by converting each row into a list and checking for the presence of "*". In another case, to filter the rows that do not include "*" in any column, you can rewrite the formula as follows:

```
= Table.SelectRows(Source, each not List.Contains(Record.ToList(_), "*"))
```

Filtering Across Multiple Columns, Part 2

Similar to the previous example, consider the sales data provided in the Source table, shown in Table 3-4, and filter the rows that contain character "*" in at least one cell.

Table 3-4. Source: Sales Info

Date	Product_ID	Customer_ID	Quantity
18/01/2024	P-5	C-03	9
19/01/2024	P-4	C-02	5
20/01/2024	P-1*	C-02	1
21/01/2024*	P-2	C-02	8*
23/01/2024	P-3	C-03	7
24/01/2024	P-2	C-01*	8
25/01/2024*	P-5	C-03	6
30/01/2024	P-1	C-03	2
31/01/2024	P-3	C-02	7

Note The data in this example is provided in an Excel file titled `02 Filtering Across Multiple Columns Part 2 .xlsx`.

In this problem, to check whether the cells in the rows contain "*" using text functions, first, select all columns. From the Home tab, convert the data type of all columns to text (this step makes the process easier, as the `Text.Contains()` function can be applied on values in the type of text). Next, click the filter icon next to the Product_ID column, choose Text Filter, select Contains, and enter *, as shown in Figure 3-8.

CHAPTER 3 SORTING AND FILTERING

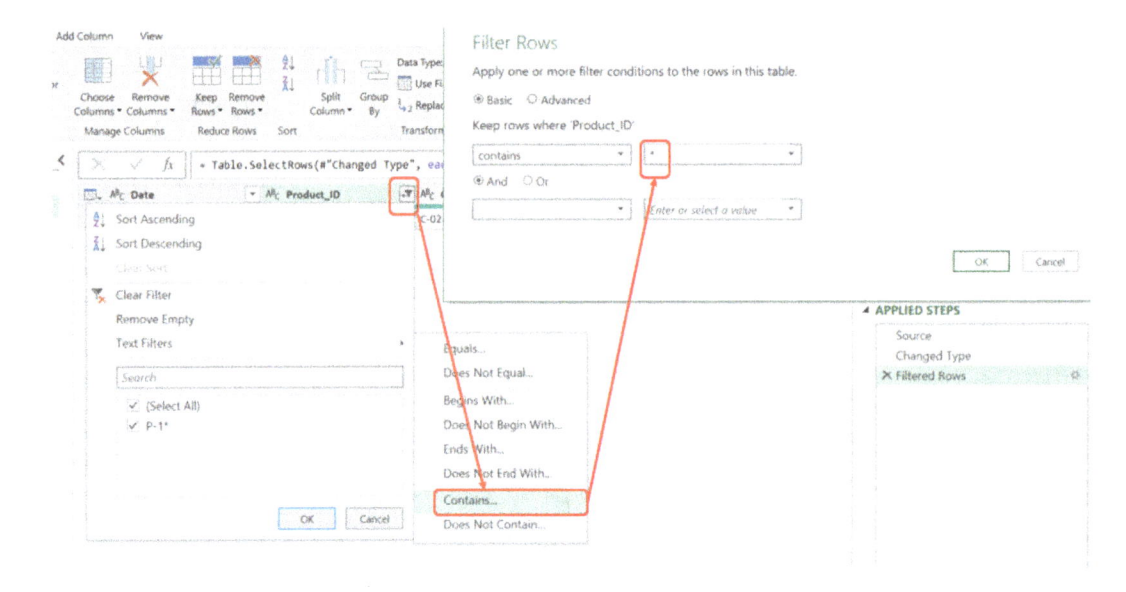

Figure 3-8. *Setting the filter*

These changes will generate the following formula in the formula bar:

= Table.SelectRows(#"Changed Type", each Text.Contains([Product_ID], "*"))

If the number of columns is limited, the previous formula can be rewritten to include additional columns in the filter criteria, ensuring that "*" is checked across all relevant columns.

= Table.SelectRows(
    #"Changed Type",
    each Text.Contains([Date], "*") or
    Text.Contains([Product_ID], "*") or
    Text.Contains([Customer_ID], "*") or
    Text.Contains([Quantity], "*"))

But if there are many, many columns, the formula can be simplified to filter rows based on the presence of "*" in any column. Do this using the following formula, which results in Figure 3-9:

= Table.SelectRows(#"Changed Type", each Text.Contains(Text.Combine(Record.ToList(_)), "*"))

CHAPTER 3 SORTING AND FILTERING

	ABC Date	ABC Product_ID	ABC Customer_ID	ABC Quantity
1	20/01/2024 12:00:00 AM	P-1*	C-02	1
2	21/01/2024*	P-2	C-02	8*
3	24/01/2024 12:00:00 AM	P-2	C-01*	8
4	25/01/2024*	P-5	C-03	6

Figure 3-9. Result of the filter

In this formula, in the Table.SelectRows() function, the result of each _ for each row is a record containing all the values for that row with field names matching the column names. For example, for the first row, it is equal to: [Date="18/01/2024 12:00:00 AM", Product_ID="P-5", Customer_ID="C-03", Quantity="9"].

Using each Record.ToList(_), the record is converted into a list of values. For the first row, this results in {"18/01/2024 12:00:00 AM", "P-5", "C-03", "9"}. Next, the Text.Combine(Record.ToList(_)) concatenates all the values in this list into a single text string. So, for the first row, this results in "18/01/2024 12:00:00 AMP-5C-039".

The Text.Contains() function is then used to check if this concatenated text contains "*" or not. Therefore, Text.Contains(Text.Combine(Record.ToList(_)), "*") will return true if at least one cell in the row contains "*", and false otherwise.

Efficiency Tips In this example, when running a query on a dataset with 500,000 rows, the execution time is approximately 4 seconds for the second solution. Additionally, adding 12 more columns to the table increases the runtime to 12 seconds. Using the or function between conditions for all column names results in faster performance, reducing the runtime to around 3 seconds for the same dataset with the additional columns.

The key issue regarding the use of or conditions is about using hardcoded column names. The code should be modified after changing the column name or adding a new column to the table.

Filtering Across Multiple Columns, Part 3

The information on yearly purchases by customers is provided in the Source table, as shown in Table 3-5. Extract the list of customer IDs who made seven or fewer purchases at least in two years.

CHAPTER 3   SORTING AND FILTERING

Table 3-5. *Source: the Purchase Info*

Customer ID	2018	2019	2020	2021	2022	2023
C-1	15	16	14	27	11	11
C-2	12	27	3	11	4	7
C-3	14	6	14	5	19	12
C-4	11	26	17	11	6	10
C-5	5	9	8	17	18	14
C-6	19	18	5	19	2	10
C-7	15	7	22	22	12	30
C-8	18	14	11	15	19	13
C-9	15	22	10	7	17	19
C-10	28	20	26	18	13	9
C-11	22	11	17	13	21	23
C-12	4	5	2	13	5	3
C-13	8	12	9	8	13	11
C-14	14	4	13	10	10	24
C-15	6	3	6	18	3	4

Note   The data in this example is provided in an Excel file titled `03 Filtering Across Multiple Columns Part 3.xlsx`.

Two different solutions are provided for this problem as follows.

Solution 1: Initial Filtering

Instead of considering all the columns for filtering, you can initially filter the rows that have a value less than or equal to 7 in the 2018 column, by using the following formula:

```
= Table.SelectRows(Source, each _[2018] <= 7)
```

CHAPTER 3 SORTING AND FILTERING

In this formula, using each _ [2018] <= 7 in the second argument filters the rows where the value in the 2018 column is less than or equal to 7. But to solve the problem, you need to consider the values of all the years (all the columns except the first one).

To extend this approach and find customers with seven or fewer purchases in at least two years, the formula can be modified as follows (this results in Figure 3-10):

```
= Table.SelectRows(
      Source,
      each List.Count(List.Select(List.Skip(Record.ToList(_)),
      (x)=> x <= 7))>=2)
```

Customer ID	1.2 2018	1.2 2019	1.2 2020	1.2 2021	1.2 2022	1.2 2023
1 C-2		12	27	3	11	4	7
2 C-3		14	6	14	5	19	12
3 C-6		19	18	5	19	2	10
4 C-12		4	5	2	13	5	1
5 C-15		6	3	6	18	3	4

Figure 3-10. The result of the filter

As presented, the selection condition is "each List.Count(List.Select(List. Skip(Record.ToList(_)), (x) => x <= 7)) >= 2". Let's break down this formula step by step.

Using each_ in the second argument results in a record for each row of the source table. For example, for the first row, this results in [Customer ID="C-1", 2018=15, 2019=16, 2020=14, 2021=27, 2022=11, 2023=11].

As it is hard to apply a condition over the values in a record, the records are converted into lists by using each Record.ToList(_). The result of this formula for the first row is { "C-1", 15, 16, 14, 27, 11, 11 }.

The first item in the result list is the Customer ID, and it is not required for creating filtering conditions, so the List.Skip() function is used in each List.Skip(Record. ToList(_)) to neglect the first items in the lists. This results in { 15, 16, 14, 27, 11, 11 } for the first row.

Out of all the values in the list, you are searching for those that are less than or equal to 7, so each List.Select(List.Skip(Record.ToList(_)), (x) => x <= 7) is used to filter the items into the list that are less than or equal to 7. For the first row, this results in {}, but for the second row, this results in { 3, 4, 7 }.

145

CHAPTER 3   SORTING AND FILTERING

In the next step, the `List.Count()` function is used, as in each `List.Count(List.Select(List.Skip(Record.ToList(_)), (x) => x <= 7))` to count the number of values less than or equal to 7. For the first row, the result of the count is 0, and for the second row, it is 3.

In the last step, the result of the count is compared by threshold 2 and it returns `true` if the count value is greater than or equal to 2. The formula solves the problem by filtering the rows that have at least two values equal to or less than 7.

Solution 2: Unpivoting and Using Group By

If the first solution seems complex, you can use this alternative approach. For the second solution, right-click the Customer ID column and select Unpivot Other Columns, resulting in Figure 3-11.

	Customer ID	Attribute	Value
1	C-1	2018	15
2	C-1	2019	16
3	C-1	2020	14
4	C-1	2021	27
5	C-1	2022	11
6	C-1	2023	11
7	C-2	2018	12
8	C-2	2019	27
9	C-2	2020	3
10	C-2	2021	11
11	C-2	2022	4
12	C-2	2023	7
13	C-3	2018	14
14	C-3	2019	6
15	C-3	2020	14

Figure 3-11. *The result of unpivoting*

In the next step, on the Value column, filter the value less than or equal to 7, to remove the years for values greater than 7 for each customer. This results in Figure 3-12.

CHAPTER 3 SORTING AND FILTERING

fx `= Table.SelectRows(#"Unpivoted Other Columns", each [Value] <= 7)`

#	Customer ID	Attribute	Value
1	C-2	2020	3
2	C-2	2022	4
3	C-2	2023	7
4	C-3	2019	6
5	C-3	2021	5
6	C-4	2022	6
7	C-5	2018	5
8	C-6	2020	5
9	C-6	2022	2
10	C-7	2019	7
11	C-9	2021	7
12	C-12	2018	4
13	C-12	2019	5

Figure 3-12. *The result of filtering values less than or equal to 7*

The resulting table includes only the years with values less than or equal to 7 for the customers. You now need to count the number of repetitions of each customer ID in this table. So, select the Customer ID column, and from the Home tab, choose the Group By command and configure the settings as shown in Figure 3-13. This will produce a table with two columns—the Customer ID and the number of its repetitions (the number of years with a value less than or equal to 7). See Figure 3-14.

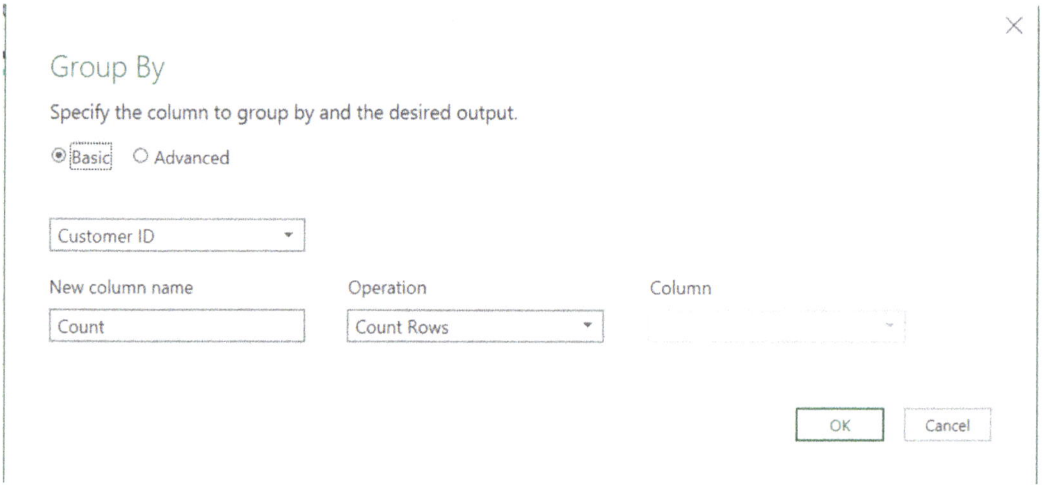

CHAPTER 3 SORTING AND FILTERING

Figure 3-13. Using Group By

	Customer ID	Count
1	C-2	3
2	C-3	2
3	C-4	1
4	C-5	1
5	C-6	2
6	C-7	1
7	C-9	1
8	C-12	5
9	C-14	1
10	C-15	5

Figure 3-14. The result of grouping

CHAPTER 3   SORTING AND FILTERING

In the next step, the problem is solved, and the Customer IDs with value less than or equal to 7 in at least two years are extracted. This is done by filtering rows where their values on the Count column is greater than or equal to 2.

Extracting a First Purchasing Date

The historical sales data for customers, sorted by the Quantity column, is provided in the Source table shown in Table 3-6. Extract the first purchase date of each customer.

Table 3-6. *Source: Student Grads*

Date	Customer_ID	Quantity
20/01/2024	C-02	1
30/01/2024	C-03	2
19/01/2024	C-02	5
25/01/2024	C-03	6
23/01/2024	C-03	7
31/01/2024	C-02	7
21/01/2024	C-02	8
24/01/2024	C-01	8
18/01/2024	C-01	9

Note The data in this example is provided in an Excel file titled `04 First Purchasing Date.xlsx`.

Two different solutions, based on sorting and grouping, are provided as outlined in this section.

Solution 1: Based on Sorting

Before exploring the solution, let's review the result of removing duplicate Customer_ID values using the `Table.Distinct()` function. To remove duplicate Customer_IDs,

CHAPTER 3   SORTING AND FILTERING

right-click this column and select the Remove Duplicates command. This generates the following formula in the formula bar and produces the table shown in Figure 3-15, which includes only the rows where each Customer_ID appears for the first time.

= Table.Distinct(Source,{"Customer_ID"})

	Date	Customer_ID	Quantity
1	20/01/2024 12:00:00 AM	C-02	1
2	30/01/2024 12:00:00 AM	C-03	2
3	24/01/2024 12:00:00 AM	C-01	8

Figure 3-15. *Removing duplicate Customer_IDs*

Based on this explanation, to solve this problem, you can sort the table in ascending order based on the Date column. Then, removing duplicate values from the Customer_ID column should ideally yield the first purchase date for each Customer_ID. However, this approach produces an unexpected result, as shown in Figure 3-16.

= Table.Distinct(#"Sorted Rows", {"Customer_ID"})

	Date	Customer_ID	Quantity
1	20/01/2024 12:00:00 AM	C-02	1
2	24/01/2024 12:00:00 AM	C-01	8
3	30/01/2024 12:00:00 AM	C-03	2

Figure 3-16. *Removing duplicate Customer_IDs*

In the provided result, it appears that duplicate rows are removed first, and then the remaining rows are sorted based on the Date column. This happens because Power Query does not execute all commands in the order they are written; instead, it optimizes the execution sequence for better performance.

To address this issue, you need to force Power Query to execute the sorting command before removing duplicates. To do this, consider the following formula generated in the formula bar after executing the Remove Duplicates command:

= Table.Distinct(#"Sorted Rows", {"Customer_ID"})

CHAPTER 3   SORTING AND FILTERING

To address the issue, you simply need to add the `Table.Buffer()` function before the name of the table (the first argument), as shown here. This results in Figure 3-17.

```
= Table.Distinct(Table.Buffer(#"Sorted Rows"), {"Customer_ID"})
```

	Date	Customer_ID	Quantity
1	18/01/2024 12:00:00 AM	C-01	9
2	19/01/2024 12:00:00 AM	C-02	5
3	23/01/2024 12:00:00 AM	C-03	7

***Figure 3-17.** The final result*

Note   To check this weird behavior of sorting in Power Query, consider another example. Consider a source table with two columns, Row and Value, containing 1,048,575 rows. The Row column lists numbers from 1 to 1,048,575 (matching Excel's row limit) in ascending order, while the Value column contains only the value A, as shown in Figure 3-18.

CHAPTER 3 SORTING AND FILTERING

row	value
1	1 A
2	2 A
3	3 A
4	4 A
5	5 A
6	6 A
7	7 A
8	8 A
9	9 A
10	10 A
11	11 A
12	12 A
13	13 A
14	14 A
15	15 A
16	16 A
17	17 A
18	18 A
19	19 A
20	20 A

Figure 3-18. *Part of the Source table*

In the first scenario, right-clicking the Value column and selecting Remove Duplicates results in a single remaining row, related to the first row of the Source table, as shown in Figure 3-19.

```
= Table.Distinct(Source, {"value"})
```

row	value
1	1 A

Figure 3-19. *The result of removing duplicates*

CHAPTER 3 SORTING AND FILTERING

In another scenario, let's sort the Row column in descending order, which results in Figure 3-20.

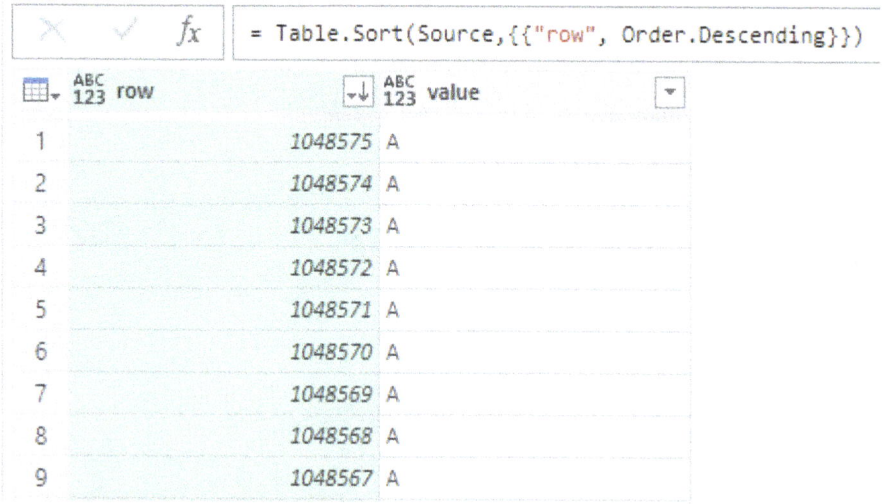

```
fx  = Table.Sort(Source,{{"row", Order.Descending}})
```

	row	value	
1		1048575	A
2		1048574	A
3		1048573	A
4		1048572	A
5		1048571	A
6		1048570	A
7		1048569	A
8		1048568	A
9		1048567	A

Figure 3-20. The result of sorting the row column in descending order

Then, by right-clicking the Value column and selecting Remove Duplicates, again the result is unexpectedly the same as in the previous scenario, as shown in Figure 3-21.

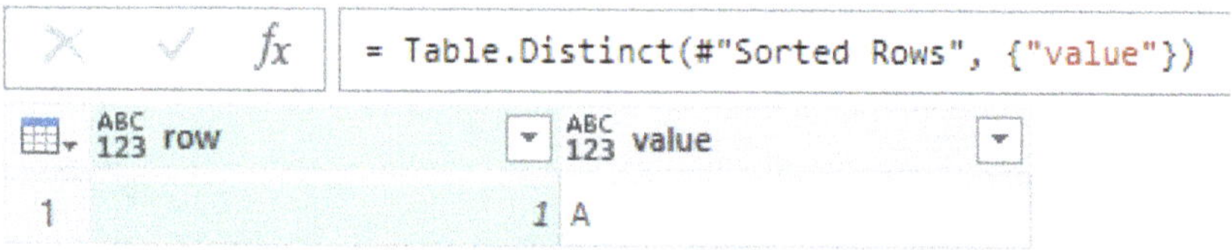

```
fx  = Table.Distinct(#"Sorted Rows", {"value"})
```

	row	value	
1		1	A

Figure 3-21. The result of removing duplicates

CHAPTER 3 SORTING AND FILTERING

This is strange, as it appears that Power Query is neglecting the sorting step first and executing the Remove Duplicates step prior to sorting. To resolve this issue, the `Table.Buffer()` function can be used to ensure the sorting command will be applied before the removing duplicate command. Instead of using this usual formula to remove duplicates:

`= Table.Distinct(#"Sorted Rows", {"value"})`

Use this formula, which results in Figure 3-22:

`= Table.Distinct(Table.Buffer(#"Sorted Rows"), {"value"})`

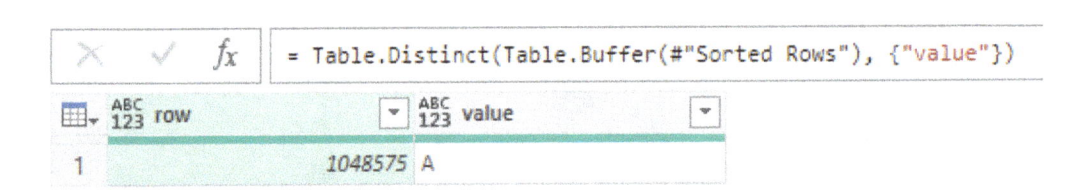

row	value
1	1048575 A

Figure 3-22. The result of removing duplicates after buffering the sorted table

Solution 2: Grouping

This problem can be solved alternatively by grouping the rows based on Customer_IDs and selecting the minimum date. To do this, right-click the Customer_ID column and choose the Group By command. Then, configure it as shown in Figure 3-23 and click OK. This results in the final table shown in Figure 3-24.

CHAPTER 3　SORTING AND FILTERING

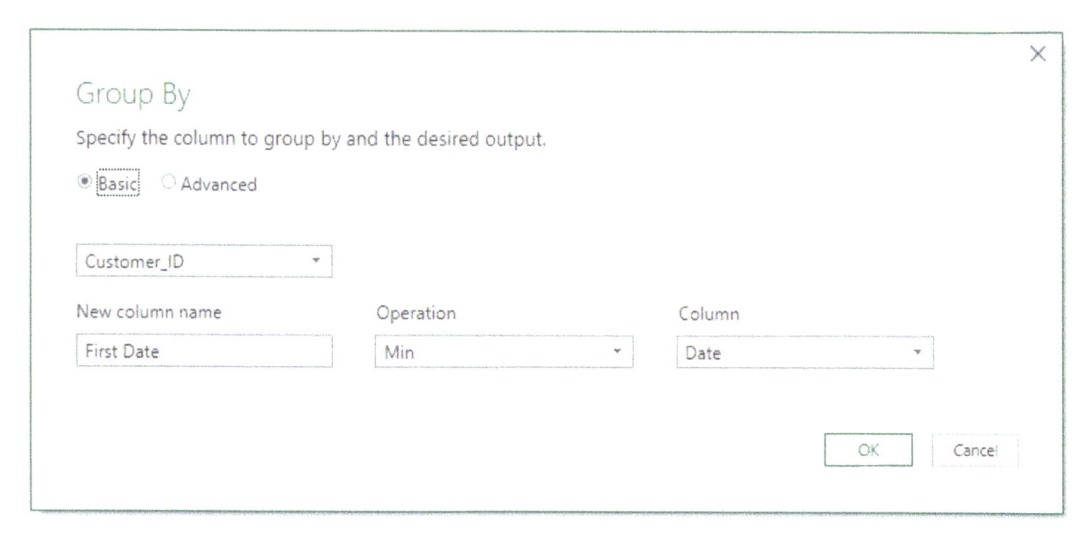

Figure 3-23. Setting Table.Group()

Figure 3-24. The result of grouping

Filtering Based on a List of Values

The Source table, shown in Table 3-7, provides a list of patients scheduled for consultations and surgeries. Filters the historical visit and surgery information of patients who have undergone surgery at least once.

CHAPTER 3 SORTING AND FILTERING

Table 3-7. *Source: Patients*

Date	Patient_ID	Gender	Referral
18/01/2024	P-01	Male	Visit
23/01/2024	P-01	Male	Surgery
8/02/2024	P-01	Male	Visit
19/01/2024	P-02	Male	Visit
20/01/2024	P-03	Female	Visit
22/01/2024	P-04	Female	Visit
24/01/2024	P-04	Female	Visit
23/01/2024	P-05	Male	Visit
7/02/2024	P-05	Male	Surgery
17/02/2024	P-05	Male	Visit
24/01/2024	P-06	Female	Visit
3/02/2024	P-06	Female	Visit
9/02/2024	P-06	Female	Visit
25/01/2024	P-07	Female	Visit
10/02/2024	P-07	Female	Surgery
14/02/2024	P-07	Female	Visit
25/01/2024	P-08	Male	Visit
31/01/2024	P-08	Male	Surgery
30/01/2024	P-09	Female	Visit
31/01/2024	P-10	Female	Visit
2/02/2024	P-11	Male	Visit
23/02/2024	P-11	Male	Visit
3/02/2024	P-12	Female	Visit
4/02/2024	P-12	Female	Visit
21/02/2024	P-12	Female	Visit

(*continued*)

Table 3-7. (*continued*)

Date	Patient_ID	Gender	Referral
4/02/2024	P-13	Female	Visit
5/02/2024	P-14	Male	Surgery
14/02/2024	P-14	Male	Surgery
28/02/2024	P-14	Male	Visit

Note The data in this example is provided in an Excel file titled `05 Filtering Based on a List of Values.xlsx`.

Before solving this challenge, assume you have a list of surgery patients identified as P-01, P-05, P-07, P-08, and P-14. Using this list, you can easily select these patients from the Filter dropdown shown in Figure 3-25, which results in the following formula in the formula bar:

```
= Table.SelectRows(Source, each
      ([Patient_ID] = "P-01" or
      [Patient_ID] = "P-05" or
      [Patient_ID] = "P-07" or
      [Patient_ID] = "P-08" or
      [Patient_ID] = "P-14"))
```

CHAPTER 3 SORTING AND FILTERING

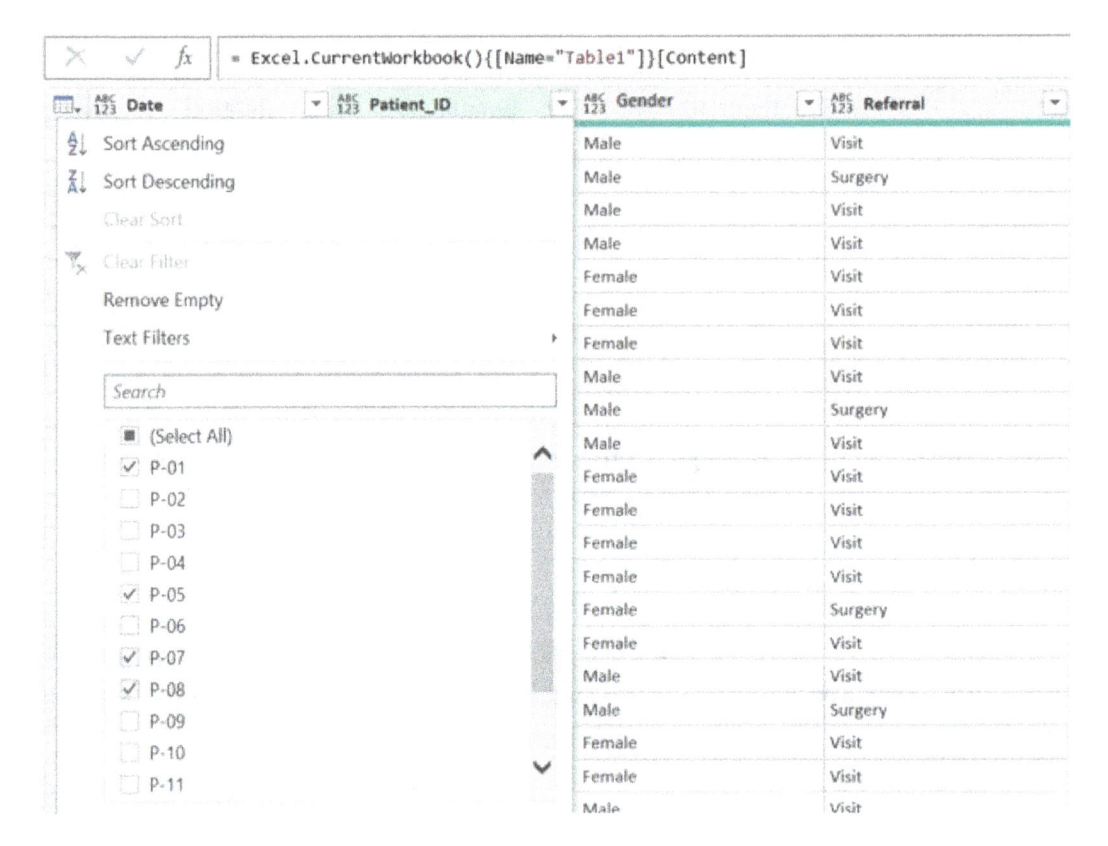

Figure 3-25. Filtering patient IDs

If you need to filter many patient IDs (like a hundred), instead of selecting each one manually, you can enter them in a list and use the List.Contains() function to filter a row, if the Patient_ID of that row is available in the defined list. The previous formula can be rewritten as follows, without changing the result:

```
= Table.SelectRows(
    Source,
    each List.Contains({"P-01", "P-05" , "P-07", "P-08",
    "P-14"},[Patient_ID]))
```

But in the question, the IDs of those who had surgery were not predefined, and you need to initially extract the list of patients who have undergone surgery and then use the previous formula to filter their historical records.

CHAPTER 3 SORTING AND FILTERING

To extract the list of patients who have undergone surgery, filter the Source table by filtering the Referral column and then select the rows with the value of Surgery, using the following formula:

= Table.SelectRows(Source, each ([Referral] = "Surgery"))

The previous formula results in a table. However, you need the patient IDs as a list. Add the column name to the end of the previous formula to obtain a list of patient IDs who had a surgery in their records. Doing so results in Figure 3-26.

= Table.SelectRows(Source, each ([Referral] = "Surgery"))[Patient_ID]

	List
1	P-01
2	P-05
3	P-07
4	P-08
5	P-14
6	P-14

Figure 3-26. *Extracting the list of patient IDs*

Now you can use this formula instead of using hardcoded patient IDs in the formula shown at the beginning of solving this problem. Use the following formula, which results in Figure 3-27:

```
= Table.SelectRows(
      Source,
      each List.Contains(
          Table.SelectRows(Source,
              each ([Referral] = "Surgery"))[Patient_ID]
              ,[Patient_ID]))
```

CHAPTER 3 SORTING AND FILTERING

	Date	Patient_ID	Gender	Referral
1	18/01/2024 12:00:00 AM	P-01	Male	Visit
2	23/01/2024 12:00:00 AM	P-01	Male	Surgery
3	8/02/2024 12:00:00 AM	P-01	Male	Visit
4	23/01/2024 12:00:00 AM	P-05	Male	Visit
5	7/02/2024 12:00:00 AM	P-05	Male	Surgery
6	17/02/2024 12:00:00 AM	P-05	Male	Visit
7	25/01/2024 12:00:00 AM	P-07	Female	Visit
8	10/02/2024 12:00:00 AM	P-07	Female	Surgery
9	14/02/2024 12:00:00 AM	P-07	Female	Visit
10	25/01/2024 12:00:00 AM	P-08	Male	Visit
11	31/01/2024 12:00:00 AM	P-08	Male	Surgery
12	5/02/2024 12:00:00 AM	P-14	Male	Surgery
13	14/02/2024 12:00:00 AM	P-14	Male	Surgery
14	28/02/2024 12:00:00 AM	P-14	Male	Visit

Figure 3-27. Final results

Efficiency Tips The problem is solved. Let's call this solution Variation 1. Go to the Home tab and choose the Advanced Editor command. All the steps of the query will be shown as follows:

```
let
    Source = Excel.CurrentWorkbook(){[Name="Table1"]}[Content],
    #"Filtered Rows" = Table.SelectRows(Source, each List.Contains
    (Table.SelectRows(Source, each ([Referral] = "Surgery"))
    [Patient_ID],[Patient_ID]))
in
    #"Filtered Rows"
```

In Variation 1, patients with a past surgery are extracted using the `Table.SelectRows(Source, each ([Referral] = "Surgery"))[Patient_ID]` formula, and this formula is directly applied to the `Table.SelectRows()` function within the step named `#"Filtered Rows"`. Let's separate these steps and create an intermediate step named PatientID before the `#"Filtered Rows"` step. This intermediate step will be equal to `Table.SelectRows(Source,`

CHAPTER 3 SORTING AND FILTERING

each ([Referral] = "Surgery"))[Patient_ID]. Then, you can use the result of this intermediate step in the #"Filtered Rows" step, as shown in the following formula. This code is Variation 2.

```
let
    Source = Excel.CurrentWorkbook(){[Name="Table1"]}[Content],
    PatientID=Table.SelectRows(Source, each ([Referral] = "Surgery"))
    [Patient_ID], #"Filtered Rows" = Table.SelectRows(Source, each List.
    Contains(PatientID,[Patient_ID]))
in
    #"Filtered Rows"
```

In another variation, called Variation 3, you could add the List.Buffer() function to the PatientID step, as follows.

```
let
    Source = Excel.CurrentWorkbook(){[Name="Table1"]}[Content],
    PatientID=List.Buffer(Table.SelectRows(Source, each ([Referral] = "Surgery"))[Patient_ID]),
    #"Filtered Rows" = Table.SelectRows(Source, each List.
    Contains(PatientID,[Patient_ID]))
in
    #"Filtered Rows"
```

To check the performance of these three variations, a test table with 10,000 rows is considered. The first variation, which did not use buffering, solved the problem in 237 seconds, while the second variation took 288 seconds. By simply applying List.Buffer() on the list of patients, as in the third variation, the runtime was drastically reduced to 0.74 seconds.

> **Note** In this example, both of the following formulas can be used to extract the rows related to patients who never had surgery:

```
let
    Source = Excel.CurrentWorkbook(){[Name="Table1"]}[Content],
    PatientID=List.Buffer(Table.SelectRows(Source, each ([Referral] =
    "Surgery"))[Patient_ID]),
    #"Filtered Rows" = Table.SelectRows(Source, each not List.
    Contains(PatientID,[Patient_ID]))
in
    #"Filtered Rows"

let
    Source = Excel.CurrentWorkbook(){[Name="Table1"]}[Content],
    #"Filtered Rows" = Table.RemoveMatchingRows( Source, Table.
    ToRecords( Table.SelectRows(Source, each ([Referral] = "Surgery"))
    [[Patient_ID]]),"Patient_ID")
in
    #"Filtered Rows"
```

Filtering Based on Sequence

Consider the previous example and extract the list of patient IDs who revisited the doctor after having surgery.

In the table, different patterns might be seen in the patient's referral. For example, if you sort the table based on the Date column in ascending order, the order of referral history for P-01 is Visit/Surgery/Visit, and for P-04, it is Visit/Visit. Among all the patients, you are searching for those who include Surgery/Visit (visiting the doctor after surgery) as part of their referral patterns. To solve this question, you initially sort the table based on the Date column, then extract the referral sequence for each patient, and finally filter those included in the desired pattern.

Initially sort the table by the Date column in ascending order. This results in the following formula in the formula bar:

=Table.Sort(Source,{{"Date", Order.Ascending}})

CHAPTER 3　SORTING AND FILTERING

Based on the information in Section 3-4, if you use the result of this sorted table in the next step, Power Query may rearrange the execution order, causing this step not to be applied first. So rewrite the previous formula as shown here, by using the Table.Buffer() function:

=Table.Buffer(Table.Sort(Source,{{"Date", Order.Ascending}}))

After sorting the table, you need to extract the sequence of referrals for each patient. To do this, you can group the rows based on the Patient IDs using the Group By command in the Home tab. So, select this command, then in the open window, switch to the Advanced settings.

The Group By window consists of two sections: the grouping section (top part) and the aggregation section (bottom part). In the grouping section, you specify which columns are used to group the rows. In the aggregation section, you define the type of calculations or summaries to be applied to the grouped data, such as counting the rows in each group.

Select Patient_ID in the grouping section. In the aggregation section, you need all the historical data; therefore, choose All Rows as the operation and name this column All. Additionally, you need to extract the sequence of referrals. To do this, add a new aggregation and name it Sequence. For this column, you need to apply a concatenation operation over the text in the Referral column. However, since there is no direct concatenation operation available, as shown in Figure 3-28, select Sum as the operation and choose Referral as the column. Clicking OK will result in Figure 3-29, where the rows are grouped based on the Patient IDs.

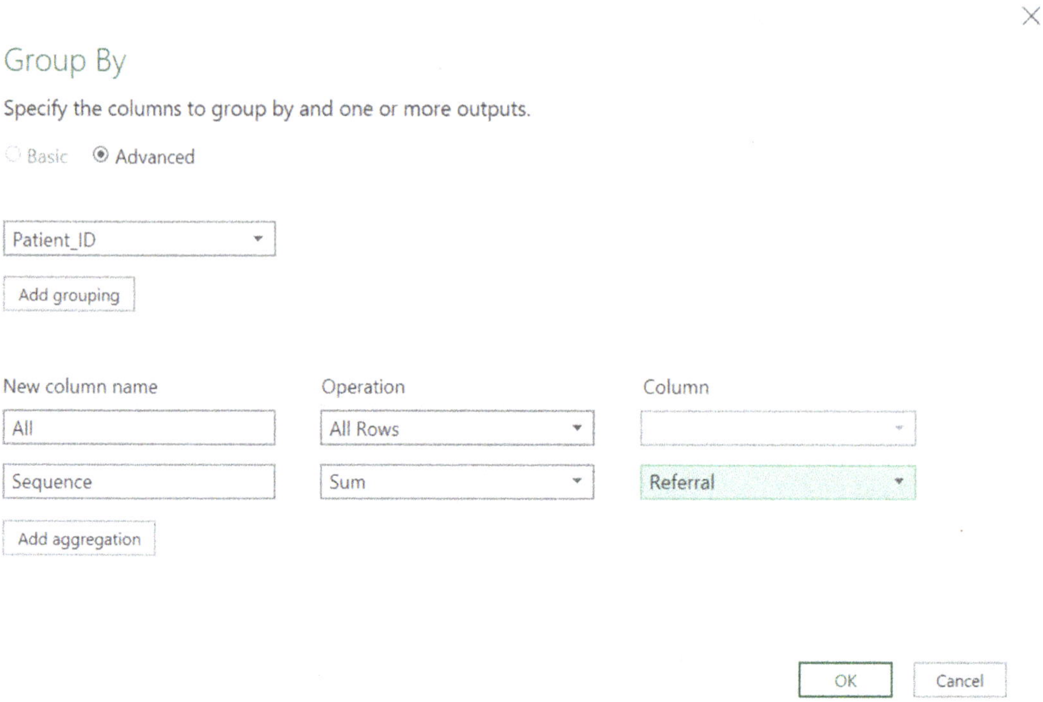

CHAPTER 3 SORTING AND FILTERING

Group By

Specify the columns to group by and one or more outputs.

○ Basic ● Advanced

Patient_ID ▼

[Add grouping]

New column name	Operation	Column
All	All Rows ▼	▼
Sequence	Sum ▼	Referral ▼

[Add aggregation]

[OK] [Cancel]

Figure 3-28. *The Group By setting*

#	Patient_ID	All	Sequence
1	P-01	Table	Error
2	P-02	Table	Error
3	P-03	Table	Error
4	P-04	Table	Error
5	P-05	Table	Error
6	P-06	Table	Error
7	P-07	Table	Error
8	P-08	Table	Error
9	P-09	Table	Error
10	P-10	Table	Error
11	P-11	Table	Error
12	P-12	Table	Error
13	P-13	Table	Error
14	P-14	Table	Error

Figure 3-29. *The result of using GroupBy()*

CHAPTER 3 SORTING AND FILTERING

The previous step used the Sum operation on the Referral column, which is in type text. It results in errors for all the values in the Sequence column. The errors can be addressed by modifying the formula. The previous steps lead to the following formula in the formula bar:

```
= Table.Group(
    #"Sorted Rows",
    {"Patient_ID"},
    {{"All", each _, type table [Date=datetime, Patient_ID=text,
    Gander=text, Referral=text]}, {"Sequence", each List.Sum([Referral]),
    type text}})
```

In the previous formula, replace the List.Sum with Text.Combine to obtain the sequence of referral for each patent. This is shown in Figure 3-30.

	Patient_ID	All	Sequence
1	P-01	Table	VisitSurgeryVisit
2	P-02	Table	Visit
3	P-03	Table	Visit
4	P-04	Table	VisitVisit
5	P-05	Table	VisitSurgeryVisit
6	P-06	Table	VisitVisitVisit
7	P-07	Table	VisitSurgeryVisit
8	P-08	Table	VisitSurgery
9	P-09	Table	Visit
10	P-10	Table	Visit
11	P-11	Table	VisitVisit
12	P-12	Table	VisitVisitVisit
13	P-13	Table	Visit
14	P-14	Table	SurgerySurgeryVisit

Figure 3-30. *The result of the replaced formula*

At this stage, you use the filter arrow next to the Sequence column. Select Text Filter and then select the Contains option. In the open window, configure the settings as shown in Figure 3-31, and click OK, which results in Figure 3-32.

165

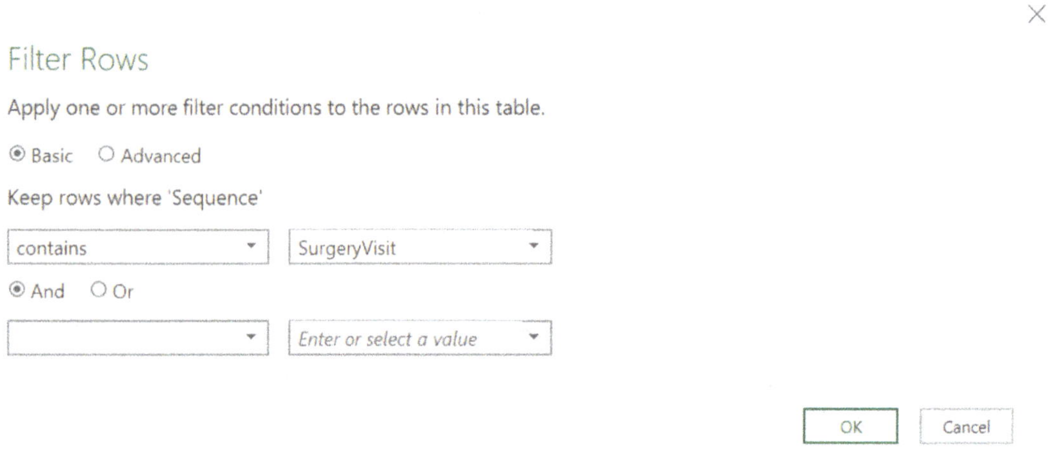

CHAPTER 3   SORTING AND FILTERING

Figure 3-31. Setting the filtering option

Figure 3-32. The result of filtering

The previous step results in the following formula:

= Table.SelectRows(#"Grouped Rows", each Text.Contains([Sequence], "SurgeryVisit"))

In this example, all the text is in the same format. However, if there are mixed cases of text (both lower- and uppercase), Text.Contains([Sequence], "SurgeryVisit") should be rewritten as Text.Contains(Text.Lower([Sequence]), "surgeryvisit") to ensure case-insensitive matching.

In the next step, remove the Sequence column and expand the All column to obtain the final result, shown in Figure 3-33.

	Patient_ID	Date	Gender	Referral
1	P-01	18/01/2024 12:00:00 AM	Male	Visit
2	P-01	23/01/2024 12:00:00 AM	Male	Surgery
3	P-01	8/02/2024 12:00:00 AM	Male	Visit
4	P-05	23/01/2024 12:00:00 AM	Male	Visit
5	P-05	7/02/2024 12:00:00 AM	Male	Surgery
6	P-05	17/02/2024 12:00:00 AM	Male	Visit
7	P-07	25/01/2024 12:00:00 AM	Female	Visit
8	P-07	10/02/2024 12:00:00 AM	Female	Surgery
9	P-07	14/02/2024 12:00:00 AM	Female	Visit
10	P-14	5/02/2024 12:00:00 AM	Male	Surgery
11	P-14	14/02/2024 12:00:00 AM	Male	Surgery
12	P-14	28/02/2024 12:00:00 AM	Male	Visit

Figure 3-33. The final result

Efficiency Tips   Despite of number of steps needed to solve this problem, this is an efficient solution in terms of execution time. For a table with 10,000 rows, its execution time is around 0.2 seconds.

Using Random Selection

Consider the Source table shown in Table 3-8, which contains staff information. Randomly select one person from each department.

Table 3-8. Source: Staff Info

Department	Staff ID
HR	S_01
Marketing	S_02
Marketing	S_03
IT	S_04
Production	S_05
R&D	S_06
IT	S_07

(continued)

CHAPTER 3   SORTING AND FILTERING

Table 3-8. (*continued*)

Department	Staff ID
IT	S_08
IT	S_09
IT	S_10
IT	S_11
IT	S_12
R&D	S_13
R&D	S_14
R&D	S_15
Production	S_16
Production	S_17
Production	S_18

Note   The data in this example is provided in an Excel file titled `07 Random Selection.xlsx`.

Two different solutions are provided for this problem.

Solution 1: Reordering Rows and Removing Duplicates

As in the first solution provided in Section 3-4, this problem can be solved by randomly reordering the rows and then removing duplicates from the Department column. To shuffle the table rows, you'll add a column with random numbers and then sort the table based on this newly added column.

To do this, go to the Add Column tab and select the Custom Column command to add a new column named Random. Use the following formula in the Custom Column window, as shown in Figure 3-34.

```
=Number.RandomBetween(1,1000)
```

CHAPTER 3 SORTING AND FILTERING

`fx` `= Table.AddColumn(Source, "Random", each Number.RandomBetween(1,1000))`

#	Department	Staff ID	Random
1	HR	S_01	616.8553187
2	Marketing	S_02	862.6337921
3	Marketing	S_03	483.3756361
4	IT	S_04	995.0719887
5	Production	S_05	535.1316794
6	R&D	S_06	760.3965426
7	IT	S_07	713.9345615
8	IT	S_08	406.7563464
9	IT	S_09	902.630204
10	IT	S_10	65.57849638
11	IT	S_11	316.6879121
12	IT	S_12	282.9183861
13	R&D	S_13	520.5669007
14	R&D	S_14	886.8731889
15	R&D	S_15	334.3354087
16	Production	S_16	248.8948102
17	Production	S_17	471.9564251
18	Production	S_18	390.285431

Figure 3-34. Adding a custom column with random values

Now sort the table based on the Random column in ascending order. Then, right-click the Department column and select the Remove Duplicates command. This will result in one row for each department and generate the following formula in the formula bar:

`= Table.Distinct(#"Sorted Rows", {"Department"})`

Based on the explanation in Section 3-4, to ensure the sorting step runs before removing any duplicates, rewrite the formula as follows:

`= Table.Distinct(Table.Buffer(#"Sorted Rows"), {"Department"})`

This results in a randomly selected row for each department, as shown in Figure 3-35.

169

CHAPTER 3   SORTING AND FILTERING

| | fx | = Table.Distinct(Table.Buffer(#"Sorted Rows"), {"Department"}) |

	Department	Staff ID	Random
1	IT	S_10	84.47831402
2	R&D	S_13	111.7939876
3	HR	S_01	335.9674438
4	Production	S_05	449.5215292
5	Marketing	S_02	573.0385599

Figure 3-35.   The result of randomly selected rows for each department

Solution 2: Shuffle the Table Rows

In this solution, you will shuffle the table rows without adding the Random column. To do this, you need to understand more about the sorting logic using the Table.Sort() function in Power Query.

Consider the Source table in this example. Sorting the table based on the Department column in ascending order will generate the following formula in the formula bar, which includes two arguments—the first is the name of the table, and the second is the sorting logic.

= Table.Sort(Source,{{"Department", Order.Ascending}})

The sorting logic can be a list, as shown in the previous formula, or it can be a custom function. For example, the following formula results in the same outcome as the previous one:

= Table.Sort(Source, each [Department])

In another case, instead of using the entire text in the Department column for sorting, you can sort the rows based on the last character of the text in this column using the following formula, which results in Figure 3-36.

= Table.Sort(Source, each Text.End([Department],1))

CHAPTER 3 SORTING AND FILTERING

	fx	= Table.Sort(Source, each Text.End([Department],1))

	Department	Staff ID
1	R&D	S_15
2	R&D	S_14
3	R&D	S_13
4	R&D	S_06
5	HR	S_01
6	IT	S_12
7	IT	S_11
8	IT	S_10
9	IT	S_09
10	IT	S_08
11	IT	S_07
12	IT	S_04
13	Marketing	S_03
14	Marketing	S_02
15	Production	S_05
16	Production	S_16
17	Production	S_17
18	Production	S_18

Figure 3-36. *Sort based on the last character of values in the Department column*

Based on this explanation, the following formula can be used to shuffle the table rows in Power Query:

= Table.Sort(Source,each Number.RandomBetween(1,1000))

This formula generates a random number for each row and sorts the table based on those values, effectively shuffling the rows.

Now, as in the previous solution, you simply need to right-click the Department column in the shuffled table and select Remove Duplicates. After that, add the Table.Buffer() function to the first argument of the resulting formula. This will

171

CHAPTER 3 SORTING AND FILTERING

solve the problem, as shown in Figure 3-37, using the following formula for all the steps shown in the Advanced Editor:

```
let
    Source = Excel.CurrentWorkbook(){[Name="Table1"]}[Content],
    #"Sorted Rows" = Table.Sort(Source,each Number.RandomBetween(1,1000)),
    #"Removed Duplicates" = Table.Distinct(Table.Buffer(#"Sorted Rows"),
    {"Department"})
in
    #"Removed Duplicates"
```

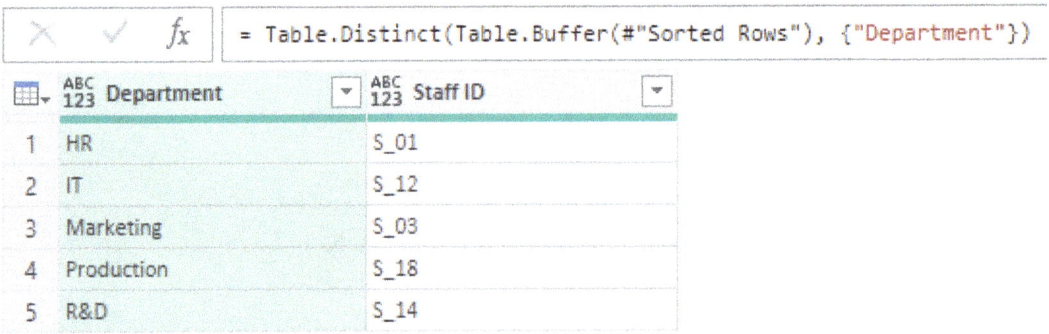

	Department	Staff ID
1	HR	S_01
2	IT	S_12
3	Marketing	S_03
4	Production	S_18
5	R&D	S_14

Figure 3-37. Randomly selected staff

Using Advanced Filtering Criteria

In multi-objective optimization models, rather than a single solution, you'll encounter a Pareto front, which includes all non-dominant solutions. Consider the solutions data provided in the Source table shown in Table 3-9. Filter out all non-dominant solutions.

CHAPTER 3 SORTING AND FILTERING

Table 3-9. *Source: Solutions*

Solution ID	Objective 1	Objective 2	Objective 3
1	32	5	32
2	84	2	20
3	91	1	73
4	29	9	78
5	52	3	30
6	21	8	77
7	80	9	41
8	74	5	73
9	57	6	94
10	74	4	95
11	92	7	93
12	76	6	11

A solution, like a, is considered non-dominant if there is no other solution, like b in the table, where all objective values of b are higher than those of a. So, Solution ID=1 is dominated by Solution ID=6, which has larger values in all three objectives.

Note The data in this example is provided in an Excel file titled 08 Advanced Filtering Criteria.xlsx.

Before solving the problem for all the solution IDs, check the condition for Solution ID=3. To verify the non-domination condition for Solution ID=3, and determine the number of solutions that dominate this solution. Then filter the Source table using the Objective 1 $\geq$ 91, Objective 2 $\geq$ 1, and Objective 3 $\geq$ 73 criteria with the following formula in the formula bar, which results in Figure 3-38:

= Table.SelectRows(Source, each [Objective 1] >= 91 and [Objective 2] >= 1 and [Objective 3] >= 73)

CHAPTER 3 SORTING AND FILTERING

	Solution ID	Objective 1	Objective 2	Objective 3
1		3	91	1	73
2		11	92	7	93

Figure 3-38. Dominant solutions for Solution ID=3

Since the formula returns two rows (more than one row), this solution (ID=3) is dominated by another (ID=11) and should be removed from the final table. As the result of the previous formula is a table and cannot be used directly as filter criteria in another filter, to convert it into a true or false value for filtering, the formula can be rewritten using the Table.RowCount() function. This will count the number of rows in the resulting table and then compare its result to the value 1, as shown here:

```
= Table.RowCount(Table.SelectRows(Source, each [Objective 1] >= 91 and
[Objective 2] >= 1 and [Objective 3] >= 73))=1
```

The previous formula checks the non-domination criteria for Solution ID=3. By replacing the objective values of other solutions in the formula, if a solution is dominated by another, the result of the formula will be false. Otherwise, it results in true. Therefore, this formula can be used as criteria for filtering non-dominant solutions.

Before proceeding further, let's replace the each _ logic in this formula with a custom function definition and rewrite the formula, as shown here, without altering the results:

```
= Table.RowCount(
    Table.SelectRows(
    Source,
    (x)=> x[Objective 1] >= 91 and x[Objective 2] >= 1 and
    x[Objective 3] >= 73
                )
  )=1
```

By considering this formula, let's return to the main question and filter the Source table by selecting only rows where Objective 1 equals 84. This results in the following formula in the formula bar:

```
= Table.SelectRows(Source, each ([Objective 1] = 84))
```

CHAPTER 3　SORTING AND FILTERING

Now, replace the filtering criteria ([Objective 1] = 84) in the previous formula with the criteria defined for ID=3 in the previous steps. Rewrite the formula as shown here:

```
= Table.SelectRows(
     Source,
     each Table.RowCount(
                  Table.SelectRows(
                       Source,(x)=>
                            x[Objective 1] >= 91 and
                            x[Objective 2] >= 1 and
                            x[Objective 3] >= 73)
                  )=1)
```

The previous formula is hardcoded for Solution ID=3, and since it is dominated, the result of the criteria is false and the whole formula results in a blank table. To make the formula dynamic and evaluate the domination criteria for every row, the formula should be adjusted to dynamically use the values of the Objective 1, Objective 2, and Objective 3 columns from the Source table, instead of the 91, 1, and 73 values.

The challenge is that the Source table is referenced twice in this formula inside two Table.SelectRows() functions: first, through the each _ definition, and second, by the (x) => definition. To refer to columns in the first Source table, add an underscore (_) before the column names. For the second Source table, mention the variable x before the column names.

Therefore, the previous formula should be rewritten as follows, resulting in Figure 3-39, including all non-dominated IDs:

```
= Table.SelectRows(
     Source,
     each Table.RowCount(
                  Table.SelectRows(
                       Source,(x)=>
                            x[Objective 1] >= _[Objective 1] and
                            x[Objective 2] >= _[Objective 2] and
                            x[Objective 3] >= _[Objective 3])
                  )=1)
```

CHAPTER 3   SORTING AND FILTERING

	Solution ID	Objective 1	Objective 2	Objective 3	
1		4	29	9	78
2		7	80	9	41
3		9	57	6	94
4		10	74	4	95
5		11	92	7	93

Figure 3-39. *The result*

Efficiency Tips   Even for a relatively small table with 10,000 rows, the code took 380 seconds to run, which is excessive. By applying the Table.Buffer() function to the Source table, the execution time was reduced to 129 seconds, but this is still quite high. Instead of buffering the entire table, buffering just the list of data, as shown here (make the changes on the Advanced Editor window), reduced the runtime to 17 seconds, making it more efficient compared to the previous solutions.

```
let
    Source = Excel.CurrentWorkbook(){[Name="Table1"]}[Content],
    S=List.Buffer(Table.ToRows(Table.RemoveColumns(Source, {"Solution ID"}))),
    #"Filtered Rows" = Table.SelectRows(
Source,
each List.Count(
                List.Select(
                    S,(x)=>
                                    x{0} >= _[Objective 1] and
                                    x{1} >= _[Objective 2] and
                                    x{2} >= _[Objective 3])
                    )=1)
in
    #"Filtered Rows"
```

Summary

Filtering and sorting are fundamental to data analysis. This chapter dived deep into the `Table.Sort()` and `Table.SelectRows()` functions, providing insights on how to apply these methods to single and multiple columns. Different filtering approaches were illustrated, including using custom functions and simple selection criteria to streamline execution. `List.Sort()` was also introduced for reordering the table rows based on custom logic. Practical examples emphasized the importance of efficient criteria in improving query performance for both functions. Remember to be careful using `Table.Buffer()` with tables.

The next chapter covers the tips related to splitting a column into several columns or merging the values over multiple columns and providing them in a column.

CHAPTER 4

Column Splitting and Merging

Splitting and merging columns are two common tasks involved in transforming data. Column splitting is the process of dividing a single column into multiple columns based on a specified delimiter or a fixed number of characters, and column merging is the process of combining multiple columns into a single column. These two tasks are useful for consolidating data, simplifying structures, and preparing data for analysis.

Consider Table 4-1 as the Source table, which includes product IDs with information about the production year, material type, color, and index, all separated by dashes.

Table 4-1. Source: Some Dates

ID
2022-Wo-Wh-12
2023-Wo-Bl-01
2024-Me-Bl-07
2024-Me-Bl-12
2024-Me-Bu-18
2024-Pl-Ye-12
2024-Wo-Re-84

To split the text in the ID column based on the - delimiter, select the column and go to the Home tab. Then choose the Split Columns command and select By Delimiter. Set the delimiter to Custom and choose Split at Each Occurrence, as shown in Figure 4-1, then click OK to achieve the result in Figure 4-2.

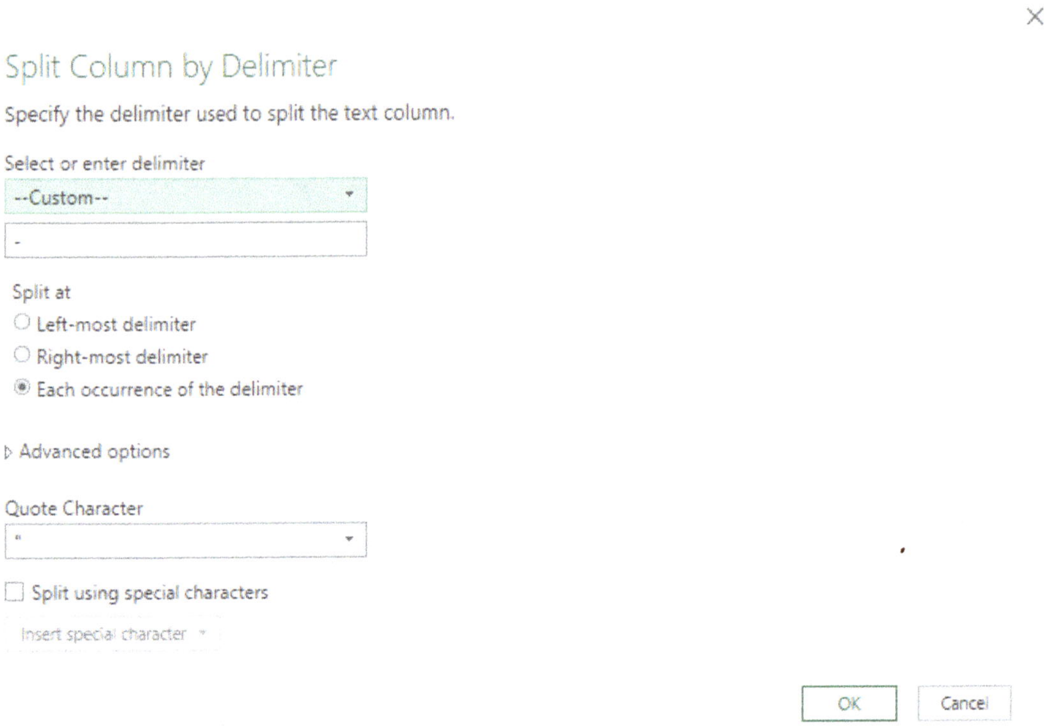

CHAPTER 4   COLUMN SPLITTING AND MERGING

Figure 4-1. Settings of the column split

	A^B_C ID.1	A^B_C ID.2	A^B_C ID.3	A^B_C ID.4
1	2022	Wo	Wh	12
2	2023	Wo	Bl	01
3	2024	Me	Bl	07
4	2024	Me	Bl	12
5	2024	Me	Bu	18
6	2024	Pl	Ye	12
7	2024	Wo	Re	84

Figure 4-2. The result of the column split

Based on the previous settings, the following formula uses the Table.SplitColumn() function and is generated in the formula bar:

```
= Table.SplitColumn(
    #"Changed Type",
    "ID",
    Splitter.SplitTextByDelimiter("-", QuoteStyle.Csv),
    {"ID.1", "ID.2", "ID.3", "ID.4"})
```

CHAPTER 4　COLUMN SPLITTING AND MERGING

Generally, the `Table.SplitColumn()` function is used to split a column into several columns based on the following six arguments (the last three arguments are optional):

```
Table.SplitColumn(
    table as table,
    sourceColumn as text,
    splitter as function,
    optional columnNamesOrNumber as any,
    optional default as any,
    optional extraColumns as any
) as table
```

In the first and second arguments, you specify the name of the table and the column to split. The third argument defines the splitting logic, which can be one of the following functions or any other custom function under specific characteristics:

- `Splitter.SplitByNothing()`
- `Splitter.SplitTextByAnyDelimiter()`
- `Splitter.SplitTextByCharacterTransition()`
- `Splitter.SplitTextByDelimiter()`
- `Splitter.SplitTextByEachDelimiter()`
- `Splitter.SplitTextByLengths()`
- `Splitter.SplitTextByPositions()`
- `Splitter.SplitTextByRanges()`
- `Splitter.SplitTextByRepeatedLengths()`
- `Splitter.SplitTextByWhitespace()`

The fourth argument in this function is optional and is used to name the resulting columns after splitting. In this example, it can be left blank, set to the number 4, or specified as a list of four items to define the column names in the result table. Modifying the formula to the following will produce a table with different column names, as shown in Figure 4-3.

```
= Table.SplitColumn(#"Changed Type",
    "ID",
```

CHAPTER 4   COLUMN SPLITTING AND MERGING

```
Splitter.SplitTextByDelimiter("-", QuoteStyle.Csv),
{"Year","Material","Color","Index"})
```

123 Year	A^B_C Material	A^B_C Color	123 Index
1	2022 Wo	Wh	12
2	2023 Wo	Bl	1
3	2024 Me	Bl	7
4	2024 Me	Bl	12
5	2024 Me	Bu	18
6	2024 Pl	Ye	12
7	2024 Wo	Re	84

Figure 4-3. Changing the column name

If the fourth argument is left blank, the function will use the first row of the table to determine the number of columns for splitting. In this example, since all rows have the same length after splitting (i.e., the same number of split values), leaving the fourth argument blank does not impact the results. However, in cases with uneven splitting results, some parts of the text might be missed if this argument is left blank.

The fifth argument of the function is optional and is known as the default value. In the previous example, if the fourth argument is set to 5, the splitting will generate five columns. Since each row contains only four parts after splitting, the fifth column will contain null values for all rows. To replace these null values with another value, you can use the fifth argument of this function.

The sixth argument of the function allows you to manage the result based on conditions using one of the following options:

ExtraValues.Error: Throws an error if extra values are found.

ExtraValues.Ignore: Ignores extra values.

ExtraValues.List: Creates a list of extra values.

Merging columns performs the reverse operation of splitting columns and is used to combine values from several columns. Consider Table 4-2 as the Source table. To create the product ID by combining the values of each row, select all the relevant columns (note that the order of selection is important). Right-click one of the selected columns and choose Merge. In the dialog that appears, use a custom separator (in this case, a dash) and name the new column Product ID, as shown in Figure 4-4. Clicking OK will result in Figure 4-5.

CHAPTER 4 COLUMN SPLITTING AND MERGING

Table 4-2. *Source: Product info*

Year	Material	Color	Index
2022	Wo	Wh	12
2023	Wo	Bl	1
2024	Me	Bl	7
2024	Me	Bl	12
2024	Me	Bu	18
2024	Pl	Ye	12
2024	Wo	Re	84

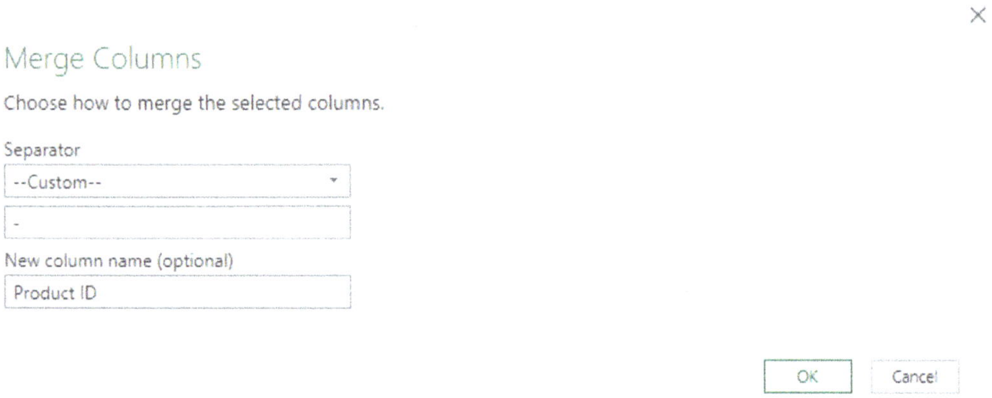

Merge Columns

Choose how to merge the selected columns.

Separator
--Custom--

-

New column name (optional)
Product ID

OK   Cancel

Figure 4-4. *Merge Columns setting*

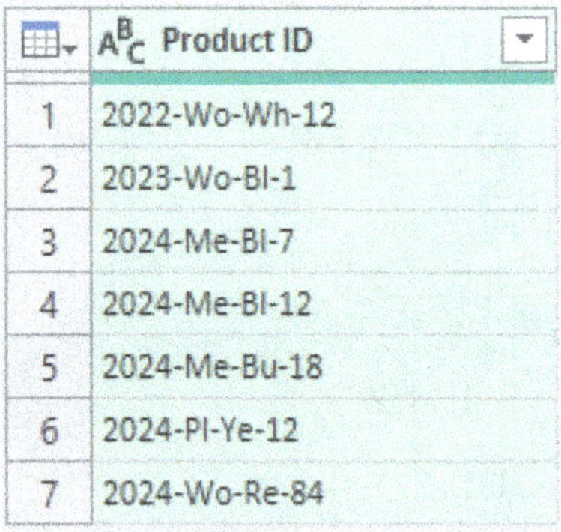

	Product ID
1	2022-Wo-Wh-12
2	2023-Wo-Bl-1
3	2024-Me-Bl-7
4	2024-Me-Bl-12
5	2024-Me-Bu-18
6	2024-Pl-Ye-12
7	2024-Wo-Re-84

Figure 4-5. *The result of merging the columns*

CHAPTER 4 COLUMN SPLITTING AND MERGING

The previous settings result in the use of the `Table.CombineColumns()` function in the formula bar with the following formula:

```
= Table.CombineColumns(
      Table.TransformColumnTypes(Source, {{"Year", type text}, {"Index", type text}}, "en-AU"),
      {"Year", "Material", "Color", "Index"},
      Combiner.CombineTextByDelimiter("-", QuoteStyle.None),
      "Product ID")
```

In the initial argument of the `Table.CombineColumns()` function, the table name is specified. In this example, since the Year and Index columns are of type number and cannot be merged with text directly, their types are first converted to text using the `Table.TransformColumnTypes()` function, then the result is used in the first argument of the function. The second argument provides a list of column names for merging, formatted as text within a list. The third argument defines the merging logic, and the final argument specifies the name of the resulting column that will contain the merged values.

This chapter explores the more advanced applications of these two functions.

Dynamic Splitting by Delimiter

The source table, as shown in Table 4-3, contains product IDs provided in a column, separated by commas. Split these product IDs into multiple columns. Ensure that your query is dynamic and can accommodate any newly added rows in the table.

Table 4-3. Source: IDs

IDs
S11
M12, N21, R81
F8
G12, S11
S11, M12
R21
F12,M11,S21,R18

CHAPTER 4 COLUMN SPLITTING AND MERGING

Note The data in this example is provided in an Excel file titled `01 Dynamic splinting by delimiter.xlsx`.

To address this problem, select the IDs column, then navigate to the Home tab and choose the Split Column by Delimiter command. Select Comma as the delimiter and click OK. This will generate the following formula in the formula bar and the result shown in Figure 4-6.

```
= Table.SplitColumn(Source, "IDs", Splitter.SplitTextByDelimiter(",",
QuoteStyle.Csv), {"IDs.1", "IDs.2", "IDs.3"})
```

#	IDs.1	IDs.2	IDs.3
1	S11		null	null
2	M12	N21	R81
3	F8		null	null
4	G12	S11		null
5	S11	M12		null
6	R21		null	null
7	F12	M11	S21

Figure 4-6. The result of splitting

Load the resulting table into Excel. It appears that this formula works correctly for the provided data; however, if you go to the Source table and add a new row containing more than two commas, such as "F12,M11,S21,R18," and then refresh the query, notice that only the first three product IDs of this code are split, while the last part is neglected. This is shown in Figure 4-7.

185

CHAPTER 4 COLUMN SPLITTING AND MERGING

	A	B	C
1	IDs.1	IDs.2	IDs.3
2	S11		
3	M12	N21	R81
4	F8		
5	G12	S11	
6	S11	M12	
7	R21		
8	F12	M11	S21
9			

Figure 4-7. *The result of splitting after adding a new row*

This issue is due to the last argument of the formula, which is {"IDs.1", "IDs.2", "IDs.3"}, indicating that the IDs column should be split into three columns. Removing this argument and rewriting the formula as follows makes the situation worse. In this case, as shown in Figure 4-8, only the first part of all the IDs will appear in the result table (where the first row of the table is considered as the pattern, and the number of columns is determined based on that).

`= Table.SplitColumn(Source, "IDs", Splitter.SplitTextByDelimiter(",", QuoteStyle.Csv))`

	IDs.1
1	S11
2	M12
3	F8
4	G12
5	S11
6	R21
7	F12

Figure 4-8. *The result of removing the fourth argument*

= Table.SplitColumn(Source, "IDs", Splitter.SplitTextByDelimiter(",", QuoteStyle.Csv))

To resolve this issue and make the formula dynamic, you need to count the number of occurrences of commas in each cell of the IDs column. Then, you take the largest count and add one to it, using that value as the fourth argument of the Table.SplitColumn() function.

To count the number of occurrences of "," in each cell, you know that the result of Source[IDs] is a list containing all the values in the IDs column. You can then apply the

CHAPTER 4　COLUMN SPLITTING AND MERGING

List.Transform() function to each item in this list to remove all characters except for commas by using the following formula, which results in Figure 4-9.

```
=List.Transform(Source[IDs], each Text.Select(_,","))
```

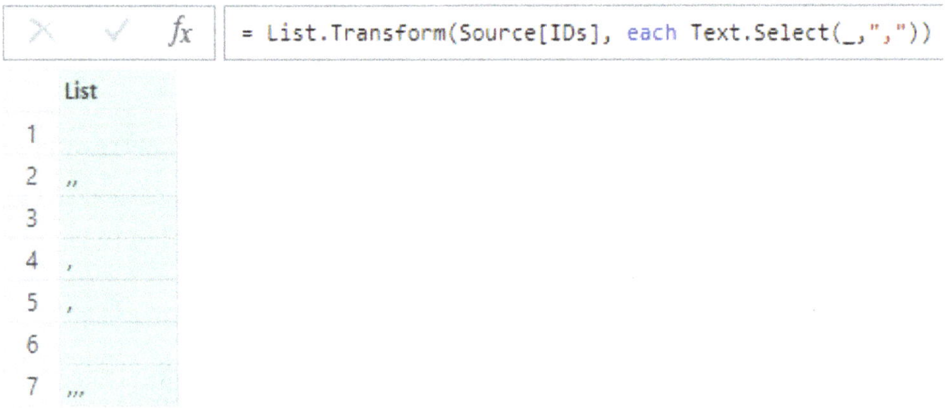

	List
1	
2	,,
3	
4	,
5	,
6	
7	,,,

Figure 4-9. *The result of List.Transform*

Instead of displaying just the commas, the formula can be rewritten to count the number of occurrences of commas in each cell of the IDs column, as follows, which results in Figure 4-10.

```
= List.Transform(Source[IDs], each Text.Length(Text.Select(_,",")))
```

	List
1	0
2	2
3	0
4	1
5	1
6	0
7	3

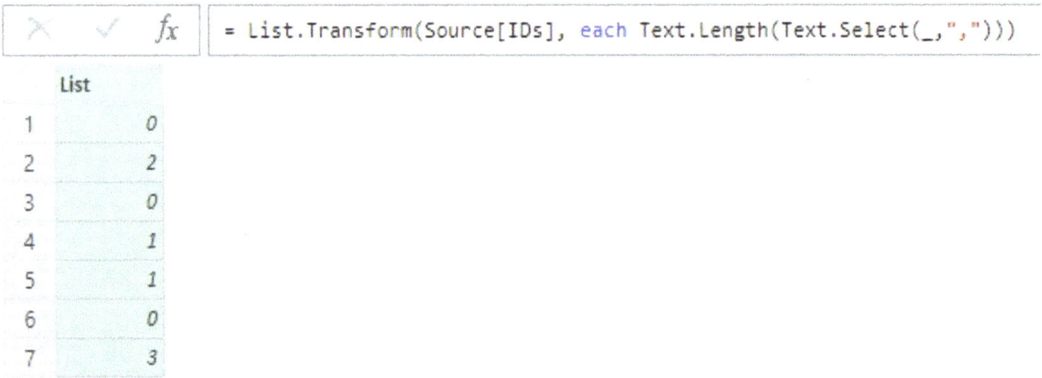

Figure 4-10. *The result of revised List.Transform*

Therefore, the maximum number of commas can be extracted using the following formula:

```
=List.Max(List.Transform(Source[IDs], each Text.Length(Text.Select(_,","))))
```

CHAPTER 4 COLUMN SPLITTING AND MERGING

In the case where a cell contains three commas, such as "F12,M11,S21,R18," it should be split into four columns, so the result of the previous formula should be added by 1one. With this in mind, the splitting function can be rewritten as follows, which is completely dynamic.

```
=Table.SplitColumn(Source, "IDs", Splitter.SplitTextByDelimiter(",",
QuoteStyle.Csv),List.Max(List.Transform(Source[IDs], each Text.Length(Text.
Select(_,","))))+1)
```

Therefore, the previous formula is dynamic and will work for any new rows added to the table, regardless of the number of commas they contain.

Splitting Text by Multiple Delimiters

Consider the Source table shown in Table 4-4, which includes sales data (Date, Product Name, and Quantity) all in one column, separated by "//" or "\\". Split this data into three separate columns.

Table 4-4. *Source: List of Transactions*

Info
2024/5/2//A//13
2024/5/3\\A\\11
2024/5/3//A//2
2024/5/6\\AA\\15
2024/5/8//B//9
2024/5/8\\C\\5
2024/5/10//B//5
2024/5/12//A//6
2024/5/12//BC//14
2024/5/12\\C\\2
2024/5/14//A//15
2024/5/19\\B\\14
2024/5/21//C//9

CHAPTER 4 COLUMN SPLITTING AND MERGING

Note The data in this example is provided in an Excel file titled `02 Splitting Text by Multiple Delimiters.xlsx`.

To split this column based on the delimiter, select the column, go to the Home tab, choose the Split Column command, and select By Delimiter. As shown in Figure 4-11, choose Custom as the delimiter type and enter "\\" as the delimiter. This will result in Figure 4-12.

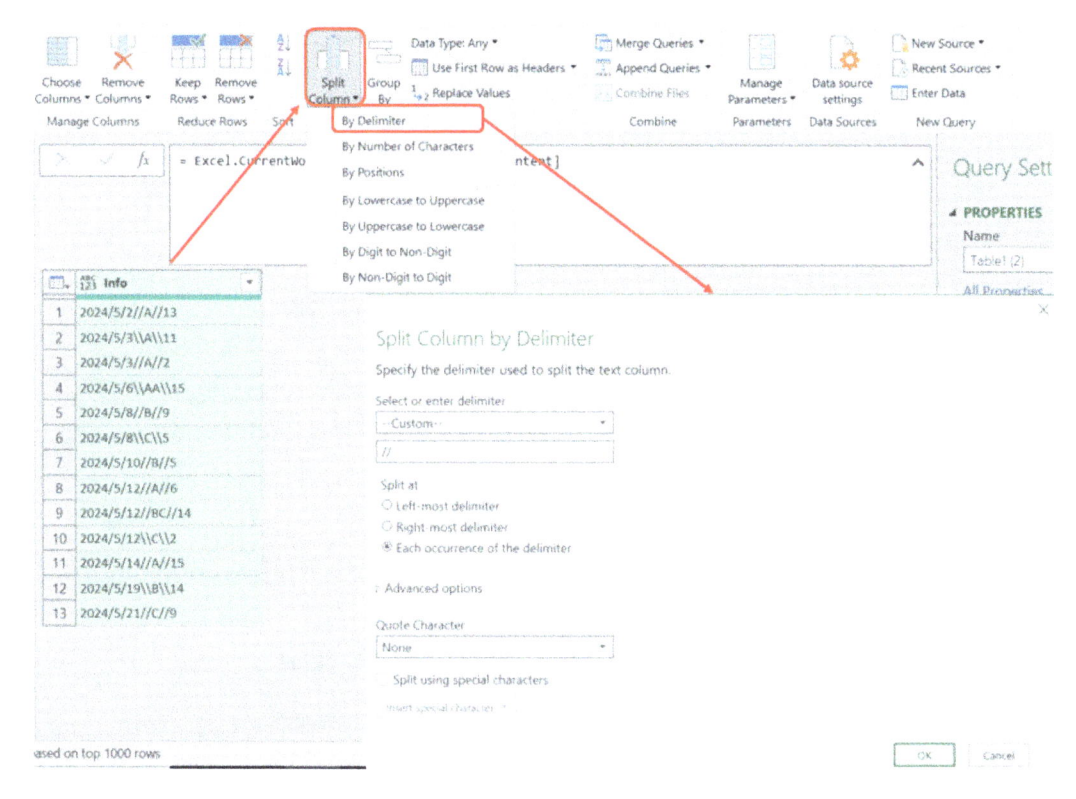

Figure 4-11. Column split setting

189

CHAPTER 4   COLUMN SPLITTING AND MERGING

	ABC Info.1	ABC Info.2	123 Info.3
1	2024/5/2	A	13
2	2024/5/3\\A\\11	null	null
3	2024/5/3	A	2
4	2024/5/6\\AA\\15	null	null
5	2024/5/8	B	9
6	2024/5/8\\C\\5	null	null
7	2024/5/10	B	5
8	2024/5/12	A	6
9	2024/5/12	BC	14
10	2024/5/12\\C\\2	null	null
11	2024/5/14	A	15
12	2024/5/19\\B\\14	null	null
13	2024/5/21	C	9

Figure 4-12. *The result of the column split*

Based on the resulting table, the current approach works for rows with the "//" delimiter but fails for rows with other delimiters. To address this, examine the formula generated in the formula bar by the previous step as follows:

```
= Table.SplitColumn(
    Source,
    "Info",
    Splitter.SplitTextByDelimiter("//", QuoteStyle.None),
    {"Info.1", "Info.2", "Info.3"})
```

After using the column split feature, two steps are added to the query: one for splitting the columns and another for changing the types of the new columns. This discussion focuses on the formula related to the splitting step.

In this code, the `Splitter.SplitTextByDelimiter()` function is used as the splitter in the third argument, which allows only a single delimiter to be defined. However, it can be replaced with the `Splitter.SplitTextByAnyDelimiter()` function to specify multiple delimiters within a list. The formula can be rewritten as follows to solve the problem by defining multiple delimiters once, resulting in Figure 4-13. (The names of the new columns are provided in the fourth argument.)

CHAPTER 4　COLUMN SPLITTING AND MERGING

```
= Table.SplitColumn(Source,
    "Info",
    Splitter.SplitTextByAnyDelimiter({"//","\\"}),
    {"Date", "Product", "Quantity"})
```

	Date	Product	Quantity
1	2024/5/2	A	13
2	2024/5/3	A	11
3	2024/5/3	A	2
4	2024/5/6	AA	15
5	2024/5/8	B	9
6	2024/5/8	C	5
7	2024/5/10	B	5
8	2024/5/12	A	6
9	2024/5/12	BC	14
10	2024/5/12	C	2
11	2024/5/14	A	15
12	2024/5/19	B	14
13	2024/5/21	C	9

Figure 4-13. The result

Note These splitter functions like, Splitter.SplitTextByAnyDelimiter(), can also used directly in the custom column or to transform the values of a column. These approaches can be useful in certain scenarios.

For example, consider the Source table in this case. Go to the Add Column tab, select the Custom Column command, and in the open window, write the following formula, which results in Figure 4-14:

```
=Splitter.SplitTextByAnyDelimiter({"//","\\"})([Info])
```

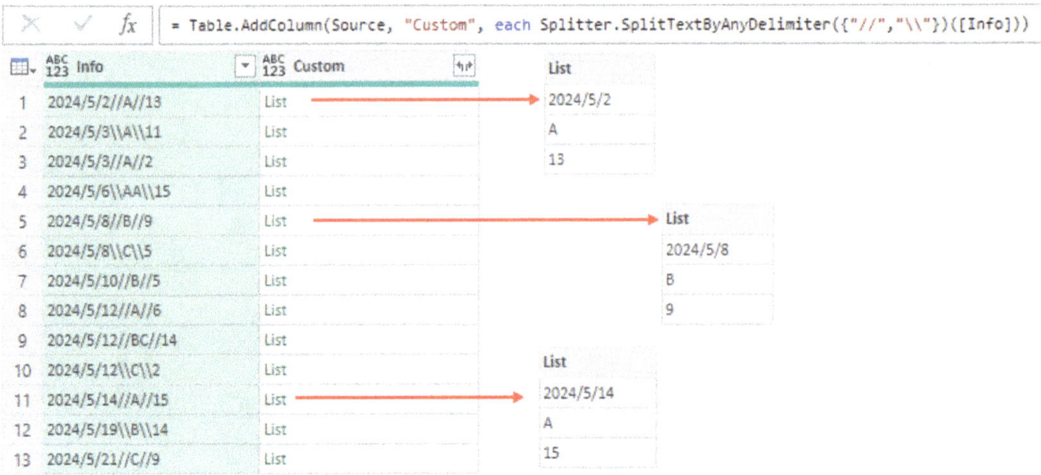

CHAPTER 4   COLUMN SPLITTING AND MERGING

Figure 4-14. The result of using Splitter.SplitTextByAnyDelimiter() in the Custom Column

Alternatively, in another scenario, you can select the Info column, then go to the Transform tab. Under the Text Column section, in the Format group, choose any case option, such as lowercase. This will generate the following formula in the formula bar, which converts all the values in the Info column to lowercase.

= Table.TransformColumns(Source,{{"Info", Text.Lower, type text}})

In this case, Text.Lower can be replaced with Splitter.SplitTextBy AnyDelimiter({"//", "\\"}). By removing the part related to the column type, type text, and rewriting the formula as follows, you will get the result in Figure 4-15.

= Table.TransformColumns(Source,{{"Info", Splitter.SplitTextByAnyDelimiter({"//","\\"})}})

CHAPTER 4   COLUMN SPLITTING AND MERGING

```
= Table.TransformColumns(Source,{{"Info", Splitter.SplitTextByAnyDelimiter({"//","\\"})}})
```

	Info	List
1	List	2024/5/2
2	List	A
3	List	13
4	List	
5	List	List
6	List	2024/5/8
7	List	B
8	List	9
9	List	
10	List	List
11	List	2024/5/14
12	List	A
13	List	15

Figure 4-15. *The result of using Splitter.SplitTextByAnyDelimiter() in column transformation*

Splitting Text by Position

Consider the Source table shown in Table 4-5, which includes different text describing product IDs in different lengths. Split the IDs into several columns with different numbers of characters following a specific pattern: {2,1,2,1,2,1,...}.

For example, with the product ID RD5FS7J, the first two characters are placed in one column, the next character in the subsequent column, and this pattern continues until the end of the ID. The result would be split into "RD," "5," "FS," "7," and "J."

Table 4-5. *Source: List of IDs*

ID
NG6GM5
UD1OP3PL
RE4EA3R
EL8DC6JK
TO1TS9RU
PN6PU

(continued)

CHAPTER 4 COLUMN SPLITTING AND MERGING

Table 4-5. (*continued*)

ID
UD8PD5
RD5FS7J
TQ4BN8
JF7
LP7U
QB6JT5SA
IH7UL2
TR7
AT7JG

Note The data in this example is provided in an Excel file titled `03 Splitting Text by Position.xlsx`.

To solve this problem, select the ID column, go to the Home tab, choose Split Column, and then select By Positions. Enter `0,2,3,5,6` as positions for splitting, as shown in Figure 4-16. This will generate the following formula in the formula bar and the resulting table shown in Figure 4-17.

```
= Table.SplitColumn(
      Source,
      "ID",
      Splitter.SplitTextByPositions({0, 2, 3, 5, 6}),
      {"ID.1", "ID.2", "ID.3", "ID.4", "ID.5"})
```

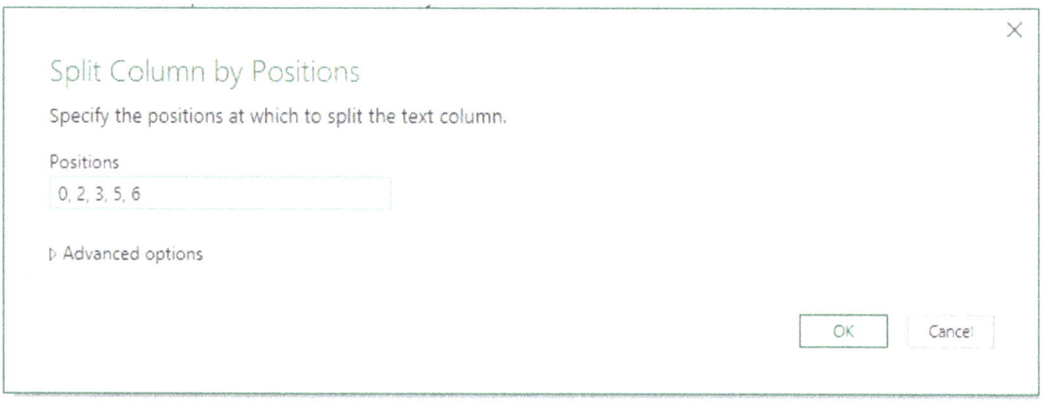

CHAPTER 4 COLUMN SPLITTING AND MERGING

Split Column by Positions

Specify the positions at which to split the text column.

Positions

0, 2, 3, 5, 6

▷ Advanced options

OK   Cancel

Figure 4-16. *Settings of the column split*

#	ID.1	ID.2	ID.3	ID.4	ID.5
1	NG	6	GM	5	
2	UD	1	OP	3	PL
3	RE	4	EA	3	R
4	EL	8	DC	6	JK
5	TO	1	TS	9	RU
6	PN	6	PU		
7	UD	8	PD	5	
8	RD	5	FS	7	J
9	TQ	4	BN	8	
10	JF	7			
11	LP	7	U		
12	QB	6	JT	5	SA
13	IH	7	UL	2	
14	TR	7			
15	AT	7	JG		

Figure 4-17. *The result of the column split*

Note The previous formula solves the problem, but the {0, 2, 3, 5, 6} list and the fourth argument are hardcoded. While it works if the maximum ID length is six, in real-world scenarios, you can't always be certain about the length of the text in a column. Therefore, at the end of this section, you learn how to make the formula dynamic.

The provided formula splits the values in the ID column of the Source table. The splitting logic is defined by the third argument, which in this example uses the Splitter.SplitTextByPositions() function.

CHAPTER 4   COLUMN SPLITTING AND MERGING

The syntax of the Splitter.SplitTextByPositions() function is as follows.

```
Splitter.SplitTextByPositions(
      positions as list,
      optional startAtEnd as nullable logical
                           ) as function
```

The first argument of this function is a list of numbers specifying the splitting positions in the text. Since Power Query indexing starts at 0, setting this argument to {0, 2, 3, 5, 6} means splitting the text after the beginning of the text, and after the second, third, fifth, and sixth characters, and then placing the resulting segments into new columns.

Additionally, according to the function definition, the second argument is optional and its default is false, so removing false from the formula will not affect the result. However, replacing it with true and rewriting the formula, as shown here, will change the splitting point starting from the end. The result is shown in Figure 4-18.

```
= Table.SplitColumn(
      Source,
      "ID",
      Splitter.SplitTextByPositions({0, 2, 3, 5, 6},true),
      {"ID.1", "ID.2", "ID.3", "ID.4", "ID.5"})
```

	ID.1	ID.2	ID.3	ID.4	ID.5
1		N	G6	G	M5
2	UD	1	OP	3	PL
3	R	E	4E	A	3R
4	EL	8	DC	6	JK
5	TO	1	TS	9	RU
6			PN	5	PU
7		U	D8	P	D5
8	R	D	5F	S	7J
9		T	Q4	B	N8
10				J	F7
11			L	P	7U
12	QB	6	JT	5	SA
13		I	H7	U	L2
14				T	R7
15			AT	7	JG

Figure 4-18. *Revising the result*

CHAPTER 4 COLUMN SPLITTING AND MERGING

In this example, besides using `Splitter.SplitTextByPositions()` in the third argument, you can use the `Splitter.SplitTextByLengths()` function to solve this problem. Rather than specifying the positions for splitting, the number of characters to include in each split should be defined for this function. Therefore, the previous formula can be rewritten as follows:

```
= Table.SplitColumn(
      Source,
      "ID",
      Splitter.SplitTextByLengths({2, 1,2,1,2}),
      {"ID.1", "ID.2", "ID.3", "ID.4", "ID.5"})
```

In this example, neglecting the last input, the following formula does also work and provides the same result with different column names.

```
= Table.SplitColumn(
      Source,
      "ID",
      Splitter.SplitTextByLengths({2, 1,2,1,2}))
```

Both of these formulas work correctly for the provided data; however, if you add a new row to the data, such as "MN2SS1FG5HR" in the source table, as shown in Figure 4-19, the characters "5HR" are ignored in the resulting table after the splitting process.

#	ID.1	ID.2	ID.3	ID.4	ID.5
1	NG	6	GM	5	
2	UD	1	OP	3	PL
3	RE	4	EA	3	R
4	EL	8	DC	6	JK
5	TO	1	TS	9	RU
6	PN	6	PU		
7	UD	8	PD	5	
8	RD	5	FS	7	J
9	TQ	4	BN	8	
10	JF	7			
11	LP	7	U		
12	QB	6	JT	5	SA
13	IH	7	UL	2	
14	TR	7			
15	AT	7	JG		
16	MN	2	SS	1	FG

Figure 4-19. *Revised splitting after adding new IDs*

197

CHAPTER 4 COLUMN SPLITTING AND MERGING

This issue arises because the splitting function `Splitter.SplitTextByLengths({2, 1, 2, 1, 2})` only accommodates the first eight characters (2+1+2+1+2=8) of the text. To make the formula dynamic, you need to extract the longest text in this column and use it to determine the number of splitting parts. Therefore, a new step, named Character, can be added to Power Query with one of the following formulas, resulting in Figure 4-20.

```
= List.Transform(Source[ID], each Text.Length(_))
```

of

```
= List.Transform(Source[ID], Text.Length)
```

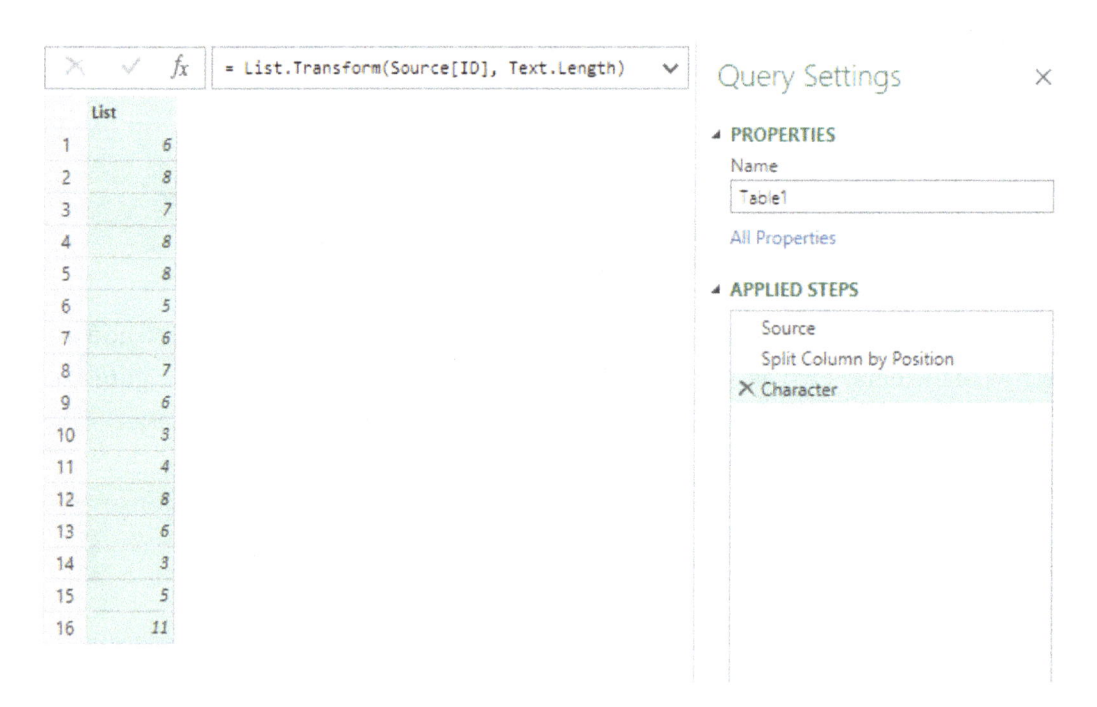

Figure 4-20. The result of the List.Transform() function

In this formula, the result of `Source[ID]` is a list that includes all the IDs from the source table, and the `List.Transform()` function is used to extract the length of each ID. To identify the largest length among all the lengths, rewrite the previous formula as follows to extract the maximum value, which is 11 for the provided data.

```
= List.Max(List.Transform(Source[ID], Text.Length))
```

198

CHAPTER 4   COLUMN SPLITTING AND MERGING

Since the Character step represents the maximum number of characters in a cell among all the cells in the ID column, the next step involves converting this value into a list, such as {2, 1} or {2,1,2}. To do this, add a new step and rename it ListofCharacters. Use the following formula for this step, which will yield a list as shown in Figure 4-21, which can be utilized in the splitter function.

= List.Repeat({2,1},Number.IntegerDivide(Character,3)) & (if Number.Mod(Character,3)=0 then {} else {2})

	List
1	2
2	1
3	2
4	1
5	2
6	1
7	2

Figure 4-21. The result of ListofCharacters

Note   The following formula is used to convert the number 11 into a list equal to {2,1,2,1,2,1,2}.

= List.Repeat({2,1},Number.IntegerDivide(Character,3)) & (if Number.Mod(Character,3)=0 then {} else {2})

As the value of Character is 11, replace it with 11, the result of Number.IntegerDivide(11,3) is 3, and the result of Number.Mod(11,3) is 2, so the formula is equal to the following:

= List.Repeat({2,1},3) & (if 2=0 then {} else {2})

List.Repeat({2,1},3) means the {2,1} list should be repeated three times, so it is equal to {2,1,2,1,2,1}, and the result of (if 2=0 then {} else {2}) is {2}, so the formula results in {2,1,2,1,2,1} & {2} which is equal to {2,1,2,1,2,1,2}.

CHAPTER 4   COLUMN SPLITTING AND MERGING

You can now proceed to the Split Column by Position step and replace its fourth argument with the name of the `ListofCharacters` step. This change results in Figure 4-22; however, the desired result will appear in an intermediate step rather than the final step. Therefore, you need to reorder the steps accordingly.

Figure 4-22. Replacing the fourth argument of Table.SplitColumn()

Go to the Home tab and choose the Advanced Editor command. The complete query including the following steps is shown in the open window:

```
let
    Source = Excel.CurrentWorkbook(){[Name="Table1"]}[Content],
    #"Split Column by Position" = Table.SplitColumn(Source,"ID",Splitter.SplitTextByLengths(Listofcharacters)),
    Character = List.Max(List.Transform(Source[ID], Text.Length)),
    Listofcharacters = List.Repeat({2,1},Number.IntegerDivide(Character,3)) & (if Number.Mod(Character,3)=0 then {} else {2})
in
    Listofcharacters
```

In the open window, reorder the steps (bring the `Character` and `ListofCharacters` steps before `#"Split Column by Position"`), then add "," to the end of the `ListofCharacters` step, and remove "," from the end of the `#"Split Column by Position"` step. Replace the `ListofCharacters` text with `#"Split Column by Position"` after the `in`, as shown here, to reach the dynamic solution, which results in Figure 4-23.

CHAPTER 4   COLUMN SPLITTING AND MERGING

```
let
    Source = Excel.CurrentWorkbook(){[Name="Table1"]}[Content],
        Character = List.Max(List.Transform(Source[ID], Text.Length)),
    Listofcharacters = List.Repeat({2,1},Number.IntegerDivide(Character,3)) & (if Number.Mod(Character,3)=0 then {} else {2}),
    #"Split Column by Position" =  Table.SplitColumn(Source,"ID",Splitter.SplitTextByLengths(Listofcharacters))
in
    #"Split Column by Position"
```

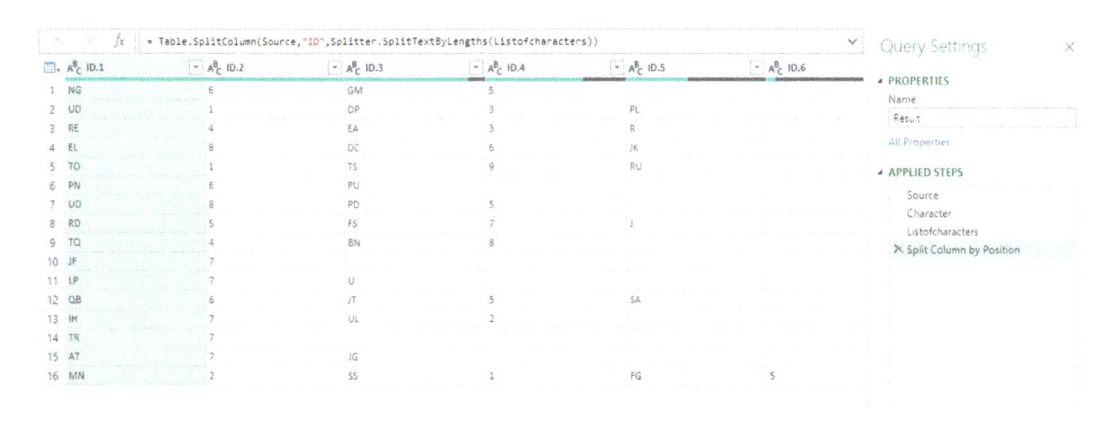

Figure 4-23. *The final result after reordering the steps*

Extracting Text Between Parentheses

Consider the text provided in the Source table, shown in Table 4-6. Extract all the values between the parameters.

201

CHAPTER 4   COLUMN SPLITTING AND MERGING

Table 4-6. *Source: Text*

Text
Renewable energy resources (5), renewable energies (RE), renewable resource (28), 81 renewable energy source (47)
Electric batteries (6), energy storage (18), 12 battery storage (52)
Photovoltaic cells (7), photovoltaic system (8)
Wind power (9), wind turbines (12), wind (24)
Solar power (SP) generation (15), 3 solar energy (32), solar power (48)
Algorithm (16), algorithms (37), genetic algorithms (19), genetic algorithm (45)
Hybrid energy system (20), hybrid renewable energy systems (21), hybrid renewable energies (41)
Related but not exactly the same terms 5
Optimization (3), Multi-objective optimization (13), particle swarm optimization (PSO) (10)
Electric power systems (EPS), 17 electric power transmission networks (40)
Energy management (EM), energy management systems (49)
26 Economic analysis (26), cost analysis (33), cost effectiveness (30), cost benefit analysis (38)

Note   The data in this example is provided in an Excel file titled `04 Extracting Text Between Parentheses.xlsx`.

Three different solutions based on splitter functions and text functions are provided for this problem.

Solution 1: Splitter-Based

At first glance, using a column splitter to split all the text after the opening parenthesis might seem like a viable solution. However, cleaning the results afterward can be quite challenging in this case. Instead, let's consider another type of splitter.

Among the available splitter functions, the `Splitter.SplitTextByRanges()` function can be useful for solving this problem. To check this function, consider the text in the

CHAPTER 4 COLUMN SPLITTING AND MERGING

first row of the Source table as variable X. The following formula extracts the character at the 28th position in X, resulting in {5} (the first value inside the parentheses).

= Splitter.SplitTextByRanges({{28,1}})(X)

Under similar conditions, the result of the following formula would be {5, "RE", 28, 47}, which is equal to all the values between the parentheses:

= Splitter.SplitTextByRanges({{28,1},{52,2},{77,2},{110,2}})(X)

As presented, the first argument used in this function is a list, including several sublists. In each sublist in {{28,1},{52,2},{77,2},{110,2}}, the first item presents the position of "(" +1 (the starting point for separation), and the second item presents the number of characters between each parentheses (the number of characters that should be extracted).

To solve the problem, you need to initially extract the position of every open parenthesis plus 1 (to reach the first character after the parentheses) and the number of characters between the parentheses to extract after the parenthesis in several sublists.

To determine the positions of the opening and closing parentheses, you can use the Text.PositionOfAny() function, as shown here. This function will return a list of the indexes for the occurrences of the ")" and "(" characters in the X variable, resulting in {27, 29, 51, 54, 76, 79, 109, 112}.

=Text.PositionOfAny(X,{"(",")"},2)

Note The Text.PositionOfAny() function is used to extract the positions of items in a list, with the following syntax:

Text.PositionOfAny(
    text as text,
    characters as list,
    optional occurrence as nullable number
) as any

203

CHAPTER 4 COLUMN SPLITTING AND MERGING

This function takes three inputs as follows:

1. The reference text.

2. A list that contains the substrings that you want to search for their positions in the reference text.

3. This input is optional. By entering the numbers 0, 1, or 2, you specify whether the smallest number (first repetition at the beginning of the text), the largest number (last repetition at the end of the text), or all the numbers should be displayed in the output.

In the next step, you can use the List.Split() function to group the positions of each occurrence of "(" and ")" into sublists. This will organize the values into sublists as follows: {{27, 29}, {51, 54}, {76, 79}, {109, 112}}.

```
=List.Split(
    Text.PositionOfAny(X,{"(",")"},2)
    ,2)
```

Considering the first sublist, the "(" is at the 27th character in X, and ")" is at the 29th character. To use these values in the splitter function, they need to be adjusted to {27 + 1, 29 - 27 - 1}, resulting in {28, 1}.

To convert the sublists into the correct format for the splitter function, you can use the List.Transform() function, and the previous formula can be rewritten as follows:

```
=List.Transform(
    List.Split(
            Text.PositionOfAny(X,{"(",")"},2),
            2),
    (y)=>{y{0}+1,y{1}-y{0}-1})
```

This transforms the values in the format {start position, number of characters}. So, the formula results in {{28, 1}, {52, 2}, {77, 2}, {110, 2}}.

To understand what happened in the previous formula, let's replace the first argument of List.Transform() with its value, which results in the following formula.

```
=List.Transform(
    {{27, 29}, {51, 54}, {76, 79}, {109, 112}},
    (y)=>{y{0}+1,y{1}-y{0}-1})
```

This means that the transformation function (y) => {y{0} + 1, y{1} - y{0} - 1} is applied to each item in the list {{27, 29}, {51, 54}, {76, 79}, {109, 112}}.

For the first item, y is {27, 29}, so y{0} is 27 and y{1} is 29. As a result, {y{0} + 1, y{1} - y{0} - 1} becomes {27 + 1, 29 - 27 - 1}, which simplifies to {28, 1}.

The same process is applied to the other items in the list, resulting in {{28, 1}, {52, 2}, {77, 2}, {110, 2}}.

After transforming the list items into the right shape, you can use this formula as the range positions for splitting in the first argument of the Splitter.SplitTextByRanges() function to extract all the values inside the parentheses from X as follows. This approach enables you to split the text at the specified ranges and retrieve the desired substrings.

```
=Splitter.SplitTextByRanges(
        List.Transform(List.Split(
                            Text.PositionOfAny(X,{"(",")"},2),
                            2),
        (y)=>{y{0}+1,y{1}-y{0}-1})
        )(X)
```

This formula is used for a single piece of text, but it can be applied to all the values on the Text column. Back to the main question—the defined custom splitter function can be applied in a new column by adding a custom column, and using the following formula in the formula bar, which will result in Figure 4-24 (producing a list of extracted values).

```
= Table.AddColumn(Source, "Custom", each Splitter.SplitTextByRanges( List.Transform(List.Split(Text.PositionOfAny([Text],{"(",")"},2),2), (y)=> {y{0}+1,y{1}-y{0}-1}))([Text]))
```

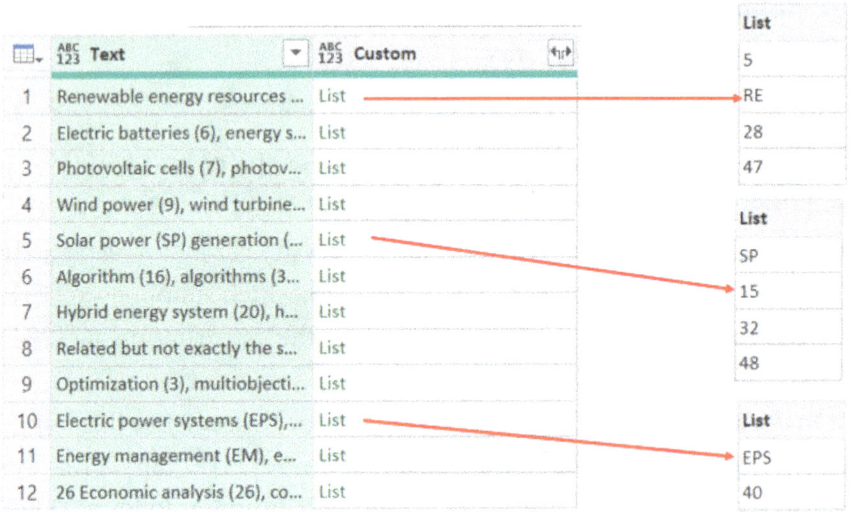

CHAPTER 4   COLUMN SPLITTING AND MERGING

Figure 4-24. The result of adding a new column

This formula can also be used in the Table.TransformColumns() function by entering the following formula in the formula bar, which results in Figure 4-25.

```
= Table.TransformColumns(
    Source,
    {
      "Text",
      each Splitter.SplitTextByRanges(
        List.Transform(
          List.Split(Text.PositionOfAny(_, {"(", ")"}), 2), 2),
          (y) => {y{0} + 1, y{1} - y{0} - 1}
        )
      )(_)
    }
)
```

CHAPTER 4 COLUMN SPLITTING AND MERGING

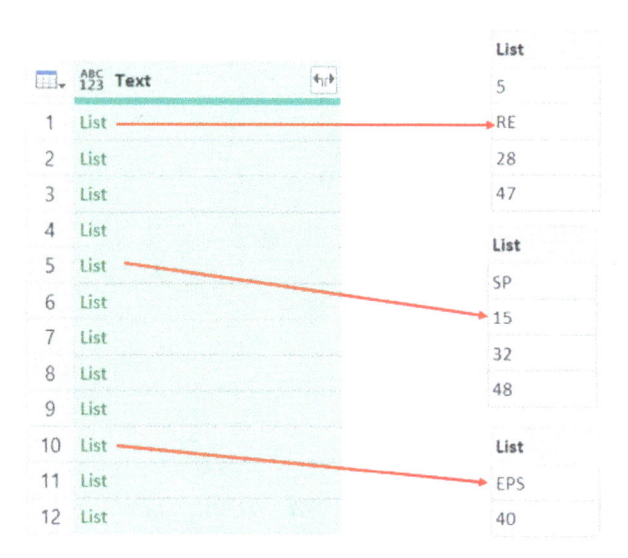

Figure 4-25. The result of the column transform

Or it can be used in the Table.SplitColumn() using the following formula in the formula bar, which results in Figure 4-26 (the number of columns after splitting is determined by the first row).

```
= Table.SplitColumn(
      Source,
      "Text",
      each Splitter.SplitTextByRanges(
                  List.Transform(
                        List.Split(
                              Text.PositionOfAny(_,{"(",")"},2)
                              ,2)
                        , (y)=> {y{0}+1,y{1}-y{0}-1})
                              )(_)
)
```

CHAPTER 4   COLUMN SPLITTING AND MERGING

	Text.1	Text.2	Text.3	Text.4
1	5	RE	28	47
2	6	18	52	null
3	7	8	null	null
4	9	12	24	null
5	SP	15	32	48
6	16	37	19	45
7	20	21	41	null
8		null	null	null	null
9	3	13	PSO	10
10	EPS	40	null	null
11	EM	49	null	null
12	26	33	30	38

Figure 4-26. Extracting all the values from parenthesis

Solution 2: Text Functions

The previous formula solved the problem, but it was not efficient. Power Query provides a useful function for extracting text between delimiters, called Text.BetweenDelimiters(). Given the previous variable X, the result of the following formula is 5, which represents the first value between the parentheses.

= Text.BetweenDelimiters(X,"(",")")

The result of the following formula is "RE", which is the value between the second parentheses:

=Text.BetweenDelimiters(X,"(",")",1)

You can use the fourth argument of this function to evaluate which parentheses you are searching for. The combination of this function and the List.Transform() function can help you solve this problem. Use the following formula to extract the values inside the first four parentheses in X, resulting in {5, "RE", 28, 47}.

= List.Transform(
    {0..3},
    (y)=>Text.BetweenDelimiters(X,"(",")",y))

The hardcoded part (the first argument that determined the number of parentheses in the text) of the previous formula can be replaced with the following formula:

CHAPTER 4   COLUMN SPLITTING AND MERGING

```
=List.Transform(
    List.Positions(Text.PositionOf(X,"(",2)),
    (y)=>Text.BetweenDelimiters(X,"(",")",y))
```

This formula dynamically generates the number of parentheses in the text and extracts the text between them.

You can use the previous formula as a custom splitter in the `Table.SplitColumn()` function by entering the following formula in the formula bar, which results in Figure 4-27, and solves the problem.

```
= Table.SplitColumn(
    Source,
    "Text",
    each List.Transform(
                        List.Positions(Text.PositionOf(_,"(",2)),
                        (y)=>Text.BetweenDelimiters(_,"(",")",y)))
```

Note Like the previous formula, the following formula can also be used to extract the values between parentheses in X using similar logic.

```
= List.Transform(Text.Split(X, "("), (y)=> Text.BeforeDelimiter (y,")"))
```

#	Text.1	Text.2	Text.3	Text.4
1	5	RE	28	47
2	6	18	52	null
3	7	8	null	null
4	9	12	24	null
5	SP	15	32	48
6	16	37	19	45
7	20	21	41	null
8		null	null	null	null
9	3	13	PSO	10
10	EPS	40	null	null
11	EM	49	null	null
12	26	33	30	38

Figure 4-27. *The final table*

Note In both of the previous solutions, the number of columns after splitting is determined by the number of parentheses in the first row of the table. In this example, since the first row contains four parentheses, the data will be split into four columns. However, if any row has more than four parentheses, the information inside the fifth and subsequent parentheses will be ignored. To resolve this and make the formula dynamic, the number of columns after splitting should be determined using the fourth argument of the function. The following formula calculates the maximum number of parentheses across all rows:

```
= List.Max( List.Transform(Source[Text],each Text.Length(Text.Select(_,"("))))
```

By adding this formula to the fourth argument of the function and rewriting it as follows, the solution becomes dynamic. This ensures the correct number of columns is generated based on the maximum number of parentheses in any row.

```
= Table.SplitColumn(
      Source,
      "Text",
      each List.Transform(
                        List.Positions(Text.PositionOf(_,"(",2)),
                        (y)=>Text.BetweenDelimiters(_,"(",")",y)),
      List.Max( List.Transform(Source[Text],each Text.Length(Text.Select(_,"(")))))
```

Solution 3: Using Text.Split

Although both of the previously mentioned solutions work correctly, this solution may be more efficient. However, it only works if the text within the parentheses is continuous, with no spaces. To try this solution, consider the source table and add a new column named Inside the Parentheses using the following formula:

```
=Text.Split([Text]," ")
```

CHAPTER 4   COLUMN SPLITTING AND MERGING

This formula splits each word in the text based on spaces, resulting in a list of individual words, as shown in Figure 4-28.

Figure 4-28. The result of Text.Split()

Out of all the items in the resulting list, you want to extract only the values between the parentheses. By rewriting the formula as follows, the result will be updated as shown in Figure 4-29 and include only the values between the parentheses:

```
=List.Transform(Text.Split([Text]," "), each Text.
BetweenDelimiters(_,"(",")"))
```

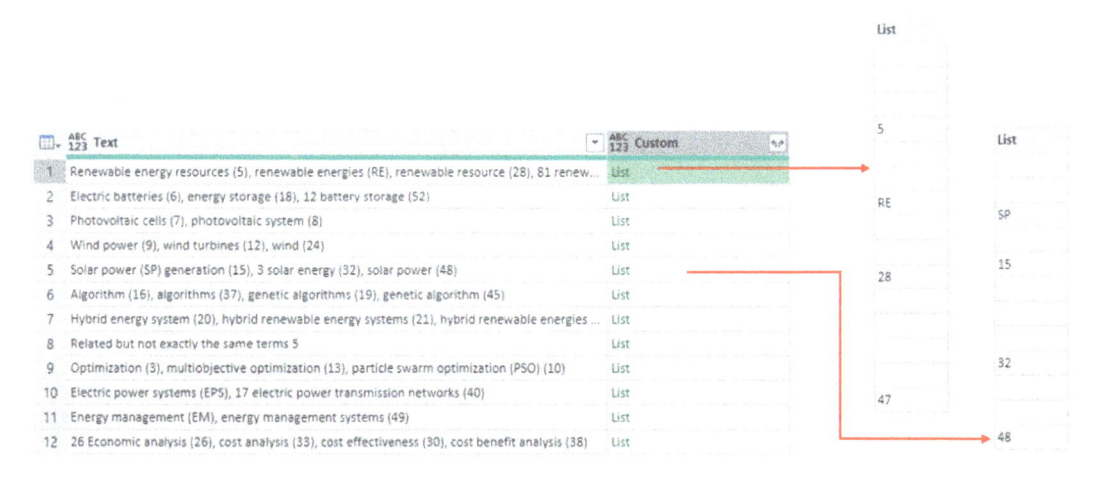

Figure 4-29. The result of the updated formula

211

To finalize this solution, you just need to remove the blank items from the list, using the `List.RemoveItems()` function, and then combine the remaining values using the `Text.Combine()` function. Replacing the formula with the following one can solve the problem and provide the final table shown in Figure 4-30:

```
=Text.Combine(List.RemoveItems(List.Transform(Text.Split([Text]," "), each
Text.BetweenDelimiters(_,"(",")")),{""}),", ")
```

#	Text	Custom
1	Renewable energy resources (5), renewable energies (RE), renewable resource (28), 81 renew...	5, RE, 28, 47
2	Electric batteries (6), energy storage (18), 12 battery storage (52)	6, 18, 52
3	Photovoltaic cells (7), photovoltaic system (8)	7, 8
4	Wind power (9), wind turbines (12), wind (24)	9, 12, 24
5	Solar power (SP) generation (15), 3 solar energy (32), solar power (48)	SP, 15, 32, 48
6	Algorithm (16), algorithms (37), genetic algorithms (19), genetic algorithm (45)	16, 37, 19, 45
7	Hybrid energy system (20), hybrid renewable energy systems (21), hybrid renewable energies ...	20, 21, 41
8	Related but not exactly the same terms 5	
9	Optimization (3), multiobjective optimization (13), particle swarm optimization (PSO) (10)	3, 13, PSO, 10
10	Electric power systems (EPS), 17 electric power transmission networks (40)	EPS, 40
11	Energy management (EM), energy management systems (49)	EM, 49
12	26 Economic analysis (26), cost analysis (33), cost effectiveness (30), cost benefit analysis (38)	26, 33, 30, 38

Figure 4-30. The final result

Extracting Email Addresses

Consider a source table containing the text (generated by ChatGPT) shown in Table 4-7. Extract all the email addresses from this text.

Table 4-7. *Source: Sample Text*

Text

Dear Team,

I hope this email finds you well. We have several important updates and announcements to share with everyone.

Firstly, please note that we have new email addresses for various departments. Kindly update your contacts accordingly:

1. Sales Department: sales@company.com

2. Support Team: support@company.com

3. HR Department: hr@company.com

4. IT Helpdesk: ithelpdesk@company.com

Secondly, we're excited to announce that we are launching a new @ProjectManagement initiative starting next month. This project aims to streamline our processes and improve efficiency across all departments.

In addition to this, please be reminded that the annual @CompanyRetreat will be held from July 15-17. Ensure you RSVP by sending an email to events@company.com no later than June 30. The itinerary will be shared soon.

We also have some exciting news about our @EmployeeRecognition program. Starting this quarter, we will be awarding the @EmployeeOfTheMonth title to outstanding performers. Nominations can be sent to recognition@company.com.

For those interested in participating in the upcoming @WorkshopSeries on digital marketing, please sign up by emailing marketing@company.com. These workshops are a great opportunity to enhance your skills and network with industry professionals.

Lastly, we have made some updates to our company policies. Please review the revised documents attached to this email and direct any questions to policy@company.com.

Thank you for your attention to these matters. If you have any questions or need further information, feel free to reach out to any of the respective departments via their new email addresses.

Best regards,

John Doe Communications Manager john.doe@company.com

CHAPTER 4   COLUMN SPLITTING AND MERGING

Note The data in this example is provided in an Excel file titled `05 Extracting Email Addresses.xlsx`.

To solve this problem, you can use the `Source[Text]{0}` formula to get the text from the first row of the Text column (instead of working on a single column and row table, it would be better to work on the text), which will result in the text shown in Figure 4-31. (If the Text column contains more than one row, use the `Text.Combine(Source[Text]," ")` formula to concatenate all rows into a single text string.)

```
Dear Team,
I hope this email finds you well. We have several important updates and announcements to share with everyone
Firstly, please note that we have new email addresses for various departments. Kindly update your contacts accordingly:
1. Sales Department: sales@company.com
2. Support Team: support@company.com
3. HR Department: hr@company.com
4. IT Helpdesk: ithelpdesk@company.com
Secondly, we're excited to announce that we are launching a new @ProjectManagement initiative starting next month. This project aims to streamline our processes and improve efficiency across all departments.
In addition to this, please be reminded that the annual @CompanyRetreat will be held from July 15-17. Ensure you RSVP by sending an email to events@company.com no later than June 30. The itinerary will be shared soon.
We also have some exciting news about our @EmployeeRecognition program. Starting this quarter, we will be awarding the @EmployeeOfTheMonth title to outstanding performers. Nominations can be sent to recognition@company.com.
For those interested in participating in the upcoming @WorkshopSeries on digital marketing, please sign up by emailing marketing@company.com. These workshops are a great opportunity to enhance your skills and network with industry professionals.
Lastly, we have made some updates to our company policies. Please review the revised documents attached to this email and direct any questions to policy@company.com.
Thank you for your attention to these matters. If you have any questions or need further information, feel free to reach out to any of the respective departments via their new email addresses.
Best regards,
John Doe Communications Manager john.doe@company.com
```

Figure 4-31. *Converting the table into text*

To solve this problem, in the first step, split the text into words based on spaces using the `Text.Split()` function as the following formula, resulting in a list containing all the words, as shown in Figure 4-32.

`= Text.Split(Source[Text]{0}," ")`

CHAPTER 4 COLUMN SPLITTING AND MERGING

 f_x = Text.Split(Source[Text]{0}," ")

	List
1	Dear
2	Team,
3	
	I
4	hope
5	this
6	email
7	finds
8	you
9	well.
10	We
11	have
12	several
13	important
14	updates
15	
16	
	and
17	announcements
18	to
19	share
20	with
21	everyone.
22	
	Firstly,

Figure 4-32. *The result of Text.Split*

To filter out the words containing "@", you can use the List.Select() function. This function takes two arguments—the reference list and the selection criteria to extract the desired items from the list. You can use Text.Split(Source[Text]{0}," ") as a reference list and then use the Text.Contains() function to define the selection criteria as follows. This results in all the items in the list including "@", resulting in Figure 4-33.

215

Chapter 4   Column Splitting and Merging

```
= List.Select(
    Text.Split(Source[Text]{0}," "),
    each Text.Contains(_,"@"))
```

	List
1	sales@company.com
2	support@company.com
3	hr@company.com
4	ithelpdesk@company.com
5	@ProjectManagement
6	@CompanyRetreat
7	events@company.com
8	@EmployeeRecognition
9	@EmployeeOfTheMonth
10	recognition@company.com.
11	@WorkshopSeries
12	marketing@company.com.
13	policy@company.com.
14	john.doe@company.com

Figure 4-33. *The result of the filtering list*

To exclude words that start with "@", you need to revise the selection criteria. You can use the Text.StartsWith() function to check the first argument of any text. So, the previous formula can be rewritten as the following formula to filter out the words starting with "@". The updated formula will result in Figure 4-34 and extract all the emails.

```
= List.Select(Text.Split(Source[Text]{0}," "),each Text.Contains(_,"@") and not Text.StartsWith(_,"@"))
```

CHAPTER 4   COLUMN SPLITTING AND MERGING

	List
1	sales@company.com
2	support@company.com
3	hr@company.com
4	ithelpdesk@company.com
5	events@company.com
6	recognition@company.com.
7	marketing@company.com.
8	policy@company.com.
9	john.doe@company.com

Figure 4-34. *Extracting all the emails*

Note   This formula works for the specific data provided here, but if the text contains words like "M@joun", it is also included in the result, even though it is not an email. In Chapter 10, this issue is addressed using advanced tools of the Regex function to account for all possible situations.

Using a Multiline Splitter

Consider the Source table shown in Table 4-8, which includes sales data (Date, Product Name, and Quantity). On a certain date, more than one transaction might happen, and they are separated by ",". Split the data into three separate columns: Date, Product Name, and Quantity.

CHAPTER 4   COLUMN SPLITTING AND MERGING

Table 4-8. *Source: Transactions*

Info
2024/04/04, A 10, B 5
2024/04/13, AS 1, A 1, M 2
2024/04/15, A 1
2024/04/22, B 3
2024/04/30, A 1, B 1
2024/05/04, AB 2
2024/05/07, AB 3, AS 4

Note   The data in this example is provided in an Excel file titled `06 Multi-Line Splitter.xlsx`.

Two separate solutions are provided to solve this problem.

Solution 1

For the first solution, select the Info column, then go to the Home tab and choose the Split Column command. Select By Delimiter and provide ", " (a comma and a space) as the delimiter, as shown in Figure 4-35. Then click OK to get resulting table, as shown in Figure 4-36.

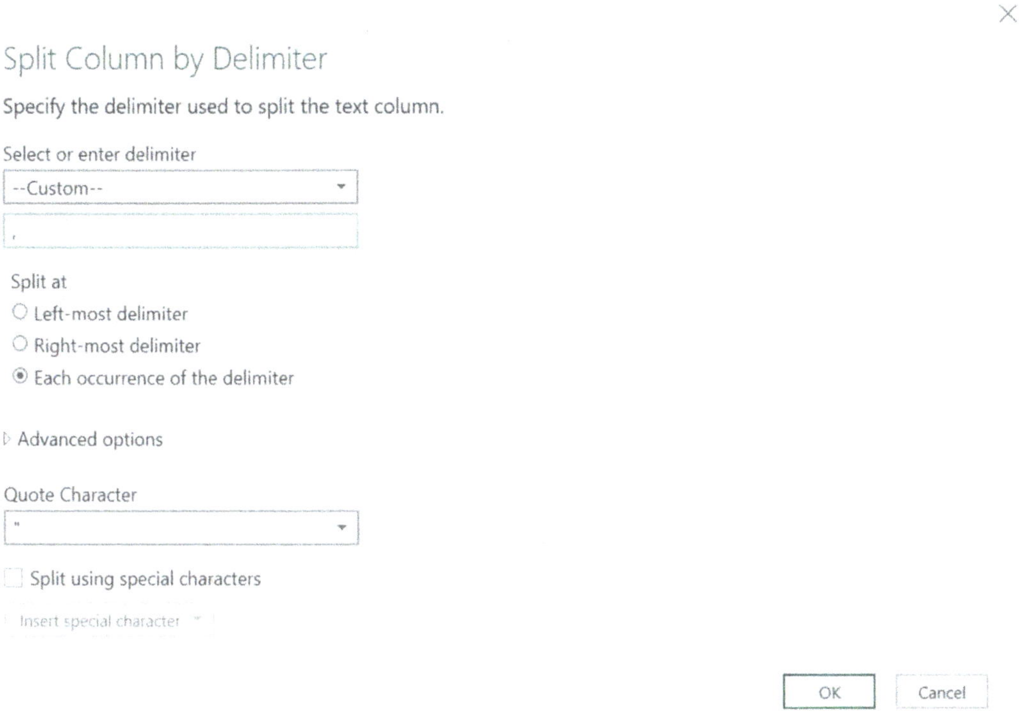

CHAPTER 4 COLUMN SPLITTING AND MERGING

Split Column by Delimiter

Specify the delimiter used to split the text column.

Select or enter delimiter

--Custom--

,

Split at
○ Left-most delimiter
○ Right-most delimiter
● Each occurrence of the delimiter

▷ Advanced options

Quote Character

"

☐ Split using special characters

Insert special character

OK   Cancel

Figure 4-35. *Setting for the splitting command*

Info.1	Info.2	Info.3	Info.4
1	4/04/2024 A 10	B 5	null
2	13/04/2024 AS 1	A 1	M 2
3	15/04/2024 A 1	null	null
4	22/04/2024 B 3	null	null
5	30/04/2024 A 1	B 1	null
6	4/05/2024 AB 2	null	null
7	7/05/2024 AB 3	AS 4	null

Figure 4-36. *The result of splitting*

Next, right-click the Info.1 column and choose Unpivot Other Columns to achieve Figure 4-37.

CHAPTER 4   COLUMN SPLITTING AND MERGING

	Info.1	Attribute	Value
1	4/04/2024	Info.2	A 10
2	4/04/2024	Info.3	B 5
3	13/04/2024	Info.2	AS 1
4	13/04/2024	Info.3	A 1
5	13/04/2024	Info.4	M 2
6	15/04/2024	Info.2	A 1
7	22/04/2024	Info.2	B 3
8	30/04/2024	Info.2	A 1
9	30/04/2024	Info.3	B 1
10	4/05/2024	Info.2	AB 2
11	7/05/2024	Info.2	AB 3
12	7/05/2024	Info.3	AS 4

Figure 4-37. The result of unpivoting

Then, select the Value column and use a space as the delimiter to obtain Figure 4-38.

	Info.1	Attribute	Value.1	Value.2
1	4/04/2024	Info.2	A	10
2	4/04/2024	Info.3	B	5
3	13/04/2024	Info.2	AS	1
4	13/04/2024	Info.3	A	1
5	13/04/2024	Info.4	M	2
6	15/04/2024	Info.2	A	1
7	22/04/2024	Info.2	B	3
8	30/04/2024	Info.2	A	1
9	30/04/2024	Info.3	B	1
10	4/05/2024	Info.2	AB	2
11	7/05/2024	Info.2	AB	3
12	7/05/2024	Info.3	AS	4

Figure 4-38. The result of splitting

Finally, remove the Attribute column and rename the remaining columns to complete the table.

CHAPTER 4　COLUMN SPLITTING AND MERGING

Solution 2

For the second solution, select the Info column, then navigate to the Home tab and choose the Split Column command. Select By Delimiter and enter ", " (a comma and a space) as the delimiter. However, in this solution, instead of selecting Each Occurrence of the Delimiter, choose Left-Most Delimiter, as shown in Figure 4-39. Then click OK to obtain Figure 4-40.

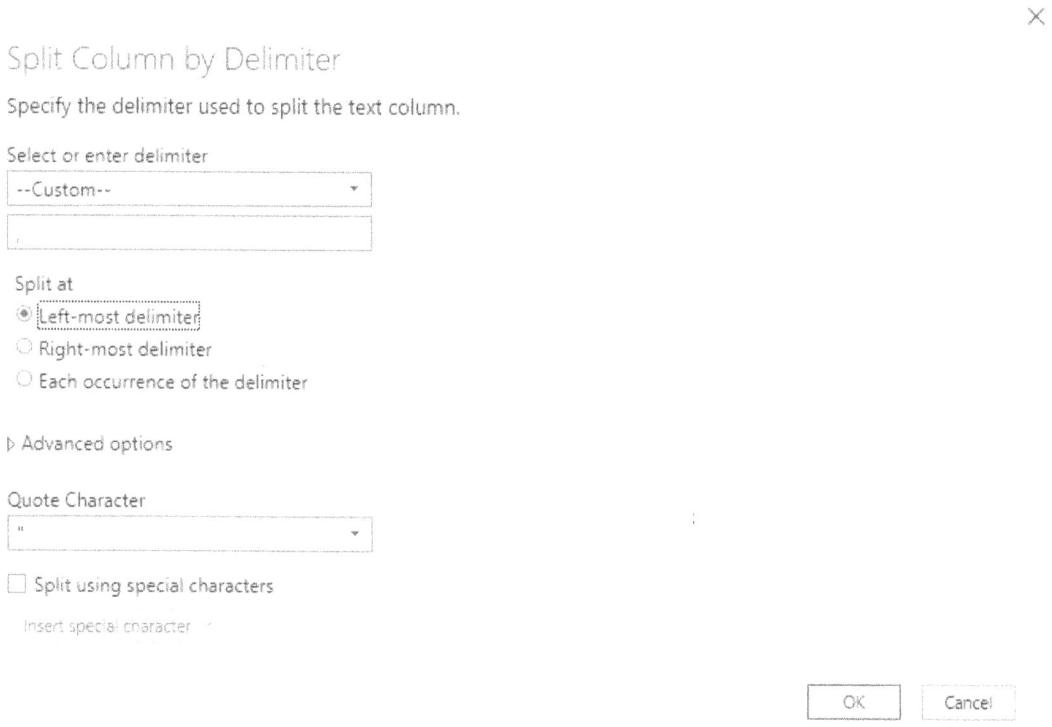

Figure 4-39. *Setting for splitting*

CHAPTER 4   COLUMN SPLITTING AND MERGING

	Info.1	Info.2
1	4/04/2024	A 10, B 5
2	13/04/2024	AS 1, A 1, M 2
3	15/04/2024	A 1
4	22/04/2024	B 3
5	30/04/2024	A 1, B 1
6	4/05/2024	AB 2
7	7/05/2024	AB 3, AS 4

Figure 4-40. *The result of splitting*

Next, select the Info.2 column, then navigate to the Home tab and choose the Split Column command. Select By Delimiter and enter " , " (a comma and a space) as the delimiter. However, this time, in the Advanced options, select Rows instead of Columns, as shown in Figure 4-41. Then click OK to obtain Figure 4-42.

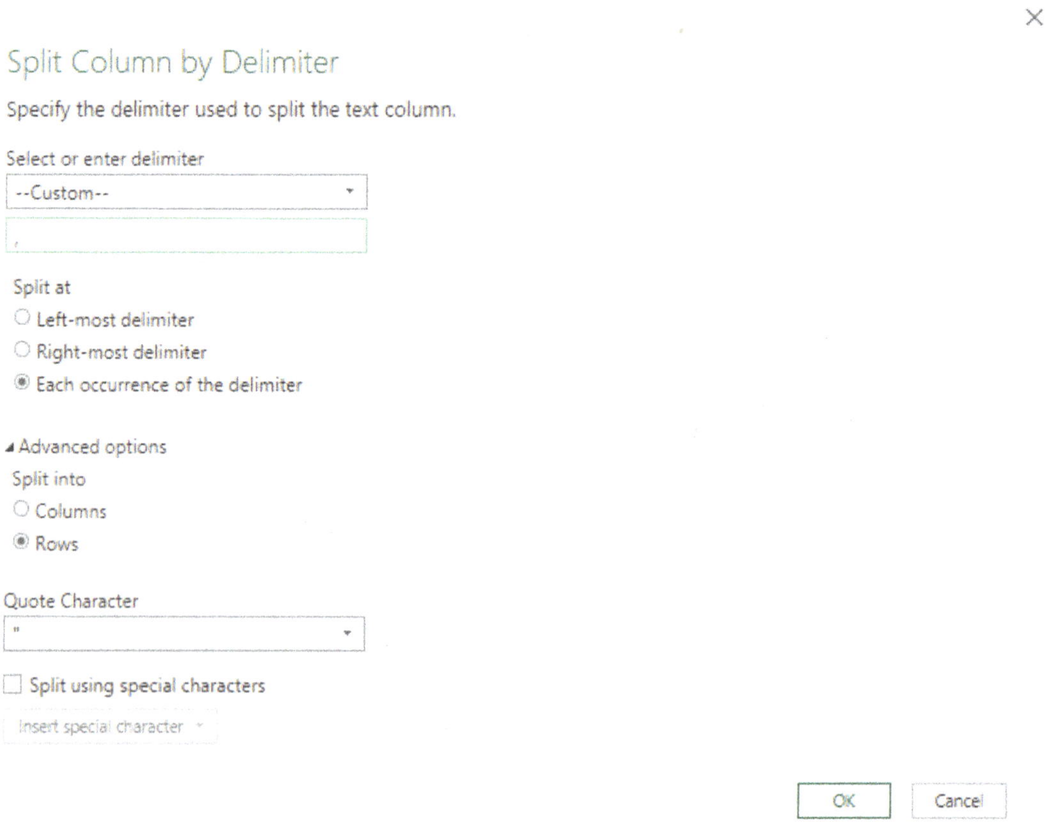

Split Column by Delimiter

Specify the delimiter used to split the text column.

Select or enter delimiter

--Custom--

Split at
○ Left-most delimiter
○ Right-most delimiter
◉ Each occurrence of the delimiter

▲ Advanced options
Split into
○ Columns
◉ Rows

Quote Character

"

☐ Split using special characters

Insert special character

OK   Cancel

Figure 4-41. *Setting of splitting*

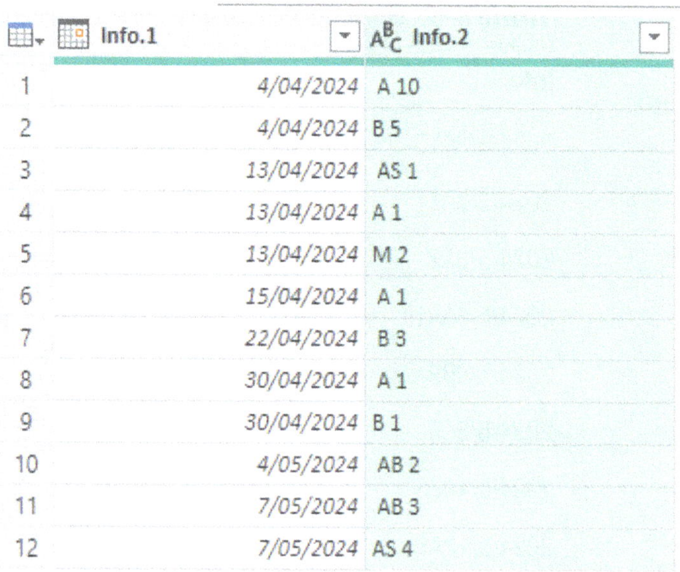

CHAPTER 4 COLUMN SPLITTING AND MERGING

	Info.1	Info.2
1	4/04/2024	A 10
2	4/04/2024	B 5
3	13/04/2024	AS 1
4	13/04/2024	A 1
5	13/04/2024	M 2
6	15/04/2024	A 1
7	22/04/2024	B 3
8	30/04/2024	A 1
9	30/04/2024	B 1
10	4/05/2024	AB 2
11	7/05/2024	AB 3
12	7/05/2024	AS 4

Figure 4-42. *The result of splitting*

As provided in the previous step, instead of placing the splitting values into different columns, the values are arranged in different rows. Therefore, in the final step, you just need to apply another splitting operation on the Info.2 column based on space to achieve the final result.

Splitting Text by Changing Character Type, Part 1

Consider the Source table in Table 4-9, which contains sales data (Date, Product Name, and Quantity) all combined into a single column. Split this data into three separate columns: Date, Product Name, and Quantity.

CHAPTER 4 COLUMN SPLITTING AND MERGING

Table 4-9. *Source: Transactions*

Info
2024/5/2A13
2024/5/3A11
2024/5/3A2
2024/5/6AA15
2024/5/8B9
2024/5/8C5
2024/5/10B5
2024/5/12A6
2024/5/12BC14
2024/5/12C2
2024/5/14A15
2024/5/19B14
2024/5/21C9

Note The data in this example is provided in an Excel file titled `07 Splitting Text by Changing Character type part 1.xlsx`.

For this task, any transition from numbers to text or reverse should be considered as splitting points. To achieve this, select the column, then go to the Home tab, and choose the Split Column command. Select By Digit to Non-Digit to split the data accordingly. This results in Figure 4-43, which shows the text split at any transition from digit to non-digit values. This also considers "/", which is part of dates, as a non-digit character, and it is used for splitting points if it comes after a digit.

CHAPTER 4 COLUMN SPLITTING AND MERGING

	Info.1	Info.2	Info.3	Info.4
1	2024	/5	/2	A13
2	2024	/5	/3	A11
3	2024	/5	/3	A2
4	2024	/5	/6	AA15
5	2024	/5	/8	B9
6	2024	/5	/8	C5
7	2024	/5	/10	B5
8	2024	/5	/12	A6
9	2024	/5	/12	BC14
10	2024	/5	/12	C2
11	2024	/5	/14	A15
12	2024	/5	/19	B14
13	2024	/5	/21	C9

Figure 4-43. *Splitting digit to non-digit type*

The previous steps lead to the following formula in the formula bar.

```
= Table.SplitColumn(
      Source,
      "Info",
      Splitter.SplitTextByCharacterTransition({"0".."9"}, (c) => not List.Contains({"0".."9"}, c)),
      {"Info.1", "Info.2", "Info.3", "Info.4"})
```

In this case, the `Splitter.SplitTextByCharacterTransition()` is used in the third argument as the splitter function.

The `Splitter.SplitTextByCharacterTransition()` function takes two arguments, typically lists or functions. To check its functionality over text, consider the first argument of this function as a list (or a function) called A, and the second argument as a list (or a function) called B. The splitting process applies to all characters in the text. For any character a at position i and its subsequent character b at position i+1, if a is in list A (or the result of function A for a is `true`) and b is in list B (or the result of function B for b is `true`), the text is split at position i+1.

In the generated formula, `{"0".."9"}`, is used as the first argument of `Splitter.SplitTextByCharacterTransition()`, and `(c) => not List.Contains({"0".."9"}, c)` is used as the second argument. So, if a is one of the items in the list `{"0".."9"}`, and its subsequent character satisfies the condition `(c) => not List.`

Contains({"0".."9"}, c), which means the subsequent character is any value except {"0".."9"}, then the split occurs between the current character and the next one. In the first row, with the value "2024/5/2A13" consider the fifth and sixth characters as "4/", as 4 is a member of {"0".."9"}, and the result of (c) => not List.Contains({"0".."9"}, c) for c="/" is true. The text is split between "4" and "/", which is not desirable.

To prevent splitting at these character transitions and only split when transitioning from numeric to alphabetic characters, the formula can be rewritten as the following formula in the formula bar:

```
= Table.SplitColumn(
    Source,
    "Info",
    Splitter.SplitTextByCharacterTransition({"0".."9"},{"A".."Z"}) ,
    {"Date","Other"})
```

If the text includes lowercase characters, the second argument should be rewritten to include both uppercase and lowercase characters as follows: {"A".."Z", "a".."z"}), which results in Figure 4-44.

CHAPTER 4   COLUMN SPLITTING AND MERGING

	Date	Other
1	2024/5/2	A13
2	2024/5/3	A11
3	2024/5/3	A2
4	2024/5/6	AA15
5	2024/5/8	B9
6	2024/5/8	C5
7	2024/5/10	B5
8	2024/5/12	A6
9	2024/5/12	BC14
10	2024/5/12	C2
11	2024/5/14	A15
12	2024/5/19	B14
13	2024/5/21	C9

Figure 4-44. *Splitting digit to non-digit type*

The values of the dates are now separated. Now it needs to split the Other column into the Product and Quantity columns. Considering the name of the previous step result was Split Column by Character Transition, apply the same process to the Other column to split it into two separate columns: Product and Quantity. Use the following formula to achieve this, resulting in Figure 4-45.

```
=Table.SplitColumn(
     #"Split Column by Character Transition",
     "Other",
     Splitter.SplitTextByCharacterTransition({"A".."Z"},{"0".."9"}),
     {"Product","Quantity"})
```

CHAPTER 4 COLUMN SPLITTING AND MERGING

	Date	Product	Quantity
1	2024/5/2	A	13
2	2024/5/3	A	11
3	2024/5/3	A	2
4	2024/5/6	AA	15
5	2024/5/8	B	9
6	2024/5/8	C	5
7	2024/5/10	B	5
8	2024/5/12	A	6
9	2024/5/12	BC	14
10	2024/5/12	C	2
11	2024/5/14	A	15
12	2024/5/19	B	14
13	2024/5/21	C	9

Figure 4-45. *The final result*

Splitting Text by Changing Character Type, Part 2

Consider the previous example, except that multiple transactions happen on each date and are presented in a cell, like the Source table shown in Table 4-10. Split the data into three separate columns—Date, Product, and Quantity.

CHAPTER 4   COLUMN SPLITTING AND MERGING

Table 4-10. *Source: Transactions*

Info
2024/5/2A13B14C10
2024/5/3A11
2024/5/3A2AA3
2024/5/6AA15B8
2024/5/8B9AA5
2024/5/8C5B2A5
2024/5/10B5
2024/5/12A6
2024/5/12BC14
2024/5/12C2AA3B18
2024/5/14A15
2024/5/19B14
2024/5/21C9

Note   The data in this example is provided in an Excel file titled `08 Splitting Text by Changing Character type part 2.xlsx`.

In this example, similar to the previous one, you can use `Splitter.SplitTextByCharacterTransition()` to split the column into several columns. However, since different transactions of products and quantities are provided for each date, some modification is required. As in the previous example, select the Info column, go to the Home tab, and choose Split Column. Then choose By Digit to Non-Digit. This will lead to the following formula in the formula bar and the result in Figure 4-46.

```
= Table.SplitColumn(Source, "Info", Splitter.
SplitTextByCharacterTransition({"0".."9"}, (c) => not List.
Contains({"0".."9"}, c)), {"Info.1", "Info.2", "Info.3", "Info.4",
"Info.5", "Info.6"})
```

CHAPTER 4 COLUMN SPLITTING AND MERGING

	Info.1	Info.2	Info.3	Info.4	Info.5
1	2024	/5	/2	A13	B14
2	2024	/5	/3	A11	
3	2024	/5	/3	A2	AA3
4	2024	/5	/6	AA15	B8
5	2024	/5	/8	B9	AA5
6	2024	/5	/8	C5	B2
7	2024	/5	/10	B5	
8	2024	/5	/12	A6	
9	2024	/5	/12	BC14	
10	2024	/5	/12	C2	AA3
11	2024	/5	/14	A15	
12	2024	/5	/19	B14	
13	2024	/5	/21	C9	

Figure 4-46. *Splitting the values*

Similar to the previous example, modify the formula in the formula bar as follows, which will result in Figure 4-47.

```
= Table.SplitColumn(Source, "Info", Splitter.
SplitTextByCharacterTransition({"0".."9"}, {"A".."Z"}))
```

	Info.1	Info.2	Info.3	Info.4	
1	2024/5/2	A13	B14	C10	
2	2024/5/3	A11		null	null
3	2024/5/3	A2	AA3		null
4	2024/5/6	AA15	B8		null
5	2024/5/8	B9	AA5		null
6	2024/5/8	C5	B2	A5	
7	2024/5/10	B5		null	null
8	2024/5/12	A6		null	null
9	2024/5/12	BC14		null	null
10	2024/5/12	C2	AA3	B18	
11	2024/5/14	A15		null	null
12	2024/5/19	B14		null	null
13	2024/5/21	C9		null	null

Figure 4-47. *The result of the revised split*

As shown, the resulting table contains information related to different transactions across different columns. Each of these columns needs to be split separately based on the transition from non-digit to digit values. However, since the number of columns is not predefined, applying this transformation to each column individually would not be efficient, especially when dealing with lots of columns. Instead, you can rewrite the previous formula as follows:

```
= Table.SplitColumn(
    Source,
    "Info",
    Splitter.SplitTextByCharacterTransition({"0".."9"}, {"A".."Z"}),
    2,
    "",
    ExtraValues.List)
```

Using 2 in the fourth argument specifies that the Info column should split into two columns and using ExtraValues.List in the sixth argument indicates that after splitting, any extra values except the first one will be provided in a list. The result is shown in Figure 4-48.

#	Info.1	Info.2	List
1	2024/5/2	List	A13
2	2024/5/3	List	B14
3	2024/5/3	List	C10
4	2024/5/6	List	
5	2024/5/8	List	List
6	2024/5/8	List	B9
7	2024/5/10	List	AA5
8	2024/5/12	List	
9	2024/5/12	List	List
10	2024/5/12	List	C2
11	2024/5/14	List	AA3
12	2024/5/19	List	B18
13	2024/5/21	List	

Figure 4-48. *The result of the revised split*

CHAPTER 4   COLUMN SPLITTING AND MERGING

Given the result of the previous step was Split Column by Character Transition, use the following formula in the formula bar to expand the Info.2 column into new rows. This will result in Figure 4-49.

= Table.ExpandListColumn(#"Split Column by Character Transition", "Info.2")

	Info.1	Info.2
1	2024/5/2	A13
2	2024/5/2	B14
3	2024/5/2	C10
4	2024/5/3	A11
5	2024/5/3	A2
6	2024/5/3	AA3
7	2024/5/6	AA15
8	2024/5/6	B8
9	2024/5/8	B9
10	2024/5/8	AA5
11	2024/5/8	C5
12	2024/5/8	B2
13	2024/5/8	A5
14	2024/5/10	B5
15	2024/5/12	A6
16	2024/5/12	BC14
17	2024/5/12	C2
18	2024/5/12	AA3
19	2024/5/12	B18
20	2024/5/14	A15

Figure 4-49. *The result of expanding the Info.2 column*

Selecting the Info.2 column and using Split Column with the By Non-Digit to Digit option will result in Figure 4-50. The problem is solved!

CHAPTER 4   COLUMN SPLITTING AND MERGING

#	ABC Info.1	ABC Info.2.1	ABC Info.2.2
1	2024/5/2	A	13
2	2024/5/2	B	14
3	2024/5/2	C	10
4	2024/5/3	A	11
5	2024/5/3	A	2
6	2024/5/3	AA	3
7	2024/5/6	AA	15
8	2024/5/6	B	8
9	2024/5/8	B	9
10	2024/5/8	AA	5
11	2024/5/8	C	5
12	2024/5/8	B	2
13	2024/5/8	A	5

Figure 4-50. *The final result*

Merging with a Custom Operation

Consider the source table in Table 4-11, including a customer's energy consumption at different times of the day (morning, evening, and night) for various dates. Convert this data to a daily table and create a table that shows the total energy consumption for each date by summing the values from the three columns.

Table 4-11. Source: Warehouse Transactions

Date	Morning	Evening	Night
1/06/2024	23	31	48
2/06/2024	46	42	73
3/06/2024	34	96	41
4/06/2024	62	35	47
5/06/2024	35	86	37
6/06/2024	26	59	36
7/06/2024	24	64	57
8/06/2024	15	49	61
9/06/2024	99	93	62

Note The data in this example is provided in an Excel file titled 09 Merging with Custom Operation.xlsx.

To solve this problem, you can add a new column by summing the available three columns and then removing these three columns. But instead of this solution, you can use Table.CombineColumns(). Select the Morning, Evening, and Night columns, then right-click one of them and choose the Merge option. In the dialog box that appears, select None as the separator. This action will generate the following formula in the formula bar. The result is in Figure 4-51.

```
= Table.CombineColumns(
    Table.TransformColumnTypes(Source, {{"Morning", type text},
    {"Evening", type text}, {"Night", type text}}, "en-AU"),
    {"Morning", "Evening", "Night"},
    Combiner.CombineTextByDelimiter("", QuoteStyle.None),
    "Merged")
```

CHAPTER 4 COLUMN SPLITTING AND MERGING

#	Date	Merged
1	1/06/2024 12:00:00 AM	233148
2	2/06/2024 12:00:00 AM	464273
3	3/06/2024 12:00:00 AM	349641
4	4/06/2024 12:00:00 AM	623547
5	5/06/2024 12:00:00 AM	358637
6	6/06/2024 12:00:00 AM	265936
7	7/06/2024 12:00:00 AM	246457
8	8/06/2024 12:00:00 AM	154961
9	9/06/2024 12:00:00 AM	999362

Figure 4-51. The result of merging columns

In this case, since Combiner.CombineTextByDelimiter() is used to combine the values in the third argument of Table.CombineColumns(), and the selected columns are of type number, the values are initially converted to text using the Table.TransformColumnTypes() function (in the first argument). The values of these columns are then concatenated. But, as you want to sum the values rather than connect them, you do not need to convert these columns to type text. So, the revised formula is shown here, resulting in Figure 4-52.

```
= Table.CombineColumns(Source,{"Morning", "Evening", "Night"},Combiner.
CombineTextByDelimiter("", QuoteStyle.None),"Merged")
```

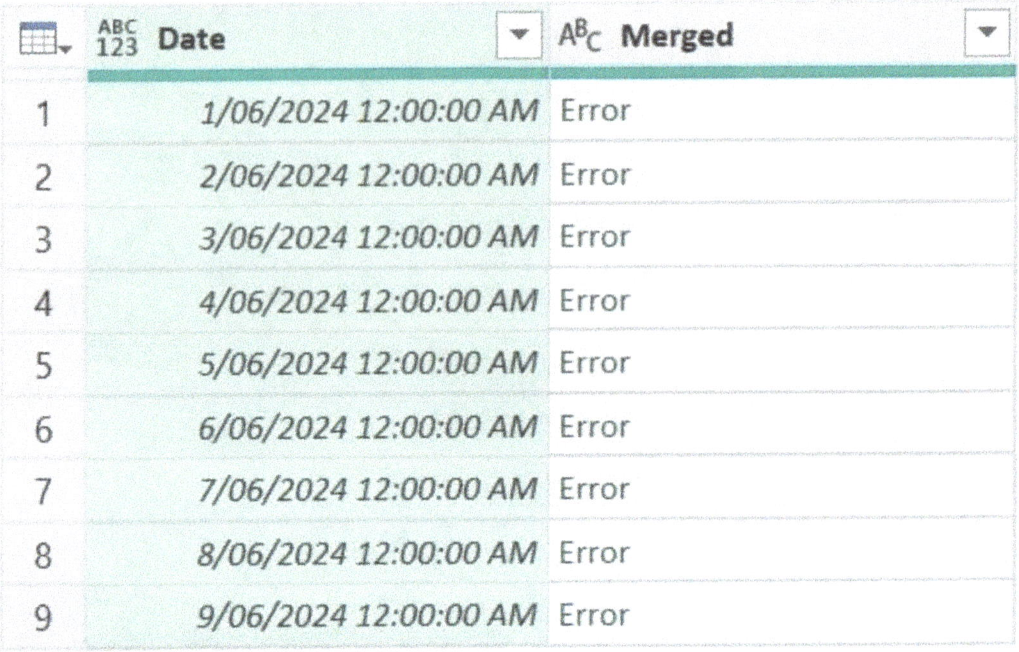

CHAPTER 4 COLUMN SPLITTING AND MERGING

#	Date	Merged
1	1/06/2024 12:00:00 AM	Error
2	2/06/2024 12:00:00 AM	Error
3	3/06/2024 12:00:00 AM	Error
4	4/06/2024 12:00:00 AM	Error
5	5/06/2024 12:00:00 AM	Error
6	6/06/2024 12:00:00 AM	Error
7	7/06/2024 12:00:00 AM	Error
8	8/06/2024 12:00:00 AM	Error
9	9/06/2024 12:00:00 AM	Error

Figure 4-52. The result of merging

Another modification is still required in the previous formula, and the combiner should be converted to summing the values instead of using Combiner.CombineTextByDelimiter(). So, replace this function with List.Sum() to sum the values of the selected columns. Additionally, update the fourth argument to a more appropriate column name. The revised formula, which results in Figure 4-53, is as follows:

```
= Table.CombineColumns(
    Source,
    {"Morning", "Evening", "Night"},
    List.Sum,
    "Energy Consumption")
```

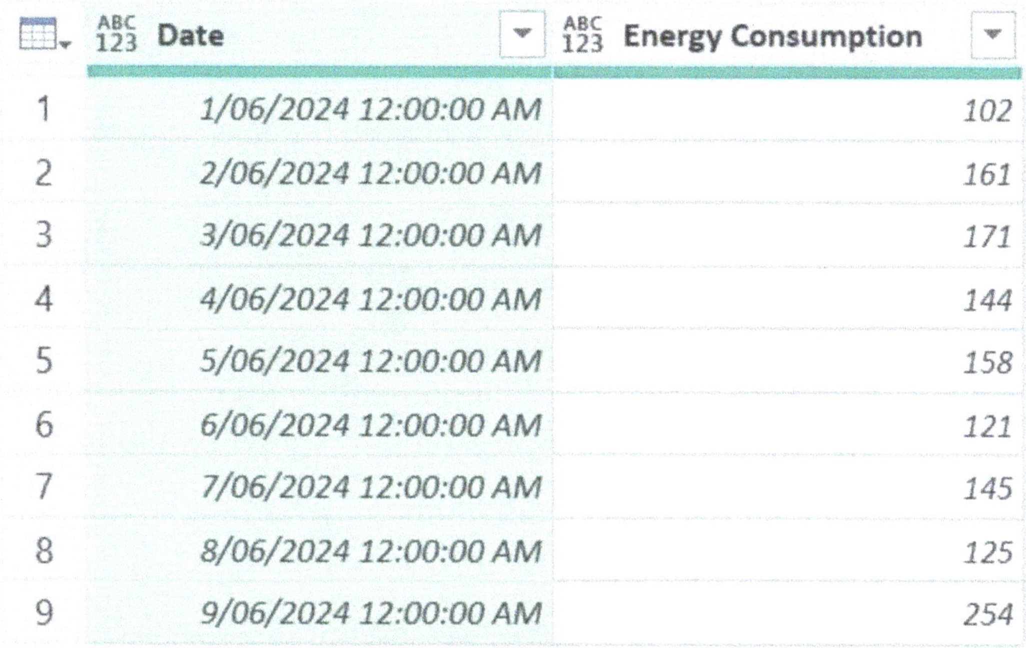

	Date	Energy Consumption
1	1/06/2024 12:00:00 AM	102
2	2/06/2024 12:00:00 AM	161
3	3/06/2024 12:00:00 AM	171
4	4/06/2024 12:00:00 AM	144
5	5/06/2024 12:00:00 AM	158
6	6/06/2024 12:00:00 AM	121
7	7/06/2024 12:00:00 AM	145
8	8/06/2024 12:00:00 AM	125
9	9/06/2024 12:00:00 AM	254

Figure 4-53. The final result

Merging Instead of Adding a Column

The Source table shown in Table 4-12 contains warehouse transactions. Calculate the final inventory of products using this formula: Final inventory = Initial value + Add - Reduce.

CHAPTER 4 COLUMN SPLITTING AND MERGING

Table 4-12. Source: Warehouse Transactions

Date	Product	Type	Quantity
1/01/2024	A	Initial value	75
1/01/2024	B	Initial value	80
1/01/2024	C	Initial value	20
5/01/2024	A	Reduce	30
10/01/2024	A	Reduce	20
15/01/2024	C	Reduce	10
20/01/2024	A	Add	20
21/01/2024	B	Reduce	60
25/01/2024	A	Add	50
25/01/2024	B	Add	50
4/02/2024	B	Reduce	30
15/02/2024	C	Reduce	5
17/02/2024	A	Reduce	70
17/02/2024	A	Reduce	20
21/02/2024	B	Reduce	25
23/02/2024	A	Reduce	2
27/02/2024	B	Reduce	10

Note The data in this example is provided in an Excel file titled 10 Merging Instead of Adding a Column.xlsx.

To solve this problem, you first need to convert the sign of the Quantity values for rows related to the Reduce transactions to negative. Then, you'll perform a grouping operation to calculate the last inventory. To adjust the signs of the quantities, you could add a new column to the table with the following formula.

if [Type]="Reduce" then -[Quantity] else [Quantity]

CHAPTER 4   COLUMN SPLITTING AND MERGING

However, in this example, the problem can be addressed by merging the existing columns instead of adding a new one (this problem is just defined to discover the feature of merging the columns). Select the Type and Quantity columns and right-click one of them. Then choose the Merge command. Use no separator to generate the following formula in the formula bar, which results in Figure 4-54.

```
= Table.CombineColumns(
    Table.TransformColumnTypes(Source, {{"Quantity", type text}},
    "en-AU"),
    {"Type", "Quantity"},
    Combiner.CombineTextByDelimiter("", QuoteStyle.None),
    "Merged")
```

#	Date	Product	Merged
1	1/01/2024 12:00:00 AM	A	Initial value75
2	1/01/2024 12:00:00 AM	B	Initial value80
3	1/01/2024 12:00:00 AM	C	Initial value20
4	5/01/2024 12:00:00 AM	A	Reduce30
5	10/01/2024 12:00:00 AM	A	Reduce20
6	15/01/2024 12:00:00 AM	C	Reduce10
7	20/01/2024 12:00:00 AM	A	Add20
8	21/01/2024 12:00:00 AM	B	Reduce60
9	25/01/2024 12:00:00 AM	A	Add50
10	25/01/2024 12:00:00 AM	B	Add50
11	4/02/2024 12:00:00 AM	B	Reduce30
12	15/02/2024 12:00:00 AM	C	Reduce5
13	17/02/2024 12:00:00 AM	A	Reduce70
14	17/02/2024 12:00:00 AM	A	Reduce20
15	21/02/2024 12:00:00 AM	B	Reduce25
16	23/02/2024 12:00:00 AM	A	Reduce2
17	27/02/2024 12:00:00 AM	B	Reduce10

Figure 4-54. The result of merging

CHAPTER 4   COLUMN SPLITTING AND MERGING

In this example, since the values in the Quantity column are of type number, by applying the merging command, `Table.TransformColumnTypes()` is used automatically to convert these values to text. Then, column merging is applied to the selected columns. As you do not want to concatenate the values of selected columns, rewrite the formula as shown here (replace the first argument with the name of the table, and the third argument with each _). This results in Figure 4-55.

```
= Table.CombineColumns(
      Source,
      {"Type","Quantity"},
      each _,
      "Merged")
```

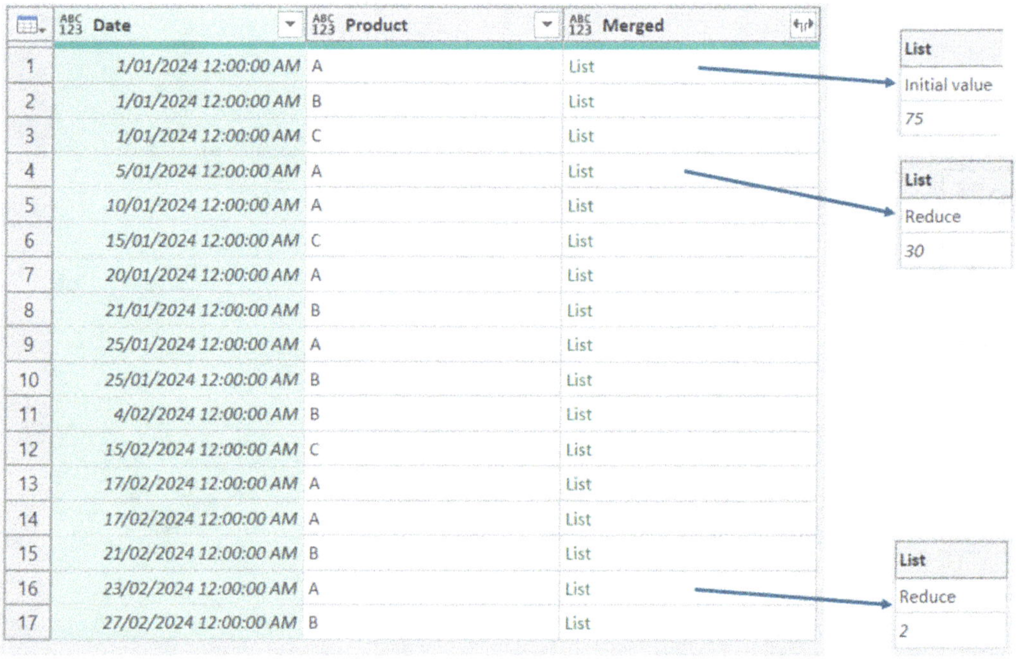

Figure 4-55.   The result of revised merging

By using each _ in the third argument of `Table.CombineColumns()` (the merging command), the values of the selected columns (Type and Quantity) are provided in a list with the selection order. The first item (_{0}) in the list determines the transaction type, and the second item (_{1}) specifies the quantity. Therefore, the formula can be

240

CHAPTER 4 COLUMN SPLITTING AND MERGING

rewritten as shown here to apply the sign to the Quantity based on the transaction type, resulting in Figure 4-56.

```
= Table.CombineColumns(
    Source,
    {"Type","Quantity"},
    each if _{0}="Reduce" then -_{1} else _{1},
    "Merged")
```

#	Date	Product	Merged
1	1/01/2024 12:00:00 AM	A	75
2	1/01/2024 12:00:00 AM	B	80
3	1/01/2024 12:00:00 AM	C	20
4	5/01/2024 12:00:00 AM	A	-30
5	10/01/2024 12:00:00 AM	A	-20
6	15/01/2024 12:00:00 AM	C	-10
7	20/01/2024 12:00:00 AM	A	20
8	21/01/2024 12:00:00 AM	B	-60
9	25/01/2024 12:00:00 AM	A	50
10	25/01/2024 12:00:00 AM	B	50
11	4/02/2024 12:00:00 AM	B	-30
12	15/02/2024 12:00:00 AM	C	-5
13	17/02/2024 12:00:00 AM	A	-70
14	17/02/2024 12:00:00 AM	A	-20
15	21/02/2024 12:00:00 AM	B	-25
16	23/02/2024 12:00:00 AM	A	-2
17	27/02/2024 12:00:00 AM	B	-10

Figure 4-56. Adding sign by merging columns

From the Home tab, select Group By and apply the settings provided in Figure 4-57. This will result in Figure 4-58, including the last inventory of products.

CHAPTER 4 COLUMN SPLITTING AND MERGING

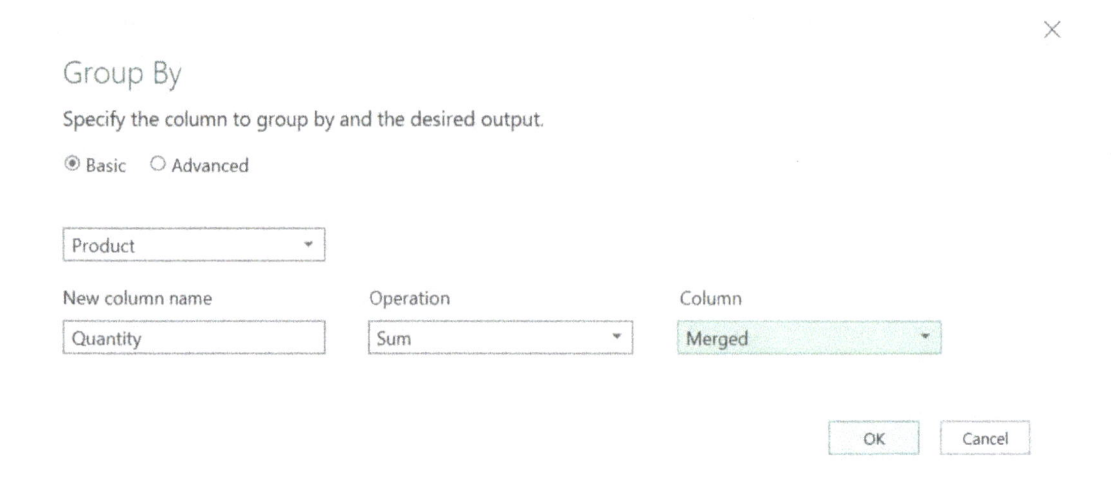

Figure 4-57. Setting of Group By

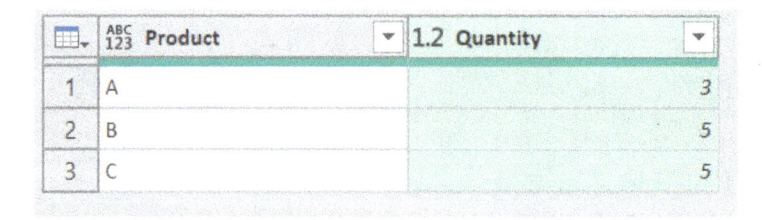

Figure 4-58. Final inventory levels of products

Merging Date Information

Consider the source table in Table 4-13, which contains date information in an inappropriate format. Extract and convert the date information for each row.

Table 4-13. Source: Sample Data

Year	Month	Day
2022	jan	7
2019	5	24
2018	february	22
2024	dec	20
2015	8	17
2010	november	21

CHAPTER 4 COLUMN SPLITTING AND MERGING

> **Note** The data in this example is provided in an Excel file titled 11 Merging Date Information .xlsx.

Similar to the previous example, select the columns in the following order: Year, Month, and Day. Right-click one of the selected columns and choose Merge. Select the custom merge option and enter "/" as the separator. This will produce the following formula and the result in Figure 4-59.

```
=Table.CombineColumns(
    Table.TransformColumnTypes(
        Source,
        {{"Year", type text}, {"Month", type text}, {"Day", type text}},
        "en-AU"
    ),
    {"Year", "Month", "Day"},
    Combiner.CombineTextByDelimiter("/", QuoteStyle.None),
    "Merged"
)
```

	ABC Merged
1	2022/jan/7
2	2019/5/24
3	2018/february/22
4	2024/dec/20
5	2015/8/17
6	2010/november/21

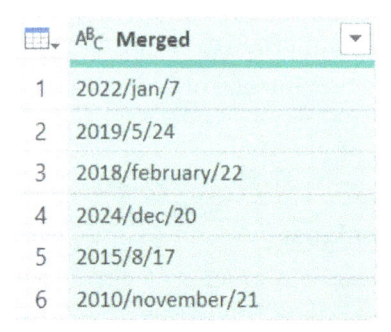

Figure 4-59. The result of merging

The previous formula results in the connected values in a mix of number and text formats, without considering that their type is Date. To address this problem, you can use the Date.From() function, as shown in the following formula, to convert the text values into a date format. This results in Figure 4-60.

243

CHAPTER 4　COLUMN SPLITTING AND MERGING

```
= Table.CombineColumns(
    Table.TransformColumnTypes(
        Source,
        {{"Year", type text}, {"Month", type text}, {"Day", type text}},
        "en-AU"
    ),
    {"Year", "Month", "Day"},
    each Date.From(Combiner.CombineTextByDelimiter("/", QuoteStyle.None)(_)),
    "Merged"
)
```

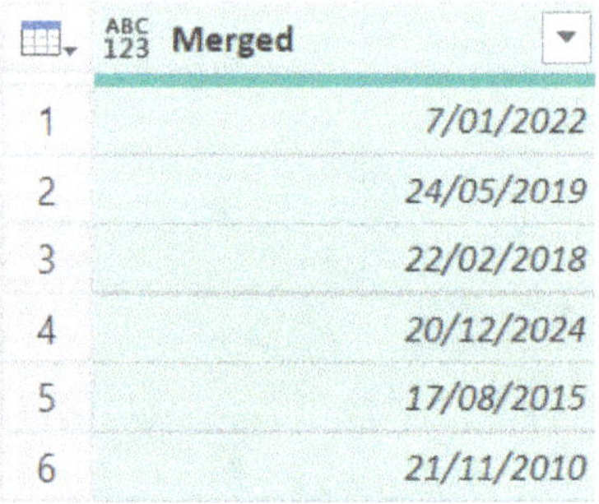

	Merged
1	7/01/2022
2	24/05/2019
3	22/02/2018
4	20/12/2024
5	17/08/2015
6	21/11/2010

Figure 4-60. *The result of merging*

It is true that the previous formula solves the problem, but it can also be rewritten using the Text.Combine() function instead of Combiner.CombineTextByDelimiter() as the combiner:

```
= Table.CombineColumns(
    Table.TransformColumnTypes(
        Source,
        {{"Year", type text}, {"Month", type text}, {"Day", type text}},
        "en-AU"
    ),
    {"Year", "Month", "Day"},
    each Date.From(Text.Combine(_, "/")),
    "Merged"
)
```

In the shortest version, instead of using `Table.TransformColumnTypes()` to convert the values to type text, you can use `List.Transform()`. The following formula can also be used to solve this problem:

```
= Table.CombineColumns(
    Source,
    {"Year", "Month", "Day"},
    each Date.From(Text.Combine(List.Transform(_,Text.From),"/")),
    "Merged")
```

To examine the formula, consider the first row of the table. The Year, Month, and Day columns are selected for merging. `each _` in the third input represents a list containing {2022, "Jan", 7}.

Using `List.Transform(_, Text.From)` converts all values for each row to text. For the first row, this results in {"2022", "Jan", "7"}. Next, `Text.Combine(List.Transform(_, Text.From), "/")` combines these text values with "/" as the separator, resulting in "2022/Jan/7". Finally, `Date.From()` converts this combined text into the date format.

Summary

This chapter explored techniques for splitting a column into several columns using `Table.SplitColumn()` and merging multiple columns into a single column with `Table.CombineColumns()`. You learned that `Table.SplitColumn()` requires six arguments: the table containing the column to be split, the name of the column to split, a custom function defining the splitting logic, the number or names of the resulting columns, as well as logic for handling extra values, and null values in rows with fewer splitting values. Among these arguments, the third and fourth are crucial for creating dynamic splitting logic.

Conversely, you discovered how to use `Table.CombineColumns()` to merge values from multiple columns. This function accepts four arguments: the name of the table, the names of the columns to be merged, the merging function, and the name of the new column that will contain the combined values. While the user interface restricts the merging function to text-related functions in the third argument, using M-code allows for more flexibility to apply different functions as needed.

The next chapter provides insights into using the `Table.Pivot()` and `Table.UnpivotColumns()` functions to transform multiple columns into rows and vice versa.

CHAPTER 5

Pivoting and Unpivoting Tables

Pivoting and unpivoting are important commands for reshaping data in order to achieve the desired structure during the cleaning process. This chapter covers the hidden features of these two amazing functions in Power Query.

As shown in Figure 5-1, pivoting in Power Query is the process of transforming data from a long format (where multiple rows contain information that should be spread across columns) into a wide format (where distinct values from a column become the headers of new columns), and unpivoting is the opposite process. In other words, if you've used Pivot Tables in Excel, pivoting is like moving a field from the Rows area (quadrant) to the Columns area (quadrant), while unpivoting is the reverse—moving the field from the Columns area back to the Rows area.

Year	ID	Quantity			Year	A	B
2010	A	10		Pivoting	2010	10	20
2010	B	20			2011	5	15
2011	A	5		Unpivoting			
2011	B	15					

Figure 5-1. *Settings of pivot columns*

To show you how to use pivoting in Power Query, this chapter uses the Source table in Table 5-1, which includes yearly data.

CHAPTER 5 PIVOTING AND UNPIVOTING TABLES

Table 5-1. *Source: Sales Info*

Year	Attribute	result
2020	Quantity	83121
2020	discount Rate	11%
2020	Sales	5437400
2021	Quantity	30293
2021	discount Rate	5%
2021	Sales	9772700
2022	Quantity	79865
2022	discount Rate	10%
2022	Sales	3137600
2023	Quantity	87445
2023	discount Rate	11%
2023	Sales	5472500
2023	Sales	45

In the Source table, each row contains information about quantity, sales, and discount rates for different years. To reshape the table and separate this information into distinct columns, select the Attribute column, then go to the Transform tab, and apply the pivot operation by clicking the Pivot Column command. Then configure the settings on the open window, by choosing Result as the value column and Sum, or any other functions as the aggregation function from advanced options, as shown in Figure 5-2. Then click OK, which results in the pivoted version of source table, as shown in Figure 5-3.

CHAPTER 5   PIVOTING AND UNPIVOTING TABLES

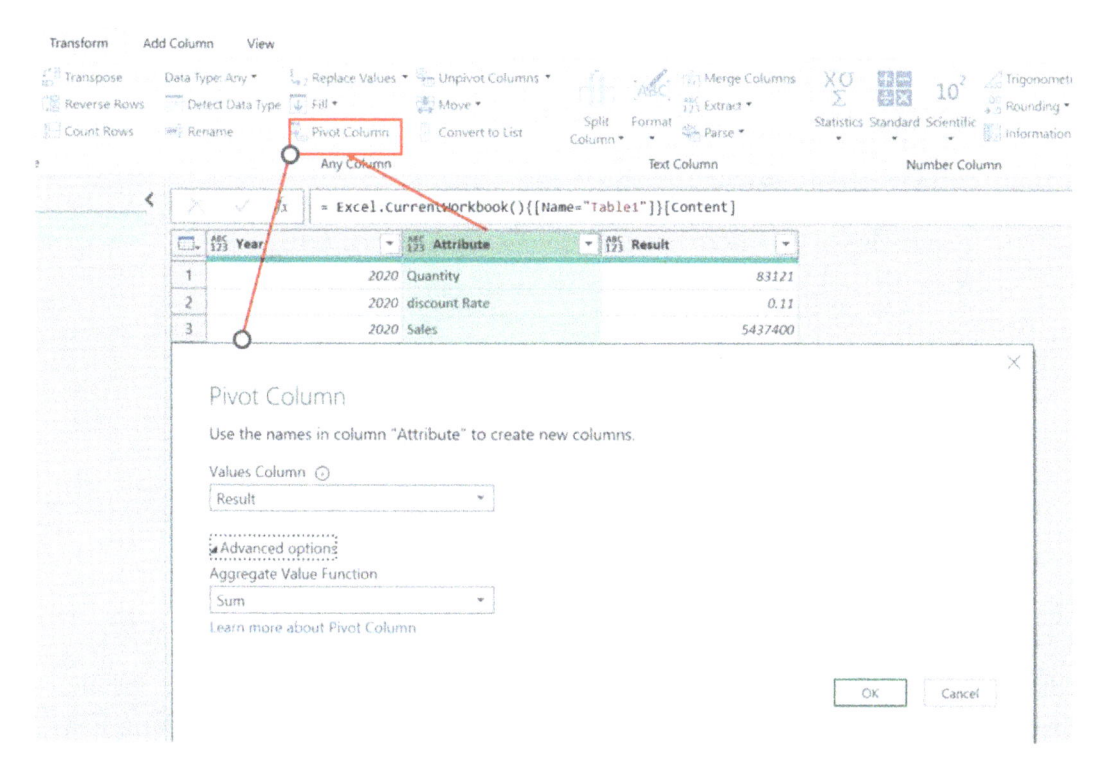

Figure 5-2. *Settings of the pivot columns*

Figure 5-3. *The result of pivot columns*

The previous steps result in the following formula in the formula bar, based on the Table.Pivot() function, which includes five key components as follows:

1. **Name of the table:** The original table being transformed is entered in the first argument.

2. **New columns:** The columns to be created in the reshaped table should be determined in the second argument.

249

CHAPTER 5 PIVOTING AND UNPIVOTING TABLES

3. **Pivot column:** The column from the original table that will be used to create the new columns.

4. **Value column:** The column whose values will be aggregated and placed under the new columns.

5. **Aggregation function:** The function used to aggregate the values, such as Sum.

```
= Table.Pivot(
    Source,
    List.Distinct(Source[Attribute]),
    "Attribute",
    "Result",
    List.Sum)
```

On the other hand, unpivoting is the process of transforming columns into rows, effectively converting a wide table with many columns into a longer, narrower format. This technique helps organize data that is structured in a tabular format, making it easier to analyze.

For example, consider the Source table shown in Table 5-2, which includes sales values across various years, presented in different columns. Unpivoting this table will consolidate the column headers into a single column and convert the associated values into rows, thus simplifying the data structure for analysis.

Table 5-2. Source: Sales info

Product	2020	2021	2022	2023
A	22	32	24	14
B	28	19	27	25
C	13	23	30	11
D	39	25	10	27

To consolidate sales data for different years into a single column, select columns 2020 to 2023, right-click one of them, and choose the Unpivot Columns command. You should get the unpivot version of the table shown in Figure 5-4.

CHAPTER 5 PIVOTING AND UNPIVOTING TABLES

#	Product	Attribute	Value
1	A	2020	22
2	A	2021	32
3	A	2022	24
4	A	2023	14
5	B	2020	28
6	B	2021	19
7	B	2022	27
8	B	2023	25
9	C	2020	13
10	C	2021	23
11	C	2022	30
12	C	2023	11
13	D	2020	39
14	D	2021	25
15	D	2022	10
16	D	2023	27

Figure 5-4. Results of unpivoting columns

Alternatively, if you select only the Product column and right-click it, then choose Unpivot Other Columns, you will achieve the same result as using the following formula:

= Table.UnpivotOtherColumns(Source, {"Product"}, "Attribute", "Value")

The rest of this chapter explains these two advanced functions in Power Query.

Managing Product IDs

The Source table contains Product IDs, as shown in Table 5-3. Generate a unique list of all Product IDs in a single column.

251

Table 5-3. Source: Product IDs

ID 1	ID 2	ID 3	ID 4
P-1112	P-1046	P-1071	P-1088
P-1130	P-1044	P-1014	P-1071
P-1150	P-1034	P-1071	P-1082
P-1108	P-1082		
P-1013	P-1082		
P-1134	P-1013	P-1030	P-1082
P-1013	P-1038	P-1007	
P-1165	P-1076	P-1089	
P-1157	P-1050		

Note The data in this example is provided in an Excel file titled 01 Managing Product IDs.xlsx.

Two different solutions, based on unpivoting and using M functions, are provided for this problem.

Solution 1: Using Unpivoting

To solve this question, you need to provide all the IDs from the four columns into a single column under each other, and then remove any duplicate values from that column. Transforming IDs from multiple columns into a single column is precisely what unpivoting is designed to do. To extract a unique list of Product IDs in a column, select all the columns, right-click one, and choose Unpivot Columns, which results in a table with two columns—one containing all the IDs, typically labeled Value, and the other, called Attribute, showing the original column names where the IDs were located. See Figure 5-5.

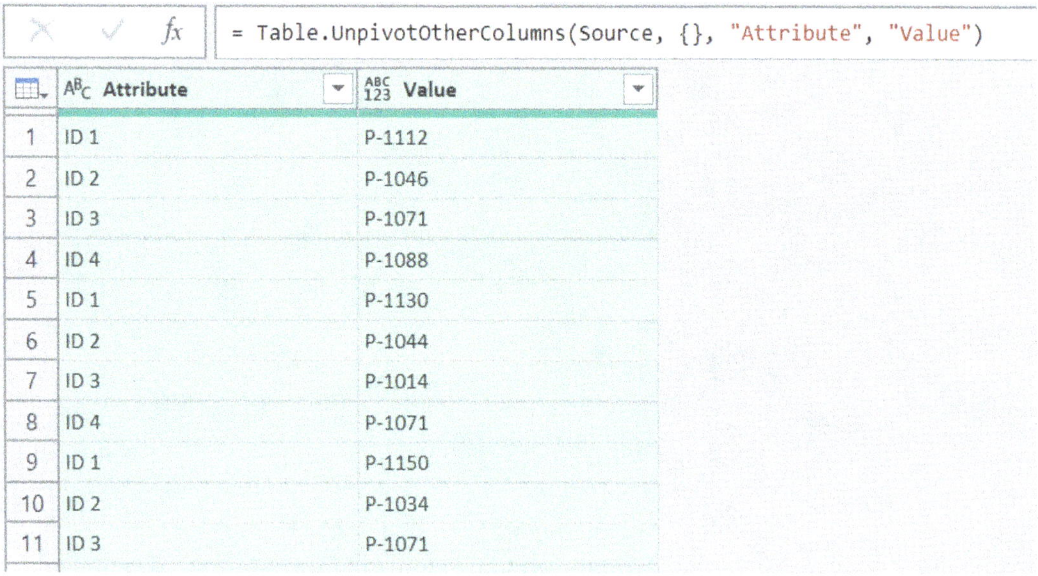

```
= Table.UnpivotOtherColumns(Source, {}, "Attribute", "Value")
```

#	Attribute	Value
1	ID 1	P-1112
2	ID 2	P-1046
3	ID 3	P-1071
4	ID 4	P-1088
5	ID 1	P-1130
6	ID 2	P-1044
7	ID 3	P-1014
8	ID 4	P-1071
9	ID 1	P-1150
10	ID 2	P-1034
11	ID 3	P-1071

Figure 5-5. *The result of unpivoting*

In this example, you do not need the Attribute column, so, remove it. Then, to remove repetitive IDs, right-click the Value column and select Remove Duplicates to obtain Figure 5-6, including all the IDs.

CHAPTER 5   PIVOTING AND UNPIVOTING TABLES

	Value
1	P-1112
2	P-1046
3	P-1071
4	P-1088
5	P-1130
6	P-1044
7	P-1014
8	P-1150
9	P-1034
10	P-1082
11	P-1108
12	P-1013
13	P-1134
14	P-1030
15	P-1038
16	P-1007
17	P-1165
18	P-1076
19	P-1089
20	P-1157
21	P-1050

Figure 5-6. Removing duplicates

Solution 2: Using M Functions

Power Query provides two powerful functions to convert all the values in a table into a list: Table.ToRows() and Table.ToColumns(). Both functions are easy to use; you only need to input the table name as the first argument. To use them, click the *fx* icon next to the formula bar to create a new step, and then use one of the following formulas. This will result in Figure 5-7.

=Table.ToRows(Source)
=Table.ToColumns(Source)

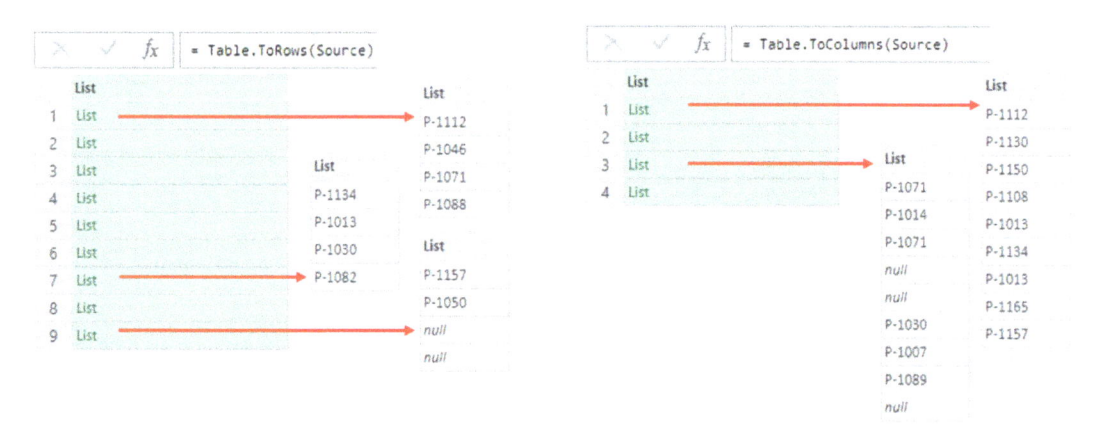

Figure 5-7. The results of using Table.ToRows() or Table.ToColumns()

No matter which formula you use, the remaining steps will be the same (I continue the explanation using `Table.ToRows()`). The result of `Table.ToRows(Source)` is a list containing several sublists, where each sublist represents the information from a single row of the source table. To extract the unique IDs, you need to combine these sublists into a single list using the `List.Combine()` function and then remove duplicates with the `List.Distinct()` function. You can rewrite the previous formula as follows to extract the unique IDs, as shown in Figure 5-8.

=List.Distinct(List.Combine(Table.ToRows(Source)))

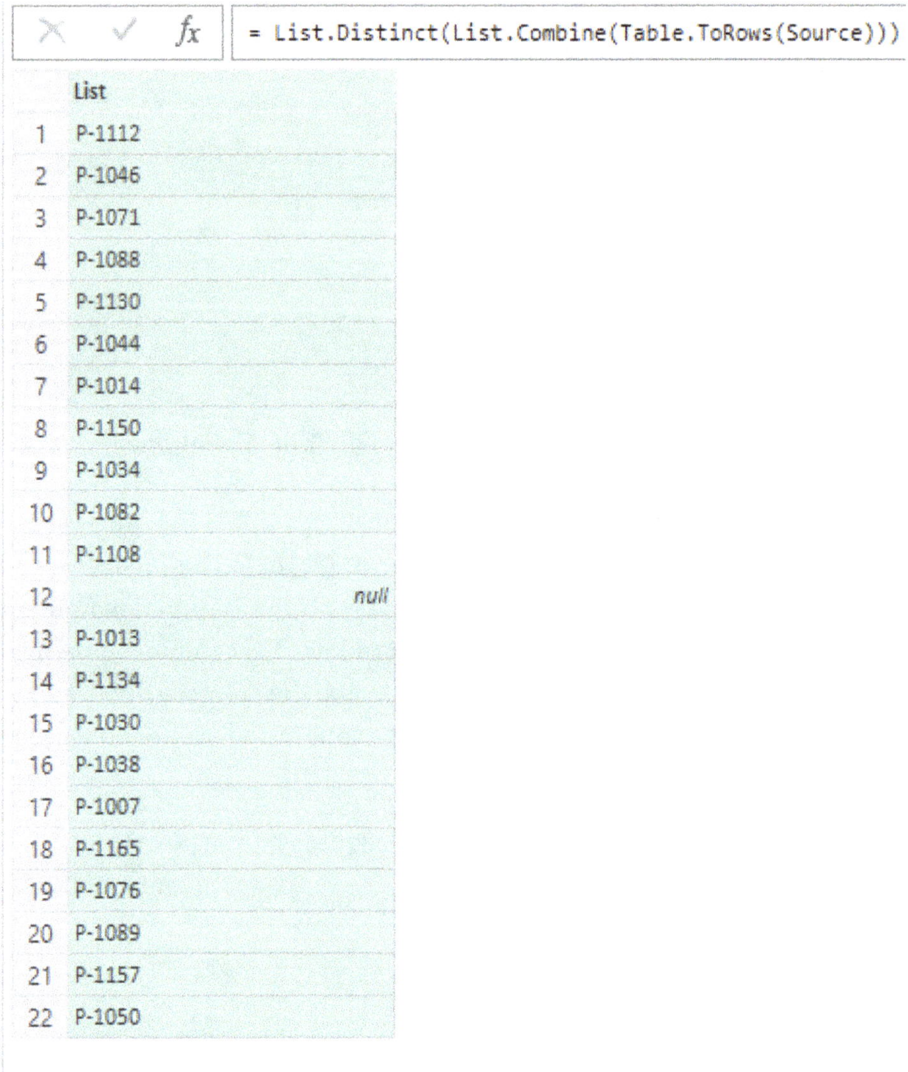

CHAPTER 5 PIVOTING AND UNPIVOTING TABLES

| | fx | = List.Distinct(List.Combine(Table.ToRows(Source))) |

	List
1	P-1112
2	P-1046
3	P-1071
4	P-1088
5	P-1130
6	P-1044
7	P-1014
8	P-1150
9	P-1034
10	P-1082
11	P-1108
12	null
13	P-1013
14	P-1134
15	P-1030
16	P-1038
17	P-1007
18	P-1165
19	P-1076
20	P-1089
21	P-1157
22	P-1050

Figure 5-8. *The result of combining the sublists and removing duplicates*

Instead of using the previous formula, which combines List.Combine() and List.Distinct(), you can use the List.Union() function as follows. This approach achieves the same result more directly.

=List.Union(Table.ToRows(Source))

CHAPTER 5   PIVOTING AND UNPIVOTING TABLES

Some of the cells in the source table are blank, so the result of the previous formula also includes null values. To remove these nulls from the list, you can use the List.RemoveNulls() function by modifying the formula as follows.

```
= List.RemoveNulls(List.Union(Table.ToRows(Source)))
```

Note In the second solution, the final result is of type list, whereas the result of the first solution is of type table.

Value Repeated in Several Columns

The data in Table 5-4 displays products sold across different seasons. Extract the following lists:

  a) Product IDs sold during all seasons.

  b) Product IDs sold during only one season.

Note The data in this example is provided in an Excel file titled 02 Value repeated in several columns.xlsx.

Table 5-4. Source: Historical Sales Value

Spring	Summer	Fall	Winter
X-005	X-004	X-020	X-015
X-017	X-002	X-025	X-011
X-011	X-003	X-012	X-002
X-023	X-017	X-025	X-022
X-015	X-012	X-012	X-017
X-004	X-023	X-012	X-006
X-015	X-019	X-010	X-022
X-008	X-008	X-019	X-018
X-012	X-016	X-016	X-003
X-021	X-020	X-025	X-013
X-012	X-009	X-014	X-023
X-014	X-004	X-025	X-003
X-013	X-016	X-024	X-021
X-004	X-001	X-015	X-012

To solve this problem, the current table structure is not ideal. Converting it into a table with two columns—one for the seasons and the other for the Product IDs—can be helpful. This is where the Unpivoting command becomes invaluable. Select all the columns in the Source table. Then, from the Transform tab, choose the Unpivot Columns command. This action will create the unpivoted table shown in Figure 5-9.

CHAPTER 5   PIVOTING AND UNPIVOTING TABLES

`= Table.UnpivotOtherColumns(Source, {}, "Attribute", "Value")`

#	Attribute	Value
1	Spring	X-005
2	Summer	X-004
3	Fall	X-020
4	Winter	X-015
5	Spring	X-017
6	Summer	X-002
7	Fall	X-025
8	Winter	X-011
9	Spring	X-011
10	Summer	X-003
11	Fall	X-012
12	Winter	X-002
13	Spring	X-023

Figure 5-9. *Unpivoted table*

The data structure is suitable for counting the number of seasons in which an ID was sold on them, and then filtering the rows with a value of 4 in the count column. This is different from counting the number of repetitions of each ID, as an ID might appear multiple times for the same season. To ensure accurate results, let's first remove duplicate entries. So, select the Attribute and Value columns. Then, as shown in Figure 5-10, go to the Home tab, choose the Remove Rows command, and then select Remove Duplicates (or right-click one of the selected columns and choose the Remove Duplicates command). This action will yield a table where each product ID appears only once per season, as shown in Figure 5-11.

259

CHAPTER 5   PIVOTING AND UNPIVOTING TABLES

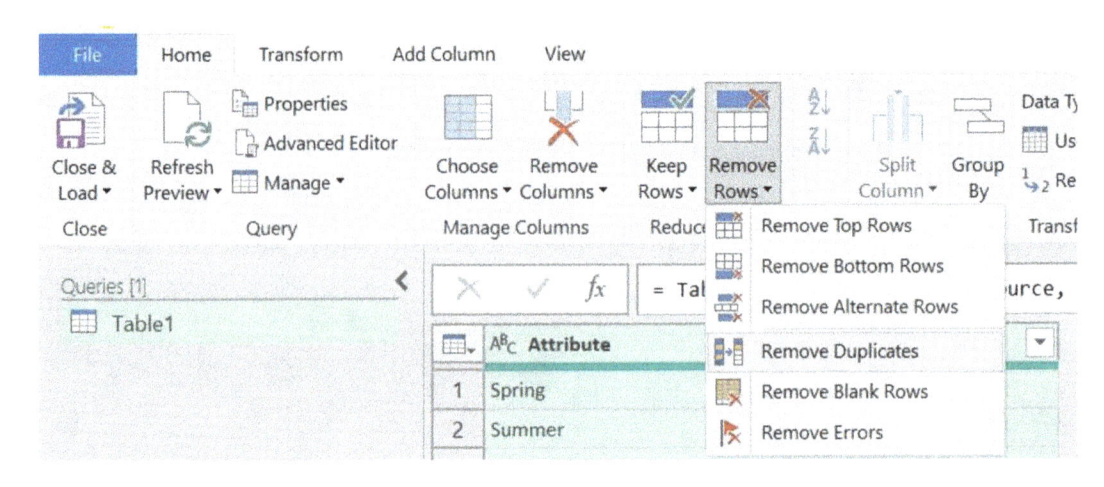

Figure 5-10.   The Remove Duplicates command

Figure 5-11.   The result of removing duplicates

After obtaining the table with unique product IDs for each season, it is time to count the number of repetitions of each ID in the table. Select the Value column. Then, right-click it and choose the Group By command. Apply the settings shown in Figure 5-12. This operation will result in the table displayed in Figure 5-13.

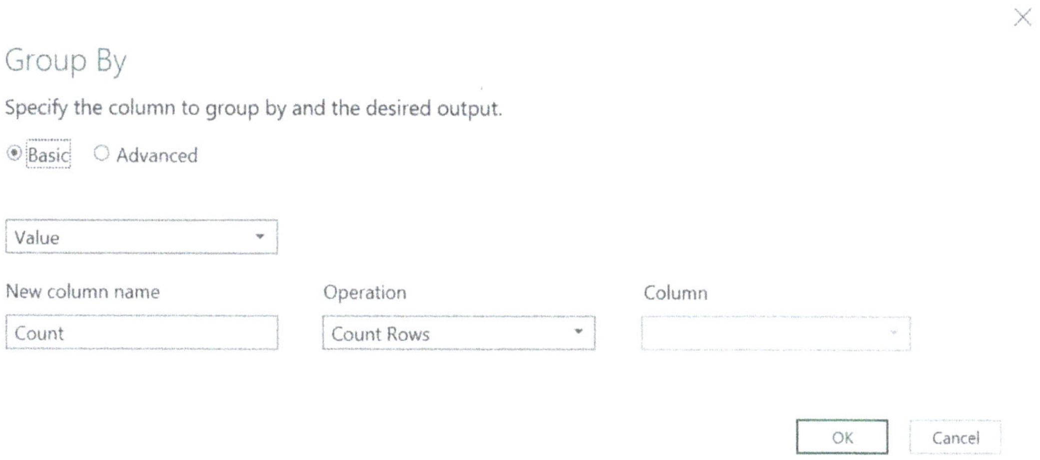

CHAPTER 5 PIVOTING AND UNPIVOTING TABLES

Group By

Specify the column to group by and the desired output.

◉ Basic   ○ Advanced

Value

New column name	Operation	Column
Count	Count Rows	

OK   Cancel

Figure 5-12. *Setting of Group By*

#	Value	Count
1	X-005	1
2	X-004	2
3	X-020	2
4	X-015	3
5	X-017	3
6	X-002	2
7	X-025	1
8	X-011	2
9	X-003	2
10	X-012	4
11	X-023	3
12	X-022	1
13	X-006	1
14	X-019	2

Figure 5-13. *The result of Group By*

CHAPTER 5   PIVOTING AND UNPIVOTING TABLES

In the resulting table, each product ID is listed along with the count of seasons it was sold in. To identify products sold in all seasons, filter the Count column for the number 4. This will give you the list of product IDs that were sold in every season, as shown in Figure 5-14.

```
= Table.SelectRows(#"Grouped Rows", each ([Count] = 4))
```

Value	Count
X-012	4

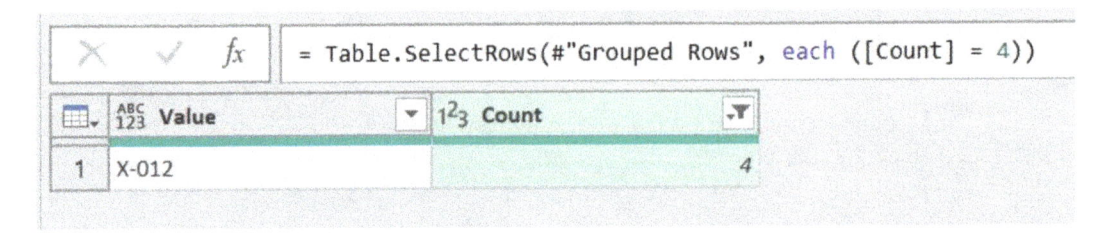

Figure 5-14. *Result of filtering 4 on the column count*

Similarly, to find product IDs sold in just one season, filter the Count column for the number 1. The resulting list of product IDs will be extracted, as shown in Figure 5-15.

```
= Table.SelectRows(#"Grouped Rows", each ([Count] = 1))
```

Value	Count
X-005	1
X-025	1
X-022	1
X-006	1
X-010	1
X-018	1
X-009	1
X-024	1
X-001	1

Figure 5-15. *The result of filtering 1 on the column count*

CHAPTER 5   PIVOTING AND UNPIVOTING TABLES

Following the steps, if you select the Advanced Editor command in the Home tab, the M-code generated by the whole steps is as follows:

```
let
    Source = Excel.CurrentWorkbook(){[Name="Table1"]}[Content],
    #"Unpivoted Columns" = Table.UnpivotOtherColumns(Source, {},
    "Attribute", "Value"),
    #"Removed Duplicates" = Table.Distinct(#"Unpivoted Columns"),
    #"Grouped Rows" = Table.Group(#"Removed Duplicates", {"Value"},
    {{"Count", each Table.RowCount(_), Int64.Type}}),
    #"Filtered Rows" = Table.SelectRows(#"Grouped Rows", each
    ([Count] = 1))
in
    #"Filtered Rows"
```

Note   While the problem can be solved using the UI, as shown in the first solution, you can use List functions to extract IDs repeated in all seasons in an easy way. Here we explore how to use such functions.

Start with the source table, then select *fx* next to the formula bar to create a new step. Use the `Table.ToColumns()` function, as follows, in the formula bar. This will convert the table into a list with four sublists, each representing a list of product IDs sold in one season (one column), as shown in Figure 5-16.

= Table.ToColumns(Source)

CHAPTER 5   PIVOTING AND UNPIVOTING TABLES

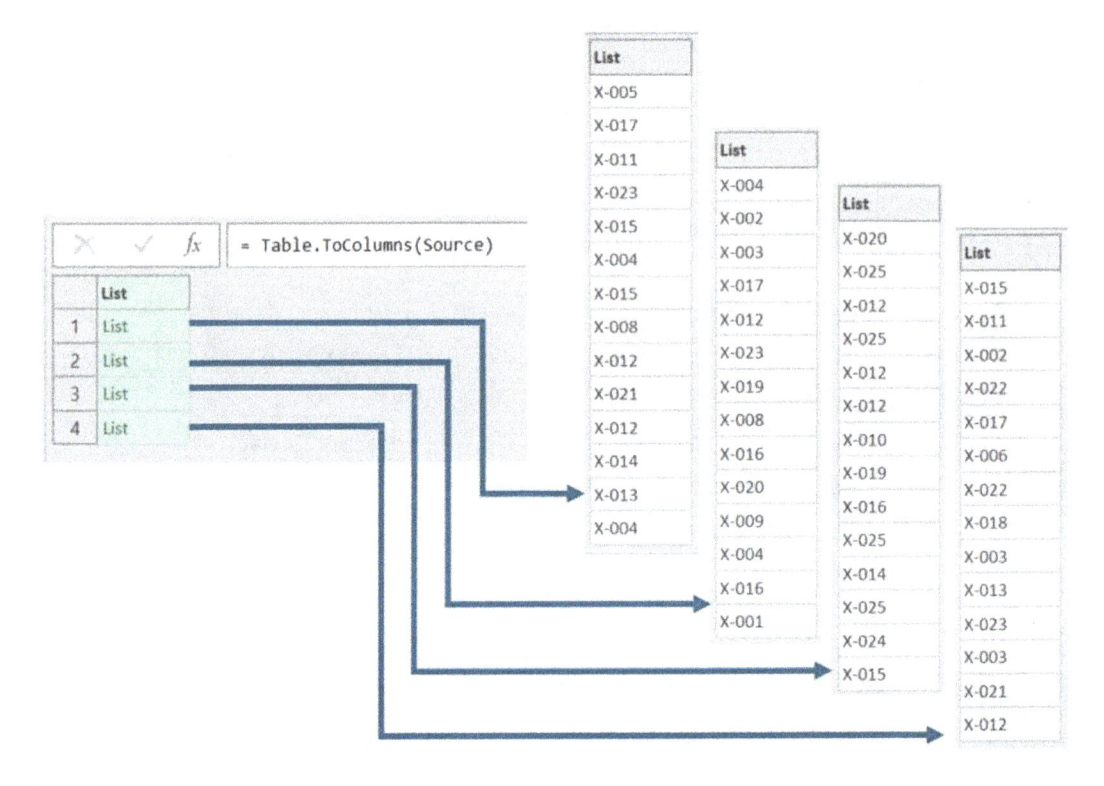

Figure 5-16. The result of Table.ToColumn

You can use List.Intersect() to extract the value that's common in all the sublists. Revising the previous formula will return the IDs repeated in all the seasons, as shown in Figure 5-17.

= List.Intersect(Table.ToColumns(Source))

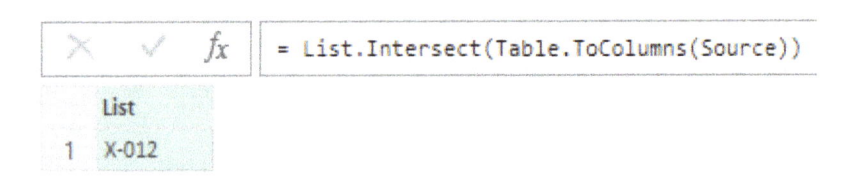

Figure 5-17. Extracting IDs sold in all the seasons

Removing Blank Columns

Table 5-5 shows the Source table imported from a CSV file into Power Query. Remove columns that contain only blank values.

Table 5-5. *Source: Product ID*

Col 1	Col 2	Col 3	Col 4	Col 5	Col 6	Col 7	Col 8
12/05/2024		C		10			8%
12/05/2024		C		20			14%
25/04/2024		A		22			9%
13/05/2024		C		10			8%

Note The data in this example is provided in an Excel file titled `03 Removing Blank Columns .xlsx`.

When you load this table into Power Query, the blank cells are shown as null, as shown in Figure 5-18.

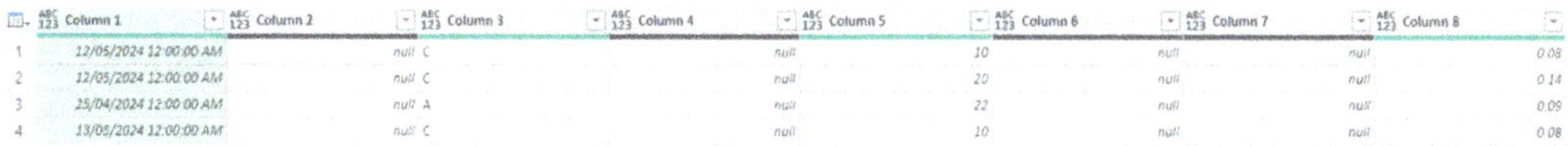

	Column 1	Column 2	Column 3	Column 4	Column 5	Column 6	Column 7	Column 8
1	12/05/2024 12:00:00 AM	null	C	null	10	null	null	0.08
2	12/05/2024 12:00:00 AM	null	C	null	20	null	null	0.14
3	25/04/2024 12:00:00 AM	null	A	null	22	null	null	0.09
4	13/05/2024 12:00:00 AM	null	C	null	10	null	null	0.08

Figure 5-18. *Loading data in Power Query*

Thanks to the unpivot and pivot commands in Power Query, removing blank columns is straightforward by following the following three steps:

1. First, add an index column to the Source table by selecting the Add Index command in the Add Column tab.

2. Then right-click the Index column and choose Unpivot Other Columns. This will result in Figure 5-19. It's important to note that after unpivoting a table, cells with null values will be ignored and will not appear in the resulting unpivoted table. Only the cells with actual data will be included in the transformation.

CHAPTER 5 PIVOTING AND UNPIVOTING TABLES

Index	Attribute	Value
1	0 Column 1	12/05/2024 12:00:00 AM
2	0 Column 3	C
3	0 Column 5	10
4	0 Column 8	0.08
5	1 Column 1	12/05/2024 12:00:00 AM
6	1 Column 3	C
7	1 Column 5	20
8	1 Column 8	0.14
9	2 Column 1	25/04/2024 12:00:00 AM
10	2 Column 3	A
11	2 Column 5	22
12	2 Column 8	0.09
13	3 Column 1	13/05/2024 12:00:00 AM
14	3 Column 3	C
15	3 Column 5	10
16	3 Column 8	0.08

Figure 5-19. The result of unpivoting

3. Next, select the Attribute column, go to the Transform tab, and select Pivot Column. In the settings, choose Value as the Value Column and Don't Aggregate as the aggregator, as shown in Figure 5-20. Click OK to obtain Figure 5-21, which is the source table without any blank columns.

CHAPTER 5 PIVOTING AND UNPIVOTING TABLES

Figure 5-20. The settings for pivoting

Index	Column 1	Column 3	Column 5	Column 8
0	12/05/2024 12:00:00 AM	C	10	0.08
1	12/05/2024 12:00:00 AM	C	20	0.14
2	25/04/2024 12:00:00 AM	A	22	0.09
3	13/05/2024 12:00:00 AM	C	10	0.08

Figure 5-21. The result of pivoting

Transforming Columns, Part 1

The Source table, shown as Table 5-6, contains a list of machinery codes and the product codes that each machinery can produce. Transform this table into a new table, with two columns, the first including product codes, and the second including corresponding machinery codes capable of producing that product.

Table 5-6. Source: Machinery-Product

Machinery Code	Products Code
M-112	P-1071,P-1082,P-1088
M-130	P-1082,P-1014,P-1088
M-150	P-1034,P-1071,P-1082
M-108	P-1082
M-106	P-1082
M-134	P-1076,P-1014,P-1082
M-102	P-1082,P-1076
M-165	P-1076,P-1034
M-157	P-1071

Note The data in this example is provided in an Excel file titled `04 Transforming Columns Part 1.xlsx`.

To address this question, you need to separate the list of products and provide them under each other. So, select the Product Code column, go to the **Home** tab, and choose the Split Column ➤ By Delimiter command. Use comma delimiter, and as shown in Figure 5-22. From Advance options, choose Rows instead of Columns to provide the results split into rows.

CHAPTER 5 PIVOTING AND UNPIVOTING TABLES

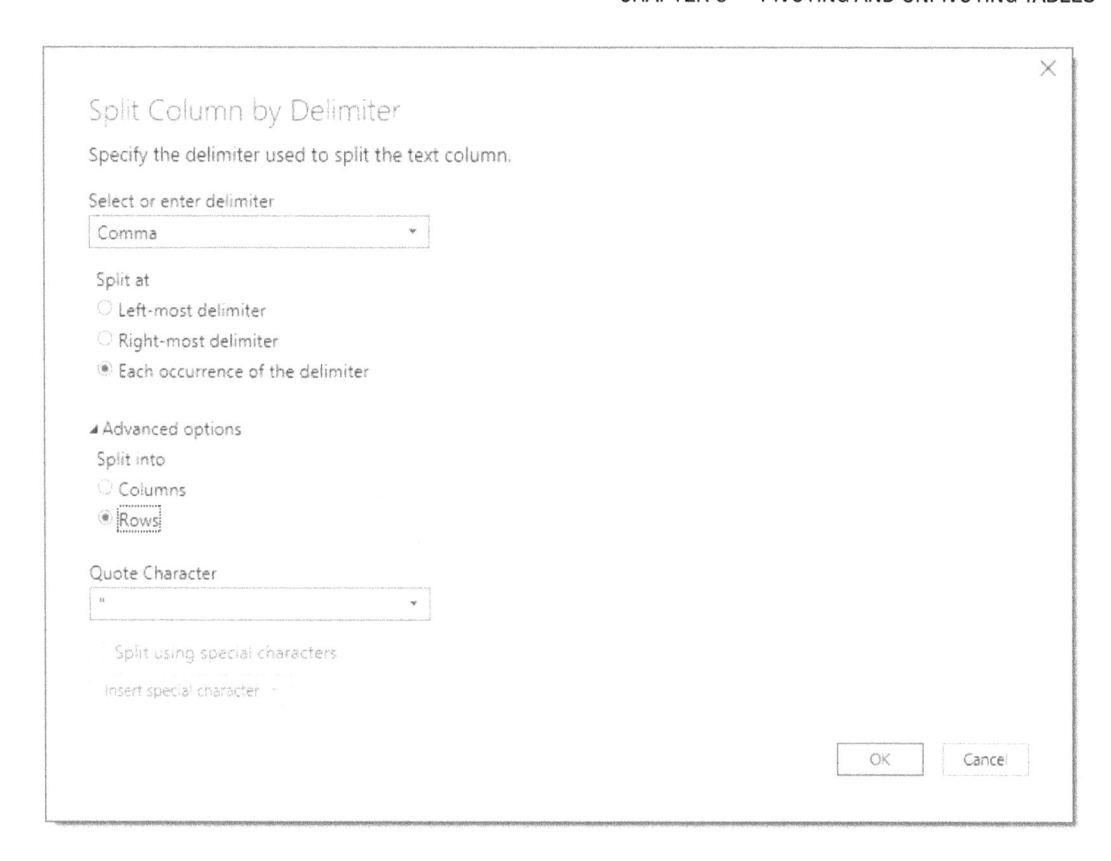

Figure 5-22. *Setting the splitting product code column*

Click OK to obtain the result shown in Figure 5-23.

CHAPTER 5 PIVOTING AND UNPIVOTING TABLES

	Machinery code	Products code
1	M-112	P-1071
2	M-112	P-1082
3	M-112	P-1088
4	M-130	P-1082
5	M-130	P-1014
6	M-130	P-1088
7	M-150	P-1034
8	M-150	P-1071
9	M-150	P-1082
10	M-108	P-1082
11	M-106	P-1082
12	M-134	P-1076
13	M-134	P-1014
14	M-134	P-1082
15	M-102	P-1082
16	M-102	P-1076
17	M-165	P-1076
18	M-165	P-1034
19	M-157	P-1071

Figure 5-23. The results of column splitting

The table structure is good to use for the Table.Group() and Table.Pivot() functions, to create a list of machinery per product code. I explain Table.Group() later in Chapter 6, but this section focused on the Table.Pivot() scenario.

To use the Pivot Column command in this example, you need a helper column with the same value for all rows. So, from the Add Column tab, choose the Custom Column command to add a new column to the table. Name the new column Helper Column and write the formula of ="X" in the Custom Column window. Then click OK, which produces the results shown in Figure 5-24.

CHAPTER 5 PIVOTING AND UNPIVOTING TABLES

#	Machinery code	Products code	Helper Column
1	M-112	P-1071	X
2	M-112	P-1082	X
3	M-112	P-1088	X
4	M-130	P-1082	X
5	M-130	P-1014	X
6	M-130	P-1088	X
7	M-150	P-1034	X
8	M-150	P-1071	X
9	M-150	P-1082	X
10	M-108	P-1082	X
11	M-106	P-1082	X
12	M-134	P-1076	X
13	M-134	P-1014	X
14	M-134	P-1082	X
15	M-102	P-1082	X
16	M-102	P-1076	X
17	M-165	P-1076	X
18	M-165	P-1034	X
19	M-157	P-1071	X

Figure 5-24. *Setting for extracting first*

Now, you can use the Helper Column for pivoting. So, select the Helper Column, go to the Transform tab, and choose Pivot Column. In the new window, set Machinery Code as the Value Column, and in the Advanced options, choose Count as the aggregation function, similar to the setting shown in Figure 5-25. (The values in the Machinery Code column are in type text, and you want to concatenate them, but there is no such aggregation function in the provided list in Advanced options, so the Count is selected and then you have to revise the formula.)

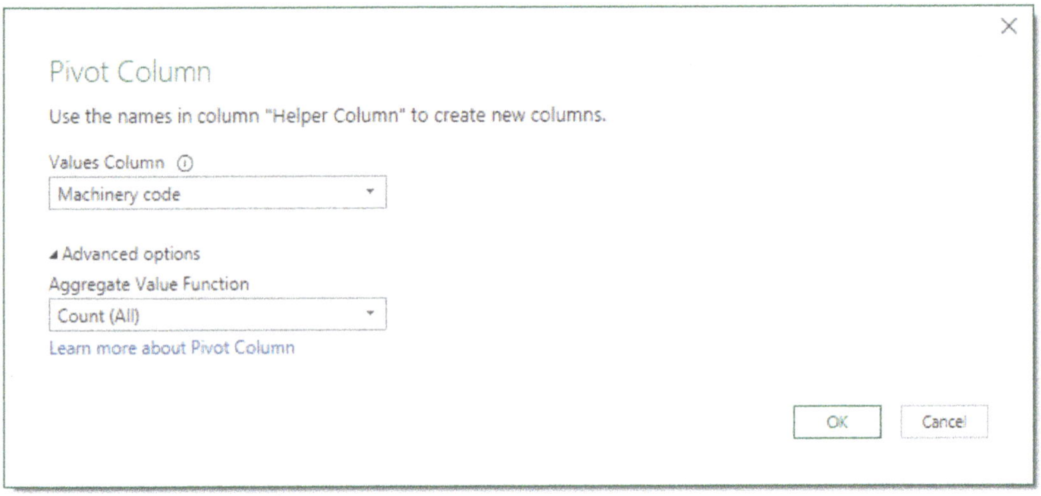

CHAPTER 5   PIVOTING AND UNPIVOTING TABLES

Figure 5-25. Setting for Table.Pivot

Click OK, leading to Figure 5-26. Since the helper column contains the same value ("X") for all rows, pivoting the table based on this column results in a new column named "X" in the pivoted table. By selecting Count as the aggregation operator, the new column will display the number of machines used for each product code.

#	Products code	X
1	P-1014	2
2	P-1034	2
3	P-1071	3
4	P-1076	3
5	P-1082	7
6	P-1088	2

Figure 5-26. The result of pivoting columns

Using the pivoting command with the previous setting, generate the following formula in the formula bar:

= Table.Pivot(#"Added Custom", List.Distinct(#"Added Custom"[#"Helper Column"]), "Helper Column", "Machinery code", List.Count)

CHAPTER 5   PIVOTING AND UNPIVOTING TABLES

Instead of using the List.Count() function as the aggregation in the previous formula, you'll use the Text.Combine() function to concatenate the machinery IDs, using "," as a separator. Replacing List.Count with Text.Combine in the previous formula and rewriting it as follows will result in Figure 5-27, which concatenates all the Machinery IDs without a separator.

= Table.Pivot(#"Added Custom", List.Distinct(#"Added Custom"[#"Helper Column"]), "Helper Column", "Machinery code", Text.Combine)

Products code	X
P-1014	M-134M-130
P-1034	M-165M-150
P-1071	M-112M-150M-157
P-1076	M-134M-102M-165
P-1082	M-130M-150M-106M-112M-134M-102M-108
P-1088	M-112M-130

Figure 5-27.   Using Text.Combine()

To use a separator in the Text.Combine() function, you can use its second argument. However, when you're using more than one argument in the aggregation function inside the Table.Pivot() function, you need to highlight the first argument as well. But what should you use for the first argument?

To clarify, consider the previous formula. Using Text.Combine or each Text.Combine(_) in the aggregation part of the formula produces the same result. However, if you only want to use one argument in the aggregation function, you can remove the each and (_) parts, to make the formula shorter and clearer. But, if you need to use the second argument of the aggregation function (like a separator), you cannot omit these parts.

Based on this explanation, you can rewrite the previous formula as follows, by replacing Text.Combine with each Text.Combine(_, ","), which will resolve the problem and produce the result shown in Figure 5-28.

= Table.Pivot(#"Added Custom", List.Distinct(#"Added Custom"[#"Helper Column"]), "Helper Column", "Machinery code", each Text.Combine(_,", "))

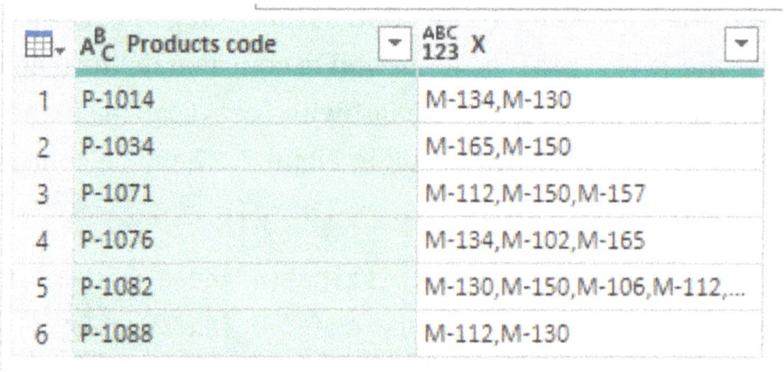

CHAPTER 5 PIVOTING AND UNPIVOTING TABLES

	Products code	X
1	P-1014	M-134,M-130
2	P-1034	M-165,M-150
3	P-1071	M-112,M-150,M-157
4	P-1076	M-134,M-102,M-165
5	P-1082	M-130,M-150,M-106,M-112,...
6	P-1088	M-112,M-130

Figure 5-28. The final result

Transforming Columns, Part 2

The Source table in Table 5-7 provides the distances between every pair of cities. Create a From-To table, as shown in Table 5-8.

Table 5-7. City Distances

From City	To City	Distance
A	B	56
A	C	73
A	D	88
A	E	84
B	C	41
B	D	10
B	E	44
C	D	28
C	E	65
D	E	54

CHAPTER 5   PIVOTING AND UNPIVOTING TABLES

Table 5-8. *The From-To Table*

	A	B	C	D	E
A	0	56	73	88	84
B	56	0	41	10	44
C	73	41	0	28	65
D	88	10	28	0	54
E	84	44	65	54	0

Note   The data in this example is provided in an Excel file titled 05 Transforming Columns Part 2.xlsx.

To solve this problem, select the To City column and use the Pivot Column command from the Transform tab. In the open window, choose Distance for the Values column and use Sum as the aggregator. Then click OK, resulting in Figure 5-29.

From City	B	C	D	E	A
A		56	73	null	null	null
B		null	41	null	null	null
C		null	null	28	65	null
D		10	null	null	54	88
E		44	null	null	null	84

Figure 5-29. *The result of pivoting*

Although based on the question, the distance from C to B is the same as from B to C, in the resulting table, the distance from C to B is reported as null, as there is no row in the Source table including the value of C, B, and 41 for the From City, To City, and Distance columns, respectively. To address this issue, you need to complete the Source table by adding rows where From City and To City are swapped.

Consider the Source table. You can use the following formula to swap the name of columns in the Source table.

=RenameColumns(Source,{{"From City","To City"},{"To City","From City"}})

CHAPTER 5   PIVOTING AND UNPIVOTING TABLES

Rewrite the previous formula as follows, to combine the modified table with the original Source table. This results in Figure 5-30:

```
= Table.Combine(
    {Source,
    Table.RenameColumns(Source,{{"From City","To City"},{"To City",
    "From City"}})})
```

#	From City	To City	Distance
1	A	B	56
2	A	C	73
3	A	D	88
4	A	E	84
5	B	C	41
6	B	D	10
7	B	E	44
8	C	D	28
9	C	E	65
10	D	E	54
11	B	A	56
12	C	A	73
13	D	A	88
14	E	A	84
15	C	B	41
16	D	B	10
17	E	B	44
18	D	C	28
19	E	C	65
20	E	D	54

Figure 5-30. *The result of combining tables*

Now you have separate rows for the distance from city C to B and the reverse. Sort the rows based on the To City column in ascending order and then pivot it in the way mentioned at the beginning of this question, to achieve Figure 5-31, based on the following formula.

From City	A	B	C	D	E
A	null	56	73	88	84
B	56	null	41	10	44
C	73	41	null	28	65
D	88	10	28	null	54
E	84	44	65	54	null

Figure 5-31. *The result of pivoting*

```
= Table.Pivot(
    #"Sorted Rows",
    List.Distinct(#"Sorted Rows"[#"To City"]),
    "To City",
    "Distance",
    List.Sum)
```

To replace null values with zeros in the resulting table, you can modify the fifth argument of the formula as follows:

```
= Table.Pivot(
    #"Sorted Rows",
    List.Distinct(#"Sorted Rows"[#"To City"]),
    "To City",
    "Distance",
    each List.Sum(_)??0)
```

Transforming Columns, Part 3

This Source table contains sales information, as shown in Table 5-9. Reshape the table to include three columns—Year, Month, and Sales—ensuring that any values related to the percentage of the grand total are removed.

CHAPTER 5　PIVOTING AND UNPIVOTING TABLES

Table 5-9. *Source: Sales Info*

Month	Sales 2020	Percent of Grand Total 2021	Sales 2021	Percent of Grand Total 2022	Sales 2022	Percent of Grand Total 2023
1	127	5%	344	5%	937	12%
2	219	8%	225	4%	831	10%
3	451	16%	601	9%	590	7%
4	77	3%	250	4%	480	6%
5	130	5%	118	2%	761	9%
6	376	13%	191	3%	869	11%
7	417	15%	810	13%	762	9%
8	135	5%	988	16%	566	7%
9	211	8%	831	13%	463	6%
10	71	3%	144	2%	596	7%
11	360	13%	936	15%	816	10%
12	216	8%	922	14%	424	5%

Note　The data in this example is provided in an Excel file titled 06 Transforming Columns Part 3.xlsx.

In this problem, if the number of percentage columns is limited and their names are constant, you can remove them directly. But if you are faced with tables in different structures for different companies, it would be better to use a more dynamic way using unpivoting commands. You can do this by right-clicking the Month column and selecting Unpivot Other Columns, which will result in Figure 5-32.

CHAPTER 5 PIVOTING AND UNPIVOTING TABLES

```
= Table.UnpivotOtherColumns(Source, {"Month"}, "Attribute", "Value")
```

Month	Attribute	Value
	1 Sales 2020	127
	1 %of Grand Total 2021	0.045519713
	1 Sales 2021	344
	1 %of Grand Total 2022	0.05408805
	1 Sales 2022	937
	1 %of Grand Total 2023	0.115750463
	2 Sales 2020	219
	2 %of Grand Total 2021	0.078494624
	2 Sales 2021	225
	2 %of Grand Total 2022	0.035377358
	2 Sales 2022	831

Figure 5-32. Unpivoting other columns

Next, use the filter option next to the Attribute column to select the text that does not contain %, achieving Figure 5-33.

Month	Attribute	Value
	1 Sales 2020	127
	1 Sales 2021	344
	1 Sales 2022	937
	2 Sales 2020	219
	2 Sales 2021	225
	2 Sales 2022	831
	3 Sales 2020	451
	3 Sales 2021	601
	3 Sales 2022	590
	4 Sales 2020	77
	4 Sales 2021	250
	4 Sales 2022	480
	5 Sales 2020	130
	5 Sales 2021	118
	5 Sales 2022	761

Figure 5-33. The result of the filter

CHAPTER 5   PIVOTING AND UNPIVOTING TABLES

To remove the Sales text in the cells of the Attribute column, select that column, go to the Home tab, choose the Replace Values command, and enter Sales in the Value To Find box while leaving the Replace With box empty, as shown in Figure 5-34. Click OK to remove this text over the cells on the Attribute column.

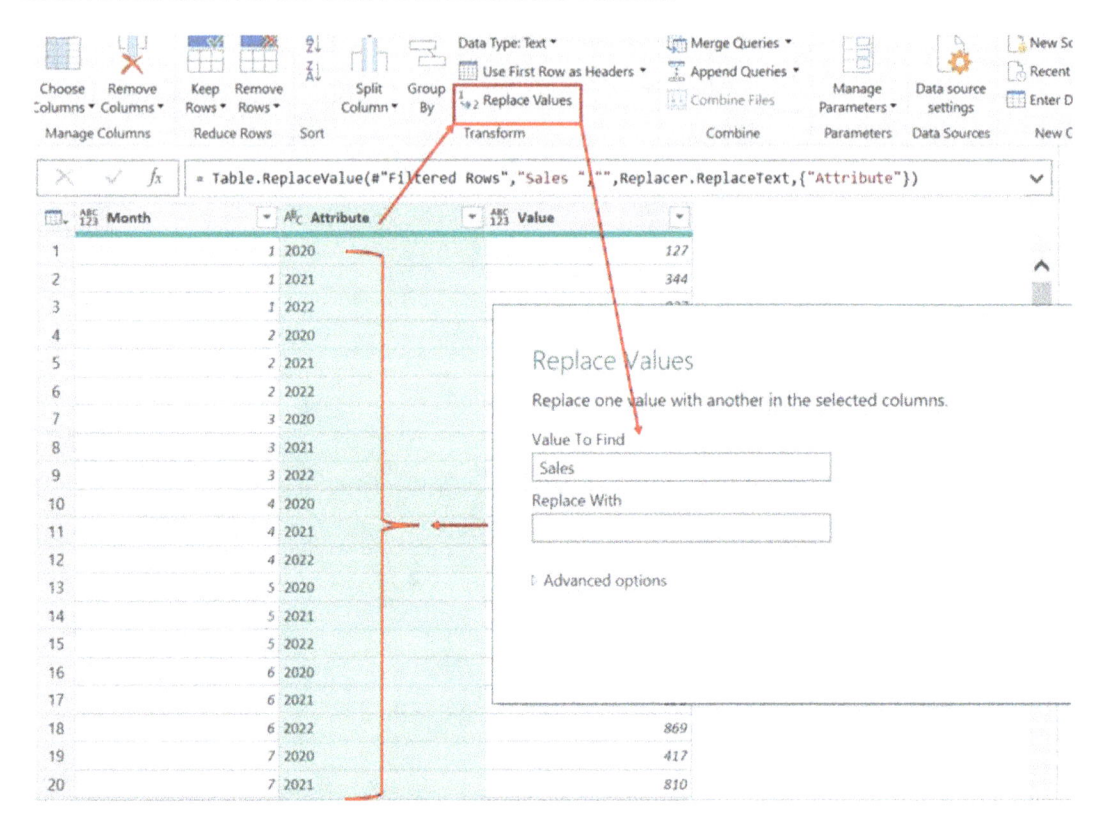

Figure 5-34. Removing the Sales text in the Attribute column

Finally, rename the Attribute and Value columns to Year and Sales, respectively, to achieve the final result shown in Figure 5-35.

	Month		Year		Sales	
1			1 2020		127	
2			1 2021		344	
3			1 2022		937	
4			2 2020		219	
5			2 2021		225	
6			2 2022		831	
7			3 2020		451	
8			3 2021		601	
9			3 2022		590	
10			4 2020		77	
11			4 2021		250	

Figure 5-35. The final result

Merging Rows

Given the historical sales data in the Source table, which is shown in Table 5-10, where sales for each product are spread across multiple rows, transform the table so that the sales for each product are consolidated into a single row.

Table 5-10. Source: Sales Info

Product	Region 1	Region 2	Region 3	Region 4
A	10			
A		12		
A				14
A			8	
B	15			
B		21		
B				23
B			30	

(continued)

Table 5-10. (*continued*)

Product	Region 1	Region 2	Region 3	Region 4
C		38		
C	12			
C				40
C			7	

> **Note** The data in this example is provided in an Excel file titled `07 Merging rows .xlsx`.

This problem can be solved either by using the Group By command or by combining unpivoting and pivoting commands over the source table. The Group By command is explained in depth in Chapter 6, so here, you see how to use the combination of unpivoting and pivoting the table.

To solve this problem, you need to load data into the Power Query Editor. As shown in Figure 5-36, loading the table into the Power Query Editor will replace the blank cells with null values.

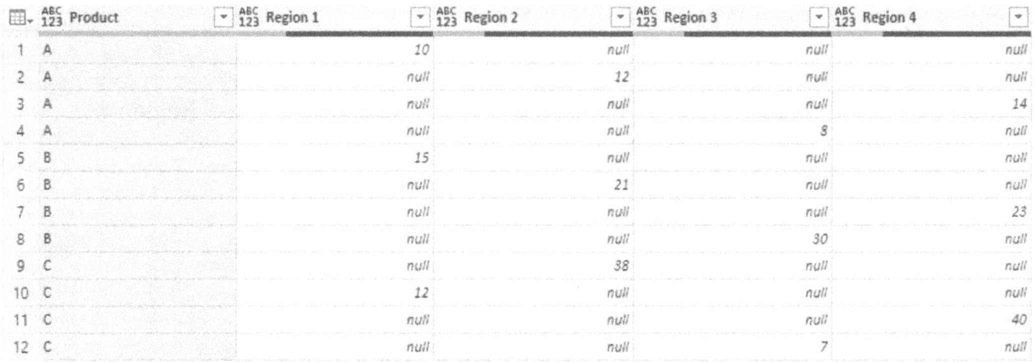

	Product	Region 1	Region 2	Region 3	Region 4
1	A	10	null	null	null
2	A	null	12	null	null
3	A	null	null	null	14
4	A	null	null	8	null
5	B	15	null	null	null
6	B	null	21	null	null
7	B	null	null	null	23
8	B	null	null	30	null
9	C	null	38	null	null
10	C	12	null	null	null
11	C	null	null	null	40
12	C	null	null	7	null

Figure 5-36. *Loading data into Power Query Editor*

As mentioned in Section 5-3, by unpivoting columns, the null values will be ignored. Right-click the Product column and choose the Unpivot Other Columns command to achieve the format shown in Figure 5-37.

CHAPTER 5 PIVOTING AND UNPIVOTING TABLES

#	Product	Attribute	Value
1	A	Region 1	10
2	A	Region 2	12
3	A	Region 4	14
4	A	Region 3	8
5	B	Region 1	15
6	B	Region 2	21
7	B	Region 4	23
8	B	Region 3	30
9	C	Region 2	38
10	C	Region 1	12
11	C	Region 4	40
12	C	Region 3	7

Figure 5-37. *Resulting table Unpivoting other columns*

Next, select the Attribute column and, from the Transform tab, choose Pivot Column with the settings shown in Figure 5-38.

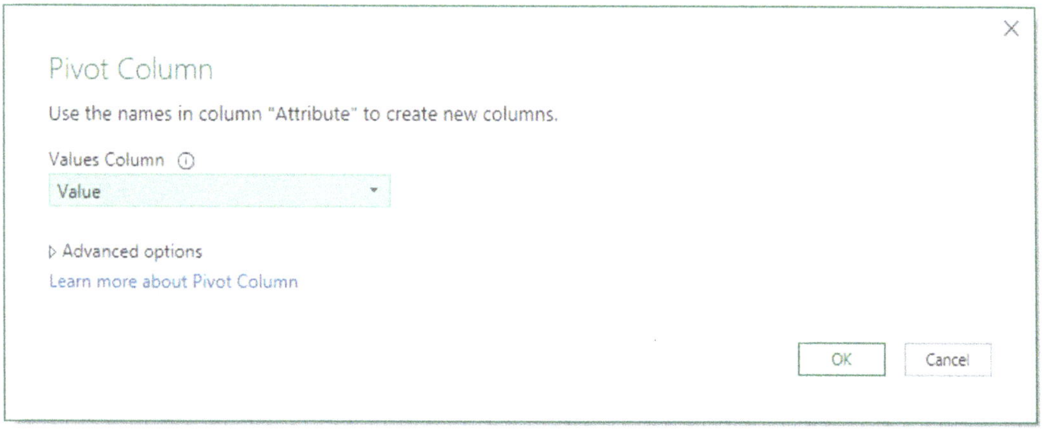

Figure 5-38. *Pivoting settings*

After clicking OK, you'll see the result shown in Figure 5-39. The following formula is in the formula bar.

```
= Table.Pivot(#"Unpivoted Other Columns", List.Distinct(#"Unpivoted Other Columns"[Attribute]), "Attribute", "Value", List.Sum)
```

283

CHAPTER 5   PIVOTING AND UNPIVOTING TABLES

Product	Region 1	Region 2	Region 4	Region 3
A		10	12	14	8
B		15	21	23	30
C		12	38	40	7

Figure 5-39. *The result of pivoting*

Merging Several Tables at Once

Consolidate the historical sales data for products across various regions, stored in multiple CSV files located in a specific directory, as shown in Figure 5-40. Each file contains sales data for different regions, and the number of files may vary. Combine these tables into a single table that presents the sales data for different products across all regions.

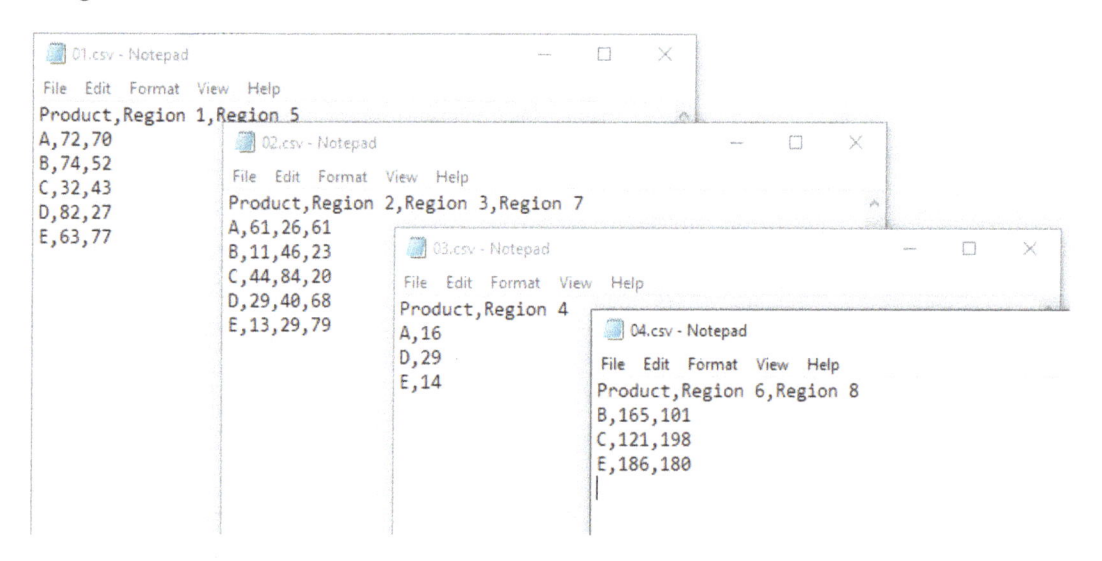

Figure 5-40. *The CSV files*

Note   The data in this example is provided in the folder with the name 08 Merging several tables once.

To solve this problem, go to the Data tab in Excel and select Get Data From File. Then choose From Folder. Navigate to the folder containing the CSV files to reach the Navigation window, as shown in Figure 5-41.

284

CHAPTER 5   PIVOTING AND UNPIVOTING TABLES

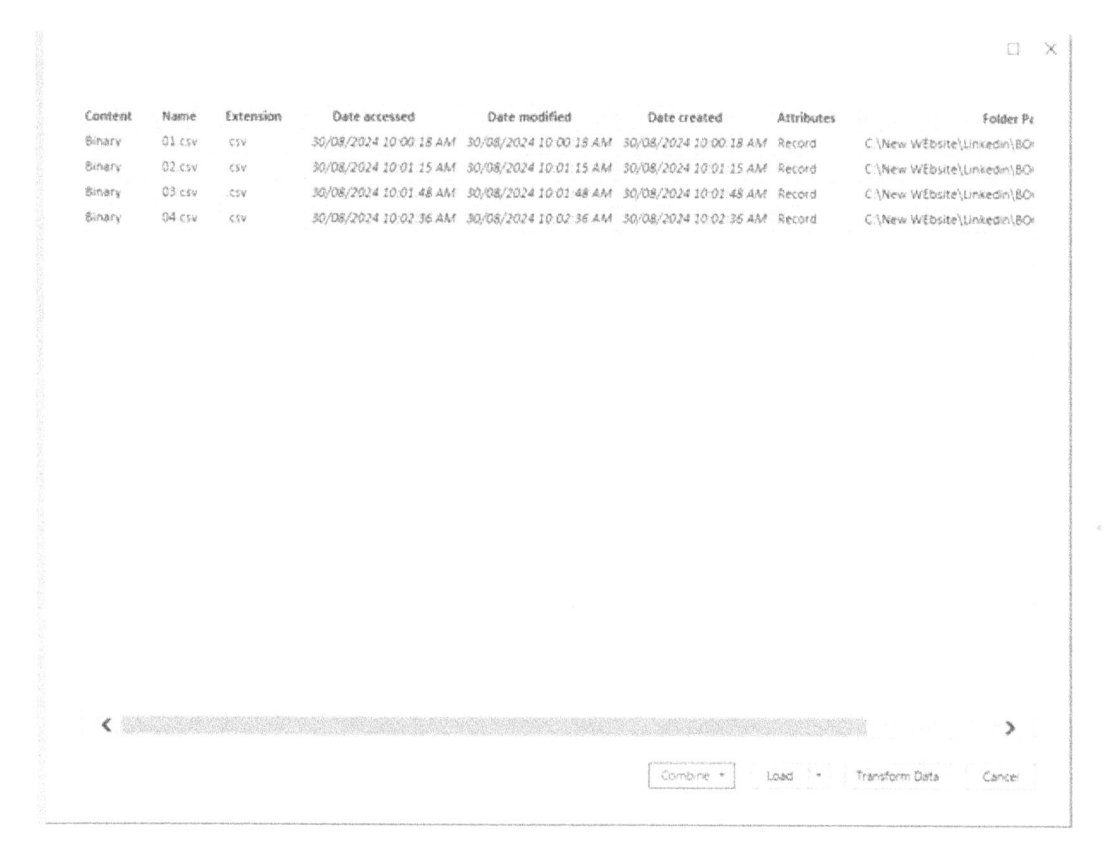

Figure 5-41. *Navigation*

From all the options under the Combine button, select Combine & Transform Data. As shown in Figure 5-42, a new window called Combine Files will appear, where you can select the sample file to combine the data.

CHAPTER 5   PIVOTING AND UNPIVOTING TABLES

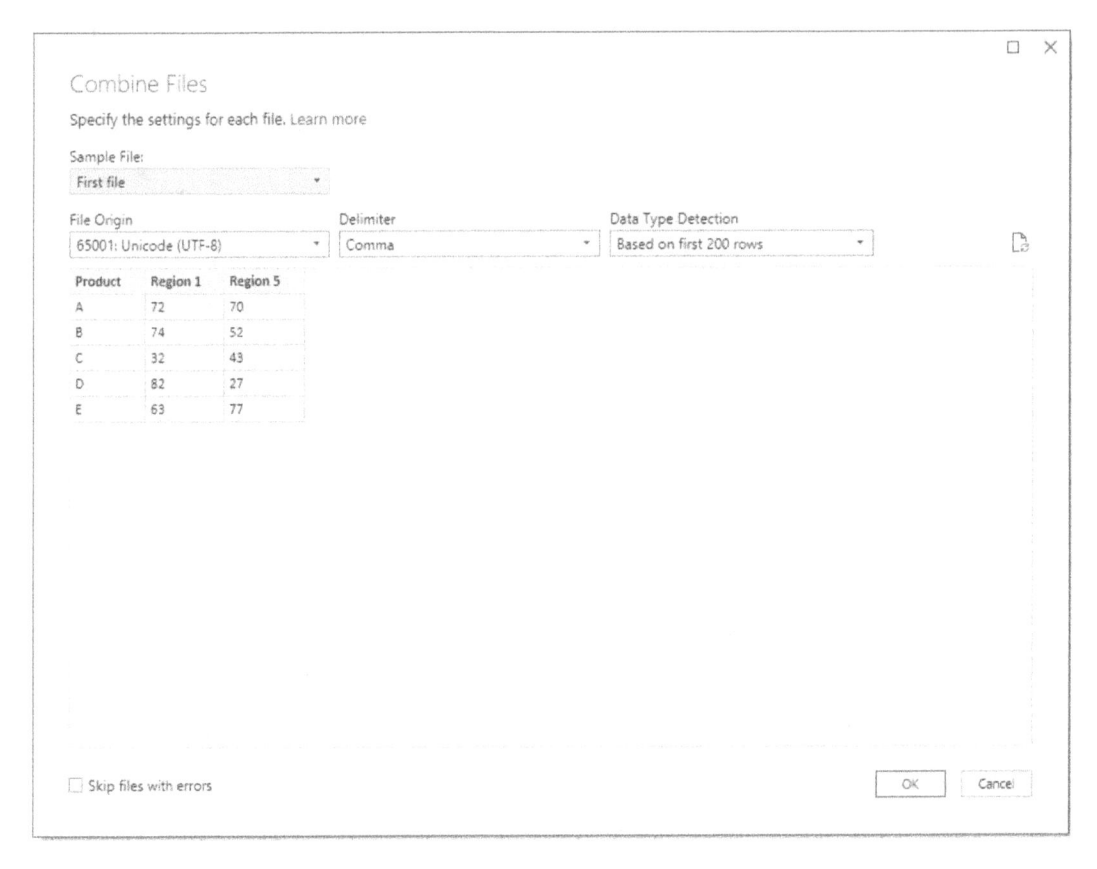

Figure 5-42. The Combine Files window

Select the first file as the sample file and click OK. This will result in two groups of queries: Helper Queries and Other Queries. The desired query will be found in the Other Queries group, and it will include seven steps, as shown in the Applied Steps section. See Figure 5-43.

CHAPTER 5   PIVOTING AND UNPIVOTING TABLES

Figure 5-43. The result of combining the files

Since the selected sample file only includes the Product, Region 1, and Region 5 columns, the resulting table will contain these three columns, along with the Source. Name column, while columns related to other regions will be excluded.

As explained in Chapter 1, you can modify the result by editing the query named Transform Sample File. As shown in Figure 5-44, this query includes two steps: Source and Promoted Headers. This means that these two steps should be applied to all the CSV files, and then their results will be combined on the main query (called 08 Merging several tables once).

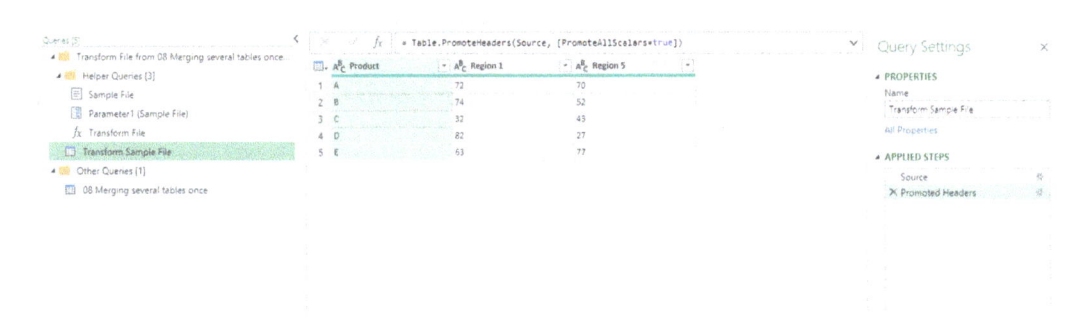

Figure 5-44. Transforming the sample file query

By selecting the Source step in this query, the following formula will appear in the formula bar, based on the sample file:

```
= Csv.Document(Parameter1,[Delimiter=",", Columns=3, Encoding=65001,
QuoteStyle=QuoteStyle.None])
```

287

CHAPTER 5 PIVOTING AND UNPIVOTING TABLES

An important issue here is that the number of columns is specified as 3 in this code. So, if a file contains more than three columns, the extra columns will be ignored. To avoid this, you can modify the formula as follows by removing the part related to specifying the number of columns, which means that the number of columns for each file should be determined separately:

```
= Csv.Document(Parameter1,[Delimiter=",", Encoding=65001, QuoteStyle=QuoteStyle.None])
```

In addition to these two predefined steps, you can add another step to this query. Select the last step, then select the Product column, right-click it, and choose Unpivot Other Columns. The result is shown in Figure 5-45. So, for all the CSV files, after promoting the headers, all columns except the Product column will be unpivoted, and the data will be organized into two columns: Attribute and Value. The columns of all the tables that came from different files are the same.

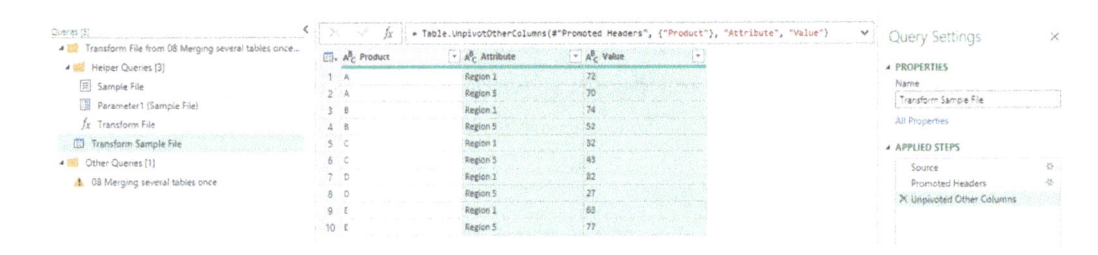

Figure 5-45. Unpivoting other columns in the sample file query

After making this change, when you select the query named 08 Merging several tables once, as shown in Figure 5-46, you'll notice that the result of the last step (Changed Type) is an error. This error occurs because the column titles were changed during the unpivoting process.

CHAPTER 5   PIVOTING AND UNPIVOTING TABLES

Figure 5-46. The result of the main query

Removing this step will result in the query proceeding without the error, as shown in Figure 5-47.

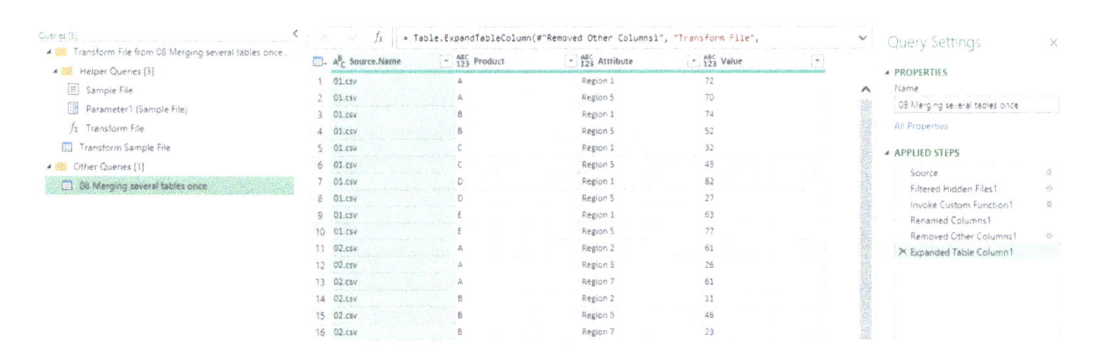

Figure 5-47. The result of main query after removing the step related to changing the type

In the resulting table, you do not need the values in the Source.Name column. Remove that table to achieve Figure 5-48.

CHAPTER 5 PIVOTING AND UNPIVOTING TABLES

Product	Attribute	Value
A	Region 1	72
A	Region 5	70
B	Region 1	74
B	Region 5	52
C	Region 1	32
C	Region 5	43
D	Region 1	82
D	Region 5	27
E	Region 1	63
E	Region 5	77
A	Region 2	61
A	Region 3	26
A	Region 7	61
B	Region 2	11
B	Region 3	46
B	Region 7	23

Figure 5-48. *Result of unpivoting*

Next, select the Value column and convert its type into the number (from the Home tab in the Transform section). Then, select the Attribute column, go to the Transform tab, and choose Pivot Column. This sets the Values column as the field to be pivoted. Click OK. This will format the data as desired, resulting in Figure 5-49.

Product	Region 1	Region 5	Region 2	Region 3	Region 7	Region 4	Region 6	Region 8
A	72	70	61	26	61	15	null	null
B	74	52	11	46	23	null	165	101
C	32	43	44	54	20	null	121	168
D	82	27	29	40	68	19	null	null
E	63	77	15	29	79	14	186	180

Figure 5-49. *Result of pivoting*

Transformations, Part 4

In a shipment company, historical data is provided in the Source table in an incorrect format, as shown in Table 5-11. Use Power Query to transform this table into a standard format with five columns: Product, Shipment Number (extract it from headers), Ship Date, PO Number, and PO Quantity.

CHAPTER 5 PIVOTING AND UNPIVOTING TABLES

Table 5-11. Source: Shipment Data

Products	Ship Date 1	Po number 1	Po Quantity 1	Ship Date 2	Po number 2	Po Quantity 2	Ship Date 3	Po number 3	Po Quantity 3	Ship Date 4	Po number 4	Po Quantity 4
A	13/01/2023	10	39	14/01/2023	10	44	15/01/2023	40	34	16/01/2023	20	18
B	17/01/2023	40	27	19/01/2023	40	39	21/01/2023	40	11			
C	26/01/2023	10	11	27/01/2023	40	48						
D	11/12/2023	10	42									

291

CHAPTER 5   PIVOTING AND UNPIVOTING TABLES

> **Note** The data in this example is provided in an Excel file titled `09 Transformations Part 4.xlsx`.

Unfortunately, there's no way to directly unpivot bulk groups of columns (for example every three columns) in Power Query so you have to find a longer way to solve this problem.

In this case, since you don't know how many columns you might encounter in the future, it's a good idea to unpivot the columns and convert them into rows. Start by right-clicking the Product column and selecting Unpivot Other Columns, leading to a table with three columns—Product, Attribute, and Value—as shown in Figure 5-50.

#	Products	Attribute	Value
1	A	Ship Date 1	13/01/2023 12:00:00 AM
2	A	Po number 1	10
3	A	Po Quantity 1	39
4	A	Ship Date 2	14/01/2023 12:00:00 AM
5	A	Po number 2	10
6	A	Po Quantity 2	44
7	A	Ship Date 3	15/01/2023 12:00:00 AM
8	A	Po number 3	40
9	A	Po Quantity 3	34
10	A	Ship Date 4	16/01/2023 12:00:00 AM
11	A	Po number 4	20
12	A	Po Quantity 4	18
13	B	Ship Date 1	17/01/2023 12:00:00 AM
14	B	Po number 1	40
15	B	Po Quantity 1	27

Figure 5-50. Unpivoted table

The Attribute column in the resulting table includes both the type of value and the shipment number, while you need these two features separately. To split the values in this column and extract the number mentioned at the end of the text in this column, select the Attribute column, and from the Home tab, choose Split Column by Delimiter.

CHAPTER 5 PIVOTING AND UNPIVOTING TABLES

In the open window, make the settings shown in Figure 5-51, and click OK, which results in Figure 5-52. (Selecting the Right-Most Delimiter option means splitting the values at the location of the last space in the cell.)

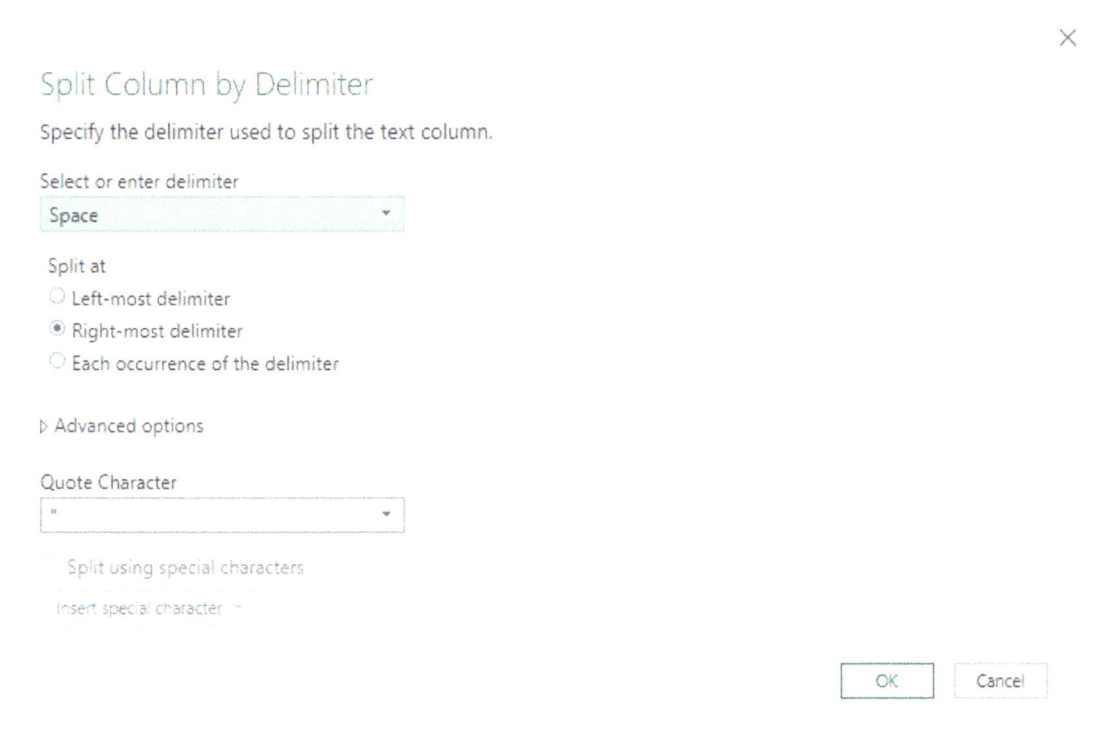

Figure 5-51. Settings for splitting

Products	Attribute.1	Attribute.2	Value
A	Ship Date	1	13/01/2023
A	Po number	1	10
A	Po Quantity	1	39
A	Ship Date	2	14/01/2023
A	Po number	2	10
A	Po Quantity	2	44
A	Ship Date	3	15/01/2023
A	Po number	3	40
A	Po Quantity	3	34
A	Ship Date	4	16/01/2023
A	Po number	4	20
A	Po Quantity	4	18
B	Ship Date	1	17/01/2023
B	Po number	1	40
B	Po Quantity	1	27

Figure 5-52. Result of splitting

293

CHAPTER 5   PIVOTING AND UNPIVOTING TABLES

Now it is time to use the Pivot command to put the values on the Attribute.1 column as the header of the new columns and provide the value on the Value column beneath them for each shipment number in each date. Select the Attribute.1 column and, from the Transform tab, choose the Pivot Column command. Then, in the open window, make the settings shown in Figure 5-53.

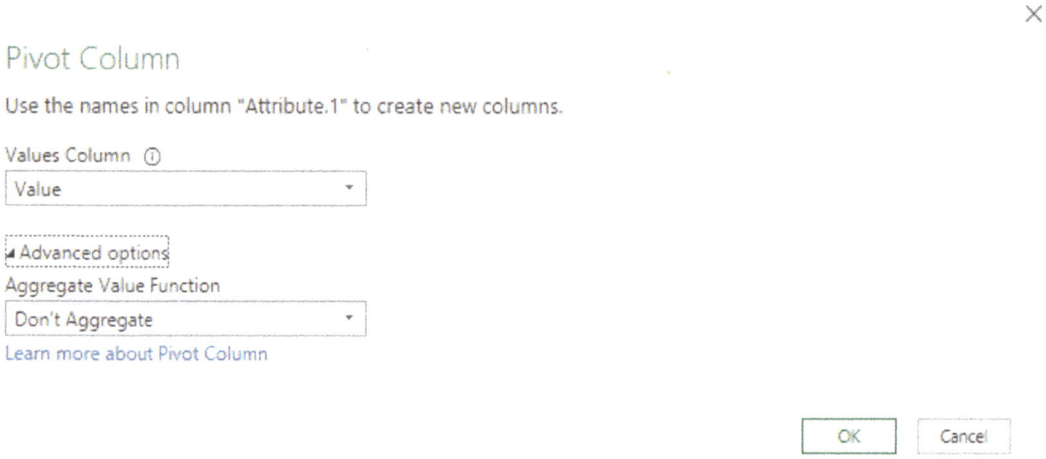

Figure 5-53. The settings of the pivot column

Clicking OK results in Figure 5-54.

Products	Attribute.2	Ship Date	Po number	Po Quantity
A	1	13/01/2023	10	39
A	2	14/01/2023	10	44
A	3	15/01/2023	40	34
A	4	16/01/2023	20	18
B	1	17/01/2023	40	27
B	2	19/01/2023	40	39
B	3	21/01/2023	40	11
B	4			
C	1	26/01/2023	10	11
C	2	27/01/2023	40	48
C	3			
C	4			
D	1	11/12/2023	10	42
D	2			
D	3			
D	4			

Figure 5-54. The result of the revised Group By

In the last step, you just need to rename the columns and filter the rows with blank values on the Ship Date column to reach the final table.

Summary

In the data-cleaning process, reshaping tables by converting several columns into rows or transforming values from a column into multiple columns is crucial. In this chapter, you learned how to use the Table.Pivot(), Table.UnpivotColumns(), and Table.UnpivotOtherColumns() functions to reshape your tables according to your needs.

Continuing your data-cleaning journey, the next chapter explains one of the most important functions in Power Query, called Table.Group(). It allows you to summarize a table with numerous rows in a more concise format.

CHAPTER 6

Grouping Rows with Table.Group()

The Group By command in Power Query is a powerful feature that allows you to aggregate and summarize data by grouping it based on one or more columns. This command is based on the `Table.Group()` function, and it is essential for performing data analysis and creating meaningful summaries from large datasets. The syntax of `Table.Group()` is:

```
=Table.Group(table, key, aggregatedColumns, groupKind, optional comparer) as table
```

The `table` is the table, the `key` is any, `aggregatedColumns` is a list, `groupKind` is option, and the `optional comparer` is a nullable function.

This function accepts five arguments, with the last two being optional. While the first three arguments can be modified through the Power Query UI, the last two must be entered manually.

In this chapter, this function and all of its arguments are explained in depth.

Introducing Table.Group()

Based on the historical sales data provided in the Source table shown in Table 6-1, calculate the total sales per product.

CHAPTER 6   GROUPING ROWS WITH TABLE.GROUP()

Table 6-1. *Source: Historical Sales Value*

Month	Week	Product	Colour	Quantity
January	W1	A	Black	6
	W1	B	Blue	9
	W1	B	Yellow	2
	W2	A	Black	6
	W2	B	Red	7
	W2	C	Red	5
	W3	B	Yellow	13
	W3	B	Red	3
	W4	A	Blue	7
	W4	C	Red	6
February	W1	A	Yellow	7
	W2	A	Red	8
	W3	B	Black	10
	W3	C	Blue	14
	W4	D	Red	9

Note   The data in this example is provided in an Excel file titled 01 Introduction to Table.Group().xlsx.

As stated in the question, in this example, you'll see how to combine the rows of the table by combining rows with the same product name into a single row and calculating the sum of their quantities. This process is precisely what is referred to as grouping in Power Query. You can explore how to use this amazing tool to solve the problem by following these steps:

CHAPTER 6 GROUPING ROWS WITH TABLE.GROUP()

1. In Power Query, select the Product column (as the column you want to grouped the rows based on), and from the Home tab, choose the Group By command (or right-click the Product column and select Group By from the list of commands). This will open a new window, as shown in Figure 6-1.

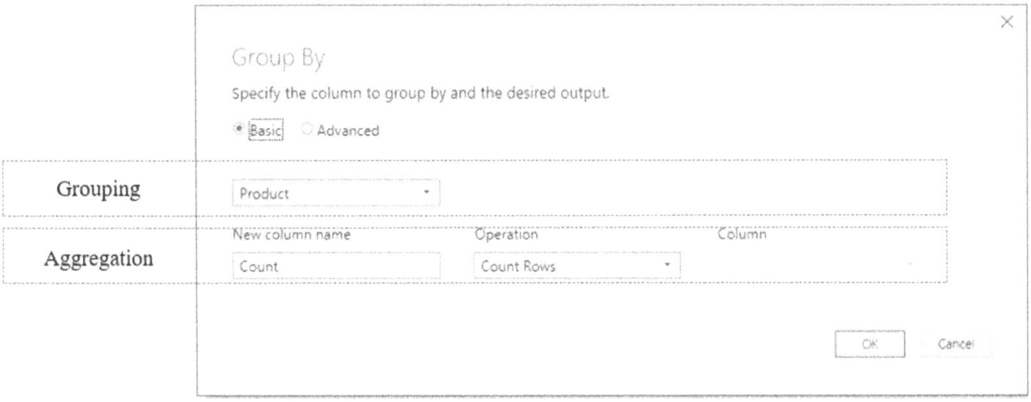

Figure 6-1. The Group By window

2. The Group By window consists of two main sections: the Grouping section, which is used to determine which column should be used to group the rows of the main table, and the Aggregation section, which is used to add calculated columns to the resulting table. In the Basic view, you can select only one item for each section. However, if you need to use multiple columns for grouping or aggregation, you can switch to the Advanced view.

You can solve the presented problem using the settings available in the Basic view. So, as shown in Figure 6-2, select the Product column in the Grouping option, and in the Aggregation part, set the name of the new column to Total Sales, the Operation to Sum, and the Column to Quantity.

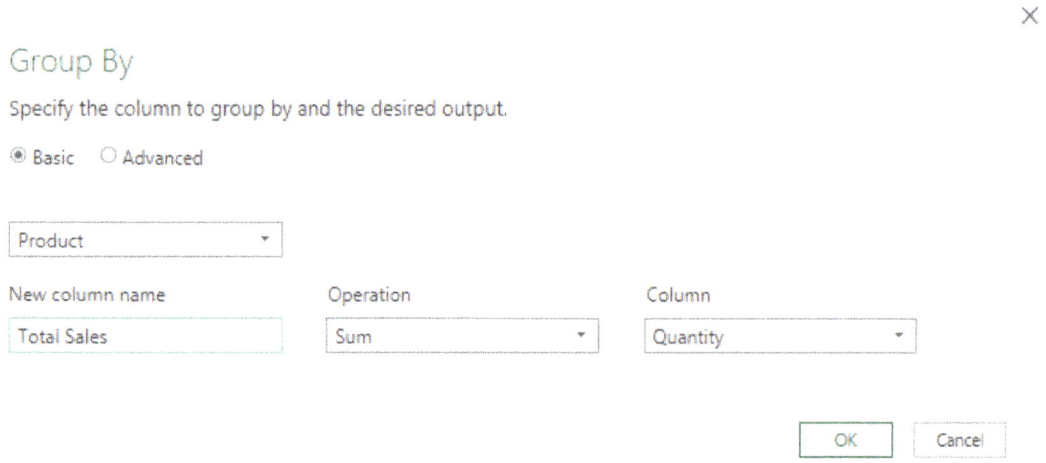

CHAPTER 6 GROUPING ROWS WITH TABLE.GROUP()

Figure 6-2. The Group By setting

By clicking OK, you'll get the result depicted in Figure 6-3, and the following formula will be shown the formula bar.

= Table.Group(Source, {"Product"}, {{"Total Sales", each List.Sum([Quantity]), type number}})

Figure 6-3. The result of Group By

The Table.Group() function in the generated formula takes three inputs:

- The table name (Source) is entered as the first argument.
- The column to group the rows based on that ({"Product"}) is entered as a list in the second argument.
- The third argument is the type of list, which includes several sublists (in this example there is just one sublist). Each sublist includes three main elements:

- The name of the new column, entered as text.

- An aggregate function. While various aggregation operations can be applied to the values of the grouped rows, in the UI settings, you can only select Sum, Average, Count, Min, Max, and All Rows. You can use other aggregations by editing the formula manually.

- The type of values in the new column (which is optional). Since determining the column type is optional, the third argument in this formula can also be written as {{"Total Sales", each List.Sum([Quantity])}}.

Note To shorten the formula and increase readability, in the rest of this chapter, the column type, which is optional, is omitted from the formula.

As mentioned earlier, the Group By window, shown in Figure 6-3 include two views of basic and advanced. In this example, by clicking the Advanced option and changing the settings shown in Figure 6-4, the rows are grouped based on the product names and colors and total sales, and maximum weekly sales are provided as new columns by applying Sum and Max over the values of the grouped rows. Clicking OK will result Figure 6-5.

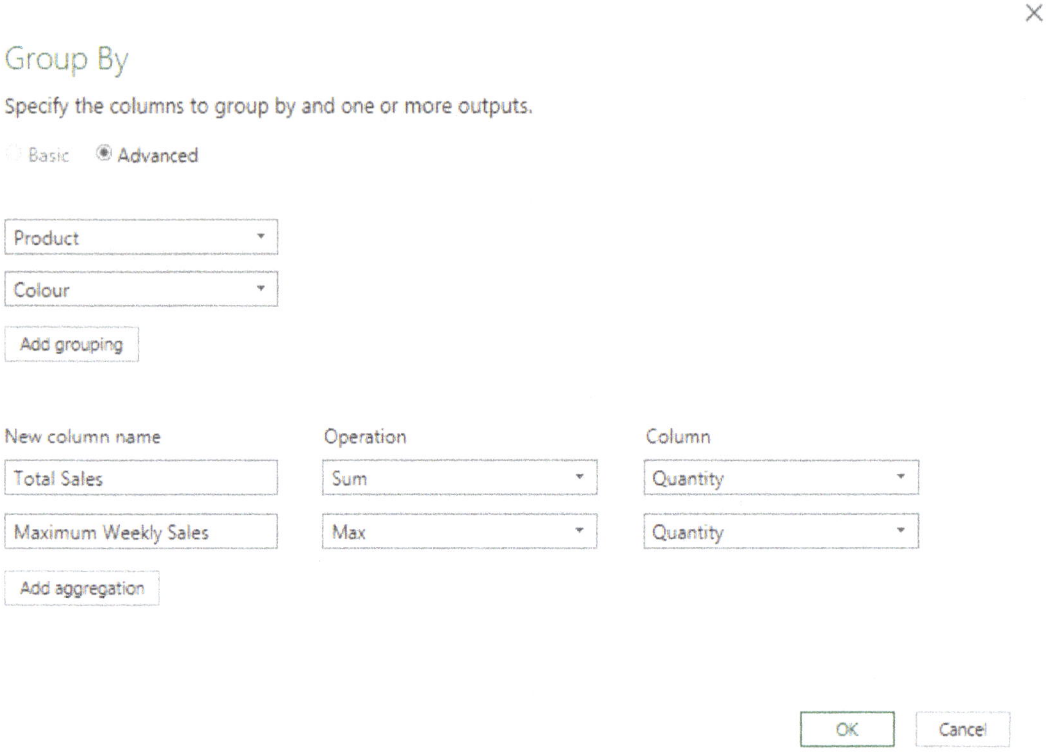

CHAPTER 6 GROUPING ROWS WITH TABLE.GROUP()

Group By

Specify the columns to group by and one or more outputs.

○ Basic   ● Advanced

Product
Colour

[Add grouping]

New column name	Operation	Column
Total Sales	Sum	Quantity
Maximum Weekly Sales	Max	Quantity

[Add aggregation]

[OK]   [Cancel]

Figure 6-4. *Advanced Group By*

#	Product	Colour	Total Sales	Maximum Weekly Sales
1	A	Black	12	6
2	B	Blue	9	9
3	B	Yellow	15	13
4	B	Red	10	7
5	C	Red	11	6
6	A	Blue	7	7
7	A	Yellow	7	7
8	A	Red	8	8
9	B	Black	10	10
10	C	Blue	14	14
11	D	Red	9	9

Figure 6-5. *The result of Advanced Group By*

With these changes, the following formula will be shown in the formula bar. This version includes two column names in the second input and two sublists in the third input: one for Total Sales and another for Maximum Weekly Sales. The `List.Sum()` and `List.Max()` functions are applied to the Quantity column in the Source table for these two new columns.

```
= Table.Group(Source,
            {"Product", "Colour"},
            {
                {"Total Sales", each List.Sum([Quantity]), type
                number},
                {"Maximum Weekly Sales", each List.Max([Quantity]),
                type number}
            })
```

As mentioned previously, without altering the result, this formula can be simplified by omitting the optional argument for column type. So, the revised formula is as follows:

```
= Table.Group(Source,
            {"Product", "Colour"},
            {
                {"Total Sales", each List.Sum([Quantity])},
                {"Maximum Weekly Sales", each List.Max([Quantity])}
            })
```

Efficiency Tips The execution time of the `Table.Group()` function depends on various factors, but in its basic use (without manually adjusting parameters), it runs quickly. In this example, for a table with 10,000 rows, it takes less than a second to complete.

Modifying the Third Input in Table.Group()

Using the historical sales data provided in the Source table shown in Table 6-2, calculate the total sales and list of colors sold (in a cell) per product.

Table 6-2. Source: Historical Sales Value

Month	Week	Product	Color	Quantity
January	W1	A	Black	6
	W1	B	Blue	9
	W1	B	Yellow	2
	W2	A	Black	6
	W2	B	Red	7
	W2	C	Red	5
	W3	B	Yellow	13
	W3	B	Red	3
	W4	A	Blue	7
	W4	C	Red	6
February	W1	A	Yellow	7
	W2	A	Red	8
	W3	B	Black	10
	W3	C	Blue	14
	W4	D	Red	9

> **Note** The data in this example is provided in an Excel file titled 02 Modifying the Third Input in Table.Group().xlsx.

This example is similar to the Example 6-1, with the difference that a new column, including all the sold colors, should also be added to the resulting table during the process of grouping. To calculate the value of this new column, the colors of the grouped rows should be concatenated. However, there is no such operation in the Group By window's operation list, so you need to use Group By first and modify it manually.

Select the Group By command and configure the settings as shown in Figure 6-6. Since there is no useful operation for text columns in the Operation list, select All Rows for the Colours column. This will produce the table in Figure 6-7.

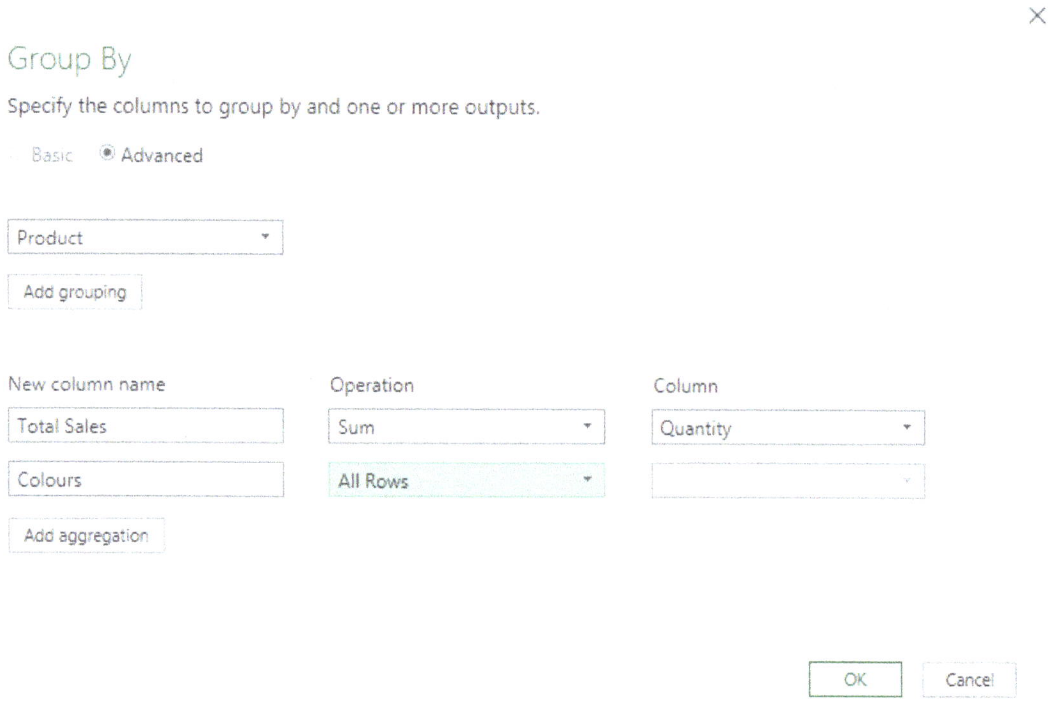

Figure 6-6. *Group By*

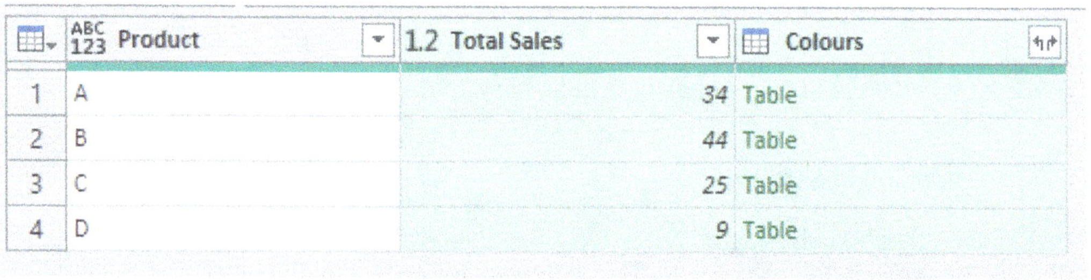

	Product	Total Sales	Colours
1	A	34	Table
2	B	44	Table
3	C	25	Table
4	D	9	Table

Figure 6-7. *The result of grouping*

The Colours column now contains Table values, which represent all the rows from the Source table related to each product, as shown in Figure 6-8.

CHAPTER 6 GROUPING ROWS WITH TABLE.GROUP()

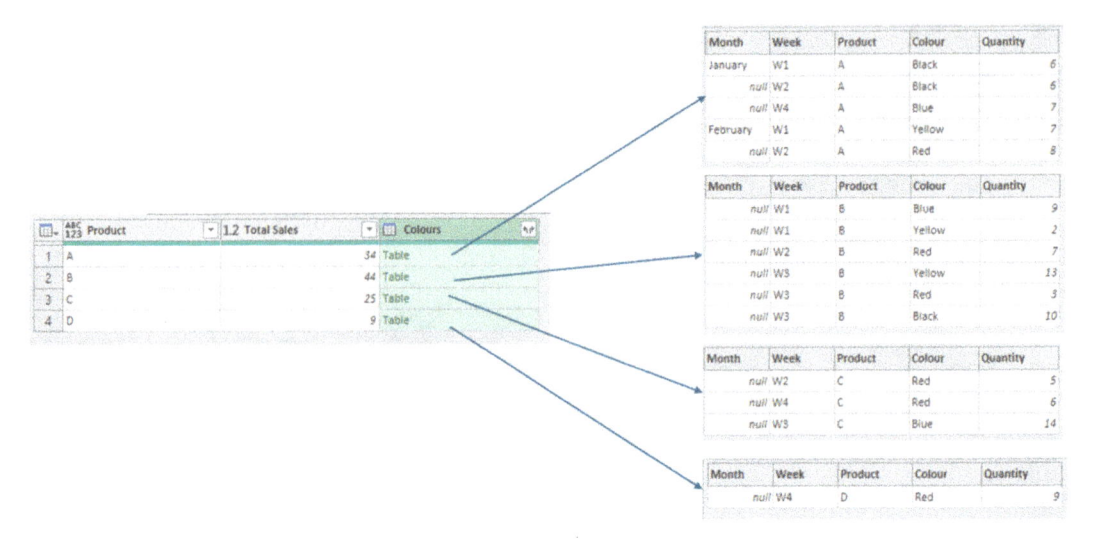

Figure 6-8. The result of the All Row operation

Instead of presenting all the values in a table format, you need the concatenated version of the colors. This can be achieved by modifying the formula. Consider the following formula displayed in the formula bar after clicking OK in the Group By window:

```
= Table.Group(Source, {"Product"},
    {
        {"Total Sales", each List.Sum([Quantity]), type number},
        {"Colours", each _, type table [Month=nullable text, Week=text,
        Product=text,
            Colour=text, Quantity=number]}
    })
```

As mentioned, without altering the result, the type of result columns can be omitted from the third item of sublists, in the third argument of the function. So, the updated formula, which is shorter, is as follows:

```
= Table.Group(Source, {"Product"},
    {
        {"Total Sales", each List.Sum([Quantity]) },
        {"Colours", each _}
    })
```

306

CHAPTER 6 GROUPING ROWS WITH TABLE.GROUP()

For the Colours column, each _ is used as an operator, leading to all the rows and columns for each product, while you only need the values from the Colours column for each product in the Source table. To extract the values from the Colours column, replace "each _" with "each _[Colour]" in the previous formula. This changes the result to Figure 6-9, where the tables are converted to lists that include the sold colors.

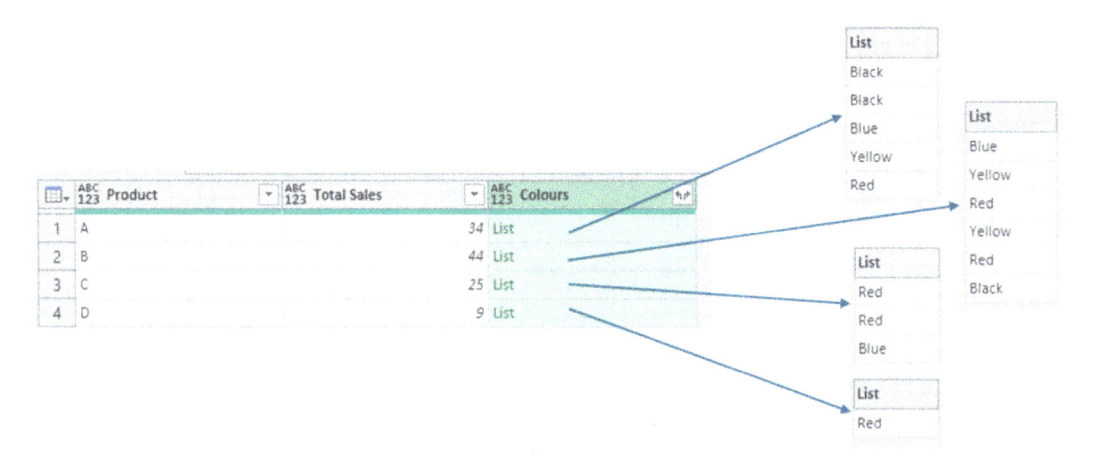

Figure 6-9. The result of each _[Colour]

To concatenate the color values and convert the lists of colors to single text, you can use the Text.Combine() function with a "," separator. Thus, each _[Colour] is replaced with each Text.Combine(_[Colour],","), resulting in Figure 6-10.

Product	Total Sales	Colours
A	34	Black,Black,Blue,Yellow,Red
B	44	Blue,Yellow,Red,Yellow,Red,Black
C	25	Red,Red,Blue
D	9	Red

Figure 6-10. The result of Text.Combine(_[Colour],",")

Since some colors, like Black for Product A, are repeated, the Colours column in the resulting table includes these repetitive colors. These duplicate colors should be removed from the list before using it inside Text.Combine(). Therefore, you need to rewrite the operation for the Colours column as each Text.Combine(List.Distinct(_[Colour]),","), resulting in Figure 6-11.

307

CHAPTER 6 GROUPING ROWS WITH TABLE.GROUP()

	ABC 123 Product		ABC 123 Total Sales		ABC 123 Colours
1	A			34	Black,Blue,Yellow,Red
2	B			44	Blue,Yellow,Red,Black
3	C			25	Red,Blue
4	D			9	Red

***Figure 6-11.** Removing the repetitive colors*

In this case, if you want to show the colors in the Colours column in alphabetic order, you can add the List.Sort() to the operation function and rewrite it as each Text.Combine(List.Sort(List.Distinct(_[Colour])),","). This results in Figure 6-12.

	ABC 123 Product		ABC 123 Total Sales		ABC 123 Colours
1	A			34	Black,Blue,Red,Yellow
2	B			44	Black,Blue,Red,Yellow
3	C			25	Blue,Red
4	D			9	Red

***Figure 6-12.** Sorting the colors*

The revised formula for solving the problem and presenting the sold colors per product next to the Total Sales is:

```
= Table.Group(Source, {"Product"},
    {
        {"Total Sales", each List.Sum([Quantity])},
        {"Colours", each Text.Combine(List.Sort(List.Distinct(_
        [Colour])),",")}
    })
```

Efficiency Tips Modifying the third argument of the Table.Group() function in this example does not increase its execution time, and for a dataset with 10,000 rows, it still runs in under a second.

Matching Items in Groups

The Source table in Table 6-3 contains product transactions between the technical and warehouse departments. Some products are returned to the warehouse in the same year or years later, indicated by the same Order No. having a negative quantity. Extract the net quantity of items sent per product in each year that aren't returned.

For example, in 2022 for product B, just on orders, Order No. 1 was issued. Based on this order, on 27/05/2022, five items of Product B were sent. Out of these, two were returned on 25/06/2023, one was returned on 14/09/2023, and the remaining two were returned on 04/10/2024. Since all items from this order were eventually returned, the net quantity of unreturned items for Product B in 2022 is 0.

For Product C in 2022, two different orders, Order No. 2 and Order No. 5, were issued with quantities of seven and three, respectively. All three items sent in Order No. 5 were returned, while none of the items from Order No. 2 were returned. Therefore, the net quantity of unreturned items for Product C in 2022 is seven, meaning 7 should be recorded for this product in that year.

Table 6-3. *Source: Product Transactions*

Date	Order No	Product	Quantity
27/05/2022	1	B	5
7/08/2022	2	C	7
8/09/2022	3	A	2
19/10/2022	4	A	3
22/12/2022	5	C	3
12/01/2023	3	A	-1
6/03/2023	6	A	7
25/06/2023	1	B	-2
28/06/2023	4	A	-3
1/08/2023	7	C	2

(*continued*)

CHAPTER 6 GROUPING ROWS WITH TABLE.GROUP()

Table 6-3. (continued)

Date	Order No	Product	Quantity
14/09/2023	1	B	-1
16/07/2024	3	A	-1
10/09/2024	5	C	-2
4/10/2024	1	B	-2
9/10/2024	6	A	-3
20/10/2024	8	B	1
22/12/2024	5	C	-1

Note The data in this example is provided in an Excel file titled 03 Matching Items in Groups.xlsx.

To solve this problem, you need to group the rows by each Order No. and calculate the total sum of the Quantity column for each order to determine the net quantity of purchases items per Order No. In addition to calculating the net quantity, you also need to extract the year in which each order was issued.

To group these rows, go to the Home tab, select Group By, switch to the Advanced mode, and configure the settings shown in Figure 6-13.

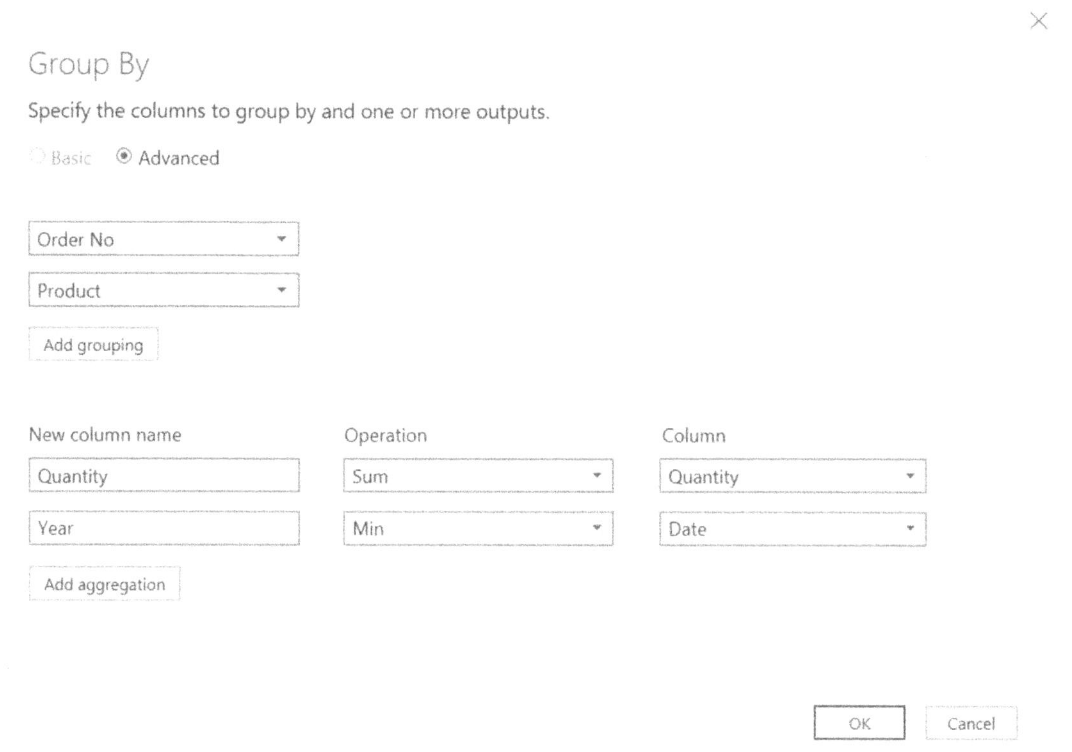

CHAPTER 6　GROUPING ROWS WITH TABLE.GROUP()

Figure 6-13. *Group By settings*

This configuration generates the following formula in the formula bar, which results in Figure 6-14.

```
= Table.Group(Source,
    {"Order No", "Product"},
    {
        {"Quantity", each List.Sum([Quantity]), type number},
        {"Year", each List.Min([Date]), type datetime}
    })
```

CHAPTER 6   GROUPING ROWS WITH TABLE.GROUP()

	Order No	Product	Quantity	Year
1		1 B	0	27/05/2022 12:00:00 AM
2		2 C	7	7/08/2022 12:00:00 AM
3		3 A	0	8/09/2022 12:00:00 AM
4		4 A	0	19/10/2022 12:00:00 AM
5		5 C	0	22/12/2022 12:00:00 AM
6		6 A	4	6/03/2023 12:00:00 AM
7		7 C	2	1/08/2023 12:00:00 AM
8		8 B	1	20/10/2024 12:00:00 AM

Figure 6-14. *The result of Table.Group*

The values in the Year column are in date format, and the year of each date can be extracted by rewriting the formula as follows:

```
= Table.Group(Source,
    {"Order No", "Product"},
    {
        {"Quantity", each List.Sum([Quantity]), type number},
        {"Year", each Date.Year(List.Min([Date])) }
    })
```

This results in Figure 6-15, which provides the net quantity of non-returned items per product, sent in each year.

	Order No	Product	Quantity	Year
1		1 B	0	2022
2		2 C	7	2022
3		3 A	0	2022
4		4 A	0	2022
5		5 C	0	2022
6		6 A	4	2023
7		7 C	2	2023
8		8 B	1	2024

Figure 6-15. *The result of the revised version*

As a final step, use the Group By command again with the settings provided in Figure 6-16, and click OK. This results in Figure 6-17.

CHAPTER 6   GROUPING ROWS WITH TABLE.GROUP()

Group By

Specify the columns to group by and one or more outputs.

○ Basic ● Advanced

Product ▼

Year ▼

[Add grouping]

New column name | Operation | Column
Total | Sum ▼ | Quantity ▼

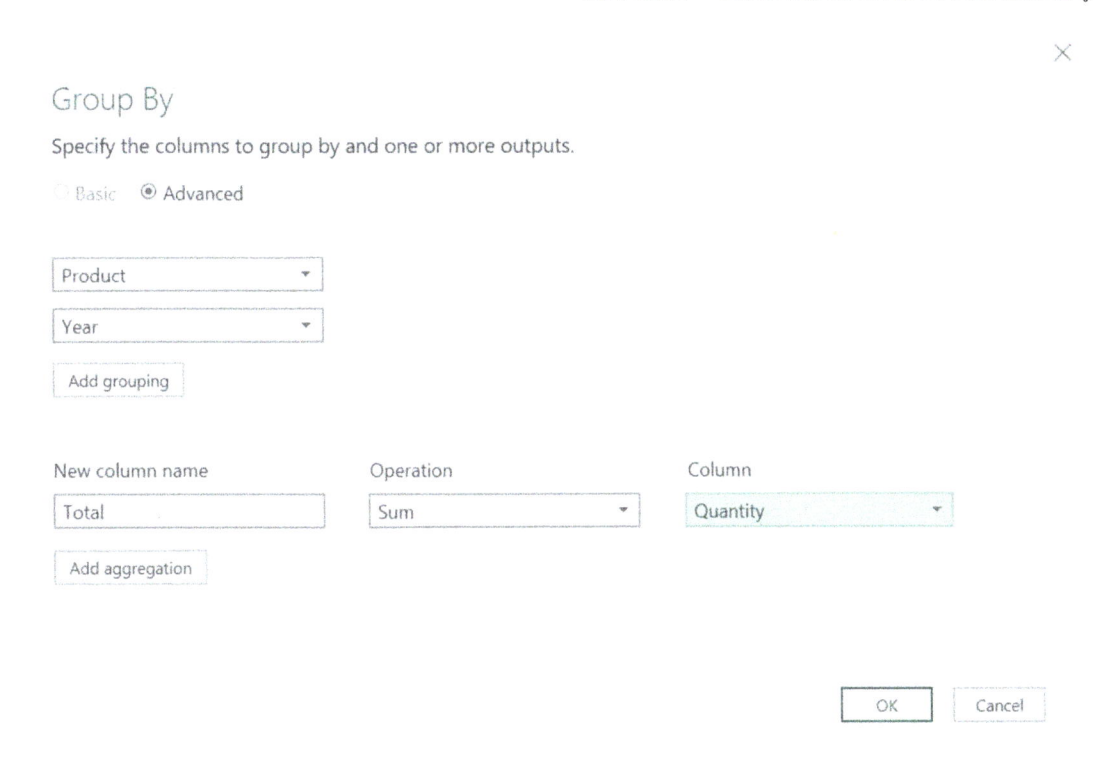

[Add aggregation]

[OK] [Cancel]

Figure 6-16. *The second use of Group By*

#	Product	Year	Total
1	B	2022	0
2	C	2022	7
3	A	2022	0
4	A	2023	4
5	C	2023	2
6	B	2024	1

Figure 6-17. *The final result*

To clean the results, filter out the rows where the quantity column has a 0 value.

CHAPTER 6   GROUPING ROWS WITH TABLE.GROUP()

Identifying All-Season Products

In the Source table, part of which is shown in Table 6-4, the sales values for different products across various dates are provided. Extract the products that have been sold at least once in each of the months.

Table 6-4. Comparison Matrix

Date	Product	Quantity
13/01/2023	A	8
14/01/2023	C	4
15/01/2023	D	3
16/01/2023	E	2
17/01/2023	J	2
19/01/2023	A	6
21/01/2023	H	7
26/01/2023	C	5
27/01/2023	B	2
30/01/2023	A	5
2/02/2023	F	2
3/02/2023	J	9
7/02/2023	G	3
10/02/2023	A	4
11/02/2023	C	5

Note   The data in this example is provided in an Excel file titled `04 Identifying All-Season Products.xlsx`.

To solve this problem, you need to determine the number of months each product was sold. To simplify the process, you can extract the month from each transaction date. This can be done by selecting the Date column, then navigating to

CHAPTER 6   GROUPING ROWS WITH TABLE.GROUP()

the Transform tab, and in the Date & Time column section, selecting Month under the Date options, as shown in Figure 6-18. This will result in the table shown in Figure 6-19.

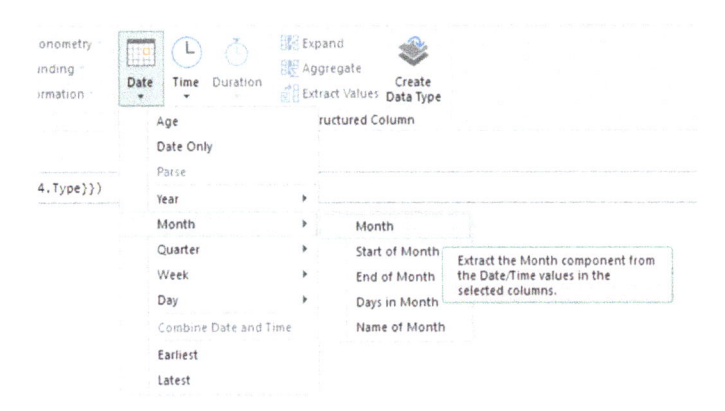

Figure 6-18. Setting for converting Date to Month

= Table.TransformColumns(Source,{{"Date", Date.Month, Int64.Type}})

Date	Product	Quantity
1	A	8
1	C	4
1	D	3
1	E	2
1	J	2
1	A	6
1	H	7
1	C	5
1	B	2
1	A	5
2	F	2
2	J	9
2	G	3
2	A	4
2	C	5
2	J	7
2	A	6

Figure 6-19. Converting dates to month

315

CHAPTER 6   GROUPING ROWS WITH TABLE.GROUP()

In the next step, you need to calculate the number of months each product was sold. To do this, select the Group By command and configure the settings shown in Figure 6-20. This will produce the results displayed in Figure 6-21.

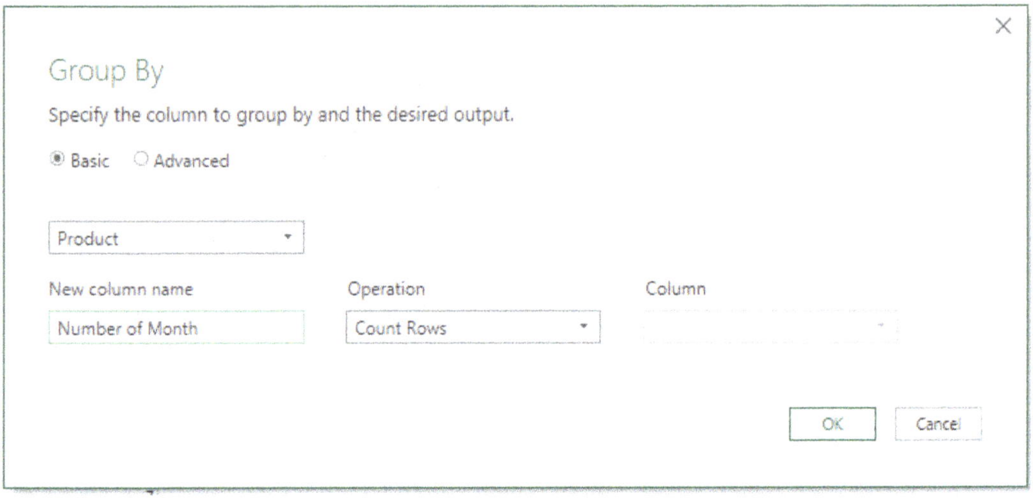

Figure 6-20. *Setting for Group By*

Product	Number of Month
A	22
C	17
D	9
E	10
J	18
H	11
B	14
F	17
G	13

Figure 6-21. *The result of group By*

In the Group By settings, Count Rows as initially selected as the operation. However, the goal is to count the number of unique months each product was sold in, rather than counting all the rows.

316

CHAPTER 6 GROUPING ROWS WITH TABLE.GROUP()

To adjust this, first examine the formula generated by the previous step in the formula bar:

```
= Table.Group(#"Extracted Month", {"Product"}, {{"Number of Month", each
Table.RowCount(_), Int64.Type}})
```

Instead of using each Table.RowCount(_), which counts all rows, you need to extract the unique values from the Date column for each product. You can achieve this by replacing it with each _[Date], which retrieves all date values per product.

To filter out duplicate months, use List.Distinct(_[Date]), and to count the unique months, wrap it with List.Count(). The revised formula is as follows:

```
= Table.Group(
    #"Extracted Month",
    {"Product"},
    {{"Number of Month", each List.Count(List.Distinct(_[Date])),
    Int64.Type}}
)
```

This updated formula provides the number of months each product was sold, as shown in Figure 6-22. Finally, to find products sold in all 12 months, simply filter the Number of Month column to keep rows where the value is 12.

	Product	Number of Month
1	A	12
2	C	7
3	D	6
4	E	7
5	J	12
6	H	7
7	B	12
8	F	10
9	G	7

Figure 6-22. The result of revised Group By

CHAPTER 6　GROUPING ROWS WITH TABLE.GROUP()

Grouping Based on the Date

Consider the sales data (sorted by the Date column) shown in Table 6-5 as the source table.

Table 6-5. *Source: Historical Sales*

Date	Quantity
25/06/2024	84
26/06/2024	23
27/06/2024	87
28/06/2024	26
30/06/2024	67
2/07/2024	42
3/07/2024	40
4/07/2024	14
5/07/2024	69
6/07/2024	32
7/07/2024	44
8/07/2024	56
9/07/2024	25
11/07/2024	15
12/07/2024	84
13/07/2024	25
14/07/2024	46
15/07/2024	38
17/07/2024	45
18/07/2024	76
19/07/2024	44

> **Note** The data in this example is provided in an Excel file titled 05 Group based on the Date.xlsx.

Group the rows based on the following scenarios:

- Group the values for each week, starting on Monday.
- Group the values for each week, starting on Wednesday.
- Group the values for every ten days, starting at the beginning of the year.
- Group the first ten days (from the 1st to the 10th of the month), the second ten days (from the 11th to the 20th), and the remaining days (from the 21st to the end of the month) into three separate groups for each month.

To solve such problems, you simply need to add a new custom column with values corresponding to the different groups. For example, to group by week across the year, you can add a new custom column using the formula provided in the Custom Column window, which determines the week number of each date, as shown in Figure 6-23. This column can then be used for grouping.

```
=Date.WeekOfYear([Date])
```

CHAPTER 6 GROUPING ROWS WITH TABLE.GROUP()

```
= Table.AddColumn(Source, "Group ID", each Date.WeekOfYear([Date]))
```

#	Date	Quantity	Group ID
1	25/06/2024 12:00:00 AM	84	26
2	26/06/2024 12:00:00 AM	23	26
3	27/06/2024 12:00:00 AM	87	26
4	28/06/2024 12:00:00 AM	26	26
5	30/06/2024 12:00:00 AM	67	26
6	2/07/2024 12:00:00 AM	42	27
7	3/07/2024 12:00:00 AM	40	27
8	4/07/2024 12:00:00 AM	14	27
9	5/07/2024 12:00:00 AM	69	27
10	6/07/2024 12:00:00 AM	32	27
11	7/07/2024 12:00:00 AM	44	27
12	8/07/2024 12:00:00 AM	56	28
13	9/07/2024 12:00:00 AM	25	28
14	11/07/2024 12:00:00 AM	15	28
15	12/07/2024 12:00:00 AM	84	28
16	13/07/2024 12:00:00 AM	25	28
17	14/07/2024 12:00:00 AM	46	28
18	15/07/2024 12:00:00 AM	38	29
19	17/07/2024 12:00:00 AM	45	29
20	18/07/2024 12:00:00 AM	76	29
21	19/07/2024 12:00:00 AM	44	29

Figure 6-23. *The result of the formula for every week*

If the table includes information related to other years, the formula can be modified as follows, resulting in Figure 6-24.

```
= DateTime.ToText([Date],"yyyy-") & Text.From(Date.WeekOfYear([Date]))
```

CHAPTER 6 GROUPING ROWS WITH TABLE.GROUP()

#	Date	Quantity	Group ID
1	25/06/2024 12:00:00 AM	84	2024-26
2	26/06/2024 12:00:00 AM	23	2024-26
3	27/06/2024 12:00:00 AM	87	2024-26
4	28/06/2024 12:00:00 AM	26	2024-26
5	30/06/2024 12:00:00 AM	67	2024-26
6	2/07/2024 12:00:00 AM	42	2024-27
7	3/07/2024 12:00:00 AM	40	2024-27
8	4/07/2024 12:00:00 AM	14	2024-27
9	5/07/2024 12:00:00 AM	69	2024-27
10	6/07/2024 12:00:00 AM	32	2024-27
11	7/07/2024 12:00:00 AM	44	2024-27
12	8/07/2024 12:00:00 AM	56	2024-28
13	9/07/2024 12:00:00 AM	25	2024-28
14	11/07/2024 12:00:00 AM	15	2024-28
15	12/07/2024 12:00:00 AM	84	2024-28
16	13/07/2024 12:00:00 AM	25	2024-28
17	14/07/2024 12:00:00 AM	46	2024-28
18	15/07/2024 12:00:00 AM	38	2024-29
19	17/07/2024 12:00:00 AM	45	2024-29
20	18/07/2024 12:00:00 AM	76	2024-29
21	19/07/2024 12:00:00 AM	44	2024-29

Figure 6-24. *The result of the formula for every week starting on Wednesday*

To change the starting date to Wednesday, simply use the second argument of the Date.WeekOfYear() function and rewrite the formula as follows.

=DateTime.ToText([Date],"yyyy-") & Text.From(Date.WeekOfYear([Date], Day.Wednesday))

To group the rows every ten days, starting from the first date of the year, you can use the formula for the Group ID as follows, resulting in Figure 6-25.

=DateTime.ToText([Date],"yyyy-") & Text.From(1+Number.IntegerDivide(Date.DayOfYear([Date])-1,10))

CHAPTER 6 GROUPING ROWS WITH TABLE.GROUP()

#	Date	Quantity	Group ID
1	25/06/2024 12:00:00 AM	84	2024-17
2	26/06/2024 12:00:00 AM	23	2024-17
3	27/06/2024 12:00:00 AM	87	2024-17
4	28/06/2024 12:00:00 AM	26	2024-17
5	30/06/2024 12:00:00 AM	67	2024-18
6	2/07/2024 12:00:00 AM	42	2024-18
7	3/07/2024 12:00:00 AM	40	2024-18
8	4/07/2024 12:00:00 AM	14	2024-18
9	5/07/2024 12:00:00 AM	69	2024-18
10	6/07/2024 12:00:00 AM	32	2024-18
11	7/07/2024 12:00:00 AM	44	2024-18
12	8/07/2024 12:00:00 AM	56	2024-18
13	9/07/2024 12:00:00 AM	25	2024-19
14	11/07/2024 12:00:00 AM	15	2024-19
15	12/07/2024 12:00:00 AM	84	2024-19
16	13/07/2024 12:00:00 AM	25	2024-19
17	14/07/2024 12:00:00 AM	46	2024-19
18	15/07/2024 12:00:00 AM	38	2024-19
19	17/07/2024 12:00:00 AM	45	2024-19
20	18/07/2024 12:00:00 AM	76	2024-19
21	19/07/2024 12:00:00 AM	44	2024-20

Figure 6-25. *The result of formula for every ten days starting from the beginning of the year*

For the last scenario, you can use the following formula, resulting in Figure 6-26.

```
DateTime.ToText([Date],"yyyy-MM-") & Text.From(List.Min({3,1+Number.IntegerDivide(Date.Day([Date])-1,10)}))
```

CHAPTER 6 GROUPING ROWS WITH TABLE.GROUP()

Date	Quantity	Group ID
25/06/2024 12:00:00 AM	84	2024-06-3
26/06/2024 12:00:00 AM	23	2024-06-3
27/06/2024 12:00:00 AM	87	2024-06-3
28/06/2024 12:00:00 AM	26	2024-06-3
30/06/2024 12:00:00 AM	67	2024-06-3
2/07/2024 12:00:00 AM	42	2024-07-1
3/07/2024 12:00:00 AM	40	2024-07-1
4/07/2024 12:00:00 AM	14	2024-07-1
5/07/2024 12:00:00 AM	69	2024-07-1
6/07/2024 12:00:00 AM	32	2024-07-1
7/07/2024 12:00:00 AM	44	2024-07-1
8/07/2024 12:00:00 AM	56	2024-07-1
9/07/2024 12:00:00 AM	25	2024-07-1
11/07/2024 12:00:00 AM	15	2024-07-2
12/07/2024 12:00:00 AM	84	2024-07-2
13/07/2024 12:00:00 AM	25	2024-07-2
14/07/2024 12:00:00 AM	46	2024-07-2
15/07/2024 12:00:00 AM	38	2024-07-2
17/07/2024 12:00:00 AM	45	2024-07-2
18/07/2024 12:00:00 AM	76	2024-07-2
19/07/2024 12:00:00 AM	44	2024-07-2

Figure 6-26. *The result of formula for every ten days in each month*

Using the Fourth Input in Table.Group()

Consider the historical sales data provided in the Source table shown in Table 6-6. Calculate the total sales per week, ensuring that the weeks from different months are grouped separately.

Table 6-6. *Source: Historical Sales Value*

Month	Week	Product	Colour	Quantity
January	W1	A	Black	6
	W1	B	Blue	9
	W1	B	Yellow	2
	W2	A	Black	6
	W2	B	Red	7
	W2	C	Red	5
	W3	B	Yellow	13
	W3	B	Red	3
	W4	A	Blue	7
	W4	C	Red	6
February	W1	A	Yellow	7
	W2	A	Red	8
	W3	B	Black	10
	W3	C	Blue	14
	W4	D	Red	9

Note The data in this example is provided in an Excel file titled `06 Using the Fourth Input in Table.Group.xlsx`.

In this problem, you want to group the rows of the table based on the values in the Week column. The challenge is that the rows for the first week of January should be grouped together and should not include the values for the first week of February, even though both are labelled as W1. In other words, you want to group the rows with the same Week value only if they are in consecutive rows; otherwise, they should be placed in different groups. This is where the fourth argument of this function comes to the rescue. (This example can be solved in different ways, but in this example you use it to learn about the fourth argument of the `Table.Group()` function.)

CHAPTER 6   GROUPING ROWS WITH TABLE.GROUP()

As in the previous examples, right-click the Week column, select the Group By command, and adjust the settings as shown in Figure 6-27.

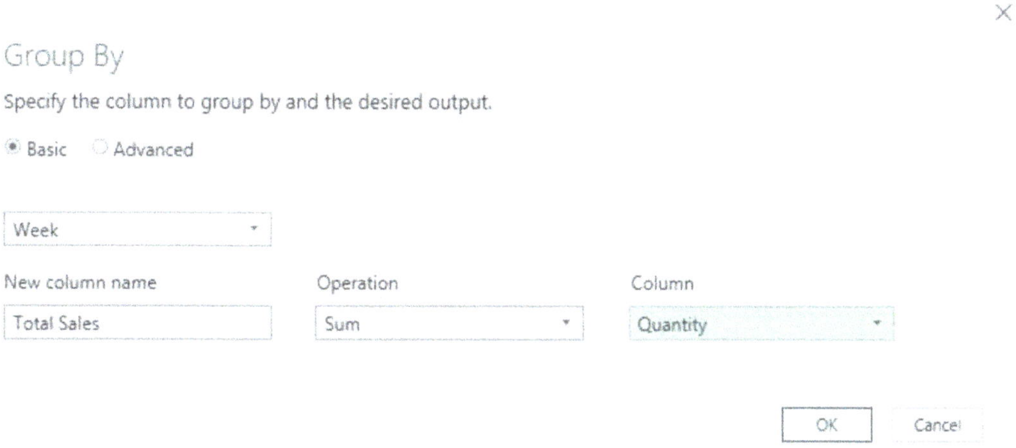

Figure 6-27. Settings for Group By week

Click OK, leading to the result shown in Figure 6-28, where weeks from different months are also grouped, and generate the following formula in the formula bar.

```
= Table.Group(Source, {"Week"}, {{"Total Sales", each List.Sum([Quantity]), 
type number}})
```

Week	Total Sales
W1	24
W2	26
W3	40
W4	22

Figure 6-28. The result of Group By week

The predefined logic of the Table.Group() function for grouping rows is global, meaning it groups all the rows in the table that have the same value in the Week column. However, this logic can be changed to a local one by manually modifying the fourth argument of the function.

325

CHAPTER 6 GROUPING ROWS WITH TABLE.GROUP()

In other words, you can use the fourth argument in the Table.Group() function to change the grouping logic by entering GroupKind.Local (or 0) or GroupKind.Global (or 1) in this argument. By default, GroupKind.Global is used, which groups similar values in the columns across the entire table. However, by entering GroupKind.Local in the fourth argument, the grouping logic is changed, and only rows with the same value that are adjacent to each other will be grouped together.

To solve this problem, add GroupKind.Local or value 0 in the fourth argument of the previous formula and rewrite it as shown here. This will result in the desired grouping, as shown in Figure 6-29, which solves the problem.

```
= Table.Group(Source, {"Week"}, {{"Total Sales", each List.Sum([Quantity]),
type number}},0)
```

#	Week	Total Sales
1	W1	17
2	W2	18
3	W3	16
4	W4	13
5	W1	7
6	W2	8
7	W3	24
8	W4	9

Figure 6-29. The result of changing the grouping logic to GroupKind.Local

---

Note When you're using the fourth input, ensure that the grouping columns are sorted correctly.

Ignoring Case Sensitivity in Grouping

Given the sales information in the Source table in Table 6-7, calculate the total quantity for each product.

Table 6-7. Source: Sales Info

Week	Product	Colour	Quantity
W1	A	Black	6
W1	B	Blue	9
W1	B	Yellow	2
W2	a	Black	6
W2	B	Red	7
W2	C	Red	5
W3	b	Yellow	13
W3	b	Red	3
W4	A	Blue	7
W4	c	Red	6

Note The data in this example is provided in an Excel file titled `07 Ignoring Case Sensitivity in Grouping .xlsx`.

To solve this problem, two different solutions are provided. The first is the easiest one, and it is based solely on the UI. The second solution is more advanced and helps you become familiar with the fifth argument in the Table.Group() function.

Solution 1: Based on UI

This is exactly the same as Example 1 in this chapter, with the difference that the product names are in uppercase and lowercase. Since Power Query is case-sensitive, "a" and "A" are considered different values. Applying the Group By command (without any modifications) directly on this table will result in two different rows for "a" and "A".

Therefore, it would be better to first convert all the product names to the same case and then apply the Group By command on the updated table.

CHAPTER 6   GROUPING ROWS WITH TABLE.GROUP()

To convert all the product names to uppercase, select the Product Name column. Then, from the Transform tab, in the Text Column section, under the Format command, choose Uppercase to convert all the product names to uppercase, as shown in Figure 6-30.

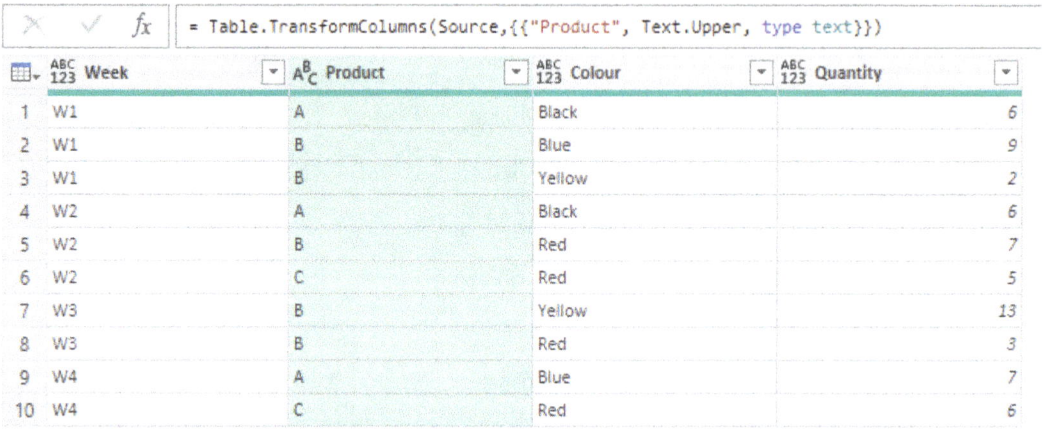

Week	Product	Colour	Quantity
W1	A	Black	6
W1	B	Blue	9
W1	B	Yellow	2
W2	A	Black	6
W2	B	Red	7
W2	C	Red	5
W3	B	Yellow	13
W3	B	Red	3
W4	A	Blue	7
W4	C	Red	6

`= Table.TransformColumns(Source,{{"Product", Text.Upper, type text}})`

Figure 6-30. *Converting product names to uppercase*

The Group By command now has the settings shown in Figure 6-31.

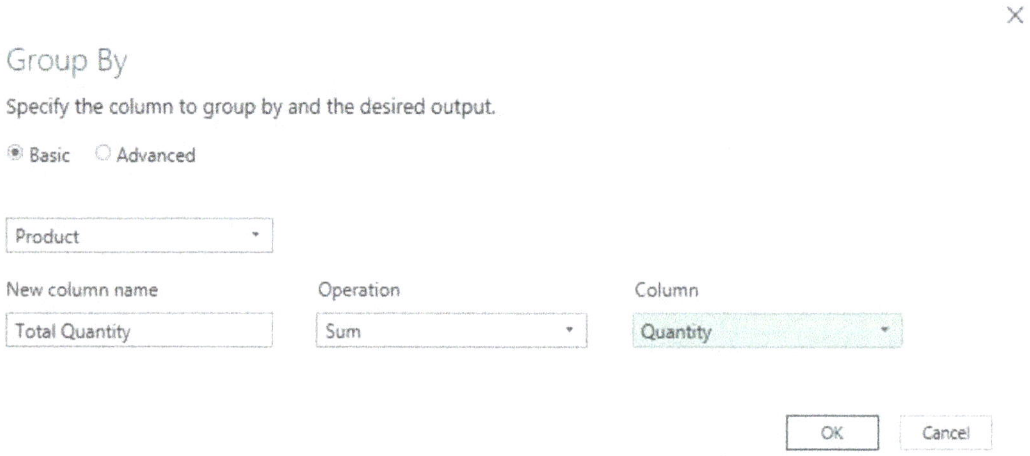

Group By

Specify the column to group by and the desired output.

● Basic   ○ Advanced

Product

New column name	Operation	Column
Total Quantity	Sum	Quantity

Figure 6-31. *Grouping settings*

CHAPTER 6　GROUPING ROWS WITH TABLE.GROUP()

Solution 2: Using the Fifth Argument of Table.Group()

Besides the previously presented solution, this problem can also be solved using the Table.Group() function without changing the product names, if you are familiar with the fifth argument of this function.

Consider the source table unchanged, then select the Product column, select the Group By command in the Home tab, and change the settings as shown in Figure 6-32, which results in Figure 6-33. Since Power Query is case-sensitive, there are different rows in the resulting table for product "a" and "A".

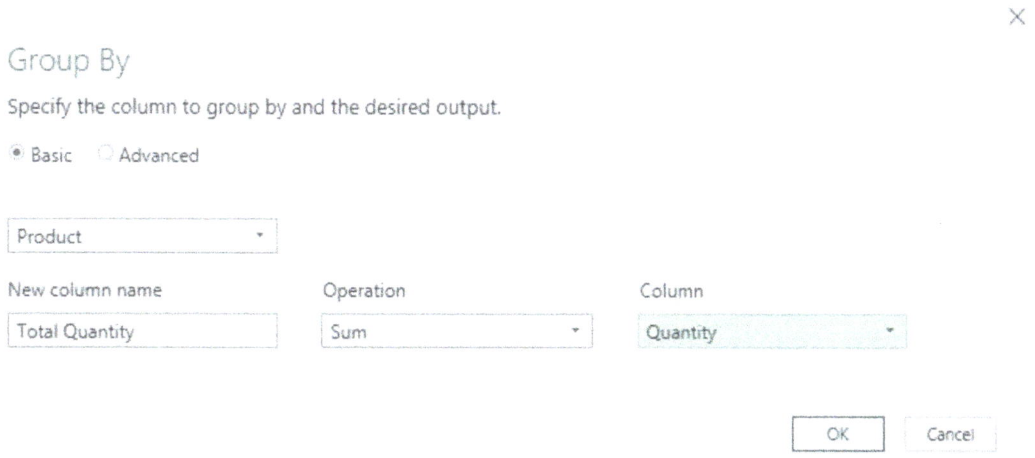

Figure 6-32. Grouping setting

Figure 6-33. Result of grouping

CHAPTER 6 GROUPING ROWS WITH TABLE.GROUP()

The previous setting for the grouping command will result in the following formula in the formula bar with three arguments:

```
= Table.Group(
    Source,
    {"Product"},
    {{"Total Quantity", each List.Sum([Quantity]), type number}})
```

As mentioned in the previous example, adding 1 to the fourth argument (or GroupKind.Global) doesn't change the result. However, to use the fifth argument, you need to define all four arguments first. So, after entering 1 in the fourth argument, you can use Comparer.OrdinalIgnoreCase in the fifth argument of this function, as shown here, to ignore the case differences. This results in Figure 6-34 and solves the problem.

```
= Table.Group(
    Source,
    {"Product"},
    {{"Total Quantity", each List.Sum([Quantity]), type number}},
    1,
    Comparer.OrdinalIgnoreCase)
```

	Product	1.2 Total Quantity
1	A	19
2	B	34
3	C	11

Figure 6-34. Final result

Note As mentioned in the syntax of the Table.Group() function, the fifth argument is the comparer, which you can use to define the condition for grouping the rows. This allows users to apply any custom logic for grouping the rows, in addition to using Comparer.OrdinalIgnoreCase.

A custom comparer, in the fifth argument of Table.Group(), can be a custom function with two input arguments, such as (s,c)=>f(s,c). The s and c are the input parameters, each representing a row of the table, and f(s,c) should be results in an integer number. You can use any notation, but s and c are generally used to stand for state and current.

Based on this description, the Value.Compare() is a useful function commonly used in this argument, instead of f(s,c). The Value.Comparer(s,c) always returns -1,0,1, based on the condition:

- Returns 0 if s and c are equal
- Returns -1 if s is less than c.
- Returns 1 if s is greater than c.

Using the (s,c)=>Value.Comparer(f(s),f(c)) indicates the values of f(s) and f(c) are compared, and if f(s) and f(c) are equal, then the rows are grouped together. This is instead of comparing the values on the column (columns) selected in the second argument.

Based on this explanation, this problem can also be solved with the following formula, by replacing Comparer.OrdinalIgnoreCase with a custom compare, which does almost the same thing (the difference is that, by using Value.Comparer(), the resulting table will be sorted based on the logic defined in this function). This formula means that, instead of comparing the rows based on the lowercase values in the Product column, the values in this column should be compared:

```
= Table.Group(
      Source,
      {"Product"},
      {{"Total Quantity", each List.Sum([Quantity]), type
      number}},
1,
      (s,c)=> Value.Compare(Text.Lower(s[Product]),Text.
      Lower(c[Product])))
```

CHAPTER 6   GROUPING ROWS WITH TABLE.GROUP()

In the previous formula, as each s and c represent a row of the table, they are in the type of record, with the number of fields equal to the number of columns entered in the second argument of `Table.Group()` function. The field titles in s and c are also the same as the name of the column entered in the second argument of `Table.Group`.

Using Value.Comparer for Grouping

Given the staff age information in the Source table in Table 6-8, group the rows by age decades and extract the staff IDs for each group.

Table 6-8. Source: Warehouse Transactions

Age	Staff ID
45	I-01
25	I-02
20	I-03
32	I-04
35	I-05
22	I-06
29	I-07
40	I-08
17	I-09
34	I-10
52	I-11
37	I-12
50	I-13
22	I-14

(*continued*)

Table 6-8. (*continued*)

Age	Staff ID
28	I-15
25	I-16
41	I-17
22	I-18
38	I-19
33	I-20
18	I-21
27	I-22
49	I-23
21	I-24
53	I-25
50	I-26
19	I-27
46	I-28
37	I-29
38	I-30
30	I-31

Note The data in this example is provided in an Excel file titled `08 Using Value.Comparer for Grouping .xlsx`.

To solve this problem, two different solutions are provided. The first solution involves adding a custom column to calculate the age decades and then grouping the rows based on this new column. The second solution uses the Group By command directly, leveraging the fifth argument in the `Table.Group()` function to achieve the desired result.

CHAPTER 6   GROUPING ROWS WITH TABLE.GROUP()

Solution 1: Using a Custom Column

In this example, the rows need to be grouped by decade of age, even though no column currently provides this information. As a first step, add a new custom column called Age Decade using the following formula in the Custom Column window, which will result in Figure 6-35.

Age	Staff ID	Age Decade
45	I-01	4
25	I-02	2
20	I-03	2
32	I-04	3
35	I-05	3
22	I-06	2
29	I-07	2
40	I-08	4
17	I-09	1
34	I-10	3
52	I-11	5
37	I-12	3
50	I-13	5
22	I-14	2
28	I-15	2
25	I-16	2

Figure 6-35. *The result of adding the decade of ages*

In the next step, right-click the Age Decade column and select the Group By command. In the window that opens, apply the settings provided in Figure 6-36. Clicking OK will result in Figure 6-37.

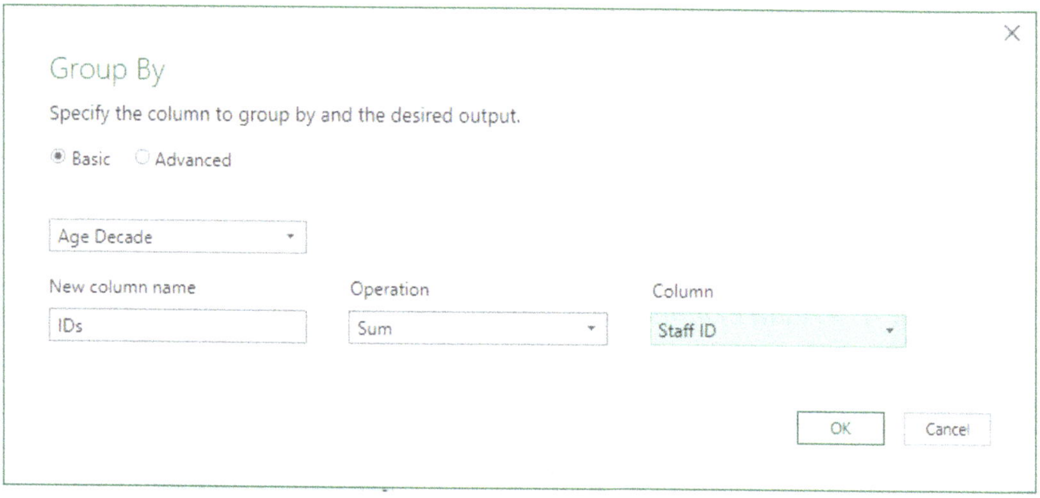

CHAPTER 6   GROUPING ROWS WITH TABLE.GROUP()

Figure 6-36.   Setting of grouping

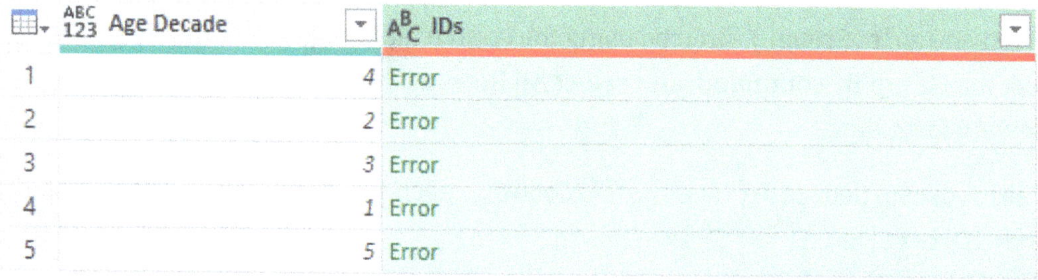

Figure 6-37.   Result of grouping

In the Group By window, you initially selected the Sum operation for the Staff ID column, which contains text values. The resulting column therefore displays an error for all the rows. To resolve this, you need to replace the Sum operation with a Concatenate operation by manually modifying the formula. Consider this generated formula in the formula bar after the previous step:

= Table.Group(#"Added Custom", {"Age Decade"}, {{"IDs", each List. Sum([Staff ID]), type text}})

Modifying this formula as shown will solve the problem and results in Figure 6-38:

= Table.Group(#"Added Custom", {"Age Decade"}, {{"IDs", each Text. Combine([Staff ID],", ")}})

335

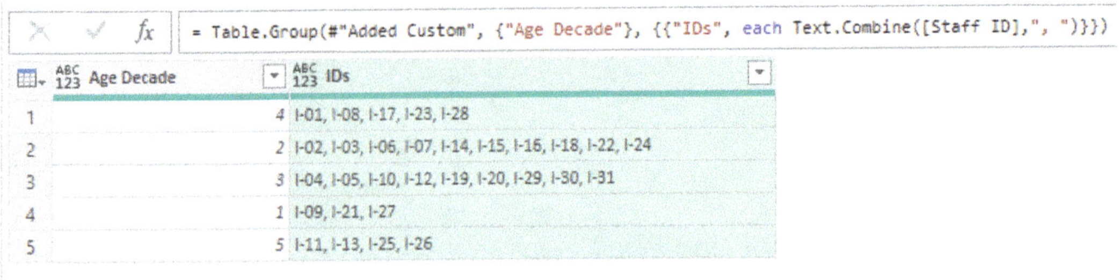

CHAPTER 6   GROUPING ROWS WITH TABLE.GROUP()

| | fx | = Table.Group(#"Added Custom", {"Age Decade"}, {{"IDs", each Text.Combine([Staff ID],", ")}}) |

	Age Decade	IDs
1	4	I-01, I-08, I-17, I-23, I-28
2	2	I-02, I-03, I-06, I-07, I-14, I-15, I-16, I-18, I-22, I-24
3	3	I-04, I-05, I-10, I-12, I-19, I-20, I-29, I-30, I-31
4	1	I-09, I-21, I-27
5	5	I-11, I-13, I-25, I-26

Figure 6-38. *The result of modified grouping*

Solution 2: Using the Fifth Argument in the Table.Group()

In the previous solution, you solved the problem using a straightforward approach by first adding a new column and then grouping the rows based on the values in that column. Alternatively, this problem can be solved directly using Table.Group() and the fifth argument in Table.Group().

To use Table.Group() directly, using the source table, right-click the Age column, select the Group By command, and select All Rows as the operation. You'll get the following formula:

= Table.Group(Source, {"Age"}, {{"Count", each _, type table [Age=number, Staff ID=text]}})

To combine the staff IDs for each age group, modify the formula to the following to reach Figure 6-39:

= Table.Group(Source, {"Age"}, {{"IDs", each Text.Combine(_[Staff ID],", ")}})

	Age	IDs
1	45	I-01
2	25	I-02, I-16
3	20	I-03
4	32	I-04
5	35	I-05
6	22	I-06, I-14, I-18
7	29	I-07
8	40	I-08
9	17	I-09
10	34	I-10
11	52	I-11
12	37	I-12, I-29
13	50	I-13, I-26
14	28	I-15
15	41	I-17

Figure 6-39. The result of grouping

In this formula, the ages of two rows are compared, and if they are equal, the rows are grouped together; otherwise, they are not grouped. However, in this example, you want to change the comparison logic from comparing the exact ages to comparing the age decades. As mentioned in the previous example, you can use the fifth argument of Table.Group() to change the logic for comparing the rows and decide whether to group those rows or not.

Staff with the same age are grouped together, but you want to group the rows based on age decades. To change the criteria for comparing the rows and decide whether to group them or not, you can use the fifth argument. The fifth argument of Table.Group() is a custom function with two arguments mostly in the type record, each one present on a row of the table. If the result of this function becomes 0, the rows will be grouped together. (An important note—using the fifth argument might change the order of the rows used in the table.)

In this example, the previous formula can be rewritten as follows:

```
= Table.Group(
    Source,
```

CHAPTER 6   GROUPING ROWS WITH TABLE.GROUP()

```
    {"Age"},
    {{"IDs", each Text.Combine(_[Staff ID],", ")}},
    1,
     (s,c)=>Value.Compare(s[Age],c[Age]))
```

The result of this formula is that the table becomes sorted based on the age decades. When you use the fifth argument, the rows represented by s and c will be grouped if s[Age] and c[Age] are equal.

In this example, instead of comparing the exact ages of s[Age] and c[Age], you want to group the rows based on the decade of ages by comparing the result of Number.IntegerDivide(s[Age],10) and Number.IntegerDivide(c[Age],10). To achieve this, rewrite the formula to group by the decade of ages. The result is shown in Figure 6-40.

```
= Table.Group(
    Source,
    {"Age"},
    {{"IDs", each Text.Combine(_[Staff ID],", ")}},
    1,
     (s,c)=>Value.Compare(
                Number.IntegerDivide(s[Age],10),
                Number.IntegerDivide(c[Age],10)
                                              )
  )
```

	Age	IDs
1	19	I-27, I-21, I-09
2	21	I-24, I-14, I-22, I-18, I-15, I-16,...
3	33	I-20, I-19, I-29, I-30, I-12, I-04,...
4	40	I-08, I-28, I-01, I-23, I-17
5	50	I-13, I-11, I-25, I-26

Figure 6-40. The result of modified grouping

In the resulting table, to clarify the age groups of each row, the formula can be rewritten to include a column that explicitly shows the age decade. This helps in understanding the grouping better. Here's how you can modify the following formula, which solves

CHAPTER 6   GROUPING ROWS WITH TABLE.GROUP()

the problem and results in Figure 6-41. In this formula, for the Age Group column, a predefined list as {"","[10-20)","[20-30)","[30-40)","[40-50)","[50-60)"} is defined, then based on the result of {Number.IntegerDivide([Age]{0},10)}, the ith item in this list will show a result. If {Number.IntegerDivide([Age]{0},10)} results in 1 (the age group between 10-20), the item with index 1 will be shown.

```
= Table.Group(
      Source,
      {"Age"},
      {
                  {"IDs", each Text.Combine(_[Staff ID],", ")},
                  {"Age Group", each {"","[10-20)","[20-30)","[30-40)",
                  "[40-50)","[50-60)"} {Number.IntegerDivide([Age]
                  {0},10)}}},
      1,
      (s,c)=>Value.Compare(Number.IntegerDivide(s[Age],10),Number.IntegerD
      ivide(c[Age],10)))
```

	Age	IDs	Age Group
1	19	I-27, I-09, I-21	[10-20)
2	25	I-16, I-02, I-03, I-06, I-07, I-24, I-22, I-14, I-15, I-18	[20-30)
3	37	I-29, I-20, I-19, I-31, I-30, I-12, I-10, I-05, I-04	[30-40)
4	49	I-23, I-08, I-28, I-17, I-01	[40-50)
5	50	I-13, I-11, I-25, I-26	[50-60)

Figure 6-41. Clarifying the age groups

Note In this example, since the rows are grouped solely based on the values in the Age column, the second input can be rewritten as text ("Age") instead of as list({"Age"}). This means that s and c in the fifth argument are no longer records and can be referenced directly. Therefore, the formula can be rewritten as follows, producing the same result.

```
= Table.Group(
      Source,
      "Age",
      {
```

339

```
                        {"IDs", each Text.Combine(_[Staff ID],", ")},
                        {"Age Group", each {"","[10-20)","[20-30)","[30-40)",
                        "[40-50)","[50-60)"} {Number.IntegerDivide([Age]
                        {0},10)}}},
    1,
    (s,c)=>Value.Compare(Number.IntegerDivide(s,10),Number.
    IntegerDivide(c,10)))
```

As in the previous example of `Table.Group()`, this one also runs 10,000 rows in less than a second.

Using the Fifth Input in Table.Group() Based on One Value

Consider the first example of this chapter and calculate the total sales per month.

Note The data in this example is provided in an Excel file titled `09 Using the Fifth Input in Table.Group Based on one Value.xlsx`.

In this case, if you apply the grouping directly based on the Month column, which includes null values, you will encounter the result shown in Figure 6-42.

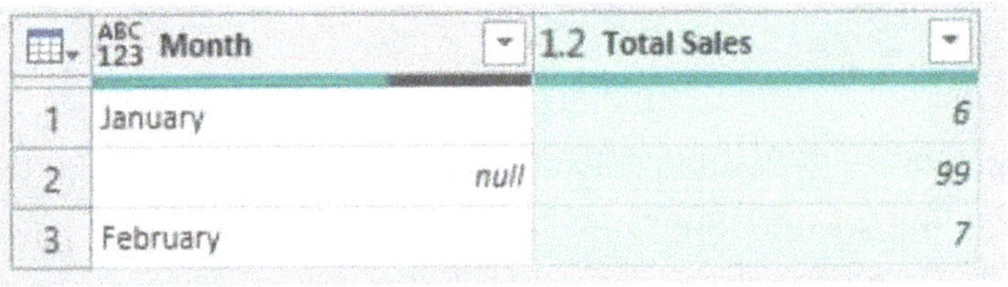

	Month	1.2 Total Sales
1	January	6
2	null	99
3	February	7

Figure 6-42. Calculation for total sales per month

To solve this problem, you must first replace the null value and then use the Group By command, or apply the Group By command directly by using its fifth argument. Both solutions are covered in this section.

CHAPTER 6 GROUPING ROWS WITH TABLE.GROUP()

Solution 1: Using Fill Down Followed by Table.Group()

In this approach, select the Month column, then go to the Transform tab and choose the Fill Down command. This will replace any null values in the column with the value from the row above it, ensuring that each row has a valid month value. You'll see the result shown in Figure 6-43.

#	Month	Week	Product	Colour	Quantity
1	January	W1	A	Black	6
2	January	W1	B	Blue	9
3	January	W1	B	Yellow	2
4	January	W2	A	Black	6
5	January	W2	B	Red	7
6	January	W2	C	Red	5
7	January	W3	B	Yellow	13
8	January	W3	B	Red	3
9	January	W4	A	Blue	7
10	January	W4	C	Red	6
11	February	W1	A	Yellow	7
12	February	W2	A	Red	8
13	February	W3	B	Black	10
14	February	W3	C	Blue	14
15	February	W4	D	Red	9

Figure 6-43. *Using Fill Down*

Now that all cells contain valid values, applying the Group By command using the settings shown in Figure 6-44 will effectively solve the problem.

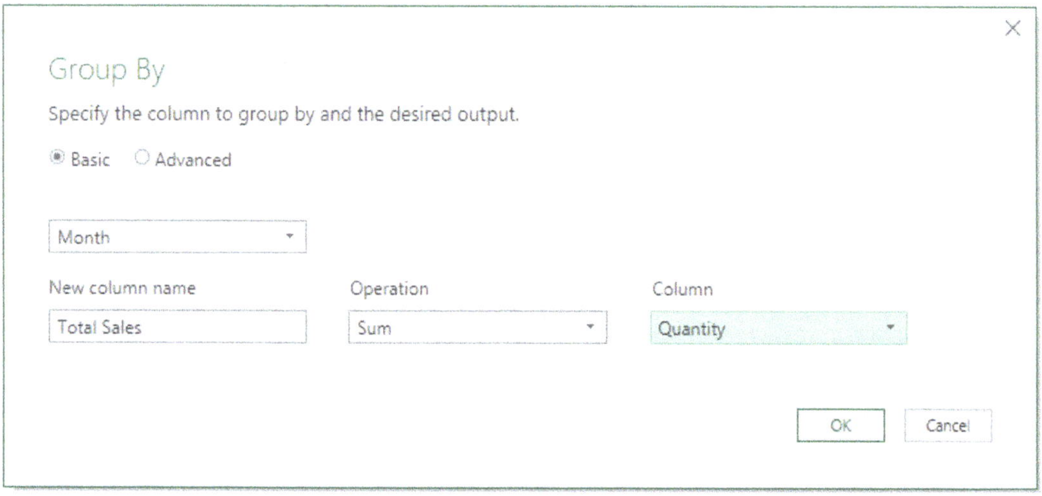

Figure 6-44. *Setting for Group By*

341

CHAPTER 6   GROUPING ROWS WITH TABLE.GROUP()

Solution 2: Using Table.Group() Directly

In this alternative approach, you use the fifth argument of the `Table.Group()` function.

> **Note** This solution is not recommended for this type of problem. Instead, the previous solution is a better approach. However, this method is included to help you become more familiar with the fifth argument of the `Table.Group()` function, which is used in later examples.

By examining the table, it seems like a good approach to start grouping from the first row and include all subsequent rows in the same group until encountering a row where the Month column contains a non-null value. When reaching such a row, you should close the previous group and start a new one. This is exactly what this example aims to achieve, using the fifth argument of the `Table.Group()` function.

Instead of writing all the formula manual, you'll use the UI and then modify its resulting formula. Select the Month column and apply the Group By command. Set the New column name to Total Sales. Select Sum as the operation and choose Quantity as the column. This will generate the following formula in the formula bar and results in Figure 6-45.

```
= Table.Group(Source, {"Month"}, {{"Total Sales", each List.
Sum([Quantity]), type number}})
```

#	Month	Total Sales
1	January	6
2	null	99
3	February	7

Figure 6-45. Calculation for total sales per month

As you start grouping from the first row and want to group the consecutive rows, change the grouping logic to local by entering 0 as the fourth input of the previous formula. The result will change to Figure 6-46.

CHAPTER 6   GROUPING ROWS WITH TABLE.GROUP()

	Month	Total Sales
1	January	6
2	null	58
3	February	7
4	null	41

Figure 6-46. *Changing the group kind to local*

Now, you can use the fifth argument in the form of (s, c) => f(s, c). In this example, since you set the fourth argument to 0 (indicating local grouping), you can define f(s, c) to return either 0 or 1.

As shown in Figure 6-47, at the first step, the first row is represented by s, and the next row is represented by c. The function f(s, c) is then calculated.

- If f(s, c) = 0, the two rows are combined into the same group. For the next iteration, s remains fixed, and c moves to the next row, as illustrated in Figure 6-48.

- If f(s, c) = 1, the current group is closed (containing only the first row), and s and c are both updated to start a new group, as shown in Figure 6-49.

	Month	Week	Product	Colour	Quantity
1	January	W1	A	Black	6
2	null	W1	B	Blue	9
3	null	W1	B	Yellow	2
4	null	W2	A	Black	6
5	null	W2	B	Red	7
6	null	W2	C	Red	5
7	null	W3	B	Yellow	13
8	null	W3	B	Red	3
9	null	W4	A	Blue	7
10	null	W4	C	Red	6
11	February	W1	A	Yellow	7

Figure 6-47. *Beginning of grouping*

343

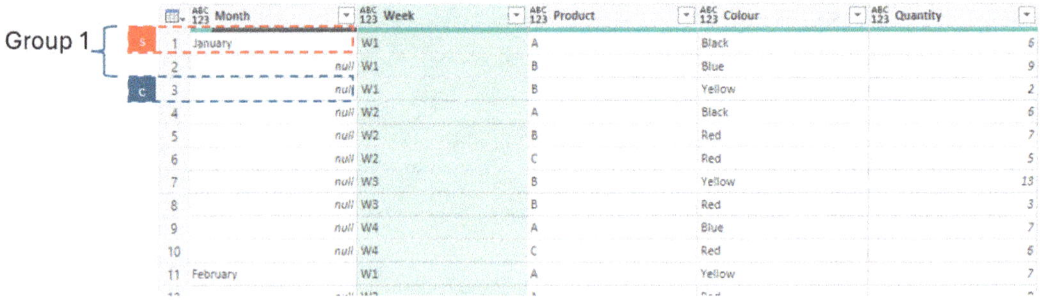

CHAPTER 6 GROUPING ROWS WITH TABLE.GROUP()

Figure 6-48. Second iteration if f(s,c) results in 0

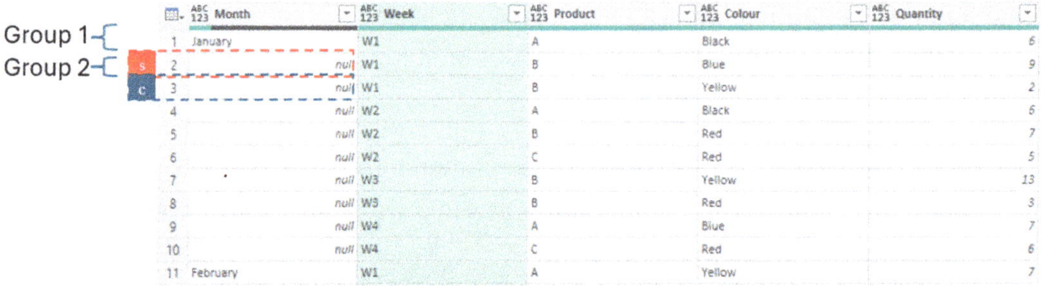

Figure 6-49. Second iteration if f(s,c) results in 1

Based on this explanation, the algorithm starts from the state shown in Figure 6-47 and the first group should continue until c reaches the row corresponding to the next month (row #11). To achieve this, f(s, c) should return 0 as long as c has not yet reached a row where the Month column contains a non-null value. In other words, grouping should continue until c[Month] <> null.

However, since f(s, c) must return 0 (to continue grouping) or 1 (to stop the current group and create a new one), you need to convert the Boolean expression c[Month] <> null, which evaluates to true or false, into a numeric value.

To achieve this conversion, you can use the Number.From() function by rewriting the formula as Number.From(c[Month] <> null), converting true to 1 and false to 0.

As you determined the f(s,c) is Number.From(c[Month] <> null), the Table.Group() formula can be rewritten as the following formula, which solves the problem and results in Figure 6-50:

```
= Table.Group(Source,
    {"Month"},
    {{"Total Sales", each List.Sum([Quantity]) }},
```

CHAPTER 6　GROUPING ROWS WITH TABLE.GROUP()

```
0,
(s,c)=>Number.From(c[Month]<>null))
```

	Month	1.2 Total Sales
1	January	64
2	February	48

Figure 6-50. *Using the fifth argument*

Note Based on the explanation in the previous example, as you use just a column for grouping, instead of writing its name as a {"Month"} list in the second argument, you can write it as "Month" text. By doing this, s and c are not in type record anymore and they are simply text. The formula can be also rewritten as follows, which leads to the same results:

```
= Table.Group(Source,
      "Month",
      {{"Total Sales", each List.Sum([Quantity]) }},
      0,
      (s,c)=>Number.From(c[Month<>,null))
```

On the other hand, you can also use Value.Comparer() in this formula.

```
= Table.Group(Source,
      "Month",
      {{"Total Sales", each List.Sum([Quantity]) }},
      0,
      (s,c)=>Value.Compare(y,null))
```

CHAPTER 6   GROUPING ROWS WITH TABLE.GROUP()

Transforming Tables

Consider the Source table, which includes the customer information shown in Table 6-9. For each customer, their data—name, family, phone, and website—is provided across four rows. Transform this table so that each customer has a single row with four columns: Name, Family, Phone, and Website.

Table 6-9. Source: Customer info

Info	Info2
Name	John
Family	Doe
Phone	555-1234
Website	www.example.com
Name	Jane
Family	Smith
Phone	555-9012
Website	www.anotherexample.com
Name	Alex
Family	Johnson
Phone	-
Website	WWW.ThirdExample.Com
Name	Emily
Family	-
Phone	-
Website	www.thirdexample.com

Note   The data in this example is provided in an Excel file titled 10 Table Transformations .xlsx.

CHAPTER 6 GROUPING ROWS WITH TABLE.GROUP()

In this question, four rows are provided per customer, so you can use the `Table.Split()` function to split the Source table into multiple smaller tables, with each table containing the information for one customer. Each sub-table will include four rows (name, family, phone, and website). On the formula bar, click *fx* and write the following formula in it:

= Table.Split(Source,4)

This will result in a list containing four items, as shown in Figure 6-51.

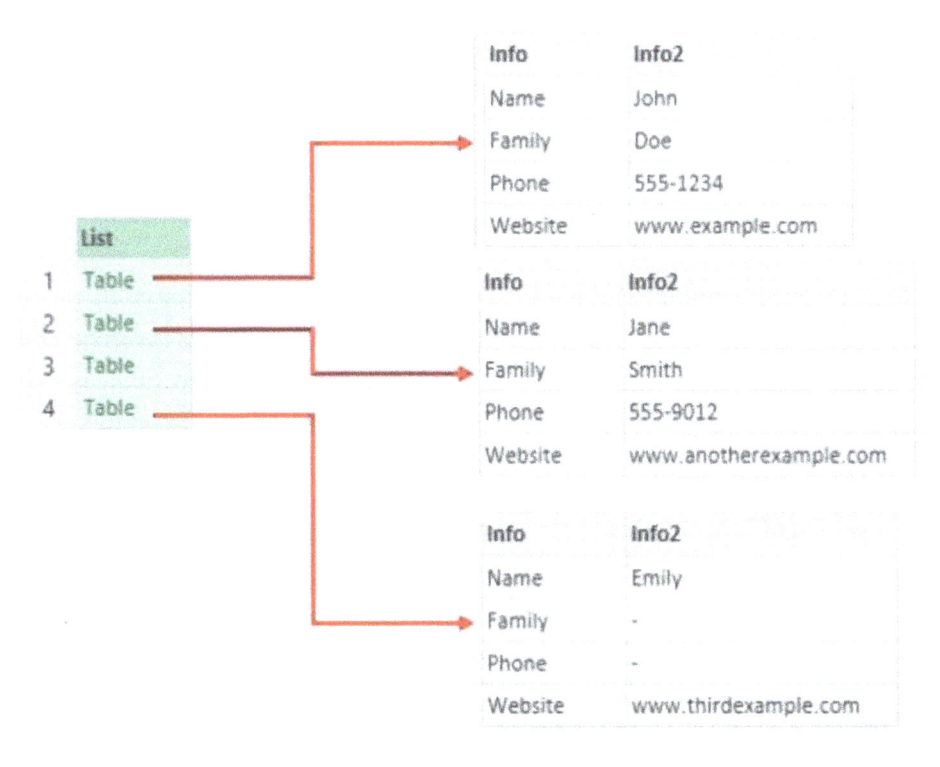

Figure 6-51. The result of Table.Split()

The previous step results in a list, including four sublists. Each sublist includes a table for the information of a customer. It would be a good idea to transpose every single in each sublist. To modify items in a list, you can use `List.Transform()`. Rewriting the previous formula as the following achieves the desired result, as shown in Figure 6-52:

= List.Transform(Table.Split(Source,4),
      each Table.Transpose(_))

CHAPTER 6   GROUPING ROWS WITH TABLE.GROUP()

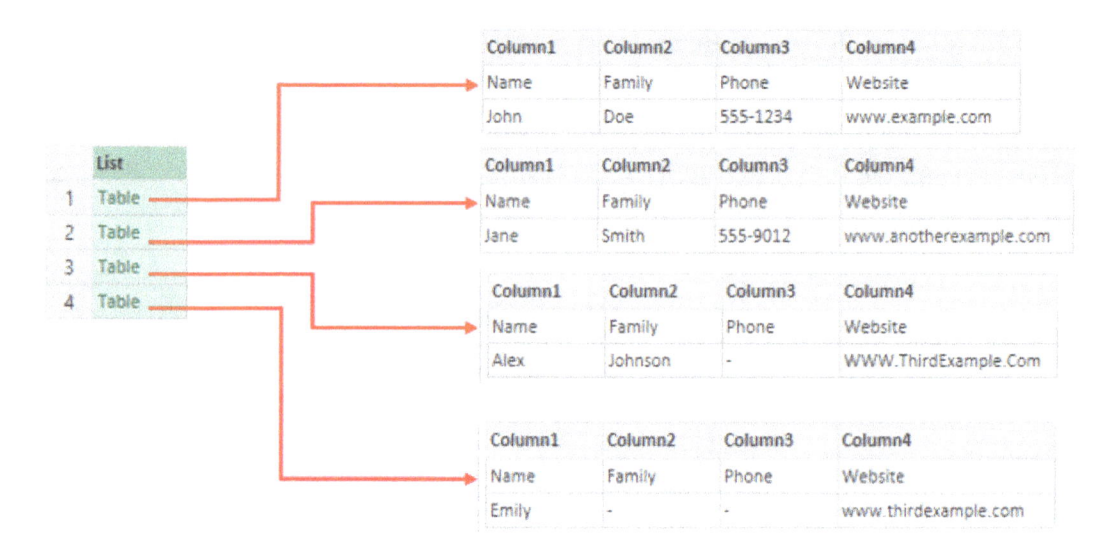

Figure 6-52. The result of List.Transform()

In the previous formula, all tables are transposed, but in addition to transposing them, you also need to promote the first row of the resulting tables as headers. These two tasks can be combined into a single step by modifying the previous formula as follows, ensuring that the first row of each transposed table is promoted to a header. The result is shown in Figure 6-53.

```
= List.Transform(Table.Split(Source,4),
      each Table.PromoteHeaders(Table.Transpose(_)))
```

Figure 6-53. The result of promoting the headers after transformation

CHAPTER 6 GROUPING ROWS WITH TABLE.GROUP()

Now it is time to convert the results into a table. You do this by selecting the To Table command from the Transform tab. This step converts the list into a structured table, leading to the final result shown in Figure 6-54.

Figure 6-54. Converting the result into a table

In the next step, expand column 1 to combine the promoted sub-tables into a single table with the desired format. This will result in a table where each row represents a customer, and the columns include name, family, phone, and website, as shown in Figure 6-55.

Figure 6-55. Expanding column 1

Note Instead of using the `List.Transform()` function to solve this problem, you can use the `Table.FromList()` function, as shown in the following formula. The key difference is that `Table.FromList()` returns a table (instead of a list), and it allows you to add multiple columns to the resulting table in a single step.

```
=Table.FromList(
    Table.Split(Source,4),
    each {Table.PromoteHeaders(Table.Transpose(_))})
```

349

CHAPTER 6   GROUPING ROWS WITH TABLE.GROUP()

Transforming Tables Within Table.Group()

Transform the Source table, provided in Table 6-10, into a new format with four columns: Name, Family, Phone, and Website. Ensure that each customer's information is organized into a single row. Note that the row related to each new customer starts with the attribute related to Name.

Table 6-10. Source: People Info

Attribute	Value
Name	John
Family	Doe
Phone	555-1234
Website	www.example.com
Name	Jane
Family	Smith
Phone	555-5678
Website	www.anotherexample.com
Name	Alex
Family	Johnson
Name	Emily
Website	www.thirdexample.com

Note   The data in this example is provided in an Excel file titled 11 Transformations within Table.Group().xlsx.

This table is similar to the one presented in the previous question, with the key difference being that there is no fixed number of rows for each customer. As a result, you cannot use Table.Split() to separate the information for each customer. Therefore, you need to find an alternative solution to handle this dynamic grouping.

CHAPTER 6   GROUPING ROWS WITH TABLE.GROUP()

Since the row of each customer starts with the Name field, you can use the fifth argument in the Table.Group() function to separate the rows related each customer and solve this problem. To solve this problem, group the table rows based on the Attribute column using the settings provided in Figure 6-56. This will result in Figure 6-57.

Figure 6-56. Grouping settings

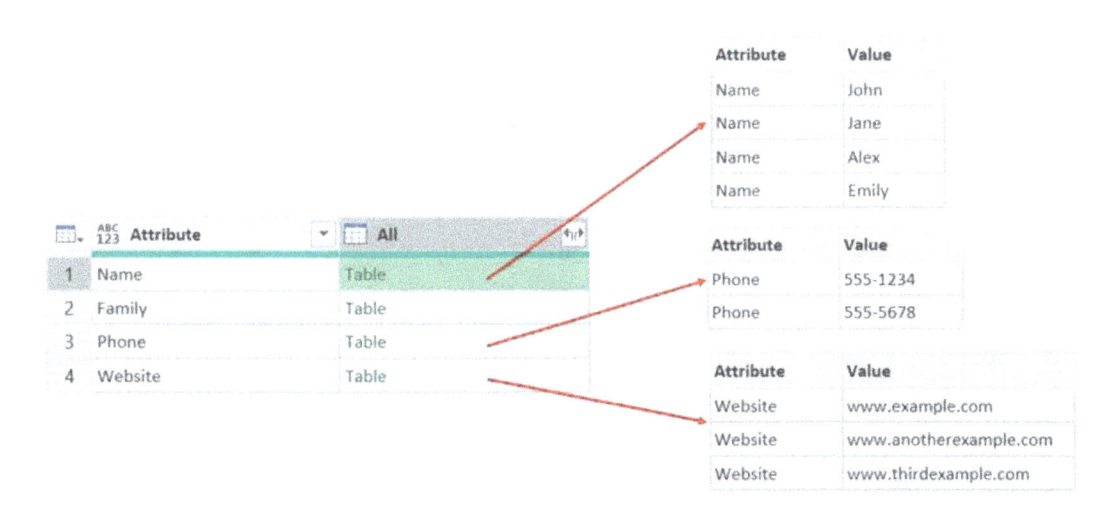

Figure 6-57. The result of grouping

The initial step generates the following formula in the formula bar:

= Table.Group(Source, {"Attribute"}, {{"All", each _, type table [Attribute=text, Value=text]}})

351

That formula can be simplified to the following one:

```
= Table.Group(Source, {"Attribute"}, {"All", each _})
```

Similar to Example 6-7, in this case, grouping will start from the first row and continue until a row with a value of Name in the Attribute column is reached. In the previous formula, enter the fourth argument as 0. To define the fifth argument in the format (s, c) => f(s, c), s initially represents the first row, and c represents the second row, as the first and second row are related to the same customer—in this case f(s,c) should result in 0 to continue grouping.

In the next iteration, s still represents the first row of the table, and c represents the third row, which is still related to the information of the first customer. Therefore, f(s, c) should return 0.

The f(s, c) should continue to return 0 for the next rows until c represents the fifth row, which is related to the next customer. At this point, f(s, c) should return 1, as it encounters the Name value in the Attribute column, signaling the start of a new group. The first group should continue until s[Attribute]="Name".

In another word, to extract all the information about the first customer, f(s, c) should return 0. That indicates that the grouping should continue until a row with the Name value in the Attribute column is encountered. At that point, the grouping should stop, and a new group can be created. The criteria for closing this group for a customer and creating a new group for the next customer can be defined as c[Attribute]="Name".

Based on this explanation, use the (s,c)=>Number.From(c[Attribute]="Name") formula as the comparer in the fifth argument of the previous formula, as shown in the following formula. This results in Figure 6-58.

```
= Table.Group(
    Source,
    {"Attribute"},
    {"All", each _},
    0,
    (s,c)=>Number.From(c[Attribute]="Name"))
```

CHAPTER 6 GROUPING ROWS WITH TABLE.GROUP()

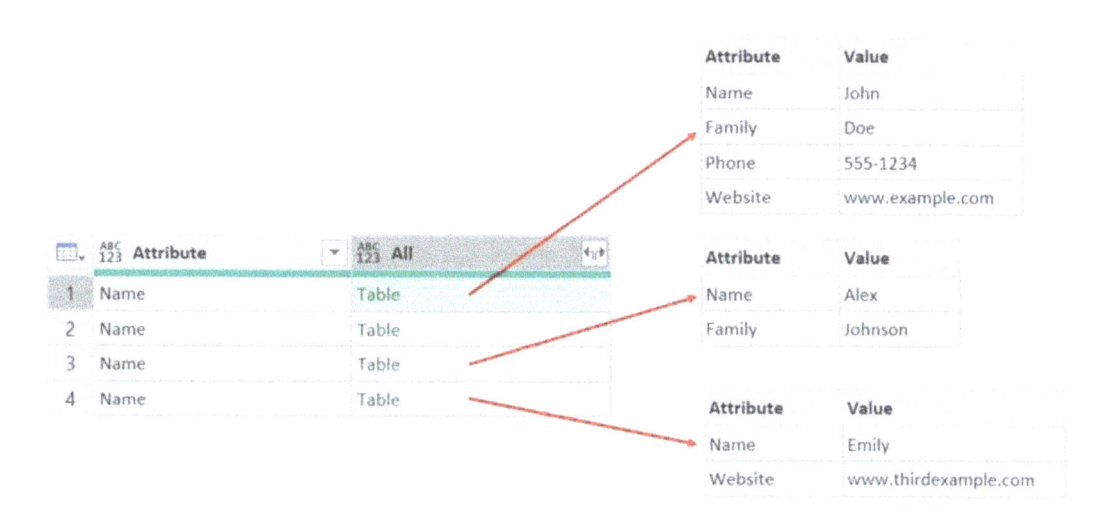

Figure 6-58. The result of grouping

Now the information of each customer is separated, and to transform its information into the right shape, you can use some functions similar to the ones used in the previous example.

In the previous formula, the second argument for the All column is defined as each _, which results in the information of each customer in a table. To transpose the values within each table in the All column, you can use the Table.Transpose() function and rewrite the formula as follows:

```
= Table.Group(5
    Source,
    {"Attribute"},
    {"All", each Table.Transpose(_)},
    0,
    (s,c)=>Number.From(c[Attribute]="Name")
```

CHAPTER 6   GROUPING ROWS WITH TABLE.GROUP()

This will transpose the values in each table within the All column, resulting in Figure 6-59.

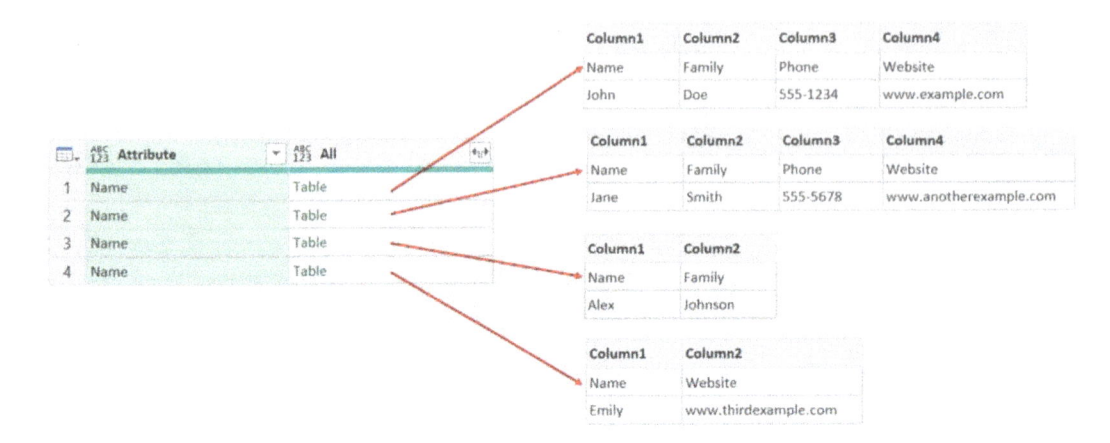

Figure 6-59. The result of adding Table.Transpose()

Based on the result, each sub-table includes two rows: one for the headers and one for the values. To promote the first row to headers and use the second row as values, add the Table.PromoteHeaders() function to the previous formula and rewrite it:

```
= Table.Group(
    Source,
    {"Attribute"},
    {"All", each Table.PromoteHeaders(Table.Transpose(_))},
    0,
    (s,c)=>Number.From(c[Attribute]="Name")
```

This will promote the first row to headers and keep the second row as values, resulting in Figure 6-60.

CHAPTER 6 GROUPING ROWS WITH TABLE.GROUP()

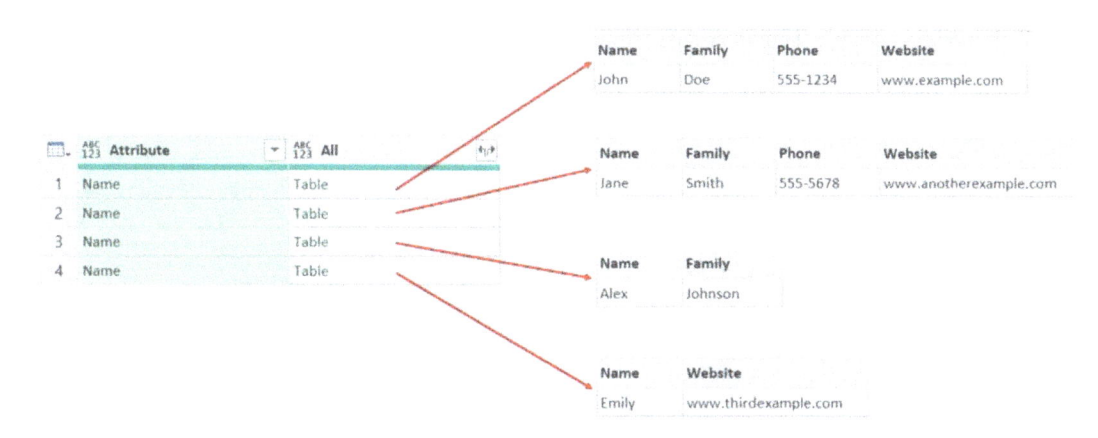

Figure 6-60. The result of permuting headers in sub-tables

The problem is almost solved. To finalize the transformation, delete the Attribute column and expand the All column. This will result in Figure 6-61.

Figure 6-61. The final result

Grouping Consecutive Dates

Consider the sales data shown in Table 6-11. Group all consecutive dates and provide a report of total sales for each group of consecutive dates. Note by loading this data into the Power Query, the values in the column Date use the `DateTime` type.

CHAPTER 6　GROUPING ROWS WITH TABLE.GROUP()

Table 6-11. Source: Historical Sales

Date	Quantity
25/06/2024	84
26/06/2024	23
27/06/2024	87
28/06/2024	26
30/06/2024	67
2/07/2024	42
3/07/2024	40
4/07/2024	14
5/07/2024	69
6/07/2024	32
7/07/2024	44
8/07/2024	56
9/07/2024	25
11/07/2024	15
12/07/2024	84
13/07/2024	25
14/07/2024	46
15/07/2024	38
17/07/2024	45
18/07/2024	76
19/07/2024	44

Note　The data in this example is provided in an Excel file titled `12 Grouping Consecutive Dates.xlsx`.

CHAPTER 6   GROUPING ROWS WITH TABLE.GROUP()

Two different solutions are provided for this problem: one using a helper column and one without it.

Solution 1: Using a Helper Column

In the first solution, you add an index column starting at 1. Then add a Custom Column called Helper Column, using the following formula in the Custom Column window to achieve Figure 6-62.

=Number.From([Date])-[Index]

	Date	Quantity	Index	Helper Column
1	25/06/2024 12:00:00 AM	84	1	45467
2	26/06/2024 12:00:00 AM	23	2	45467
3	27/06/2024 12:00:00 AM	87	3	45467
4	28/06/2024 12:00:00 AM	26	4	45467
5	30/06/2024 12:00:00 AM	67	5	45468
6	2/07/2024 12:00:00 AM	42	6	45469
7	3/07/2024 12:00:00 AM	40	7	45469
8	4/07/2024 12:00:00 AM	14	8	45469
9	5/07/2024 12:00:00 AM	69	9	45469
10	6/07/2024 12:00:00 AM	32	10	45469
11	7/07/2024 12:00:00 AM	44	11	45469
12	8/07/2024 12:00:00 AM	56	12	45469
13	9/07/2024 12:00:00 AM	25	13	45469
14	11/07/2024 12:00:00 AM	15	14	45470
15	12/07/2024 12:00:00 AM	84	15	45470
16	13/07/2024 12:00:00 AM	25	16	45470
17	14/07/2024 12:00:00 AM	46	17	45470
18	15/07/2024 12:00:00 AM	38	18	45470
19	17/07/2024 12:00:00 AM	45	19	45471
20	18/07/2024 12:00:00 AM	76	20	45471
21	19/07/2024 12:00:00 AM	44	21	45471

Figure 6-62. *The result of adding the custom column*

The helper column for consecutive dates contains the same value for each group of consecutive dates, and you can use this column to group the rows. Select this column, right-click it, and apply the settings shown in Figure 6-63. When you click OK, you'll get Figure 6-64.

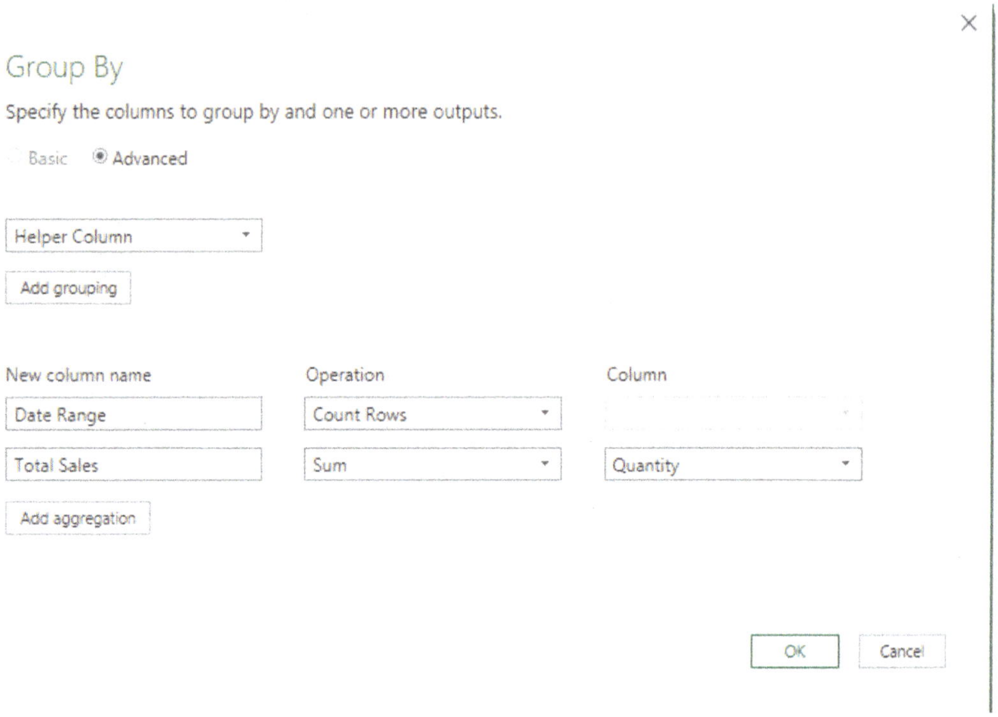

CHAPTER 6 GROUPING ROWS WITH TABLE.GROUP()

Figure 6-63. Settings for Table.Group()

Helper Column	Date Range	Total Sales
1	45467	4	220
2	45468	1	67
3	45469	8	322
4	45470	5	208
5	45471	3	165

Figure 6-64. The result of grouping

The previous step leads to the following simplified formula:

```
= Table.Group(
    #"Added Custom",
    {"Helper Column"},
    {{"Date Range", each Table.RowCount(_)},
    {"Total Sales", each List.Sum([Quantity])}})
```

CHAPTER 6 GROUPING ROWS WITH TABLE.GROUP()

At this step, the values in the Date Range column are calculated using `Table.RowCount(_)`, which returns the number of rows for each group of consecutive dates. To replace these values with the actual date range, modify this part of the formula with the following updated formula. This will result in Figure 6-65, and by removing the helper column, the problem will be solved.

```
each DateTime.ToText(List.First(_[Date]),"yyyy/MM/dd") & " - " & DateTime.ToText(List.Last(_[Date]),"yyyy/MM/dd")
```

Helper Column	Date Range	Total Sales
45467	2024/06/25 - 2024/06/28	220
45468	2024/06/30 - 2024/06/30	67
45469	2024/07/02 - 2024/07/09	322
45470	2024/07/11 - 2024/07/15	208
45471	2024/07/17 - 2024/07/19	165

Figure 6-65. The final result of grouping

Solution 2: Using the Fifth Argument

Although I recommend using the previous solution for similar problems, the problem can also be solved without using a helper column. To do so, you need to identify from which row a new group should be created.

By examining the data, it is clear that the first group starts at the first row and continues until the fifth row. However, the fifth row does not belong to the first group, as there is a gap between it and the data in the previous row. In other words, the table does not include the date related to the previous day of 2024/06/30.

Therefore, for each date, if the table does not include the date that corresponds to the previous day, a new grouping should begin. To solve this problem, you initially need to determine which dates aren't mentioned in the table.

To extract missing dates, you first need to determine all the dates within the surveyed period. You can use `List.Min(Source[Date])`, `List.Max(Source[Date])`, and `Duration.Days(List.Max(Source[Date])-List.Min(Source[Date]))`, respectively, to extract minimum date, maximum date, and duration between the minimum and maximum date.

After clicking *fx* in the formula bar, write the following formula to list all the dates within the surveyed period, as shown in Figure 6-66.

```
= List.DateTimes(
    List.Min(Source[Date]),
    Duration.Days(List.Max(Source[Date]) - List.Min(Source[Date])),
    #duration(1, 0, 0, 0)
)
```

	List
1	25/06/2024 12:00:00 AM
2	26/06/2024 12:00:00 AM
3	27/06/2024 12:00:00 AM
4	28/06/2024 12:00:00 AM
5	29/06/2024 12:00:00 AM
6	30/06/2024 12:00:00 AM
7	1/07/2024 12:00:00 AM
8	2/07/2024 12:00:00 AM
9	3/07/2024 12:00:00 AM
10	4/07/2024 12:00:00 AM
11	5/07/2024 12:00:00 AM
12	6/07/2024 12:00:00 AM
13	7/07/2024 12:00:00 AM
14	8/07/2024 12:00:00 AM
15	9/07/2024 12:00:00 AM
16	10/07/2024 12:00:00 AM
17	11/07/2024 12:00:00 AM
18	12/07/2024 12:00:00 AM
19	13/07/2024 12:00:00 AM
20	14/07/2024 12:00:00 AM
21	15/07/2024 12:00:00 AM
22	16/07/2024 12:00:00 AM
23	17/07/2024 12:00:00 AM
24	18/07/2024 12:00:00 AM

Figure 6-66. *List of all the dates and times*

To extract the missing dates, rewrite the previous formula using the following updated version, which results in Figure 6-67.

CHAPTER 6   GROUPING ROWS WITH TABLE.GROUP()

```
=List.Difference(
  List.DateTimes(
    List.Min(Source[Date]),
    Duration.Days(List.Max(Source[Date]) - List.Min(Source[Date])),
    #duration(1, 0, 0, 0)
  ),
  Source[Date]
)
```

	List
1	29/06/2024 12:00:00 AM
2	1/07/2024 12:00:00 AM
3	10/07/2024 12:00:00 AM
4	16/07/2024 12:00:00 AM

Figure 6-67. Extracting the missing dates

Let's call the list resulting from the previous formula MissingDates and define the custom comparer as (s, c) => f(s, c), which works as follows.

As shown in Figure 6-68, s initially represents the first row, and c represents the second row. Since MissingDates does not include the day before the date in the second row (represented by c), f(s, c) should return 0, meaning that the second row becomes part of the first group.

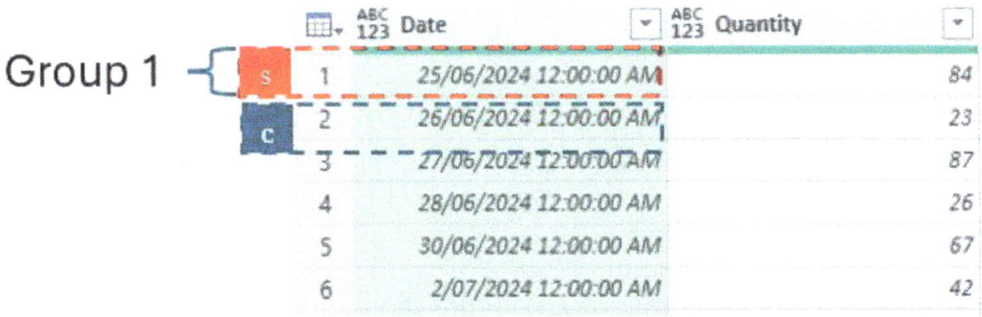

Figure 6-68. Beginning of grouping

Then, as shown in Figure 6-69, in the next iteration, c represents the third row. Again, as MissingDates does not include the day before the date represented by c,

361

CHAPTER 6 GROUPING ROWS WITH TABLE.GROUP()

f(s, c) should return 0. This process continues until c reaches the fifth row, as shown in Figure 6-70. At this point, the date in c is 30/06/2024 12:00:00 AM. One day before this date is 29/06/2024 12:00:00 AM, which is in the MissingDates list. So, here, f(s, c) should return 1, signaling the closure of the first group and the start of the next group. See Figure 6-71.

Figure 6-69. Second iteration of the grouping

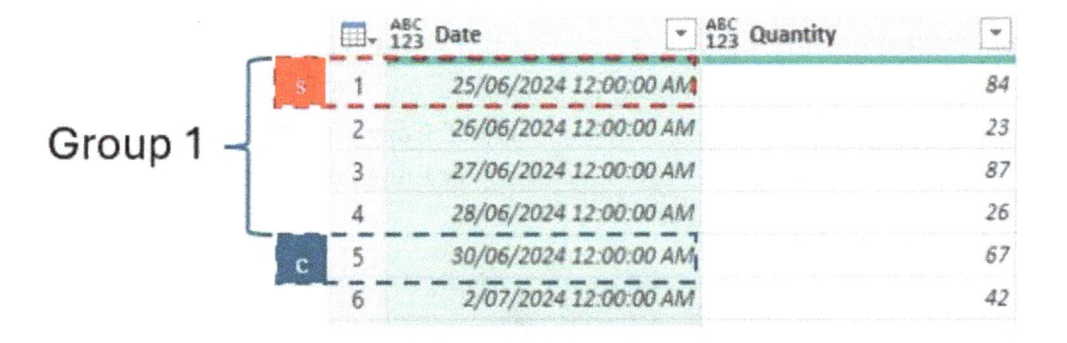

Figure 6-70. Fourth iteration of the grouping

CHAPTER 6 GROUPING ROWS WITH TABLE.GROUP()

	Date	Quantity
1	25/06/2024 12:00:00 AM	84
2	26/06/2024 12:00:00 AM	23
3	27/06/2024 12:00:00 AM	87
4	28/06/2024 12:00:00 AM	26
5	30/06/2024 12:00:00 AM	67
6	2/07/2024 12:00:00 AM	42

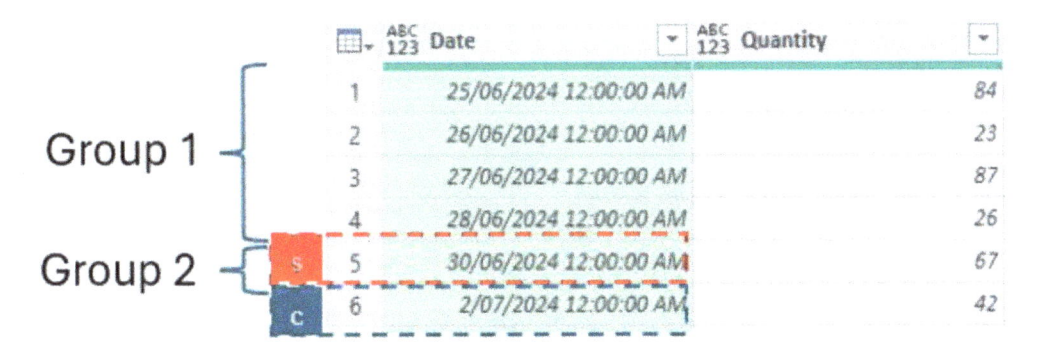

Group 1: rows 1–4. Group 2: rows 5–6.

Figure 6-71. Fifth iteration of the grouping

To implement this, the grouping should close if the formula List.Contains(MissingDates, one day before c[Date]) evaluates to true. This can be written as List.Contains(MissingDates, c[Date] - #duration(1, 0, 0, 0)). Thus, the fifth argument of the Table.Group() function will be (s, c) => Number.From(List.Contains(MissingDates, c[Date] - #duration(1, 0, 0, 0))).

By replacing MissingDates with its formula and incorporating it into the fifth argument of the Table.Group() function, the full formula becomes as follows, which results in Figure 6-72.

```
Table.Group(Source, "Date",
  {{"Date Range",Table.RowCount(_)},
   {"Total Sales", each List.Sum([Quantity])}},
  0,
  (s,c) =>
    Number.From(
      List.Contains(
        List.Difference(
          List.DateTimes(
            List.Min(Source[Date]),
            Duration.Days(List.Max(Source[Date]) - List.Min(Source[Date])),
            #duration(1, 0, 0, 0)
          ),
```

363

CHAPTER 6   GROUPING ROWS WITH TABLE.GROUP()

```
            Source[Date]
        ),
        c - #duration(1, 0, 0, 0)
      )
    )
)
```

	Date	Date Range	Total Sales
1	25/06/2024 12:00:00 AM	4	220
2	30/06/2024 12:00:00 AM	1	67
3	2/07/2024 12:00:00 AM	8	322
4	11/07/2024 12:00:00 AM	5	208
5	17/07/2024 12:00:00 AM	3	165

Figure 6-72. Result of the grouping

Similar to the first solution, the second argument can be modified to display date ranges instead of the number of rows in each group.

Efficiency Tip   Both previously mentioned solutions produce the same result, but their execution times differ significantly. While the first solution solves the problem quickly, the second solution takes around 17 seconds even for a small table with 1,000 rows, which is excessive. So it is recommended to use the first solution.

In case you have to use the second solution, let's check the cause of its slow performance. The delay is caused by the calculation of the MissingDates, which is part of the Table.Group() formula, and will be calculated several times. To improve performance when using such a formula, it's recommended to separate the XXX part into its own step and apply List.Buffer() to it. Rewriting the code in the Advanced Editor, as shown here, reduces the execution time for 1,000 rows to 0.08 seconds and for 10,000 rows to 4.7 seconds (the first solution still outperforms it by solving the 10,000-row table in less than a second).

```
let
Source = Excel.CurrentWorkbook(){[Name = "Question"]}[Content],
XXX = List.Buffer(
        List.Difference(
      List.DateTimes(
        List.Min(Source[Date]),
        Duration.Days(List.Max(Source[Date]) - List.Min(Source[Date])),
         Source[Date]
    ),
    each _ + #duration(1, 0, 0, 0)
  )
),
GroupBy = Table.Group(
  Source,
  "Date",
  {
    {
      "Date Range",
      each DateTime.ToText(List.First(_[Date]), "yyyy/MM/dd")
        & " - "
        & DateTime.ToText(List.Last(_[Date]), "yyyy/MM/dd")
    },
    {"Total Sales", each List.Sum([Quantity])}
  },
  0,
  (x, y) => Number.From(List.Contains(XXX, y-#duration(1, 0, 0, 0)))
  )
in
  GroupBy
```

CHAPTER 6 GROUPING ROWS WITH TABLE.GROUP()

Using the Fifth Input in Table.Group Based on Two Values

Consider the Source table shown in Table 6-12. Group the rows, starting at the first row, under the condition that the difference between the first and last date of each group is fewer than ten days.

Table 6-12. *Source: Historical Sales*

Date	Quantity
6/03/2024	32
7/04/2024	44
9/04/2024	25
12/04/2024	67
25/05/2024	84
26/06/2024	23
27/06/2024	87
28/06/2024	26
2/07/2024	42
3/07/2024	40
4/07/2024	14
5/07/2024	69
8/07/2024	56
11/07/2024	15
12/07/2024	84
13/07/2024	25
14/07/2024	46
15/07/2024	38
17/07/2024	45
18/07/2024	76
19/07/2024	44

CHAPTER 6   GROUPING ROWS WITH TABLE.GROUP()

Note The data in this example is provided in an Excel file titled `13 Using the Fifth Input in Table.Group Based on Two Values.xlsx`.

You can solve this problem using the fifth argument of the `Table.Group()` function in the form of `(s, c) => f(s, c)`. However, this problem is different from the previous ones that were solved using the fifth argument of `Table.Group()`. In those cases, the condition for stopping the current group was determined based solely on the row represented by `c`. In this case, however, you need to compare the starting date and the ending date within the group to decide whether to continue the current group or start a new one.

Consider the first iteration of grouping shown in Figure 6-73, where `s[Date]` and `c[Date]` should be compared. If the difference between these dates is fewer than ten days, `f(s, c)` should return 0. Otherwise, it should return 1 to close the current group and create the next one. To calculate the difference between these two dates, you can use the `Duration.Days()` function as `Duration.Days(c[Date] - s[Date])`. To compare the result with 10, the formula is `Duration.Days(c[Date] - s[Date]) >= 10`.

However, as mentioned earlier, the comparer used with the local grouping should return 0 or 1. To convert the Boolean result (`True` or `False`) into a 1 or 0, use the `Number.From()` function. The entire comparer can be written as `(s,c)=> Number.From(Duration.Days(c[Date] - s[Date]) >= 10)`. See Figure 6-73.

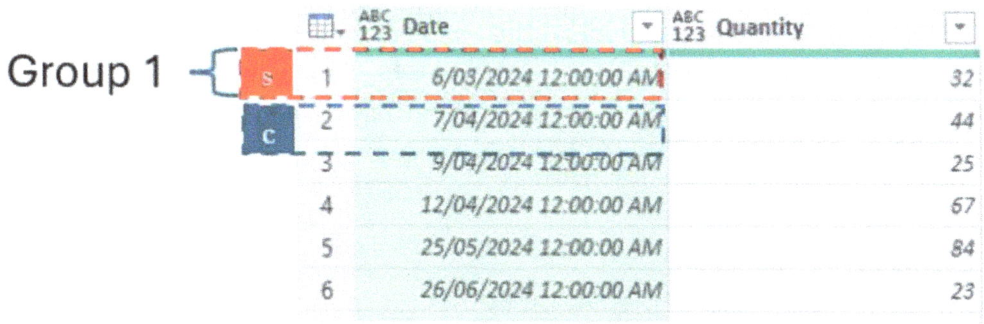

Figure 6-73. The first iteration of grouping

CHAPTER 6   GROUPING ROWS WITH TABLE.GROUP()

Based on this introduction and using the source table, select the Group By command. Then, apply the settings shown in Figure 6-74 and click OK, which will result in the following formula in the formula bar:

```
= Table.Group(Source, {"Date"}, {{"Total Sales", each List.Sum([Quantity]),
type number}})
```

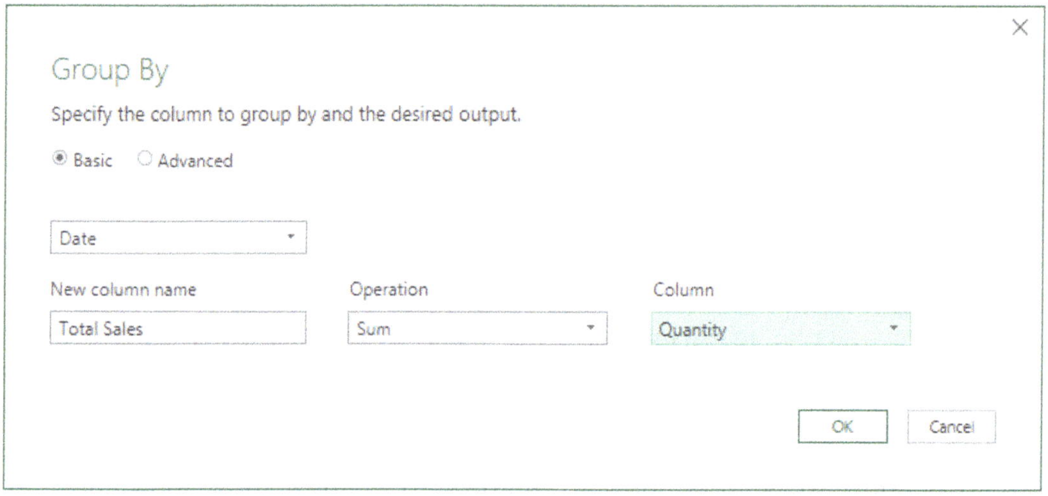

Figure 6-74. Grouping settings

In the generated formula, insert 0 as the fourth argument and use the comparer defined earlier as the fifth argument to reach the following formula. This results in Figure 6-75.

```
= Table.Group(Source, {"Date"}, {{"Total Sales", each List.Sum([Quantity]),
type number}},0,(s,c)=> Number.From(Duration.Days(c[Date] -
s[Date]) >= 10))
```

#	Date	Total Sales
1	6/03/2024 12:00:00 AM	32
2	7/04/2024 12:00:00 AM	136
3	25/05/2024 12:00:00 AM	84
4	26/06/2024 12:00:00 AM	301
5	8/07/2024 12:00:00 AM	309
6	18/07/2024 12:00:00 AM	120

Figure 6-75. The result of revised formula

In the resulting table, the Date column only shows the starting date of each group. To display the range of dates for each group, the previous formula can be rewritten as follows, which results in Figure 6-76.

```
= Table.Group(Source, {"Date"}, {{"Total Sales", each List.Sum([Quantity]),
type number},{"Date Range", each DateTime.ToText(List.First(_[Date]),
"yyyy/MM/dd") & " - " & DateTime.ToText(List.Last(_[Date]),"yyyy/MM/
dd")}},0,(s,c)=> Number.From(Duration.Days(c[Date] - s[Date]) >= 10))
```

Date	Total Sales	Date Range
6/03/2024 12:00:00 AM	32	2024/03/06 - 2024/03/06
7/04/2024 12:00:00 AM	136	2024/04/07 - 2024/04/12
25/05/2024 12:00:00 AM	84	2024/05/25 - 2024/05/25
26/06/2024 12:00:00 AM	301	2024/06/26 - 2024/07/05
8/07/2024 12:00:00 AM	309	2024/07/08 - 2024/07/17
18/07/2024 12:00:00 AM	120	2024/07/18 - 2024/07/19

Figure 6-76. The final result

Using the Fifth Input in Table.Group Based on All the Group items

Consider the historical complaint values shown in the Source table in Table 6-13. All the complaints need to be inspected by different people, and each person can inspect five complaints (No.). Group the rows of the table, from the top, into different groups, each including a maximum of five complaints (the sum of the values on the Complaint No. column in each group should be less than or equal to 5).

CHAPTER 6　GROUPING ROWS WITH TABLE.GROUP()

Table 6-13. *Source: Historical Complaint*

Date	Complaint ID	Complaint No.
10/01/2024	C-1	1
25/01/2024	C-2	1
27/01/2024	C-3	2
27/01/2024	C-4	1
10/02/2024	C-5	1
3/03/2024	C-6	4
14/03/2024	C-7	1
11/04/2024	C-8	3
17/05/2024	C-9	1
17/05/2024	C-10	1
1/06/2024	C-11	2
17/06/2024	C-12	1
21/06/2024	C-13	1
24/06/2024	C-14	1
11/07/2024	C-15	1
20/08/2024	C-16	1
22/09/2024	C-17	2
26/09/2024	C-18	1
30/09/2024	C-19	1

Note　The data in this example is provided in an Excel file titled `14 Using the Fifth Input in Table.Group Based on All the Group items.xlsx`.

In the previous example, the rows were grouped based on the first and last row of each group. However, in this example, the grouping logic is determined by all the rows within the group. Despite the difficulty of this problem, it can be solved with the fifth

CHAPTER 6　GROUPING ROWS WITH TABLE.GROUP()

argument of Table.Group(), which allows for more complex grouping logic. The idea is to group the rows from the top row, ensuring that each group contains five or fewer complaints.

As in the previous example, you need to use local grouping and define the fifth argument as (s,c) => f(s,c). However, before you start the solution, consider the second iteration of grouping shown in Figure 6-77.

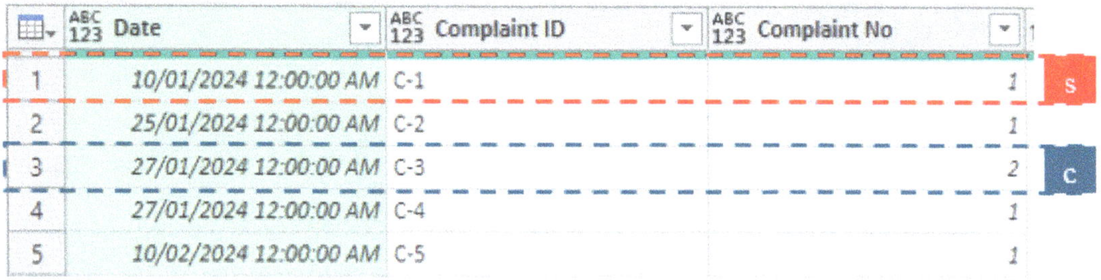

#	Date	Complaint ID	Complaint No	
1	10/01/2024 12:00:00 AM	C-1	1	s
2	25/01/2024 12:00:00 AM	C-2	1	
3	27/01/2024 12:00:00 AM	C-3	2	c
4	27/01/2024 12:00:00 AM	C-4	1	
5	10/02/2024 12:00:00 AM	C-5	1	

Figure 6-77. *Second iteration of grouping*

As presented, to determine the grouping, you need to consider the first three rows, where s represents the first row and c represents the third row. However, you don't have direct access to the rows between these two.

To address this issue and simplify the process, add an index column, which will help you later access the intermediate rows between the starting and ending rows of the group. Select the Index column from the Add Column tab, which creates a new column with sequential numbers starting from 1, as shown in Figure 6-78.

CHAPTER 6   GROUPING ROWS WITH TABLE.GROUP()

	Date	Complaint ID	Complaint No	Index
1	10/01/2024 12:00:00 AM	C-1	1	0
2	25/01/2024 12:00:00 AM	C-2	1	1
3	27/01/2024 12:00:00 AM	C-3	2	2
4	27/01/2024 12:00:00 AM	C-4	1	3
5	10/02/2024 12:00:00 AM	C-5	1	4
6	3/03/2024 12:00:00 AM	C-6	4	5
7	14/03/2024 12:00:00 AM	C-7	1	6
8	11/04/2024 12:00:00 AM	C-8	3	7
9	17/05/2024 12:00:00 AM	C-9	1	8
10	17/05/2024 12:00:00 AM	C-10	1	9
11	1/06/2024 12:00:00 AM	C-11	2	10
12	17/06/2024 12:00:00 AM	C-12	1	11
13	21/06/2024 12:00:00 AM	C-13	1	12
14	24/06/2024 12:00:00 AM	C-14	1	13
15	11/07/2024 12:00:00 AM	C-15	1	14
16	20/08/2024 12:00:00 AM	C-16	1	15
17	22/09/2024 12:00:00 AM	C-17	2	16
18	26/09/2024 12:00:00 AM	C-18	1	17
19	30/09/2024 12:00:00 AM	C-19	1	18

Figure 6-78. *The result of adding an Index column*

After adding this new column, reconsider the second iteration, as shown in Figure 6-79.

	Date	Complaint ID	Complaint No	Index	
1	10/01/2024 12:00:00 AM	C-1	1	0	s
2	25/01/2024 12:00:00 AM	C-2	1	1	
3	27/01/2024 12:00:00 AM	C-3	2	2	c
4	27/01/2024 12:00:00 AM	C-4	1	3	

Figure 6-79. *Second iteration of grouping after adding a custom column*

In this case, s[Index] is 0, which represents the starting row of the grouping, and c[Index] is 2, which represents the ending row for the grouping. To decide about the grouping, you need to extract all the values from the Complain No. column in the Source table, from s[Index] to c[Index]. This can be done using the following formula:

List.Range(Source[Complaint No],s[Index],c[Index]-s[Index]+1)

CHAPTER 6 GROUPING ROWS WITH TABLE.GROUP()

To calculate the sum of complaints, you can rewrite it as follows:

```
List.Sum(List.Range(Source[Complaint No],s[Index],c[Index]-s[Index]+1))
```

Since you have a cap on the number of complaints in each group (five), the formula can be further rewritten as follows:

```
List.Sum(List.Range(Source[Complaint No],s[Index],c[Index]-s[Index]+1))>5
```

Finally, to convert the Boolean value into a 0-1 value, you modify the formula and write the comparer as follows:

```
F(s,c)=>Number.From(List.Sum(List.Range(Source[Complaint No],s[Index],c[Index]-s[Index]+1))>5)
```

You can use this comparer in the Group By to solve the problem. Consider the table after adding the Index column. Right-click the Index column, apply the Group By operation, and choose the All Rows option. The following M-code will then be generated in the formula bar:

```
= Table.Group(#"Added Index", {"Index"}, {{"IDs", each _, type table [Date=datetime, Complaint ID=text, Complaint No=number, Index=number]}})
```

This can be shortened to the following formula:

```
= Table.Group(#"Added Index", "Index", {{"IDs", each }})
```

To revise the grouping criteria, enter 0 in the fourth input and use the defined comparer in the fifth input as follows. This adjustment will result in Figure 6-80, which includes the groups where the complaint number is less than or equal to five.

```
= Table.Group(
      #"Added Index",
      {"Index"},
      {{"IDs", each _}},
      0,
       (s,c)=>Number.From(
                    List.Sum(
                         List.Range(Source,s[Index],c[Index]
                         -s[Index]+1)
                                  )>5))
```

373

CHAPTER 6 GROUPING ROWS WITH TABLE.GROUP()

Figure 6-80. *The result of advanced grouping*

Table 6-14 summarizes the results of each part of the formula in different iterations. Review each iteration for grouping based on this table. In the following steps, Source[Complaint No] refers to the values in the Complaint Number column shown in Figure 6-81.

CHAPTER 6 GROUPING ROWS WITH TABLE.GROUP()

	List
1	1
2	1
3	2
4	1
5	1
6	4
7	1
8	3
9	1
10	1
11	2
12	1
13	1
14	1
15	1
16	1
17	2
18	1
19	1

Figure 6-81. *#"Added Index"[Complaint No]*

Group 1, Step 1:

The second argument of Table.Group() is provided as a list, so s and c in the fifth argument are of type record. Since the list in the second argument of Table.Group() contains only one column name (Index), s and c are both records with a single field named Index. (If the second argument of Table.Group() were written as the text "Index" instead of the list {"Index"}, then s and c would both be of type number.)

Figure 6-82 shows s and c in the first step, where s is the record [Index = 0], and c is the record [Index = 1]. The result of s[Index] is 0 and the result of c[Index] is 1, and c[Index] - s[Index] + 1 is equal to 2.

CHAPTER 6   GROUPING ROWS WITH TABLE.GROUP()

Based on these values, `List.Range(Source[Complaint No], s[Index], c[Index] - s[Index] + 1)` can be rewritten as `List.Range(Source[Complaint No], 0, 1-0+ 1)`, which equals to the first two values from the complaint list (shown on Figure 6-81), which are {1, 1}.

So, `List.Sum(List.Range(Source[Complaint No], s[Index], c[Index] - s[Index] + 1))` in this step is equal to `List.Sum({1,1})`, which is 2. Because the result of `List.Sum()` is not greater than five, the result of `Number.From()` is 0, so the grouping continues, and c moves to the next row. See Figure 6-83.

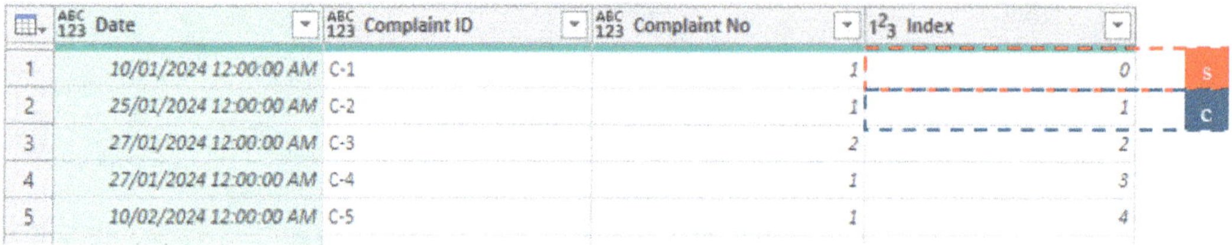

Figure 6-82. The s and c in step 1

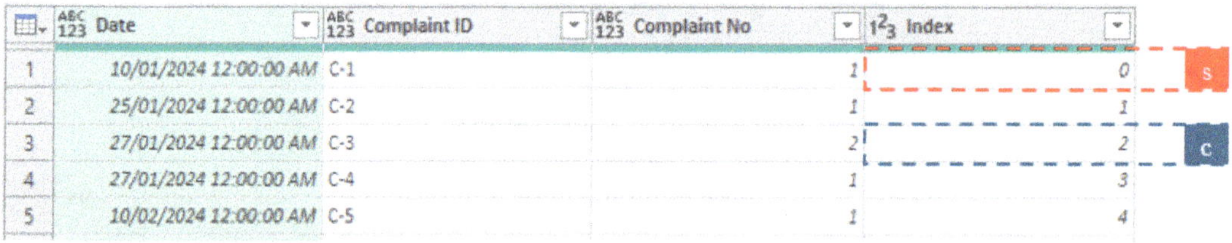

Figure 6-83. The s and c in step 2

Group 1. Step 2:

In this step, `s[Index] = 0`, `c[Index] = 2` and `c[Index] - s[Index] + 1 = 3`. Applying these values to `List.Range(Source[Complaint No], s[Index], c[Index] - s[Index] + 1)` results in {1, 1, 2}. Since the result of `List.Sum()` for the resulting list is 4, which is not greater than five, the result of `Number.From()` is 0. Therefore, the grouping continues, and c moves to the next row. See Figure 6-84.

CHAPTER 6   GROUPING ROWS WITH TABLE.GROUP()

	Date	Complaint ID	Complaint No	Index	
1	10/01/2024 12:00:00 AM	C-1	1	0	s
2	25/01/2024 12:00:00 AM	C-2	1	1	
3	27/01/2024 12:00:00 AM	C-3	2	2	
4	27/01/2024 12:00:00 AM	C-4	1	3	c
5	10/02/2024 12:00:00 AM	C-5	1	4	

Figure 6-84. *The s and c in step 3*

Group 1. Step 3:

In this step, `s[Index] = 0`, `c[Index] = 3`, and `c[Index] - s[Index] + 1 = 4`. Applying these values to `List.Range(Source[Complaint No], s[Index], c[Index] - s[Index] + 1)`, you get {1, 1, 2, 1}. Since `List.Sum()` equals five, which is not greater than five, the result of `Number.From()` is 0. Therefore, the grouping continues, and c moves to the next row, as shown in Figure 6-85.

	Date	Complaint ID	Complaint No	Index	
1	10/01/2024 12:00:00 AM	C-1	1	0	s
2	25/01/2024 12:00:00 AM	C-2	1	1	
3	27/01/2024 12:00:00 AM	C-3	2	2	
4	27/01/2024 12:00:00 AM	C-4	1	3	
5	10/02/2024 12:00:00 AM	C-5	1	4	c
6	3/03/2024 12:00:00 AM	C-6	4	5	

Figure 6-85. *The s and c in step 4*

Moving to Group 2:

In this step, `s[Index] = 0`, `c[Index] = 4`, and `c[Index] - s[Index] + 1 = 5`. The result of `List.Range(Source[Complaint No], s[Index], c[Index] - s[Index] + 1)` is {1, 1, 2, 1, 1}. Since `List.Sum()` over the items in the resulting list equals six, which is greater than five, the result of `Number.From()` is 1. This means Group 1 should be closed, and the row presented by c becomes the starting row for Group 2.

Consequently, as shown in Figure 6-86, s and c are updated, and `s[Index]`, `c[Index]`, and `c[Index] - s[Index] + 1` are now 4, 5, and 2, respectively.

377

CHAPTER 6   GROUPING ROWS WITH TABLE.GROUP()

	Date	Complaint ID	Complaint No	Index
1	10/01/2024 12:00:00 AM	C-1	1	0
2	25/01/2024 12:00:00 AM	C-2	1	1
3	27/01/2024 12:00:00 AM	C-3	2	2
4	27/01/2024 12:00:00 AM	C-4	1	3
5	10/02/2024 12:00:00 AM	C-5	1	4
6	3/03/2024 12:00:00 AM	C-6	4	5
7	14/03/2024 12:00:00 AM	C-7	1	6

Figure 6-86. The s and c in step 1 for Group 2

As in the previous step, this process will continue until the last row of Source table. Table 6-14 summarizes this process.

Table 6-14. Summarizing the Steps of Running the Fifth Input

Step	s[Index]	c[Index]	s[Index]-c[Index]+1	List.Range (…)	List.Sum (…)	Number.From (…)	Group
1	0	1	2	{1,1}	2	0	1
2	0	2	3	{1,1,2}	4	0	1
3	0	3	4	{1,1,2,1}	5	0	1
4	0	4	5	{1,1,2,1,1}	6	1	-
4	4	5	2	{1,4}	5	0	2
5	4	6	3	{1,4,1}	6	1	-
5	6	7	2	{1,3}	4	0	3

Now that the grouping is functioning correctly, you can include the Complaint IDs in the resulting table. To achieve this, modify the formula by revising the third argument, to present Groups and Complaint IDs within each group. The updated M-code to accomplish this is as follows, which results in Figure 6-87.

```
= Table.Group(
    #"Added Index",
    {"Index"},
    {{"IDs", each Text.Combine(_[Complaint ID],",")}},
    0,
```

```
(s,c)=>Number.From(
            List.Sum(
                    List.Range(Source[Complaint No],s[Index],
                    c[Index]-s[Index]+1)
                            )>5))
```

Index		IDs
1	0	C-1,C-2,C-3,C-4
2	4	C-5,C-6
3	6	C-7,C-8,C-9
4	9	C-10,C-11,C-12,C-13
5	13	C-14,C-15,C-16,C-17
6	17	C-18,C-19

Figure 6-87. *The resulting table*

Note In this example, since one column is used in the second input of the function, the name of the column can be directly inserted as text instead of using list syntax. Therefore, for the fifth argument, instead of using s[Index] and c[Index], you can simply use s and c. The revised version of the formula is as follows:

```
= Table.Group(
      #"Added Index",
      "Index",
      {{"IDs", each Text.Combine(_[Complaint ID],",")}},
      0,
      (s,c)=>Number.From(
                    List.Sum(
                            List.Range(Source[Complaint
                            No],s,c-s+1)
                                    )>5))
```

Additionally, in this example, the values in the Date column in the source table are unique, so instead of adding an Index column, you can use this column to extract the values between the starting row and ending row of groupings. Here's how you can modify the approach to use the Date column without adding an Index column (this can be used only when the Date column is unique):

```
= Table.Group(
    Source,
    "Date",
                    {{"IDs", each Text.Combine(_[Complaint ID],",")}},
     0,
      (s,c)=>Number.From(
                    List.Sum(
                        Table.SelectRows(
                        Source,each [Date]>=s and [Date]<=c)
                        [Complaint No]
                                )>=5))
```

Efficiency Tip To check the execution time of the proposed formula, a table with 3,000 rows was used. Without buffering, the execution time was 26 seconds. However, by buffering Source[Complaint No], the execution time was reduced to less than a second for the same table, and for a table with 100,000 rows, it took 21 seconds, which is high.

The whole formula using buffering is provided here:

```
let
    Source = Excel.CurrentWorkbook(){[Name="Table2"]}
    [Content],
    #"Added Index" = Table.AddIndexColumn(Source, "Index", 0,
    1, Int64.Type),
    Buffer=List.Buffer(Source[Complaint No]),
    #"Grouped Rows" = Table.Group(
#"Added Index",
"Index",
```

CHAPTER 6 GROUPING ROWS WITH TABLE.GROUP()

```
    {{"IDs", each Text.Combine(_[Complaint ID],",")}},
0,
(s,c)=>Number.From(
                List.Sum(
                    List.Range(Buffer,s,c-s+1)
                                )>5))
in
    #"Grouped Rows"
```

In the provided solution, during each iteration of grouping, all the values in the group are examined using `List.Sum(List.Range(Buffer, s, c - s + 1)`, which increases execution time. An alternative solution is proposed that determines grouping by comparing the cumulative complaints for the row related to the start and end of each group, instead of evaluating a range of complaints for all the rows inside each group.

To implement this solution, first add a new index column to the source table, starting at 0. Then click the *fx* button to add a new step called Custom1. Then use the following formula in the formula bar, which generates a list of all complaints, resulting in Figure 6-88.

```
= List.Buffer(#"Added Index"[Complaint No])
```

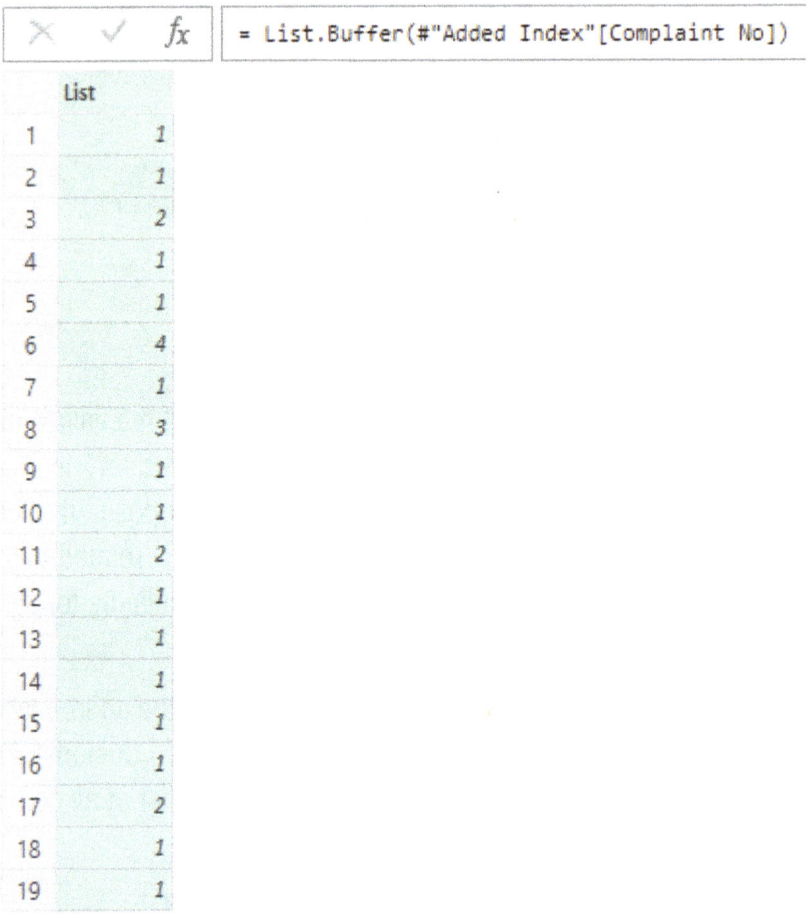

CHAPTER 6 GROUPING ROWS WITH TABLE.GROUP()

	List
1	1
2	1
3	2
4	1
5	1
6	4
7	1
8	3
9	1
10	1
11	2
12	1
13	1
14	1
15	1
16	1
17	2
18	1
19	1

= List.Buffer(#"Added Index"[Complaint No])

Figure 6-88. *List of complains*

Rename the new step to Complaint. In the next step, you need a list starting from 0 that includes the cumulative values from the complaint list. There are several ways to achieve this, but one of the most efficient methods is by using the following formula, using the List.Generate() function (this function is explained in depth in Chapter 9), which results in Figure 6-89.

```
= List.Buffer((List.Generate(
        () => {0,0},
        each _{0} <= List.Count(Complaint),
        each {_{0}+1,_{1}+ Complaint{_{0}}},
        each _{1})))
```

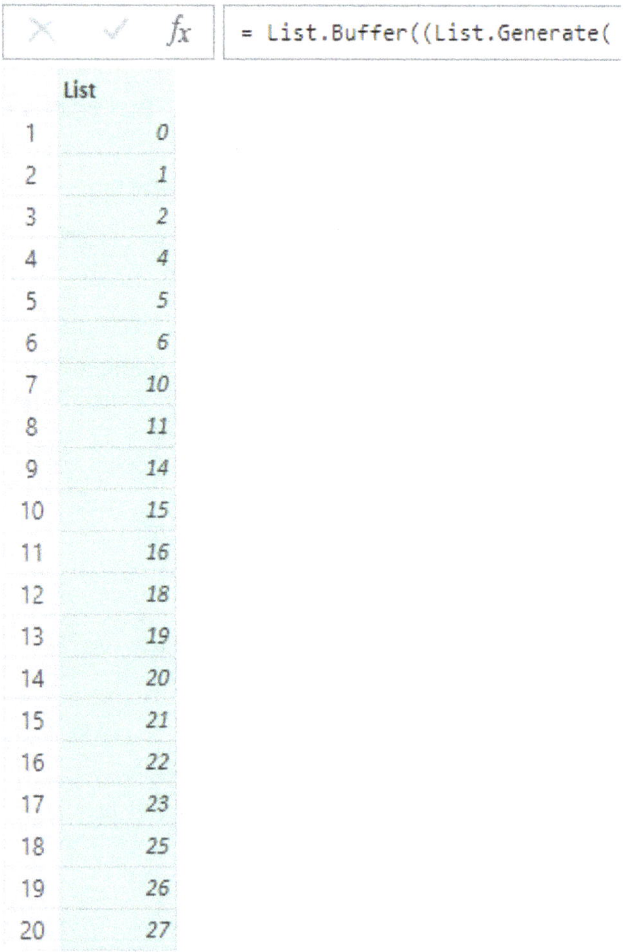

CHAPTER 6 GROUPING ROWS WITH TABLE.GROUP()

	List
1	0
2	1
3	2
4	4
5	5
6	6
7	10
8	11
9	14
10	15
11	16
12	18
13	19
14	20
15	21
16	22
17	23
18	25
19	26
20	27

= List.Buffer((List.Generate(

Figure 6-89. *Cumulative list of complaints*

Let's call the previous step Buffer. By using the following formula, you can solve the problem in a more efficient way:

```
= Table.Group(
        #"Added Index",
        "Index",
```

383

CHAPTER 6 GROUPING ROWS WITH TABLE.GROUP()

```
{{"IDs", each Text.Combine(_[Complaint ID],",")}},
0,
(s,c)=>Number.From((Buffer{c+1}-Buffer{s})>5))
```

The initial steps of this formula are provided in Table 6-15.

Table 6-15. *Summary of the Steps*

Step	s	c	Buffer{c+1}	Buffer{s}	Number.From(..)	Group
1	0	1	2	0	0	1
2	0	2	4	0	0	1
3	0	3	5	0	0	1
4	0	4	6	0	1	-
4	4	5	6	5	0	2
5	4	6	10	5	0	2
6	4	7	11	5	1	-
6	7	8	15	11	0	3
7	7	9	16	11	0	3
7	7	10	18	11	1	-

The complete code for solving this problem is provided here, and it executes in under a second for a table with 1 million rows.

```
let
  Source = Excel.CurrentWorkbook(){[Name = "Table2"]}[Content],
  #"Added Index" = Table.AddIndexColumn(Source, "Index", 0, 1, Int64.Type),
  Complaint = List.Buffer(#"Added Index"[Complaint No]),
  Buffer = List.Buffer(
    (
      List.Generate(
```

```
      () => {0, 0},
      each _{0} <= List.Count(Complaint),
      each {_{0} + 1, _{1} + Complaint{_{0}}},
      each _{1}
    )
  )
),
#"Grouped Rows" = Table.Group(
  #"Added Index",
  "Index",
  {{"IDs", each Text.Combine(_[Complaint ID], ",")}},
  0,
  (s, c) => Number.From((Buffer{c + 1} - Buffer{s}) > 5)
)
in
  #"Grouped Rows"
```

Summary

The advanced Table.Group() function in Power Query is presented in this chapter as a tool for effectively summarizing rows within a table. Using the UI, the function's first three arguments allow users to specify the table name, the column used for grouping, and a list of new column names with their respective operations.

These three arguments alone can address numerous real-world challenges. However, the fourth and fifth arguments significantly enhance the function's versatility. The fourth argument allows you to switch the grouping logic from global (across all rows) to local (among neighboring rows), while the fifth enables you to use custom grouping criteria. In this fifth argument, you can define a custom function. The custom function should include two arguments (usually in the type of record) that represent rows from the source table. For every two rows represented by the custom function arguments, when the custom function returns a value of 1, the rows are grouped together in the result; otherwise, they are placed in separate groups.

The next chapter covers essential tips for merging and appending multiple tables.

CHAPTER 7

Merging and Appending Tables

When working with multiple tables, you might need to combine them in different ways by using append or merge. The *append* process involves stacking tables on top of each other, essentially putting rows from multiple tables under each other in a single table. This is useful when you have similar datasets across different tables and want to consolidate them into one unified dataset. The *merge* process, on the other hand, involves combining columns from multiple tables based on one (or more) common key or column. This allows you to enrich one table with data from another table by aligning them side by side based on matching values and selected merging logic.

Consider the Source1 and Source2 tables, which contain historical sales data for the years 2022 and 2023, respectively. They are shown in Table 7-1 and Table 7-2.

Table 7-1. Source1: Sales in 2022

Year	Product	Sales
2022	A	140
2022	B	210
2022	C	410

CHAPTER 7 MERGING AND APPENDING TABLES

Table 7-2. Source1: Sales in 2023

Year	Product	Sales
2023	A	25
2023	B	360
2023	C	800
2024	D	51

In this example, the tables contain data from different years, but they have the same columns. To append the tables and stack them vertically, follow these steps.

Select one of the tables, go to the Home tab, and choose Append Queries, as shown in Figure 7-1. In the dialog that appears, configure the settings as shown in Figure 7-2. This will result in a combined table, as illustrated in Figure 7-3.

Figure 7-1. Choosing Append Queries as New

Figure 7-2. Setting the Append query

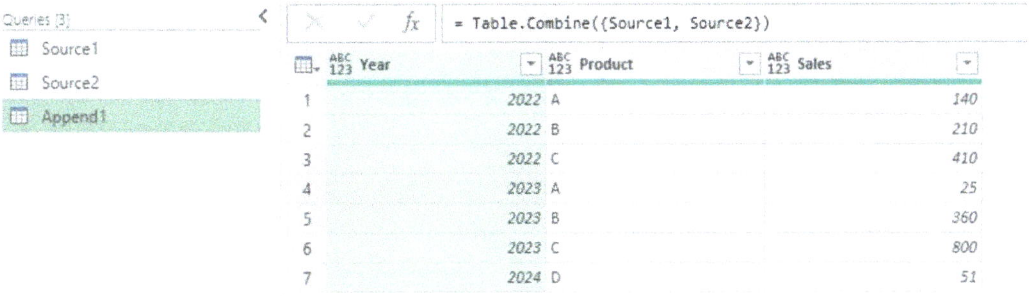

CHAPTER 7 MERGING AND APPENDING TABLES

	Year	Product	Sales
1	2022	A	140
2	2022	B	210
3	2022	C	410
4	2023	A	25
5	2023	B	360
6	2023	C	800
7	2024	D	51

Figure 7-3. The result of the "Append Queries as New" option

Note As shown in Figure 7-1, there are two options for appending queries: Append Queries and Append Queries as New. Selecting Append Queries as New creates a new query, where the appended table is provided as the result, as shown in Figure 7-3. Selecting Append Queries adds the appended table as a new step within the existing selected query.

The previous steps result in the following formula in the formula bar, which combines (appends) two or more tables vertically:

= Table.Combine({Source1, Source2})

This example uses the Table.Combine() function to append tables in Power Query. It takes two arguments—the first argument is a list containing the names of the tables to be combined, and you can use the second argument to limit the resulting table to specific columns. You do this by specifying the column names in the second argument of the Table.Combine() functions in the type list. Rewriting the previous formula as shown here will result in an appended table that includes only the Product and Year columns (see Figure 7-4):

= Table.Combine({Source1,Source2},{"Product","Sales"})

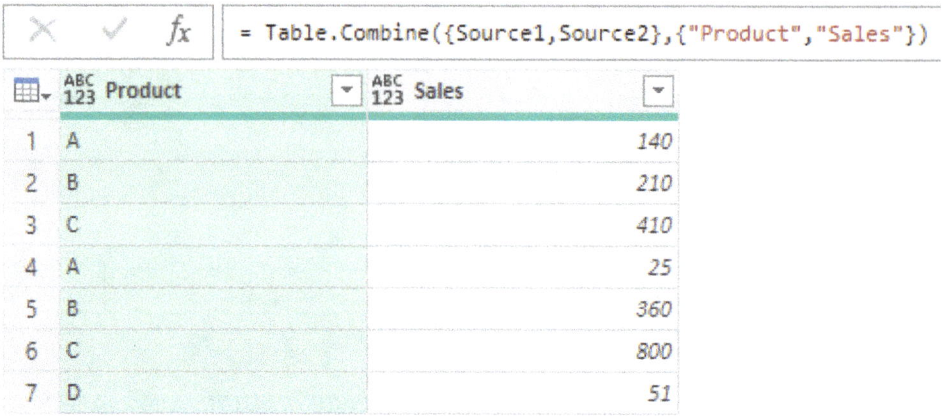

CHAPTER 7 MERGING AND APPENDING TABLES

| | fx | = Table.Combine({Source1,Source2},{"Product","Sales"}) |

	ABC 123 Product	ABC 123 Sales
1	A	140
2	B	210
3	C	410
4	A	25
5	B	360
6	C	800
7	D	51

Figure 7-4. Selecting the column list for appending

Note In addition to using the Table.Combine() function, the & operator can also be used to append tables. These formulas produce the same result:

= Table.Combine({Source1, Source2})

=Source1 & Source2

In this case, as explained in Chapter 2, you can limit the result to specific columns by specifying the desired column names in brackets. The following formula returns only the Product and Sales columns in the resulting table:

= (Source1 & Source2)[[Product],[Sales]]

In another scenario, you may need to extract information from one table and add it as a new column to another table. For example, consider the Historical_Sales and Product_Info tables, as shown in Table 7-3 and Table 7-4.

CHAPTER 7 MERGING AND APPENDING TABLES

Table 7-3. Historical_Sales Table

Date	Product	Quantity
2/21/2024	A	2
2/22/2024	B	2
2/23/2024	A	1
2/23/2024	C	3

Table 7-4. Product_Info Table

Product Name	Price
A	100
B	150
C	200

To extract product prices from the Product_Info table and add them as a new column to the Historical_Sales table, follow these steps:

1. Select the Historical_Sales table.

2. From the Home tab, select the Merge Queries command. This opens the Merge window, where the Historical_Sales table is automatically selected at the top.

3. Next, in the bottom part, choose the table from which you want to extract information—in this case, Product_Info.

4. Then, select the common column(s) that exist in both tables. In this example, the common column is the product name, which appears as the Product column in the Historical_Sales table and as the Product Name column in the Product_Info table. Configure the settings as shown in Figure 7-5 by selecting the mentioned columns and clicking OK. This results in Figure 7-6.

CHAPTER 7   MERGING AND APPENDING TABLES

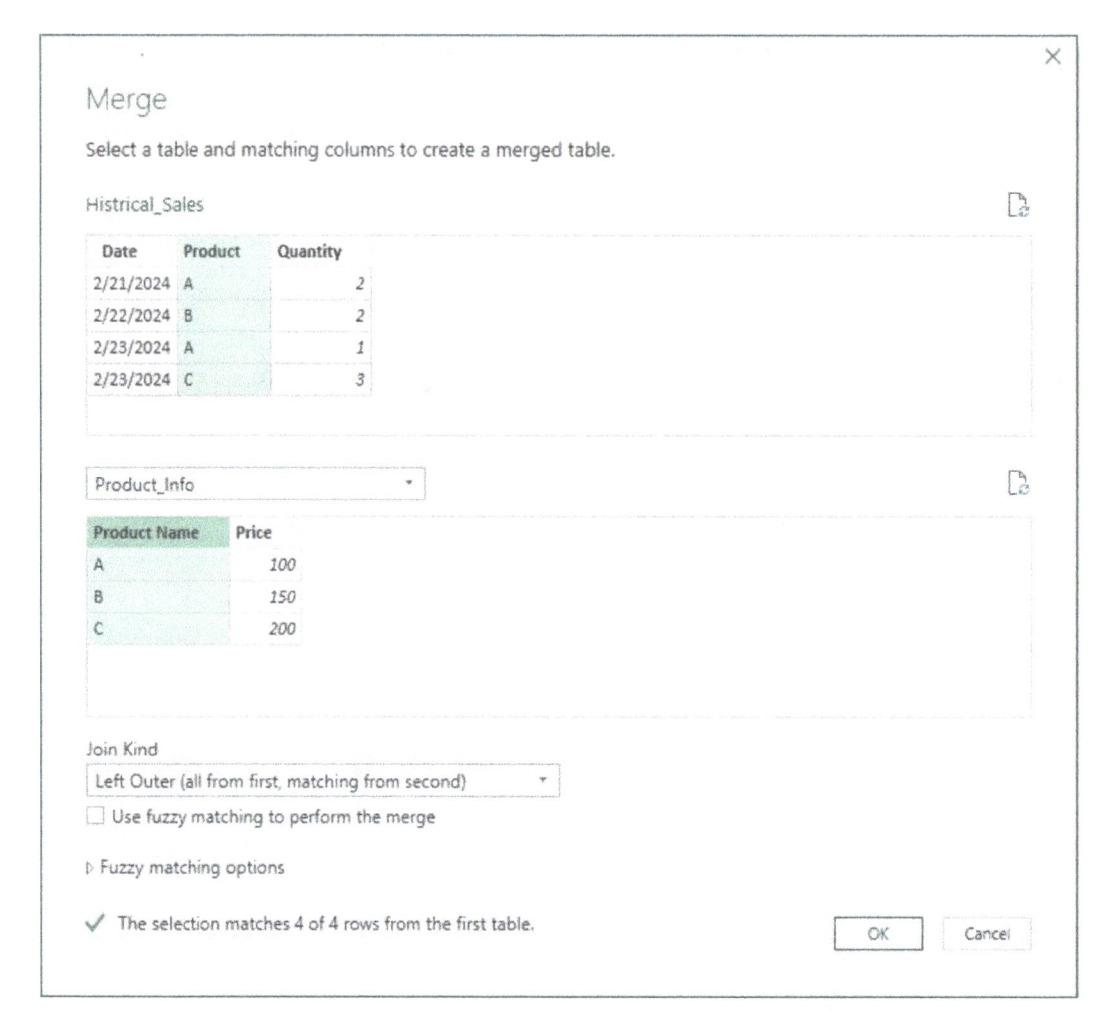

Figure 7-5. Setting the merging query

Figure 7-6. The result of the merging query

CHAPTER 7 MERGING AND APPENDING TABLES

In the resulting table, a new column called Product_Info, including the information of the matched rows in the `Product_Info` table, will be added to the `Historical_Sales` table. You can then extract the product price by expanding this new column. After applying this step, the formula for merging the tables generated in the formula bar is as follows:

```
= Table.NestedJoin(Source, {"Product"}, Product_Info, {"Product Name"}, "Product_Info", JoinKind.LeftOuter)
```

As shown in Figure 7-5, the Merge window includes a setting for Join Kind, which offers various options, including Left Outer, Right Outer, Full Outer, Inner, Left Anti, and Right Anti. Each option affects the merging logic differently, determining how matched and unmatched rows are handled. (In this example, the `Historical_Sales` table is the left table, and the `Product_Info` table is the right table.)

Now revise the `Product_Info` table, as shown in Table 7-5, and consider the `Historical_Sales` table as previously shown. In this case:

- Product B appears only in the left table.
- Product A is repeated twice in the left table, and once in the right table.
- Product D appears only in the right table and is listed twice.
- Product C appears twice in the right table and once in the left table.

The resulting tables of applying different Join Kind settings under each merge logic are shown in Figure 7-7 to Figure 7-12:

- **Left Outer Join:** In the Left Outer Join, the merge keeps all rows from the left table and brings in matching rows from the right table wherever possible. If a match exists, the corresponding data from the right table is included; otherwise, NULL values appear for unmatched rows. In this case, Product B has no match in the right table, so it remains in the result with NULL values in the merged columns. Product A appears twice in the left table but has only one corresponding row in the right table, meaning both instances of A will get the same match. Product C, however, appears twice in the right table but only once in the left table, causing it to be duplicated in the result.

393

- **Right Outer Join:** This merge keeps all rows from the right table, ensuring that every row from it appears in the final result. Any matching rows from the left table are brought in, while NULL values appear where no match exists. In this scenario, Product D, which is only present in the right table, appears in the result with NULLs from the left table. Product B doesn't appear in the resulting table.

- **Full Outer Join:** This merge includes all rows from both tables, regardless of whether a match exists. If a product appears in both tables, the corresponding values are merged; otherwise, NULL values fill the gaps. This ensures that Product B, which only exists in the left table, and Product D, which only exists in the right table, both appear in the result with NULL values for the missing side. Products A and C, which exist in both tables, are merged based on matching logic, leading to multiple rows when necessary.

- **Inner Join:** This merge keeps only the rows that have a match in both tables, effectively filtering out any records that don't exist in both datasets. This means that Product B, which only appears in the left table, and Product D, which only appears in the right table, will be completely excluded. The remaining products, A and C, will be matched based on their occurrences, ensuring that every possible combination of left and right matches appears in the final result.

- **Left Anti Join:** This merge returns only the rows from the left table that do not have a match in the right table. It essentially filters out all products that appear in both tables. In this scenario, Product B is the only product unique to the left table, meaning it is the only row that remains in the final result. All other products are excluded since they have corresponding matches in the right table.

- **Right Anti Join:** This merge works in the opposite way to the Left Anti Join, keeping only rows from the right table that have no match in the left table. Here, Product D is the only product unique to the right table, so it is the only row that appears in the final result. All other products, which have at least one match in the left table, are filtered out.

CHAPTER 7 MERGING AND APPENDING TABLES

Table 7-5. Product_Info table

Product Name	Price
A	100
C	200
D	50
D	25
C	120

Figure 7-7. The resulting table under the Left Outer logic

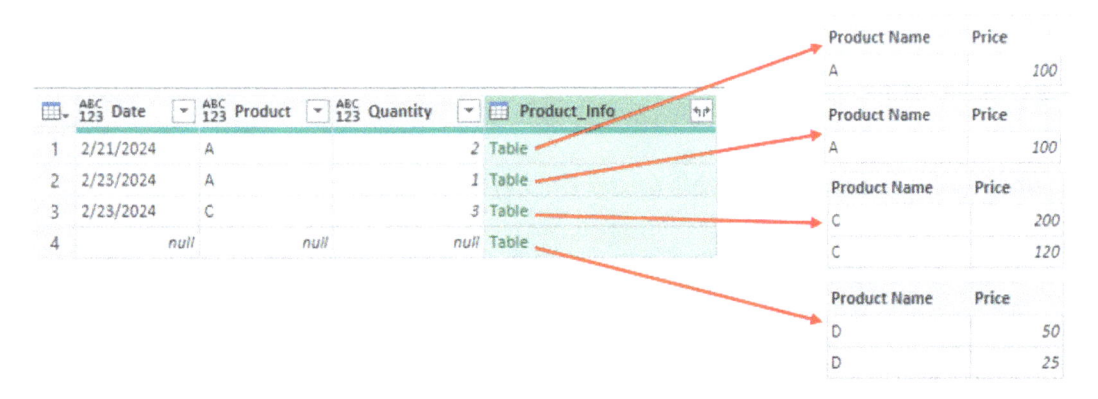

Figure 7-8. The resulting table under the Right Outer logic

395

CHAPTER 7   MERGING AND APPENDING TABLES

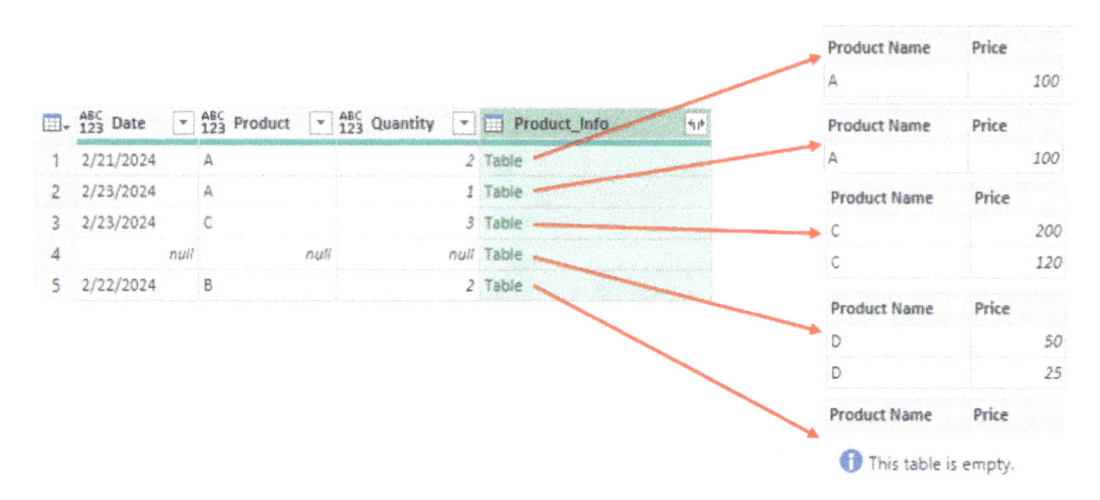

Figure 7-9. *The resulting table under the Full Outer logic*

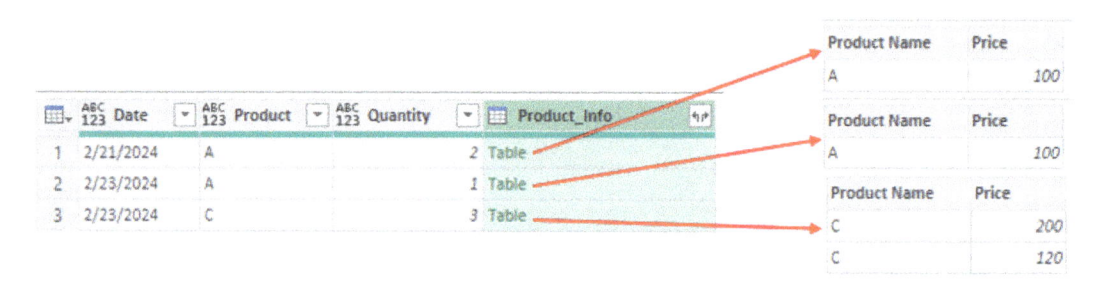

Figure 7-10. *The resulting table under the Inner logic*

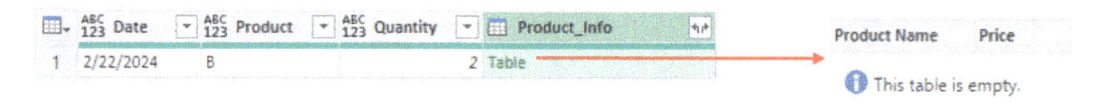

Figure 7-11. *The resulting table under the Left Anti logic*

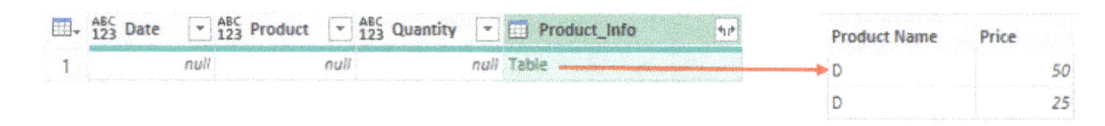

Figure 7-12. *The resulting table under the Right Anti logic*

The rest of this chapter explores more tips about using append and merge queries.

Combining Tables

Consider the monthly sales data for Spring provided in Table 7-6, Table 7-7, and Table 7-8. Combine all these tables to create a unified table for Spring, where each row represents a region, each column represents a product, and the values show the total sales of each product in that region across different months.

Table 7-6. Table1: Sales in March

Regions	Product A	Product B	Product E
Region 1	98	45	91
Region 2	37	71	23
Region 3	92	39	90

Table 7-7. Table2: Sales in April

Regions	Product A	Product D	Product C	Product E
Region 1	90	30	95	74
Region 4	51	41	80	17
Region 3	88	37	69	70

Table 7-8. Table3: Sales in May

Regions	Product D	Product B	Product E
Region 3	77	22	37
Region 2	98	66	59
Region 4	32	57	29

CHAPTER 7   MERGING AND APPENDING TABLES

Note The data in this example is provided in an Excel file titled 01 Combining Tables.xlsx.

As mentioned in the introduction, tables can be appended using the Table. Combine() function or the & operator. To solve this problem, create a blank query and write the following formula in the formula bar, resulting in the appended version of the tables shown in Figure 7-13:

= Table1 & Table2 & Table3

#	Regions	Product A	Product B	Product E	Product D	Product C
1	Region 1	98	45	91	null	null
2	Region 2	37	71	23	null	null
3	Region 3	92	39	90	null	null
4	Region 1	90	null	74	30	95
5	Region 4	51	null	17	41	80
6	Region 3	88	null	70	37	69
7	Region 3	null	22	37	77	null
8	Region 2	null	66	59	98	null
9	Region 4	null	57	29	32	null

Figure 7-13. Combining tables

In the next step, rows belonging to the same region need to be aggregated. For example, rows 1 and 4 represent Region 1 and should be combined accordingly using the Group By command (or unpivoting the table and then using pivoting, as explained in Chapter 5, which is a better solution when faced with several column names). See Figure 7-14 for the proper settings. Click OK to get the result in Figure 7-15.

CHAPTER 7 MERGING AND APPENDING TABLES

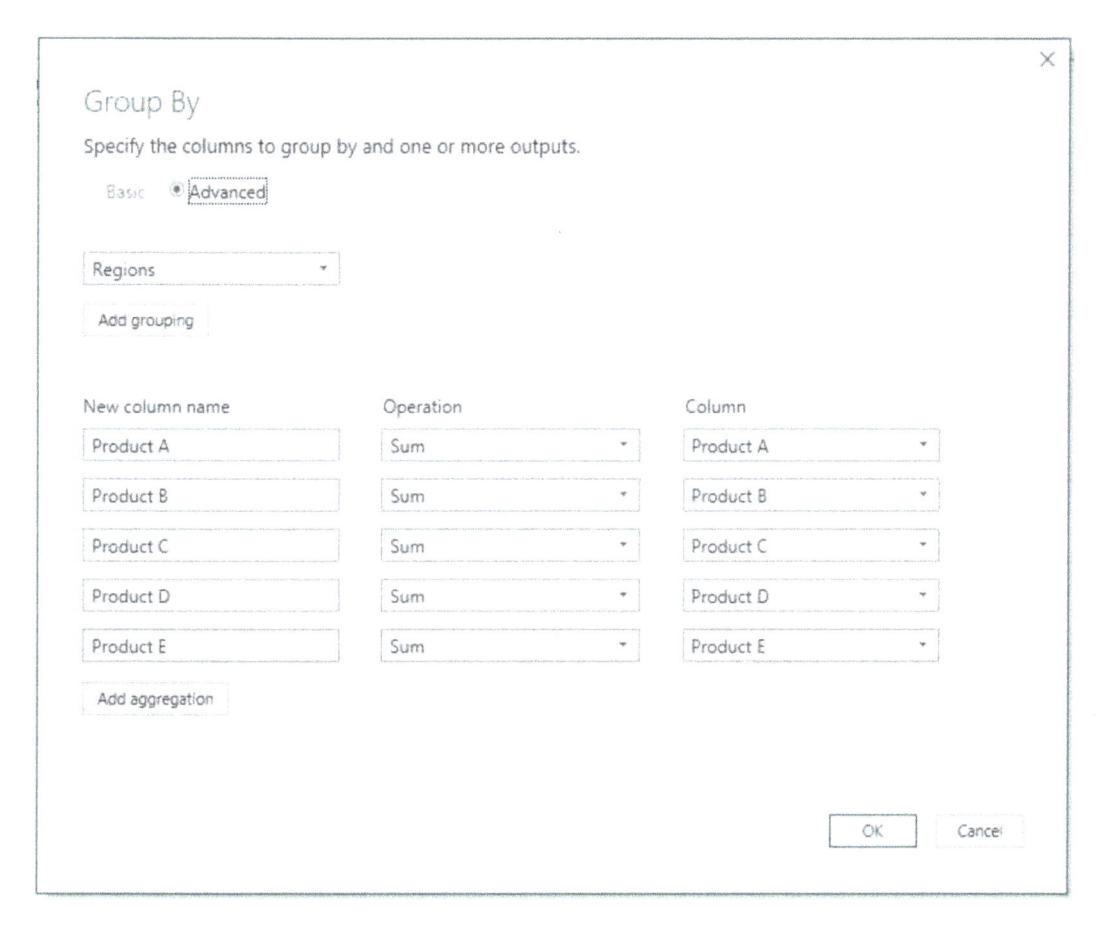

Figure 7-14. Settings of Group By

Figure 7-15. The results of Group By

Calculating Weighted Averages

The Production table includes monthly production figures (in meters) for various machines. It's shown in Table 7-9. The Sample table lists the weight (kg/m) of product samples produced by different machines and is shown Table 7-10. Calculate the average weight of products (kg/m) produced each month using these tables.

399

CHAPTER 7 MERGING AND APPENDING TABLES

Table 7-9. *Production: Monthly Production by Meter by Different Machinery*

Month	Machine Code	Production (m)
1	A	100
2	A	183
3	A	55
1	B	220
3	B	231
2	C	100
3	C	220

Table 7-10. *Sample: Weight of Samples*

Machine Code	Month	Sample	Weight (kg/Meter)
A	1	1	1.25
A	1	2	1.2
B	1	1	1.25
A	1	3	1.22
A	1	4	1.24
B	1	2	1.25
C	2	1	1.29
C	2	2	1.22
A	2	1	1.33
C	2	3	1.39
A	2	2	1.26
C	2	4	1.21
C	3	1	1.32
A	3	1	1.28
A	3	2	1.33
B	3	1	1.27

CHAPTER 7 MERGING AND APPENDING TABLES

> **Note** The data in this example is provided in an Excel file titled 02 Calculating Weighted Averages.xlsx.

To address this problem for Month 1, follow these steps:

1. **Calculate Average Weights (kg/m):** First, compute the average weights of a meter for the sample products produced by each machine in each month presented in the Sample table:

   – For machinery A in month 1: Average weight of samples per meter = (1.25+1.2+1.22+1.24)/4= 1.2275

   – For machinery B in month 1: Average weight of samples per meter = (1.25+1.25)/2=1.25

2. Calculate the average of Production Weight (kg/m) for each month. For example for month 1:

   – Machinery A produced 100 meters of products. The average weight per meter, calculated in the previous step, is 1.2275 kg/m.

   – Machinery B produced 220 meters with an average weight per meter of 1.25 kg/m.

   – The average weight of each meter of products (kg/m) produced in this month is calculated by (100*1.2275+220*1.25)/(100+220)=397/320=1.242

To solve the problem according to the first step and calculate the average weight of each meter of product produced by each machine in each month, you can use the Group By command. Select the Sample table, and from the Home tab, choose the Group By command. Then apply the settings shown in Figure 7-16 to group the Sample table by Month and Machine Code. Use the Average operation over the Weight column to achieve the table shown in Figure 7-17.

401

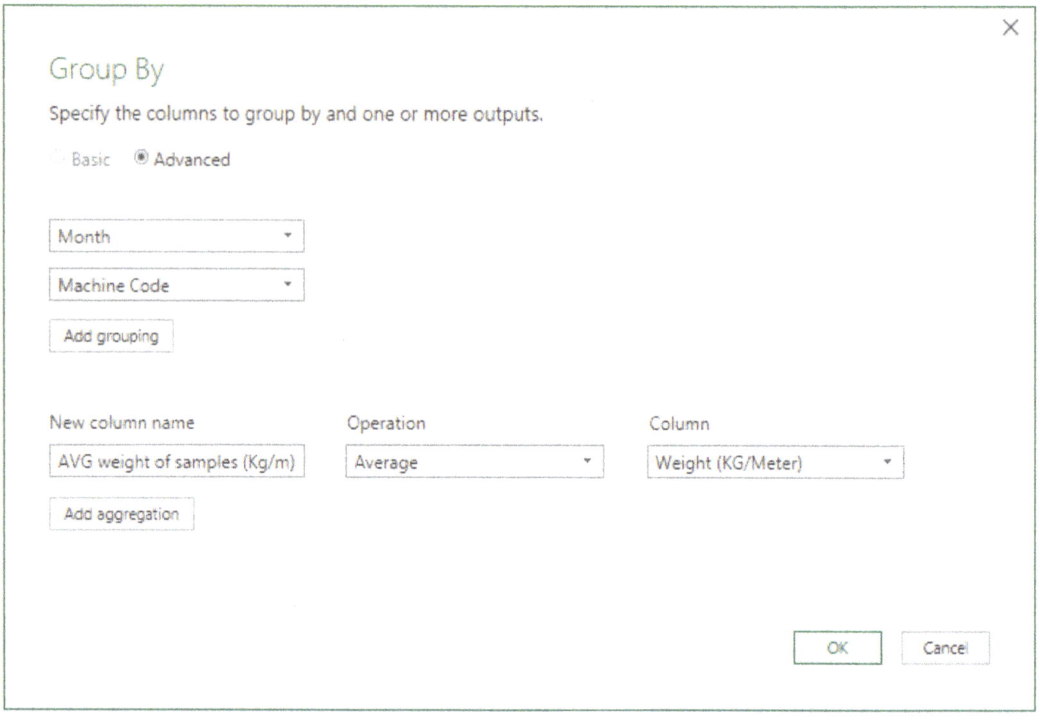

CHAPTER 7 MERGING AND APPENDING TABLES

Figure 7-16. Settings of Group By

Month	Machine Code	AVG weight of samples (Kg/m)
1	A	1.2275
1	B	1.25
2	C	1.2775
2	A	1.295
3	C	1.32
3	A	1.305
3	B	1.27

Figure 7-17. The results of Group By

The resulting table shows the average weight of samples (kg/m) produced by each machine in different months. This information needs to be merged with the data from the Production table based on the Month and Machine Code columns. To merge the tables, select the Sample table. Then go to the Home tab and click Merge Queries. In the Merge window, select the Production code for the right table. In this example,

402

CHAPTER 7 MERGING AND APPENDING TABLES

two columns should be considered for merging, so in the left table, first select Month column, then hold Ctrl and select the Machine Code column as the second column. Repeat this process on the right table, ensuring the selection is in the same order (Month and Machine Code). This will show the numbers 1 and 2 next to the column names, as shown in Figure 7-18. Clicking OK results in the table shown in Figure 7-19.

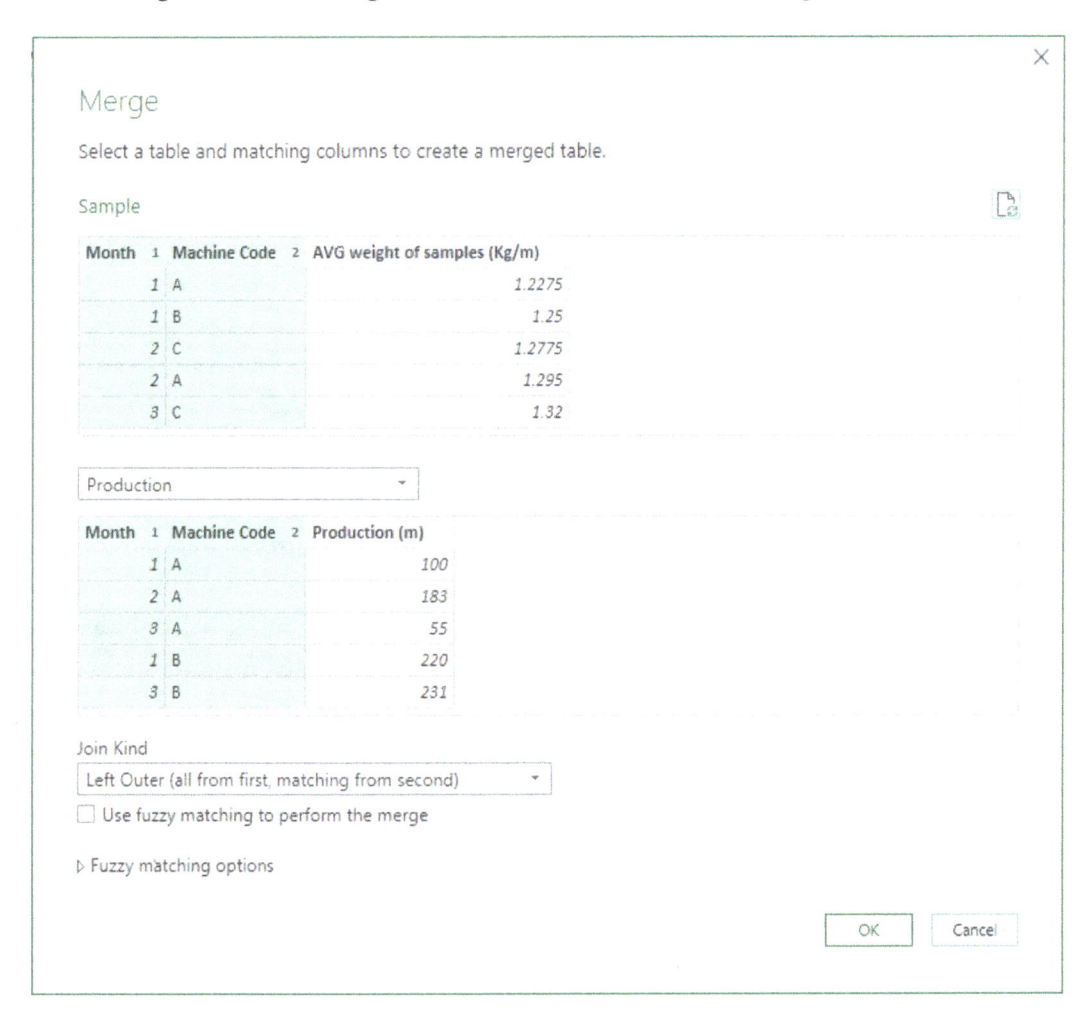

Figure 7-18. Settings of merging queries

CHAPTER 7 MERGING AND APPENDING TABLES

Month	Machine Code	AVG weight of samples (Kg/m)	Grouped Rows
1	A	1.2275	Table
1	B	1.25	Table
2	C	1.295	Table
2	A	1.2775	Table
3	C	1.305	Table
3	A	1.32	Table
3	B	1.27	Table

Month	Machine Code	Production (m)
1	A	100

Month	Machine Code	Production (m)
2	A	183

Month	Machine Code	Production (m)
3	B	231

Figure 7-19. *Results of merging queries*

Expand the new column named Grouped Rows by selecting only the Production (m) column to obtain Figure 7-20.

Month	Machine Code	AVG weight of samples (Kg/m)	Production (m)
1	A	1.2275	100
1	B	1.25	220
2	A	1.295	183
2	C	1.2775	100
3	A	1.305	55
3	C	1.32	220
3	B	1.27	231

Figure 7-20. *The result of expanding the Grouped Rows column*

The resulting table includes both the average weight of samples (kg/m) and the total production (m) for each machine in each month. To calculate the total weight of production for each machine in each month, multiply the values in these two columns (average weight and total production). Add a new column called Avg Production Weight (Kg) using the following formula in the Custom Column window.

=[#"AVG weight of samples (Kg/m)"]*[#"Production (m)"]

In the next step, you can group the rows by month and calculate the total production in meters and kilograms for each month. Using the Group By command with the settings shown in Figure 7-21 results in the table shown in Figure 7-22.

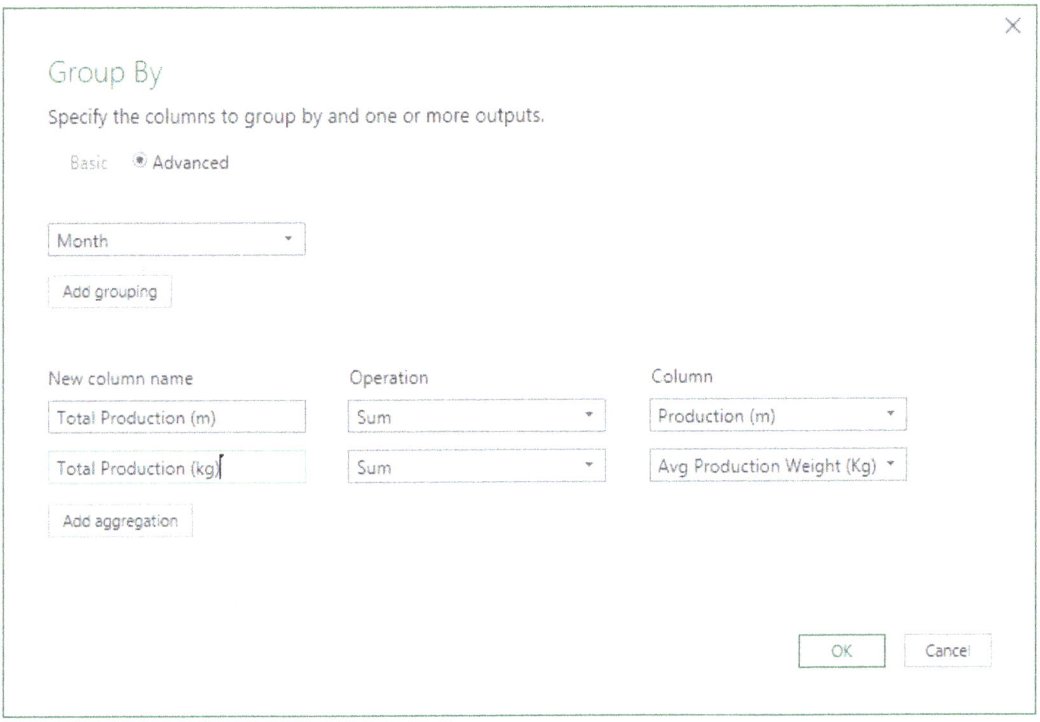

CHAPTER 7   MERGING AND APPENDING TABLES

Figure 7-21. Setting for Group By

Figure 7-22. The result of grouping

As the final step, add a new column called AVG Weight of Monthly Production (Kg/m) with the following formula in the Custom Column window.

=[#"Total Production (kg)"]/[#"Total Production (m)"]

This formula calculates the average weight of monthly production, as shown in Figure 7-23. Remove any extra columns to achieve the result.

405

CHAPTER 7 MERGING AND APPENDING TABLES

Figure 7-23. The final result

Reconciliation, Part 1

Consider Table 7-11, including the bank statement, and Table 7-12, including the finance department's records, for the same period. Reconcile these two tables and identify any mismatched rows. (A row is considered a mismatch if there is no corresponding transaction in the other table with the same amount on the same date.)

Table 7-11. Bank: Including Bank Statements

Date	Transaction Type	Amount	Transaction Category	Source
19/02/2024	Online	700	Flights	Bank
19/02/2024	Online	150	Transportation	Bank
19/02/2024	Online	120	Transportation	Bank
19/02/2024	In-person	250	Food	Bank
19/02/2024	In-person	160	Lodging	Bank
20/02/2024	Online	150	Official	Bank
20/02/2024	Online	115	Official	Bank
20/02/2024	Online	5	Official	Bank
20/02/2024	In-person	180	Transportation	Bank
20/02/2024	Online	2	Food	Bank
20/02/2024	In-person	160	Food	Bank
20/02/2024	Online	10	Food	Bank
21/02/2024	Online	250	Lodging	Bank
21/02/2024	In-person	90	Official	Bank
21/02/2024	Online	160	Official	Bank
21/02/2024	Online	10	Food	Bank

Table 7-12. Finance: Records on Company

Date	Department Budget	Amount	Source
19/02/2024	HR	700	Finance
19/02/2024	Sales	150	Finance
19/02/2024	HR	120	Finance
19/02/2024	Finance	250	Finance
19/02/2024	HR	160	Finance
19/02/2024	Sales	10	Finance
20/02/2024	HR	150	Finance
20/02/2024	Sales	120	Finance
20/02/2024	Finance	250	Finance
20/02/2024	HR	160	Finance
20/02/2024	HR	10	Finance
21/02/2024	Sales	150	Finance
21/02/2024	Finance	120	Finance
21/02/2024	HR	250	Finance
21/02/2024	HR	160	Finance
21/02/2024	Sales	10	Finance

In this example, for simplicity, the column names are the same in both tables, and both tables include a column indicating the source of each table. It is also assumed that there is no transaction with the similar date and amount. (This assumption is removed in the next example.)

CHAPTER 7   MERGING AND APPENDING TABLES

Note   The data in this example is provided in an Excel file titled `03 Reconciliation Part 1.xlsx`.

In finance, reconciliation refers to the process of ensuring that two sets of financial records are in agreement. The goal is to verify that the amounts in one set of records match those in another, typically comparing transactions or balances across different systems or accounts. For example:

Bank reconciliation   Comparing a company's internal financial records with the bank statement to ensure both sets match and to identify any discrepancies (such as missing transactions or errors).

Account reconciliation   Ensuring that the balances in different accounts (e.g., accounts payable, accounts receivable) are consistent and correct.

In short, reconciliation ensures that financial data is accurate, complete, and consistent across different sources, helping to prevent errors and detect fraud.

In practice, reconciliation can be a challenging task because a row in one table might be split into multiple rows in another table. This situation cannot be easily handled by simply merging the tables. Advanced functions like `List.Generate()` and `List.Accumulate()` are often required to address such cases.

In this example, to identify the rows that are common in both tables based on the transaction date and amount, you can use the Merge command. Select the Bank table and use the Merge Queries as New option. Then apply the settings shown in Figure 7-24, ensuring that the Date and Amount columns are both selected in the same order for both tables. Set the Join Kind to Left Anti and click OK to reach Figure 7-25.

CHAPTER 7 MERGING AND APPENDING TABLES

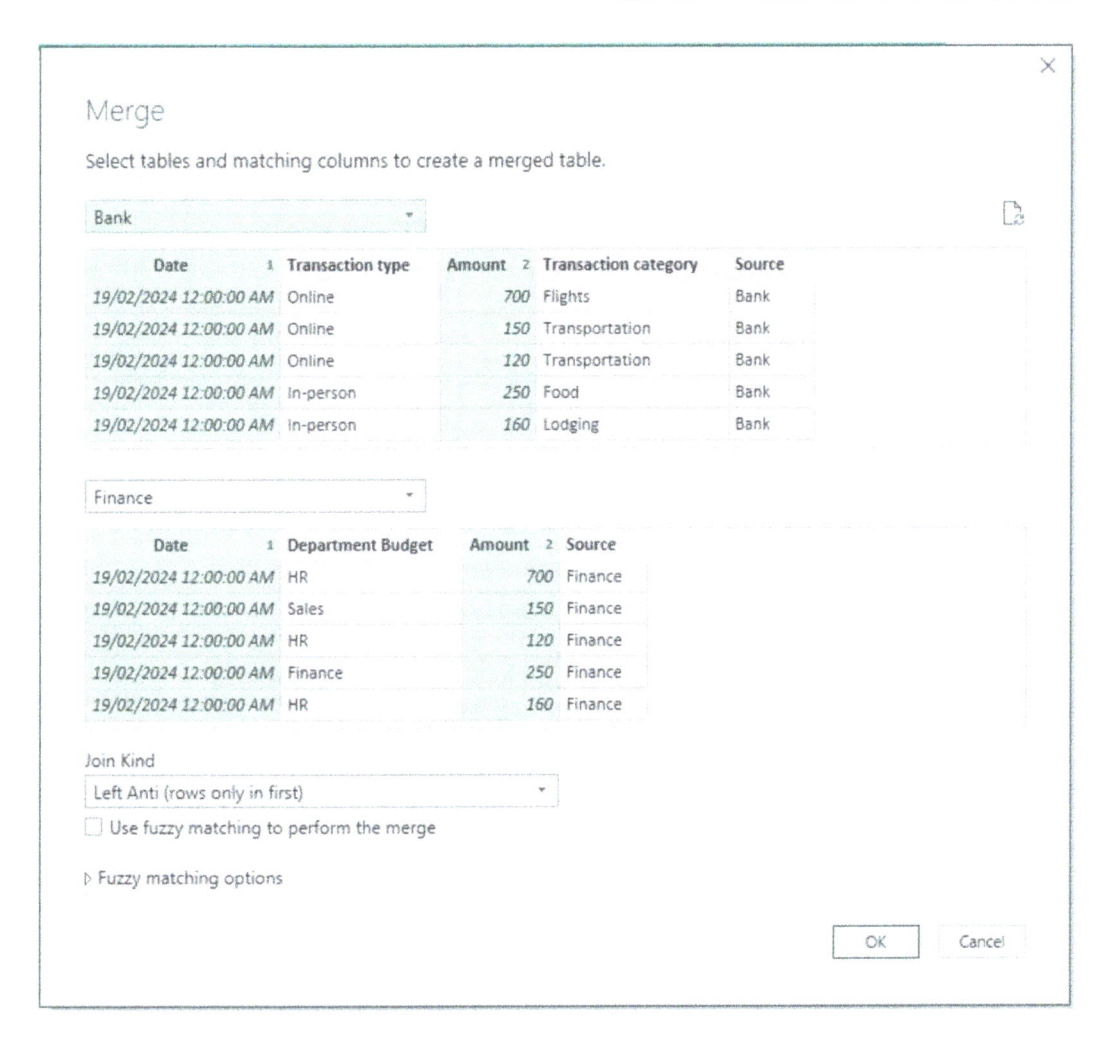

Figure 7-24. Merge setting for Left Anti

Figure 7-25. The result of merge for Left Anti

409

CHAPTER 7 MERGING AND APPENDING TABLES

This will allow you to extract the transactions that are present in the bank statement (the Bank table) but not in the company records (the Finance table).

Although the resulting rows in the new Finance column are marked as Table, they all contain a null row for all the rows, as shown in Figure 7-25.

The previous steps lead to the following formula in the formula bar. It's used to merge both the tables—Bank and Finance—based on the Date and Amount columns on both the tables.

```
= Table.NestedJoin(Bank, {"Date", "Amount"}, Finance, {"Date", "Amount"}, "Finance", JoinKind.LeftAnti)
```

In the previous formula, by swapping the first and third arguments (and if the column names in both tables don't match exactly, the second argument should be swapped with the fourth argument as well), the result will change to display rows that are in the company file but not in the bank statement, as shown in Figure 7-26.

```
= Table.NestedJoin(Finance, {"Date", "Amount"}, Bank, {"Date", "Amount"}, "Finance", JoinKind.LeftAnti)
```

#	Date	Department Budget	Amount	Source	Finance
1	19/02/2024 12:00:00 AM	Sales		10 Finance	Table
2	20/02/2024 12:00:00 AM	Sales		120 Finance	Table
3	20/02/2024 12:00:00 AM	Finance		250 Finance	Table
4	21/02/2024 12:00:00 AM	Sales		150 Finance	Table
5	21/02/2024 12:00:00 AM	Finance		120 Finance	Table

Date	Transaction type	Amount	Transaction category	Source	
null	null	null	null	null	null

Figure 7-26. *The result of swapping arguments on the merge function*

CHAPTER 7 MERGING AND APPENDING TABLES

Note In the previous step, instead of swapping the tables, changing the merge logic to Right Anti and expanding the generated column will also lead to the same result.

You have two formulas: one returns the transactions that are in the Bank table but not in the Finance table, and the other returns the transactions that are in the Finance table but not in the Bank table. Appending these two tables will result in a complete list of all mismatched rows. Using the following formula in the formula bar will produce the output shown in Figure 7-27.

```
= Table.Combine(
    {Table.NestedJoin(Bank, {"Date", "Amount"}, Finance, {"Date",
    "Amount"}, "Finance", JoinKind.LeftAnti),
    Table.NestedJoin(Finance, {"Date", "Amount"}, Bank, {"Date",
    "Amount"}, "Finance", JoinKind.LeftAnti)},
    {"Date","Amount","Source"})
```

#	Date	Amount	Source
1	20/02/2024 12:00:00 AM	115	Bank
2	20/02/2024 12:00:00 AM	5	Bank
3	20/02/2024 12:00:00 AM	180	Bank
4	20/02/2024 12:00:00 AM	2	Bank
5	21/02/2024 12:00:00 AM	90	Bank
6	19/02/2024 12:00:00 AM	10	Finance
7	20/02/2024 12:00:00 AM	120	Finance
8	20/02/2024 12:00:00 AM	250	Finance
9	21/02/2024 12:00:00 AM	150	Finance
10	21/02/2024 12:00:00 AM	120	Finance

Figure 7-27. The result of reconciliation

In the resulting table, the first five rows represent transactions that appear on the bank statements but not in the company records. The remaining rows correspond to transactions that are recorded in the company files but are missing from the bank statements.

CHAPTER 7   MERGING AND APPENDING TABLES

Reconciliation, Part 2

As in the previous example, this example considers the bank statement and company records tables, shown in Table 7-13 and Table 7-14, with the difference that the tables are included the rows with the same Date and Amount values. The goal is to reconcile these two tables and identify any mismatched records. For simplicity, the column names are the same in both tables, and there is a column called Source, which represents the source of table.

Table 7-13. Bank: Including Bank Statements

Date	Transaction Type	Amount	Transaction Category	Source
19/02/2024	Online	700	Flights	Bank
19/02/2024	Online	700	Transportation	Bank
19/02/2024	Online	120	Transportation	Bank
19/02/2024	In-person	250	Food	Bank
19/02/2024	In-person	160	Lodging	Bank
20/02/2024	Online	150	Official	Bank
20/02/2024	Online	115	Official	Bank
20/02/2024	Online	115	Official	Bank
20/02/2024	In-person	115	Transportation	Bank
20/02/2024	Online	2	Food	Bank
20/02/2024	In-person	160	Food	Bank
20/02/2024	Online	10	Food	Bank
21/02/2024	Online	250	Lodging	Bank
21/02/2024	In-person	90	Official	Bank
21/02/2024	Online	160	Official	Bank
21/02/2024	Online	10	Food	Bank

Table 7-14. Finance: Records on Company

Date	Department Budget	Amount	Source
19/02/2024	HR	700	Finance
19/02/2024	Sales	700	Finance
19/02/2024	HR	700	Finance
19/02/2024	Finance	250	Finance
19/02/2024	HR	160	Finance
19/02/2024	Sales	10	Finance
20/02/2024	HR	150	Finance
20/02/2024	Sales	115	Finance
20/02/2024	Finance	115	Finance
20/02/2024	HR	160	Finance
20/02/2024	HR	10	Finance
21/02/2024	Sales	150	Finance
21/02/2024	Finance	120	Finance
21/02/2024	HR	250	Finance
21/02/2024	HR	160	Finance
21/02/2024	Sales	10	Finance

Note The data in this example is provided in an Excel file titled `04 Reconciliation Part 2.xlsx`.

The key difference between this problem and the previous one is that, in the previous scenario, you assumed that the values of rows in the Amount column for each date were unique (i.e., no rows with duplicate amounts and dates). However, in this example, the amount of 700 on the date 19/02/2024 appears twice in the Bank table and three times in the Finance table.

CHAPTER 7   MERGING AND APPENDING TABLES

Applying the solution in the previous example to these two tables results in the table shown in Figure 7-28. Although the transaction of 19/02/2024 with an amount of 700 is recorded more frequently in the Finance table, the resulting table does not show it as a mismatch row. This means it does not properly handle cases where amounts are repeated, such as 700 on 19/02/2024 and 115 on 20/02/2024.

#	Date	Amount	Source
1	19/02/2024 12:00:00 AM	120	Bank
2	20/02/2024 12:00:00 AM	2	Bank
3	21/02/2024 12:00:00 AM	90	Bank
4	19/02/2024 12:00:00 AM	10	Finance
5	21/02/2024 12:00:00 AM	150	Finance
6	21/02/2024 12:00:00 AM	120	Finance

Figure 7-28. *The result of reconciliation*

Merging the tables presented in this chapter does not resolve the issue in this case. However, there is a powerful function called List.Difference() that can help extract mismatched items by considering the number of repetitions, but it just works on lists.

The List.Difference() function takes three arguments, the last being optional and for changing the matching criteria. In the first two arguments, two lists will be entered. The function returns all the items that are in the first list but not in the second list. For example, List.Difference({1,2,3},{1,2,4}) results in {3}, and List. Difference({1,2,3,1},{1,2,4}) results in {3,1}.

In the advanced version of this function, the lists in the first two arguments can be in type record (or even list and table), so the field of records will be compared and the ones in the first list and not in the second list will be returned. So the following formula results in {[X=2,Y=1],[X=1,Y=2]}:

= List.Difference({[X=1,Y=1],[X=2,Y=1],[X=1,Y=2]},{[X=1,Y=1],[X=1,Y=10]})

In this case, the first list include three items all in type record with two fields of X and Y, and the second list include two items in type record, and the function results in the records that are in the first list but not in the second list. In Power Query, two records are equal if they have the same number of fields with the same field name and equal field values.

414

CHAPTER 7 MERGING AND APPENDING TABLES

In the previous example, to adjust the logic for comparing the records and compare only the values of the X field (ignoring the other fields), you can use the third argument of the List.Difference() function. The formula can be rewritten as follows, which results in {[X=2, Y=1]}:

= List.Difference({[X=1,Y=1], [X=2,Y=1], [X=1,Y=2]},
{[X=1,Y=1],[X=1,Y=1]},each _[X])

In this case, using each _[X] as a custom equality means, that only the values on the field of X are considered for comparison. In this case, the records of [X=1,Y=2] are equal to the record of [X=1,Y=10], as they have the same number in the X field. As a result, from the first list, [X=1,Y=1] is removed because it is already present in the second list. Similarly, [X=1,Y=2] is removed because there is a record in the second list, [X=1,Y=10], that has the same value for X.

Based on this explanation, this problem can be solved by converting each table into a list of records, where each record represents a row from the table. These lists can then be used in the List.Difference() function, with the third argument specifying that only the Date and Amount fields should be considered for comparison.

To reshape the tables into the appropriate format, you can use the Table.ToRecords() function, converting the rows of the table into a record which is presented in a list. Create a new query, and in the formula bar, enter the following formula to represent each row of the Bank table as a record, all provided in a list, as shown in Figure 7-30.

=Table.ToRecords(Bank)

CHAPTER 7 MERGING AND APPENDING TABLES

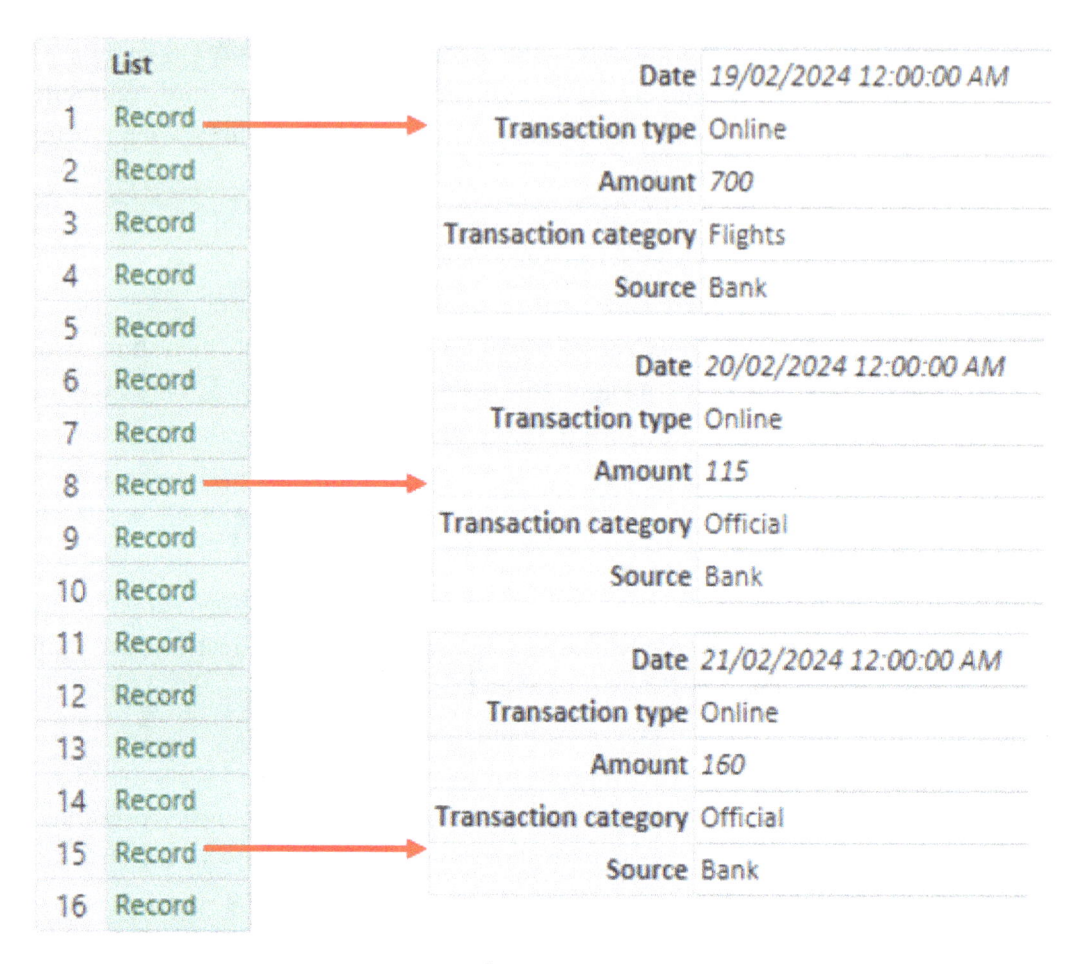

Figure 7-29. *Using Table.ToRecords()*

Based on the result of `Table.ToRecords()`, rewriting the previous formula as follows will compare the rows of the two tables based on all their fields:

```
= List.Difference(Table.ToRecords(Bank),Table.ToRecords(Finance))
```

To limit the comparison to just the Date and Amount fields, you can adjust the formula by using the third argument of the `List.Difference()` function. This modified formula will return all the rows available in the Bank table that are not present in the Finance table, based on the values in the Date and Amount columns, as shown in Figure 7-30.

```
= List.Difference(Table.ToRecords(Bank),Table.ToRecords(Finance), each 
{_[Date],_[Amount]})
```

CHAPTER 7 MERGING AND APPENDING TABLES

Figure 7-30. The result of using List.Difference()

Swapping the Bank and Finance tables will return the rows that exist in the Finance table, but not in the Bank table. By combining the previous formula with its swapped version and rewriting it as follows in the formula bar, you can retrieve all mismatched rows from both tables. The result is shown in Figure 7-31.

```
= List.Difference(Table.ToRecords(Bank),Table.ToRecords(Finance), each
{_[Date],_[Amount]}) & List.Difference(Table.ToRecords(Finance),Table.
ToRecords(Bank), each {_[Date],_[Amount]})
```

CHAPTER 7   MERGING AND APPENDING TABLES

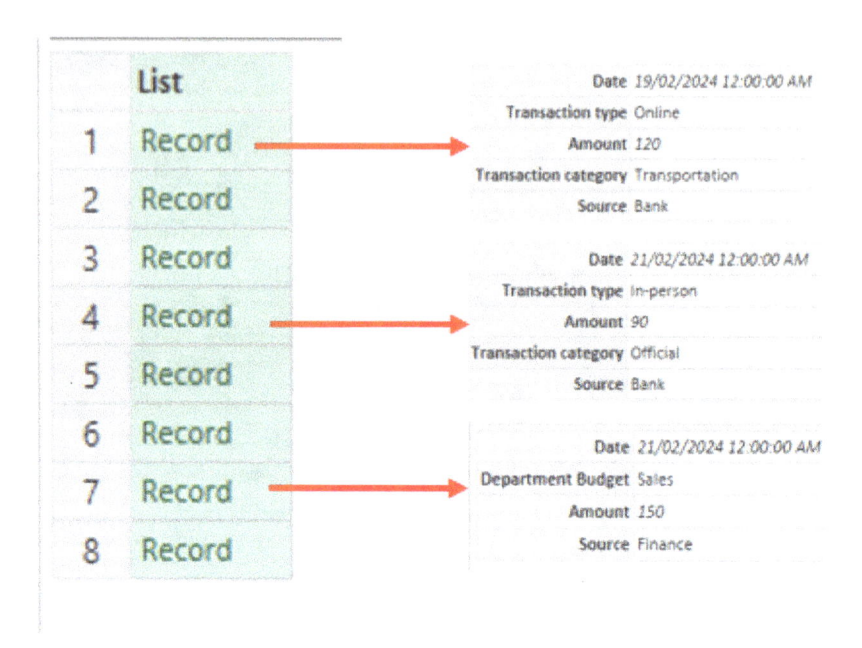

Figure 7-31. List of all mismatched items

In the next step, to convert the result from a list to a table, go to the Transform tab and select the To Table command. In the dialog window that appears, choose None as the delimiter and click OK to obtain the final result, shown in Figure 7-32.

Figure 7-32. Converting the result to a table

In the final step, expand Column1 to extract the individual fields from the records. This will transform the data into a structured table, solving the problem and producing the final results, as shown in Figure 7-33.

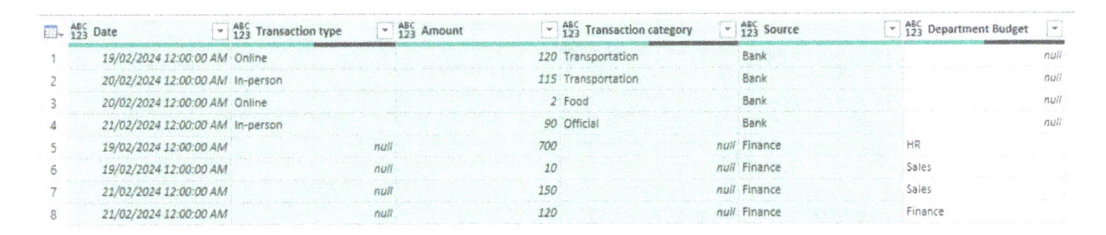

Figure 7-33. *The final table*

Fuzzy Merging

Consider the Historical Sales info and Product Info tables provided on Table 7-15 and Table 7-16. Add the product price from the Product Info table into the Historical Sales info. The product IDs do not exactly match in the tables, so you have to extract the similar information.

Table 7-15. Sales: Historical Sales Info

Date	Product ID	Quantity
24/07/2024	PNX4	2
24/07/2024	LMYL1	7
25/07/2024	PN-X	5
25/07/2024	PNX41	1
28/07/2024	nc	2
29/07/2024	PNX6	6
29/07/2024	LMYL-pnx	3
29/07/2024	NC2	3
29/07/2024	PNX5	2
30/07/2024	LMYLL	2
30/07/2024	NC6	2

Table 7-16. Info: Product Price Info

Product ID	Price
Pnx	10
LMYL	7
NC-2	5

> **Note** The data in this example is provided in an Excel file titled 05 Fuzzy Merging.xlsx.

In this example, the IDs are not clean. For instance, in the Info table, an ID like NC-2 appears in different variations in the Sales table, such as nc, NC2, and NC6. Similarly, for LMYL, multiple variations like LMYL1, LMYLL, and LMYL-pnx exist. This leads to several challenges, including:

- Extra characters in some ID variations
- Inconsistent character casing (uppercase vs. lowercase)
- Combinations of IDs in different formats

Handling these inconsistencies requires a robust approach to standardize and correctly match the IDs across both tables.

Since the IDs follow inconsistent patterns and variations, it is difficult to clean them automatically and use them directly in a merge process. The lack of a uniform structure makes it challenging to apply simple transformations like trimming, case conversion, or substring extraction to standardize the IDs. As a result, a more advanced approach, called fuzzy matching or custom mapping, may be required to correctly align the IDs across both tables.

> **Note** In the *fuzzy logic*, instead of comparing two values like nc and NC2 and saying they are equal or not, a similarity value is defined based on a threshold defined by user. This determines whether they are the same. However, in Power Query, it works like a black box and you might be faced with unexpected results.

CHAPTER 7 MERGING AND APPENDING TABLES

To use fuzzy merge, the common column in the right-side table must be of type text. The Product ID column in the Info table needs to be converted to text. This can be done by selecting the Info table, navigating to the Transform tab, and using the Detect Data Type option to ensure the column is recognized as text. It is not required but it is better to do the same for the Info table.

Once the column type is set correctly, the merge process can be performed. Selecting the Sales table and using the Merge Queries option from the Home tab allows for merging with the Product Info table. In the merge window, the Product ID column should be selected from both tables to establish the relationship. However, as shown in Figure 7-34, no matching rows appear due to inconsistencies in the Product ID formatting across the tables.

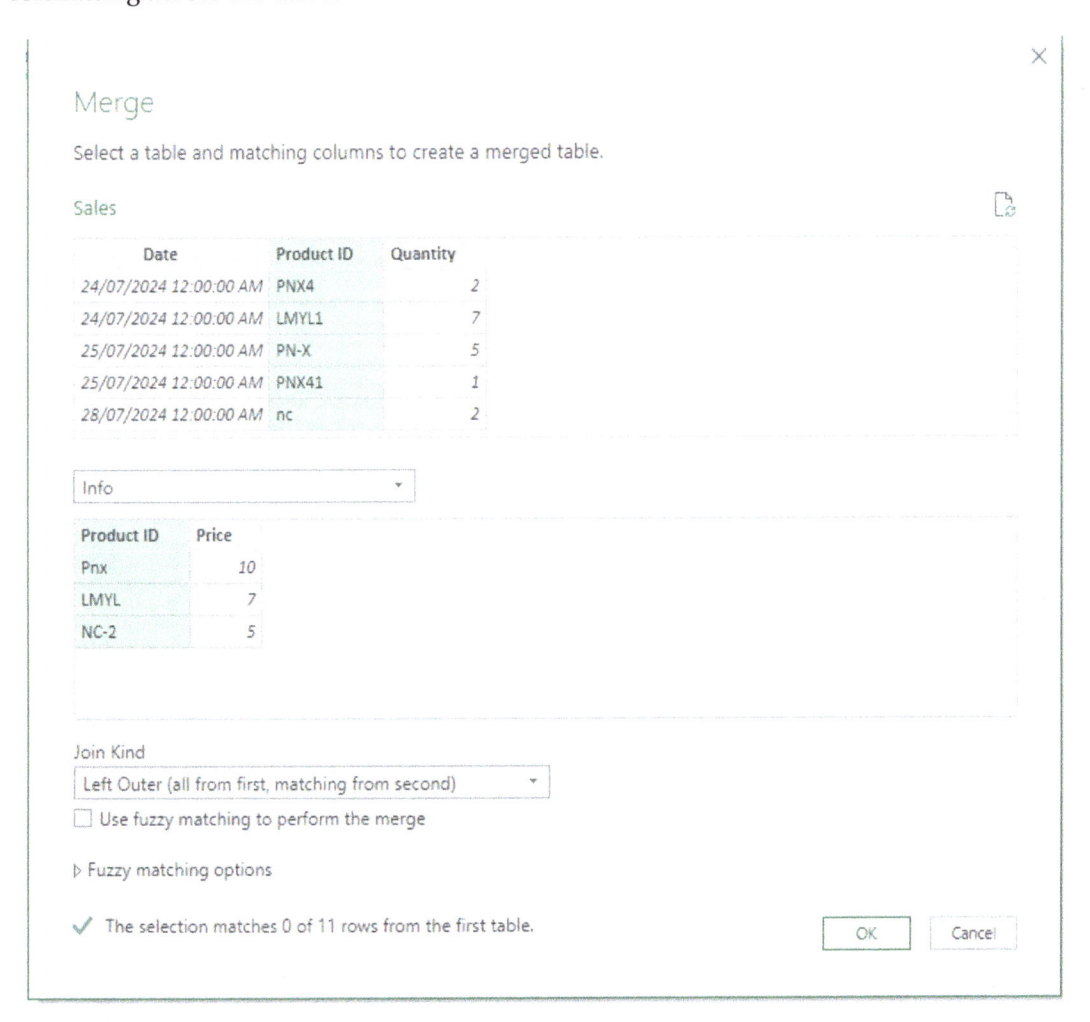

Figure 7-34. Merging setting

Instead of using a simple merge, fuzzy matching should be enabled, allowing adjustments to its parameters and settings. After enabling the Fuzzy Matching option, you can adjust its settings and observe the number of matching rows. By tweaking parameters like the similarity threshold and the matching methods, you can fine-tune the merge process. As you make these adjustments, Power Query will display the updated number of rows that match based on the defined criteria, allowing you to evaluate the effectiveness of the fuzzy matching configuration

In this example, selecting Ignore Case and Match by Combining Text Parts, along with setting the similarity threshold to 0, ensures the highest possible match (10 out of 11 rows), as shown in Figure 7-35. These settings help account for variations in ID formatting, thus improving the accuracy of the merge process.

CHAPTER 7 MERGING AND APPENDING TABLES

Merge

Select a table and matching columns to create a merged table.

Sales

Date	Product ID	Quantity
24/07/2024 12:00:00 AM	PNX4	2
24/07/2024 12:00:00 AM	LMYL1	7
25/07/2024 12:00:00 AM	PN-X	5
25/07/2024 12:00:00 AM	PNX41	1
28/07/2024 12:00:00 AM	nc	2

Info

Product ID	Price
Pnx	10
LMYL	7
NC-2	5

Join Kind

Left Outer (all from first, matching from second)

☑ Use fuzzy matching to perform the merge

▲ Fuzzy matching options

Similarity threshold (optional)

0

☑ Ignore case

☑ Match by combining text parts

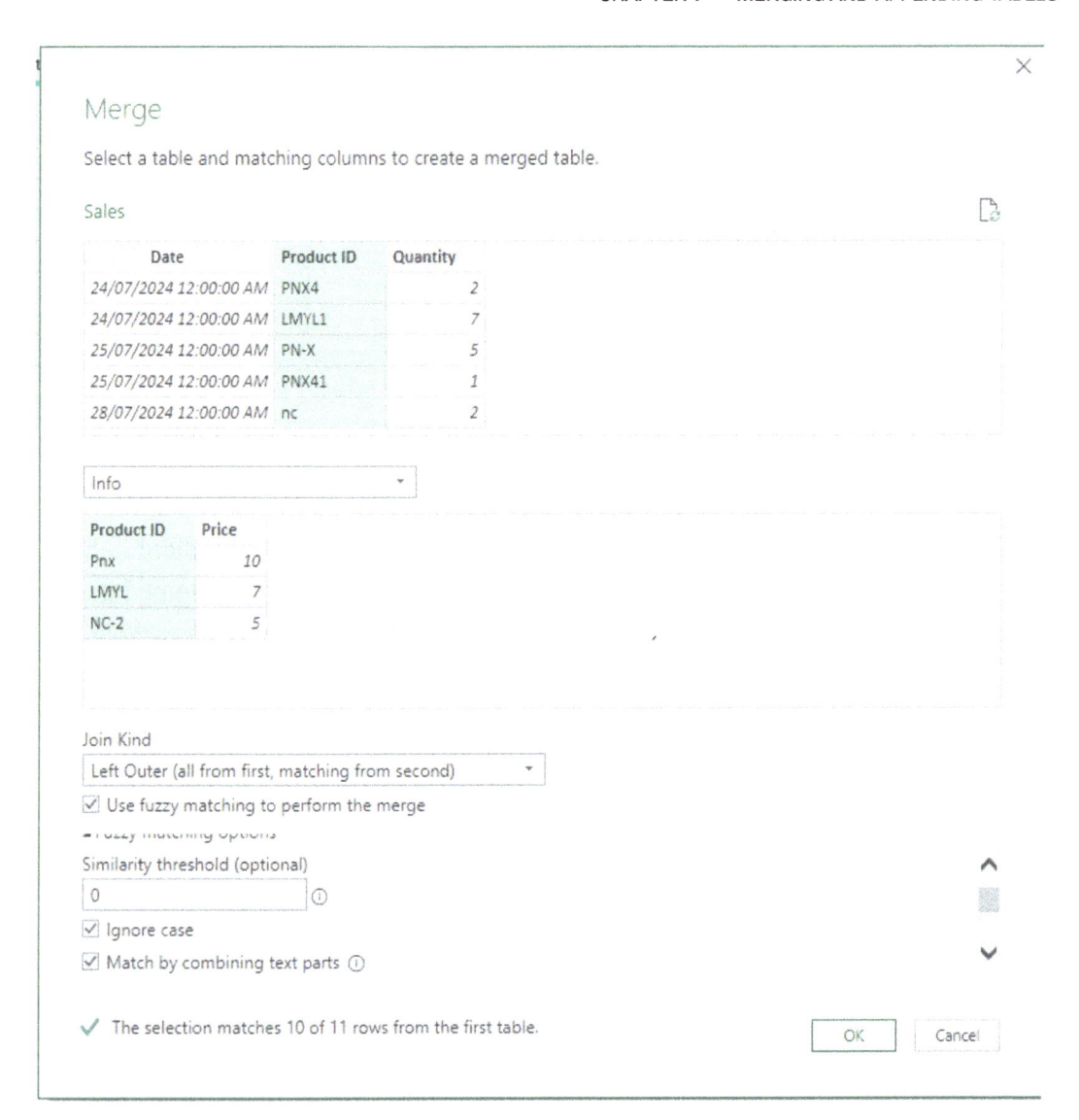

✓ The selection matches 10 of 11 rows from the first table.

[OK] [Cancel]

Figure 7-35. *Fuzzy matching setting*

Clicking OK and expanding the result column will produce the table shown in Figure 7-36. As seen, LMYL-pnx is matched to both LYML and Pnx IDs. Additionally, the row with PNX41 does not match any ID.

CHAPTER 7　MERGING AND APPENDING TABLES

#	Date	Product ID	Quantity	Info.Product ID	Info.Price
1	24/07/2024 12:00:00 AM	PNX4	2	Pnx	10
2	24/07/2024 12:00:00 AM	LMYL1	7	LMYL	7
3	25/07/2024 12:00:00 AM	PN-X	5	Pnx	10
4	25/07/2024 12:00:00 AM	PNX41	1	null	null
5	28/07/2024 12:00:00 AM	nc	2	NC-2	5
6	29/07/2024 12:00:00 AM	PNX6	6	Pnx	10
7	29/07/2024 12:00:00 AM	LMYL-pnx	3	Pnx	10
8	29/07/2024 12:00:00 AM	LMYL-pnx	3	LMYL	7
9	29/07/2024 12:00:00 AM	NC2	3	NC-2	5
10	29/07/2024 12:00:00 AM	PNX5	2	Pnx	10
11	30/07/2024 12:00:00 AM	LMYLL	2	LMYL	7
12	30/07/2024 12:00:00 AM	NC6	2	NC-2	5

Figure 7-36. *The result of fuzzy merging*

Note　Fuzzy matching is highly beneficial when working with inconsistent data, such as slight variations in spelling, case, or formatting. It enables merging tables even when values in the common columns are not exact matches, for example, matching NY to New York or NC2 to nc. It also allows for flexibility in controlling the matching criteria through adjustable similarity thresholds, ensuring that users can customize how strict or lenient the matching process should be. Additionally, fuzzy matching automates the merging process, saving time and reducing the need for manual data cleaning, especially when handling large datasets with variations.

Despite its advantages, fuzzy matching can yield unpredictable results. Since the algorithm works by calculating similarity scores, it may sometimes incorrectly match records that appear similar but are not actually the same. Furthermore, the fuzzy matching process in Power Query lacks transparency, as the exact algorithm used for calculating similarity is not visible or adjustable. This can make troubleshooting difficult when the results don't meet your expectations. Additionally, fuzzy merging can be performance-intensive, especially with large datasets, and may cause delays or slowdowns, particularly when a low similarity threshold is set, making the matching criteria more lenient.

Conditional Merging

Historical sales transactions are stored in the Sales table as shown in Table 7-17, and customer location, which may change over time, is recorded in the Info table, as illustrated in Table 7-18. Based on the information provided, calculate the total sales per state.

Table 7-17. *Sales: Historical Sales Info*

Date	Customer ID	Quantity
18/07/2023	C-2	40
31/07/2023	C-3	31
31/07/2023	C-3	35
3/08/2023	C-3	25
30/08/2023	C-2	11
31/08/2023	C-3	25
3/09/2023	C-1	36
8/09/2023	C-3	28
14/09/2023	C-1	12
2/10/2023	C-1	34
2/10/2023	C-1	25
21/10/2023	C-1	33
23/10/2023	C-3	23
10/11/2023	C-2	35
26/12/2023	C-3	15
1/01/2024	C-2	21
10/01/2024	C-2	30
14/01/2024	C-3	24
26/02/2024	C-2	23
28/02/2024	C-3	10
1/03/2024	C-2	15
12/04/2024	C-3	37
27/04/2024	C-3	18

CHAPTER 7 MERGING AND APPENDING TABLES

Table 7-18. Info: Customer Info

From	To	Customer ID	States
1/07/2023	now	C-1	TA
1/07/2023	22/11/2023	C-2	NSW
1/07/2023	30/10/2023	C-3	NSW
30/10/2023	3/01/2024	C-3	TA
22/11/2023	now	C-2	WA
3/01/2024	12/02/2024	C-3	NSW
12/02/2024	now	C-3	QLD

Note The data in this example is provided in an Excel file titled `06 Conditional Merging .xlsx`.

This problem can be solved using the techniques presented in Chapter 3, but in this case, you will solve it using the Merge command. Before merging the tables, you'll replace the "now" text in the To column of the Info table with more meaningful values. To do this, select the column, then from the Home tab, click the Replace Values command. As shown in Figure 7-37, in the Value to Find box, enter now, and in the Replace with box, enter `DateTime.LocalNow()` (or alternatively, you can choose a future date, such as 2050/01/01).

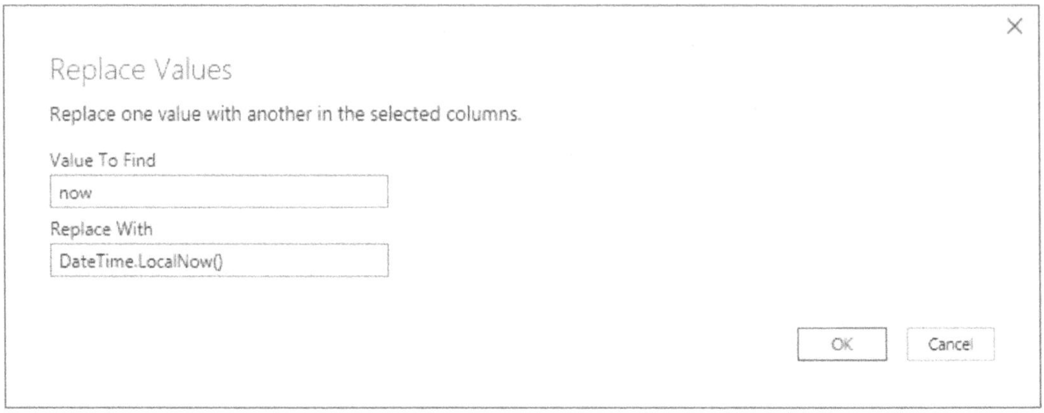

Figure 7-37. Replacement setting

CHAPTER 7 MERGING AND APPENDING TABLES

This process will replace "now" with DateTime.LocalNow(), as shown in the Figure 7-38.

= Table.ReplaceValue(Source,"now","DateTime.LocalNow()",Replacer.
ReplaceValue,{"To"})

	From	To	Customer ID	States
1	1/07/2023 12:00:00 AM	DateTime.LocalNow()	C-1	TA
2	1/07/2023 12:00:00 AM	22/11/2023 12:00:00 AM	C-2	NSW
3	1/07/2023 12:00:00 AM	30/10/2023 12:00:00 AM	C-3	NSW
4	30/10/2023 12:00:00 AM	3/01/2024 12:00:00 AM	C-3	TA
5	22/11/2023 12:00:00 AM	DateTime.LocalNow()	C-2	WA
6	3/01/2024 12:00:00 AM	12/02/2024 12:00:00 AM	C-3	NSW
7	12/02/2024 12:00:00 AM	DateTime.LocalNow()	C-3	QLD

Figure 7-38. *The result of replacement*

Removing the double quotation marks around "DateTime.LocalNow()" and rewriting the formula as follows will result in today's date and current time, as shown in Figure 7-39.

= Table.ReplaceValue(Source,"now",DateTime.LocalNow(),Replacer.
ReplaceValue,{"To"})

	From	To	Customer ID	States
1	1/07/2023 12:00:00 AM	4/02/2025 3:08:28 PM	C-1	TA
2	1/07/2023 12:00:00 AM	22/11/2023 12:00:00 AM	C-2	NSW
3	1/07/2023 12:00:00 AM	30/10/2023 12:00:00 AM	C-3	NSW
4	30/10/2023 12:00:00 AM	3/01/2024 12:00:00 AM	C-3	TA
5	22/11/2023 12:00:00 AM	4/02/2025 3:08:28 PM	C-2	WA
6	3/01/2024 12:00:00 AM	12/02/2024 12:00:00 AM	C-3	NSW
7	12/02/2024 12:00:00 AM	4/02/2025 3:08:28 PM	C-3	QLD

Figure 7-39. *The result of modified formula*

Now select the From and To columns in the Info table and change the type of values on them to Date. Then perform the same action for the Date column in the Sales table.

In this next step, you need to extract the customer location from the Info table and add it to the Sales table. Select the Sales table. Then, from the Home tab, select Merge Queries and choose the Info table as the second table. Choose Customer ID as the linked column between the two tables, using the settings provided in Figure 7-40.

CHAPTER 7   MERGING AND APPENDING TABLES

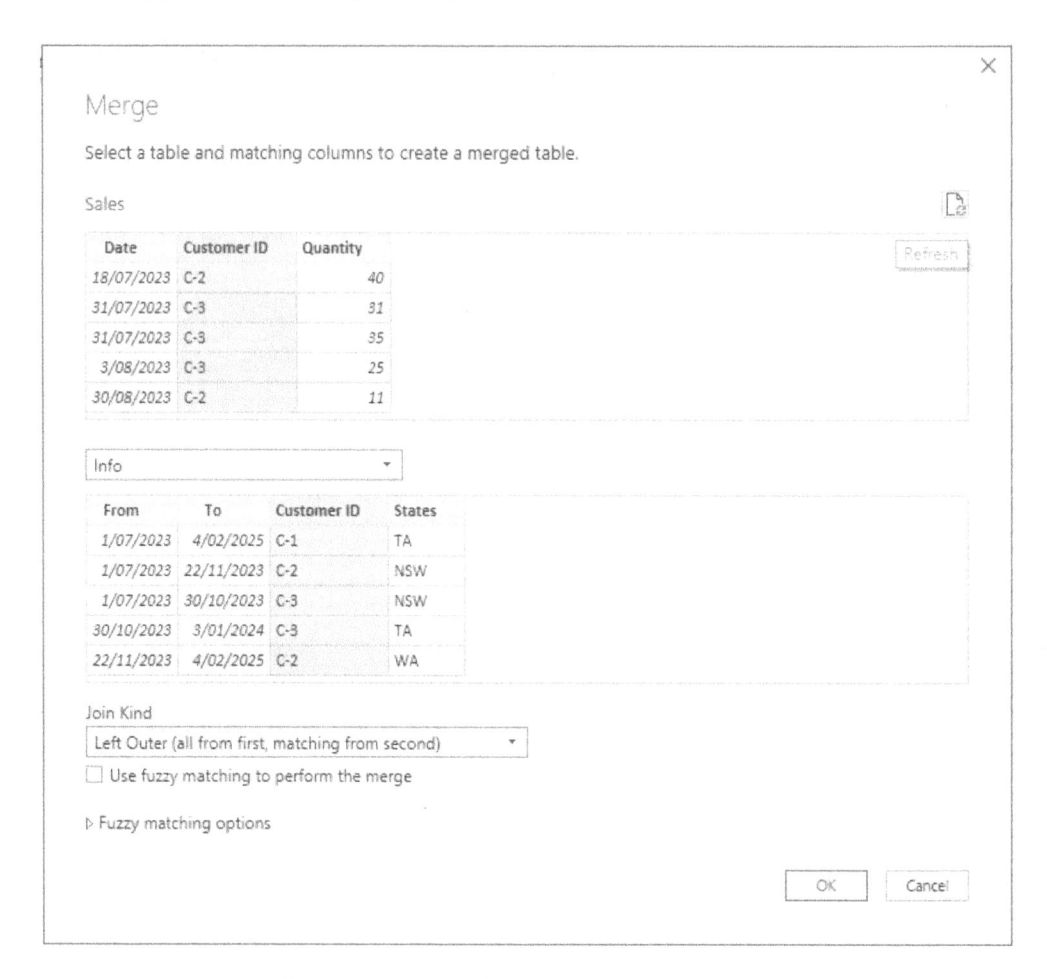

Figure 7-40. Settings for merging tables

After clicking OK, you will see the merged table shown in Figure 7-41. In this example, since the Customer ID C-3 is repeated multiple times in the Info table, the resulting column includes several rows from the Info table being matched with the row in the Sales table. You need to filter the rows in the resulting table based on the transaction date to select the correct location data.

CHAPTER 7 MERGING AND APPENDING TABLES

#	Date	Customer ID	Quantity	Info
1	18/07/2023	C-2	40	Table
2	31/07/2023	C-3	31	Table
3	31/07/2023	C-3	35	Table
4	3/08/2023	C-3	25	Table
5	30/08/2023	C-2	11	Table
6	31/08/2023	C-3	25	Table
7	3/09/2023	C-1	36	Table
8	8/09/2023	C-3	28	Table
9	14/09/2023	C-1	12	Table
10	2/10/2023	C-1	34	Table
11	2/10/2023	C-1	25	Table
12	21/10/2023	C-1	33	Table
13	23/10/2023	C-3	23	Table

From	To	Customer ID	States
1/07/2023	22/11/2023	C-2	NSW
22/11/2023	4/02/2025	C-2	WA

From	To	Customer ID	States
1/07/2023	30/10/2023	C-3	NSW
30/10/2023	3/01/2024	C-3	TA
3/01/2024	12/02/2024	C-3	NSW
12/02/2024	4/02/2025	C-3	QLD

From	To	Customer ID	States
1/07/2023	4/02/2025	C-1	TA

Figure 7-41. The results of merging

To extract the customer location from the transaction date, you can use the method presented in the Chapter 3, but this section shows a solution based on the UI. Expand all the items on the newly added column called Info to reach the result presented in Figure 7-42.

As shown in Figure 7-42, only the rows where the value in the Date column falls between the values in the From and To columns are considered valid for the location. All other rows should be excluded.

#		Date	Customer ID	Quantity	From	To	Customer ID.1	States
1	✓	18/07/2023	C-2	40	1/07/2023	22/11/2023	C-2	NSW
2	✗	18/07/2023	C-2	40	22/11/2023	4/02/2025	C-2	WA
3	✓	30/08/2023	C-2	11	1/07/2023	22/11/2023	C-2	NSW
4	✗	30/08/2023	C-2	11	22/11/2023	4/02/2025	C-2	WA
5	✓	3/09/2023	C-1	36	1/07/2023	4/02/2025	C-1	TA
6	✓	31/07/2023	C-3	31	1/07/2023	30/10/2023	C-3	NSW
7	✗	31/07/2023	C-3	31	30/10/2023	3/01/2024	C-3	TA
8	✗	31/07/2023	C-3	31	3/01/2024	12/02/2024	C-3	NSW
9	✗	31/07/2023	C-3	31	12/02/2024	4/02/2025	C-3	QLD

Figure 7-42. Filtering the previous date

To extract the valid rows, apply a filter on the Date column and select a specific date. This results in the following formula:

```
= Table.SelectRows(#"Expanded Info", each ([Date] = #date(2023, 8, 3)))
```

429

CHAPTER 7 MERGING AND APPENDING TABLES

To modify the condition and filter rows where the value in the Date column is less than the To column value and greater than or equal to the From column value, you can rewrite the formula as follows, which results in Figure 7-43:

= Table.SelectRows(#"Expanded Info", each ([Date] >=[From] and [Date]<[To]))

Figure 7-43. Extracting the last row

The state of each transaction has now been determined. Applying the Group By command with the settings shown in Figure 7-44 will resolve the issue, resulting in the table shown in Figure 7-45.

CHAPTER 7 MERGING AND APPENDING TABLES

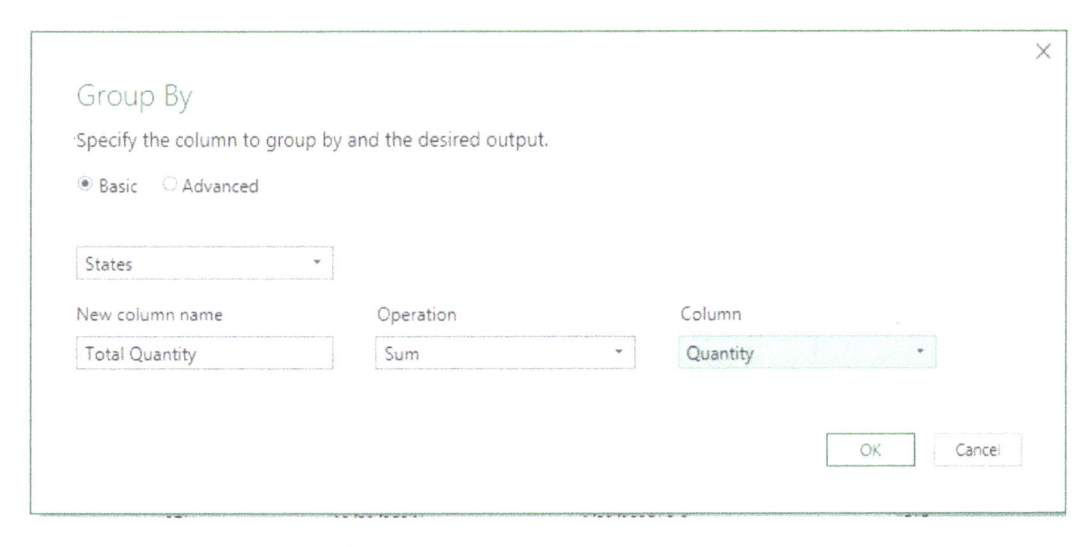

Figure 7-44. Extracting the states

Figure 7-45. The final table

Self-Merging

Historical sales transactions are shown in the Sales table in Table 7-19, and you'll calculate the sales per customer. However, the Customer ID may change over time, and these changes are recorded in the Info table shown in Table 7-20. Based on the Info table, the ID of Customer C-1 was first changed to C-7, then to C-9, and finally to C-13. Thus, all these IDs (C-1, C-7, C-9, and C-13) refer to the same customer, so you need to sum all the values for these IDs and present it as the Total Quantity for C-13. Initially extract the last Customer ID for each customer, then, calculate the total quantity per customer using the latest Customer ID.

Table 7-19. *Sales: Historical Sales Info*

Date	Customer ID	Quantity
18/07/2023	C-2	40
19/07/2023	C-5	22
26/07/2023	C-3	24
27/07/2023	C-2	12
31/07/2023	C-1	31
31/07/2023	C-1	35
3/08/2023	C-3	25
19/08/2023	C-10	10
30/08/2023	C-4	11
31/08/2023	C-15	25
9/09/2023	C-11	11
13/10/2023	C-11	24
21/10/2023	C-1	33
23/10/2023	C-15	23
10/11/2023	C-10	35
16/11/2023	C-7	27
2/12/2023	C-8	30
4/12/2023	C-12	13
16/12/2023	C-9	22
24/12/2023	C-13	34
26/12/2023	C-14	15
1/01/2024	C-13	21
10/01/2024	C-13	30
14/01/2024	C-14	24

Table 7-20. Info: Customer Info

Old ID	New ID
C-1	C-7
C-5	C-8
C-7	C-9
C-9	C-13
C-2	C-12
C-12	C-14

Note The data in this example is provided in an Excel file titled 07 Self-Merging.xlsx.

The complexity of this problem lies within the Info table. If there were an additional column, say Last ID, that displayed the last ID for each customer (e.g., C-13 for all the IDs C-1, C-7, and C-9), you could easily solve this problem, but as there is no such column, you need to add it first and then use merging to solve the problem. Two different solutions based on merging and using the List.Generate() function are proposed to determine the last IDs.

Solution 1: Based on Merging Logic

At first glance, one way to solve this problem is through recursion, where the Info table is repeatedly merged with itself multiple times, in each iteration, until it finds the last IDs for all customers. Create a new query called Repetitive_Self_Merge and write the following formula in its formula bar as the first step, as shown in Figure 7-46. This refers to the result of the Info query (at this step is exactly the same as the Info table).

= Info

CHAPTER 7 MERGING AND APPENDING TABLES

OLD ID	New ID
C-1	C-7
C-5	C-8
C-7	C-9
C-9	C-13
C-2	C-12
C-12	C-14

Queries [3]: Sales, Info, Repetitive_Self_Merge

Query Settings — PROPERTIES — Name: Repetitive_Self_Merge — All Properties — APPLIED STEPS — Source

Figure 7-46. New query

Consider the first row in this table. Based on this row, the ID of customer C-1 is updated to C-7. To find its next update, you need to search for its last ID, which was presented on the New ID column (C-7) in the Old ID column across other rows. If you find C-7 in a row, the value in the New ID column of that row will provide the updated ID for this customer. If C-7 is not found, it indicates that this is the final ID for this customer. To achieve this, you need to recursively merge the table with itself to track the sequence of ID updates.

With the Repetitive_Self_Merge query selected, go to the Home tab and click the Merge Queries command. In the open window, select Repetitive_Self_Merge for the top and bottom tables. To extract the next ID, you need to search for values in the New ID column against the values in the Old ID column. So, in the top table, select the New ID column, and in the bottom table, select the Old ID column as the common columns, as shown in Figure 7-47. By clicking OK, you will get the result shown in Figure 7-48, which provides a table for rows where the IDs have changed again and a blank table for those rows where the IDs have not changed further.

434

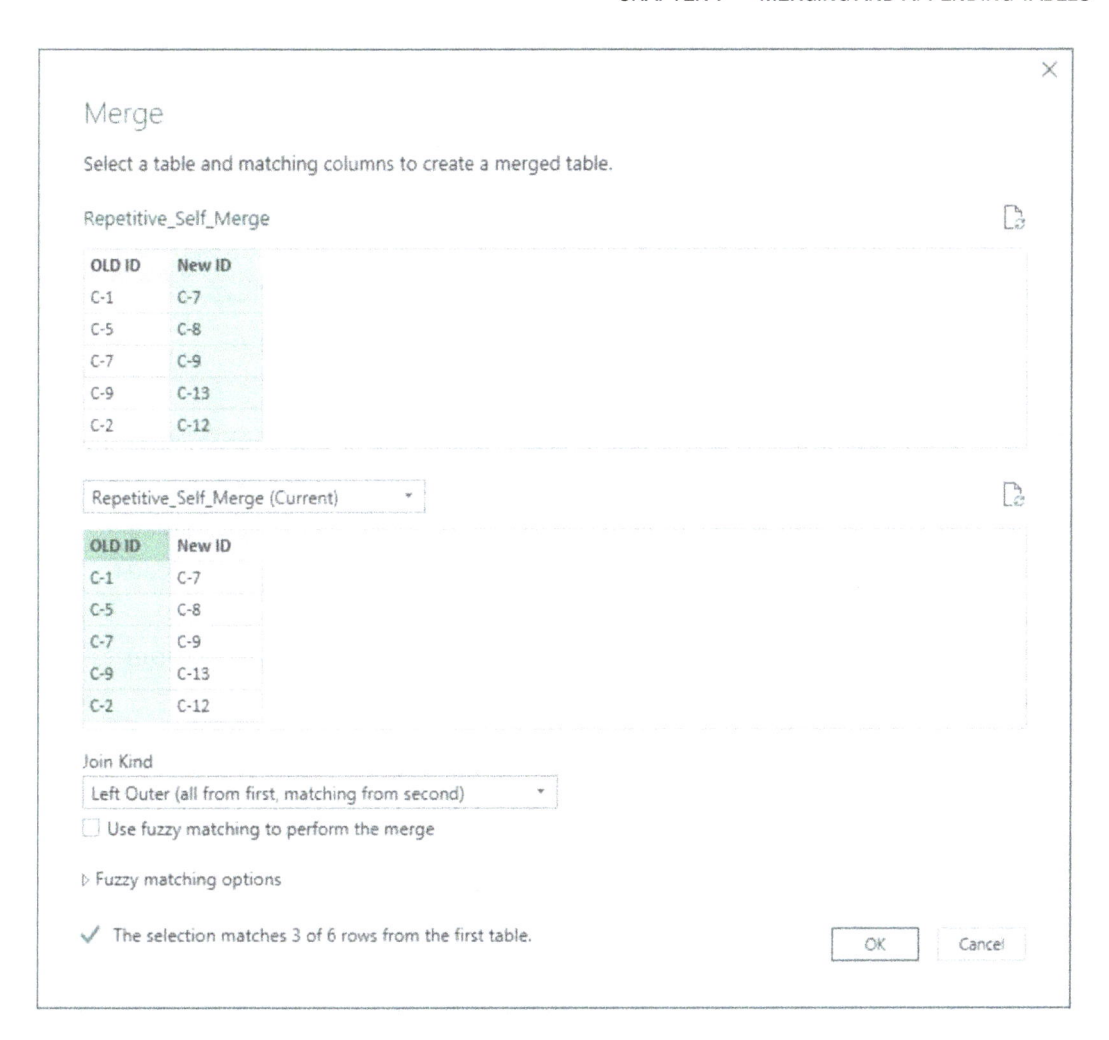

Figure 7-47. Merge settings

CHAPTER 7 MERGING AND APPENDING TABLES

	OLD ID		New ID		Source		OLD ID	New ID
1	C-1		C-7		Table		C-7	C-9
2	C-5		C-8		Table			
3	C-7		C-9		Table		OLD ID	New ID
4	C-9		C-13		Table		C-9	C-13
5	C-2		C-12		Table			
6	C-12		C-14		Table		OLD ID	New ID
							This table is empty.	

***Figure 7-48.** Merge results*

If the Source column contains an empty table (as in row 4), it means that the New ID in this row is the final ID for that customer. However, if the Source column contains a non-empty table, it does not guarantee that you've reached the last ID. Instead, it indicates that you've only found the next ID for that customer, and you will need to perform the self-merging process again to continue the sequence.

Add a new column called Next ID using the following formula in the Custom Column window:

```
= if Table.IsEmpty([Source]) then [New ID] else [Source][New ID]{0}
```

This column will show the value from the New ID column if the Source column is blank; otherwise, it will extract the value from the New ID column in the table is present in the Source column, and produces the result shown in Figure 7-49.

	OLD ID	New ID	Source	Next ID
1	C-1	C-7	Table	C-9
2	C-5	C-8	Table	C-8
3	C-7	C-9	Table	C-13
4	C-9	C-13	Table	C-13
5	C-2	C-12	Table	C-14
6	C-12	C-14	Table	C-14

***Figure 7-49.** Merge results*

CHAPTER 7 MERGING AND APPENDING TABLES

In the first row of the resulting table, the customer ID was initially C-1, and its New ID became C-7, which was later changed to C-9 (as shown in the Next ID column). However, C-9 is not the final ID, as it is changed to C-13 next. Therefore, you need to repeat this self-merge process again.

The number of times the self-merging process needs to be repeated depends on the structure of the data. This process should continue until a stop condition is met. For example, the process can stop once all the tables in the merged column are blank, indicating that no further IDs need to be updated.

Since the number of times this process needs to be repeated is not always clear, you need to create a loop using a recursive function to repeat this process until reaching the last ID for all the customers. Since this process will be repeated multiple times, it's helpful to convert the output table back to the same structure as the input table. This will ensure that the process can continue smoothly without having to adjust for changes in the table structure with each iteration.

In this example, the initial table contains only two columns: Old ID and New ID. To transform the resulting table into this structure, remove the New ID and Source columns, then rename the Next ID column to New ID. You will then have a table with the same column names as in the first step, as shown in Figure 7-50.

```
= Table.RenameColumns(#"Removed Columns",{{"Next ID", "New ID"}})
```

OLD ID	New ID
C-1	C-9
C-5	C-8
C-7	C-13
C-9	C-13
C-2	C-14
C-12	C-14

Figure 7-50. *Changing the table*

Next, open the Advanced Editor, where the steps are shown in Figure 7-51.

437

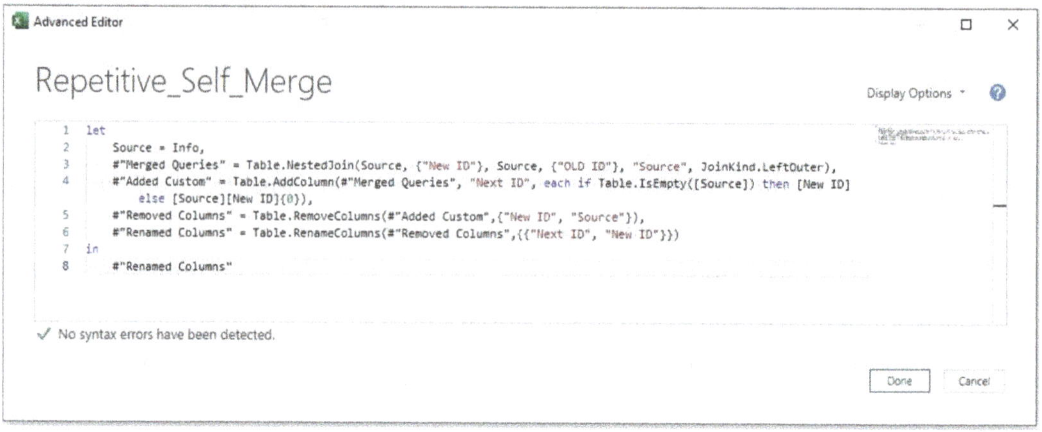

CHAPTER 7   MERGING AND APPENDING TABLES

Figure 7-51. Advanced Editor

All the steps you followed up to now are presented here. In the first step, you defined the Source as the result of the Info query, and all subsequent steps were applied to this table. Instead of directly using this table, you can convert it into a parameter. By doing this, this query will be transformed into a function that takes a table as input, applies all the steps to it, and returns the resulting table.

To convert this query into a function and make it dynamic, you need to remove the first step (Source = Info) and define Source as an input parameter. You do this by entering (Source)=> before the let expression, as shown in Figure 7-52.

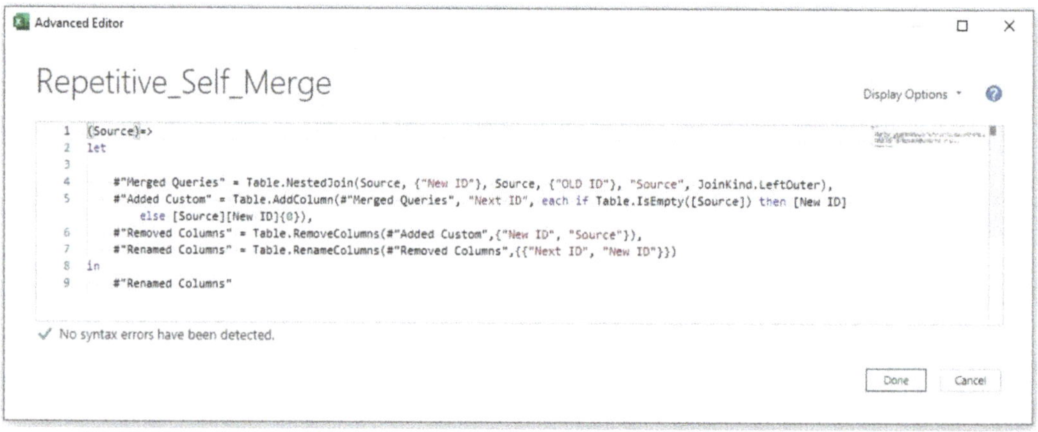

Figure 7-52. Converting the query into a function

CHAPTER 7 MERGING AND APPENDING TABLES

The query has been converted into a function, as shown in Figure 7-53, so that it takes a table like Info and performs a self-merge on it once. To repeat this process until the last IDs for all the customers are found using a recursive cycle, you need to define a stop condition.

In this example, you reach the last IDs for all the customers when none of the text in the New ID column is present in the Old ID column. So, the condition can be written as follows (since the last step in the defined function is named #"Renamed Columns", I use that for the table name):

```
= List.ContainsAny(#"Renamed Columns"[New ID],#"Renamed Columns" [OLD ID])
```

If the result of the previous formula is true, it means that there is at least one value in the New ID column that is also found in the Old ID column, so the cycle should be repeated. Otherwise, you have reached the final table, and it should be presented as the result.

In the function steps shown in Figure 7-52, after the in expression, the result of #"Renamed Columns" is currently returned. However, since you have now defined a stop condition, you need to modify this logic. You need to write it as, if the stop condition evaluates to true, it means you have not yet reached the final table and must apply self-merging again to #"Renamed Columns". If the stop condition is false, the process is complete, and #"Renamed Columns" represents the final table.

To implement this logic, write the formula as follows:

```
if [stop condition] then Repetitive_Self_Merge(#"Renamed Columns") else #"Renamed Columns"
```

The revised recursive custom function is defined as follows (see Figure 7-53):

```
(Source)=>
let
    #"Merged Queries" = Table.NestedJoin(Source, {"New ID"}, Source, {"OLD ID"}, "Source", JoinKind.LeftOuter),
    #"Added Custom" = Table.AddColumn(#"Merged Queries", "Next ID", each if Table.IsEmpty([Source]) then [New ID] else [Source][New ID]{0}),
```

CHAPTER 7 MERGING AND APPENDING TABLES

```
    #"Removed Columns" = Table.RemoveColumns(#"Added Custom",{"New ID",
    "Source"}),
    #"Renamed Columns" = Table.RenameColumns(#"Removed Columns",{{"Next
    ID", "New ID"}})
in
    if List.ContainsAny(#"Renamed Columns"[New ID],#"Renamed Columns" [OLD
        ID]) then Repetitive_Self_Merge(#"Renamed Columns") else #"Renamed
        Columns"
```

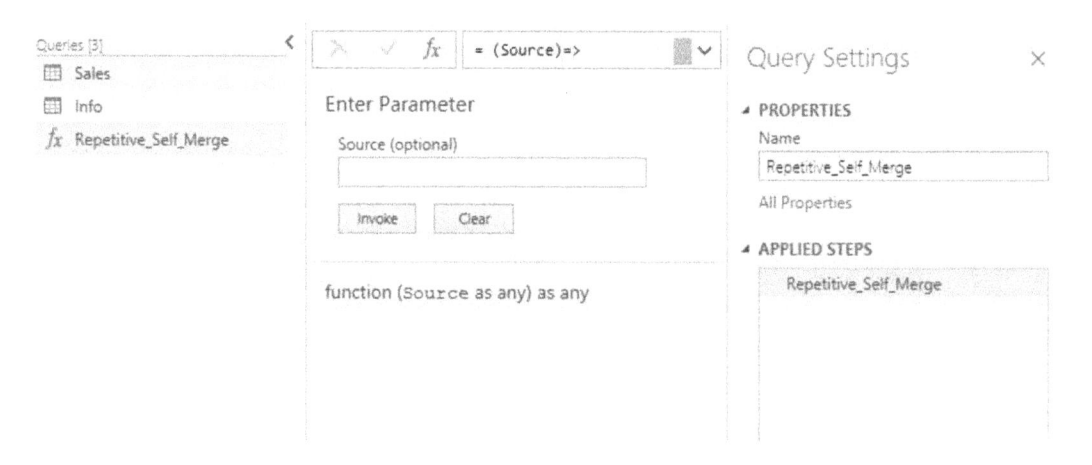

Figure 7-53. Defining the recursive function

By creating a new query named `Revised_Info` and using the following formula, you obtain the desired table. This table includes the latest IDs for customers who have undergone ID changes. This includes all the changed IDs and their last IDs for merging with the Sales table, as shown in Figure 7-54:

`= Repetitive_Self_Merge(Info)`

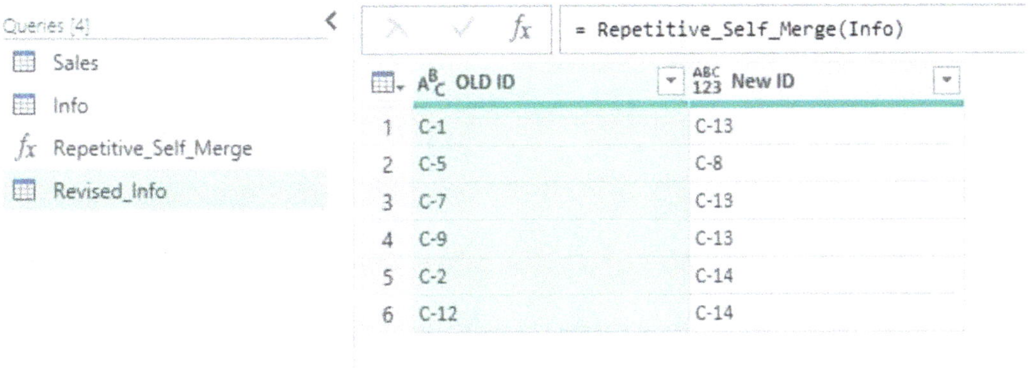

CHAPTER 7   MERGING AND APPENDING TABLES

#	OLD ID	New ID
1	C-1	C-13
2	C-5	C-8
3	C-7	C-13
4	C-9	C-13
5	C-2	C-14
6	C-12	C-14

Figure 7-54. Revised Info table

After reaching the last IDs for all the customers, select the Sales table and perform a merge with the Revised_Info table based on the settings shown in Figure 7-55. Then, expand the new column by selecting only New ID to achieve the result shown in Figure 7-56.

CHAPTER 7 MERGING AND APPENDING TABLES

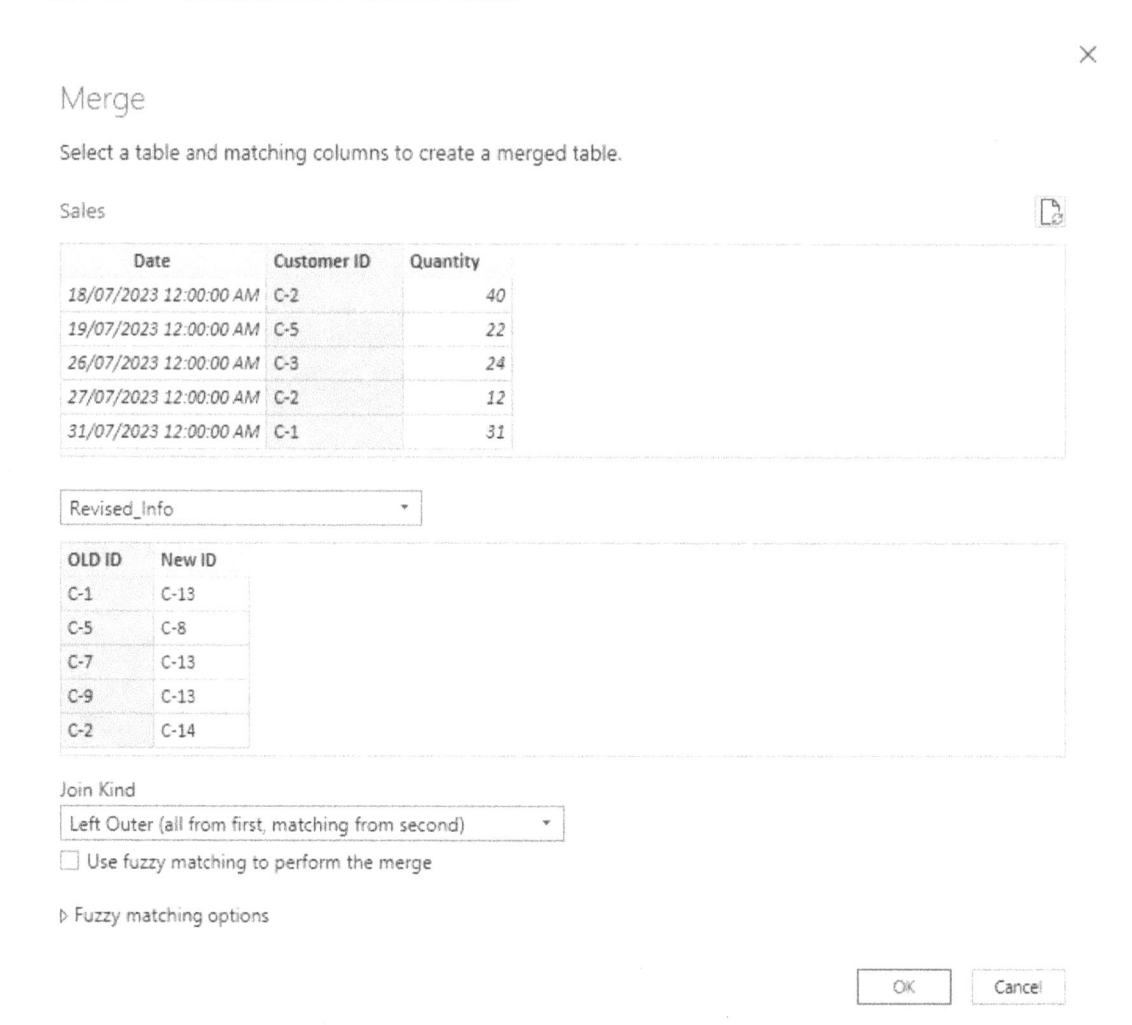

Figure 7-55. Setting for merging

CHAPTER 7 MERGING AND APPENDING TABLES

	Date	Customer ID	Quantity	New ID
1	18/07/2023 12:00:00 AM	C-2	40	C-14
2	27/07/2023 12:00:00 AM	C-2	12	C-14
3	31/07/2023 12:00:00 AM	C-1	31	C-13
4	31/07/2023 12:00:00 AM	C-1	35	C-13
5	19/07/2023 12:00:00 AM	C-5	22	C-8
6	26/07/2023 12:00:00 AM	C-3	24	null
7	3/08/2023 12:00:00 AM	C-3	25	null
8	19/08/2023 12:00:00 AM	C-10	10	null
9	30/08/2023 12:00:00 AM	C-4	11	null
10	31/08/2023 12:00:00 AM	C-15	25	null
11	9/09/2023 12:00:00 AM	C-11	11	null
12	13/10/2023 12:00:00 AM	C-11	24	null
13	21/10/2023 12:00:00 AM	C-1	33	C-13
14	23/10/2023 12:00:00 AM	C-15	23	null
15	10/11/2023 12:00:00 AM	C-10	35	null
16	16/11/2023 12:00:00 AM	C-7	27	C-13
17	2/12/2023 12:00:00 AM	C-8	30	null
18	4/12/2023 12:00:00 AM	C-12	13	C-14
19	16/12/2023 12:00:00 AM	C-9	22	C-13
20	24/12/2023 12:00:00 AM	C-13	34	null
21	26/12/2023 12:00:00 AM	C-14	15	null
22	1/01/2024 12:00:00 AM	C-13	21	null
23	10/01/2024 12:00:00 AM	C-13	30	null
24	14/01/2024 12:00:00 AM	C-14	24	null

Figure 7-56. *Result of merging*

Since the Info table only includes customers who have experienced at least one ID change, some customers may have a null value in the **New ID** column. For these customers, you should use the value from the **Customer ID** column. Add a new column named Final ID using one of the following formulas to reach the result shown in Figure 7-57:

=if [New ID]=null then [Customer ID] else [New ID]

=[New ID]??[Customer ID]

CHAPTER 7   MERGING AND APPENDING TABLES

#	Date	Customer ID	Quantity	New ID	Final ID
1	18/07/2023 12:00:00 AM	C-2	40	C-14	C-14
2	27/07/2023 12:00:00 AM	C-2	12	C-14	C-14
3	31/07/2023 12:00:00 AM	C-1	31	C-13	C-13
4	31/07/2023 12:00:00 AM	C-1	35	C-13	C-13
5	19/07/2023 12:00:00 AM	C-5	22	C-8	C-8
6	26/07/2023 12:00:00 AM	C-3	24	null	C-3
7	3/08/2023 12:00:00 AM	C-3	25	null	C-3
8	19/08/2023 12:00:00 AM	C-10	10	null	C-10
9	30/08/2023 12:00:00 AM	C-4	11	null	C-4
10	31/08/2023 12:00:00 AM	C-15	25	null	C-15
11	9/09/2023 12:00:00 AM	C-11	11	null	C-11
12	13/10/2023 12:00:00 AM	C-11	24	null	C-11
13	21/10/2023 12:00:00 AM	C-1	33	C-13	C-13
14	23/10/2023 12:00:00 AM	C-15	23	null	C-15
15	10/11/2023 12:00:00 AM	C-10	35	null	C-10
16	16/11/2023 12:00:00 AM	C-7	27	C-13	C-13
17	2/12/2023 12:00:00 AM	C-8	30	null	C-8
18	4/12/2023 12:00:00 AM	C-12	13	C-14	C-14
19	16/12/2023 12:00:00 AM	C-9	22	C-13	C-13
20	24/12/2023 12:00:00 AM	C-13	34	null	C-13
21	26/12/2023 12:00:00 AM	C-14	15	null	C-14
22	1/01/2024 12:00:00 AM	C-13	21	null	C-13
23	10/01/2024 12:00:00 AM	C-13	30	null	C-13
24	14/01/2024 12:00:00 AM	C-14	24	null	C-14

Figure 7-57. *Calculating the final ID*

You can use this new column to calculate the sales per customer. Select the Quantity column and change its type to number and then select the Group By command and applying the settings shown in Figure 7-58. Click OK to reach the result shown in Figure 7-59.

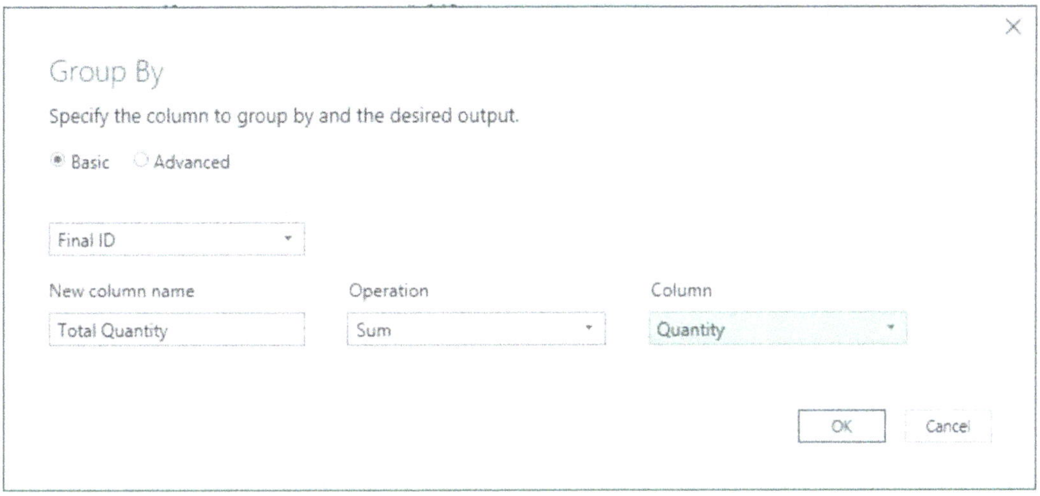

CHAPTER 7   MERGING AND APPENDING TABLES

Figure 7-58.   Setting for Group By

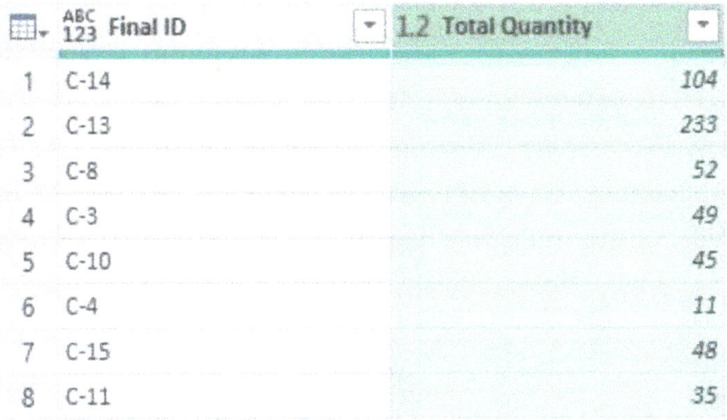

Figure 7-59.   Result of Group By

Solution 2: Using the List.Generate() Function

The previous solution solves the problem, but for large-scale scenarios, it may be time-consuming due to repeated self-merging. This solution introduces an alternative that is more efficient compared to the previous approach.

CHAPTER 7   MERGING AND APPENDING TABLES

To verify the logic of this solution, consider the customer with the ID C-1 as an example. You can use a formula to search for it in the Info table's Old ID column. If found, it chooses the corresponding New ID and repeats the search process using this new ID in the Old ID column until the last ID is found, as illustrated in Figure 7-60.

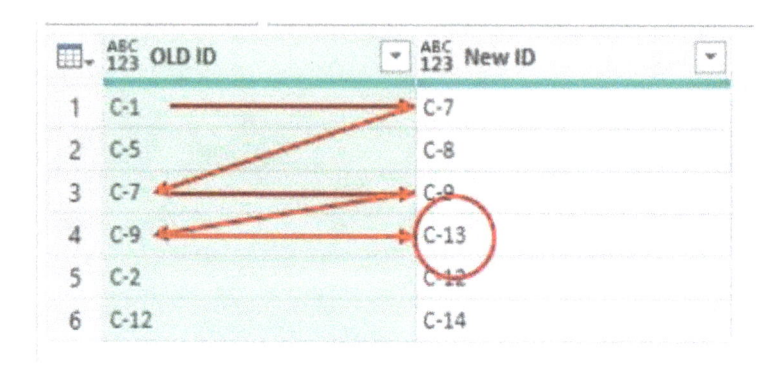

	OLD ID	New ID
1	C-1	C-7
2	C-5	C-8
3	C-7	C-9
4	C-9	C-13
5	C-2	C-12
6	C-12	C-14

Figure 7-60. *Searching for the last ID of customer C-1*

To perform this loop until the last ID of customers is found, you can use the List.Generate() function, (Chapter 9 explains this function and another way of defining a loop in Power Query.) To prepare the formula, create a new query called Test and write the following formula for customer ID C-1 to retrieve all the historical IDs of C-1. As shown in Figure 7-61, this formula produces all the historical IDs of the C-1 customer.

```
= List.Generate(
      ()=> "C-1",
      each _<>0,
      each try Info{[OLD ID=_]}[New ID] otherwise 0)
```

To clarify this formula, consider a variable named x (in the formula it is _, but since x is more easy to follow, let's assume the variable name is x), initially set to C-1 in the first argument. The second argument, which defines the stop condition, states that if x is not equal to 0, the loop should continue; otherwise, the loop should stop. In the third argument, x is updated using the following formula, which means searching for the value of x in the Old ID column. If a matching row is found, the corresponding value in

CHAPTER 7 MERGING AND APPENDING TABLES

the New ID column on that row is assigned the new value of x; otherwise, x is set to 0. The stop condition is then checked again, and based on the result, the loop continues or terminates.

```
try Info{[OLD ID=_]}[New ID] otherwise 0
```

Changing C-1 to C-2 or C-3 in the first input of the previous formula will yield all the historical IDs of C-2 and C-3, as shown in Figure 7-62 and Figure 7-63.

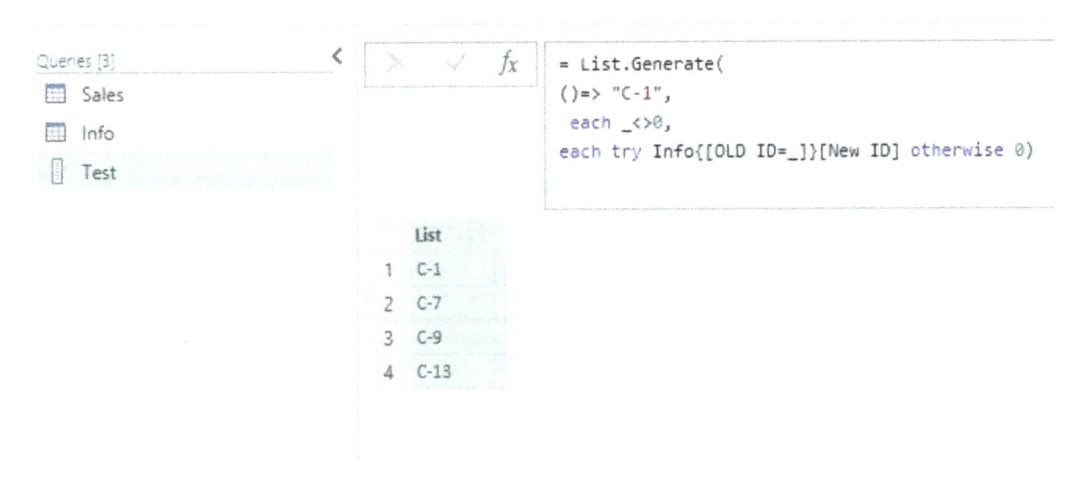

Figure 7-61. Result for the last ID of customer C-1

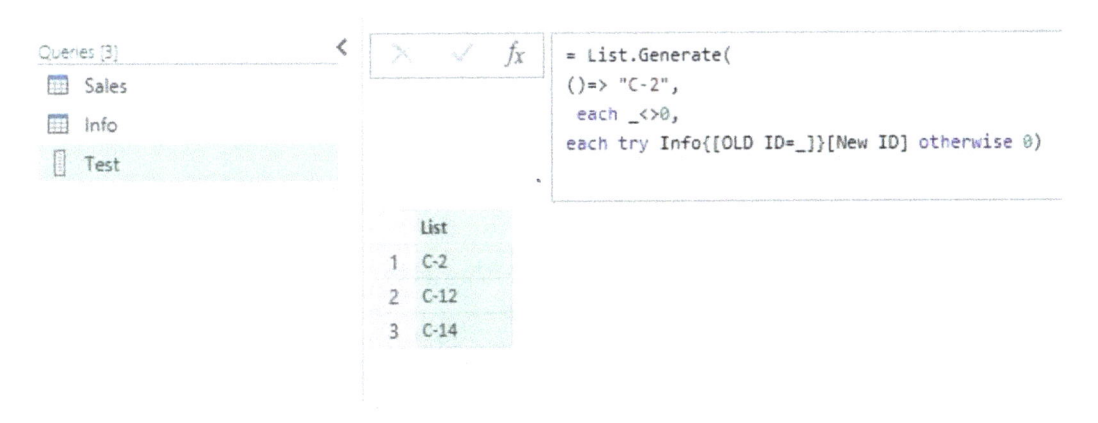

Figure 7-62. The result for the last ID of customer C-2

447

CHAPTER 7 MERGING AND APPENDING TABLES

```
= List.Generate(
    ()=> "C-3",
    each _<>0,
    each try Info{[OLD ID=_]}[New ID] otherwise 0)
```

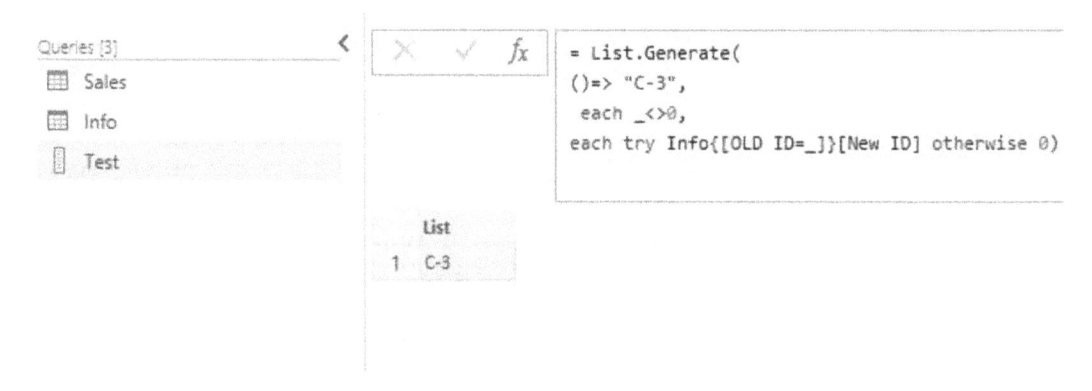

Figure 7-63. The result for the last ID of customer C-3

Since this formula returns a list of all changes in the customer IDs, the last value in the list represents the final ID for that customer. Therefore, the following formula will yield the last ID for the customer with ID = C-1:

```
= List.Last(List.Generate(
    ()=> "C-1",
    each _<>0,
    each try Info{[OLD ID=_]}[New ID] otherwise 0))
```

Based on this explanation, go to the Sales table and add a new column named Last ID using the following formula. This will extract the last IDs for each customer, as shown in Figure 7-64, and these IDs can then be used for grouping the data, similar to the previous solution.

```
=List.Last(List.Generate(
    ()=> [Customer ID],
    each _<>0,
    each try Info{[OLD ID=_]}[New ID] otherwise 0))
```

CHAPTER 7 MERGING AND APPENDING TABLES

	Date	Customer ID	Quantity	Last ID
1	18/07/2023 12:00:00 AM	C-2	40	C-14
2	19/07/2023 12:00:00 AM	C-5	22	C-8
3	26/07/2023 12:00:00 AM	C-3	24	C-3
4	27/07/2023 12:00:00 AM	C-2	12	C-14
5	31/07/2023 12:00:00 AM	C-1	31	C-13
6	31/07/2023 12:00:00 AM	C-1	35	C-13
7	3/08/2023 12:00:00 AM	C-3	25	C-3
8	19/08/2023 12:00:00 AM	C-10	10	C-10
9	30/08/2023 12:00:00 AM	C-4	11	C-4
10	31/08/2023 12:00:00 AM	C-15	25	C-15
11	9/09/2023 12:00:00 AM	C-11	11	C-11
12	13/10/2023 12:00:00 AM	C-11	24	C-11
13	21/10/2023 12:00:00 AM	C-1	33	C-13
14	23/10/2023 12:00:00 AM	C-15	23	C-15
15	10/11/2023 12:00:00 AM	C-10	35	C-10
16	16/11/2023 12:00:00 AM	C-7	27	C-13
17	2/12/2023 12:00:00 AM	C-8	30	C-8
18	4/12/2023 12:00:00 AM	C-12	13	C-14
19	16/12/2023 12:00:00 AM	C-9	22	C-13
20	24/12/2023 12:00:00 AM	C-13	34	C-13
21	26/12/2023 12:00:00 AM	C-14	15	C-14
22	1/01/2024 12:00:00 AM	C-13	21	C-13
23	10/01/2024 12:00:00 AM	C-13	30	C-13
24	14/01/2024 12:00:00 AM	C-14	24	C-14

Figure 7-64. Extracting the last ID for customers

Note Although this solution is more efficient compared to the first approach, it can be slow in real-world scenarios, especially when dealing with a large Info table, as it queries the table multiple times. To improve performance, similar to the technique presented in Chapter 2, it is recommended that you introduce an intermediate step. In this step, apply `Table.Buffer(Info)` to cache the table, and then reference this buffered table in the formula to reduce redundant lookups.

Summary

In this chapter, you learned how to manage multiple tables by either stacking them vertically (*appending*) or aligning them horizontally (*merging*), which are known as unite and joint in SQL. To append tables, you can use the Table.Combine() function, which takes two arguments—the first is a list of tables to be stacked, and the optional second argument specifies columns to include after appending, and it keeps the data types of the combined columns.

To merge tables, you use Table.Join() function to align two tables based on shared columns. This function supports various join types, such as inner and outer joins, to combine tables according to specific needs. Additionally, if the common columns are not exact matches, you can apply *fuzzy matching* to approximate and join similar values.

Your journey with Power Query continues! In the next chapter, you explore techniques for handling missing values in Power Query.

CHAPTER 8

Handling Missing Values

During the data-cleaning process, you might have to deal with missing values, which arise from various reasons, including the data-collection process, human mistakes, and technical issues. For example, if you create a form for job applicants where they can enter their date of birth in various formats (e.g., year, year-month, year/month/day), you might encounter missing values during analysis because some parts of the information are not provided. In another scenario, if you store your data in Excel files by year and inadvertently remove the data for 2012, that data will become missing for future analysis. Alternatively, if you want to use a government index in your prediction model, but the value of that index was not reported for a specific period in the past, it will be treated as a missing value in your analysis.

There are different scenarios in which you might encounter missing values, and handling missing values is a critical step in the data-cleaning process because it ensures data integrity and accuracy. Properly addressing missing values significantly improves model performance and enhances the overall quality and usability of the data. High-quality data is essential for making informed decisions, and addressing missing values ensures that the dataset is both complete and accurate. This chapter explains how to handle missing values in several scenarios.

Note Missing values and zeros are often confused, but they are fundamentally different. Consider the process of collecting data via a questionnaire. After conducting five interviews, the decision is made to add a question asking participants how many children they have. For the individuals interviewed before this question was added, there is no data available on this field, meaning it is a missing value. This does not imply that these individuals have no children—it simply means the information wasn't collected. Therefore, you cannot enter a value of 0 for these individuals. However, for future interviews, if a participant answers 0, that is a valid response indicating they have no children, rather than a missing value.

© Omid Motamedisedeh 2025
O. Motamedisedeh, *96 Common Challenges in Power Query*, https://doi.org/10.1007/979-8-8688-1288-0_8

CHAPTER 8   HANDLING MISSING VALUES

Filling Nulls with Previous Values

Table 8-1 shows the project progress reports at the end of the month for projects A and B. In some months, the progress is missing, indicated by a null value in the Actual Progress column (the cells in the Excel files are blank, which will be converted to null after loading them into Power Query). Replace the null values with the last reported progress from the previous month.

Table 8-1. Source: Monthly Project Progress

Date	Project	Actual Progress
31/01/2023	A	0.05
28/02/2023	A	0.07
31/03/2023	A	0.09
30/04/2023	A	null
31/05/2023	A	null
30/06/2023	A	null
31/07/2023	A	0.24
31/08/2023	A	null
30/09/2023	A	0.28
31/10/2023	A	null
30/11/2023	A	null
31/12/2023	A	0.35
31/01/2023	B	0.02
28/02/2023	B	0.05
31/03/2023	B	null
30/04/2023	B	null
31/05/2023	B	0.16

(*continued*)

Table 8-1. (*continued*)

Date	Project	Actual Progress
30/06/2023	B	0.21
31/07/2023	B	null
31/08/2023	B	0.24
30/09/2023	B	null
31/10/2023	B	null
30/11/2023	B	null
31/12/2023	B	0.41

Note The data in this example is provided in an Excel file titled `01 Filling with Previous Values.xlsx`.

The rows are sorted for each project based on Date column, so to replace null values with the last reported progress from the previous month, you just need to replace the null values with the previous non-null value on that column. Select the Actual Progress column, then from the Transform tab, use the Fill command. Choose Fill Down to solve the problem and reach Figure 8-1 based on the following formula:

```
= Table.FillDown(Source,{"Actual Progress"})
```

CHAPTER 8   HANDLING MISSING VALUES

#	Date	Project	Actual Progress
1	31/01/2023	A	0.05
2	28/02/2023	A	0.07
3	31/03/2023	A	0.09
4	30/04/2023	A	0.09
5	31/05/2023	A	0.09
6	30/06/2023	A	0.09
7	31/07/2023	A	0.24
8	31/08/2023	A	0.24
9	30/09/2023	A	0.28
10	31/10/2023	A	0.28
11	30/11/2023	A	0.28
12	31/12/2023	A	0.35
13	31/01/2023	B	0.02
14	28/02/2023	B	0.05
15	31/03/2023	B	0.05
16	30/04/2023	B	0.05
17	31/05/2023	B	0.16
18	30/06/2023	B	0.21
19	31/07/2023	B	0.21
20	31/08/2023	B	0.24
21	30/09/2023	B	0.24
22	31/10/2023	B	0.24
23	30/11/2023	B	0.24
24	31/12/2023	B	0.41

Figure 8-1. *The result of Fill Down*

Note If you plan to load the result table into the data model, instead of filling null values with the previous value in Power Query before loading, you can remove the rows with null values and then use DAX to extract the last available values after loading the table into the data model.

CHAPTER 8   HANDLING MISSING VALUES

Handling Missing Rows

Similar to previous examples, the project progress reports at the end of the month for projects A and B are shown in the table called Source in Table 8-2. Some months are missing. Add the missing months to the table and then fill them with the last reported progress.

Table 8-2. Source: Monthly Project Progress

Date	Project	Actual Progress
31/01/2023	A	5%
28/02/2023	A	7%
31/03/2023	A	9%
31/07/2023	A	24%
30/09/2023	A	28%
31/12/2023	A	35%
31/01/2023	B	2%
28/02/2023	B	5%
31/05/2023	B	16%
30/06/2023	B	21%
31/08/2023	B	24%
31/12/2023	B	41%

Note The data in this example is provided in an Excel file titled `02 Handling Entirely Missing Rows.xlsx`.

To solve this problem, two different solutions—one based on merging and the other on appending—are provided. In both solutions, you need a table including all relevant dates (in this example, the last days of each month in 2023) for both projects.

CHAPTER 8   HANDLING MISSING VALUES

You can use the `Table.FromList()` function to generate this table efficiently (for more details on this function, see the Example 11 in Chapter 1). In the `AllRowsData` query, you can click the *fx* button next to the formula bar to create a new step and write the following formula in the formula bar:

```
=Table.FromList({1..12}, each {Date.EndOfMonth(#date(2023,_,1)),
{"A","B"}}, {"Date","Project"})
```

This results in Figure 8-2.

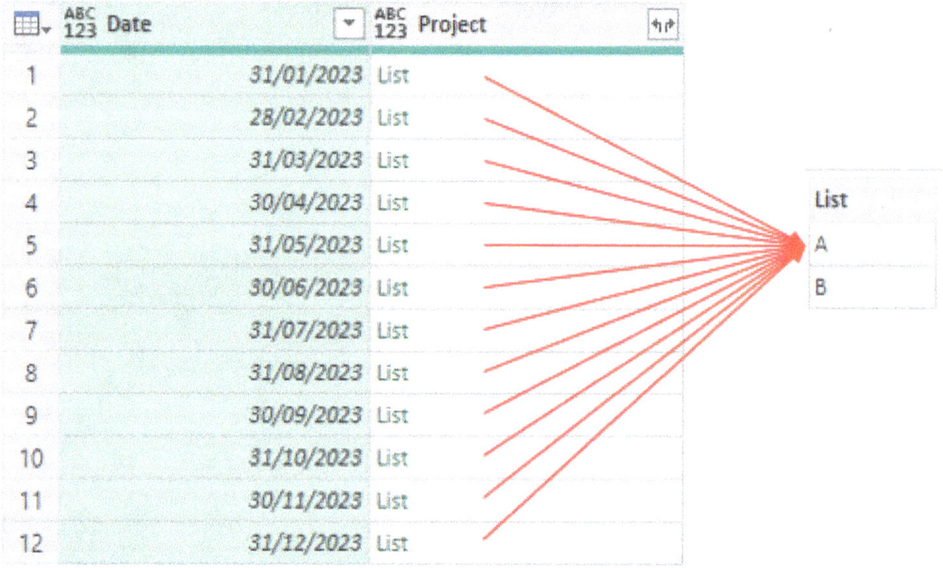

Figure 8-2. *Result of using Table.FromList*

Expanding the values in the Project column and changing the data type of the Date column will result in Figure 8-3.

CHAPTER 8 HANDLING MISSING VALUES

#	Date	Project
1	31/01/2023	A
2	31/01/2023	B
3	28/02/2023	A
4	28/02/2023	B
5	31/03/2023	A
6	31/03/2023	B
7	30/04/2023	A
8	30/04/2023	B
9	31/05/2023	A
10	31/05/2023	B
11	30/06/2023	A
12	30/06/2023	B
13	31/07/2023	A
14	31/07/2023	B
15	31/08/2023	A
16	31/08/2023	B
17	30/09/2023	A
18	30/09/2023	B
19	31/10/2023	A
20	31/10/2023	B
21	30/11/2023	A
22	30/11/2023	B
23	31/12/2023	A
24	31/12/2023	B

Figure 8-3. The result of expanding the Project column

CHAPTER 8   HANDLING MISSING VALUES

> **Note** In this example, the following formula is used to create a table that includes all valid dates for two projects—A and B:
>
> =Table.FromList({1..12}, each {Date.EndOfMonth(#date(2023,_,1)), {"A","B"}}, {"Date","Project"})
>
> In practice, if you are working with multiple projects, instead of hardcoding {"A", "B"}, you can dynamically retrieve the list of projects using List.Distinct(Info[Project]). This ensures that all the project names from the Info[Project] column are included.
>
> Additionally, if you need a wider range of dates—such as the last day of each month from 2023 to 2025—after changing the first argument from {1..12} to {1..36} (as you need 36 rows), you can use the following formula to generate the correct dates dynamically:
>
> Date.EndOfMonth(Date.AddMonths(#date(2023,1,1),_-1))

In the next step, load the Source table into the Power Query Editor as a query named Info, as Figure 8-4.

#	Date	Project	Actual Progress
1	31/01/2023 12:00:00 AM	A	0.05
2	28/02/2023 12:00:00 AM	A	0.07
3	31/03/2023 12:00:00 AM	A	0.09
4	31/07/2023 12:00:00 AM	A	0.24
5	30/09/2023 12:00:00 AM	A	0.28
6	31/12/2023 12:00:00 AM	A	0.35
7	31/01/2023 12:00:00 AM	B	0.02
8	28/02/2023 12:00:00 AM	B	0.05
9	31/05/2023 12:00:00 AM	B	0.16
10	30/06/2023 12:00:00 AM	B	0.21
11	31/08/2023 12:00:00 AM	B	0.24
12	31/12/2023 12:00:00 AM	B	0.41

Figure 8-4. *Loading the source table*

CHAPTER 8　HANDLING MISSING VALUES

As shown, the Date column includes the date and time. Select this column and change its type to Date to obtain Figure 8-5.

	Date	Project	Actual Progress
1	31/01/2023	A	0.05
2	28/02/2023	A	0.07
3	31/03/2023	A	0.09
4	31/07/2023	A	0.24
5	30/09/2023	A	0.28
6	31/12/2023	A	0.35
7	31/01/2023	B	0.02
8	28/02/2023	B	0.05
9	31/05/2023	B	0.16
10	30/06/2023	B	0.21
11	31/08/2023	B	0.24
12	31/12/2023	B	0.41

Figure 8-5. Converting the data type in the Dates column

You have two queries—`Info`, which contains reported progress for specific months, and `AllRowsData`, which includes all the dates for the projects but does not have any progress values. To generate a complete table that ensures valid progress values are available for all dates, you can use two different solutions—by merging and by appending the tables. These are presented in the following sections.

Solution 1: Using the Merge Command

In this solution, select AllRowsData query, and from the Home tab, use the Merge Queries command. Select Merge Queries to open a new window for merging the queries. As shown in Figure 8-6, for the second table, select the `Info` query, and then in the tables, select the Date and Project columns by holding Ctrl. Then click OK to obtain Figure 8-7.

CHAPTER 8   HANDLING MISSING VALUES

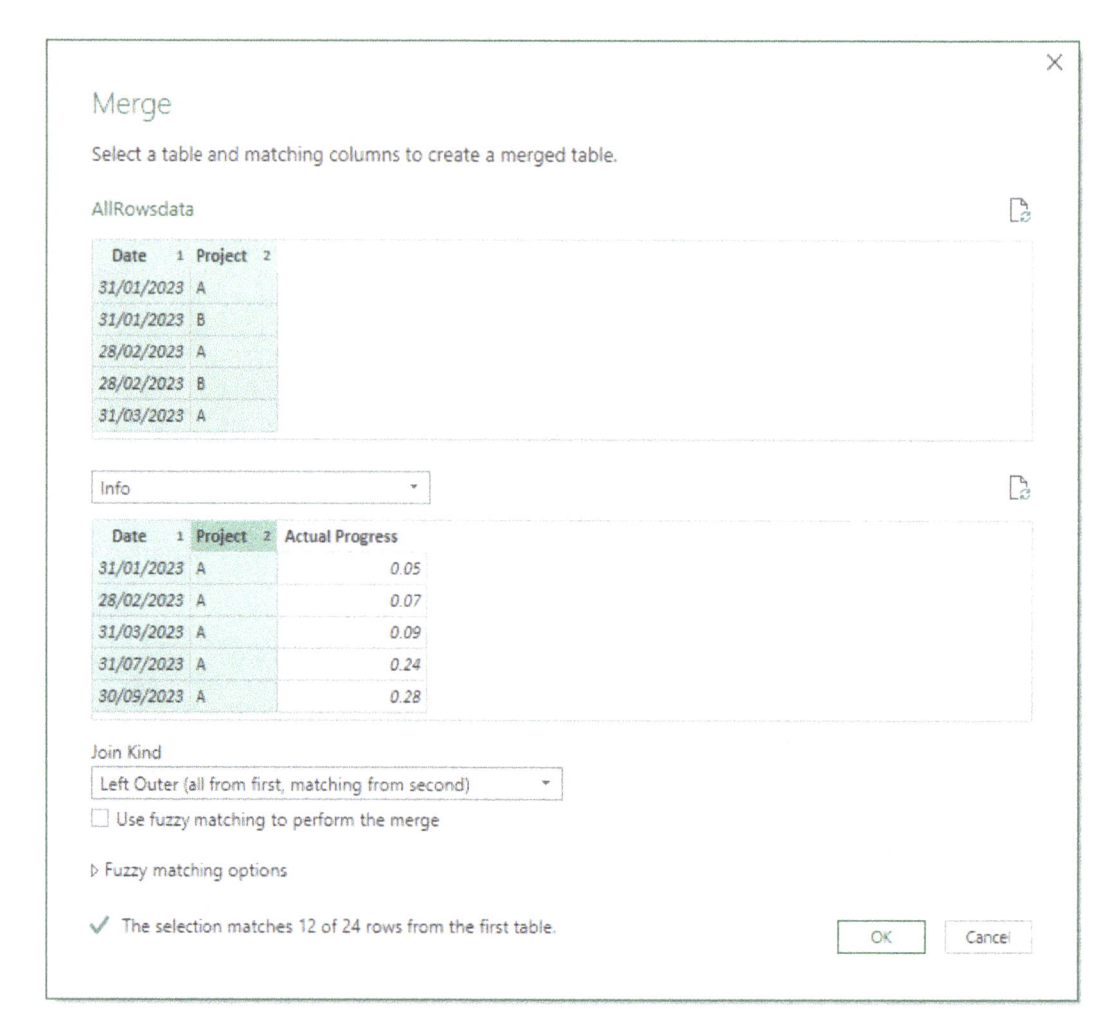

Figure 8-6. Merging settings

Figure 8-7. The result of merging

CHAPTER 8   HANDLING MISSING VALUES

In this next step, from the expand icon next to the new column called Info, select Actual Progress and expand it to obtain Figure 8-8.

	Date	Project	Actual Progress
1	31/01/2023	A	0.05
2	31/01/2023	B	0.02
3	28/02/2023	A	0.07
4	31/03/2023	A	0.09
5	28/02/2023	B	0.05
6	31/07/2023	A	0.24
7	31/03/2023	B	null
8	30/04/2023	A	null
9	30/04/2023	B	null
10	31/05/2023	A	null
11	31/05/2023	B	0.16
12	30/06/2023	B	0.21
13	30/06/2023	A	null
14	31/07/2023	B	null
15	31/08/2023	A	null
16	31/08/2023	B	0.24
17	30/09/2023	A	0.28
18	30/09/2023	B	null
19	31/10/2023	A	null
20	31/10/2023	B	null
21	30/11/2023	A	null
22	30/11/2023	B	null
23	31/12/2023	A	0.35
24	31/12/2023	B	0.41

Figure 8-8. *Expanding the Actual Progress column*

CHAPTER 8 HANDLING MISSING VALUES

By using merge, the row orders might be changed, so sort the table initially based on the project name and then based on the Date column to reorder the rows. This way, you can use the Fill Down command. Then, as in the previous example, use the Fill Down function to replace null values with the last values from the previous rows.

Solution 2: Based on Appending the Queries

In the previous solution, you used merge to extract the progress values from the Info query into the AllRowsData query. Alternatively, you can solve this problem by stacking the tables on top of each other and then removing the rows from AllRowsData that already exist in the Info query with the same Date and Project name.

So, first create a blank query. Then, click the *fx* button next to the formula bar to create a new step. In the formula bar, use the following formula to append the results from both queries (since the tables have the same column names):

= Info & AllRowsdata

This will append the rows from the Info query to the AllRowsData query, as shown in Figure 8-9.

CHAPTER 8 HANDLING MISSING VALUES

#	Date	Project	Actual Progress
1	31/01/2023	A	0.05
2	28/02/2023	A	0.07
3	31/03/2023	A	0.09
4	31/07/2023	A	0.24
5	30/09/2023	A	0.28
6	31/12/2023	A	0.35
7	31/01/2023	B	0.02
8	28/02/2023	B	0.05
9	31/05/2023	B	0.16
10	30/06/2023	B	0.21
11	31/08/2023	B	0.24
12	31/12/2023	B	0.41
13	31/01/2023	A	null
14	31/01/2023	B	null
15	28/02/2023	A	null
16	28/02/2023	B	null
17	31/03/2023	A	null
18	31/03/2023	B	null
19	30/04/2023	A	null
20	30/04/2023	B	null
21	31/05/2023	A	null
22	31/05/2023	B	null

Formula bar: `= Info & AllRowsdata`

***Figure 8-9.** Combining the tables*

Now, since the rows with actual progress are at the top and those with null values in the Actual Progress column are at the bottom, removing duplicates based on the Date and Project columns will eliminate the common rows with null values in Actual Progress (be careful when removing duplicates in more complex scenarios due to Power Query's execution order, as this can affect the results).

Select the Date and Project columns, right-click one of them, and choose Remove Duplicates to obtain Figure 8-10.

CHAPTER 8   HANDLING MISSING VALUES

Date	Project	Actual Progress
31/01/2023	A	0.05
28/02/2023	A	0.07
31/03/2023	A	0.09
31/07/2023	A	0.24
30/09/2023	A	0.28
31/12/2023	A	0.35
31/01/2023	B	0.02
28/02/2023	B	0.05
31/05/2023	B	0.16
30/06/2023	B	0.21
31/08/2023	B	0.24
31/12/2023	B	0.41

Formula: `= Table.Distinct(Source, {"Date", "Project"})`

Figure 8-10. Removing duplicates

Now sort the table in ascending order based on the Project column first, and then based on the Date column, and finally use the Fill Down command.

Extracting Missing Values

Consider the previous example and extract a list of dates with missing values for each project. Three different solutions—based on appending, merging, and grouping—are provided in this section.

Solution 1: Based on Appending/Merging

Consider all the steps in the previous example that lead to the table shown in Figure 8-10. Selecting the rows with null values in the Actual Progress column will leave you with only the dates for the projects that haven't reported values.

CHAPTER 8 HANDLING MISSING VALUES

Solution 2: Using Merging

Consider the steps that lead to the queries shown in Figure 8-4. In this case, selecting the `AllRowsData` query and using the Merge command with the Left Anti Join kind, as shown in Figure 8-11, will result in the missing data, as demonstrated in Figure 8-12.

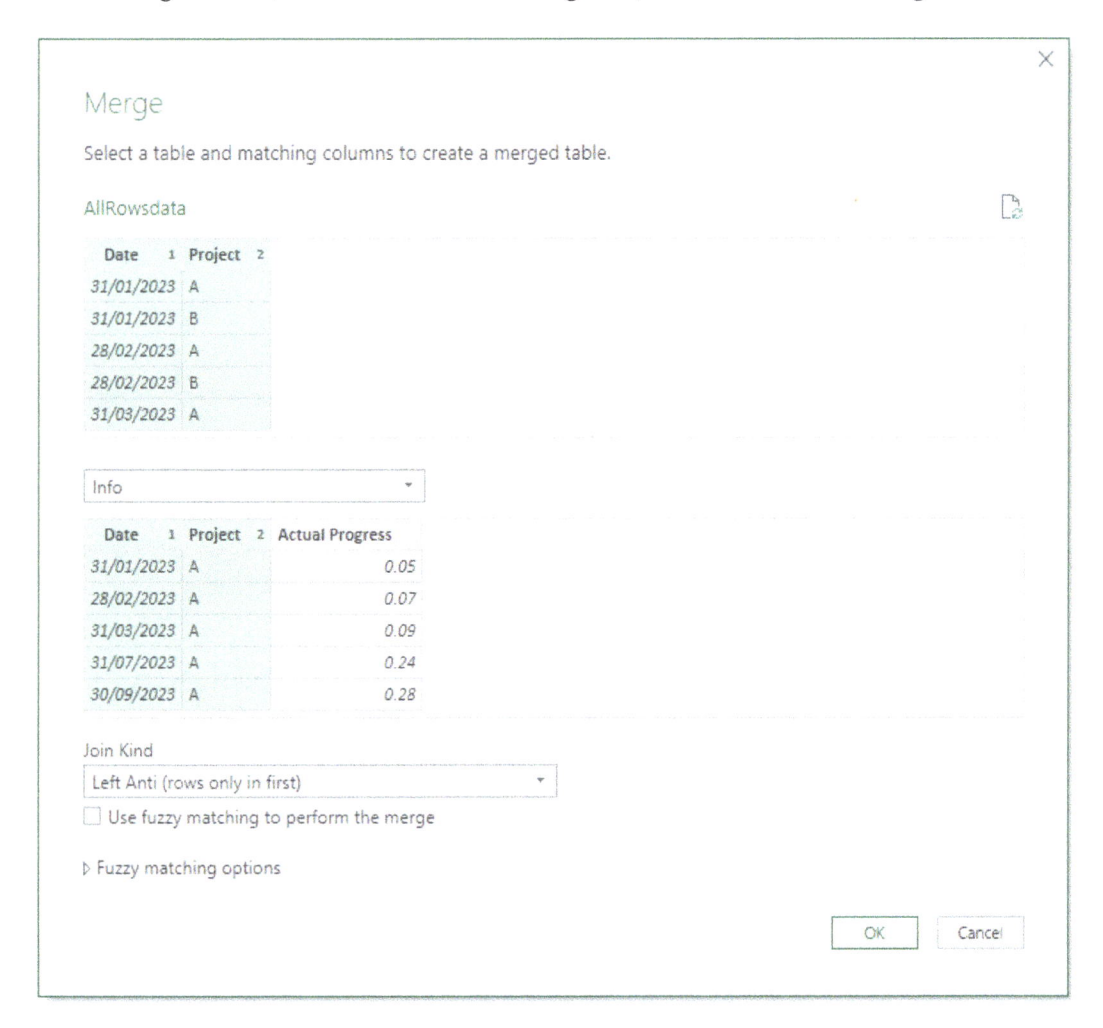

Figure 8-11. Configuration for merging

CHAPTER 8   HANDLING MISSING VALUES

#	Date	Project	Info
1	31/03/2023	B	Table
2	30/04/2023	A	Table
3	30/04/2023	B	Table
4	31/05/2023	A	Table
5	30/06/2023	A	Table
6	31/07/2023	B	Table
7	31/08/2023	A	Table
8	30/09/2023	B	Table
9	31/10/2023	A	Table
10	31/10/2023	B	Table
11	30/11/2023	A	Table
12	30/11/2023	B	Table

Figure 8-12. *The result of merging*

Solution 3: Based on Grouping the Rows

In this solution, the Table.Group() function extracts the list of reported dates, and then List.Difference() is applied to determine the missing dates. To achieve the table shown in Figure 8-13, load the data into Power Query and set the data types for the Date, Project, and Actual Progress columns as Date, Text, and Number, respectively.

CHAPTER 8   HANDLING MISSING VALUES

#	Date	Project	1.2 Actual Progress
1	31/01/2023 12:00:00 AM	A	0.05
2	28/02/2023 12:00:00 AM	A	0.07
3	31/03/2023 12:00:00 AM	A	0.09
4	31/07/2023 12:00:00 AM	A	0.24
5	30/09/2023 12:00:00 AM	A	0.28
6	31/12/2023 12:00:00 AM	A	0.35
7	31/01/2023 12:00:00 AM	B	0.02
8	28/02/2023 12:00:00 AM	B	0.05
9	31/05/2023 12:00:00 AM	B	0.16
10	30/06/2023 12:00:00 AM	B	0.21
11	31/08/2023 12:00:00 AM	B	0.24
12	31/12/2023 12:00:00 AM	B	0.41

Figure 8-13. *Loading data into Power Query and changing their types*

In the next step, select the Project column and use Group By. Select All Rows as the operation. The settings are provided in Figure 8-14. This will result in a table with a row for each project, as shown in Figure 8-15.

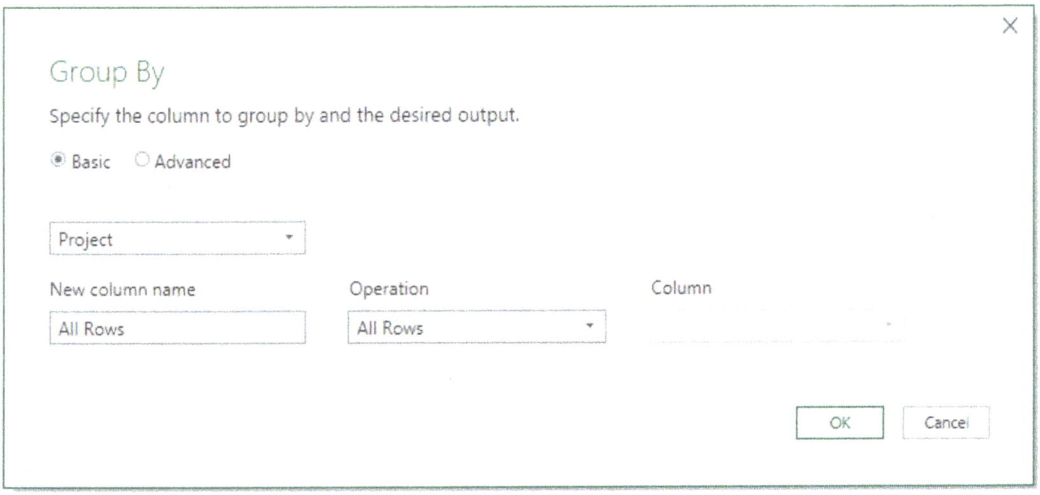

Figure 8-14. *Settings for grouping*

467

CHAPTER 8   HANDLING MISSING VALUES

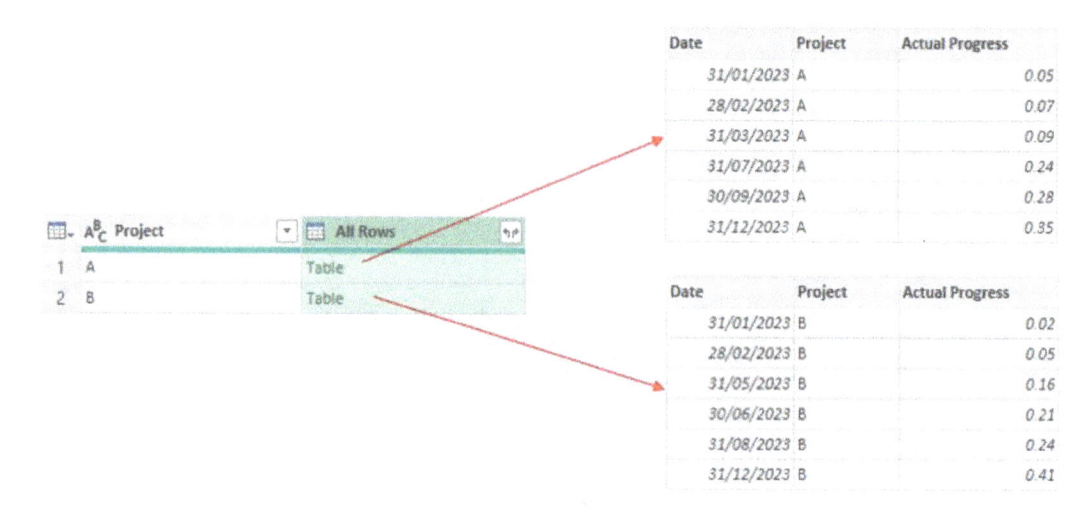

Figure 8-15. The result of grouping

In this example, since you are searching for the missing dates, you only need the Date values from all the columns presented in the tables in the All Rows column. This can be achieved by revising the formula. Consider the following formula, generated in the formula bar after grouping the rows based on the Project names.

= Table.Group(#"Changed Type", {"Project"}, {{"All Rows", each _, type table [Date=nullable date, Project=nullable text, Actual Progress=nullable number]}})

As mentioned in Chapter 6, this formula can be simplified as follows:

= Table.Group(#"Changed Type", {"Project"}, {{"All Rows", each _}})

As explained in Chapter 6, in this formula, each _ generates a table for each row. To extract the value from a specific column in the resulting tables, you can rewrite the formula as each _[Column Names]. By rewriting the previous formula as follows, the result will change as shown in Figure 8-16.

= Table.Group(Source, {"Project"}, {"All Rows", each _[Date]})

CHAPTER 8 HANDLING MISSING VALUES

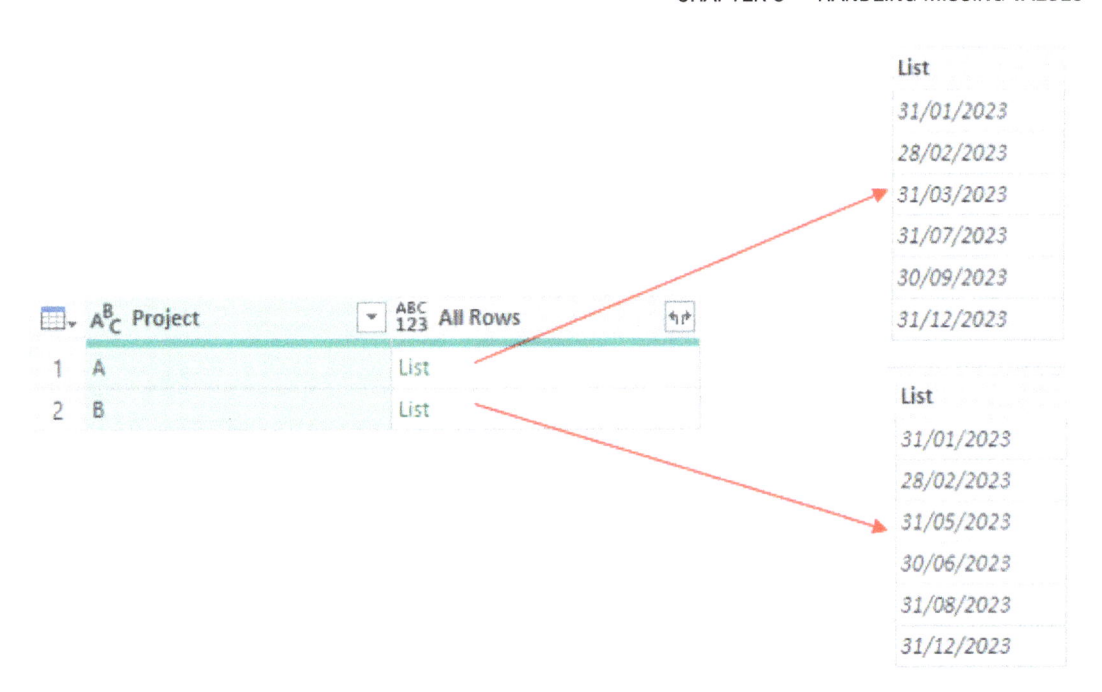

Figure 8-16. The result of the revised grouping

In the previous formula, _[Date] results in a list for each row (project), containing all the dates with reported values for Actual Progress. So, if you have a complete list of dates, you can use List.Difference(alldates, _[Date]) to extract the missing dates. You can use several formulas, like the following one (for more dynamic formula, see the recommendation in the Example 2 in this chapter) to extract the list of dates at the end of each month in 2023:

```
List.Transform({1..12}, (X)=> Date.EndOfMonth(#date(2023,X, 1)))
```

Rewriting the previous grouping formula as follows will present the list of missing dates for each project, as shown in Figure 8-17.

```
= Table.Group(#"Changed Type", {"Project"}, {{"All Rows", each List.Difference(List.Transform({1..12}, (X)=> Date.EndOfMonth(#date(2023,X, 1))),_[Date])}})
```

CHAPTER 8 HANDLING MISSING VALUES

Figure 8-17. *Converting the dates to the number*

By expanding the All Rows column, the problem is solved and all the missing dates per projects are extracted.

Linear Interpolation for Missing Data

Consider the project progress reports at the end of each month for projects A and B, as shown in the Source table in Table 8-3. Fill in the missing values using linear interpolation between the known values before and after each missing period (after you load data into Power Query, the blank cells will be shown as null).

Table 8-3. Source Table: Project Progress

Month	Project	Actual Progress
1	A	0.05
2	A	0.07
3	A	0.09
4	A	
5	A	
6	A	
7	A	0.24
8	A	
9	A	0.28
10	A	
11	A	
12	A	0.35
1	B	0.02
2	B	0.05
3	B	
4	B	
5	B	0.16
6	B	0.21
7	B	
8	B	0.24
9	B	
10	B	
11	B	
12	B	0.41

CHAPTER 8   HANDLING MISSING VALUES

> **Note** The data in this example is provided in an Excel file titled `04 Linear Interpolation for Missing Data.xlsx`.

Before addressing this problem, it's important to mention that interpolated values are not actual values; they provide an estimation that might be inaccurate. Treating both real and estimated values as the same in a table and later using them as input for other models, such as prediction models, can affect the results. In cases where null values are replaced by other values, it is recommended to distinguish them, for example, by adding a column that indicates which rows contain real values and which contain estimated values. This can be helpful for further analysis.

Interpolation is a method used to estimate unknown values that fall between known values in a dataset (for more detail, visit www.johndcook.com/interpolator.html). There are several models for interpolation, but in this example, you use linear interpolation, which assumes that the change between two known values is constant. The estimated value is found by drawing a straight line between two known values.

Generally, linear interpolation is calculated based on the following formula:

$$y = y_1 + (x - x_1) * (y_2 - y_1) / (x_2 - x_1)$$

Where:
x_1, y_1 are the coordinates of the first known data point.
x_2, y_2 are the coordinates of the second known data point.
x is the value for which you want to estimate the corresponding y.

In this example, x comes from the column Month and y comes from the column Actual Progress. So for the project B in month 3, x=3, x1=2, y1= 0.05 , x2 =5, and y2=0.16. So y is 0.05+(3-2)*(0.16-0.05)/(5-2), which is equal to 0.867. To calculate each month, you need the month and the actual progress values from the nearest previous and next rows that contain known actual progress.

Based on the data structure (where data is sorted by month for each project and the first and last month of each project are not null), selecting the Actual Progress column and applying Fill Down will replace null values with the previous non-null actual progress values (y1). Similarly, using Fill Up will replace nulls with the next non-null actual progress values (y2). By creating a similar column for the month, you can extract x1 and x2 in the same way.

To solve this problem, load the data into Power Query and change the column types for Month and Actual Progress to Number. Next, extract the values of x1, y1, x2, and y2 for each row. Instead of adding four separate columns individually, use record definitions to define all the columns at once (as demonstrated in Example 4 of Chapter 2). To do this, go to the Add Column tab, select Custom Column, and enter the following formula in the open window. You'll get the result shown in Figure 8-18.

```
=[y1=[Actual Progress],y2=y1,x1=if [Actual Progress] = null then null else [Month],x2=x1]
```

	Month	Project	Actual Progress	Custom
1	1	A		0.05 Record
2	2	A		0.07 Record
3	3	A		0.09 Record
4	4	A		null Record
5	5	A		null Record
6	6	A		null Record
7	7	A		0.24 Record
8	8	A		null Record
9	9	A		0.28 Record
10	10	A		null Record
11	11	A		null Record
12	12	A		0.35 Record
13	1	B		0.02 Record
14	2	B		0.05 Record
15	3	B		null Record
16	4	B		null Record
17	5	B		0.16 Record
18	6	B		0.21 Record
19	7	B		null Record
20	8	B		0.24 Record
21	9	B		null Record
22	10	B		null Record
23	11	B		null Record
24	12	B		0.41 Record

Figure 8-18. The result of adding custom column

Expanding the custom column will result in the table shown in Figure 8-19.

CHAPTER 8   HANDLING MISSING VALUES

#	1.2 Month	ABC Project	1.2 Actual Progress	ABC y1	ABC y2	ABC x1	ABC x2
1	1	A	0.05	0.05	0.05	1	1
2	2	A	0.07	0.07	0.07	2	2
3	3	A	0.09	0.09	0.09	3	3
4	4	A	null	null	null	null	null
5	5	A	null	null	null	null	null
6	6	A	null	null	null	null	null
7	7	A	0.24	0.24	0.24	7	7
8	8	A	null	null	null	null	null
9	9	A	0.28	0.28	0.28	9	9
10	10	A	null	null	null	null	null
11	11	A	null	null	null	null	null
12	12	A	0.35	0.35	0.35	12	12
13	1	B	0.02	0.02	0.02	1	1
14	2	B	0.05	0.05	0.05	2	2
15	3	B	null	null	null	null	null
16	4	B	null	null	null	null	null
17	5	B	0.16	0.16	0.16	5	5

Figure 8-19. *The result of expanding the column*

In the next step, select the y1 and x1 columns, then go to the Transform tab and apply the Fill Down command. Next, select the y2 and x2 columns and apply the Fill Up command. This will populate each row with the nearest previous and next known data for Month and Actual Progress, requiring for linear interpolation, as shown in Figure 8-20

CHAPTER 8 HANDLING MISSING VALUES

#	1.2 Month	ABC Project	1.2 Actual Progress	ABC y1	ABC y2	ABC x1	ABC x2
1	1	A	0.05	0.05	0.05	1	1
2	2	A	0.07	0.07	0.07	2	2
3	3	A	0.09	0.09	0.09	3	3
4	4	A	null	0.09	0.24	3	7
5	5	A	null	0.09	0.24	3	7
6	6	A	null	0.09	0.24	3	7
7	7	A	0.24	0.24	0.24	7	7
8	8	A	null	0.24	0.28	7	9
9	9	A	0.28	0.28	0.28	9	9
10	10	A	null	0.28	0.35	9	12
11	11	A	null	0.28	0.35	9	12
12	12	A	0.35	0.35	0.35	12	12
13	1	B	0.02	0.02	0.02	1	1
14	2	B	0.05	0.05	0.05	2	2
15	3	B	null	0.05	0.16	2	5
16	4	B	null	0.05	0.16	2	5
17	5	B	0.16	0.16	0.16	5	5

Figure 8-20. *The result of applying Fill Down and Up over the columns*

Now that all the required information for applying the interpolation formula is available for each row, add a Custom Column named Interpolation and enter the following formula in the Custom Column window. After clicking OK, remove any extra columns to obtain the final table, as shown in Figure 8-21.

```
=if [Actual Progress] = null then [y1]+([Month]-[x1])*([y2]-[y1])/([x2]-[x1]) else [Actual Progress]
```

CHAPTER 8 HANDLING MISSING VALUES

1.2 Month	ABC Project	ABC interpolation
1	1 A	0.05
2	2 A	0.07
3	3 A	0.09
4	4 A	0.1275
5	5 A	0.165
6	6 A	0.2025
7	7 A	0.24
8	8 A	0.26
9	9 A	0.28
10	10 A	0.303333333
11	11 A	0.326666667
12	12 A	0.35
13	1 B	0.02
14	2 B	0.05
15	3 B	0.086666667
16	4 B	0.123333333
17	5 B	0.16
18	6 B	0.21
19	7 B	0.225
20	8 B	0.24
21	9 B	0.2825
22	10 B	0.325
23	11 B	0.3675
24	12 B	0.41

Figure 8-21. *The final table*

Note The presented solution is simple and efficient in terms of time. However, for those interested in exploring Power Query further, this problem can also be solved without using Fill Down and Fill Up and instead by utilizing the Filter function (which is not recommended). To do this, add a Custom Column and use the following formula:

```
=[
  Non_null_rows = Table.SelectRows(
    Source,
    (X) => X[Actual Progress] <> null and X[Project] = [Project]
  ),
  Previous_Month = Table.Last(Table.SelectRows(Non_null_rows, (X) =>
  X[Month] <= [Month])),
```

```
    Next_Month = Table.First(Table.SelectRows(Non_null_rows, (X) =>
X[Month] >= [Month])),
    Result = [Actual Progress]
        ?? (
            Previous_Month[Actual Progress]
                + ([Month] - Previous_Month[Month])
                * (Next_Month[Actual Progress] - Previous_Month[Actual
                  Progress])
                / (Next_Month[Month] - Previous_Month[Month])
        )
][Result]
```

K-Nearest Neighbors (K-NN) for Imputation

K-nearest neighbors (KNN) is a supervised machine learning algorithm used for classification and regression tasks, which you can use to handle missing values. In this example, the goal is to use this technique to replace the missing values.

In the Source table shown in Table 8-4, the values of each row are represented by x, y, and z, but some values are missing. Fill in the missing values using the K-NN method with K=2 by following this process:

1. Consider set P, which includes all rows without any missing values, and set S, which includes all rows with at least one missing value.

2. For any row, like i, in set S (rows with missing values), calculate the distance of that row from all rows in set S based on non-missing values. For example, if x in row i is missing, the distance is calculated using $(y_i-y_p)^2+(z_i-z_p)^2$, and if both x and y in the ith row are missing, the distance is calculated using $(z_i-z_p)^2$.

3. Select the two rows from set P with the smallest distances from the ith rows in set S and designate them as r1 and r2.

4. Replace the missing value in the ith row with the average of the corresponding values in r1 and r2.

CHAPTER 8   HANDLING MISSING VALUES

Table 8-4. Source Table: Sample Data

Row ID	X	Y	Z
1	11	12	89
2	32	36	78
3	78	50	10
4	65	67	94
5	94	84	82
6	57	68	
7		30	12
8	40		
9	34		10
10	10	70	

Note The data in this example is provided in an Excel file titled `05 K-Nearest Neighbors (K-NN) for Imputation.xlsx`.

For example, consider the row ID=6 with x=57, y=68, and z=null (z is a missing value). To apply the KNN method and estimate the missing z value, you first need to extract the rows that have no missing values, as shown in Figure 8-22.

Row ID	X	Y	Z
1	11	12	89
2	32	36	78
3	78	50	10
4	65	67	94
5	94	84	82

Figure 8-22. Selecting the rows without a null value

CHAPTER 8 HANDLING MISSING VALUES

Next, calculate the distance between row ID=6 and every row in the table resulting from the previous step, using the values on Columns x and y. You do this using the $(x_i-x_6)^2+(y_i-y_6)^2$ formula, as shown in Figure 8-23.

Row ID	X	Y	Z	Distance
1	11	12	89	5252
2	32	36	78	1649
3	78	50	10	765
4	65	67	94	65
5	94	84	82	1625

Figure 8-23. Calculating distances

In the final step, you identify the two nearest rows with the smallest distances and take the average of their z values. This average (average of 10 and 94) is then assigned as the estimated z value for row ID=6, as shown in Figure 8-24.

Row ID	X	Y	Z	Distance	
1	11	12	89	5252	
2	32	36	78	1649	
3	78	50	10	765	✓
4	65	67	94	65	✓
5	94	84	82	1625	

Figure 8-24. Extracting the nearest rows

Note There are rare situations where applying such mathematical algorithms directly in Power Query is necessary. In most cases, it is easier to use Python or R within the Power BI version of Power Query (explained in Chapter 10). However, this example demonstrates that even advanced transformations can be performed with just a few steps in Power Query.

To solve this problem, first load the data into Power Query and rename the query MainTable, ensuring that all numerical columns (X, Y, and Z) are set to the number data type. If not, do this manually.

CHAPTER 8   HANDLING MISSING VALUES

The table is now ready to apply the steps of KNN over it. Instead of solving the problem for all rows at once, you begin by applying the method to a single row with missing values—like the row related to Row ID=6. This allows you to construct a solution that can later be converted into a function applicable to all rows with missing values.

Create a new blank query, named KNN, where you simulate the process for a single row before generalizing it. To work on Row 6, extract its values using the following formula in the formula bar, which serves as a reference for subsequent calculations:

= MainTable{5}

If you follow these steps, you will reach two queries: MainTable and KNN. In the KNN query, the first step, named Source, extracts the details of the sixth row from MainTable, as shown in Figure 8-25.

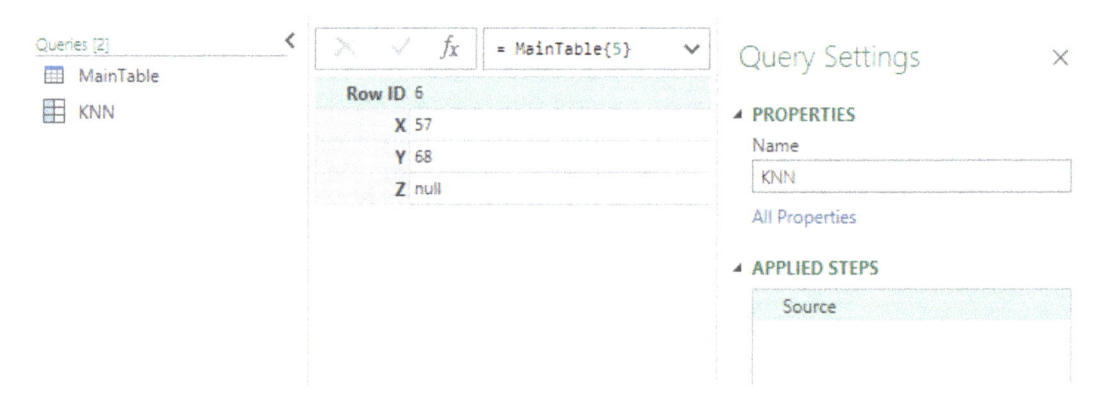

Figure 8-25. *The result of referring to the sixth row in MainTable*

In addition to the information in row 6, you need the entire dataset, which you'll later use to compute distances. So, in the KNN query, click the *fx* button to create a new step, which will be named Custom1 by default. In the formula bar, enter = MainTable, which will load the full dataset into the KNN query, as shown in Figure 8-26.

CHAPTER 8 HANDLING MISSING VALUES

Figure 8-26. Result of referring to Maintable

Before proceeding with the solution, you'll refine the approach by renaming the steps for better clarity. To do this, navigate to the Home tab, select Advanced Editor, and review all the steps, as shown in Figure 8-27.

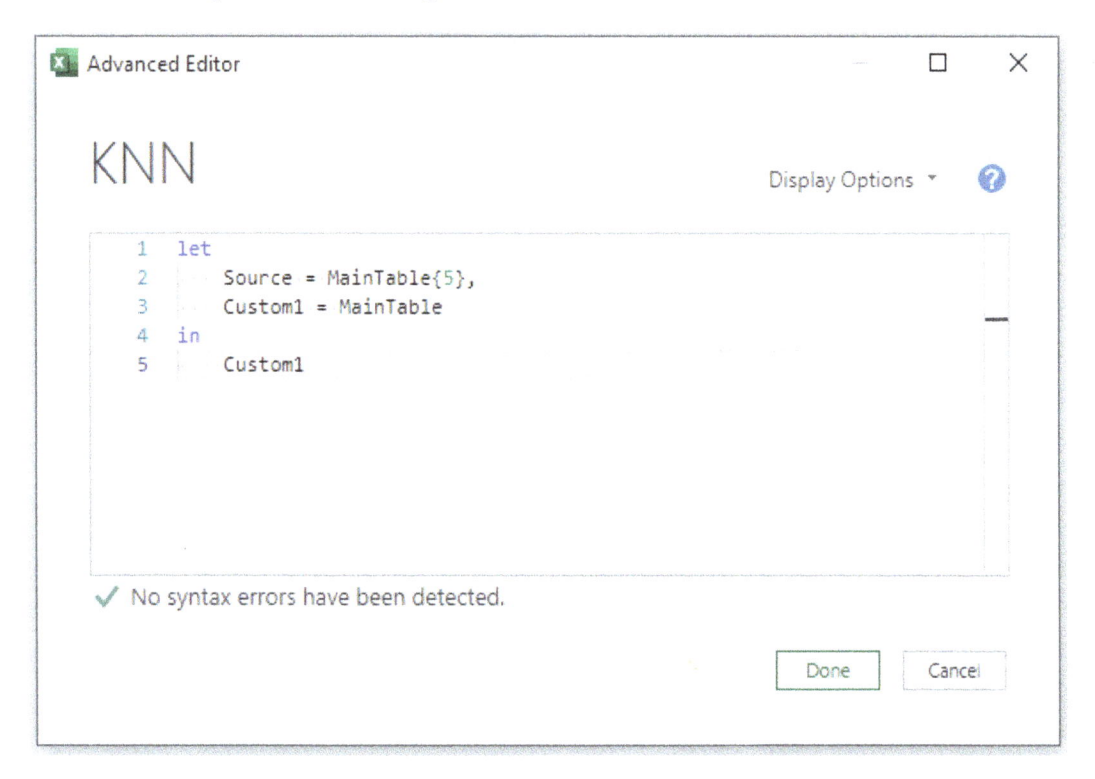

```
let
    Source = MainTable{5},
    Custom1 = MainTable
in
    Custom1
```

Figure 8-27. Query steps before changing

In the open window, rename Source to Row6 and Custom1 to InputTable, as shown in Figure 8-28.

481

CHAPTER 8   HANDLING MISSING VALUES

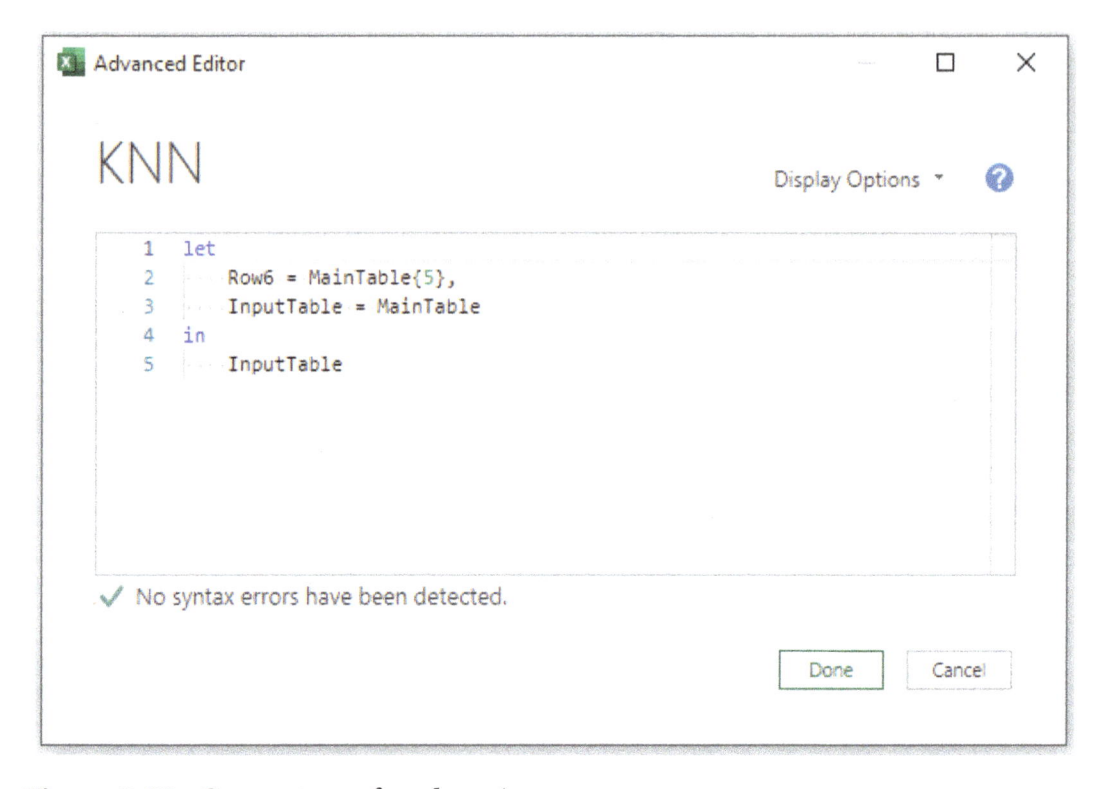

```
1  let
2      Row6 = MainTable{5},
3      InputTable = MainTable
4  in
5      InputTable
```

Figure 8-28. Query steps after changing

Now you can apply the KNN steps. The first step is to filter out rows that contain null values in any column. To achieve this, use the filter option next to a column, such as column X, and deselect the null values. This results in the following formula:

= Table.SelectRows(InputTable, each ([X] <> null))

Applying the same filter to other columns or rewriting the formula shown here will remove all rows that contain null values in any column. (If you are working with a large number of columns, refer to the technique presented in Example 1 of Chapter 3.) This process results in the table shown in Figure 8-29.

= Table.SelectRows(InputTable, each ([X] <> null) and ([Y] <> null) and ([Z] <> null))

CHAPTER 8 HANDLING MISSING VALUES

Row ID	1²₃ X	1²₃ Y	1²₃ Z	
1	1	11	12	89
2	2	32	36	78
3	3	78	50	10
4	4	65	67	94
5	5	94	84	82

Figure 8-29. *The result of selecting rows without null values*

The next step involves computing the Euclidean distance between Row6 and rows in the filtered dataset. Since you know that Row6 has a missing value in column Z, you can use a formula to calculate the squared differences between corresponding values in the X and Y columns using the following formula in the Custom Column window.

```
=Number.Power(Row6[X]-[X],2)+Number.Power(Row6[Y]-[Y],2)
```

The previous formula only works for rows where the missing value is in column Z. If it were applied to a row with a null value in column X, the term Number.Power(Row6[X] - [X], 2) would return null. Since any operation involving null results in null, the entire formula would also return null. To prevent this, you can modify the formula by using Number.Power(Row6[X] - [X], 2) ?? 0, which ensures that if the value in column X is null, it is replaced with 0.

Since any of columns X, Y, and Z may contain null values, you can use the following formula in a custom column to create a new column named Distance. This formula ensures that the Euclidean distance can be calculated for any row, even if some fields contain null values, resulting in the table shown in Figure 8-30.

```
(Number.Power(Row6[X]-[X],2)??0)+(Number.Power(Row6[Y]-[Y],2)??0)+(Number.Power(Row6[Z]-[Z],2)??0)
```

Row ID	1²₃ X	1²₃ Y	1²₃ Z	Distance
1	1	11	12	89	5252
2	2	32	36	78	1649
3	3	78	50	10	765
4	4	65	67	94	65
5	5	94	84	82	1625

Figure 8-30. *The result of calculating distance*

CHAPTER 8 HANDLING MISSING VALUES

Once the distances are calculated, you can identify the two nearest neighbors using the Table.MinN() function, which extracts the rows with the smallest distance values to the selected row. After the previous step, click the *fx* button to create a new step named Custom1. Then Table.MinN() function, as shown here, to identify the two rows with the smallest distance. This will produce the desired result shown in Figure 8-31.

= Table.MinN(#"Added Custom","Distance",2)

Row ID	X	Y	Z	Distance	
1	4	65	67	94	65
2	3	78	50	10	765

Figure 8-31. *The result of selecting two nearest neigbours*

Since you have identified the two nearest rows without any null values for Row6, you can now replace the null values in Row6. For each field in Row6, if a value except null is present, it should be used as is. Otherwise, it should be replaced with the average of that field from the two nearest rows. The following formula, entered in the formula bar, creates a record containing X, Y, and Z fields, where each field takes its value from Row6 if it is not null; otherwise, it uses the average value of that field from the nearest rows (see Figure 8-32):

= [X=Row6[X]??List.Average(Custom1[X]),Y=Row6[Y]??List.Average(Custom1[Y]), Z=Row6[Z]??List.Average(Custom1[Z])]

X	57
Y	68
Z	52

Figure 8-32. *The result of replacing the null values in Row6*

At this point, the method successfully imputes the missing value for Row6. To generalize the approach, you can transform the query into a function with two arguments: the row containing a missing value and the full dataset. To convert the query to a function, from the Home tab, select the Advanced Editor command to see all the steps of the query, as shown in Figure 8-33.

CHAPTER 8 HANDLING MISSING VALUES

```
let
    Row6 = MainTable{5},
    InputTable = MainTable,
    #"Filtered Rows" = Table.SelectRows(InputTable, each ([X] <> null) and ([Y] <> null) and ([Z] <>
        null)),
    #"Added Custom" = Table.AddColumn(#"Filtered Rows", "Distance", each (Number.Power(Row6[X]-[X],2)??
        0)+(Number.Power(Row6[Y]-[Y],2)??0)+(Number.Power(Row6[Z]-[Z],2)??0)),
    Custom1 = Table.MinN(#"Added Custom","Distance",2),
    Custom2 = [X=Row6[X]??List.Average(Custom1[X]),Y=Row6[Y]??List.Average(Custom1[Y]),Z=Row6[Z]??
        List.Average(Custom1[Z])]
in
    Custom2
```

Figure 8-33. *Query steps before converting to a function*

The first two steps, which define Row6 and the InputTable value, can be removed and instead passed as function arguments. To achieve this, define them at the beginning of the formula using (Row6, InputTable) =>, before the let expression, as shown in Figure 8-34.

```
(Row6,InputTable)=>
let
    #"Filtered Rows" = Table.SelectRows(InputTable, each ([X] <> null) and ([Y] <> null) and ([Z] <>
        null)),
    #"Added Custom" = Table.AddColumn(#"Filtered Rows", "Distance", each (Number.Power(Row6[X]-[X],2)??
        0)+(Number.Power(Row6[Y]-[Y],2)??0)+(Number.Power(Row6[Z]-[Z],2)??0)),
    Custom1 = Table.MinN(#"Added Custom","Distance",2),
    Custom2 = [X=Row6[X]??List.Average(Custom1[X]),Y=Row6[Y]??List.Average(Custom1[Y]),Z=Row6[Z]??
        List.Average(Custom1[Z])]
in
    Custom2
```

Figure 8-34. *Query steps after converting it into a function*

485

CHAPTER 8 HANDLING MISSING VALUES

By applying this step, the KNN query is converted into a function, as shown in Figure 8-35, which can be applied to other queries. This transformation allows you to apply the same logic to different rows or datasets, making the process more flexible and efficient.

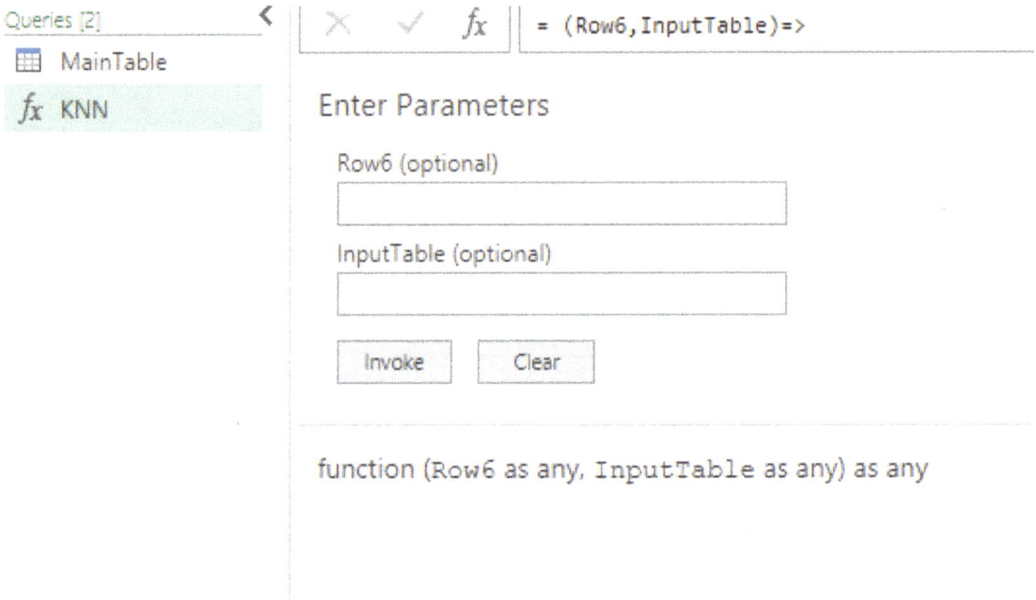

Figure 8-35. The result of converting the query to a function

This function can then be applied across all rows of `MainTable` by adding a new custom column. To do this, go to `MainTable`, add a custom column, and use the following formula in the Custom Column window. This will apply the KNN function to each row, calculating the missing values based on the logic you defined earlier, and will return the updated table shown in Figure 8-36.

```
=KNN(_,#"Changed Type")
```

CHAPTER 8 HANDLING MISSING VALUES

Row ID	X	Y	Z	Custom
1	1	11	12	89 Record
2	2	32	36	78 Record
3	3	78	50	10 Record
4	4	65	67	94 Record
5	5	94	84	82 Record
6	6	57	68	null Record
7	7	null	30	12 Record
8	8	40	null	null Record
9	9	34	null	10 Record
10	10	10	70	null Record

X 11
Y 12
Z 89

X 65
Y 67
Z 94

X 57
Y 68
Z 52

X 40
Y 51.5
Z 86

Figure 8-36. *The result of applying KNN for the table*

It is true that the previous formula solves the problem, but it executes all the steps of the KNN function for every row in the MainTable, even for those rows that do not have any null values. To optimize this, it would be better to revise the formula to apply the KNN function only for rows with null values. This can be achieved by checking if any of the fields (X, Y, or Z) in a row are null. If none of them are null, the row should be left unchanged. The revised formula would look like the following formula:

=if ([X]+[Y]+[Z])= null then KNN(_,#"Changed Type") else _

This revised formula ensures that the KNN function is applied only to rows where one or more fields have a null value (if one of them is null, the result of ([X]+[Y]+[Z]) is null), reducing unnecessary calculations for rows with complete data.

In the final step, you need to remove the original X, Y, and Z columns from the table. After that, expand the custom column by selecting only the X, Y, and Z fields. This will replace the missing values in the original X, Y, and Z columns with the results from the KNN function, and you'll achieve the desired outcome, as shown in Figure 8-37.

CHAPTER 8   HANDLING MISSING VALUES

Row ID	X	Y	Z
1	1	11	12	89
2	2	32	36	78
3	3	78	50	10
4	4	65	67	94
5	5	94	84	82
6	6	57	68	52
7	7	55	30	12
8	8	40	51.5	86
9	9	34	43	10
10	10	10	70	86

Figure 8-37. The result of replacing null values in all the rows

Summary

Missing values are an unavoidable aspect of the data-cleaning process. This chapter covered strategies for managing these gaps, such as replacing missing values with previous entries, applying linear interpolation, and using advanced methods like K-Nearest Neighbors (KNN). The chapter discussed scenarios in which replacing missing values can beneficial and where it can be detrimental, in terms of general business logic.

The next chapter introduces the important topic of looping in Power Query, which enables the automation of repetitive tasks across tables.

In Chapter 10, you explore how to integrate Python and R into Power Query. These tools are particularly useful for running machine learning models on data with complex scenarios, offering a more efficient and flexible approach compared to methods within Power Query.

CHAPTER 9

Looping in Power Query

Loops are fundamental control structures in programming that enable code to run repeatedly based on specified conditions. They are essential for automating repetitive tasks, handling large datasets, and simplifying complex operations. The most commonly used loops include the `For-Each` loop, the `For-Next` loop, and the `Do-While` loop. Each type serves a specific purpose in different scenarios. (For more information, visit www.tutorialspoint.com/computer_programming/computer_programming_loops.htm).

The For-Each Loop

A `For-Each` Loop is designed to iterate through each element in a collection, such as a list, array, or table, without requiring an explicit counter. This makes it particularly useful for working with datasets where the number of elements is unknown or may change dynamically. A `For-Each` loop retrieves elements one by one, ensuring a simple and readable approach to handling data.

For example, in Excel VBA, you can use a `For-Each` loop to iterate through various elements, such as all the cells in a selected range, all the sheets in a workbook, or all the shapes on a worksheet. This loop simplifies the process of performing actions on multiple objects efficiently.

The For-Next Loop

A `For-Next` Loop executes a block of code a fixed number of times, using a counter variable that increments or decrements with each iteration. This loop is particularly useful when the number of iterations is predetermined. It allows control over the step size, meaning that you can iterate in different increments, such as by twos or fives, rather than the default step of one. This loop structure is commonly used in scenarios like filling an array, applying formulas to multiple cells, or processing datasets with a known number of elements.

For example, in Excel VBA, you can use a `For-Next` loop to insert values into cells A1 to A10 or apply changes across Sheet1 to Sheet10. This loop is ideal for executing a set of instructions a specific number of times.

The Do-While Loop

A `Do-While` Loop executes a block of code as long as a specified condition remains true. Unlike a `For-Next` loop, the number of iterations is not fixed beforehand. Instead, it depends on the condition, which is evaluated before each iteration. If the condition is false from the start, the loop may not run at all. This makes `Do-While` loops useful for scenarios where an operation should continue until a certain condition is met, such as applying a change from the top rows until reaching an empty cell.

For example, in Excel VBA, you can use a `Do-While` loop to continuously add numbers to a column until a specific value is reached. This loop is useful when the number of iterations depends on a condition rather than a fixed count.

Looping in Power Query

Although Power Query does not include looping functions like for, while, or do-while, it offers alternative functions to achieve similar results. Functions like `List.Transform()`, `List.TransformMany()`, `List.Accumulate()`, and `List.Generate()` enable iterative operations in Power Query. This chapter provides an in-depth exploration of these powerful functions, showcasing their applications in various scenarios.

List.Transform()

`List.Transform()` is a versatile function for applying transformations to items in a list and has been used many previous examples (including Examples 4-1, 4-3, and 4-4). The syntax of `List.Transform()` is presented as follows:

CHAPTER 9 LOOPING IN POWER QUERY

```
List.Transform(
    list as list,
    transform as function) as list
```

This function takes two arguments:

- The first argument is in the type of list and includes the items that you want to transform.

- The second argument is in the type of function and defines the transformation function to be applied to the items in the list specified by the first argument.

In this function, the transformation function defined as its second argument will be applied to each item in the list specified as its first argument, and it will return a new list containing the transformed items.

In other words, the List.Transform() function in Power Query operates similarly to a For-Each Loop. As mentioned, a For-Each loop iterates through each item in a collection, processing them one by one. Similarly, List.Transform() applies a specified transformation to each item in a given list.

In this function, the collection of items is provided in the first argument as a list. The items in the list can be of any data type, including numbers, text, records, or even tables. The transformation function is then applied to all the items in the list, and the resulting transformed items are returned in a new list.

For the first example, consider a list of monthly incomes for four months: {4200, 3871, 3910, 3800}. You want to calculate the tax value, which is 10 percent of the income. To do this, you need to multiply each salary by 0.1, representing 10 percent of the amount.

This can be easily accomplished using the List.Transform() function in Power Query. In this case, the list of items is {4200, 3871, 3910, 3800} and the transformation function is defined as each _ * 0.1, where _ represents each item in the list.

You can type the following formula in the formula bar to apply the transformation to each item, resulting in {420, 387.1, 391, 380}.

```
=List.Transform({4200, 3871, 3910, 3800}, each _ * 0.1)
```

CHAPTER 9 LOOPING IN POWER QUERY

In the formula, you created a For-*Each* loop that iterates over the items in the list {420, 387.1, 391, 380}. During each iteration, the transformation function (provided as the second argument) is applied to the selected item (in this case, the numbers representing the salary). The transformed value is then included in the final result. In the first iteration, _ is 4200, and its transformed value is calculated as 4200 * 0.1, resulting in 420. In the second iteration, _ becomes 3871, and its transformed value is 3871 * 0.1, which equals 387.1. This process continues for all the items in the defined list, applying the same transformation (_ * 0.1) to each item and producing the corresponding results for each iteration.

For the second example, say you want to extract the first day of each month in 2023. This can be done using the List.Transform() function as well.

In this case, you need to iterate over the month number, and in each iteration use the #date() function to extract the first date of that month. So, you define the month numbers as the list of items in the first input and use each #date(2023, _, 1) as the transformation function to transform any month number to its first date in 2023.

You can type the following formula in the formula bar, which results in Figure 9-1.

```
= List.Transform({1..12}, each #date(2023,_,1))
```

	List
1	1/01/2023
2	1/02/2023
3	1/03/2023
4	1/04/2023
5	1/05/2023
6	1/06/2023
7	1/07/2023
8	1/08/2023
9	1/09/2023
10	1/10/2023
11	1/11/2023
12	1/12/2023

Figure 9-1. Extracting the first dates of months using List.Transform()

CHAPTER 9 LOOPING IN POWER QUERY

Note The #date() function in Power Query takes three arguments—year, month, and day—and returns the corresponding date based on the input values.

In another example, to extract the last day of each month in 2023, you can use similar logic but the last date of each month is not fixed like 31. So, in this case, you need to extract a day of each month and then use the Date.EndOfMonth() function to extract the last date of that month. This can be done by modifying the transformation function in the previous formula. and This results in Figure 9-2.

= List.Transform({1..12}, each Date.EndOfMonth(#date(2023,_,1)))

Alternatively, you can break the process into multiple steps using a record definition. In the first step, you extract the first date of each month, and in the second step, you apply Date.EndOfMonth() to extract the last date of that month. In this scenario, the transformation would look like this:

each [Step1=#date(2023,_,1), Step2=Date.EndOfMonth(Step1)]

However, this transformation will result in a record for each item, but you only need the value of Step2 (the last date). To fix this, you simply select Step2, by adding [Step2] to the end of the transformation function and rewrite the formula as follows:

each [Step2 = Date.EndOfMonth(#date(2023, _, 1))][Step2]

The full formula in the formula bar looks like following, which results in Figure 9-2:

= List.Transform({1..12}, each [Step1=#date(2023,_,1), Step2=Date.EndOfMonth(Step1)][Step2])

CHAPTER 9 LOOPING IN POWER QUERY

| | fx | = List.Transform({1..12}, each Date.EndOfMonth(#date(2023,_,1))) |

	List
1	31/01/2023
2	28/02/2023
3	31/03/2023
4	30/04/2023
5	31/05/2023
6	30/06/2023
7	31/07/2023
8	31/08/2023
9	30/09/2023
10	31/10/2023
11	30/11/2023
12	31/12/2023

Figure 9-2. *Extracting the last dates of months using List.Transform()*

Similarly, to extract the list of month names, you can type the following formula, which results in Figure 9-3.

```
= List.Transform({1..12}, each Date.MonthName(#date(2023,_,1)))
```

| | fx | = List.Transform({1..12}, each Date.MonthName(#date(2023,_,1))) |

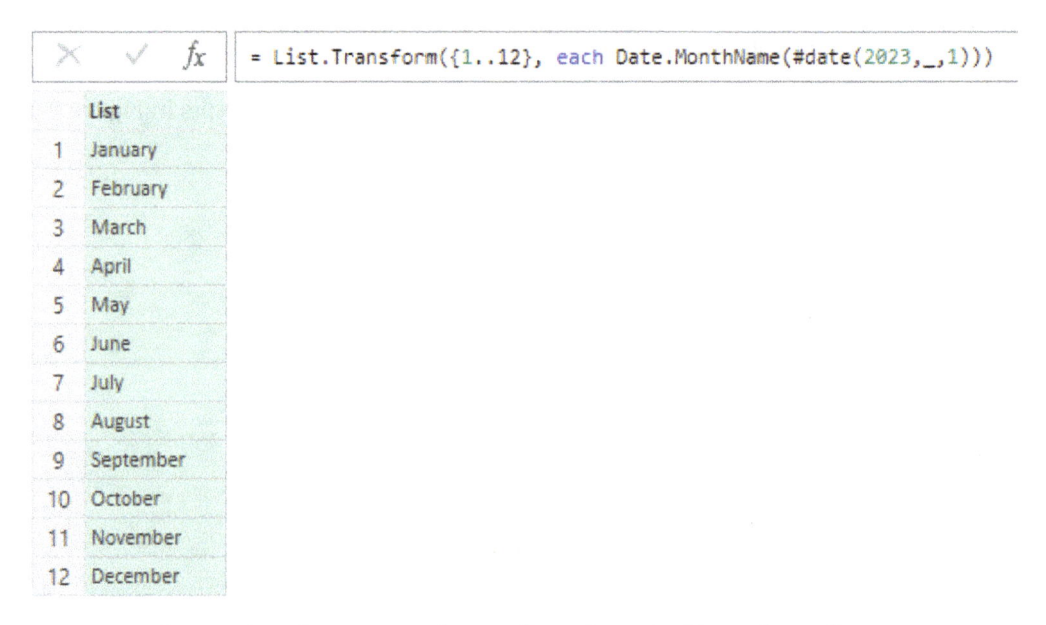

	List
1	January
2	February
3	March
4	April
5	May
6	June
7	July
8	August
9	September
10	October
11	November
12	December

Figure 9-3. *Extracting the name of months using List.Transform()*

CHAPTER 9 LOOPING IN POWER QUERY

Additionally, to create a list of ten consecutive dates starting at #date(2023, 05, 10), you can use the List.Transform() function with the {0..9} list. The transformation will add each value from this list (representing the number of days to be added) to the initial date #date(2023, 05, 10). The formula can be written as follows and results in Figure 9-4:

= List.Transform({0..9}, each Date.AddDays(#date(2023,05,10),_))

	List
1	10/05/2023
2	11/05/2023
3	12/05/2023
4	13/05/2023
5	14/05/2023
6	15/05/2023
7	16/05/2023
8	17/05/2023
9	18/05/2023
10	19/05/2023

Figure 9-4. The range of dates using List.Transform()

In the previous examples, you used a list of numbers as the first argument of the List.Transform() function. However, it's important to note that this function can also be applied to other types of data, such as tables. In this case, a list of tables can be defined as the first argument. The transformation function will then be applied to each table separately, and the transformed tables will be presented in the resulting list. Each table in the list will undergo the specified transformation individually, and the output will be a list of the transformed tables.

For example, consider three tables—Table1, Table2, and Table3—shown in Figure 9-5. They contain sales data for each product in various regions over the spring months. These tables are loaded into Power Query and are named Table1, Table2, and Table3, respectively.

CHAPTER 9 LOOPING IN POWER QUERY

Table1: March

Regions	Product A	Product B	Product E
Region 1	98	45	91
Region 2	37	71	23
Region 3	92	39	90

Table2: April

Regions	Product A	Product D	Product C	Product E
Region 1	90	30	95	74
Region 4	51	41	80	17
Region 3	88	37	69	70

Table3: May

Regions	Product D	Product B	Product E
Region 3	77	22	37
Region 2	98	66	59
Region 4	32	57	29

Figure 9-5. *Loaded tables*

Since the tables have different column names, directly combining them will not yield the desired result. However, combining the unpivoted version of the tables (where all columns except for Region are unpivoted) will produce better results. One approach is to unpivot each table separately and then combine them using the Table.Combine() function. Alternatively, you can use List.Transform() to create a loop over each table and apply the unpivot transformation for each table.

To do this, create a blank query and define the list by entering the following formula in the formula bar, which will result in Figure 9-6.

= {Table1,Table2,Table3}

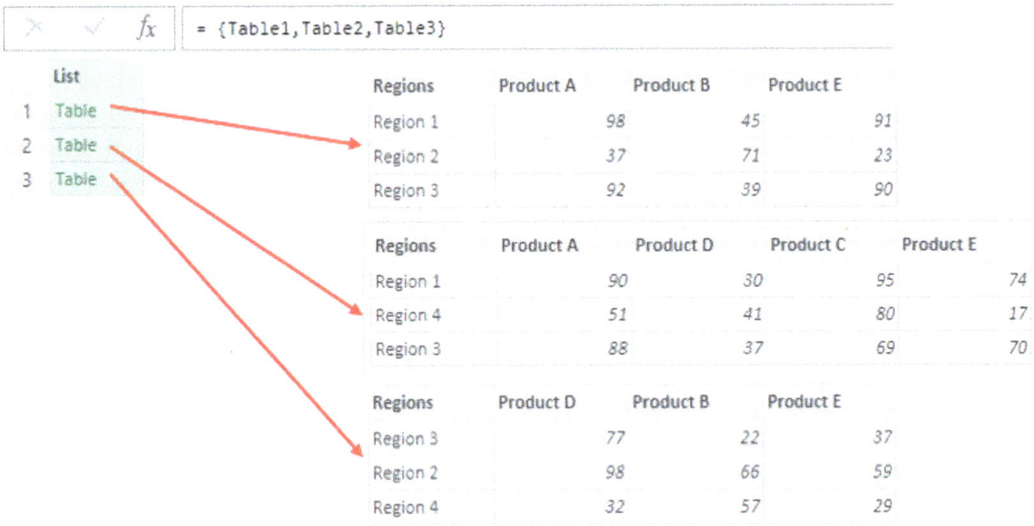

CHAPTER 9 LOOPING IN POWER QUERY

Figure 9-6. Creating a list of tables

In this case, the list of tables can be placed in the first argument of List. Transform(), and un-pivoting transformation function can be defined to apply a transformation to any table in this list. Since the items in this list are of type table, using *e*ach _ in the second argument means that _ represents each table item in the list.

As explained in Chapter 4, to unpivot the columns in a table (let's call it _), excluding the Regions column, you can use the following formula:

= Table.UnpivotOtherColumns(_, {"Regions"}, "Attribute", "Value")

So, the transformation function in this example can be defined as follows:

each Table.UnpivotOtherColumns(_, {"Regions"}, "Attribute", "Value")

The full formula to unpivot each table in the list is as follows and it results in Figure 9-7.

= List.Transform({Table1,Table2,Table3},each Table.UnpivotOtherColumns (_, {"Regions"}, "Attribute", "Value"))

497

CHAPTER 9 LOOPING IN POWER QUERY

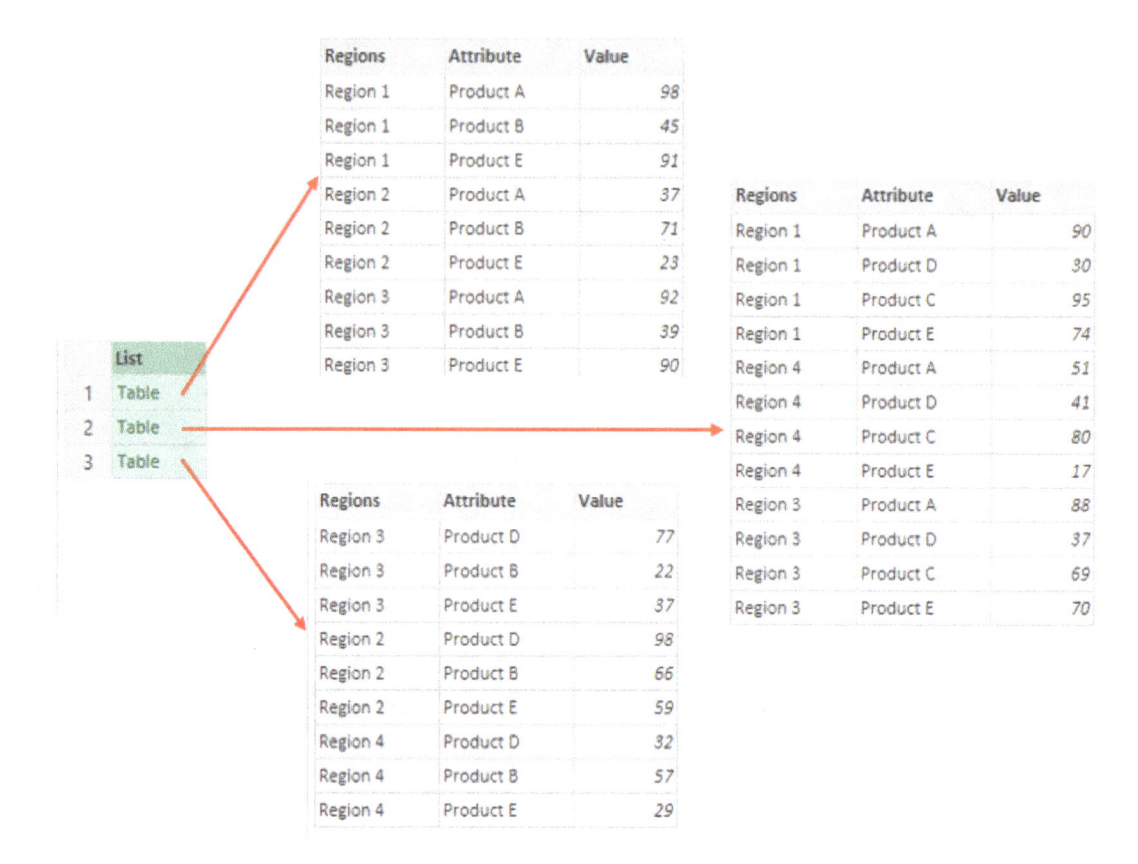

List	
1	Table
2	Table
3	Table

Regions	Attribute	Value
Region 1	Product A	98
Region 1	Product B	45
Region 1	Product E	91
Region 2	Product A	37
Region 2	Product B	71
Region 2	Product E	23
Region 3	Product A	92
Region 3	Product B	39
Region 3	Product E	90

Regions	Attribute	Value
Region 3	Product D	77
Region 3	Product B	22
Region 3	Product E	37
Region 2	Product D	98
Region 2	Product B	66
Region 2	Product E	59
Region 4	Product D	32
Region 4	Product B	57
Region 4	Product E	29

Regions	Attribute	Value
Region 1	Product A	90
Region 1	Product D	30
Region 1	Product C	95
Region 1	Product E	74
Region 4	Product A	51
Region 4	Product D	41
Region 4	Product C	80
Region 4	Product E	17
Region 3	Product A	88
Region 3	Product D	37
Region 3	Product C	69
Region 3	Product E	70

Figure 9-7. *Transformed version of tables*

Based on the examples presented, you can see that `List.Transform()` is a powerful function in Power Query that allows you to apply a `For-Each` loop over items of various types.

List.TransformMany()

`List.TransformMany()` is an advanced version of `List.Transform()` and can be thought of as two nested `For-Each` loops. For example, in Excel, you might create a `For-Each` loop over the sheets, and inside that loop, define another `For-Each` loop over the cells in a specific range. Similarly, `List.TransformMany()` in Power Query allows you to create a `For-Each` loop over the items in a list. For each item in the list, it creates a nested `For-Each` loop for its sub-collections, applying transformations to each of the sub-items.

CHAPTER 9 LOOPING IN POWER QUERY

This function in Power Query comes with the following syntax:

```
List.TransformMany(
    list as list,
    collectionTransform as function,
    resultTransform as function) as list
```

The arguments of this function are as follows:

- The first argument defines the list of items for the first For-Each loop.

- The list of items for the second For-Each loop is defined in the second argument. This argument is different than the first one and should be in the type of function, which results in a list.

- The third argument is the transformation function that is applied to both items from the first and second lists. Since there are two lists, the transformation function must be a custom function with two arguments, such as (L1, L2) => F(L1, L2), where L1 comes from the first list (first argument) and L2 comes from the second list (second argument).

This function returns a list containing the transformed items from both lists.

List.TransformMany() initially iterates over the items in the first list. For each item in the first list, it then iterates over the items in the second list and applies the transformation function to every combination of items from the first and second lists. This means that List.TransformMany() works like two nested For-Each loops. In contrast, List.Transform() creates a single For-Each loop over the items in a list only. Therefore, List.TransformMany() is similar to using two nested List.Transform() functions. This will become more clear in the following example.

In this example, you want to create the first date of each quarter in the years 2022 to 2025. You have two lists of items: one for the years {2022..2025}, and one for the first month of each quarter, {1, 4, 7, 10}.

Before solving this problem using List.TransformMany(), let's try to solve it by nested List.Transform().

Initially, to extract the first date of each quarter in 2022, you can type the following formula, which results in Figure 9-8.

```
= List.Transform({1,4,7,10}, each #date(2022,_,1))
```

499

CHAPTER 9 LOOPING IN POWER QUERY

```
= List.Transform({1,4,7,10}, each #date(2022,_,1))
```

	List
1	1/01/2022
2	1/04/2022
3	1/07/2022
4	1/10/2022

Figure 9-8. *Extracting the first dates of the quarters using List.Transform()*

In the previous formula, you created a loop to iterate over the months using each #date(2022, _, 1) as the transformation function. In the next step, you want to add another List.Transform() to iterate over the years. However, since you are nesting two List.Transform() functions, you cannot use each _ for both loops (as it is not clear which _ came from the list of years and which one came from the list of months). So, you need to replace the each _ logic in the previous formula with custom function logic and rewrite it as follows:

```
= List.Transform({1,4,7,10}, (m)=> #date(2022,m,1))
```

To create a loop over the years, you can define another List.Transform({2022..2025}, (y) => f(y)), where y iterates over the years. This allows you to create a nested loop using the following formula, which results in Figure 9-9.

```
= List.Transform({2022..2025}, (y)=> List.Transform({1,4,7,10}, (m)=> #date(y,m,1)))
```

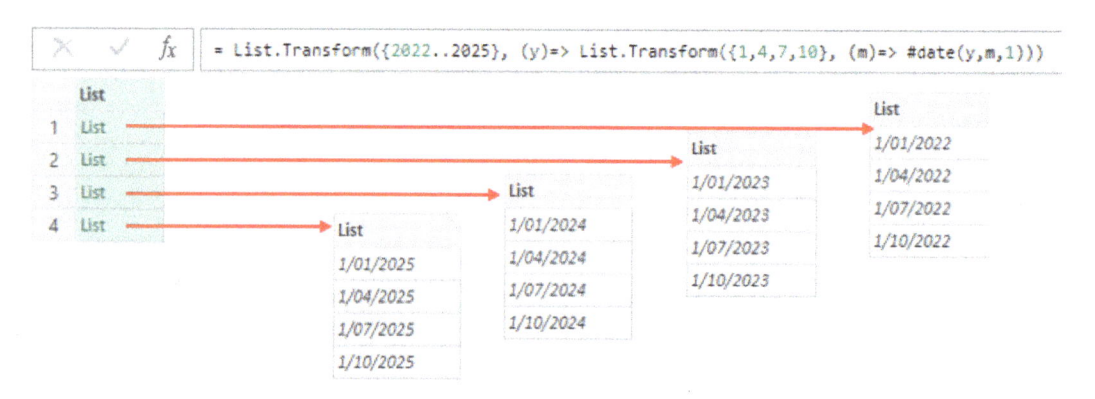

Figure 9-9. *The result of a nested List.Transform()*

CHAPTER 9 LOOPING IN POWER QUERY

In this case, y iterates over the items in the list of years. Initially, y becomes 2022. In the transformation function, for y = 2022, m will iterate over the list of months. It starts with 1, then goes through 4, 7, and finally 10. For each value of m and y=2022, #date(y, m, 1) will be calculated. So, for y=2022, a list of dates will be generated. Then, y will be updated to the next value in the list of years and become 2023. Again, for this value of y, m will iterate over the months, and four new dates will be generated. This process continues until y iterates over all the years in the list.

To combine the results into a single list, you can wrap the formula inside the List.Combine() function, as shown in following formula, which results in Figure 9-10.

```
= List.Combine(List.Transform({2022..2025}, (y)=> List.
Transform({1,4,7,10}, (m)=> #date(y,m,1))))
```

	List
1	1/01/2022
2	1/04/2022
3	1/07/2022
4	1/10/2022
5	1/01/2023
6	1/04/2023
7	1/07/2023
8	1/10/2023
9	1/01/2024
10	1/04/2024
11	1/07/2024
12	1/10/2024
13	1/01/2025
14	1/04/2025
15	1/07/2025
16	1/10/2025

Figure 9-10. *The result of combining the nested List.Transform()*

Instead of using a nested List.Transform() and then wrapping it with List.Combine(), you can directly use List.TransformMany(). In this case, the list of years {2022..2025} will be placed in the first argument, and a function that generates the list of months, such as {1, 4, 7, 10}, will be placed in the second argument as each {1, 4, 7, 10}.

501

CHAPTER 9 LOOPING IN POWER QUERY

The transformation function can be defined as (y, m) => f(y, m), where y iterates over the items in the first list (years) and m iterates over the items in the second list (months). So, the transformation function can be defined as (y,m)=> #date(y,m,1).

The formula becomes as follows and using it in the formula bar results in Figure 9-11.

```
= List.TransformMany({2022..2025}, each {1,4,7,10}, (y,m)=> #date(y,m,1))
```

	List
1	1/01/2022
2	1/04/2022
3	1/07/2022
4	1/10/2022
5	1/01/2023
6	1/04/2023
7	1/07/2023
8	1/10/2023
9	1/01/2024
10	1/04/2024
11	1/07/2024
12	1/10/2024
13	1/01/2025
14	1/04/2025
15	1/07/2025
16	1/10/2025

Figure 9-11. *The result of List.TransformMany()*

In the presented solution, y will iterate over the items in the first list, {2022..2025}. For each selected value of y, the function in the second argument will be evaluated. In this case, the function is defined as each {1,4,7,10}, meaning that regardless of the value of y, it will always return the list {1,4,7,10}. For the selected y=2022, the second list will be generated as {1,4,7,10}, and m will start iterating over the items in this list. So:

CHAPTER 9 LOOPING IN POWER QUERY

- Iteration 1: y=2022 and m=1, the transformation function produces #date(2022, 1, 1).

- Iteration 2: y=2022 and m=4, the transformation function produces #date(2022, 4, 1).

- Iteration 3: y=2022 and m=7, the transformation function produces #date(2022, 7, 1).

- Iteration 4: y=2022 and m=10, the transformation function produces #date(2022, 10, 1).

At this iteration, m is iterated over all the items in the second list. Once m finishes iterating, y will be updated to the next item in the first list and become 2023. The second argument will then be evaluated for this selected y, but since it is independent of the selected value of y, it will still result in {1,4,7,10}. m will then start iterating over these values again. So, the next iterations are as follows:

- Iteration 5: y=2023 and m=1, the transformation function produces #date(2023, 1, 1).

- Iteration 6: y=2023 and m=4, the transformation function produces #date(2023, 4, 1).

- Iteration 7: y=2023 and m=7, the transformation function produces #date(2023, 7, 1).

- Iteration 8: y=2023 and m=10, the transformation function produces #date(2023, 10, 1).

This process continues for each value of y in the {2022..2025} list.

In the presented solution, in the second argument of List.TransformMany(), you use a function such as each {1,4,7,10}, which means that for every item from the first list (every selected y), this function should be executed. The result of this function does not depend on the selected item in the first list (selected y), and it always returns {1, 4, 7, 10}. However, in practice, you may encounter situations where the second list needs to be defined dynamically based on the selected value in the first list.

Let's consider an example where you want to extract all the dates in 2023 using List.TransformMany(). The first list you should iterate over is the list of months {1..12}, and the second list is the list of days. However, the number of days varies in each month.

503

CHAPTER 9 LOOPING IN POWER QUERY

For the first month (January), the list of days is {1..31} and for the second month (February), the list is {1..28}. Therefore, the second list is dependent on the value selected from the first list.

Note While there may be more efficient solutions for generating a list of all dates in a year, I use this example simply to explore the capabilities of `List.TransformMany()`.

In this example, the first argument for the `List.TransformMany()` function is the list of months {1..12} representing each month in the year. The second argument requires a function that generates a list of days based on the selected month. For instance:

- If the first item (January) is selected, the list should be {1..31}.
- If the second item (February) is selected, the list should be {1..28}, and so on for the other months.

To achieve this, you can use `Date.DaysInMonth(#date(2023, _, 1))` in the second argument to get the number of days in the selected month. However, this results in a number (e.g., 31 for January or 28 for February), but you need a value in the type of list in this argument. To create this list, you can define the second argument as follows:

`each {1..Date.DaysInMonth(#date(2023,_,1))}`

In this case, the selected item from the first list is represented by _. If _ = 1, that means the selected month is January, so the second argument will result in {1..31} (the number of days in January). If _ = 2, this means the selected month is February, and the second argument will result in {1..28} (the number of days in February).

This dynamic selection based on the month number will ensure that the correct number of days is generated for each month in the second argument.

After defining the first two arguments, the third argument can be defined as `(m, d) => #date(2023, m, d)`, where m iterates over the items in the first list (the months) and d iterates over the items in the second list (the days in each month). With this setup, writing the following formula in the formula bar will generate a list of all the dates in 2023, as shown in Figure 9-12.

`= List.TransformMany({1..12}, each {1..Date.DaysInMonth(#date(2023,_,1))}, (m,d)=> #date(2023,m,d))`

CHAPTER 9 LOOPING IN POWER QUERY

	List
1	1/01/2023
2	2/01/2023
3	3/01/2023
4	4/01/2023
5	5/01/2023
6	6/01/2023
7	7/01/2023
8	8/01/2023
9	9/01/2023
10	10/01/2023
11	11/01/2023
12	12/01/2023
13	13/01/2023
14	14/01/2023
15	15/01/2023
16	16/01/2023
17	17/01/2023
18	18/01/2023
19	19/01/2023
20	20/01/2023
21	21/01/2023
22	22/01/2023
23	23/01/2023
24	24/01/2023

Figure 9-12. Extracting dates in a year using List.TransformMany()

List.Accumulate()

List.Accumulate() is another function in Power Query that's used to perform a For-Each loop, similar to List.Transform(). However, the key difference is that, while List.Transform() produces separate, independent results for each iteration, List.Accumulate() allows you to aggregate (or combine) the results in different ways during the iteration.

Like other list functions, List.Accumulate() doesn't have a built-in graphical interface and must be written manually. It uses the following syntax:

List.Accumulate(**list** as list, **seed** as any, **accumulator** as function) as any

As proposed by its syntax, this function receives three arguments:

- Similar to List.Transform(), the first argument in List.Accumulate() is a list, which contains the items that you want to iterate over.

- With List.Accumulate(), the results of each iteration are combined into a defined variable, starting with an initial value. This initial value, known as the *seed*, is defined in the second argument of the function. The seed can be a number, record, list, or even a table.

- The third argument is an accumulator, which is a custom function that takes two inputs, typically written as (s, c) => f(s, c). Here, s represents the state, and c represents the current value. This accumulator function is applied to each iteration to determine how the results of iterations should be combined. In the first iteration, s starts with the seed value, and c is the first item in the list (from the first argument). The function f(s, c) is evaluated and updates s with the result. For each subsequent iteration, s is replaced with the updated value from the previous iteration, and c becomes the next item in the list. This process continues until c has iterated over all the items in the list, and the final value of f(s, c) is returned as the result.

This function can produce any type of value, but in most cases, the result will have the same type as the seed (the second argument). This is because the seed value defines the starting type for the accumulation process, and the accumulator function (f(s, c)) ensures that the state (s) is updated in a way that maintains this type consistency throughout the iterations.

As presented, List.Accumulate() and List.Transform() both perform a For-Each loop over the items in the list defined in their first argument. The difference is that in List.Transform(), the result of each iteration is independent, while in List.Accumulate(), the results of each iteration can be combined. To explore this difference, calculate the sum of the squares of values from 1 to 5 using both functions.

CHAPTER 9　LOOPING IN POWER QUERY

Using List.Transform(), you can define the list of numbers as {1..5}, iterate over them, and calculate the square of each number (see Figure 9-13):

=List.Transform({1..5}, each _*_)

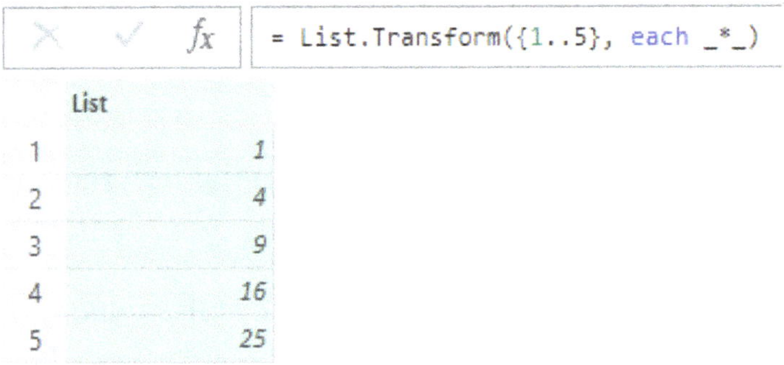

Figure 9-13. Extracting the square of 1 to 5 using List.Transform()

In the formula, a For-Each loop is defined over the items in the {1..5} list, and then the transformation function each _*_ is applied to each item independently. To sum the transformed values, you need to use List.Sum() to calculate the sum of the squares of the numbers. The formula would be rewritten as following:

=List.Sum(List.Transform({1..5}, each _*_))

Using List.Accumulate(), you can combine (in this case, sum) the results of iterations. You do not need to transform the values first and then use List.Sum() to calculate the sum of transformed values.

To use List.Accumulate() in this example, you want to iterate over the {1..5} list, so the first argument is {1..5}. You aim to sum the results of the iterations, and this sum will be stored in a variable. The initial value of this variable is defined in the second argument (the *seed*). So, the initial value of the variable can be defined as 0.

You now define the accumulator function as (s, c) => f(s, c). Here:

- s represents the accumulated value, starting at 0.
- c is the current item in the {1..5} list.

507

CHAPTER 9 LOOPING IN POWER QUERY

For each iteration, you want to add the square of the current item (c * c) to the accumulated value s. The f(s, c) function is defined as s + c * c. This ensures that, for each iteration, the square of the current value of c will be added to s.

Using the following formula in the formula bar, you can solve the problem, as shown in Figure 9-14.

= List.Accumulate({1..5},0, (s,c)=> s+c*c)

```
fx  = List.Accumulate({1..5},0, (s,c)=> s+c*c)

55
```

Figure 9-14. *Extracting the square of 1 to 5 using List.Accumulate()*

In this formula, the initial value of the seed is 0, so the accumulator function starts with s = 0. The variable c iterates over the items in the {1..5} list, and in each iteration, the function (s, c) => s + c * c is applied.

- In the first iteration, s is 0 and c is 1 (the first item in the list). The function calculates 0 + 1 * 1 = 1, so the value of s becomes 1. This updated value of s is then used in the next iteration.

- In the second iteration, s is 1 and c is 2 (the second item in the list). The function calculates 1 + 2 * 2 = 5, so the value of s becomes 5.

- In the third iteration, s is 5 and c is 3. The function calculates 5 + 3 * 3 = 14, so s becomes 14.

- In the fourth iteration, s is 14, and c is 4. The function calculates 14 + 4 * 4 = 30, updating s to 30.

- Finally, in the fifth iteration, s is 30 and c is 5. The function calculates 30 + 5 * 5 = 55, giving the final value of s as 55.

At the end of all iterations, the final result of the List.Accumulate() function is 55. This process is summarized in Table 9-1.

CHAPTER 9   LOOPING IN POWER QUERY

Table 9-1. Iterations

Iteration Number	s	c	s+c*c
1	0	1	1
2	1	2	1+2*2=5
3	5	3	5+3*3=14
4	14	4	14+4*4=30
5	30	5	30+5*5=55

Note In the previous example, if you want to save the result of each iteration separately, you can use the List.Accumulate() function with a different seed and accumulator function. In this case, the initial value of the seed should be defined as a blank list {}, and in each iteration, a new item (the result of transforming items in the list in the first argument) should be added to it.

To achieve this, instead of summing the result of c * c with s, you convert the result of c * c into a list and combine it with s, which is now a list. This can be done using the accumulator function (s, c) => s & { c * c }. The operator & is used to append the result of each iteration to the accumulated list s.

You can use this formula:

= List.Accumulate({1..5},{}, (s,c)=> s & {c*c})

It is true that List.Accumulate() iterates over the item in the list entered in its first argument, like a For-Each loop, but it can also be used to simulate a For-Next loop. For example, say you have a variable x equal to 2 and you want to repeatedly square it for five iterations. In other words, you want to calculate x = x * x repeatedly for five steps.

You can accomplish this using List.Accumulate() by defining a list with five elements (e.g., {1..5}), which will act as the counter for the loop. The initial value of x is set as the seed, so the seed will be 2. Then, the transformation function (s, c) => f(s, c) can be defined as (s, c) => s * s, where s is the current value of x, and c iterates through the list (though in this case c is not being used, as you are just repeating the operation).

509

CHAPTER 9　LOOPING IN POWER QUERY

You can type the following formula in the formula bar to solve this problem:

`= List.Accumulate({1..5},2, (s,c)=> s*s)`

This formula will start with s = 2 (the seed value), and in each iteration, s will be squared. It passes five iterations as presented here:

> Iteration 1: s = 2, so s * s = 2 * 2 = 4
>
> Iteration 2: s = 4, so s * s = 4 * 4 = 16
>
> Iteration 3: s = 16, so s * s = 16 * 16 = 256
>
> Iteration 4: s = 256, so s * s = 256 * 256 = 65536
>
> Iteration 5: s = 65536, so s * s = 65536 * 65536 = 4294967296

The result of five iterations is 4294967296.

List.Generate()

List.Generate() is another function in Power Query used to create loops. Unlike the previous functions (List.Transform() and List.Accumulate()), which iterate over a fixed set of items, List.Generate() allows you to create a Do-While loop. This means the loop will continue to iterate until a specified condition is met. If you are unsure about the number of iterations, you can use this function to define a stop condition.

The function syntax is:

```
List.Generate(
    initial as function,
    condition as function,
    next as function,
    optional selector as nullable function) as list
```

This function takes four arguments, all of which are functions, with the following specific applications:

- The first argument, called initial, defines the starting value or state of the loop. It is a function with no input variables, and it is defined as ()=>. For example, ()=>0 sets the initial value to 0.

CHAPTER 9 LOOPING IN POWER QUERY

- The second argument, called condition, is a function with one input parameter, which is the result from the previous iteration. This function is evaluated to determine whether the loop should continue or stop. The condition returns true to continue the loop and false to stop it. For example, each _ < 5 means the loop continues if the result of the previous iteration is less than five; otherwise, the loop stops, and the result is returned.

- The third argument, called next, is a function with one input parameter. It receives the result from the previous iteration and updates it based on the defined logic. For example, each _ + 1 adds one to the result of the previous iteration for the next iteration.

- The fourth argument, called selector, is optional. If provided, it applies a transformation or selection process to the final output of each iteration. If it's not provided, the current value of the iteration is used. This function determines what is added to the resulting list.

To demonstrate how to use List.Generate(), in the first example, you'll use it to extract all the dates between two specific dates, such as #date(2004, 1, 10) and #date(2004, 2, 05). Follow these steps:

- In this case, the loop should start at #date(2004, 1, 10), so the first argument will be ()=> #date(2004, 1, 10).

- The loop should continue until you reach a date larger than #date(2004, 2, 05). So, the second argument (the condition) will be each _ <= #date(2004, 2, 05).

- In each iteration, you need to calculate the next date by adding one day to the current date. This can be done using the Date.AddDays() function, so the third argument will be each Date.AddDays(_, 1).

The formula can be written as follows, and this will generate the list of dates shown in Figure 9-15:

```
= List.Generate(()=> #date(2004, 1, 10),each _ <= #date(2004, 2, 05) , each Date.AddDays(_,1))
```

	List
1	10/01/2004
2	11/01/2004
3	12/01/2004
4	13/01/2004
5	14/01/2004
6	15/01/2004
7	16/01/2004
8	17/01/2004
9	18/01/2004
10	19/01/2004
11	20/01/2004
12	21/01/2004
13	22/01/2004
14	23/01/2004
15	24/01/2004
16	25/01/2004
17	26/01/2004
18	27/01/2004
19	28/01/2004
20	29/01/2004
21	30/01/2004
22	31/01/2004
23	1/02/2004
24	2/02/2004
25	3/02/2004
26	4/02/2004
27	5/02/2004

Figure 9-15. Extracting dates using List.Generate()

CHAPTER 9 LOOPING IN POWER QUERY

Note In the previous solution, instead of using Date.AddDays(), you can use other functions like Date.AddWeeks(), Date.AddMonths(), Date.AddQuarters(), and Date.AddYears() to generate a date list with different levels of granularity. For example, using Date.AddWeeks(_,1) will create a list of dates increasing by one week, while Date.AddMonths(_,1) will generate a list of dates increasing by one month.

As another example, say you want to extract all even numbers starting at 0 but less than 10 using List.Generate(). The parameters for this function are as follows:

- Initial value: Since you start at 0, the first argument is ()=>0.

- Condition: The loop should continue as long as the value remains less than 10, so the second argument is each _ < 10.

- Next value: In each iteration, you need to generate the next even number by adding two to the previous value, so the third argument is each _ + 2.

The formula can be written as follows, and it results in a list of even numbers from 0 to 8, as shown in Figure 9-16:

```
=List.Generate(()=>0,each _<10 , each _+2)
```

List
0
2
4
6
8

Figure 9-16. Extracting even numbers less than 10 using List.Generate()

CHAPTER 9 LOOPING IN POWER QUERY

In the previous example, if you wanted to extract the square values of even numbers less than 10, you could use the fourth argument (selector) in the previous formula. You define it as each _ * _, which means that after applying the loop, instead of displaying the iteration results directly, show their squares as the final output.

The revised formula is as follows, and it results in a list of squared even numbers as shown in Figure 9-17:

= List.Generate(()=>0,each _<10 , each _+2, each _*_)

	List
1	0
2	4
3	16
4	36
5	64

Figure 9-17. *Extracting the square of even numbers less than 10 using List.Generate()*

Again using the previous example, say you wanted to generate a list of even numbers starting at 0 and continuing until the sum of the extracted values reaches 100. To achieve this, you need to track two values simultaneously—the current even number, (call it E) and the cumulative sum of the previous even numbers (call it S). Thus, you would define the arguments as follows:

- The initial value should be a record containing both E and S, defined as ()=> [E=0, S=0].

- The stop condition is based on S, because the loop should continue as long as S is less than 100. The second argument is therefore each _[S] < 100.

- The iteration step updates both values: E increases by 2, and S is updated by adding the new E. This is expressed as each [E = _[E] + 2, S = _[S] + _[E]].

CHAPTER 9 LOOPING IN POWER QUERY

Using these parameters, the formula can be written as follows, and it results in a list including the records, as shown in Figure 9-18.

= List.Generate(()=>[E=0, S=0],each _[S]<100 , each [E=_[E]+2, S=_[S]+E])

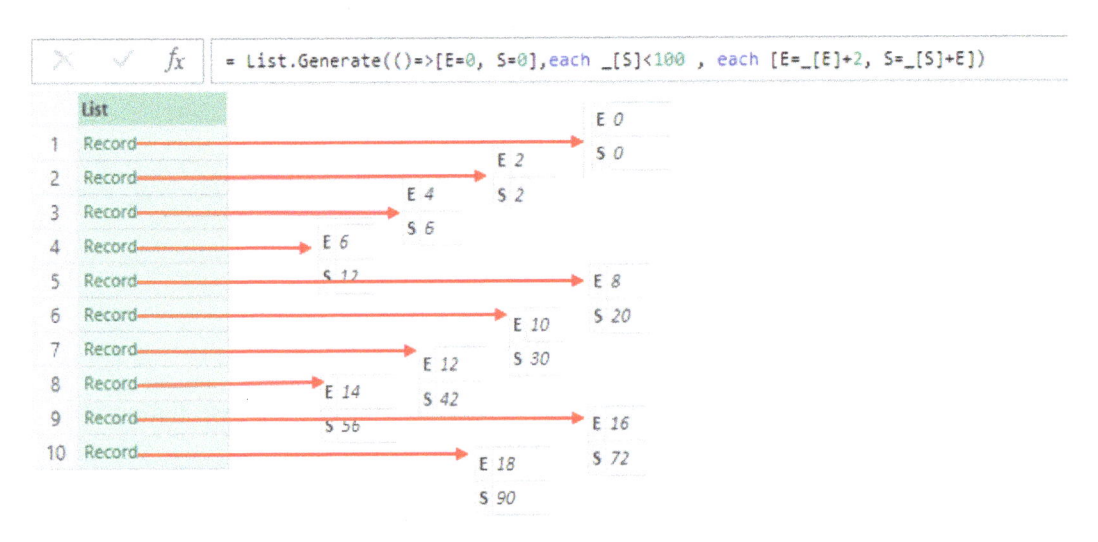

Figure 9-18. Extracting even numbers with a sum less than 100 using List.Generate()

Since you only need the even numbers as output, and the sum (S) is used only for the stop condition, and you can utilize the fourth argument (selector) of List.Generate() to return only the E values. This simplifies the formula as follows, which results in Figure 9-19.

= List.Generate(()=>[E=0, S=0],each _[S]<100 , each [E=_[E]+2, S=_[S]+E], each _[E])

515

CHAPTER 9 LOOPING IN POWER QUERY

`= List.Generate(()=>[E=0, S=0],each _[S]<100 , each [E=_[E]+2, S=_[S]+E], each _[E])`

	List
1	0
2	2
3	4
4	6
5	8
6	10
7	12
8	14
9	16
10	18

Figure 9-19. *Extracting the even numbers using List.Generate()*

The remainder of this chapter explores all the hidden features of these remarkable functions.

Running Totals by List.Accumulate()

Calculate the running total for items in the Source list {1, 10, 50, 100, 150} using the List.Accumulate() function.

You can solve this problem using List.Accumulate() in different ways, and two possible solutions are provided here. In both solutions, based on the question, the result of the formula should be in the type of list equal to {1, 11, 61, 161, 311}. Therefore, it is better to use an item in the type of list in the second argument of List.Accumulate().

Solution 1: Based on the For-Each Loop

In this first solution, you use a For-Each loop approach, where the Source list is directly used as the first argument of List.Accumulate(). The seed is initialized as {0}, and in each iteration, a new item is added to the seed. This new item is calculated as the sum of the current item from the Source list and the last item in the seed. So, in the iterations seed is updated as follows:

CHAPTER 9 LOOPING IN POWER QUERY

- Iteration 1: The seed becomes {0, 0 + 1} → {0, 1}
- Iteration 2: It becomes {0, 1, 1 + 10} → {0, 1, 11}
- Iteration 3: It becomes {0, 1, 11, 11 + 50} → {0, 1, 11, 61}

This process continues for the remaining items in the Source list.

In the formula, the first argument is the Source list and the second argument (seed) is {0}. Now it is time to define the accumulator function in the form (s, c) => f(s, c). To determine f(s, c), consider the first iteration:

- s represents the current state and is {0}
- c is the first element of the Source list, which is 1
- f(s, c) should produce {0, 1}

The result of f(s, c) is equal to adding a new item (1) to the s, and this new item is calculated as the sum of the last item in s (0) and the value of c (1). So, in general, the formula is f(s, c) is s & {List.Last(s) + c}, which ensures that each new value is derived from the sum of the last item in s and the current item c. Using this approach, the formula to solve this problem is as follows. Using this formula in the formula bar results in {0, 1, 11, 61, 161, 311}:

= List.Accumulate(Source,{0},(s,c)=>s & {List.Last(s)+c})

To remove the first item in the result {0, 1, 11, 61, 161, 311}, the formula can be modified using the List.Skip() function. This function removes the first item from the resulting list, ensuring that the final output starts with the desired values. By applying this change, the final result becomes {1, 11, 61, 161, 311}.

= List.Skip(List.Accumulate(Source,{0},(s,c)=>s & {List.Last(s)+c}))

While the previous formula solves the problem, it initially adds 0 to the list by defining the seed as {0}, and removes it later using the List.Skip() function. Instead of this approach, you can redefine the seed as an empty list {} from the beginning. However, doing so introduces a challenge: in the first iteration, List.Last(s) returns null since s is empty, causing all subsequent calculations to also result in null.

To handle this, you can replace null with 0 using List.Last(s) ?? 0 or using the second argument in the List.Last() function as List.Last(s,0). This ensures that when s is empty, List.Last() returns 0 instead of null, preventing errors in the calculations. By applying this adjustment and writing the formula as follows in the formula bar, you achieve the same final result without needing to add and later remove an extra value.

```
= List.Accumulate(Source,{},(s,c)=>s & {List.Last(s,0)+c})
```

In this formula, during each iteration, the last value of s (which represents the accumulated value from the previous iteration) is retrieved using `List.Last(s,0)`, then added to c (the next value in the Source list). The result is then converted to a list and appended to s. Since the initial value of s is `{}`, using `List.Last(s)` will return `null` in the first iteration, while using `List.Last(s,0)` returns 0 instead of `null`.

The iterations of this formula are detailed in Table 9-2.

Table 9-2. Iterations of List.Accumulate

iteration	s	c	List.Last(s)??0	{List.Last(s,0)+c}	s&{List.Last(s,0)+c}
1	{}	1	0	{1}	{1}
2	{1}	10	1	{11}	{1,11}
3	{1,11}	50	11	{61}	{1,11,61]
4	{1,11,61]	100	61	{161}	{1,11,61,161}
5	{1,11,61,161}	150	161	{311}	{1,11,61,161,311}

Solution 2: Based on the For-Next Loop

In this second scenario, you use a `For-Next` loop approach. Here, the iterator is c, and for each value of c, you calculate the sum of the first c items in the Source list. For example, if c is equal to 3 (the third iteration), you extract the sum of the first three items, such as `List.Sum({1, 10, 50})`, which is equal to `List.Sum(List.FirstN(Source,c))`.

Since the Source list contains five items, the counter should start at 1 and end at 5, meaning the first input is `{1..5}`. The second input should match the type of the result, so it is initialized as an empty list `{}`.

For the accumulator function `(s, c) => f(s, c)`, in each iteration, you concatenate the list s with the sum of the first c items from the Source list. This can be expressed as `s & {List.Sum(List.FirstN(Source, c))}`.

CHAPTER 9 LOOPING IN POWER QUERY

The whole formula can be written as follows:

= List.Accumulate({1..5},{},(s,c)=>s&{List.Sum(List.FirstN(Source,c+1))})

Since the dimension of the Source might vary in different examples, instead of hardcoded values, the first argument can be rewritten using List.Positions(Source), which results in {0..4}. Because the replaced list starts at 0, in the revised formula, c should be replaced with c+1 in the accumulator argument, and the revised formula will be:

= List.Accumulate(List.Positions(Source),{},(s,c)=>s&{List.Sum(List.FirstN(Source,c+1))})

Table 9-3 illustrates the result of this formula across different iterations.

Table 9-3. Iterations of List.Accumulate

iteration	s	c	List.FirstN(Source,c+1)	{List.Sum(....)}	s&{List.Sum(....)}
1	{}	0	{1}	{1}	{1}
2	{1}	1	{1,10}	{11}	{1,11}
3	{1,11}	2	{1,10,50}	{61}	{1,11,61]
4	{1,11,61]	3	{1,10,50,100}	{161}	{1,11,61,161}
5	{1,11,61,161}	4	{1,10,50,100,150}	{311}	{1,11,61,161,311}

Note For those familiar with VBA, in the second solution, c acts as a counter ranging from 0 to 4, similar to For c = 1 To 4. In contrast, in the first solution, c represents the elements within the Source list, analogous to For c In Range in VBA.

Efficiency Tip Let's evaluate the performance of the formula proposed in Solution 1. For a list with 4,000 items, the first solution (without using List.Buffer()) takes 137 seconds to execute, which is too long. However, applying List.Buffer() to the source list (e.g., Source = List.Buffer({1..4000})) outside of the List.Accumulate() arguments does not significantly impact execution time, as the Source list is just used once in the first argument of the formula and is not directly part of the accumulator function (third argument).

In contrast, using `List.Buffer()` in the third argument of `List.Accumulate()`, and then rewriting the formula as follows, reduces the execution time to under one second.

```
= List.Accumulate(Source,{},(s,c)=>List.Buffer(s & {List.Last(s,0)+c}))
```

On the other hand, Solution 2, without using `List.Buffer()`, outperformed solution 1, but as the Source list is called several times in the accumulator functions in this solution, using `List.Buffer()` for the source list can improve its execution time.

Running Totals by List.Generate()

Calculate the running total using `List.Generate` from the Source list {1, 10, 50, 100, 150}.

You can solve this problem by creating a loop using `List.Generate()`. Two different solutions—a basic one and an efficient one—are provided using the `List.Generate()` function.

Solution 1: Basic Option

In this approach, in the `List.Generate()`, the counter starts at 1, so the first argument of `List.Generate()` is defined as ()=>1. In each iteration, the counter is incremented by one, making the third argument each _ + 1. Since the source list contains five items, the loop should runs five times. Therefore, the second argument of the function can be defined as each _ <= 5 or more dynamically as each _ <= List.Count(Source).

Using these arguments inside the `List.Generate()` function will create a loop starting at 1 and ending at 5, resulting in {1, 2, 3, 4, 5}.

CHAPTER 9 LOOPING IN POWER QUERY

```
= List.Generate(
    ()=>1,
    each _<=List.Count(Source),
    each _+1)
```

In this example, instead of returning the value of i in each iteration, you want to extract the sum of the first i items in the Source list. To achieve this, you need to convert i into the sum of the first i items from the Source list. This can be done by using List.Sum(List.FirstN(Source, _)) as the fourth argument of the List.Generate() function. By applying this modification and rewriting the formula as follows, you get the result as {1, 11, 61, 161, 311}.

```
= List.Generate(
    ()=>1,
    each _<=List.Count(Source),
    each _+1,
    each List.Sum(List.FirstN(Source, _)))
```

Solution 2: Efficient Option

The previous solution solves the problem, but it is not the most efficient approach for handling large datasets. As shown, in each iteration, the cumulative sum is calculated separately from scratch. For example, in the 1,000th iteration, the sum of the first 1,000 items in the list is computed, even though the sum of the first 999 items was already determined in the previous iteration. This redundant recalculation increases computational cost significantly.

Instead of recomputing the sum each time, you can optimize the approach by using the previously calculated sum to determine the next value, reducing unnecessary calculations and improving performance.

In this solution, each iteration requires two values: C, which represents the iteration index (counter), and M, which represents the sum of the first C items in the source list. To save the information of C and M into each iteration, you can use a record with two fields called C and M.

The initial value of C is 1, and in each iteration, C is incremented by one. The initial value of M is Source{0}, and in each iteration, M is updated by adding the Cth item from the source list to its previous value.

521

CHAPTER 9 LOOPING IN POWER QUERY

Based on these initial values, the first argument of List.Generate() is defined as follows:

()=>[C=1, M=Source{0}]

As in the previous solution, the number of iterations is limited to List.Count(Source). However, since C and M are both maintained in each iteration, the second argument is defined as follows:

each [C] <= List.Count(Source)

Additionally, as C is incremented by one and M is updated by adding Source{[C]}, the third argument is defined as follows:

each [C=[C]+1, M=[M] + Source{[C]}]

By inserting these arguments into List.Generate(), the final formula will produce the result shown in Figure 9-20.

= List.Generate(
    ()=>[C=1,M=Source{0}],
    each [C]<=List.Count(Source),
    each [C=[C]+1,M=[M]+Source{[C]}])

Figure 9-20. The result of List.Generate()

CHAPTER 9 LOOPING IN POWER QUERY

In the formula used here, the C and M values are both maintained and updated during each iteration. The result of this formula is a list containing records, with each record having two fields: C and M.

Since you are interested in extracting the values of M from the output, you can use the fourth argument of the List.Generate() function to select the M value from each record. This can be done by referring to [M] in the fourth argument.

To update the formula, which extracts only the M values from the result, the formula can be rewritten as follows. This will result in the output {1, 11, 61, 161, 311}, as expected.

```
= List.Generate(
    ()=>[C=1,M=Source{0}],
    each [C]<=List.Count(Source),
    each [C=[C]+1,M=[M]+Source{[C]}],
    each [M])
```

In this formula, as shown in the third argument of the List.Generate() function, the value of M is updated by adding Source{[C]} to the previous value of M. This approach eliminates the need to recalculate the sum of the first C items from the Source list for each iteration.

Instead of calculating the sum from scratch in each iteration, the formula efficiently builds the cumulative sum by adding the current item from the Source list to the running total. This significantly improves performance, especially for larger datasets, since only the new item in each iteration is added to the previous cumulative sum.

Note Instead of using a record to store the values of C and M in the previous solution, you can use a list with two items. The first item will represent C, and the second item will represent M. This approach simplifies the structure. The formula can be rewritten as follows, yielding the same result.

```
= List.Generate(
    ()=>{1,Source{0}},
    each _{0}<=List.Count(Source),
    each {_{0}+1,_{1}+Source{_{0}}},
    each _{1})
```

523

CHAPTER 9   LOOPING IN POWER QUERY

Calculating the Running Total by List.Transform()

Calculate the running total using List.Transform() from the Source list {1, 10, 50, 100, 150}.

Besides using List.Accumulate() and List.Generate(), this problem can also be solved with the List.Transform() function. In this case, for each item in the list defined in the first argument, the transformation function will be applied.

If you define the first argument as {1..5}, the transformation function should replace each number n in this list with the sum of the first *n* items in the Source list. For this, you can use each List.Sum(List.FirstN(Source, _)) as a transformation function, where the underscore _ represents the current item in the list.

Using the following formula in the formula bar will solve the problem:

= List.Transform(List.Positions(Source), each List.Sum(List.FirstN(Source, _+1)))

In the previous formula, the first argument is hardcoded as {1..5}, which can be replaced with List.Positions(Source) to dynamically handle the position of each item in the list. The formula can be rewritten as follows:

= List.Transform(List.Positions(Source), each List.Sum(List.FirstN(Source, _+1)))

Generating the Fibonacci Sequence by List.Accumulate()

Calculate the first ten terms of the Fibonacci sequence using List.Accumulate().

Note for more information about the Fibonacci sequence, visit this page: www.mathsisfun.com/numbers/fibonacci-sequence.html.

In the Fibonacci sequence, the initial values are $x_0 = 0$ and $x_1 = 1$. Each subsequent term is the sum of the two preceding terms: So $x_2 = x_0 + x_1 = 1$ and $x_3 = x_2 + x_1 = 2$ and so on, where $x_n = x_{n-1} + x_{n-2}$.

Since you are looking for the first ten numbers in the Fibonacci sequence in the

CHAPTER 9 LOOPING IN POWER QUERY

form of a list, it is convenient to define the seed as a list, and as you know the first two numbers in the sequence, you can define the seed as {0, 1}. In the process of using List.Accumulate() to solve this problem, starting with the initial values {0, 1} as the seed, you calculate the next Fibonacci number in each iteration and update the seed accordingly.

In the Fibonacci sequence, each number is the sum of the two preceding numbers. Therefore, the next number can be calculated using List.Sum(List.LastN(s, 2)), where s represents the current state. To continue the process, this value should be added to the list of previous numbers. Thus, the accumulator function can be written as follows.

(s,c)=>s&{List.Sum(List.LastN(s,2))}

On the other hand, with each run of the accumulator, a new number in the sequence is calculated and added. Since the seed includes the first two items of the sequence, to extract the first ten numbers, you need to iterate this process ten times. Therefore, the first argument can be any list with a length of eight, such as {1..8}. The whole formula to solve this problem is as follows. It results in {0,1,1,2,3,5,8,13,34}.

```
= List.Accumulate(
    {1..8},
    {0,1},
    (x,y)=>x&{List.Sum(List.LastN(x,2))})
```

Table 9-4 illustrates the values of x and y during different iterations of this formula.

Table 9-4. Iterations of List.Accumulate for the Fibonacci Series

iteration	s	c	List.LastN(s,2)	List.Sum(....)	s& {List.Sum(..)}
1	{0,1}	1	{0,1}	1	{0,1,1}
2	{0,1,1}	2	{1,1}	2	{0,1,1,2}
3	{0,1,1,2}	3	{1,2}	3	{0,1,1,2,3}
4	{0,1,1,2,3}	4	{2,3}	5	{0,1,1,2,3,5}
5	{0,1,1,2,3,5}	5	{3,5}	6	{0,1,1,2,3,5,8}
6	{0,1,1,2,3,5,8}	6	{5,8}	13	{0,1,1,2,3,5,8,13}
7	{0,1,1,2,3,5,8,13}	7	{8,13}	13	{0,1,1,2,3,5,8,13}
8	{0,1,1,2,3,5,8,13}	8	{8,13}	34	{0,1,1,2,3,5,8,13,34}

Generating the Fibonacci Sequence with List.Generate

Calculate the first ten terms of the Fibonacci series using `List.Generate`.

The Fibonacci sequence has been previously created using `List.Accumulate()`, but here, to better understand the arguments in the `List.Generate()` function, you will solve this problem using `List.Generate()`.

This problem can be solved using `List.Generate()` in various ways, but an efficient approach is to keep track of the last two values in the series and use them to generate the next value by simply adding them together. In each iteration, you need C (the counter), Xn_2 (the second-to-last value in the series), and Xn_1 (the last value in the series).

To start, you set the initial value of C to 1, which indicates the first iteration. For Xn_2, you start with 0, which is the first value in the series, and for Xn_1, you start with 1, which is the second value in the series. These initial values are set using the first argument of `List.Generate()`, as follows:

```
()=>[C=1,Xn_2=0,Xn_1=1]
```

The number of iterations should be repeated ten times, so the second argument of the function will define the stopping condition. This ensures that the iteration stops after ten iterations. The condition is simply [C] <= 10.

In each iteration, the counter C is incremented by one, while Xn_2 is updated to the previous value of Xn_1 (since the value of Xn_1 in the next iteration corresponds to the value of Xn-2), and Xn_1 is updated by adding the current values of Xn_1 and Xn_2. This logic is defined in the third argument of `List.Generate()`:

```
each [C=[C]+1,xn_2=[xn_1],xn_1=[xn_1]+[xn_2]]
```

Combining all the parts, you can type the formula in the formula bar as follows. This results in Figure 9-21.

```
= List.Generate(()=>[C=0,xn_2=0,xn_1=1],each [C]<10,each [C=[C]+1,xn_2=[xn_1],xn_1=[xn_1]+[xn_2]])
```

CHAPTER 9 LOOPING IN POWER QUERY

Figure 9-21. *The result of List.Generate() for the Fibonacci sequence*

In the presented result, all the values of C, Xn_2, and Xn_1 are presented in the result in the type of record. If you want to extract only the values of Xn_2 from the result to get the Fibonacci sequence from the initial item, you can use the fourth argument of List. Generate(). This argument specifies what you want to return in each iteration. The formula can then be rewritten as follows and results in {1, 1, 2, 3, 5, 8, 13, 21, 34, 55}:

= List.Generate(()=>[C=0,xn_2=0,xn_1=1], each [C]<10, each [C=[C]+1,xn_2=[xn_1],xn_1=[xn_1]+[xn_2]], each [xn_2])

Note In addition to the previously presented solution, you can use another variation with List.Generate(), as shown here.

In this variation, instead of defining separate fields for Xn_2 and Xn_1, you can combine them into a single field called X, which will store them as a list. The first item in the list will represent Xn_2, and the second item will represent Xn_1.

527

This variation simplifies the logic by grouping these two values together in a list. As a result, the formula can be rewritten as follows:

```
= List.Generate(
    ()=>[C=0,x={0,1}],
    each [C]<10,
    each [C=[C]+1,x={List.Last([x]),List.Sum([x])}],
    each List.First([x]))
```

Implementing Sumproduct

The SUMPRODUCT function in Excel is a versatile and powerful function that multiplies corresponding components in given arrays or ranges and then sums the results. Calculate the SUMPRODUCT of two lists S1={1,3,5,2,7} and S2={0,1,2,1,1} in Power Query using List.Accumulate() and List.Transform().

Solution 1: Using List.Transform()

The List.Transform() function alone cannot solve the entire problem; it only handles the part of multiplying corresponding items from the two lists and provides a list of the multiplication results. To obtain the final SUMPRODUCT, you need to use List.Sum() to sum the results of the multiplication.

To handle the multiplication part, you can use the index {0..4} as the first argument in the List.Transform() function, since you have five items in the lists. In the second argument, you can use the expression each S1{_} * S2{_} to calculate the product of the corresponding items from S1 and S2. The following formula can be rewritten in the formula bar:

```
= List.Transform({0..4}, each S1{_}*S2{_})
```

This formula results in the {0, 3, 10, 2, 7} list. To get the final result of SUMPRODUCT, you apply List.Sum() to the result of List.Transform(), which will give the final result, 25.

```
= List.Sum(List.Transform({0..4}, each S1{_}*S2{_}))
```

CHAPTER 9 LOOPING IN POWER QUERY

Alternatively, you can approach the solution in a different way. Instead of using indexes, you can create a list of sublists, where each sublist contains the corresponding values from S1 and S2, such as {{1, 0}, {3, 1}, {5, 2}, {2, 1}, {7, 1}}. Using this list in the first argument of List.Transform() can help you apply the multiplication of corresponding items, by using each _{0}*_{1} as a transformation function in the second argument of List.Transform().

You can use List.Zip({S1, S2}) to create this list of corresponding pairs. Then, you can use List.Transform() with the transformation function each _{0} * _{1} to calculate the product of each pair. The formula for this approach is as follows:

= List.Transform(List.Zip({S1, S2}), each _{0} * _{1})

This will give the same intermediate list {0, 3, 10, 2, 7}, and to get the final result, you apply List.Sum():

= List.Sum(List.Transform(List.Zip({S1, S2}), each _{0} * _{1}))

This approach also results in the final SUMPRODUCT value of 25.

Solution 2: Using List.Accumulate()

Using List.Accumulate(), you can solve this problem directly without the need for another function like List.Sum(). In this case, similar to the first variation provided earlier, you can use {0..4} (since you have five items in the lists) as the first argument of List.Accumulate(), with the seed value set to 0. Then, in each iteration, you add the result of multiplying the corresponding items in S1 and S2 to the accumulated value using the accumulator function (s, c) => s + S1{c} * S2{c}.

You can type the following formula in the formula bar to solve the problem:

= List.Accumulate (List.Positions(S1), 0,(x,y)=> x+S1{y}*S2{y})

Table 9-5 summarizes the iterations of the proposed code.

Table 9-5. Iterations of List.Accumulate()

iteration	s	c	S1{c}*S2{c}	s+ S1{c}*S2{c}
1	0	0	1*0	0
2	0	1	3*1	3
3	3	2	5*2	13
4	13	3	2*1	15
5	15	4	7*1	22

Although the previous formula solves the problem, it can lead to incorrect results if the two lists have different lengths. Specifically, if the shorter list is used to create the first input, the formula will produce incorrect results instead of throwing an error. To handle this situation more robustly, it's recommended you use the second variation based on List.Zip() and then use the following formula.

= List.Accumulate (List.Zip({S1,S2}), 0,(s,c)=> s+c{0}*c{1})

In this case, if one list is shorter than the other, the zipped version will pair corresponding elements, and for the shorter list, null will be used for the missing values. After multiplying the corresponding numbers, the presence of null will result in a null value being generated. This will cause the final result of the formula to be null.

Applying Transformation Over the Columns

The data collected from a questionnaire is provided in the Source table, as shown in Table 9-6. To normalize the table, divide the values of each column by the sum of the values in that column.

CHAPTER 9 LOOPING IN POWER QUERY

Table 9-6. Comparison Matrix

Criteria 1	Criteria 2	Criteria 3	Criteria 4	Criteria 5	Criteria 6
36	78	11	83	93	63
79	21	54	89	18	71
58	75	85	33	44	67
72	12	56	54	81	59
11	54	27	42	91	29
18	33	20	10	97	19

Note The data in this example is provided in an Excel file titled `07 Apply Transformation Over the Columns.xlsx`.

Two different solutions using `List.Accumulate()` and `List.Transform()` are presented here, but before starting the solutions, you need to know how to change the values of a column once.

To divide all the values of a column like Criteria 1 by a specific number, initially select that column. Then, from the Transform tab, in the Number Column section, choose Standard and then the Divide command, as shown in Figure 9-22.

CHAPTER 9 LOOPING IN POWER QUERY

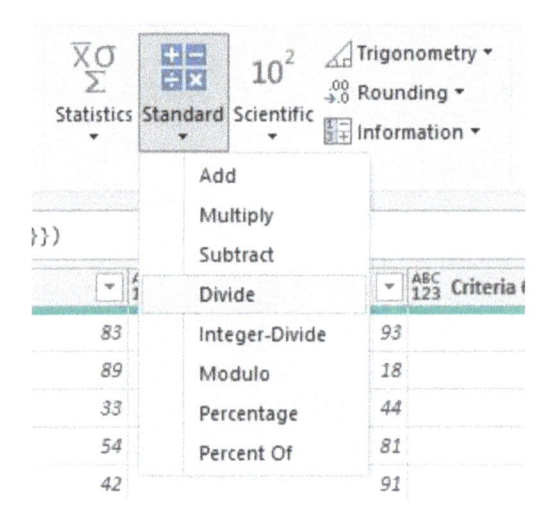

Figure 9-22. Transforming a table column

In the dialog box that appears, enter a value such as 100, so each value in the Criteria 1 column is divided by 100, using the generated formula in the formula bar as follows:

= Table.TransformColumns(Source, {{"Criteria 1", each _ / 100, type number}})

In this formula, 100 can be replaced with List.Sum(Source[Criteria 1]) or List.Sum(Table.Column(Source,"Criteria 1")), to divide each value of the Criteria 1 column by the sum of the values on that column.

To normalize all the columns, the same process can be applied to other columns, or the previous formula can be rewritten as follows, resulting in the table where all the columns are normalized, shown in Figure 9-23:

```
= Table.TransformColumns(Source, {
    {"Criteria 1", each _ / List.Sum(Table.Column(Source,"Criteria 1"))},
    {"Criteria 2", each _ / List.Sum(Table.Column(Source,"Criteria 2"))},
    {"Criteria 3", each _ / List.Sum(Table.Column(Source,"Criteria 3"))},
    {"Criteria 4", each _ / List.Sum(Table.Column(Source,"Criteria 4"))},
    {"Criteria 5", each _ / List.Sum(Table.Column(Source,"Criteria 5"))},
    {"Criteria 6", each _ / List.Sum(Table.Column(Source,"Criteria 6"))}
})
```

CHAPTER 9 LOOPING IN POWER QUERY

Criteria 1	Criteria 2	Criteria 3	Criteria 4	Criteria 5	Criteria 6
0.131386861	0.285714286	0.043478261	0.266881029	0.219339623	0.204545455
0.288321168	0.076923077	0.213438735	0.286173633	0.04245283	0.230519481
0.211678832	0.274725275	0.335968379	0.106109325	0.103773585	0.217532468
0.262773723	0.043956044	0.221343874	0.173633441	0.191037736	0.191558442
0.040145985	0.197802198	0.106719368	0.135048232	0.214622642	0.094155844
0.065693431	0.120879121	0.079051383	0.032154341	0.228773585	0.061688312

Figure 9-23. *Normalization result*

The previous formula is not dynamic, and it will result in an error if the column names change. It will not be applied to any newly added columns. Additionally, when dealing with a table that has many columns, instead of applying the previous formula, you can use List.Accumulate() and List.Transform() to normalize the entire table by iterating through the columns in a loop.

Solution 1: Using List.Accumulate()

As presented, you can use the following formula to apply the transformation on a column (Criteria 1).

```
=Table.TransformColumns(Source, {{"Criteria 1", each _ / List.Sum(Table.Column(Source,"Criteria 1"))}})
```

Using List.Accumulate(), you can create a For-Each loop to apply this transformation to all columns in the source table. In this case, the first argument of List.Accumulate() is a list containing all the column names, and the seed is the source table. In the third argument, you use the transformation formula, meaning that for each column name, this transformation will be applied to the corresponding column. The formula can be written as follows:

```
List.Accumulate(
    {"Criteria 1","Criteria 2","Criteria 3","Criteria 4","Criteria 5",
    "Criteria 6"}, Source, (s,c)=>Table.TransformColumns(s, {c,
    each _/List.Sum(Table.Column(s,c))}
))
```

CHAPTER 9   LOOPING IN POWER QUERY

In this formula:

- Initially, s is the source table, and c represents the name of the first column.

- For the column represented by c, Table.TransformColumns() is applied to normalize the value of that column, by dividing each value by the sum of values on that column.

- The result of this iteration becomes the s for the next iteration and c will be updated to the name of the next column.

- Then, this process continues until all specified columns in the first argument are normalized, producing a table where all the columns have been normalized.

In the previous formula, the column named are defined manually. The formula can indeed be more dynamic by replacing the first input with Table.ColumnNames(Source). This way, you can dynamically apply the normalization to all columns in any table:

```
= List.Accumulate(
    Table.ColumnNames(Source), Source, (s,c)=>Table.TransformColumns(s,
    {c, each _/List.Sum(Table.Column(s,c))}
))
```

Solution 2: Using List.Transform()

The previous formula solves the problem, but it is not the most efficient approach, as the column transformations are applied separately in each iteration. Instead, you can use List.Transform() to apply all the transformations at once in a single formula.

Consider the following hardcoded formula for transforming the columns from Criteria 1 to Criteria 6:

```
= Table.TransformColumns(Source, {
    {"Criteria 1", each _ / List.Sum(Table.Column(Source,"Criteria 1"))},
    {"Criteria 2", each _ / List.Sum(Table.Column(Source,"Criteria 2"))},
    {"Criteria 3", each _ / List.Sum(Table.Column(Source,"Criteria 3"))},
    {"Criteria 4", each _ / List.Sum(Table.Column(Source,"Criteria 4"))},
```

CHAPTER 9 LOOPING IN POWER QUERY

```
    {"Criteria 5", each _ / List.Sum(Table.Column(Source,"Criteria 5"))},
    {"Criteria 6", each _ / List.Sum(Table.Column(Source,"Criteria 6"))}
})
```

In the previous formula, the second argument is a list containing several sublists, one sublist for each column transformation. Each sublist consists of two parts (the third part, which determines the result type, is omitted for simplicity). The first part is the column name, and the second part is a function that applies the transformation to the values of the specified column.

In this solution, you want to use List.Transform() to generate the second argument of Table.TransformColumns(). Since Table.ColumnNames(Source) returns a list of all the column names from the source table, you can use the following formula to create sublists containing the column name as the first argument and the number 1 as the second argument, as shown in Figure 9-24.

```
=List.Transform( Table.ColumnNames(Source), (x)=> {x, 1})
```

Figure 9-24. The first step of creating the sublists

At this point, the second argument of the sublists is the number 1. However, you need to use a function instead. To convert the second item in the sublists to a function, you can modify the formula. Replace the 1 with a function, as shown in Figure 9-25.

```
=List.Transform( Table.ColumnNames(Source), (x)=> {x, each 1})
```

CHAPTER 9   LOOPING IN POWER QUERY

Figure 9-25. Creating the sublists in the right format

As presented, the result of the previous formula is a list containing several sublists, where the first item in each sublist is a column name and the second item is a function. As the result is in the right format, you can use this formula as the second argument in the Table.TransformColumns() function, using the following formula.

```
= Table.TransformColumns(Source, 
List.Transform(Table.ColumnNames(Source), (x)=> {x,   each 1 })  )
```

In this case, the transformation function is defined as each 1, which converts all the values in the columns to the number 1, as shown in Figure 9-26.

Figure 9-26. Replacing all the values of a table with 1

Instead of applying each 1 to all values, you can use the previously defined transformation function and rewrite the formula as follows to achieve the desired normalized table.

```
= Table.TransformColumns(
    Source,
    List.Transform(
      Table.ColumnNames(Source),
      (x)=> {x,  each _/List.Sum(Table.Column(Source, x)) }
    )
  )
```

Adding Multiple Columns Simultaneously

The actual cost in 2023 for different departments is provided in the Source table in Table 9-7. Define the budget columns for each department in three different scenarios, with increasing cost rates equal to 3, 7, and 10 percent.

Table 9-7. Department Cost

Department	Cost 2023
Sales	30,462.00
Marketing	40,289.00
Purchase	47,141.00
Finance	23,826.00
HR	40,415.00
Production	10,371.00
Technical Support	37,704.00
CRM	34,269.00

Note The data in this example is provided in an Excel file titled `08 Adding Multiple Columns Simultaneously .xlsx`.

CHAPTER 9 LOOPING IN POWER QUERY

In Example 4 of Chapter 2, you learned how to use record definitions to add multiple columns at once. However, in this case, since the columns follow a specific pattern, you can use the functions to generate the required record and then expand it.

Following the approach from Example 4 in Chapter 2, applying the following formula in the Custom Column window and then expanding the resulting column will solve the problem.

```
=[#"by 3%"=[Cost 2023]*1.03,
#"by 5%"=[Cost 2023]*1.05,
#"by 7%"=[Cost 2023]*1.07
]
```

To create this record in the rest of this section, three solutions based on List.Transform() and List.Accumulate() are provided.

Solution 1: Using List.Transform()

In this example, three different scenarios are defined. To represent them dynamically, you use the {3,5,7} list as the first input for List.Transform(). Then you will use a transformation function, converting each item into a record with a specific field name and value. To create a record, you'll use the Record.AddField() function, which takes three arguments: the base record (which, in this case, can be an empty record), the field name, and the field value.

For instance, using =Record.AddField([], "X", 1) in the formula bar results in a [X=1] record. Applying this as the transformation function in List.Transform(), using the following formula in the formula bar, produces a list of three records, each identical to [X=1]:

```
=List.Transform({3,5,7},(i)=> Record.AddField([],"X",1))
```

Instead of using X as the field name, you can dynamically generate field names by concatenating By with Text.From(i), making each record's field name unique. So the revised formula is presented as follows, which results in Figure 9-27:

```
=List.Transform({3,5,7},(i)=> Record.AddField([],"By "&Text.From(i)
  & "%" ,1))
```

CHAPTER 9 LOOPING IN POWER QUERY

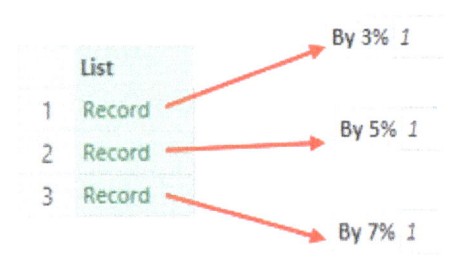

Figure 9-27. The result of modifying the field names

The previous formula generates three single-field records within a list. To combine them into a single record with three fields, you can use the Record.Combine() function. By passing the previous formula as its input, you obtain the record shown in Figure 9-28:

= Record.Combine(List.Transform({3,5,7},(i)=> Record.AddField([],"By "&Text.From(i) & "%" ,1)))

Figure 9-28. The result of combining the records

Returning to the main problem, adding a custom column with the previous formula results in the same record (with tree fields) for all rows. Now that you have structured the records correctly, you need to replace the placeholder value 1 with the percentage-based calculation using the Cost in 2023 column. The percentages originate from the list used in List.Transform(), indexed by *i*. Since *i* is in the type of number, to convert it to percentages, it should be divided 100.

The values for different growth rates, for example, a 3 percent increase in Cost in 2023, is reached by multiplying the cost by 1.03, which translates to [Cost 2023] * (1 + i / 100).

Thus, the revised formula for the Custom Column window is as follows:

=Record.Combine(List.Transform({3,5,7},(i)=> Record.AddField([],"By "&Text.From(i) & "%" ,[Cost 2023]*(1+i/100))))

After applying this formula and expanding the newly created column, you can obtain the final result.

Solution 2: Using List.Accumulate(), Variation 1

This solution follows the same logic as presented in Solution 1. However, since `List.Accumulate` provides an accumulator function, you do not need to transform the values into records and then combine them using `Record.Combine()`. Instead, you can add fields to the record one by one.

Here, the seed is considered a blank record, and the first argument remains the same as in `List.Transform()`. When you use `Record.AddField()` in the third argument of `List.Accumulate`, new fields are added to the existing record iteratively. Therefore, the following formula can also be used to solve this problem.

```
List.Accumulate({3,5,7},[],(s,c)=> Record.AddField(s,"By "&Text.From(c) &
"%" ,[Cost 2023]*(1+c/100)))
```

Solution 3: Using List.Accumulate(), Variation 2

Besides the first two solutions, which involved adding a column using a record, this problem can also be solved by adding each column separately within a loop using `List.Accumulate()`. In this approach, the seed is the Source table, and with each iteration, a new column is added to it.

Before starting the solution, recall the formula for adding a column to a table. In Power Query, you can add a new column by selecting the Custom Column command from the Add Column tab and configuring the settings shown in Figure 9-29 to create a new column named By 3%.

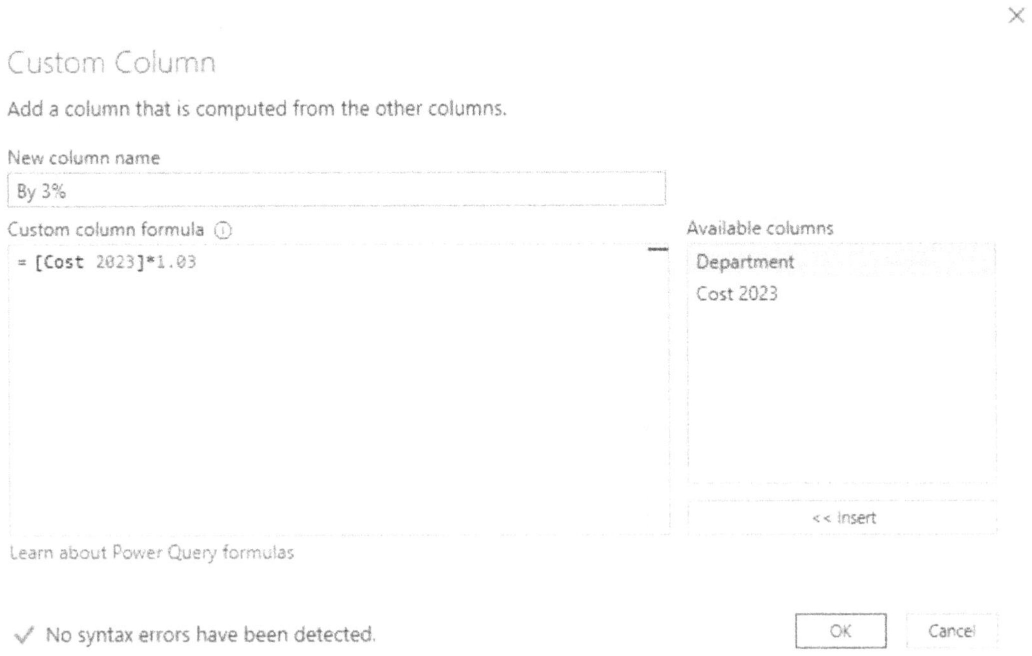

CHAPTER 9 LOOPING IN POWER QUERY

Figure 9-29. Adding a column

The formula bar will generate the following expression to create a new column named By 3%, which you will use later to add the columns:

= Table.AddColumn(Source, "By 3%", each [Cost 2023]*1.03)

To solve this problem with new logic, you need to loop through the values {3, 5, 7} and, in each iteration, add a new column to the source table by multiplying the Cost 2023 column by a specific percentage. So, the {3, 5, 7} list serves as the first argument of List.Accumulate(), and in each iteration, you apply modifications to the Source table, so the Source table is used as the second argument.

To update the table during each iteration, you need to define a function called (s, c) => f(s, c), where:

- s represents the table at the current step.
- c is a value from the {3, 5, 7} list.

Using the formula for adding a column, the original table (Source) should be replaced with s, and the multiplication factor 1.03 should be replaced with (1 + c / 100). Additionally, the column name should dynamically reflect the percentage, so By 3% is replaced with "By " & Text.From(c) & "%".

CHAPTER 9   LOOPING IN POWER QUERY

Thus, the function inside `List.Accumulate()` becomes:

`(s,c)=>Table.AddColumn(s, "By "&Text.From(c) & "%", each [Cost 2023]*(1+c/100))`

And the complete formula for solving this problem is as follows (see Figure 9-30):

```
= List.Accumulate(
      {3,5,7},
      Source,
      (s,c)=>Table.AddColumn(s, "By "&Text.From(c) & "%", each
      [Cost 2023]*(1+c/100)))
```

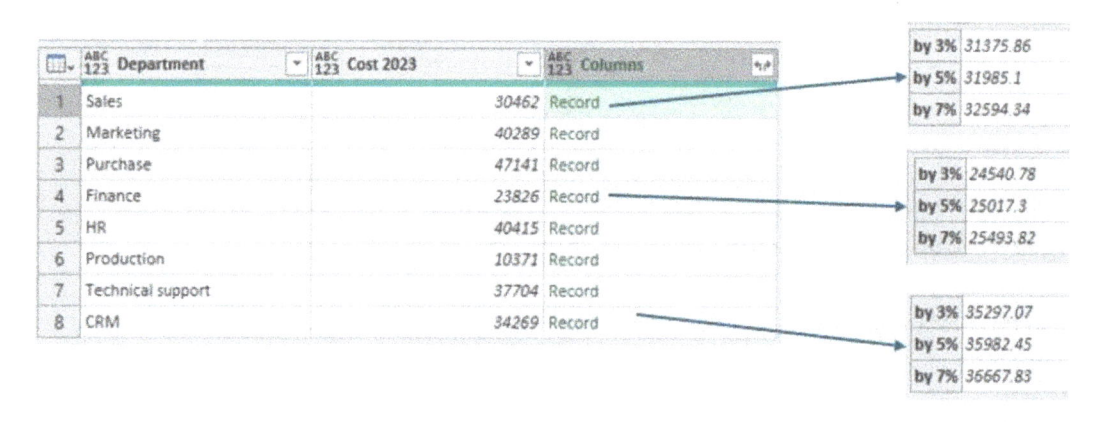

Figure 9-30. The result of Group By

Note This problem can be also solved using the splitting function as follows:

`= Table.SplitColumn(Source, "Cost 2023", each List.Transform({0,3,5,7},(i)=> _*(1+i/100)))`

In this case, you need to rename the column names after modification. The revised version that will define the column names is as follows:

`= Table.SplitColumn(Source, "Cost 2023", each List.Transform({0,3,5,7},(i)=> _*(1+i/100)),{"Cost 2023"}& List.Transform({3,5,7},(i)=> "By "&Text.From(i) & "%" ))`

CHAPTER 9　LOOPING IN POWER QUERY

Handling the Sequences

Consider a company with four branches in four different locations. The distances between the branches are provided in the Distance table, as in Table 9-8. (The distance from Branch X to Branch Y is the same as the distance from Branch Y to Branch X.) The historical trips of staff between these branches on different dates are presented in the Travel table, as shown in Table 9-9. To calculate staff commissions, the distance traveled is required. So, add a new column to the Source table to calculate the distance traveled for each row.

Note　The data in this example is provided in an Excel file titled 09 List. Accumulate with Memory Handling.xlsx.

Table 9-8. Distance: Distance Matrix

Place 1	Place 2	Value
A	B	73
A	C	85
A	D	13
B	C	91
B	D	41
C	D	31

CHAPTER 9 LOOPING IN POWER QUERY

Table 9-9. *Travel: Travel History*

Date	Staff ID	Path
6/04/2024	s-2	C,B
12/04/2024	s-2	D,C
12/04/2024	s-3	D,C,D
15/04/2024	s-3	A,C,B,A,B,A,C
16/04/2024	s-1	A,B
21/04/2024	s-1	A,C,B,A
21/04/2024	s-3	A,B,C,A,B,A
22/04/2024	s-2	A,B,C,D
26/04/2024	s-1	A,B
28/04/2024	s-2	A,B
29/04/2024	s-1	A,C
30/04/2024	s-1	A,B,C

Note If the distances are stored in the format shown in Figure 9-31, right-click the first column and select Unpivot Other Columns to convert the data into the format used in this example.

From-To	A	B	C	D
A		0	73	85	13
B		73	0	91	41
C		85	91	0	31
D		13	41	31	0

Figure 9-31. *Another format of the Distance table*

To solve this problem, first load both tables into Power Query by different queries. Then, rename the first query to Distance and the second to Travel.

CHAPTER 9 LOOPING IN POWER QUERY

As explained in Chapter 3, to retrieve the distance between two branches (e.g., A to B), filter the Distance table where Place 1 is A and Place 2 is B. Then, extract the value from the Distance column using the following formula:

```
= Table.SelectRows(Distance, each ([Place 1] = "A") and ([Place 2] = "B"))
[Distance]{0}
```

This formula can be rewritten using the function notation (x) => as follows. As presented in the Chapter 3, this modification is required, as this formula will later be used in another formula with an each _ definition.

```
= Table.SelectRows(Distance, (x)=> (x[Place 1] = "A") and (x[Place 2] = "B"))[Distance]{0}
```

For the reverse case (calculating the distance from B to A), while the result should be the same, filtering Place 1 for B and Place 2 for A returns a blank table. As you know, the distances from A to B and from B to A are the same, and the Distance table just includes one way. To handle both cases, you need to use an or condition in the formula and rewrite it as follows:

```
= Table.SelectRows(Distance, (x)=> (x[Place 1] = "A" and x[Place 2] = "B")
or (x[Place 1] = "B" and x[Place 2] = "A"))[Distance]{0}
```

Now that you have a formula to extract the distance between two branches, let's apply it to solve the problem.

In the Travel table, the Path column contains branch sequences in text format (e.g., "A,C,B,A,B,A,C"). To work with these values as separate entries, you add a Custom Column using the Text.Split() function. Add a custom column called Path List to the Travel table using the following formula in the Custom Column window:

```
= Text.Split([Path],",")
```

This converts each path from text into a list of visited branches. So for the first row, the value for path column is C,B and the result of path list become {"C", "B"}. For the fourth row, the value of the Path column is "A,C,B,A,B,A,C", and the Path list becomes {"A", "C", "B", "A", "B", "A", "C"}. Based on this new column, in the rest of this section, three different solutions based on List.Transform() and List.Accumulate() are presented.

CHAPTER 9 LOOPING IN POWER QUERY

Solution 1: Using List.Transform()

Before solving the problem for all rows, first consider the value in the Path List column for the fourth row, which is {"A", "C", "B", "A", "B", "A", "C"}. You'll calculate the total distance for this journey first, then extend the solution to all rows. Let's name this list ListX.

In this list, the sequence of branches visited during the journey is provided. However, you need to break it down into individual trips, each with a starting and ending branch. In other words, instead of representing the journey as {"A", "C", "B", "A", "B", "A", "C"}, it would be more useful to structure it as {{"A", "C"}, {"C", "B"}, {"B", "A"}, {"A", "B"}, {"B", "A"}, {"A", "C"}}. This format clearly shows each leg of the journey—for example, the first trip is from A to C, the second is from C to B, and so on.

To generate the revised list, you need to create sublists where each element at index i in ListX is paired with the element at index $i+1$. This means that for each i (starting at 0 and including all valid indexes of ListX), you extract ListX{i} and ListX{i+1} and place them together in a sublist as {ListX{i}, ListX{i+1}}.

To achieve this transformation, you can use the List.Transform() function over the {0..6} range, applying the transformation to convert ListX into the desired format by the following formula:

= List.Transform({0..6},(i)=> {ListX{i},ListX{i+1}})

In the previous formula, the {0..6} range can be replaced with List.Positions(ListX) to make the transformation more dynamic. However, before making this change, let's analyze what happens when i = 6.

If you apply the transformation function at i = 6, it results in {ListX{6}, ListX{7}}, but since there is no element at index 7, an error occurs. To prevent this issue, you can either:

- Use the range {0..5} instead of {0..6}, thus ensuring that ListX{i+1} always exists.

- Use the range {1..6} and modify the transformation function to {ListX{i-1}, ListX{i}}, effectively shifting the indexing logic.

CHAPTER 9　LOOPING IN POWER QUERY

Thus, you can use either of the following formulas to dynamically transform ListX into the required format, as shown in Figure 9-32.

= List.Transform(List.RemoveLastN(List.Positions(ListX),1),(i)=>
{ListX{i},ListX{i+1}})

= List.Transform(List.Skip(List.Positions(ListX)),(i)=>
{ListX{i-1},ListX{i}})

Figure 9-32. The result of transforming ListX

In this case, the formula results in a list of sublists, where each sublist contains two items:

- The first item represents the departure branch for each sub-trip.
- The second item represents the destination branch for each sub-trip.

Instead of keeping them as separate values, you can directly use these two branches in the formula you developed for extracting the distance between two branches as follows:

=Table.SelectRows(Distance, (x)=> (x[Place 1] = "A" and x[Place 2] = "B")
or (x[Place 1] = "B" and x[Place 2] = "A"))[Distance]{0}

CHAPTER 9 LOOPING IN POWER QUERY

To do this, replace A in the formula with ListX{i-1} (the departure branch) and B with ListX{i} (the destination branch), ensuring that the transformation dynamically computes the distances for each leg of the journey.

The revised formula is as follows, which results in Figure 9-33.

```
=List.Transform(
  List.Skip(List.Positions(ListX)),
  (i) =>
    Table.SelectRows(
      Distance,
      (x) => (x[Place 1] = ListX{i - 1} and x[Place 2] = ListX{i})
        or (x[Place 1] = ListX{i} and x[Place 2] = ListX{i - 1})
    )[Distance]{0}
)
```

	List
1	85
2	91
3	73
4	73
5	73
6	85

Figure 9-33. Distance of the travel legs

In this case, 85 represents the distance traveled from A to C, and 91 represents the distance from C to the next branch, and the same for other numbers.

To calculate the total traveled distance, you can use List.Sum() to sum up all the individual distances.

Thus, the formula can be rewritten as follows to dynamically compute the total distance for the entire journey in ListX:

```
= List.Sum(
    List.Transform(
      List.Skip(List.Positions(ListX)),
      (i) =>
        Table.SelectRows(
          Distance,
          (x) => (x[Place 1] = ListX{i - 1} and x[Place 2] = ListX{i})
            or (x[Place 1] = ListX{i} and x[Place 2] = ListX{i - 1})
        )[Distance]{0}
    )
  )
```

This formula can be applied to all rows in the Travel table. So, after adding the Path List column, you introduce another column called Distance. Then, you use the previously developed formula in the Custom Column window, by replacing `ListX` with `[Path List]`, as shown here:

```
= List.Sum(
    List.Transform(
      List.Skip(List.Positions([Path List])),
      (i) =>
        Table.SelectRows(
          Distance,
          (x) => (x[Place 1] = [Path List]{i - 1} and x[Place 2] = [Path List]{i}) or (x[Place 1] = [Path List]{i} and x[Place 2] = [Path List]{i - 1})
        )[Distance]{0}
    )
  )
```

This transformation dynamically computes the total travel distance for each row, resulting in the final table displayed in Figure 9-34.

CHAPTER 9   LOOPING IN POWER QUERY

#	Date	Staff ID	Path	Path List	Total Distance
1	6/04/2024 12:00:00 AM	s-2	C,B	List	91
2	12/04/2024 12:00:00 AM	s-2	D,C	List	31
3	12/04/2024 12:00:00 AM	s-3	D,C,D	List	62
4	15/04/2024 12:00:00 AM	s-3	A,C,B,A,B,A,C	List	480
5	16/04/2024 12:00:00 AM	s-1	A,B	List	73
6	21/04/2024 12:00:00 AM	s-1	A,C,B,A	List	249
7	21/04/2024 12:00:00 AM	s-3	A,B,C,A,B,A	List	395
8	22/04/2024 12:00:00 AM	s-2	A,B,C,D	List	195
9	26/04/2024 12:00:00 AM	s-1	A,B	List	73
10	28/04/2024 12:00:00 AM	s-2	A,B	List	73
11	29/04/2024 12:00:00 AM	s-1	A,C	List	85
12	30/04/2024 12:00:00 AM	s-1	A,B,C	List	164

Figure 9-34. List.Accumulate

Solution 2: Using List.Accumulate(), Variation 1

List.Accumulate() can also be used to solve this problem. However, since it utilizes an accumulator function instead of a transformation function, you can define an initial seed value of 0 and create a loop where, in each iteration, the distance of the next leg of the journey is calculated and added to the accumulated value.

The first argument of this function remains the same as the first input of List. Transform(). The second argument is set to 0 (the initial seed value). In the third argument, instead of using (i) => f(i), you can modify it to (s, i) => s + f(i), meaning that in each iteration, the function calculates the distance using f(i) and adds it to the accumulated sum s.

The revised formula is as follows. You can use this in the Custom Column window for the table after adding the Path List column to solve the problem efficiently.

```
= List.Accumulate(
  List.Skip(List.Positions([Path List])),
  0,
  (s, i) =>
    s
      + Table.SelectRows(
        Distance,
```

CHAPTER 9　LOOPING IN POWER QUERY

```
    (x) => (x[Place 1] = [Path List]{i - 1} and x[Place 2] = [Path
    List]{i}) or (x[Place 1] = [Path List]{i} and x[Place 2] =
    [Path List]{i - 1})
  )[Distance]{0}
)
```

To maintain consistency with the notation, replace i with c and rewrite the formula as follows:

```
= List.Accumulate(
  List.Skip(List.Positions([Path List])),
  0,
  (s, c) =>
    s
      + Table.SelectRows(
        Distance,
        (x) => (x[Place 1] = [Path List]{c - 1} and x[Place 2] = [Path
        List]{c}) or (x[Place 1] = [Path List]{c} and x[Place 2] =
        [Path List]{c - 1})
      )[Distance]{0}
)
```

Solution 3: Using List.Accumulate(), Variation 2

As in the previous solutions, instead of solving the entire problem at once, let's first consider ListX and solve the problem for this specific case. Once you derive the correct formula, you can generalize it and apply it to all rows in the dataset. By focusing on ListX first, you can verify that the logic works correctly before extending it to the entire table.

In the previous solution, you initially calculated the Path List in a helper column, then used indexes to convert the sequence of trips into a list of sublists, where each sublist represented a departure and destination pair for a leg of the journey. You then applied this list to the distance calculation formula.

In this approach, however, you aim to solve the problem without using a helper column. Instead of relying on indexes (e.g., List.Skip(List.Positions(ListX)), which

CHAPTER 9   LOOPING IN POWER QUERY

results in {1..6}), you will work directly with the trip sequence {"A","C","B","A","B","A","C"}.

If you use this list as the first input in List.Accumulate(), each iteration will pass only a single branch to the accumulator function. However, you need two branches in each step (departure and destination) to compute the distance.

To illustrate, consider the following formula:

=List.Accumulate(ListX, seed, (s,c)=>f(s,c))

Here, c represents only one city at a time, which is insufficient for calculating distances.

To address this issue, you modify the seed to store not just the accumulated distance but also the previous branch. Instead of defining the seed as a single number (starting at 0), you define it as a record with two fields:

- D: The total accumulated distance (initially set to 0).
- P: The previously visited branch (initially set to ListX{0}, the starting branch of the trip).

Since the first element of ListX is stored in P, you replace ListX in the first argument of List.Accumulate() with List.Skip(ListX) to exclude the first branch from iteration. Thus, the revised formula becomes:

=List.Accumulate(List.Skip(ListX), [D=0,P=ListX{0}], (s,c)=>f(s,c))

Which is equal to the following formula:

=List.Accumulate({"C","B","A","B","A","C"}, [D=0,P="A"], (s,c)=>f(s,c))

To define the (s, c) => f(s, c) function, let's analyze the first iteration:

- s starts as [D = 0, P = "A"]
- c is C

In this step, the departure branch comes from s[P] (which is A), and the destination branch is c (which is C).

Thus, you can update the value of D (total accumulated distance) using the same formula from the previous solution with small modifications as follows.

552

CHAPTER 9 LOOPING IN POWER QUERY

- Instead of using ListX{c-1}, you use s[P] as the departure branch.
- Instead of using ListX{c}, you use c as the destination branch.
- Instead of using s directly, you update only s[D] (the accumulated distance).

With these adjustments, the formula for updating D becomes:

D=s[D]+Table.SelectRows(Distance, (x)=> (x[Place 1] = s[P] and x[Place 2] =c) or (x[Place 1] = c and x[Place 2] = s[P]))[Distance]{0}))

Besides updating D, the value of P in the seed should also be updated to store the departure branch for the next iteration. This value is exactly the same as c, meaning that for P, the update formula is P = c.

Thus, the accumulator function can be defined as follows:

```
(s, c) => [
  D = s[D]
    + Table.SelectRows(
      Distance,
      (x) => (x[Place 1] = s[P] and x[Place 2] = c) or (x[Place 1] = c and
      x[Place 2] = s[P])
    )[Distance]{0},
  P = c
]
```

Using the following formula, you can extract the total traveled distance for ListX:

```
=List.Accumulate(
  List.Skip(ListX),
  [D = 0, P = ListX{0}],
  (s, c) => [
    D = s[D]
      + Table.SelectRows(
        Distance,
        (x) => (x[Place 1] = s[P] and x[Place 2] = c) or (x[Place 1] = c
        and x[Place 2] = s[P])
```

CHAPTER 9 LOOPING IN POWER QUERY

```
    )[Distance]{0},
  P = c
  ]
)
```

However, since the seed value in this example is a record, the formula returns a record as well. Since you only need the value of the D field (which represents the traveled distance), you can extract it by appending [D] to the end of the formula as follows. This ensures that the result is just the total traveled distance for ListX.

```
=List.Accumulate(
  List.Skip(ListX),
  [D = 0, P = ListX{0}],
  (s, c) => [
    D = s[D]
      + Table.SelectRows(
        Distance,
        (x) => (x[Place 1] = s[P] and x[Place 2] = c) or (x[Place 1] = c and x[Place 2] = s[P])
      )[Distance]{0},
    P = c
  ]
)[D]
```

Before applying this formula to all rows, you can refine it further. Instead of setting the seed as [D=0, P=ListX{0}] and using List.Skip(ListX) as the first argument, you can define the seed as [D=0, P=""] and use ListX directly in the first argument.

However, this change introduces an issue: in the first iteration, since P="", the filtering table for P="" returns an error. To handle this, you need to modify the accumulator function by adding an if condition. This condition checks if s[P] is "", and assigns a 0 instead of causing an error. Otherwise, the function proceeds with the distance calculation as follows:

```
(s, c) => [
  D = s[D]
```

CHAPTER 9   LOOPING IN POWER QUERY

```
    + (
      if s[P] = "" then
        0
      else
        Table.SelectRows(
          Distance,
          (x) => (x[Place 1] = s[P] and x[Place 2] = c) or (x[Place 1] =
          c and x[Place 2] = s[P])
        )[Distance]{0}
    ),
  P = c
]
```

The whole formula is as follows:

```
=List.Accumulate(
  ListX,
  [D = 0, P = ""],
  (s, c) => [
    D = s[D]
      + (
        if s[P] = "" then
          0
        else
          Table.SelectRows(
            Distance,
            (x) => (x[Place 1] = s[P] and x[Place 2] = c) or (x[Place 1] =
            c and x[Place 2] = s[P])
          )[Distance]{0}
      ),
    P = c
  ]
)[D]
```

This formula can be applied directly in the Custom Column window of the Travel table, even before adding the Path List column. Simply replace `ListX` with `Text.Split([Path], ",")` as follows, to dynamically generate the list from the Path column.

```
=List.Accumulate(
  Text.Split([Path], ","),
  [D = 0, P = ""],
  (s, c) => [
    D = s[D]
      + (
        if s[P] = "" then
          0
        else
          Table.SelectRows(
            Distance,
            (x) => (x[Place 1] = s[P] and x[Place 2] = c) or (x[Place 1] = c and x[Place 2] = s[P])
          )[Distance]{0}
      ),
    P = c
  ]
)[D]
```

Implementing Stepped Tax Calculations

Given the tax rates in Table 9-10 and the income values in Table 9-11, add a new column to the people's income table to calculate the tax for each person using stepped tax logic.

Note In stepped tax logic, different tax rates apply to various segments of income. For instance, based on the Tax_Rates table, individuals with an income less than $18,200 are taxed at 0%. For incomes exceeding $18,200, different rates apply to different income ranges: 0% for the first $18,200, 19% for the portion from $18,201 to $45,000, 33% for the portion from $45,001 to $120,000, and 37% for the amount above $120,000. For example, the tax calculation for a person with an income of $142,566 (person E) is as follows:

=0*(18200-0)+0.19*(45000-18201)+0.33*(120000-45001)+
0.37*(142566-120001)

Table 9-10. Tax_Rates: TaxRates

From	To	Tax Rate
$0	$18,200	0%
$18,201	$45,000	19%
$45,001	$120,000	33%
$120,001	$180,000	37%
$180,001	Over	45%

Table 9-11. People_Income: People Incomes

Person ID	Income
A	199,920
B	26,068
C	106,439
D	28,521
E	142,566

CHAPTER 9   LOOPING IN POWER QUERY

> **Note** The data in this example is provided in an Excel file titled 10 Implementing Stepped Tax Calculations.xlsx.

To solve this problem in Power Query, load both tables into separate queries named Tax_Rates and People_Income. Then, you can address the problem using any of the following three solutions.

Solution 1: Using a Nested if

In the first solution, select the People_Income query and change the type of column Income to number. Then, from the Add Column tab, add a Custom Column called Tax. Then use the following nested if formula in the Custom Column window to add a new column for calculating the tax:

```
=if [Income]<18201
     then 0
else if [Income]<45001
     then 0.19*([Income]-18201)
else if [Income]<120001
     then 0.19*(45000-18201)+0.325*([Income]-45001)
else if [Income]<180001
     then 0.19*(45000-18201)+0.325*(120000-45001)+0.37*([Income]-120001)
else 0.19*(45000-18201)+0.325*(120000-45001)+0.37*(180000-120001)+
0.45*([Income]-180001)
```

The previous formula can be simplified by calculating the results of the arithmetic operations as follows:

```
=if [Income]<18201
     then 0
else if [Income]<45001
     then 0.19*([Income]-18201)
else if [Income]<120001
     then 5091.81+0.325*([Income]-45001)
```

CHAPTER 9   LOOPING IN POWER QUERY

```
else if [Income]<180001
    then 5091.81+24374.675+0.37*([Income]-120001)
else 5091.81+24374.675+22199.63+0.45*([Income]-180001)
```

Solution 2: Using List.Transform()

The first solution was not dynamic as it hardcoded the tax rate information. Additionally, using a nested if statement might work for a Tax_Rates table with only a few rows (e.g., up to four), but as the table grows, the formula becomes too long and difficult to manage.

A better approach is to use List.Transform() to calculate the applied tax for each row of the Tax_Rates table dynamically. However, since the tax rate information is stored in a table, you need to convert it into a list format that List.Transform() can process.

To achieve this conversion, you can use the Table.ToRows() function, which transforms the Tax_Rates table into a list where each row is represented as a sublist. The following formula in the formula bar performs this transformation, as shown in Figure 9-35.

```
= Table.ToRows(Tax_Rates)
```

Figure 9-35. *The result of Table.ToRows()*

CHAPTER 9 LOOPING IN POWER QUERY

You can use the result of the `Table.ToRows(Tax_Rates)` formula as the first input of `List.Transform()` to calculate the tax amount applied at each tax bracket.

Instead of calculating the tax for all individuals at once, first compute the tax for Person A, whose income is 199,920, with the following formula:

`=List.Transform(Table.ToRows(Tax_Rates),(x)=>f(x))`

To determine f(x), consider an example tax bracket from the transformed Tax_Rates table, related to the second row of the table as {18201, 45000, 0.19}:

- 18201: Lower bound of the tax bracket, which is equal to x{0}.
- 45000: Upper bound of the tax bracket, which is equal to x{0}.
- 0.19: Tax rate for this bracket, which is equal to x{0}.

So, the tax calculation logic for this bracket is:

- If income < 18201, the tax for this bracket is 0.
- If income > 45000, the tax for this bracket is (45000 - 18201) * 0.19.
- If 18201 ≤ income ≤ 45000, the tax for this bracket is (income - 18201) * 0.19.

Which simplifies to:

`if income<18201 then 0 else (List.Min({Income,45000})-18201)*0.19`

And is further refactored using `List.Max()` to ensure non-negative values:

`List.Max({0,(List.Min({Income,45000})-18201)*0.19})`

In the transformation function, you replace the static values with the corresponding list elements:

- 45000 → x{1} (upper bound)
- 18201 → x{0} (lower bound)
- 0.19 → x{2} (tax rate)
- Income → 199,920 (for Person A)

Thus, the transformation function becomes:

```
(x)=>List.Max({0,(List.Min({199920,x{1}})-x{0})*x{2}})
```

Finally, the complete formula that calculates the tax at each tax level for Person A is:

```
= List.Transform(Table.ToRows(Tax_Rates),(x)=>List.Max({0,(List.Min({199920,x{1}})-x{0})*x{2}}))
```

This will return a list of tax amounts for each tax bracket, which can be summed up to determine the total tax payable, as shown in Figure 9-36.

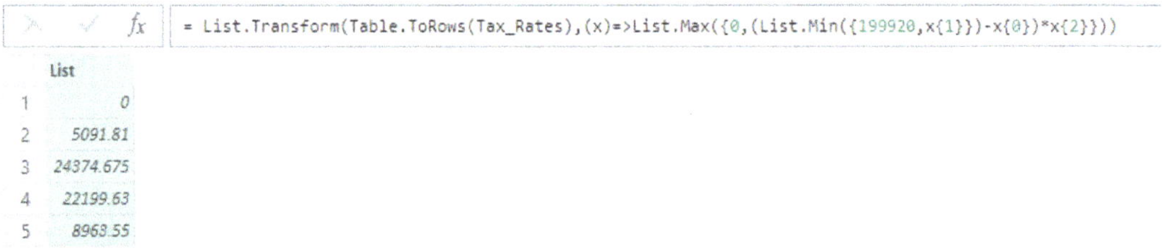

	List
1	0
2	5091.81
3	24374.675
4	22199.63
5	8968.55

Figure 9-36. Calculating the tax for each level

Note In the Tax_Rates table, the last value in the To column is a text value called Over, instead of a numeric value. Interestingly, the formula still works correctly because `List.Min({199920, "Over"})` returns 199,920, treating the text as a higher value. However, this behavior might not always be reliable in similar cases, so caution is advised.

To get the total tax amount for Person A, you sum the tax amounts for each bracket using `List.Sum()`. The revised formula is as follows:

```
= List.Sum(
    List.Transform(
      Table.ToRows(Tax_Rates),
      (x) => List.Max({0, (List.Min({199920, x{1}}) - x{0}) * x{2}})
    )
  )
```

This formula applies the tax calculation logic to each bracket and sums the results to determine the total tax payable for Person A.

To calculate the tax for all individuals, select the People Income table and add a Custom Column named Tax using the revised formula (replacing the hardcoded income value (199,920) with the [Income] column reference). This will solve the problem and results in Figure 9-37.

```
= List.Sum(
    List.Transform(
      Table.ToRows(Tax_Rates),
      (x) => List.Max({0, (List.Min({[Income], x{1}}) - x{0}) * x{2}})
    )
  )
```

	Person ID	Income	Tax
1	A	199920	60629.665
2	B	26068	1494.73
3	C	106439	25059.16
4	D	28521	1960.8
5	E	142566	37815.535

Figure 9-37. Adding a Tax column

Solution 3: Using List.Accumulate()

In addition to using List.Transform(), you can also use List.Accumulate() to solve this problem, following a similar logic. However, the key difference is that with List.Accumulate(), you don't need to calculate the tax for each bracket separately and then sum the results. Instead, you can accumulate the tax directly from the initial tax bracket and, for each subsequent bracket, add the tax calculated for that bracket to the total accumulated tax.

For the third input as an accumulator function, you can use the transformation function in List.Transform() with some modification. In List.Transform(), you used (x) => f(x), where f(x) calculates the tax for each bracket. In List.Accumulate(), the accumulator function is written as (s, x) => s + f(x), where s represents the accumulated tax, x is the current tax bracket, and f(x) is used in List.Transform().

CHAPTER 9 LOOPING IN POWER QUERY

The formula is as follows:

```
= List.Accumulate(
  Table.ToRows(Tax_Rates),
  0,
  (s, x) => s + List.Max({0, (List.Min({[Income], x{1}}) - x{0}) * x{2}})
)
```

Using consistent notation, you can replace x with c in the accumulator function. The revised formula becomes:

```
= List.Accumulate(
  Table.ToRows(Tax_Rates),
  0,
  (s, c) => s + List.Max({0, (List.Min({[Income], c{1}}) - c{0}) * c{2}})
)
```

This formula can be used in the Custom Column window for the People Income table to calculate the tax of each person, as shown in Figure 9-38.

#	Person ID	Income	Tax
1	A	199920	60629.665
2	B	26068	1494.73
3	C	106439	25059.16
4	D	28521	1960.8
5	E	142566	37815.535

Figure 9-38. Adding a Tax column using List.Accumulate()

Changing Data Granularity

The power consumption data of a house recorded every 30 minutes for different dates is listed in the Source table, as shown in Table 9-12. Convert this data into hourly energy consumption by merging every two columns and summing their values. For example, in the results table, the values in columns E_0000 and E_0030 for each row should be summed and presented in a single column named E_0000.

Table 9-12. Source: Power Consumption

Date	E_0000	E_0030	E_0100	E_0130	E_0200	E_0230	E_0300	E_0330
1/04/2012	426	396	340	392	348	378	362	356
2/04/2012	1872	1920	1620	304	230	268	198	248
3/04/2012	766	528	320	474	384	338	326	356
4/04/2012	696	546	408	390	362	384	186	198
5/04/2012	632	490	506	330	364	308	352	318
6/04/2012	734	802	716	246	166	244	202	244
7/04/2012	220	234	170	234	172	228	182	184
8/04/2012	1094	870	1720	1338	534	498	484	528
9/04/2012	834	682	686	664	682	588	516	556
10/04/2012	378	358	304	302	354	304	304	350

Note The data in this example is provided in an Excel file titled `11 Changing Data Granularity.xlsx`.

You can use several approaches to solve this problem, and this section explains four different solutions. The first approach is suitable for cases where the column naming follows a specific logic (like this example), while the other solutions are more general and based on unpivoting the `List.Transform()` and `List.Accumulate()` functions. Before talking about the solutions, select all the columns that start with E and change their types into `Number`.

Note As mentioned, the first proposed solution relies on a specific column name pattern, meaning that even small changes to column names could lead to unintended results. Therefore, in practice, it is recommended to use more dynamic approaches, such as those presented in Solutions 2 and 3.

CHAPTER 9 LOOPING IN POWER QUERY

Solution 1: Column Name-Based Approach

By looking more closely at the column names, it becomes clear that any pair of columns that should be merged share the same first four characters. By extracting these first four characters, you can identify and group columns with the same prefix. However, this operation cannot be directly applied to columns, as it is impossible to have multiple columns with identical names. Instead, you need to transform the data structure so that these names are represented in rows.

Right-click the Date column and select Unpivot Other Columns to transform the table, as shown in Figure 9-39.

	Date	Attribute	Value
1	1/04/2012 12:00:00 AM	E_0000	426
2	1/04/2012 12:00:00 AM	E_0030	396
3	1/04/2012 12:00:00 AM	E_0100	340
4	1/04/2012 12:00:00 AM	E_0130	392
5	1/04/2012 12:00:00 AM	E_0200	348
6	1/04/2012 12:00:00 AM	E_0230	378
7	1/04/2012 12:00:00 AM	E_0300	362
8	1/04/2012 12:00:00 AM	E_0330	356
9	2/04/2012 12:00:00 AM	E_0000	1872
10	2/04/2012 12:00:00 AM	E_0030	1920
11	2/04/2012 12:00:00 AM	E_0100	1620
12	2/04/2012 12:00:00 AM	E_0130	304
13	2/04/2012 12:00:00 AM	E_0200	230
14	2/04/2012 12:00:00 AM	E_0230	268
15	2/04/2012 12:00:00 AM	E_0300	198
16	2/04/2012 12:00:00 AM	E_0330	248
17	3/04/2012 12:00:00 AM	E_0000	766
18	3/04/2012 12:00:00 AM	E_0030	528

Figure 9-39. Unpivoting columns.

Then, select the Attribute column. From the Transform tab, under the Text Column section, choose Extract and then First Characters. In the open window, select four characters to get the result shown in Figure 9-40.

CHAPTER 9 LOOPING IN POWER QUERY

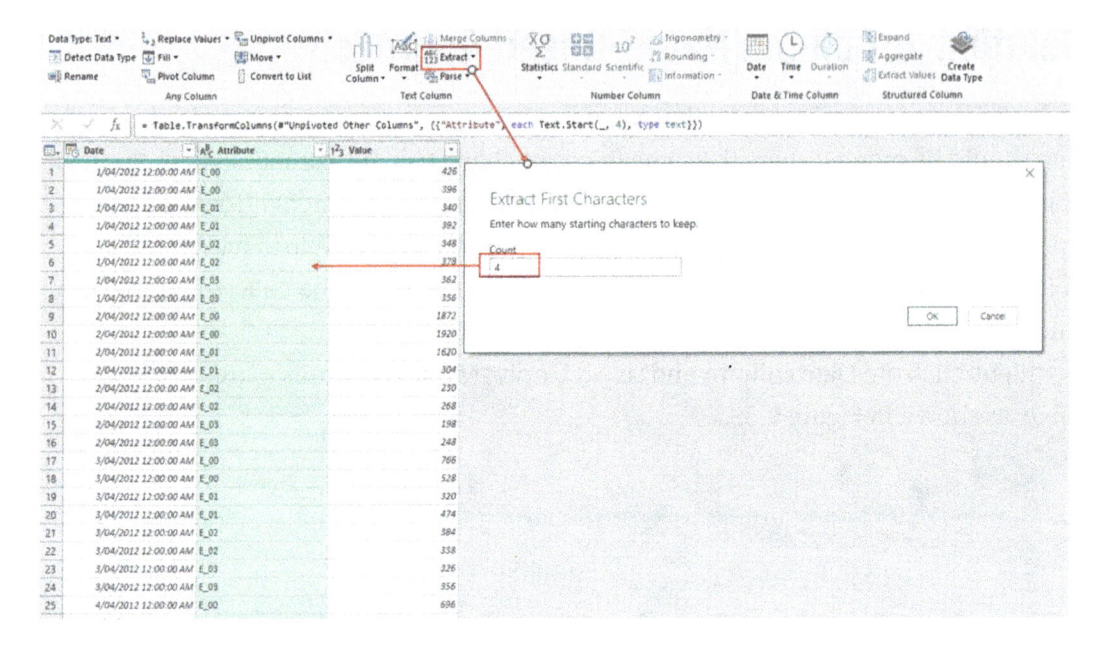

Figure 9-40. Select the first four characters

In the result table, the values on the Attribute column for every two rows are the same. Select the Attribute column. From the Transform tab, choose Pivot Column. In the Pivot Column window, set Value as the Value column, and in the Advanced tab, select Sum as the aggregation method to produce the final table shown in Figure 9-41.

CHAPTER 9 LOOPING IN POWER QUERY

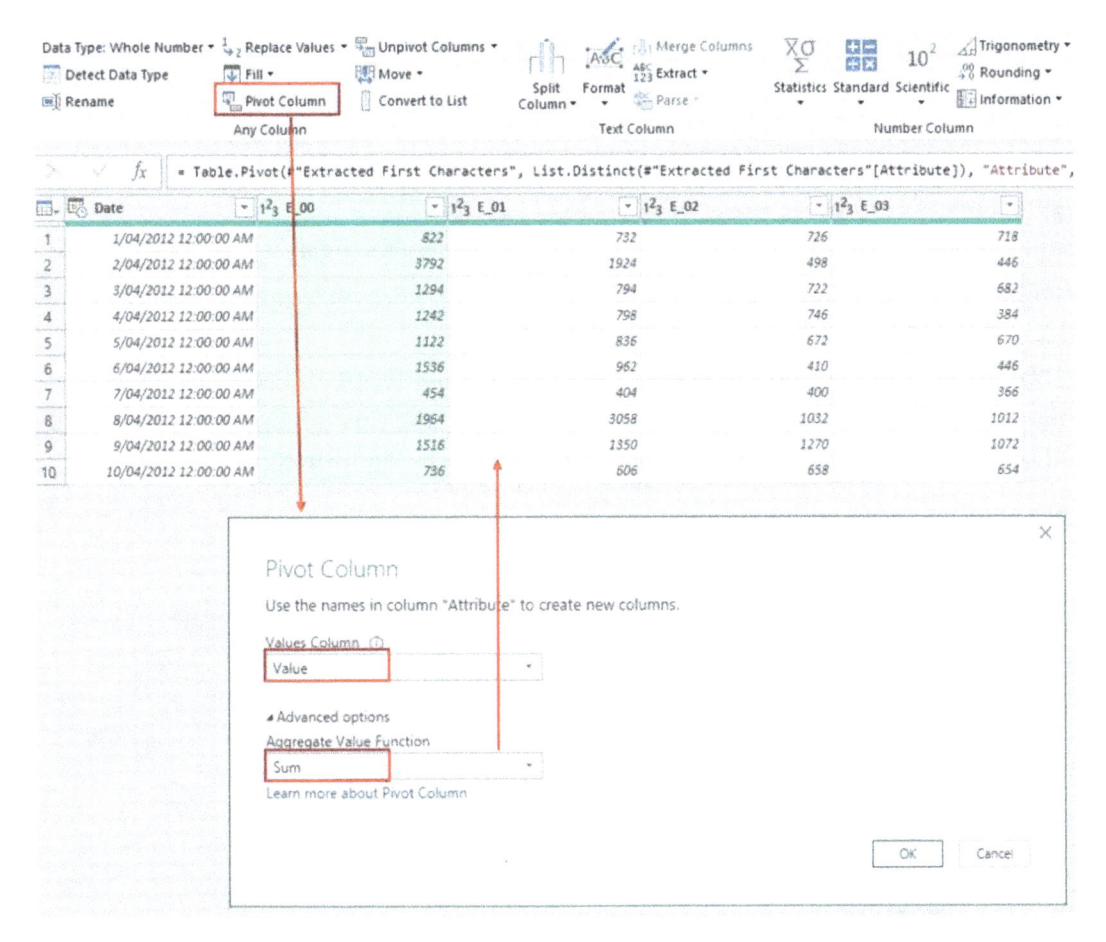

Figure 9-41. *The result of pivoting*

This method works well if the column naming is consistent and follows a specific pattern.

Note This approach works, and the output data is pivoted—making it human-readable, which is good. However, for machine processing and BI, unpivoted data is generally preferred (i.e., a structure with three columns: Date, Time, and Consumption). Additionally, creating a table with hundreds of columns is considered poor practice for data analysts, as it can lead to column limits and significant performance slowdowns when processing large datasets.

567

CHAPTER 9 LOOPING IN POWER QUERY

Solution 2: Using the Unpivoting Column

The previous solution works when the column names follow a specific pattern. However, this solution is based on unpivoted columns. Consider the unpivoted table shown in Figure 9-39.

If there is no specific pattern in the column names, in the next step, you can use the group command to combine every two rows together. For grouping, you need a column with a unique value for every pair of rows.

To create this new column, add an Index column starting at 0. Then, add a custom column named Unique using the following formula in the Custom Column window, to generate a unique value for every other row, as shown in Figure 9-42.

```
=Number.IntegerDivide([Index], 2)
```

	Date	Attribute	Value	Index	Unique
1	1/04/2012 12:00:00 AM	E_0000	426	0	0
2	1/04/2012 12:00:00 AM	E_0030	396	1	0
3	1/04/2012 12:00:00 AM	E_0100	340	2	1
4	1/04/2012 12:00:00 AM	E_0130	392	3	1
5	1/04/2012 12:00:00 AM	E_0200	348	4	2
6	1/04/2012 12:00:00 AM	E_0230	378	5	2
7	1/04/2012 12:00:00 AM	E_0300	362	6	3
8	1/04/2012 12:00:00 AM	E_0330	356	7	3
9	2/04/2012 12:00:00 AM	E_0000	1872	8	4
10	2/04/2012 12:00:00 AM	E_0030	1920	9	4
11	2/04/2012 12:00:00 AM	E_0100	1620	10	5
12	2/04/2012 12:00:00 AM	E_0130	304	11	5
13	2/04/2012 12:00:00 AM	E_0200	230	12	6
14	2/04/2012 12:00:00 AM	E_0230	268	13	6
15	2/04/2012 12:00:00 AM	E_0300	198	14	7
16	2/04/2012 12:00:00 AM	E_0330	248	15	7
17	3/04/2012 12:00:00 AM	E_0000	766	16	8
18	3/04/2012 12:00:00 AM	E_0030	528	17	8
19	3/04/2012 12:00:00 AM	E_0100	320	18	9
20	3/04/2012 12:00:00 AM	E_0130	474	19	9
21	3/04/2012 12:00:00 AM	E_0200	384	20	10
22	3/04/2012 12:00:00 AM	E_0230	338	21	10

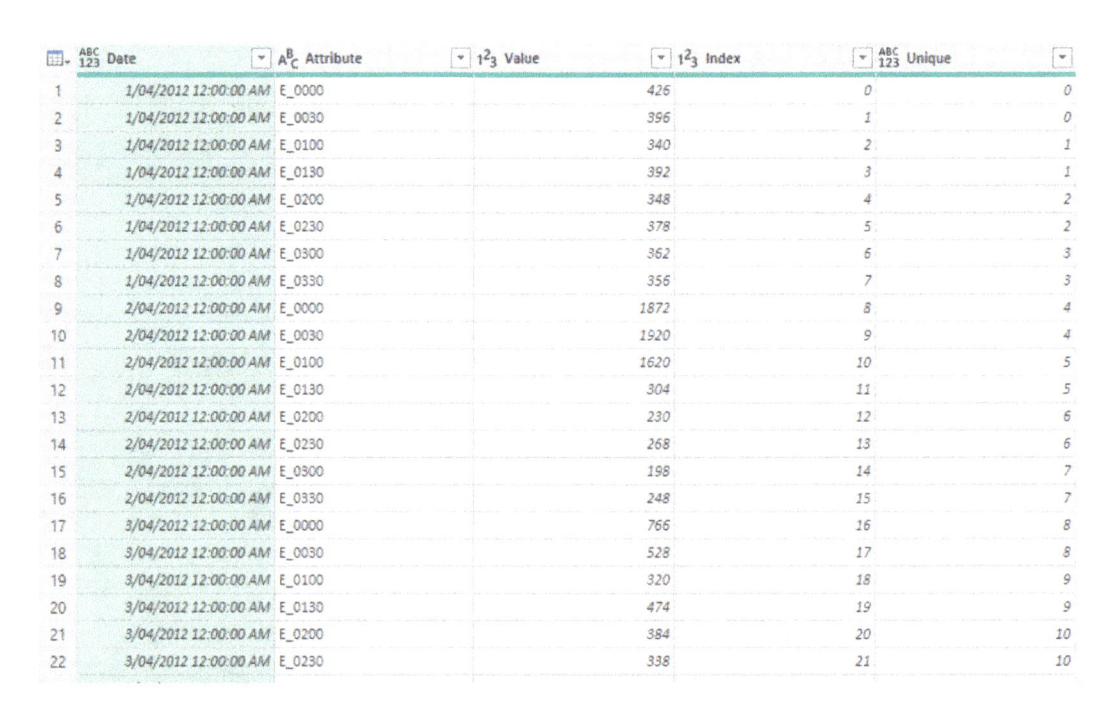

Figure 9-42. Adding the Unique column

Next, right-click the Unique column and select the Group By command, using the settings shown in Figure 9-43.

CHAPTER 9 LOOPING IN POWER QUERY

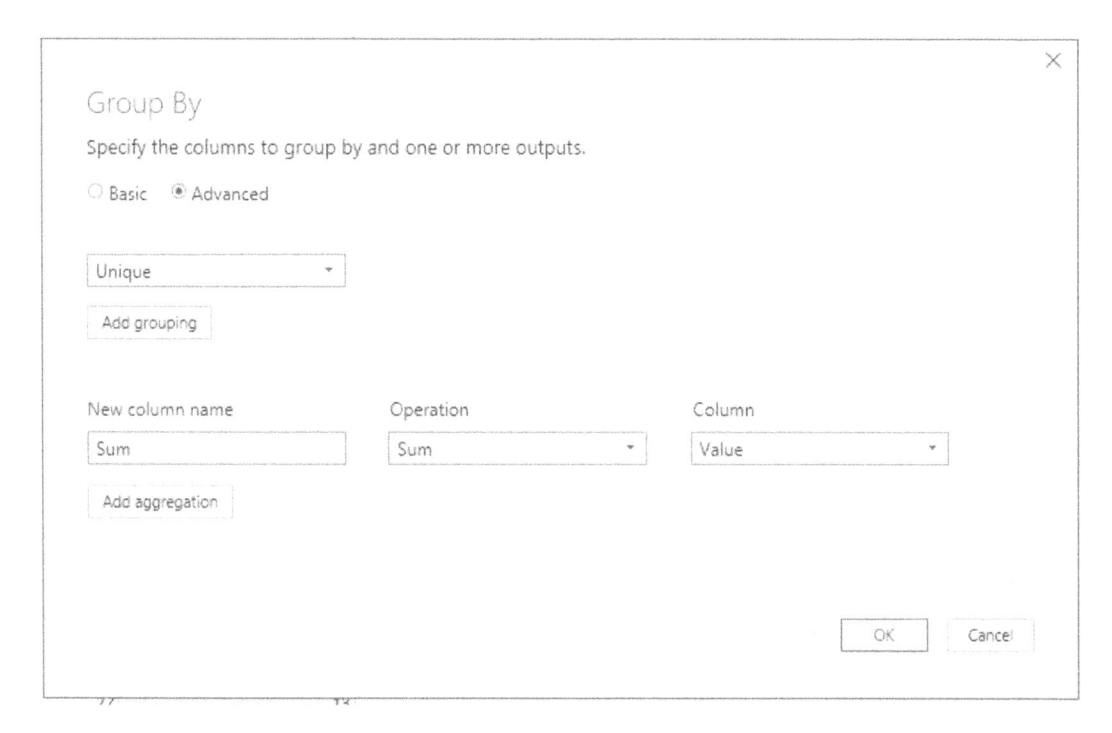

Figure 9-43. Settings for the grouping

Clicking OK will result in Figure 9-44 and generate the following formula in the formula bar:

= Table.Group(#"Added Custom", {"Unique"}, {{"Sum", each List.Sum([Value]), type number}})

CHAPTER 9 LOOPING IN POWER QUERY

Unique	Sum
0	822
1	732
2	726
3	718
4	3792
5	1924
6	498
7	446
8	1294
9	794
10	722
11	682
12	1242
13	798
14	746
15	384
16	1122
17	836
18	672
19	670
20	1536
21	962
22	410
23	446
24	454
25	404

Figure 9-44. *The result of grouping*

As presented in Chapter 6, to extract the Date value and the column name value, rewrite the previous formula as follows, which results in Figure 9-45.

```
= Table.Group(
    #"Added Custom",
    {"Unique"},
```

CHAPTER 9 LOOPING IN POWER QUERY

```
{{"Sum", each List.Sum([Value])}, {"Date", each _[Date]{0}},
{"Attribute", each _[Attribute]{0}}}
)
```

Unique	Sum	Date	Attribute
	0	822	1/04/2012 12:00:00 AM	E_0000
	1	732	1/04/2012 12:00:00 AM	E_0100
	2	726	1/04/2012 12:00:00 AM	E_0200
	3	718	1/04/2012 12:00:00 AM	E_0300
	4	3792	2/04/2012 12:00:00 AM	E_0000
	5	1924	2/04/2012 12:00:00 AM	E_0100
	6	498	2/04/2012 12:00:00 AM	E_0200
	7	446	2/04/2012 12:00:00 AM	E_0300
	8	1294	3/04/2012 12:00:00 AM	E_0000
	9	794	3/04/2012 12:00:00 AM	E_0100
	10	722	3/04/2012 12:00:00 AM	E_0200
	11	682	3/04/2012 12:00:00 AM	E_0300
	12	1242	4/04/2012 12:00:00 AM	E_0000
	13	798	4/04/2012 12:00:00 AM	E_0100
	14	746	4/04/2012 12:00:00 AM	E_0200
	15	384	4/04/2012 12:00:00 AM	E_0300
	16	1122	5/04/2012 12:00:00 AM	E_0000
	17	836	5/04/2012 12:00:00 AM	E_0100
	18	672	5/04/2012 12:00:00 AM	E_0200
	19	670	5/04/2012 12:00:00 AM	E_0300
	20	1536	6/04/2012 12:00:00 AM	E_0000
	21	962	6/04/2012 12:00:00 AM	E_0100
	22	410	6/04/2012 12:00:00 AM	E_0200
	23	446	6/04/2012 12:00:00 AM	E_0300

Figure 9-45. The result of revised grouping

In the next step, remove the Unique column. Then, similar to the previous solution, select the Attribute column and apply the Pivot command to solve the problem. This will rearrange the data by turning the unique values from the Attribute column into new columns, resulting in the desired output.

CHAPTER 9   LOOPING IN POWER QUERY

Solution 3: Using List.Transform()

Besides what was presented in Solutions 1 and 2, the List.Transform() function can also be used to solve this problem. In this approach, after changing the column types to numbers, you can select all the columns that need to be merged (all except the first one), right-click one of them, and choose Merge Columns. In the dialog box that appears, select None as the separator and click OK. This will concatenate the values, as shown in Figure 9-46.

	Date	Merged
1	1/04/2012 12:00:00 AM	4263963403923483783 62356
2	2/04/2012 12:00:00 AM	1872192016203042302681982...
3	3/04/2012 12:00:00 AM	7665283204743843383 26356
4	4/04/2012 12:00:00 AM	6965464083903623841 86198
5	5/04/2012 12:00:00 AM	6324905063303643083 52318
6	6/04/2012 12:00:00 AM	7348027162461662442 02244
7	7/04/2012 12:00:00 AM	2202341702341722281 82184
8	8/04/2012 12:00:00 AM	1094870172013385344984845...
9	9/04/2012 12:00:00 AM	8346826866646825885 16556
10	10/04/2012 12:00:00 AM	3783583043023543043 04350

Figure 9-46.   Combining the columns

The generated formula in the formula bar will be as follows:

```
= Table.CombineColumns(
  Table.TransformColumnTypes(
    #"Changed Type",
    {
      {"E_0000", type text},
      {"E_0030", type text},
      {"E_0100", type text},
      {"E_0130", type text},
      {"E_0200", type text},
      {"E_0230", type text},
```

```
      {"E_0300", type text},
      {"E_0330", type text}
    },
    "en-AU"
  ),
  {"E_0000", "E_0030", "E_0100", "E_0130", "E_0200", "E_0230", "E_0300", "E_0330"},
  Combiner.CombineTextByDelimiter("", QuoteStyle.None),
  "Merged"
)
```

As what was presented in Example 9 in Chapter 4, you can replace the first argument called Table.TransformColumnTypes(...) with the name of the previous step, such as #"Changed Type". Additionally, replace the combiner in the fourth argument Combiner.CombineTextByDelimiter("", QuoteStyle.None) with each _ and rewrite the formula as follows:

```
=Table.CombineColumns(
  #"Changed Type",
  {"E_0000", "E_0030", "E_0100", "E_0130", "E_0200", "E_0230", "E_0300", "E_0330"},
  each _,
  "Merged"
)
```

This formula will present all the values of the merged column into a list, as shown in Figure 9-47.

CHAPTER 9 LOOPING IN POWER QUERY

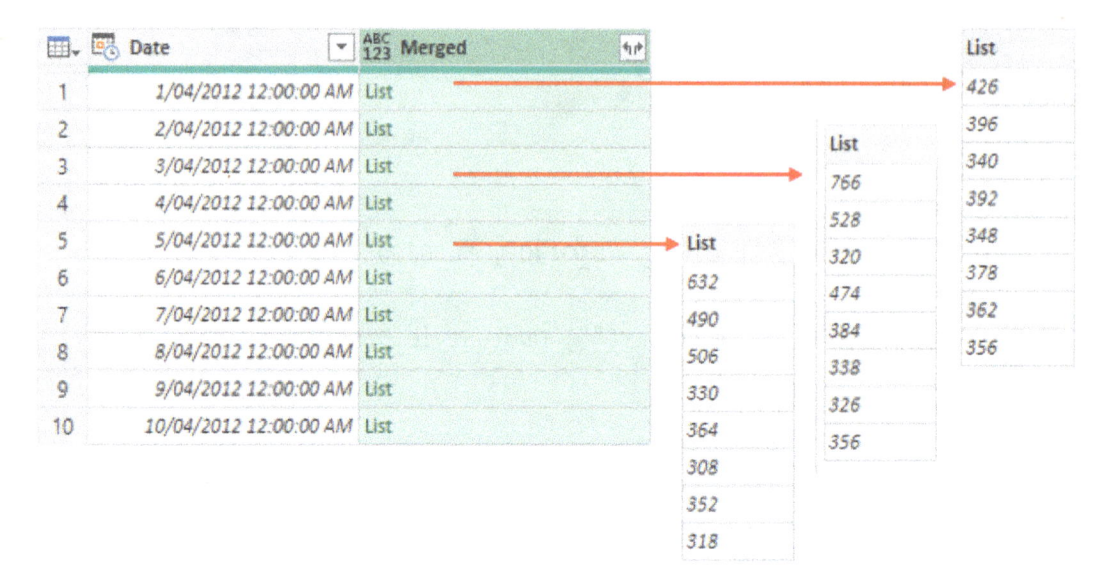

Figure 9-47. Combining the column after the revised formula

To make the solution more dynamic without changing the result, you can replace the second argument with `List.Skip(Table.ColumnNames(#"Changed Type"))` and rewrite the formula as follows:

```
= Table.CombineColumns(
  #"Changed Type",
  {"E_0000", "E_0030", "E_0100", "E_0130", "E_0200", "E_0230", "E_0300",
  "E_0330"},
  each _,
  "Merged"
)
```

Here, the result of each _ is a list that includes the values of the row. Replacing each _ with each `List.Split(_,2)` will change the result and provide every two values in a sublist, as shown in Figure 9-48.

574

CHAPTER 9 LOOPING IN POWER QUERY

Figure 9-48. The result of using List.Split()

So each _ for the first row results in {426,396,340,392,348,378,362,356}, and each List.Split(_,2) will change the result to {{426,396},{340,392},{348,378}, {362,356}}.

Here, you can use List.Transform() to replace each sublist with the sum of its values. Using each List.Transform(List.Split(_,2), (x)=>List.Sum(x)) means replace each sublist by the sum of the values in it.

Revising the formula as shown here will result in Figure 9-49.

```
= Table.CombineColumns(
  #"Changed Type",
  List.Skip(Table.ColumnNames(#"Changed Type")),
  each List.Transform(List.Split(_, 2), (x) => List.Sum(x)),
  "Merged"
)
```

575

CHAPTER 9 LOOPING IN POWER QUERY

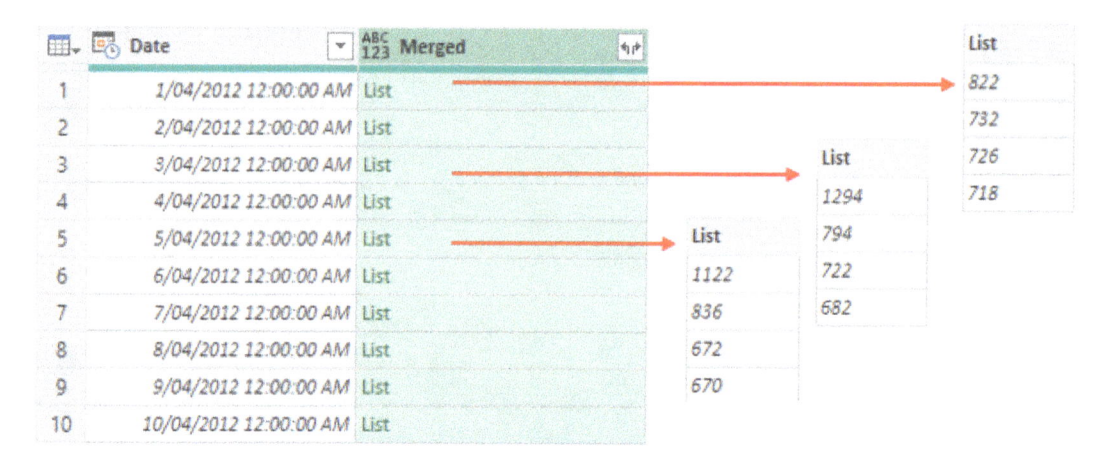

	Date	Merged				List
1	1/04/2012 12:00:00 AM	List				822
2	2/04/2012 12:00:00 AM	List				732
3	3/04/2012 12:00:00 AM	List			List	726
4	4/04/2012 12:00:00 AM	List			1294	718
5	5/04/2012 12:00:00 AM	List		List	794	
6	6/04/2012 12:00:00 AM	List		1122	722	
7	7/04/2012 12:00:00 AM	List		836	682	
8	8/04/2012 12:00:00 AM	List		672		
9	9/04/2012 12:00:00 AM	List		670		
10	10/04/2012 12:00:00 AM	List				

Figure 9-49. *The result of adding List.Transform()*

The splitting command can be applied to the Merged column in the result table to separate the values into individual columns. However, it is often more efficient to first convert the list values into records with meaningful names, and then expand the new column to include these records.

To achieve this, you can use the Record.FromList() function, which takes two arguments: the list of values and the corresponding field names. The list of values is already generated using List.Transform(), as demonstrated earlier. For the field names, instead of manually specifying a list like {"E_0000", "E_0100", "E_0200", "E_0300"}, you can dynamically generate the names.

To do this, you can use List.Skip(Table.ColumnNames(#"Changed Type")) to get all the column names (e.g., {"E_0000","E_0030", "E_0100", "E_0130", "E_0200", "E_0230", "E_0300", and "E_0330"}). Then, you use List.Alternate() to select every other item in this list, resulting in the desired field names, such as {"E_0000", "E_0100", "E_0200", "E_0300"}.

List.Alternate(List.Skip(Table.ColumnNames(#"Changed Type")),1,1,1)

The revised formula is as follows and results in Figure 9-50:

```
= Table.CombineColumns(
  #"Changed Type",
  List.Skip(Table.ColumnNames(#"Changed Type")),
  each Record.FromList(
    List.Transform(List.Split(_, 2), (x) => List.Sum(x)),
```

CHAPTER 9 LOOPING IN POWER QUERY

```
    List.Alternate(List.Skip(Table.ColumnNames(#"Changed Type"))), 1, 1, 1)
),
"Merged"
)
```

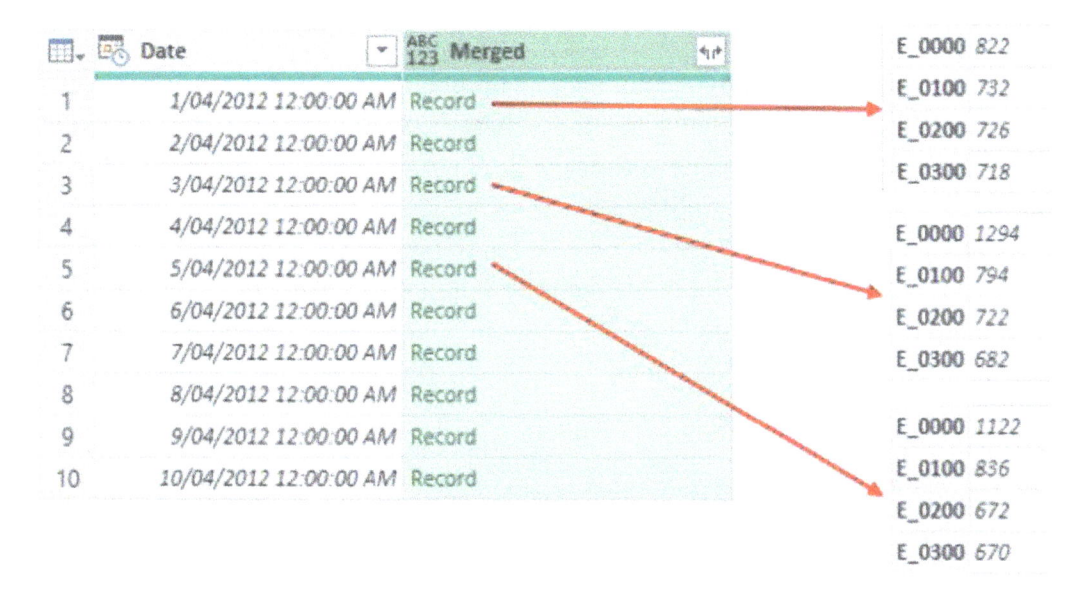

Figure 9-50. Converting the items to a record

By expanding the Merged column, you solve the problem.

Note In this solution, you first combine the columns, and the values of selected columns are provided in the list using each _ as a combiner. However, when you add a custom column and using _ as the formula in the Custom Column window, all the values of that row will be presented as a list. Using List.Skip(_) will exclude the value from the first column, and then you can apply the same solution as before in the Custom Column window to solve the problem.

577

CHAPTER 9 LOOPING IN POWER QUERY

Solution 4: Using List.Accumulate()

Besides the solution presented earlier, where all columns are combined at once, you can use List.Accumulate() to combine every two columns in separate iterations. To achieve this, let's first combine two sample columns and extract the formula for combining them in Power Query.

After converting the values of columns into number, select the E_0000 and E_0030 columns, right-click one of them, and choose Merge Columns. However, as shown in Figure 9-51, you cannot select Sum as a merging operation, so like the previous solution, select None as the separator and click OK.

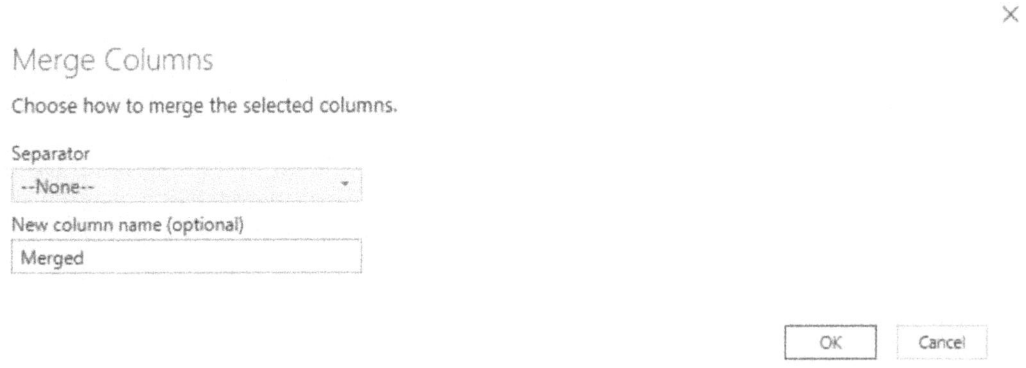

Figure 9-51. Merge setting

This action concatenates the values of the selected columns and presents the result in a new column called Merged, as demonstrated in Figure 9-52 and based on the following formula generated in the formula bar.

```
= Table.CombineColumns(
    Table.TransformColumnTypes(#"Changed Type", {{"E_0000", type text},
    {"E_0030", type text}}, "en-AU"),
    {"E_0000", "E_0030"},
    Combiner.CombineTextByDelimiter("", QuoteStyle.None),
    "Merged")
```

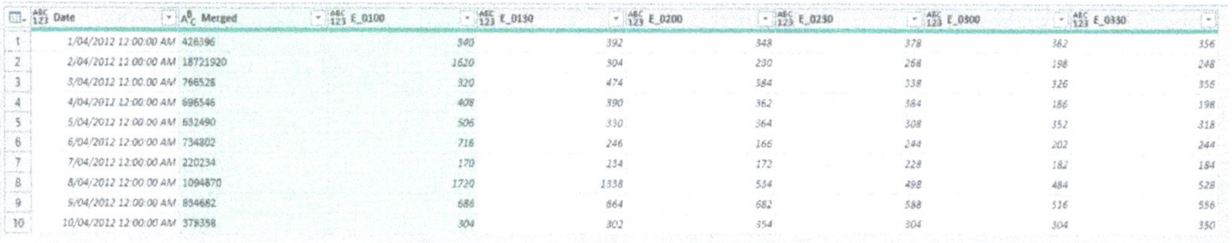

CHAPTER 9 LOOPING IN POWER QUERY

Figure 9-52. The result of merge

Since the selected columns are of type number and the merging logic specified in the third argument is Combiner.CombineTextByDelimiter, the initial step involves converting the column types to text using Table.TransformColumnTypes. After that, the values are combined.

However, in this example, the values need to be summed rather than concatenated. Therefore, the step to convert the values type to text is unnecessary, and the formula can be modified to directly summing the values, as shown here and resulting in Figure 9-53.

```
= Table.CombineColumns(
    #"Changed Type",
    {"E_0000", "E_0030"},
    List.Sum,
    "Merged")
```

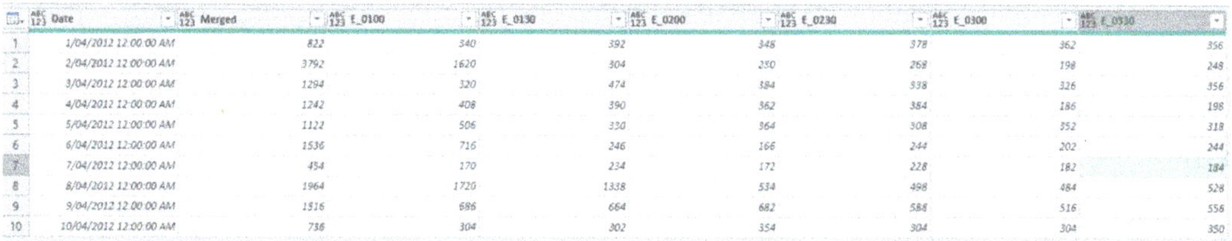

Figure 9-53. The result of the revised formula

This formula summed the values from the E_0000 and E_0030 columns by summing their values and placing the result in a new column named Merged, which the column name can and will be changed by modifying the fourth argument in the formula.

To solve this problem, you need to apply a similar action for other pairs of columns as {"E_0100", "E_0130"}, {"E_0200", "E_0230"}, and { "E_0300", "E_0330"}. To automate the process, you can identify the pairs of columns that need to be merged as sublists of a min list, and repeat the merging process for each pair of column names.

579

CHAPTER 9 LOOPING IN POWER QUERY

Use the following formula in the formula bar to extract all column names as {"Date","E_0000", "E_0030", "E_0100", "E_0130", "E_0200", "E_0230", "E_0300", "E_0330"}:

=Table.ColumnNames(Source)

Since the Date column should not be processed, you need to filter it out from the to-be-processed-columns. Because the date column is the first one, List.Skip() will do the job. Rewrite the formula as follows:

=List.Skip(Table.ColumnNames(Source))

In the next step, to convert the list of column names for merging into several sublists for the pair of columns, you can use the List.Split() function with the page of 2 (second argument). So, rewrite the formula as shown here, which results in pairs like {{"E_0000", "E_0030"}, {"E_0100", "E_0130"}, {"E_0200", "E_0230"}, {"E_0300", "E_0330"}}:

```
= List.Split(
      List.Skip(Table.ColumnNames(Source)),
      2)
```

The previous formula results in the {{"E_0000", "E_0030"}, {"E_0100", "E_0130"}, {"E_0200", "E_0230"}, {"E_0300", "E_0330"}} list, which you can use as the first argument of List.Accumulate().

In each iteration of List.Accumulate(), two columns from the main table should be combined, so #"Changed Type" (the name of last step) serves as the initial table (seed) in the second argument.

To create the accumulator function, such as (s,c) => f(s,c), where s is the table and c is the pair of column names, you can use the formula for combining two columns, which was presented earlier in this section, and is shown here:

```
= Table.CombineColumns(
      #"Changed Type",
      {"E_0000", "E_0030"},
      List.Sum,
      "Merged")
```

CHAPTER 9 LOOPING IN POWER QUERY

In this case, #"Changed Type" can be replaced with s, {"E_0000", "E_0030"} can be replaced with c, and "Merged" can be replaced with c{0} to represent the meaningful name after merging. The accumulator formula becomes:

(s,c)=> Table.CombineColumns(s,c,List.Sum,c{0})

The entire formula for List.Accumulate() can be written as flows:

```
= List.Accumulate(
    List.Split(List.Skip(Table.ColumnNames(Source)),2),
    #"Changed Type",
    (s,c)=>Table.CombineColumns(s,c,List.Sum,c{0})
)
```

Writing this formula in the formula bar will iterate through each pair of columns, combine them, and assign a meaningful name to the merged column, updating the table with each iteration.

This will generate the final table, where every pair of columns in the Source table are merged, as shown in Figure 9-54.

	Date	E_0000	E_0100	E_0200	E_0300
1	1/04/2012 12:00:00 AM	822	732	726	718
2	2/04/2012 12:00:00 AM	3792	1924	498	446
3	3/04/2012 12:00:00 AM	1294	794	722	682
4	4/04/2012 12:00:00 AM	1242	798	746	384
5	5/04/2012 12:00:00 AM	1122	836	672	670
6	6/04/2012 12:00:00 AM	1536	962	410	446
7	7/04/2012 12:00:00 AM	454	404	400	366
8	8/04/2012 12:00:00 AM	1964	3058	1032	1012
9	9/04/2012 12:00:00 AM	1516	1350	1270	1072
10	10/04/2012 12:00:00 AM	736	606	658	654

Figure 9-54. The final table

Efficiency Tips   Four different solutions are provided for this problem. To evaluate their performance, a table with 10,000 rows and 101 columns was used. The execution times for the four solutions were measured as 6.9 seconds, 34 seconds, 3.1 seconds, and 0.6 seconds, respectively.

CHAPTER 9 LOOPING IN POWER QUERY

Product Combinations

Imagine a store with products defined by the set S = {"A","B","C","D","E"}. Generate all possible combinations of products in a customer's basket, ignoring the order of the products.

The expected solution for this problem is:

{"A","B","C","D","E","AB","AC","AD","AE","BC","BD","BE","CD"," CE", "DE","ABC","ABD","ABE"," ACD","ACE","ADE","BCD","BCE","BDE","CDE","ABCD", "ABCE","ABDE","ACDE","BCDE","ABCDE"}

To solve this problem, you can use a combination of the List.Accumulate() and List.Transform() functions, as shown in the following formula:

= List.Accumulate({"A".."E"}, {""},(s,c)=>s&List.Transform(s,each _&c))

To discover the logic behind this formula, the result of different elements in this formula for the first three iterations is illustrated in Table 9-13. It begins with an initial list {""}. In each iteration, it adds all possible combinations of the new product to each previously selected product in the list, thereby building the complete set of combinations.

Table 9-13. *Source: Solutions*

iteration	s	c	List.Transform(s,each _&c)	s&List.Transform(s,each _&c)
1	{""}	"A"	"A"	{"","A"}
2	{"","A"}	"B"	{"B","AB"}	{"","A","B","AB"}
3	{"","A","B","AB"}	"C"	{"C","AC","BC","ABC"}	{"","A","B","AB","C","AC","BC","ABC"}
...				

To remove the initial empty string from the result list, the formula can be adjusted as follows, which results in Figure 9-55:

=List.Skip(List.Accumulate({"A".."E"}, {""},(s,c)=>s&List.Transform(s,each _&c)))

CHAPTER 9 LOOPING IN POWER QUERY

	List
1	A
2	B
3	AB
4	C
5	AC
6	BC
7	ABC
8	D
9	AD
10	BD
11	ABD
12	CD
13	ACD

Figure 9-55. *All the product combinations*

To sort the result list based on the number of characters, you can place the formula inside the List.Sort() function and use Text.Length() to define the sorting logic by the following formula:

= List.Sort(List.Skip(List.Accumulate({"A".."E"}, {""},(a,b)=>a&List. Transform(a,each _&b))), Text.Length)

To sort items with the same length in ascending order, in addition to sorting by Text. Length, you can apply a secondary sorting logic as follows, resulting in Figure 9-56:

= List.Sort(List.Skip(List.Accumulate({"A".."E"}, {""},(a,b)=>a&List. Transform(a,each _&b))), {Text.Length,each _})

	List
1	A
2	B
3	C
4	D
5	E
6	AB
7	AC
8	AD
9	AE
10	BC
11	BD

Figure 9-56. *Sorting the product combinations*

Note In the previous formula, product names are combined into a single text string. To create combinations as lists instead, perhaps to use the result for other application, the formula can be rewritten as follows:

= List.Skip(List.Accumulate({"A".."E"}, {{}},(a,b)=>a&List. Transform(a,each _&{b})))

Working with Set Combinations (Cartesian Product)

Consider a company that produces three products—A, B, and C—using two formulations—Eco and Pro—with two colors—Black and Blue—and in three sizes—X, XL, and XXL. Generate the names of all possible product combinations, such as "A Pro Black XXL".

CHAPTER 9 LOOPING IN POWER QUERY

> **Note** This full combination is known as a cartesian product.

Three different solutions based on combining the table column, using `List.Accumulate()` to expand the columns, and using a combination of `List.Accumulate()` and `List.TransformMany()` are provided for this problem, as outlined in this section.

Solution 1: Merging the Table Columns

The first solution involves creating a table with one row and four columns, where each column contains a list of specific product features. Expanding these lists will generate all possible combinations of the features.

To create a table with all possible product combinations, use the following formula to generate the results shown in Figure 9-57.

```
= #table(
    {"Name","Formulation","Colour","Size"},
    {
        {{"A","B","C"},{"Eco","Pro"},{"Black","Blue"},
        {"X","XL","XXL"}}
    })
```

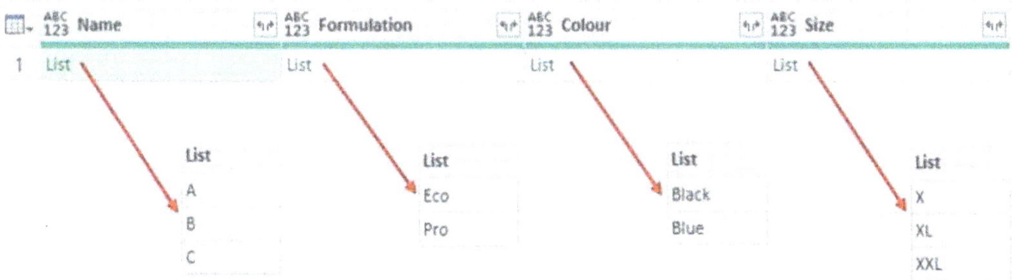

Figure 9-57. The #table function

585

CHAPTER 9 LOOPING IN POWER QUERY

Note #table is a function in Power Query used to create a table, with the syntax:

#table(columns as any, rows as any) as any

In the simplest form, as used in this example, the column names are provided as a list in the first argument, and the row data is entered as sublists within a general list in the second argument.

In the next step, expanding the Name column into new rows results in Figure 9-58.

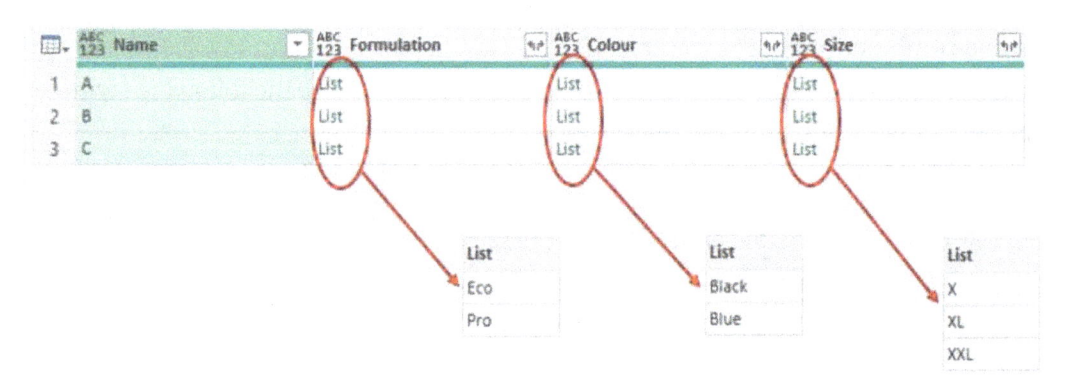

Figure 9-58. Expanding the Name column

CHAPTER 9 LOOPING IN POWER QUERY

Expanding all the other columns will result in Figure 9-59.

#	Name	Formulation	Colour	Size
1	A	Eco	Black	X
2	A	Eco	Black	XL
3	A	Eco	Black	XXL
4	A	Eco	Blue	X
5	A	Eco	Blue	XL
6	A	Eco	Blue	XXL
7	A	Pro	Black	X
8	A	Pro	Black	XL
9	A	Pro	Black	XXL
10	A	Pro	Blue	X
11	A	Pro	Blue	XL
12	A	Pro	Blue	XXL
13	B	Eco	Black	X
14	B	Eco	Black	XL
15	B	Eco	Black	XXL
16	B	Eco	Blue	X
17	B	Eco	Blue	XL
18	B	Eco	Blue	XXL
19	B	Pro	Black	X
20	B	Pro	Black	XL
21	B	Pro	Black	XXL
22	B	Pro	Blue	X
23	B	Pro	Blue	XL
24	B	Pro	Blue	XXL
25	C	Eco	Black	X
26	C	Eco	Black	XL
27	C	Eco	Black	XXL
28	C	Eco	Blue	X
29	C	Eco	Blue	XL
30	C	Eco	Blue	XXL
31	C	Pro	Black	X
32	C	Pro	Black	XL
33	C	Pro	Black	XXL
34	C	Pro	Blue	X
35	C	Pro	Blue	XL
36	C	Pro	Blue	XXL

Figure 9-59. Expanding all the columns

CHAPTER 9 LOOPING IN POWER QUERY

In this next step, select all the columns (the selection order is important), right-click one of them, choose Merge Columns, select space as the separator, enter the new column name as Product Names, and click OK. Figure 9-60 shows the final table.

#	Product Names
1	A Eco Black X
2	A Eco Black XL
3	A Eco Black XXL
4	A Eco Blue X
5	A Eco Blue XL
6	A Eco Blue XXL
7	A Pro Black X
8	A Pro Black XL
9	A Pro Black XXL
10	A Pro Blue X
11	A Pro Blue XL
12	A Pro Blue XXL
13	B Eco Black X
14	B Eco Black XL
15	B Eco Black XXL
16	B Eco Blue X
17	B Eco Blue XL
18	B Eco Blue XXL
19	B Pro Black X
20	B Pro Black XL
21	B Pro Black XXL
22	B Pro Blue X
23	B Pro Blue XL
24	B Pro Blue XXL
25	C Eco Black X
26	C Eco Black XL
27	C Eco Black XXL
28	C Eco Blue X
29	C Eco Blue XL
30	C Eco Blue XXL
31	C Pro Black X
32	C Pro Black XL
33	C Pro Black XXL
34	C Pro Blue X
35	C Pro Blue XL
36	C Pro Blue XXL

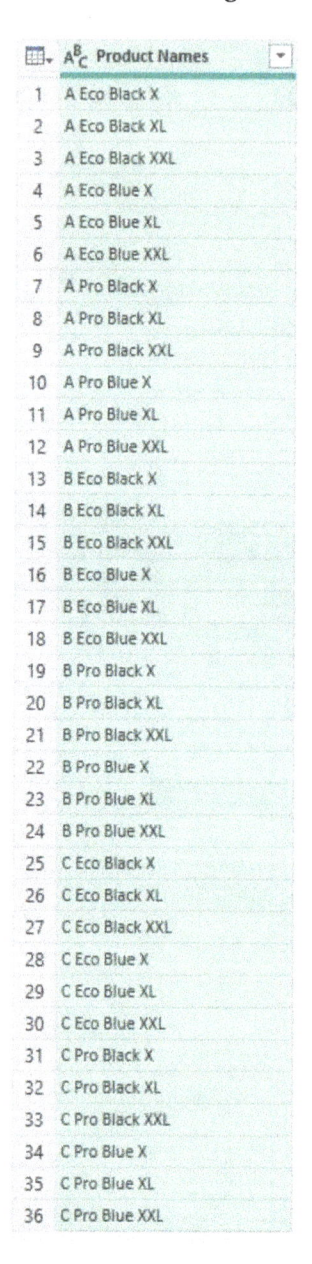

Figure 9-60. *The result of merging*

Solution 2: Based on List.Accumulate()

In the previous solution, where all the columns were expanded manually, this task can be automated using `List.Accumulate()`.

After applying all the steps in the previous solution, select the Advanced Editor to see the steps, as follows:

```
let
    Source = #table({"Name","Formulation","Colour","Size"},{{{"A","B","C"},
    {"Eco","Pro"},{"Black","Blue"},{"X","XL","XXL"}}}),
    #"Expanded Name" = Table.ExpandListColumn(Source, "Name"),
    #"Expanded Formulation" = Table.ExpandListColumn(#"Expanded Name",
    "Formulation"),
    #"Expanded Colour" = Table.ExpandListColumn(#"Expanded Formulation",
    "Colour"),
    #"Expanded Size" = Table.ExpandListColumn(#"Expanded Colour", "Size"),
    #"Merged Columns" = Table.CombineColumns(#"Expanded Size",{"Name",
    "Formulation", "Colour", "Size"},Combiner.CombineTextByDelimiter(" ",
    QuoteStyle.None),"Product Names")
in
    #"Merged Columns"
```

In this code, the expansion of columns is applied in four steps, each over a different column name using the `Table.ExpandListColumn()` function. However, by defining the column names as a list in the first argument of `List.Accumulate()` and considering the source table as the seed, the expansion can be performed through a loop over the column names, making the process more efficient and dynamic. So, by using `List.Accumulate()`, the code can be rewritten as follows:

```
let
    ColNames={"Name","Formulation","Colour","Size"},
    Source =List.Accumulate(
        ColNames,
        #table(ColNames,{{{"A","B","C"},{"Eco","Pro"},{"Black","Blue"},
        {"X","XL","XXL"}}}),
         (x,y)=>Table.ExpandListColumn(x, y)),
```

```
    #"Merged Columns" = Table.CombineColumns(
        Source,ColNames,
        Combiner.CombineTextByDelimiter(" ", QuoteStyle.None),
        "Product Names")
in
    #"Merged Columns"
```

Solution 3: Combining List.Accumulate() and List.TransformMany()

In this solution, a combination of `List.Accumulate()` and `List.TransformMany()` is used to solve the problem.

Before addressing the problem for all product features (Name, Formulation, Color, and Size), let's first focus on just the Name and Color features and explore how to generate their Cartesian combination. This will help simplify the process and establish the method for handling the full set of product features later.

In this case, you need two nested loops: one for iterating over all the Names and the other for iterating over the Colors, and as a function, you can concatenate the name and colors of all iterations. This can be achieved using the `List.TransformMany()` function.

To do this:

- The first list (Names) will be placed as the first argument.

- The second list (Colours) will be placed as the second argument.

- A concatenation function will be applied to combine each Name with every Colour, creating the desired combinations.

You can use the following formula:

```
= List.TransformMany(
    {"A","B","C"},
    each {"Black","Blue"},
    (Product,Colour)=>Product &" - "& Colour)
```

In this example, `{"A", "B", "C"}` is the list of product names in the initial argument, and each `{"Black", "Blue"}` is a function in the second argument. This function specifies that for each product, you should consider the list `{"Black", "Blue"}`

CHAPTER 9 LOOPING IN POWER QUERY

list of colors. The third argument is also a function as (Product, Colour) => Product & " - " & Colours. This function combines each product with each color to generate the final strings.

For each product in {"A", "B", "C"}, the each {"Black", "Blue"} function generates the list of colors {"Black", "Blue"}, and the third argument function (Product, Colour) => Product & " - " & Colour then combines each product with each color.

So, the output is a list, combining all products with colors as follows: {"A - Black","A - Blue","B - Black","B - Blue","C - Black","C - Blue"}.

List.TransformMany() can combine two lists, but in this case, you are dealing with four lists: Product Name, Formulation, Color, and Size. To handle all four lists and generate all possible combinations, you can use List.Accumulate() in combination with List.TransformMany().

Here's how this combination works:

- Each of the four lists (Name, Formulation, Color, and Size) is provided as a sublist within the first argument of List.Accumulate().

- At the beginning, a list with one blank item is considered the seed, as {""}.

- In each iteration, a sublist of the first argument and the seed are passed to List.TransformMany().

- List.TransformMany() combines this sublist with the seed value (which is equal to all the combinations generated so far) and provides the new combination as a new seed.

The formula for solving this problem is as follows:

```
= List.Accumulate(
    {{"A","B","C"},{"Eco","Pro"},{"Black","Blue"},{"X","XL","XXL"}},
    {""}, (s, c) => List.TransformMany(s, each  c, (L1, L2) =>
    L1 & " "& L2))
```

CHAPTER 9 LOOPING IN POWER QUERY

You can use this formula in the formula bar; it results in Figure 9-61.

	List
1	A Eco Black X
2	A Eco Black XL
3	A Eco Black XXL
4	A Eco Blue X
5	A Eco Blue XL
6	A Eco Blue XXL
7	A Pro Black X
8	A Pro Black XL
9	A Pro Black XXL
10	A Pro Blue X
11	A Pro Blue XL
12	A Pro Blue XXL
13	B Eco Black X
14	B Eco Black XL
15	B Eco Black XXL
16	B Eco Blue X
17	B Eco Blue XL
18	B Eco Blue XXL
19	B Pro Black X
20	B Pro Black XL
21	B Pro Black XXL
22	B Pro Blue X
23	B Pro Blue XL
24	B Pro Blue XXL
25	C Eco Black X
26	C Eco Black XL
27	C Eco Black XXL
28	C Eco Blue X
29	C Eco Blue XL
30	C Eco Blue XXL
31	C Pro Black X
32	C Pro Black XL
33	C Pro Black XXL
34	C Pro Blue X
35	C Pro Blue XL
36	C Pro Blue XXL

Figure 9-61. *The result of List.Accumulate and List.TransformMany*

CHAPTER 9 LOOPING IN POWER QUERY

Let's examine how this formula operates. Initially, s (state) in List.Accumulate() is {" "}, and c (current) is {"A", "B", "C"}. By substituting s and c into List.TransformMany(), the function becomes:

```
=List.TransformMany(
     {""},
     each {"A","B","C"},
     (L1, L2) => a & " "& b)
```

In the third argument of this formula, L1 is "" and L2 is {"A", "B", "C"}, resulting in a list that combines L1 with each item in L2, which yields {"A", "B", "C"}.

In the subsequent step, where s is {"A", "B", "C"} (the result of the previous aggregator) and c is {"Eco", "Pro"}, substituting s and c into List.TransformMany() results in the following formula:

```
=List.TransformMany(
     {"A","B","C"},
     each {"Eco","Pro"},
     (L1, L2) => L1 & " "& L2)
```

This formula produces {"A Eco", "A Pro", "B Eco", "B Pro", "C Eco", "C Pro"}.

In the next iteration, where s is {"A Eco", "A Pro", "B Eco", "B Pro", "C Eco", "C Pro"} and c is {"Black", "Blue"}, substituting s and c into List.TransformMany() results in the following formula:

```
=List.TransformMany(
     {"A Eco","A Pro" "B Eco","B Pro" "C Eco","C Pro"},
     each {"Black","Blue"},
     (L1, L2) => L1 & " "& L2)
```

And results in this list: {"A Eco Black", "A Pro Black", "B Eco Black", "B Pro Black", "C Eco Black", "C Pro Black", "A Eco Blue", "A Pro Blue", "B Eco Blue", "B Pro Blue", "C Eco Blue", "C Pro Blue"}.

The same process is then repeated in the next iterations for the sizes and provides a list including all the combinations of product names.

CHAPTER 9 LOOPING IN POWER QUERY

Summary

This chapter introduced looping concepts in Power Query, covering how to implement For-Next, For-Each, and Do-While loops. Since Power Query lacks a user interface for loops, they are executed through M-code functions like List.Transform(), List.TransformMany(), List.Accumulate(), and List.Generate().

List.Transform() works like a For-Each loop and applies a transformation function to each item in a list. It iterates through the list and returns a new list with the transformed values. On the other hand, List.TransformMany() is an advanced version of List.Transform(). It functions similarly to having two nested List.Transform() calls, providing two levels of iteration (nested loops). This allows you to apply a transformation to one list, and within each transformation, you can apply another transformation to another list or to nested items, making it ideal for handling more complex combinations or multi-level operations.

List.Accumulate() is a more flexible function because it allows you to carry forward the result of each iteration into the next iteration. This means that you can build upon the results from previous steps as you move through the list. It operates by taking an initial value (the seed) and applying a function iteratively to each item in the list, accumulating the result. This feature makes it ideal for scenarios when you need to maintain state or accumulate value for performing complex transformations that require previous results to influence the next steps.

Similarly, List.Generate() is a powerful function for loops in Power Query. It accepts four function-type arguments: the initial value, a condition defining when the loop continues, a "next" function to update the value per iteration, and an optional selector for transforming or selecting each iteration's output.

The next chapter explores external integrations with Power Query, including the use of R, Python, and JavaScript.

CHAPTER 10

Leveraging Scripting and External Integrations in Power Query

This chapter addresses additional common challenges in Power Query and demonstrates solutions using APIs and scripting with R, Python, and JavaScript.

Using a Regex Function Based on JavaScript in Power Query

Consider the Source table, which contains a single column called Text, as shown in Table 10-1. Extract all emails, dates, numbers, and times from the text.

Table 10-1. Source: Text

Text
On 2023-05-14, John Doe (john.doe@example.com) received an email from his colleague, Jane Smith (jane_smith@workplace.org). The email mentioned a meeting scheduled for 2024-07-20 at 2:30 PM. During the meeting, they planned to discuss the budget, which had a preliminary figure of $150,000.
Jane also mentioned that the project's milestones needed to be reviewed by the end of the fiscal year on 2024-12-31. John replied with a confirmation: "Let's meet @ 2:30 PM sharp and make sure we cover all agenda items." He also added: "Please cc to mark.spencer@department.gov and finance@office.com for their input."

(continued)

CHAPTER 10 LEVERAGING SCRIPTING AND EXTERNAL INTEGRATIONS IN POWER QUERY

Table 10-1. (*continued*)

Text
John had a note in his calendar to call the supplier at +1-800-555-1234 and inquire about the order #987654321.
Meanwhile, the team was informed via the internal messaging system that the server maintenance would be conducted on 2024-08-15 @ 10:00 PM.
The project management tool also sent automatic reminders to everyone involved, highlighting the importance of completing their tasks by the specified deadlines.

> **Note** The general idea of this solution came from the website of TheBICCOUNTANT, written by Microsoft MVP Imke Feldmann. See `https://www.thebiccountant.com/2018/04/25/regex-in-power-bi-and-power-query-in-excel-with-java-script/`.

To address such problems, most software uses Regular Expression (*regex* or *regexp*) functions to extract sequences of characters that match a specific search pattern. Unfortunately, Power Query does not natively support regex functions. While Power BI users can utilize regex through Python or R scripts, this code is not yet supported directly within Power Query inside Excel.

If you are an Excel user, the good news is that you can use JavaScript within Power Query to achieve regex functionality, using the `Web.Page()` function in Power Query, which allows you to execute JavaScript code.

> **Note** To learn more about regex, check out this website: `https://regex101.com/`.

Here is a simple JavaScript example that defines a variable x and provides it as a result value:

```
x = ' My email Address is Example@Outlook.Com';
document.write(x);
```

CHAPTER 10   LEVERAGING SCRIPTING AND EXTERNAL INTEGRATIONS IN POWER QUERY

To use this JavaScript code within Power Query, you can embed it using the Web.Page() function. The Power Query formula for this looks like the following and results in Figure 10-1.

```
= Web.Page( "<script>
x = ' My email Address is Example@Outlook.Com ';
document.write(x);
</script>")
```

Figure 10-1. Example of JaveScript code processed by Power Query

To achieve the desired result, you need to navigate through the first row under the Data column. The navigation path is started by appending {0}[Data] to the previous formula. However, this navigation alone is not sufficient, and further steps are required. The final result is obtained after the following navigation: {0}[Data]{0}[Children]{1}[Children]{0}[Text].

Rewriting the formula as follows will result in a table where the output matches the text contained in variable x, as shown in Figure 10-2:

```
= Web.Page( "<script>
x = 'My email Address is Example@Outlook.Com';
document.write(x);
</script>"){0}[Data]{0}[Children]{1}[Children] {0}[Text]
```

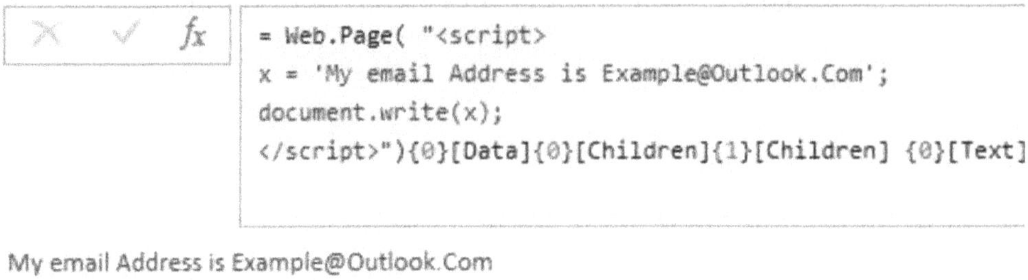

CHAPTER 10 LEVERAGING SCRIPTING AND EXTERNAL INTEGRATIONS IN POWER QUERY

```
= Web.Page( "<script>
x = 'My email Address is Example@Outlook.Com';
document.write(x);
</script>"){0}[Data]{0}[Children]{1}[Children] {0}[Text]
```

My email Address is Example@Outlook.Com

Figure 10-2. *Result of the x variable (bottom), addressed in Web.Page() output hierarchy (top)*

To extract only the email addresses from the text, you can modify the JavaScript code within the Web.Page() function to focus solely on extracting emails. Here's the revised formula, which results in Figure 10-3.

```
= Web.Page( "<script>
x = 'My email address is Example@Outlook.Com';
document.write(x.match(RegExp('^ [A-Za-z._%+-]+@[A-Za-z]+.[A-Za-z]
{2,}$', 'g')));
</script>"){0}[Data]{0}[Children]{1}[Children]{0}[Text]
```

```
= Web.Page( "<script>
x = 'My email address is Example@Outlook.Com';
document.write(x.match(RegExp('[A-Za-z._%+-]+@[A-Za-z.-]+.[A-Za-z]{2,}', 'g')));
</script>"){0}[Data]{0}[Children]{1}[Children]{0}[Text]
```

Example@Outlook.Com

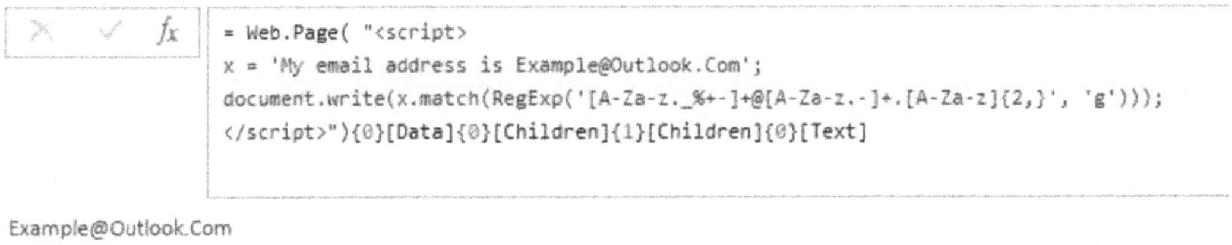

Figure 10-3. *Regexp that extracts an email address from some text, wrapped in Power Query code*

By changing the value of the variable x to include two email addresses, the formula will return both email addresses, as shown in Figure 10-4.

```
= Web.Page( "<script>
x = 'My email address is Example@Outlook.Com & anotheremail@outlook.com';
```

Chapter 10 Leveraging Scripting and External Integrations in Power Query

```
document.write(x.match(RegExp('^ [A-Za-z._%+-]+@[A-Za-z]+.[A-Za-z]
{2,}$', 'g')));
</script>"){0}[Data]{0}[Children]{1}[Children]{0}[Text]
```

```
fx   = Web.Page( "<script>
       x = 'My email address is Example@Outlook.Com & anotheremail@outlook.com';
       document.write(x.match(RegExp('[A-Za-z._%+-]+@[A-Za-z.-]+.[A-Za-z]{2,}', 'g')));
       </script>"){0}[Data]{0}[Children]{1}[Children]{0}[Text]
```

Example@Outlook.Com,anotheremail@outlook.com

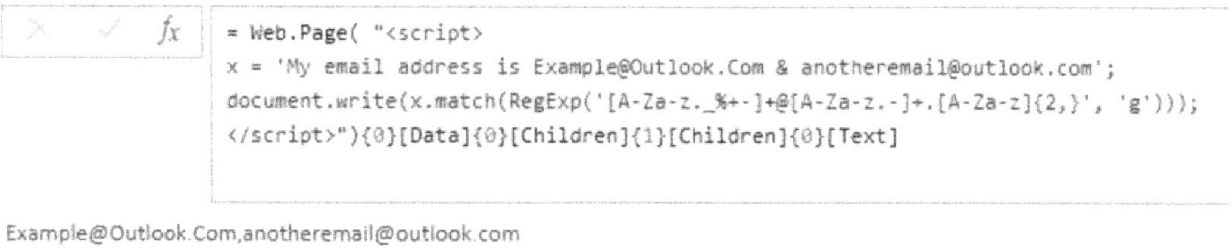

Figure 10-4. *Extracting all the email address*

This formula can be converted into a custom function in Power Query by defining an input parameter. Here's how you can rewrite the formula to include an input parameter, as shown in Figure 10-5:

```
= (input)=> Web.Page( "<script> var x='"&input&"';
document.write(x.match(RegExp('^ [A-Za-z._%+-]+@[A-Za-z]+.[A-Za-z]
{2,}$', 'g')));
</script>"){0}[Data]{0}[Children]{1}[Children]{0}[Text]
```

Using a single line of text, such as "My email address is Example@Outlook.Com & anotheremail@outlook.com," works with the proposed function. However, it does not handle multiline text or text that includes single quotes ('). To address these issues, you can modify the formula to replace line breaks (which usually appear as #(lf) in Power Query and are equal to Character.FromNumber(10), but other line breaks can also appear in the text) and single quotes with spaces. Here's the updated formula:

```
= (input)=> Web.Page(
        "<script> var x='"
        & Text.Replace(Text.Replace(input,"#(lf)"," "),"'"," ") &
        "'; document.write( x.match(RegExp('^ [A-Za-z._%+-]+@[A-Za-z]+.
        [A-Za-z]{2,}$', 'g')));
</script>"){0}[Data]{0}[Children]{1}[Children]{0}[Text]
```

CHAPTER 10 LEVERAGING SCRIPTING AND EXTERNAL INTEGRATIONS IN POWER QUERY

```
= (input)=> Web.Page( "<script> var x='"&input&"';
document.write(x.match(RegExp('[A-Za-z._%+-]+@[A-Za-z.-]+.[A-Za-z]{2,}', 'g')));
</script>"){0}[Data]{0}[Children]{1}[Children]{0}[Text]
```

Enter Parameter

input (optional)

[Invoke] [Clear]

function (input as any) as any

Figure 10-5. Converting the formula into function

The defined custom function takes a text input and returns all the email addresses found within that text. You can use this function to extract emails from the text in Table 10-1.

For the example with a single-row table, you can use Source[Text]{0} as the input for the custom function. (As long as it does not exceed Power Query's ability to handle approximately 30,000 ASCII characters per cell.) Alternatively, you can add a new column to the Source table using the following formula, which results in Figure 10-6:

```
=Web.Page( "<script> var x='"
        & Text.Replace(Text.Replace([Text],"#(lf)"," "),"'"," ") &
        "'; document.write(x.match(RegExp('^ [A-Za-z._%+-]+@[A-Za-z]+.
        [A-Za-z]{2,}$', 'g')));
</script>"){0}[Data]{0}[Children]{1}[Children]{0}[Text]
```

```
= Table.AddColumn(Source, "Custom", each Web.Page( "<script> var x='"& Text.Replace(Text.Replace([Text],"#(lf)"," "),"'"," ") &"';
document.write(x.match(RegExp('[A-Za-z._%+-]+@[A-Za-z]+.[A-Za-z]{2,}', 'g')));
</script>"){0}[Data]{0}[Children]{1}[Children]{0}[Text])
```

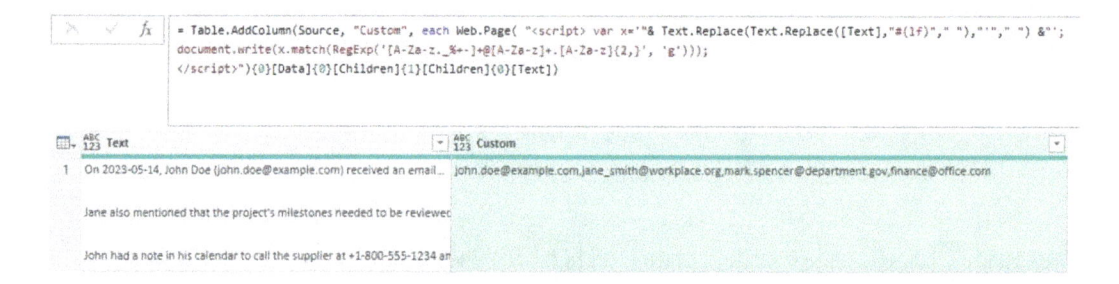

ABC Text	ABC Custom
1 On 2023-05-14, John Doe (john.doe@example.com) received an email... Jane also mentioned that the project's milestones needed to be reviewed John had a note in his calendar to call the supplier at +1-800-555-1234 an	john.doe@example.com,jane_smith@workplace.org,mark.spencer@department.gov,finance@office.com

Figure 10-6. Extracting the emails of text

This formula adds a new column named Emails to the Source table, displaying the extracted email addresses.

In this example, the pattern `'^ [A-Za-z._%+-]+@[A-Za-z]+\\.[A-Za-z]{2,}$'` defines common email formats. Here's a breakdown of the pattern:

- ^ and $ are used to mark the beginning and end of the pattern, ensuring that the entire string conforms to the format.
- `[A-Za-z._%+-]+@` matches the local part of the email address, which includes any uppercase or lowercase letters, as well as the ., _, %, +, and - characters. In practical scenarios, numbers can also be included.
- `@[A-Za-z]+\\.` specifies that after the @ character, there should be one or more uppercase or lowercase letters followed by a dot.
- `\\.[A-Za-z]{2,}$` indicates that after the dot, there must be at least two uppercase or lowercase letters, representing the domain suffix.

This pattern ensures that the string matches the typical structure of email addresses.

You can use such functions to extract text with regular formats by replacing the relevant part of the formula with the appropriate regex pattern for each data type, as shown in Table 10-2.

Table 10-2. Regex Pattern Examples

Purpose	Pattern
Email	^[A-Za-z0-9._%+-]+@[A-Za-z0-9.-]+\.[A-Za-z]{2,}$
Date	^(?:19|20)\d\d-(?:0[1-9]|1[0-2])-(?:0[1-9]|[12][0-9]|3[01])$
Number	^\d+(?:\.\d+)?$
Time	^(1[0-2]|0?[1-9]):[0-5][0-9] (AM|PM)$
ZIP Code	^\d{5}(?:[-\s]\d{4})?$
File Extension	^.+\.(jpg|jpeg|png|gif|pdf)$

CHAPTER 10 LEVERAGING SCRIPTING AND EXTERNAL INTEGRATIONS IN POWER QUERY

Integrating Python with Power Query

Consider the Source table, which contains several sentences, as shown in Table 10-3. Extract the names of cities and countries from each row.

Table 10-3. *Source: Texts*

Sentences
Tokyo is the capital of Japan.
Sydney is a major city in Australia.
Berlin is the capital of Germany.
New York is located in the United States.
Paris is known as the city of love in France.
Rio de Janeiro is a famous city in Brazil.
Toronto is a large city in Canada.
Moscow is the capital of Russia.

Solving this problem without using an API or additional tools in Power Query is quite challenging. Therefore, this example uses Python to address it. At the time of writing this book, Python is not available in Power Query for Excel, but you can use Power BI to tackle this issue.

To use Python in Power Query, you need to complete some setup, including installing Python and the required libraries (such as pandas and spacy), and configuring Python scripting options in Power Query, as explained at https://learn.microsoft.com/en-us/power-bi/connect-data/desktop-python-in-query-editor.

Before tackling the main problem, let's explore a smaller example and see how to use Python in Power Query. Select the Source table, then from the Transform tab, select Run Python Script to open the window for entering Python script, as illustrated in Figure 10-7.

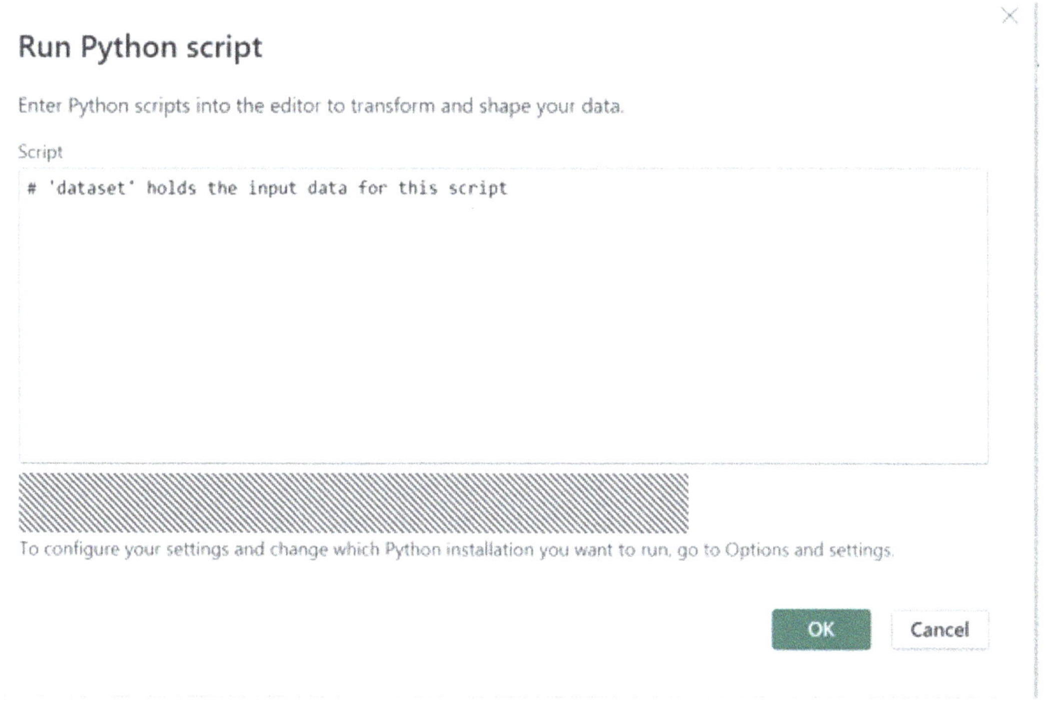

CHAPTER 10 LEVERAGING SCRIPTING AND EXTERNAL INTEGRATIONS IN POWER QUERY

Figure 10-7. The Run Python script dialog box in Power Query, a place for entering Python code

The first line of the open window states, `# 'dataset' holds the input data for this script`. This means you can refer to the result of the previous step of Power Query in the Python script using the name `dataset` (which can be changed by modifying the script).

Consider the following script. The first line imports the `pandas` library. The second line converts the Source table (referred to as `dataset`) into a structured data format in Python, named `df`. The last line adds a new column to the `df`, called `WordCount`, by applying the `len` function to the `text.split()` version of the text. Enter the following script in the open window and click OK, which will result in Figure 10-8.

```
import pandas as pd
df = pd.DataFrame(dataset)
df['WordCount'] = df['Sentences'].apply(lambda text: len(text.split()))
```

CHAPTER 10   LEVERAGING SCRIPTING AND EXTERNAL INTEGRATIONS IN POWER QUERY

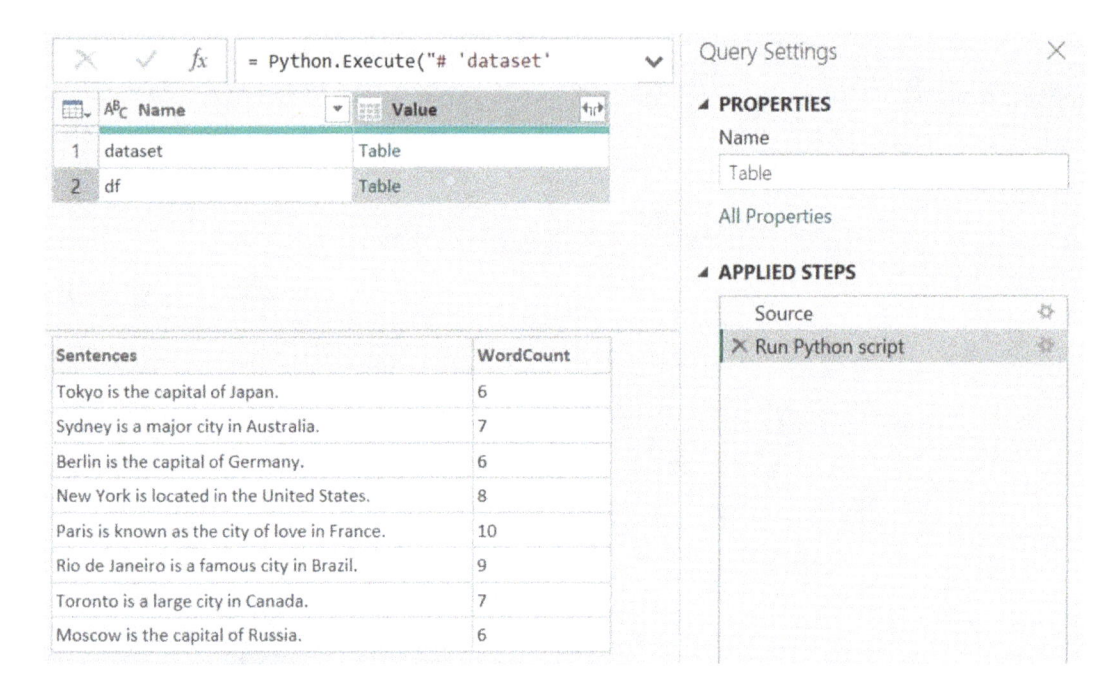

Figure 10-8. The result of Python code that counts words in a sentence

The result of this script is a table with two columns, named Name and Value. In this table, the Value column for the row with the name dataset is identical to the Source table. However, the table where the value is df represents the result of executing the Python code on the Source table. The code adds a new column called WordCount to the Source table, which displays the number of words in each row.

Now, let's update the Python script with the following script, which will result in Figure 10-9.

```
import pandas as pd
import spacy
nlp = spacy.load('en_core_web_sm')
df = pd.DataFrame(dataset)
df['Locations'] = df['Sentences'].apply(lambda text: ', '.join([ent.text for ent in nlp(text).ents if ent.label_ in ['GPE']]))
```

	Name	Value
1	dataset	Table
2	df	Table

Sentences	Locations
Tokyo is the capital of Japan.	Tokyo, Japan
Sydney is a major city in Australia.	Sydney, Australia
Berlin is the capital of Germany.	Berlin, Germany
New York is located in the United States.	New York, the United States
Paris is known as the city of love in France.	Paris, France
Rio de Janeiro is a famous city in Brazil.	Rio de Janeiro, Brazil
Toronto is a large city in Canada.	Toronto, Canada
Moscow is the capital of Russia.	Moscow, Russia

Figure 10-9. The result of Python-based extraction of geopolitical entities (city name, country name) by extracting the city names from text

In this script, the spacy library is used to extract labels related to GPE (geopolitical entities), which include cities, countries, and states from the sentences (to use this code, make sure the spacy library is installed). The output is a table with two columns and two rows. By selecting the table in the row with the name df, you can view the desired result, which is shown in Figure 10-10.

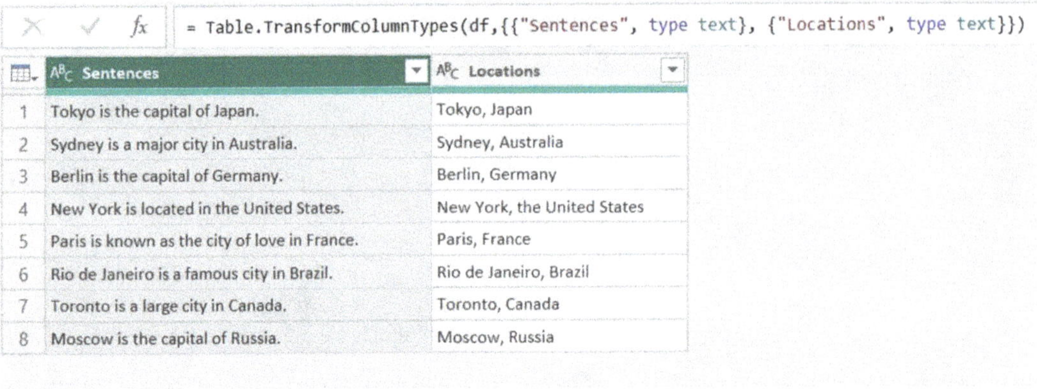

```
= Table.TransformColumnTypes(df,{{"Sentences", type text}, {"Locations", type text}})
```

#	Sentences	Locations
1	Tokyo is the capital of Japan.	Tokyo, Japan
2	Sydney is a major city in Australia.	Sydney, Australia
3	Berlin is the capital of Germany.	Berlin, Germany
4	New York is located in the United States.	New York, the United States
5	Paris is known as the city of love in France.	Paris, France
6	Rio de Janeiro is a famous city in Brazil.	Rio de Janeiro, Brazil
7	Toronto is a large city in Canada.	Toronto, Canada
8	Moscow is the capital of Russia.	Moscow, Russia

Figure 10-10. The final results

Note When working with Power Query, it is important to note that you can leverage external tools like R, Python, and JavaScript multiple times within a single query. For instance, you can access external data via Power Query, preprocess it using Python, join the result with other data in Power Query, apply post-processing in Python, and finally utilize the output from Python in an R statistical package for further analysis.

Integrating R with Power Query

Consider the Source table, which includes X and Y values, as shown in Table 10-4. Some values in the Y column are missing. Use the rows with complete Y values and create a regression model based on the selected data. Apply it over the rows with missing Ys and define new values for the missing Ys.

CHAPTER 10 LEVERAGING SCRIPTING AND EXTERNAL INTEGRATIONS IN POWER QUERY

Table 10-4. Source: Parameters

X	Y
126	73
150	85
210	
420	229
500	
810	430
900	500

This problem can be addressed in various ways, but this example demonstrates how to use R scripts in Power Query to solve it.

Like Python, R can be utilized in Power Query within Power BI as of the time of writing this book. This requires some setup, which is outlined in https://learn.microsoft.com/en-us/power-bi/connect-data/desktop-r-in-query-editor.

In this example, after loading the data into Power Query, go to the Transform tab and select Run R Script to open a new window for entering R code, as shown in Figure 10-11 (at this time R can be applied to Power Query in Power BI, but not in the Excel version).

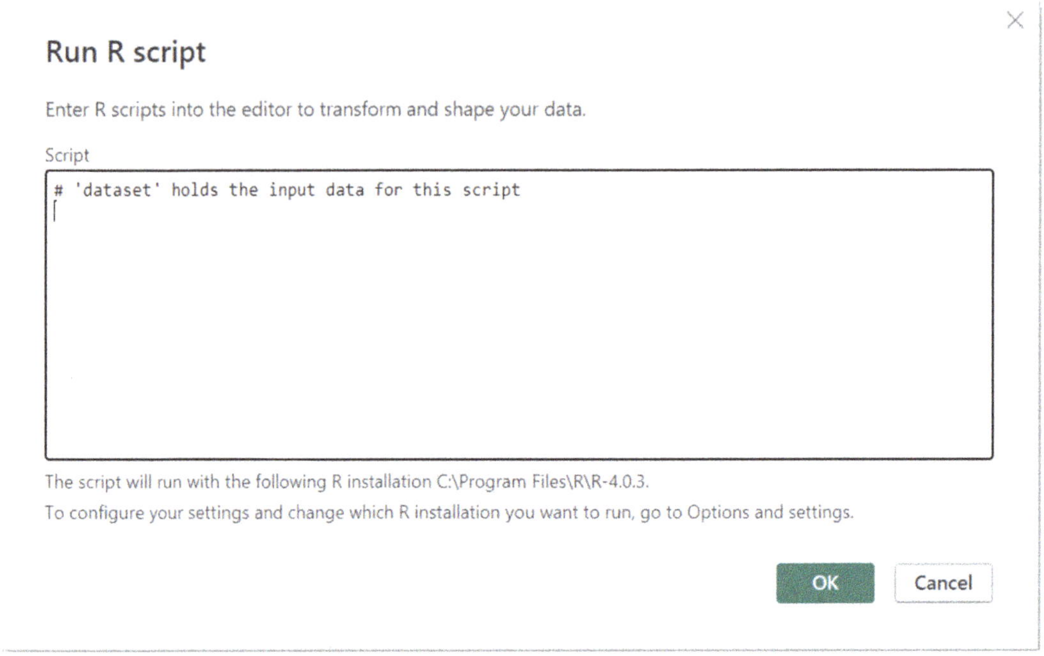

CHAPTER 10 LEVERAGING SCRIPTING AND EXTERNAL INTEGRATIONS IN POWER QUERY

Figure 10-11. The Run R Script dialog box, a place for writing R scripts

As with Python, the last table is referred to as the dataset. Enter the following script into the Run R Script window and click OK, which will result in Figure 10-12.

```
dataset <- dataset
model_data <- na.omit(dataset)
model <- lm(Y ~ X, data = model_data)
X_missing_row <- dataset[is.na(dataset$Y), "X", drop = FALSE]
predictions <- predict(model, X_missing_row)
result <- cbind(X_missing_row , Y = predictions)
```

	ABC Name	123 Value
1	model_data	Table
2	result	Table
3	X_missing_row	Table

X	Y
210	116.8437251
500	273.5595058

Figure 10-12. The result of running the R script that fits missing data points (using linear interpolation) to the data input

In this script, the second line filters out rows with blank values in the Y column, and the remaining data is used in the third line to determine the regression model. Rows with missing Y values are extracted into a vector named X_missing_row. In the fifth line, the predicted Y values for these X values are calculated based on the regression model, and in the final line, the X and Y values are combined.

The output of running the R script in this example is a table that includes three variables: mode_data, result, and X_missing_row. You only need the data from mode_data and result, so filter out the rows related to X_missing_row using the filter command in Power Query. Expanding the tables in the Value column in the last row of the resulting table will yield the rows for missing the Ys (which came from the result step) and the other rows (which came from the model_data step). This is shown in Figure 10-13.

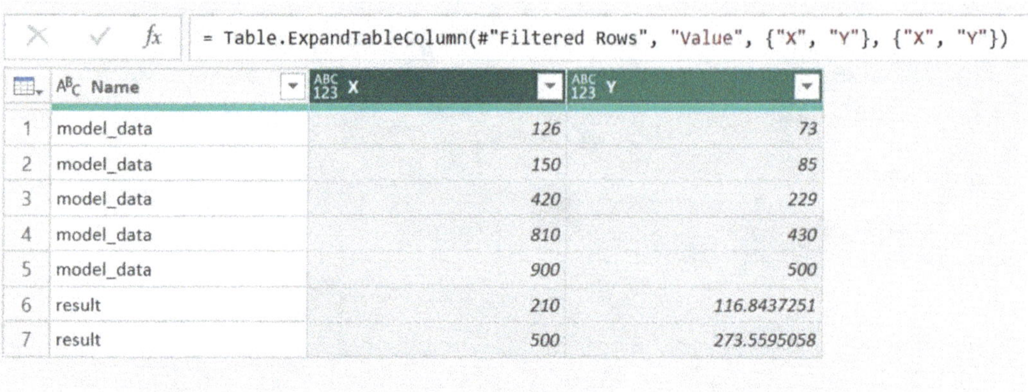

CHAPTER 10 LEVERAGING SCRIPTING AND EXTERNAL INTEGRATIONS IN POWER QUERY

```
= Table.ExpandTableColumn(#"Filtered Rows", "Value", {"X", "Y"}, {"X", "Y"})
```

	Name	X	Y
1	model_data	126	73
2	model_data	150	85
3	model_data	420	229
4	model_data	810	430
5	model_data	900	500
6	result	210	116.8437251
7	result	500	273.5595058

Figure 10-13. *The result of expanding the column value*

By removing the Name column, the program replaces the missing values with the predicted regression values.

Translating Text Using the Google Translate API

Consider the Source table shown in Table 10-5, which contains customer comments for an online shop in various languages. Use Power Query to translate these comments into English.

Table 10-5. *Source: Customer Comments*

Customer ID	Comments
C-094	The product is great, but the delivery was too slow
C-052	No estoy satisfecho con la calidad del producto
C-055	商品の品質は素晴らしいです。
C-065	El producto es bueno, pero la caja llegó dañada
C-091	Je ne suis pas content du service après-vente
C-069	خیلی راضی هستم، دقیقاً همان چیزی است که نیاز داشتم
C-094	The product didn't meet my expectations
C-069	محصول خوب است، اما قیمت کمی بالاست

In Power Query, you can use APIs to modify tables. This example uses the Google Translate API for translation. To use this API frequently, you'll need to log in to the Google Cloud Platform, activate the Google Cloud Translation API, and create an API key for use in Power Query. This example uses the free version of the API, which has some limitations.

Note It is crucial to be well aware of the potential risks of sending data to third parties through API calls. This issue is not specific to Power Query, but rather pertains to data security, and for such situations, consider your company policies.

The free version can be accessed using the following URL format, where parameters are indicated with XXX:

```
https://translate.googleapis.com/translate_a/single?client=gtx&sl=XXX&tl=XXX&dt=t&q=XXX
```

There are three parameters for using this API, called sl, tl, and q. Here, sl specifies the source language, tl specifies the target language, both in ISO codes, and q is the text to be translated.

For instance, to translate "Hello World!" from English to French, you would use the parameters sl=en, tl=fr, and q=Hello World! So, the URL would be:

```
https://translate.googleapis.com/translate_a/single?client=gtx&sl=en&tl=fr&dt=t&q=Hello World!
```

In Power Query, you can use the Web.Contents() function to apply APIs. Since the result will be in JSON format, use Json.Document() function to process JSON output to Power Query-friendly data structure. So, to translate "Hello World!" into French, you use the following formula in the formula bar, which results in Figure 10-14.

```
= Json.Document(
    Web.Contents(
    "https://translate.googleapis.com/translate_a/single?client=gtx&sl=en&tl=fr&dt=t&q=Hello World!"))
```

```
= Json.Document(Web.Contents("https://translate.googleapis.com/translate_a/single?client=gtx&
  sl=en&tl=fr&dt=t&q=Hello World!"))
```

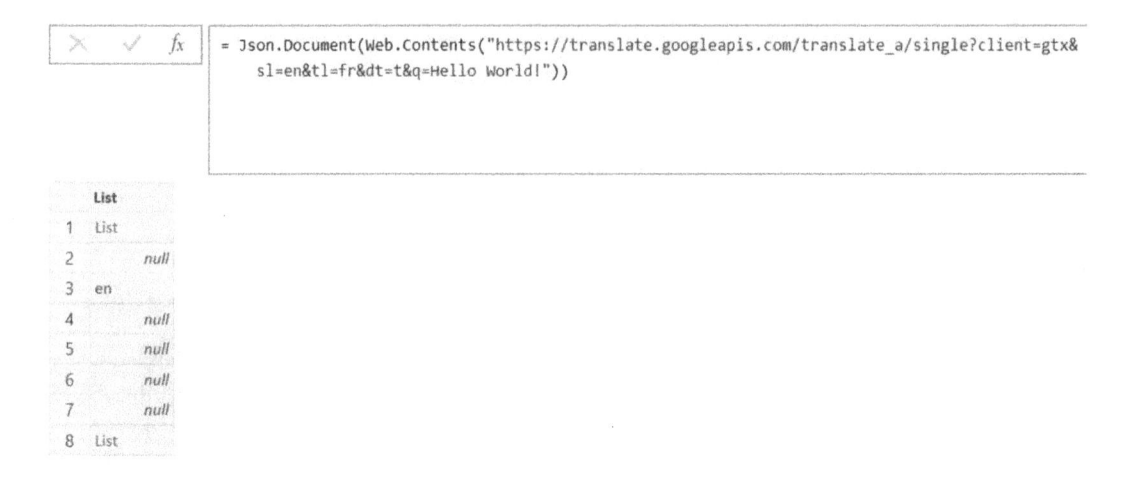

	List
1	List
2	null
3	en
4	null
5	null
6	null
7	null
8	List

Figure 10-14. The result of calling the API

Given the result from the previous formula as Source, the following formula will extract the translated text by navigating over the result list, as shown in Figure 10-15.

```
= Source{0}{0}
```

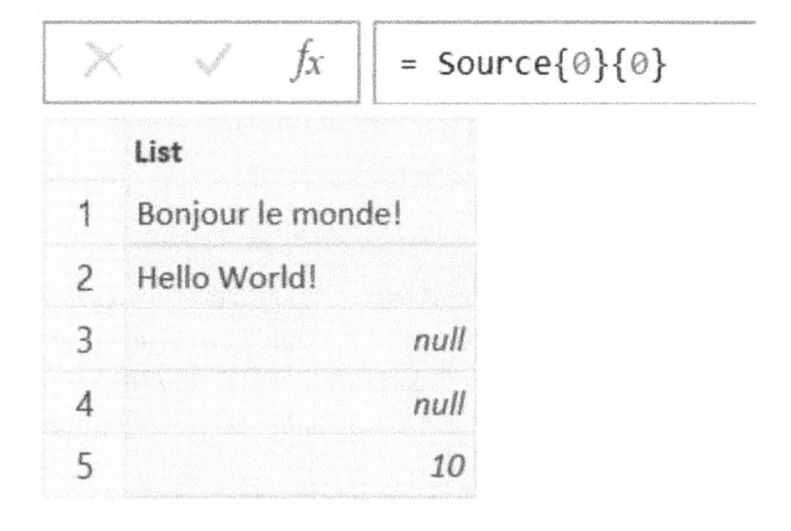

	List
1	Bonjour le monde!
2	Hello World!
3	null
4	null
5	10

Figure 10-15. The result of calling the API

To directly get the translated text, use the following formula:

```
= Json.Document(
    Web.Contents(
    "https://translate.googleapis.com/translate_a/single?client=gtx&sl=
    en&tl=fr&dt=t&q=Hello World!")){0}{0}{0}
```

If you encounter any credential warnings during this process, such as the one shown in Figure 10-16, edit the credentials and connect, as shown in Figure 10-17.

Figure 10-16. *The Access Web Content window*

Figure 10-17. *Credentials warning from the first connection to a source*

Returning to the original problem, if you have a table with text in various languages and the source languages are not predefined, you can set `sl` to `auto-detect` so it can determine the language.

Based on this explanation, let's return to the main problem. Add a new column to the Source table named Translated Text and use the following formula to solve the problem and get the translated text.

```
=Json.Document(Web.Contents("https://translate.googleapis.com/translate_a/
single?client=gtx&sl=auto&tl=en&dt=t&q="&[Comments])){0}{0}{0}
```

CHAPTER 10 LEVERAGING SCRIPTING AND EXTERNAL INTEGRATIONS IN POWER QUERY

This formula will populate the new column with the auto-translated text, as shown in Figure 10-18.

```
= Table.AddColumn(Source, "Translated text", each Json.Document(Web.Contents("https://
    translate.googleapis.com/translate_a/single?client=gtx&sl=auto&tl=en&dt=t&q="&[Comments]))
    {0}{0}{0})
```

	Customer ID	Comments	Translated text
1	C-094	The product is great, but the delivery was too slow	The product is great, but the delivery was too slow
2	C-052	No estoy satisfecho con la calidad del producto	I am not satisfied with the quality of the product
3	C-055	商品の品質は素晴らしいです。	The quality of the product is excellent.
4	C-065	El producto es bueno, pero la caja llegó dañada	The product is good, but the box arrived damaged
5	C-091	Je ne suis pas content du service après-vente	I am not happy with the after-sales service
6	C-069	خیلی راضی هستم، دقیقاً همان چیزی است که نیاز داشتم	Very satisfied, exactly what I needed
7	C-094	The product didn't meet my expectations	The product didn't meet my expectations
8	C-069	محصول خوب است، اما قیمت کمی بالاست	The product is good, but the price is a bit high

Figure 10-18. *The result of auto-translated text (the input language is automatically detected)*

In this problem, rather than adding a new column, you can directly apply the translation to the existing Comments column using the Table.TransformColumns() function. If you are a seasoned Power Query user, you can add a new transformation step directly, where you'll transform the column (Source[Comments]) using Google API translation. However, I recommend using a "lazy dev" approach, where you call an arbitrary transformation on the column of your choice and then adapt the automatically generated Power Query code to run the auto-translation.

To see this function setting, right-click the Comments column and choose a transformation option, such as converting text to uppercase. In this example, using the uppercase transformation will result in the following formula in the formula bar:

= Table.TransformColumns(Source,{{"Comments", Text.Upper, type text}})

This formula applies the Text.Upper() function as the transformation function over all the values in this column.

CHAPTER 10 LEVERAGING SCRIPTING AND EXTERNAL INTEGRATIONS IN POWER QUERY

Instead of changing the text to uppercase, you want to translate the text. You can achieve this by creating a custom function for translation and applying it to the Comments column. To convert the translation formula into a function with one input parameter named text, use the following formula:

```
(text)=>Json.Document(Web.Contents("https://translate.googleapis.com/translate_a/single?client=gtx&sl=auto&tl=en&dt=t&q="& text)){0}{0}{0}
```

Now replace Text.Upper with this translation function in the Table.TransformColumns() formula. The updated formula will look like this:

```
= Table.TransformColumns(
    Source,
    {{"Comments",
    (text)=>Json.Document(
                    Web.Contents( "https://translate.googleapis.com/
                    translate_a/single?client=gtx&sl=auto&tl=en&dt=
                    t&q="& text)){0}{0}{0}, type text}})
```

This formula will directly translate the text in the Comments column and provide the translated result, as shown in Figure 10-19.

#	Customer ID	Comments
1	C-094	The product is great, but the delivery was too slow
2	C-052	I am not satisfied with the quality of the product
3	C-055	The quality of the product is excellent.
4	C-065	The product is good, but the box arrived damaged
5	C-091	I am not happy with the after-sales service
6	C-069	Very satisfied, exactly what I needed
7	C-094	The product didn't meet my expectations
8	C-069	The product is good, but the price is a bit high

Figure 10-19. *The result of the translation*

CHAPTER 10   LEVERAGING SCRIPTING AND EXTERNAL INTEGRATIONS IN POWER QUERY

Automating Query Export to CSV Files

Add a query step to export the results from the previous step into a CSV file.

For Power BI users, solving this task is straightforward with the use of R and Python scripts. To save the previous query results to a file named `test` in the `C:/other/` directory as a TXT or CSV file, you can use the following R scripts in the Power BI version of Power Query:

```
write.table(dataset, "C:/other/test.txt", sep = "\t", row.names = FALSE, quote = FALSE)
```

```
write.table(dataset, "C:/other/test.csv", sep = "\t", row.names = FALSE, quote = FALSE)
```

Alternatively, to achieve the same result using a Python script, you can use the following scripts:

```
import pandas as pd
data = pd.DataFrame(dataset)
data.to_csv('C:/other/test.csv', index=False)
```

```
import pandas as pd
data = pd.DataFrame(dataset)
data.to_csv('C:/other/test.txt', index=False)
```

For Excel users, who cannot use Python or R scripts (as of the time this book was written), JavaScript must be utilized instead. However, this requires changing ActiveX control settings, which can involve certain risks (it is not recommended and in most of companies can be changed by IT only). Proceed with these changes only if necessary for saving the data as a CSV file.

The process of enabling ActiveX controls might be different in different versions of Windows. In Windows 10, go to the Internet Options settings, navigate to the Security tab and select Custom Level. In the Security Settings, locate "Initialize and Script ActiveX Controls Not Marked As Safe..." and set it to Enable, as shown in Figure 10-20.

CHAPTER 10 LEVERAGING SCRIPTING AND EXTERNAL INTEGRATIONS IN POWER QUERY

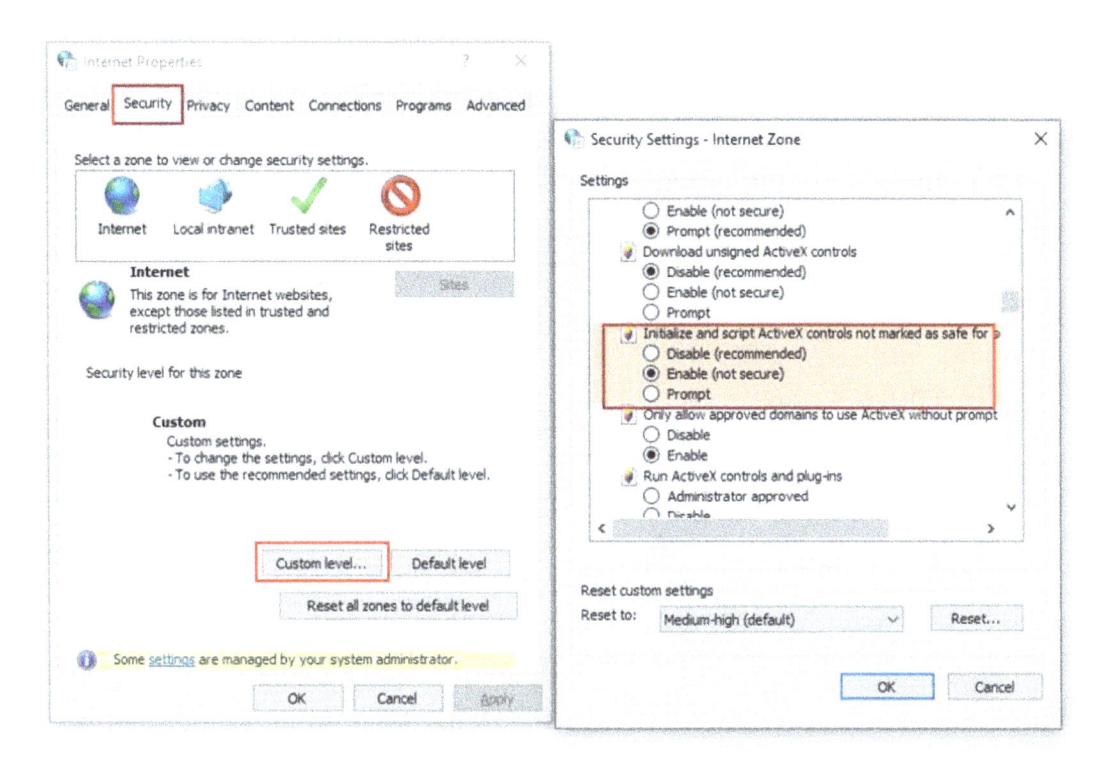

Figure 10-20. *ActiveX-specific security settings*

After applying these settings, a warning window like Figure 10-21 will appear. Click Yes.

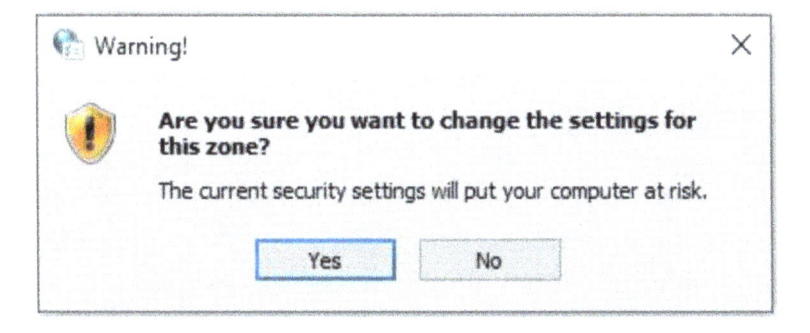

Figure 10-21. *Warning alarms*

Once the initial settings are configured, you need to convert the Power Query table to JSON before saving it in a CSV file. Assuming the previous step of Power Query is named dataset, use the following formula to convert it to the JSON format. Create a new step, rename it JSON, and type the following formula in the formula bar.

```
= Text.FromBinary(Json.FromValue(Table.ToRows
  (Table.DemoteHeaders(dataset)))),
```

Next, use the following formula to export the JSON table to a CSV file.

```
Export = Web.Page("<script>
                    var fso=new ActiveXObject('Scripting.
                    FileSystemObject');
                    var f1=fso.CreateTextFile('C:/other/test.
                    csv',true);
                    var arr="&Json&";
                    f1.WriteLine(arr.join('\n'));
                    f1.WriteBlankLines(1);
                    f1.Close();
            </script>")
```

Summary

This chapter explored how to run Python, JavaScript, and R scripts within Power Query to extend its functionality. Using Python and the spacy library, you extracted city names from text data, while R was employed to predict and replace missing values through regression. JavaScript enabled you to use regular expressions (regex) to extract email addresses from text. Additionally, you learned how to export the output of a Power Query step as a CSV file. Beyond these scripting techniques, you also integrated Google Translate APIs to automatically translate text from various languages into English.

The next chapter explains the techniques related to error handling in Power Query.

CHAPTER 11

Error-Handling Strategies

Dealing with errors is an inseparable part of the data-cleaning process, and Power Query provides several functions to handle them. Errors in Power Query can be categorized into two groups: step-level errors and cell-level errors.

A common cause of step-level errors is referencing a column, table, data source or a query that does not exist. For example, consider the Source table in Table 11-1.

Table 11-1. Source: Historical sales value

Date	Sales
4/07/2024	21
7/07/2024	10
12/07/2024	X
15/07/2024	22
21/07/2024	7

If a Power Query developer addresses the Sales column by the wrong name (e.g., Sale or sales, because Power Query is case-sensitive), like in the following formula, it leads to error, as shown in Figure 11-1:

= Table.RenameColumns(Source,{{"Sale", "Daily Sales"}})

```
= Table.RenameColumns(Source,{{"Sale", "Daily Sales"}})

Expression.Error: The column 'Sale' of the table wasn't found.
Details:
    Sale
```

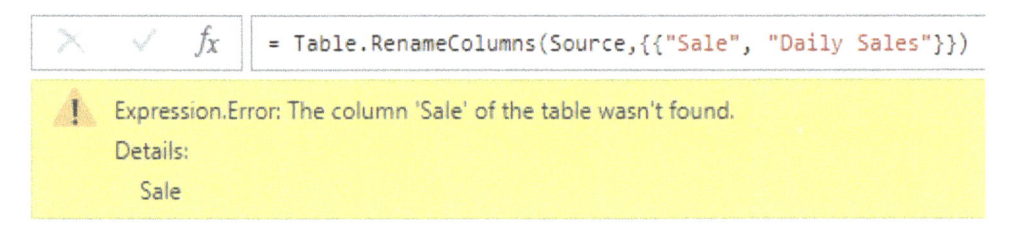

Figure 11-1. Step-level error example

CHAPTER 11 ERROR-HANDLING STRATEGIES

A step-level error prevents the query from loading and consists of three parts:

– Reason for the error (the part before the colon)

– Message (the part after the colon on the first line)

– Details (the section following the message)

Given the variety of situations that can lead to step-level errors, there is no universal solution for handling all of them. However, most of the time, step-level errors are caused by hardcoding or mismatched column names, so be mindful of these situations.

In the case of mismatch column names, you can use `MissingField.Error` (or value 1) and `MissingField.UseNull` (or value 2) as an additional argument in some functions to prevent errors.

The previous formula leads to an error, and rewriting it using `MissingField.UseNull`, as shown in the next formula, results in Figure 11-2. This says that if there is a column called sale, rename it Daily Sale. Otherwise, ignore it.

```
= Table.RenameColumns(Source,{{"sales", "Daily Sales"}},MissingField.Ignore)
```

	Date	Sales
1	4/07/2024 12:00:00 AM	21
2	7/07/2024 12:00:00 AM	10
3	12/07/2024 12:00:00 AM	X
4	15/07/2024 12:00:00 AM	22
5	21/07/2024 12:00:00 AM	7

Figure 11-2. Using MissingField.Ignore

The `MissingField.Ignore` argument can also be used to rename and remove columns, including:

- `Record.RemoveFields()`
- `Record.RenameFields()`
- `Record.ReorderFields()`
- `Record.SelectFields()`

CHAPTER 11 ERROR-HANDLING STRATEGIES

- `Record.TransformFields()`
- `Table.FromRecords()`
- `Table.RemoveColumns()`
- `Table.RenameColumns()`
- `Table.ReorderColumns()`
- `Table.SelectColumns()`
- `Table.TransformColumns()`

Cell-level errors typically occur due to a data type mismatch. For instance, consider the Source table from the earlier example. To add a new column for calculating tax equal to 10 percent of sales, add a Custom column using the following formula in the Custom Column window Since the value in the third row is non-numeric (x), the result for that row in the new column will be an error, as shown in Figure 11-3:

```
= 0.1*[Sales]
```

#	Date	Sales	Tax
1	4/07/2024 12:00:00 AM	21	2.1
2	7/07/2024 12:00:00 AM	10	1
3	12/07/2024 12:00:00 AM X		Error
4	15/07/2024 12:00:00 AM	22	2.2
5	21/07/2024 12:00:00 AM	7	0.7

Figure 11-3. Cell-level error

In such conditions, you can use the `try-otherwise` function to handle errors. By rewriting the formula in the Custom Column window as shown here, the error for non-numeric values will be replaced with a placeholder value, resulting in Figure 11-4:

```
= try 0.1*[Sales] otherwise "-"
```

CHAPTER 11 ERROR-HANDLING STRATEGIES

Note This example uses a placeholder to replace the errors, but this approach is not recommended. Using non-numerical placeholder values (such as "N/A", "-", or "Missing") in numerical columns can lead to several issues in data processing and reporting, including:

- **Calculation errors:** In some cases, functions expecting numerical inputs (e.g., aggregations, arithmetic operations) will fail or produce incorrect results if non-numeric placeholders are present.

- **Performance overhead:** Additional transformations (e.g., replacing placeholders, handling errors) might be required in the later steps or after loading data into the Data Model.

- **Visualization problems:** BI tools like Power BI might struggle with mixed data types, affecting sorting, filtering, and chart rendering.

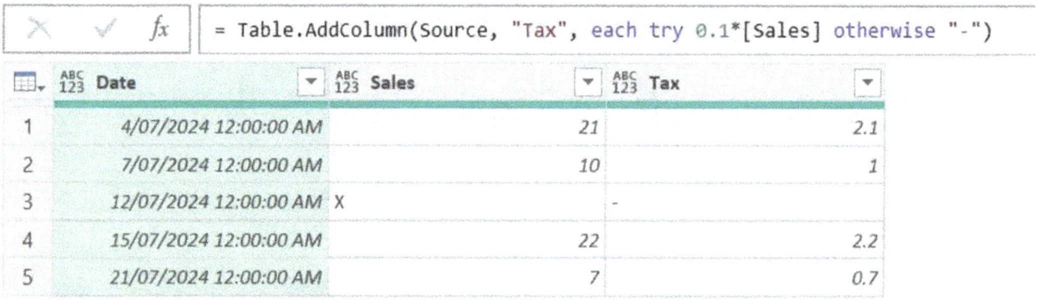

Date	Sales	Tax
4/07/2024 12:00:00 AM	21	2.1
7/07/2024 12:00:00 AM	10	1
12/07/2024 12:00:00 AM X		-
15/07/2024 12:00:00 AM	22	2.2
21/07/2024 12:00:00 AM	7	0.7

`= Table.AddColumn(Source, "Tax", each try 0.1*[Sales] otherwise "-")`

Figure 11-4. Using try-otherwise

Note In the Custom Column window, this example used the `try 0.1 * [Sales] otherwise "-"` formula. However, using just `try 0.1 * [Sales]` changes the results, as shown in Figure 11-5.

CHAPTER 11 ERROR-HANDLING STRATEGIES

*Figure 11-5. Result of using try 0.1 * [Sales]*

As demonstrated, this formula returns a record with two fields:

- The HasError field, which is present in all rows.
- A second field, which is either Value (for rows where 0.1 * [Sales] does not result in an error) or Error (for rows where 0.1 * [Sales] results in an error).

For rows where 0.1 * [Sales] does not result in an error, HasError is false, and the Value field contains the calculated result of 0.1 * [Sales]. But, for rows where 0.1 * [Sales] does result in an error, HasError is true, and the Error field is a record containing details about the error.

If you drill down into the Error record for the third row (which causes an error), you can view the error details, as shown in Figure 11-6.

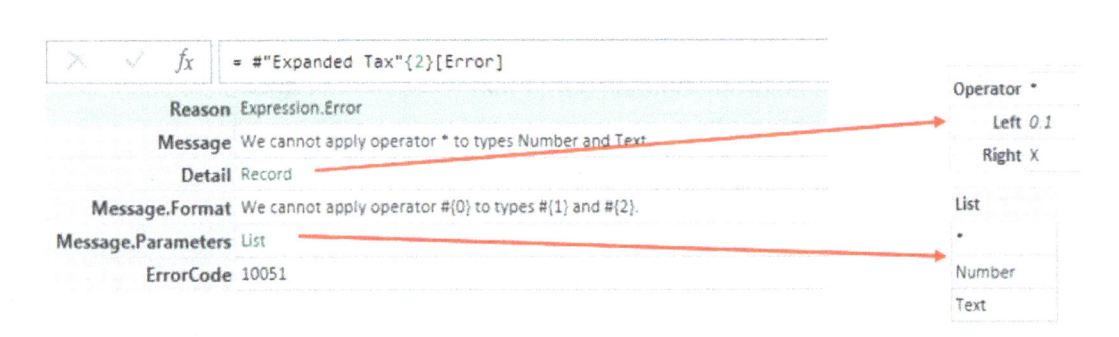

Figure 11-6. Values of the Error field

623

CHAPTER 11 ERROR-HANDLING STRATEGIES

Besides using the `try-otherwise` combination, you can also use `try-catch`. In this approach, the expression after the `try` keyword is evaluated and returned as the result. However, if it results in an error, the value of the `Error` field is passed as input to the function defined after the `catch` keyword.

So, in the previous example, if you use the following formula to calculate the tax, it will result in Figure 11-7.

```
=try 0.1*[Sales] catch (x)=>x
```

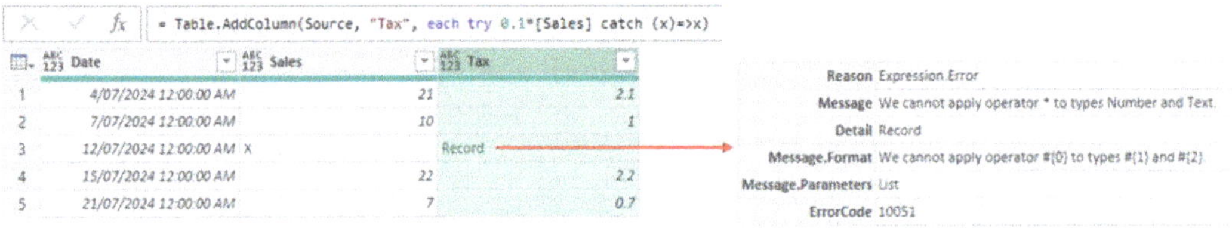

Figure 11-7. Using try-catch

Note While the `try` keyword can be useful for handling errors by converting them into alternative results, it might come to your mind to use it for all the formulas to reach error-free results. But this would significantly impact query performance, especially when working with large datasets.

To demonstrate the performance impact, I expanded the Source table to 1 million rows and tested three different scenarios. In each case, I added a column to calculate the tax value and then summed all the tax amounts:

Scenario 1: The Sales column contains some text values, and I added a Tax column using the following formula:

```
= try 0.1*[Sales] otherwise "-"
```

Scenario 2: The same table of scenario 1 was used, but instead of "-", I replaced errors with `null` using the following formula:

```
= try 0.1*[Sales] otherwise null
```

CHAPTER 11 ERROR-HANDLING STRATEGIES

Scenario 3: The Sales column contained only numeric values, so I used the following formula:

= try 0.1*[Sales] otherwise null

The results showed a significant performance difference. Execution time for the different scenarios were as follows:

Scenario 1: 27 seconds

Scenario 2: 18 seconds

Scenario 3: 3 seconds

As you can see, using try-otherwise increases processing time considerably.

In real-world scenarios, where tables contain millions of records, it is crucial to remove rows with errors and to determine the reasons for cell-level errors in queries. However, for the purpose of this chapter and to enhance readability, small tables are used in the rest of this chapter.

Removing Rows with Errors

Consider the Source table, which includes historical sales transactions, as shown in Table 11-2. Calculate the average daily sales for each row (without cleaning the data) and remove the rows with errors from the resulting table.

Table 11-2. Source: Historical Sales Value

Start Date	End Date	Sales
4/07/2024 12:00:00 AM	6/07/2024 12:00:00 AM	21
7/07/2024 12:00:00 AM	11/07/2024 12:00:00 AM	10
12/07/2024 12:00:00 AM	16/07/2024 12:00:00 AM	24*
17/07/2024 12:00:00 AM	07/20/2024	22
21/07/2024 12:00:00 AM	23/07/2024 12:00:00 AM	7
24/07/2024 12:00:00 AM	29/07/2024 12:00:00 AM	5

CHAPTER 11 ERROR-HANDLING STRATEGIES

To calculate the daily sales without cleaning the data, you can add a new column to the Source table named AVG Daily Sale using the following formula in the Custom Column window. This results in Figure 11-8:

=[Sales]/Number.From([End Date]-[Start Date])

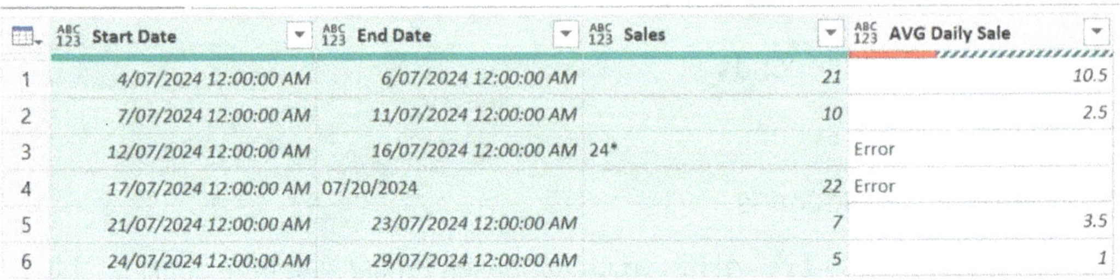

	Start Date	End Date	Sales	AVG Daily Sale
1	4/07/2024 12:00:00 AM	6/07/2024 12:00:00 AM	21	10.5
2	7/07/2024 12:00:00 AM	11/07/2024 12:00:00 AM	10	2.5
3	12/07/2024 12:00:00 AM	16/07/2024 12:00:00 AM 24*	Error	
4	17/07/2024 12:00:00 AM	07/20/2024	22	Error
5	21/07/2024 12:00:00 AM	23/07/2024 12:00:00 AM	7	3.5
6	24/07/2024 12:00:00 AM	29/07/2024 12:00:00 AM	5	1

***Figure 11-8.** Result of daily sales*

In this case, the defined formula results in errors in rows 3 and 4. In row 3, the sales value is entered as 24*, which is not a number. Since the formula attempts to divide this value by the duration, it results in an error. On the other hand, in row 4, the value in the Start Date column is in the format of DD/MM/yyyy hh:mm:ss and the value in the End Date column is in the format of MM/DD/YY. Because these values are entered in different formats, subtracting [Start Date] from [End Date] causes an error in this row.

To remove rows with errors from the resulting table, select all columns in the table, then as shown in Figure 11-9, go to the Home tab. Under the Reduce Rows section, click the Remove Rows command, then select Remove Errors to produce Figure 11-10.

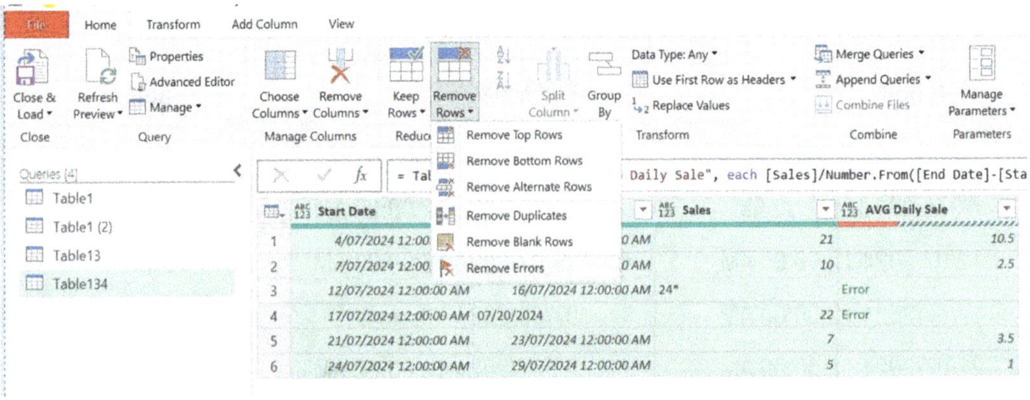

***Figure 11-9.** Removing errors*

626

CHAPTER 11   ERROR-HANDLING STRATEGIES

	Start Date	End Date	Sales	AVG Daily Sale
1	4/07/2024 12:00:00 AM	6/07/2024 12:00:00 AM	21	10.5
2	7/07/2024 12:00:00 AM	11/07/2024 12:00:00 AM	10	2.5
3	21/07/2024 12:00:00 AM	23/07/2024 12:00:00 AM	7	3.5
4	24/07/2024 12:00:00 AM	29/07/2024 12:00:00 AM	5	1

Figure 11-10. *The result of removing the errors*

The final step removes all the rows containing errors in any column, which generates the following formula:

```
= Table.RemoveRowsWithErrors(#"Added Custom", {"Start Date", "End Date", "Sales", "AVG Daily Sale"})
```

In this example, you can simplify the formula by omitting the list of column names to check for errors in all the columns and rewrite it as following:

```
= Table.RemoveRowsWithErrors(#"Added Custom")
```

Extracting the Causes of Errors

In the previous example, instead of removing the rows with errors, extract all the rows with errors and identify the causes of those errors.

Note   In the previous example, after adding the Custom column, if you load the data (with the errors) into Excel (or Power BI), you may notice that the resulting table contains two errors, as shown in Figure 11-11.

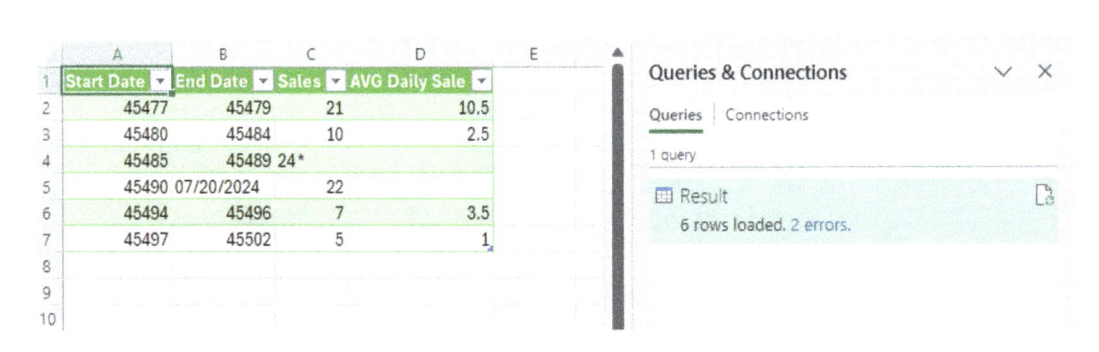

Figure 11-11. *Loading a table with an error in Power Query*

627

CHAPTER 11   ERROR-HANDLING STRATEGIES

If you click the error message text, a query will be generated, which will display the rows that cause the errors, as shown in Figure 11-12.

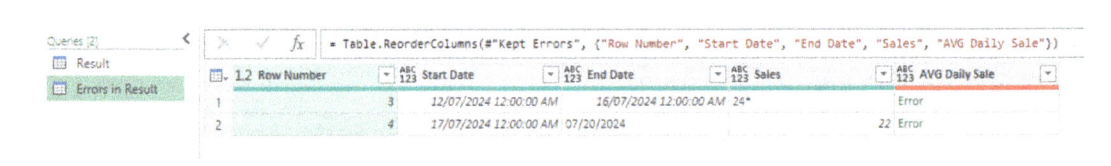

Figure 11-12. Automatically generated query showing the error

In the previous example, after adding the AVG Daily Sale column, instead of removing errors, you can extract rows with errors and identify their causes. To do this, you would select all the columns. (Although in this example, the errors are caused by the AVG Daily Sale column, so instead of selecting all the columns, you can select this column only.) Go to the Home tab, under the Reduce Rows section, click Keep Rows and select Keep Errors, as shown in Figure 11-13. This will result in all the rows with an error value in any of selected columns being shown, as in Figure 11-14.

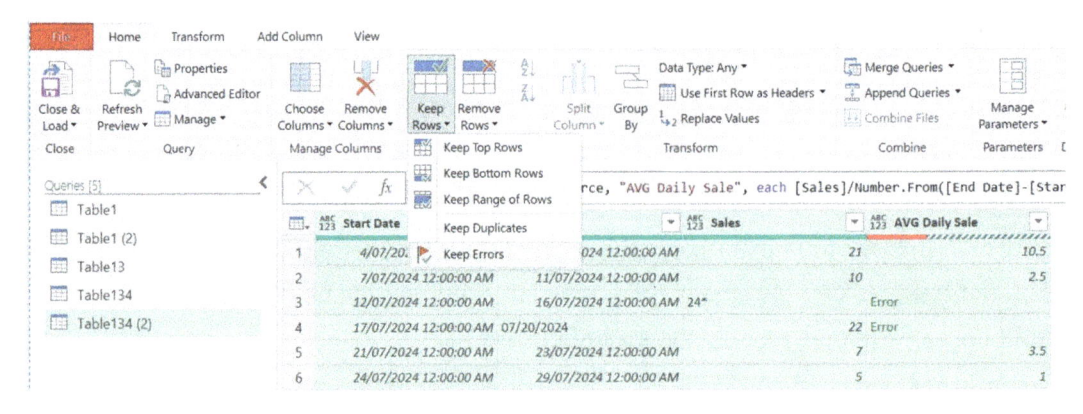

Figure 11-13. Using the Keep Error command

Figure 11-14. The result of using Keep Errors

CHAPTER 11 ERROR-HANDLING STRATEGIES

After extracting the rows with errors, you can extract the cause of the errors. In the next step, add a new column named Err using the following formula, resulting in Figure 11-15:

```
=try [AVG Daily Sale]
```

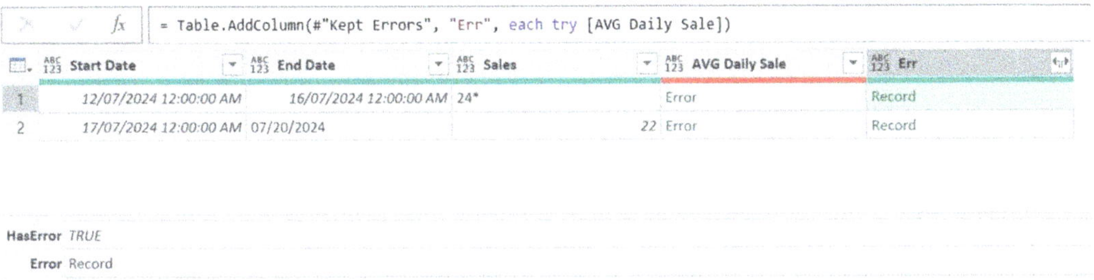

Figure 11-15. Results of try

The formula used for each row results in a value of type record, which contains information about the cause of the error. This record has two fields: HasError and Error. The HasError field is set to true if the expression following try leads to an error; otherwise, it is set to false. If HasError is true, the details of the error are stored in the Error field within the record.

To extract the information about the errors, expand the Err column. You'll see the table shown in Figure 11-16.

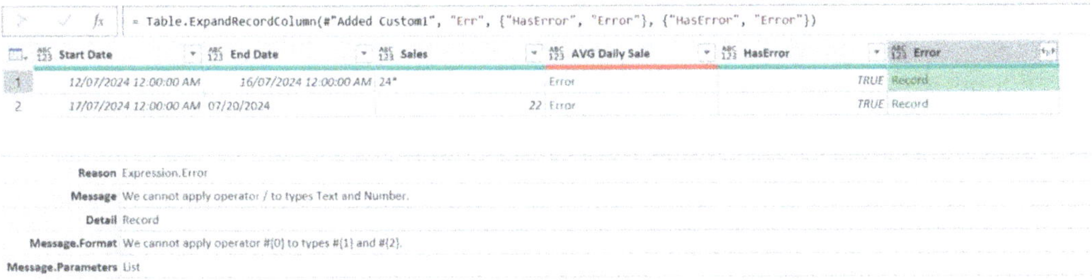

Figure 11-16. Results of expanding the Err column

The values in the Error column are of type record and contain several fields related to the error. Expanding this column will result in the table shown in Figure 11-17.

629

CHAPTER 11   ERROR-HANDLING STRATEGIES

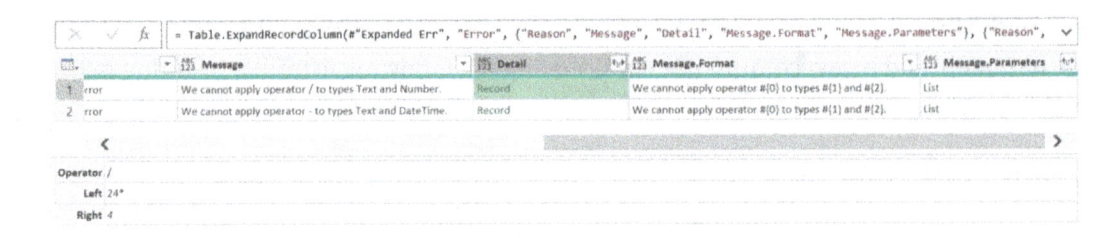

Figure 11-17. Expanding the Error column and extracting the error message

Over the expanded fields, the Detail column is in the type record. To extract its values and convert them to text, you need to add a new Custom Column called Detailed Text. Do this using the following formula in the Custom Column window:

```
=Text.Combine(List.Transform(Record.FieldNames([Detail]),
(x)=> x &": " & Text.From(Record.Field([Detail],x))))
```

Finally, by removing all columns except Start Date, End Date, Reason, Message, and Detail Text, you will obtain Figure 11-18.

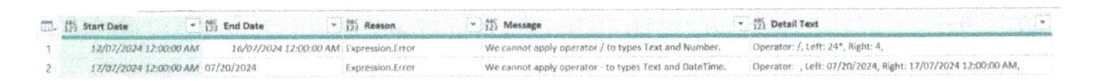

Figure 11-18. The result of extracting rows

Note   In this example, adding a custom column introduces errors in some rows, so all the errors appear in a single column. However, in practice, errors may occur in multiple columns.

To extract the cause of errors across different columns for multiple rows, follow these steps before removing the rows without errors:

1. Add an Index column to your table.

2. Right-click the newly added column and select Unpivot Other Columns.

Applying this step leads to a table with three columns related to the index value (representing the origin row), column titles, and row values.

Applying these steps in the example presented in this section results in the table shown in Figure 11-19.

CHAPTER 11 ERROR-HANDLING STRATEGIES

Index	Attribute	Value
1	0 Start Date	4/07/2024 12:00:00 AM
2	0 End Date	6/07/2024 12:00:00 AM
3	0 Sales	21
4	0 AVG Daily Sale	10.5
5	1 Start Date	7/07/2024 12:00:00 AM
6	1 End Date	11/07/2024 12:00:00 AM
7	1 Sales	10
8	1 AVG Daily Sale	2.5
9	2 Start Date	12/07/2024 12:00:00 AM
10	2 End Date	16/07/2024 12:00:00 AM
11	2 Sales	24*
12	2 AVG Daily Sale	Error
13	3 Start Date	17/07/2024 12:00:00 AM
14	3 End Date	07/20/2024
15	3 Sales	22
16	3 AVG Daily Sale	Error

Figure 11-19. Result of unpivoting columns

In the transformed table, the errors are now on a column, and you can continue with the steps presented in this example. If, in the final table, the Index column is not useful for tracking the original rows, you can merge the final result table with the original table (before unpivoting) using the Index column as a key. This will extract all the information of the row represented by each index.

Summary

This chapter explained that, during the data-cleaning process, certain actions can lead to errors in Power Query. These errors fall into two categories: step-level errors and cell-level errors. Step-level errors stop the entire query from running, whereas cell-level errors allow the query to complete, although some cells may display errors.

CHAPTER 11   ERROR-HANDLING STRATEGIES

As presented, to handle cell-level errors, you can use the `try-otherwise` function to catch errors and replace them with appropriate values. For step-level errors, it's best to avoid hardcoded values and take advantage of functions that allow flexibility, such as those that can ignore mismatched column names or define the column names dynamically.

CHAPTER 12

Custom Functions

Despite Power Query offering over 700 built-in functions, there are instances where creating custom functions is necessary. There were many situations in the previous chapters where you used custom functions, such as using the fifth argument of `Table.Group()` in Chapter 6, Example 7 in Chapter 7, Example 5 in Chapter 8, and using the third arguments of `List.Accumulate()` and `List.Generate()` in Chapter 9. In this chapter, you learn more about custom functions in Power Query.

When you think about custom functions, it doesn't necessarily mean you need to put in a lot of effort to create a complex function. There are many scenarios—such as filtering, splitting a column, or combining columns—where simply applying a command through the UI automatically generates a custom function in the formula of that command. For example, consider the historical sales transactions in the Source table shown in Table 12-1.

Table 12-1. Source: Historical Sales Value

Date	Customer ID	Quantity
18/07/2023	C-2	40
31/07/2023	C-3	31
31/07/2023	C-3	35
3/08/2023	C-3	25
30/08/2023	C-2	11
31/08/2023	C-3	25
3/09/2023	C-1	36
8/09/2023	C-3	28

(continued)

CHAPTER 12　CUSTOM FUNCTIONS

Table 12-1. (continued)

Date	Customer ID	Quantity
14/09/2023	C-1	12
2/10/2023	C-1	34
2/10/2023	C-1	25
21/10/2023	C-1	33
23/10/2023	C-3	23
10/11/2023	C-2	35
26/12/2023	C-3	15
1/01/2024	C-2	21
10/01/2024	C-2	30
14/01/2024	C-3	24
26/02/2024	C-2	23
28/02/2024	C-3	10
1/03/2024	C-2	15
12/04/2024	C-3	37
27/04/2024	C-3	18

If you select the Customer ID column and filter for C-2, the following formula will be generated to filter the rows of the table related to Customer ID equal to C-2:

= Table.SelectRows(Source, each ([Customer ID] = "C-2"))

Examining the syntax of the Table.SelectRows() function on the Microsoft website (https://learn.microsoft.com/en-us/powerquery-m/table-selectrows), presented as the following, reveals that its second argument is a condition, and it is in the type of function.

Table.SelectRows(**table** as table, **condition** as function) as table

So, in the generated formula, each ([Customer ID] = "C-2") is a (custom) function used within the Table.SelectRows() function.

CHAPTER 12 CUSTOM FUNCTIONS

As you know, every function in Power Query has its own characteristics, defined for a specific purpose. Some functions accept arguments of type number, while others take arguments of type table, list, record, date, text, or other data types. Additionally, some functions require a single argument, while others accept multiple arguments, and there are also functions like DateTime.LocalNow() that do not require any arguments at all. In Power Query, function arguments can be optional or mandatory.

Similarly, custom functions in Power Query follow the same principles. They are designed for a specific purpose, and depending on that purpose, they may take no arguments, a single argument, or multiple arguments of different types.

At this point, the question arises: If each ([Customer ID] = "C-2") is a custom function tailored for the second argument of the Table.SelectRows() function in this example, what is its argument? How many arguments does it have, and what should the argument type be? Additionally, how can you address its argument?

Some of these questions have been answered implicitly when using the formulas in the previous chapters. However, this chapter discusses these issues in greater depth. To address these questions, you first need to explore custom functions in Power Query. Then the chapter will return to these questions and answer them.

Let's build a basic custom function. Go the Power Query Editor and create a blank query. Then type the following formula in the formula bar, which results in Figure 12-1.

= each 1

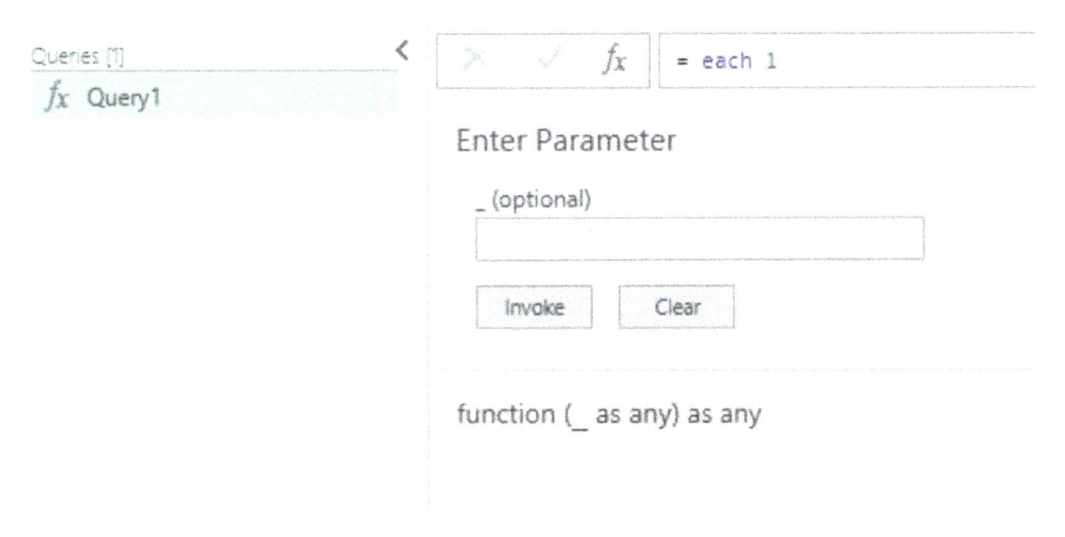

Figure 12-1. Creating a basic custom function

CHAPTER 12 CUSTOM FUNCTIONS

As shown, after you press Enter, the query icon changes from a standard query icon to a function icon, indicated by the *fx* symbol next to the function name (in this example, the name of the function is Query1). Additionally, the details of the created function are displayed in the preview window.

In the Enter Parameter section, there is a box where you can write a value as the input of the defined function. You can then see the function's result for the entered value by clicking the Invoke button. Above this box, the parameter name is highlighted as an underscore (_) followed by "(optional)". This indicates that the name of this argument in the defined function is _ and this argument for the defined function is optional.

Note Number.Abs() is a predefined Power Query function. If you open a blank query and write the following formula (without closing the parentheses and entering any input) in the formula bar, and click OK, it results in Figure 12-2. This is similar to the result when you write =each 1 in the formula bar, but Number.Abs() is a predefined function. More detailed documentation for this function is provided.

= Number.Abs

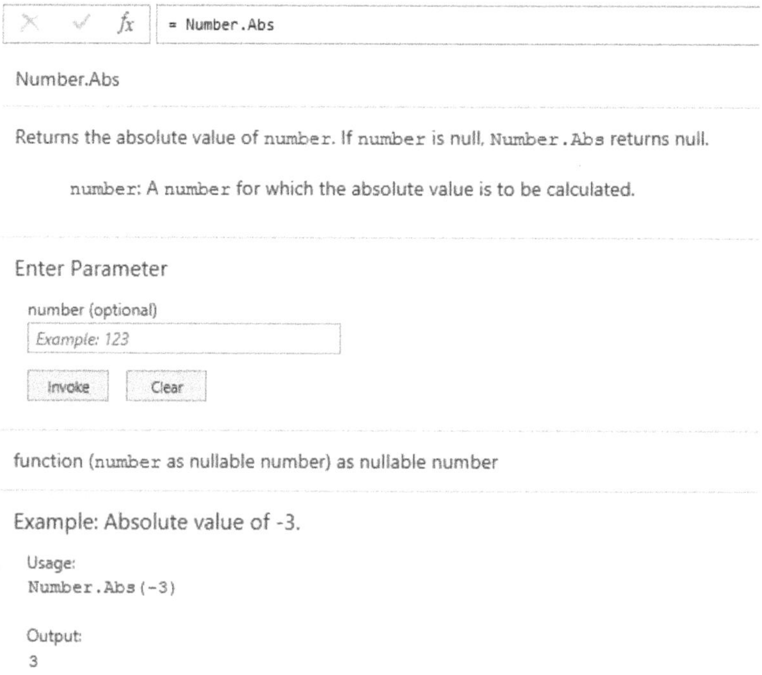

Figure 12-2. Documentation of Number.Abs()

CHAPTER 12   CUSTOM FUNCTIONS

To check the result of the defined function, over different inputs, insert 1234 in the function box shown in Figure 12-1 and click Invoke. This generates a new query, which presents the result of a defined function for the value 1234, as shown in Figure 12-3 (see the formula bar).

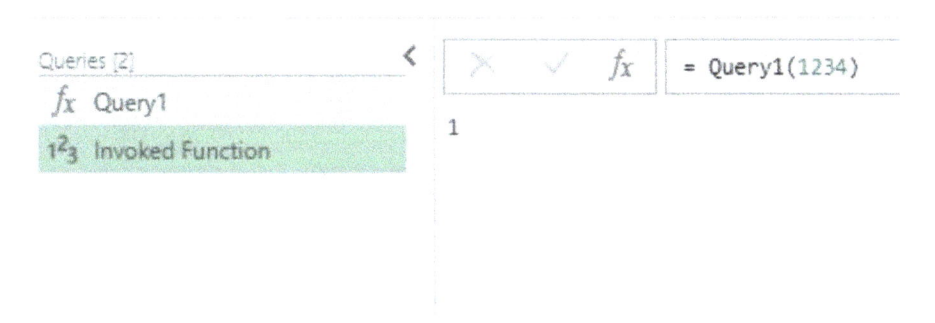

Figure 12-3. *The result of invoking a function*

If you change the input value, even if you do not enter a value as input and invoke the function again, it results in 1, as shown in Figure 12-3.

In this case, you've defined a function with one optional argument. Regardless of the input type or value entered, the function will always return 1 in all cases.

In the defined function, the result of invoking does not relate to the input parameter. Now let's define a custom function whose result depends on the input value. Write the following formula in the formula bar of a blank query.

= each _

In this case, entering the number 1234 as the input for the defined custom function will lead to 1234 as the result, as shown in Figure 12-4.

Figure 12-4. *The result of invoking 1234 in the custom function*

When you're trying to invoke the function with other inputs, you will notice that it returns the same value as whatever you input. For example, entering 2 as the input will result in 2, and entering a list such as {1,2,3} will result in the same list as output.

CHAPTER 12 CUSTOM FUNCTIONS

Note Entering {1,2,3,4} in the input box and invoking it will result in the text "{1,2,3,4}", as shown in Figure 12-5. This is because, after invoking the function, the input value is treated as text, not as a list.

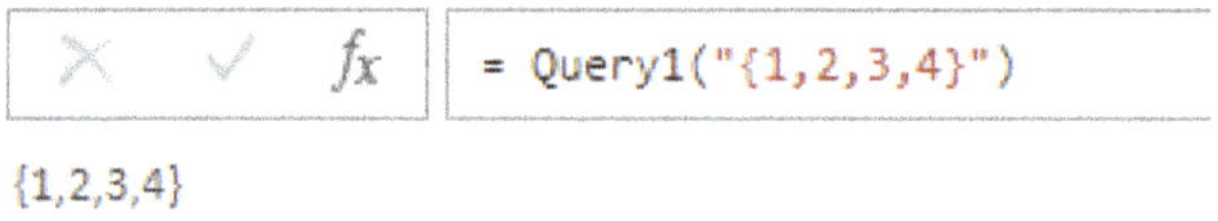

Figure 12-5. The result of invoking {1,2,3,4}

Revising the input value in the formula bar and removing the text sign will change the result into a list, as shown in Figure 12-6.

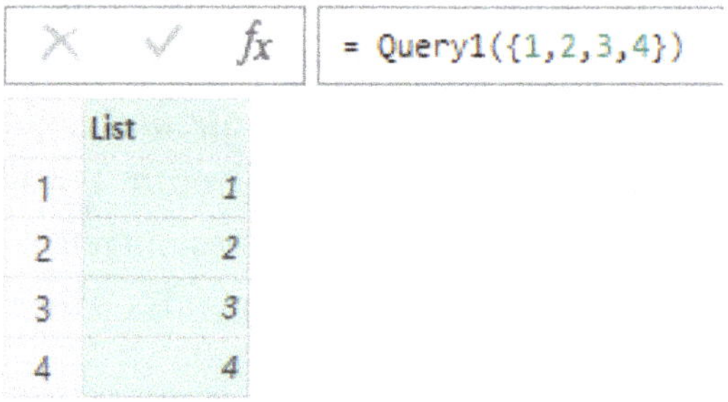

Figure 12-6. The result of revised formula after invoking {1,2,3,4}

In the previous step, the defined function simply returned the exact input value. Now, it's time to create a custom function that performs some modifications on the input value. Create a blank query and write the following formula in the formula bar:

= each "Hello: " & _

In this case, if you invoke the function after entering a name like Omid in the parameter box, the result will be Hello: Omid, as shown in Figure 12-7. But if you invoke the function for the input record like [Name= "Omid", Family= "Motamedi"], an error is returned, as shown in Figure 12-8. This is because the & operation cannot be used to concatenate the text ("Hello") shown a record ([Name= "Omid", Family= "Motamedi"]).

CHAPTER 12 CUSTOM FUNCTIONS

> = Query1("Omid")
>
> Hello: Omid

Figure 12-7. *Invoking the custom function for Omid*

> = Query1([Name= "Omid", Family= "Motamedi"])
>
> ! An error occurred in the 'Query1' query. Expression.Error: We cannot apply operator & to types Text and Record.
> Details:
>   Operator=&
>   Left=Hello:
>   Right=
>   Name=Omid
>   Family=Motamedi

Figure 12-8. *Invoking the custom function for a record*

To define a custom function that extracts the Name field from a record and concatenates Hello to it, you need to use this formula:

= each "Hello: " & _[Name]

Now you can use [Name= "Omid", Family= "Motamedi"] as the input value of the defined function, which results in Figure 12-9.

> = Query1([Name= "Omid", Family= "Motamedi"])
>
> Hello: Omid

Figure 12-9. *Invoking the revised custom function for a record*

You can try to revise the function by removing the underscore and rewriting it as follows:

= each "Hello: " & [Name]

Unexpectedly, the result of invoking this function for the record does not change. It seems that when you use the each _ expression to define a custom function, if the input value is of type record, the underscore can be omitted, and Power Query automatically knows how to handle it.

CHAPTER 12 CUSTOM FUNCTIONS

Based on the defined custom functions you've seen so far, this list sums up what you have learned about the each _ expression:

- You can use each to define a custom function.
- When using each to define a custom function, you can define up to one optional argument for the function.
- If each is used to create a custom function, the argument is represented with the underscore (_).
- When creating a custom function to handle data of type record, the underscore can be omitted without affecting the result.

Based on this explanation, let's return to the initial example of this section, where each ([Customer ID] = "C-2") was used as a custom function within the Table.SelectRows() function. Based on the Table.SelectRows() logic, the defined custom function in its second argument will be evaluated for all the rows separately. If the custom function returns true for a row, it will remain in the final result after filtering. Otherwise, that row will be removed.

The custom function will be evaluated for each row separately, and in Power Query, each single row in the evaluation process is considered as type record. Therefore, the input of the defined custom function is in type record. Based on these tips, when you define a custom function using each _ logic for the case with input parameter in type record, the underscore can be omitted without affecting the results.

In another words, the whole version of the custom function in this example is each (_[Customer ID] = "C-2"), whereby the underscore is removed. In this custom function, for each row each _[Customer ID] extracts the value of the Customer ID of that row, and each _[Customer ID] = "C-2" returns true if the value of Customer ID is C-2 and false otherwise.

For instance, consider the first row of the Source table as a record [Date=18/07/2023, Customer ID="C-2", Quantity=40]. Using each _ will result in the same record. Using each _[Customer ID] will return C-2, and each _[Customer ID] = "C-2" will return true, so this row will be presented in the final table.

Despite all the advantages of using the each _ expression to create a custom function, it has a limitation—it can only be used when your custom function requires just one argument. There are situations, such as when defining the fifth argument of

CHAPTER 12 CUSTOM FUNCTIONS

the Table.Group() function, where you need to create a custom function with multiple arguments. In such situations, you need to use the general definition of the custom function, as shown here:

(input 1, input 2,….., input n) => calculation logic

In this definition, the function is indicated by the => sign, with inputs defined before it and the calculation logic defined after. For example, the following formula defines a custom function that receives two inputs, called A and B, as shown in Figure 12-10, and results in the sum of inputs.

=(A,B)=>A+B

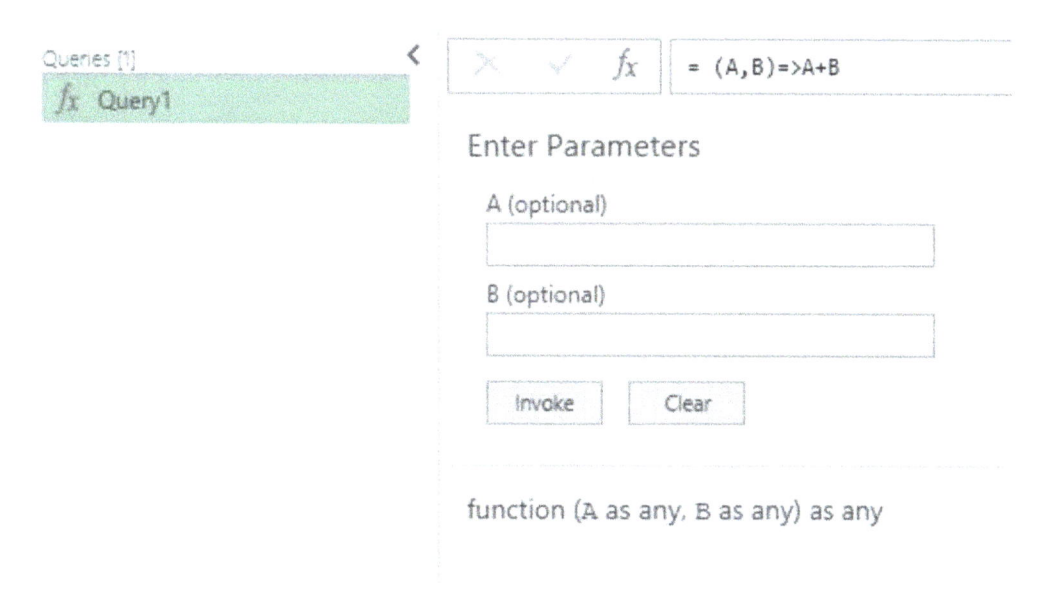

Figure 12-10. Custom function with two inputs

Given this general definition, you can say that the each _ syntax presented at the beginning of this chapter is a shorthand version for defining a custom function with a single input argument named _. So, all the previous custom functions defined with each _ in this section can be rewritten using this general definition, as provided in Table 12-2.

641

Table 12-2. *Comparing each _ and the General Definition of the Custom Function*

each	=>
= each 1	()=> 1
=each _	(A)=>A
=each "Hello: " & _	(A)=> "Hello: " & A
= each "Hello: " & _[Name]	(A)=> "Hello: " & A[Name]
= each "Hello: " & [Name]	(A)=> "Hello: " & A[Name]

Besides what's mentioned in the introduction of this chapter, in the custom functions, you can define the type of input parameters as well as the type of result, and define optional parameters. Additionally, custom functions can perform multi-step calculations, which you explore further later in this chapter.

Implementing Sumproduct as a Custom Function

Define the Sumproduct function in Power Query, which receives two lists as input and returns the sum of the products of the corresponding items in both lists (similar to the Sumproduct function in Excel, but here it's applied to just two inputs).

To define a Sumproduct function in Power Query, create a blank query. Name it Sumproduct and use the following formula to define the function that leads to Figure 12-11, assuming the lists have the same length.

```
(L1 as list ,L2 as list) as number =>
    List.Sum(
            List.Transform(List.Positions(L1), each L1{ _ } *
        L2{ _ })
                )
```

CHAPTER 12 CUSTOM FUNCTIONS

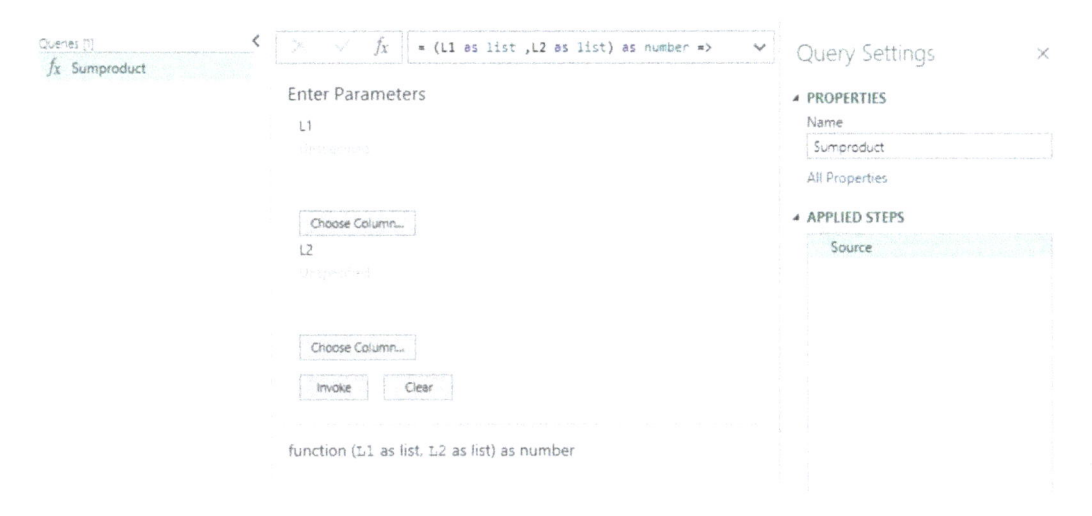

Figure 12-11. Defining Sumproduct

In this function, the input parameters L1 and L2 are defined as type lists. (When using the function in the Power Query UI, you need to select a column from a table as input, as the parameter type should be set to list.) The function's output type is specified as a number, just by entering a number after the list of input parameters.

The defined function can be written on a single line, but for better readability, it can be broken into several steps using records, as the following:

```
(L1 as list ,L2 as list) as number =>
    [
    Step1=List.Positions(L1),
    Step2=List.Transform(Step1, each L1{_} * L2{_}),
    Step3=List.Sum(Step2)
    ][Step3]
```

You can also use the let expression, as shown in the following formula, where the Power Query snippets are identical in output:

```
(L1 as list ,L2 as list) as number => let
    Step1=List.Positions(L1),
    Step2=List.Transform(Step1, each L1{_} *L2{_}),
    Step3=List.Sum(Step2)
    in
    Step3
```

CHAPTER 12   CUSTOM FUNCTIONS

To understand this custom function, consider the example where L1 = {1,0,4} and L2 = {4,5,6}. Here's the breakdown:

Step 1: List.Positions({1,0,4}) returns {0,1,2}.

Step 2: List.Transform({0,1,2}, each L1{_} * L2{_}) calculates the products of corresponding elements: {L1{0} * L2{0}, L1{1} * L2{1}, L1{2} * L2{2}}, resulting in {1*4, 0*5, 4*6} = {4,0,24}.

Step 3: All the items in the list from the previous step are summed and the result is presented as the final result of defined custom function.

If you create a new blank query and use the Sumproduct({1,0,4},{2,5,6}) formula, the function will calculate the Sumproduct of these two lists, resulting in 28. Similarly, if you use Sumproduct({1,0,4},{2,5,6,8}), you will reach the same result. While the lists have different lengths, the function should ideally result in an error.

Since in the defined function, the dimension is determined by L1 (using List.Positions()), the function does not consider the extra elements in L2 and presents the same result as Sumproduct({1,0,4},{2,5,6}). To address this issue, the function can be modified to use the list with the largest dimension for calculations as follows.

```
(L1 as list ,L2 as list) as number => let
    Step1={0..(List.Max({List.Count(L1),List.Count(L2)})-1)},
    Step2=List.Transform(Step1, each L1{_} *L2{_}),
    Step3=List.Sum(Step2)
    in
    Step3
```

In the revised version, using the =Sumproduct({1,0,4},{2,5,6,8}) formula in a blank query will result in an error, as shown in Figure 12-12. However, the error message provided is not very helpful or meaningful. It doesn't give clear information about the cause of the issue.

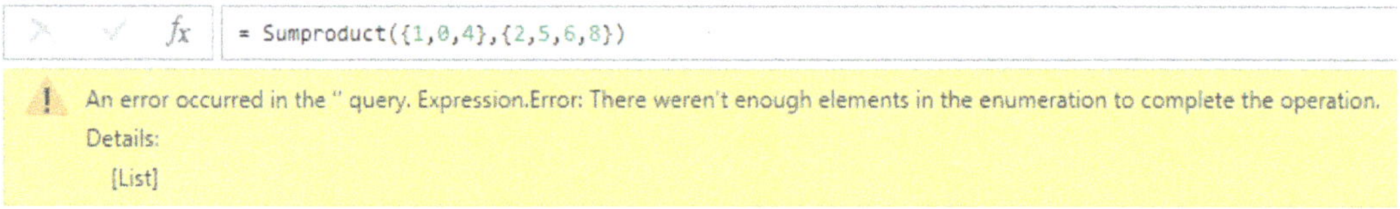

CHAPTER 12　CUSTOM FUNCTIONS

Figure 12-12. The result of using =Sumproduct({1,0,4},{2,5,6,8})

To provide a more meaningful error when entering lists of different lengths, the formula can be revised by modifying the term after the expression:

```
(L1 as list ,L2 as list) as number =>
let
    Step1={0..(List.Max({List.Count(L1),List.Count(L2)})-1)},
    Step2=List.Transform(Step1, each L1{_} *L2{_}),
    Step3=List.Sum(Step2)
In
    if List.Count(L1) <> List.Count(L2) then error "The lists have
    different lengths" else Step3
```

Now, instead of the generic error, if the lengths of the lists do not match, the formula will return a more descriptive error, as shown in Figure 12-13.

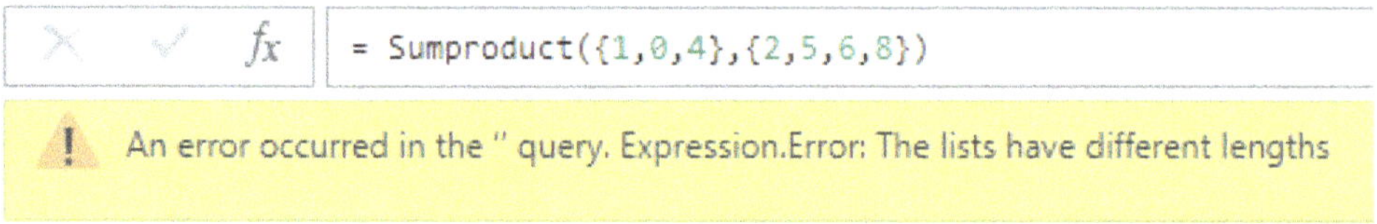

Figure 12-13. The result of revised formula for =Sumproduct({1,0,4},{2,5,6,8})

Documenting Custom Functions

Consider the previous custom function and define its documentation.

First, let's review what function documentation looks like and why it's important to add it to your custom functions, which you and your colleagues use frequently.

Documentation provides important information about the function, including its input parameters, calculation logic, expected results, examples of how to use it, and more. Without documentation, if you share a custom function with others, you will need to explain its application, parameters, and how to use it verbally (e.g., in an

645

CHAPTER 12　CUSTOM FUNCTIONS

email or a meeting). However, if you create documentation that explains the function's characteristics, this documentation will always be available with the function, allowing users to refer to it whenever they need more information. It also helps you in the future when you revisit the function and need to modify it. Therefore, it's best to add documentation to your most frequently used custom functions.

All predefined Power Query functions have their own documentation as well. To see the function documentation, create a blank query and write a predefined function like `List.Sum` without parentheses in the formula bar. Press Enter to display the documentation, as shown in Figure 12-14.

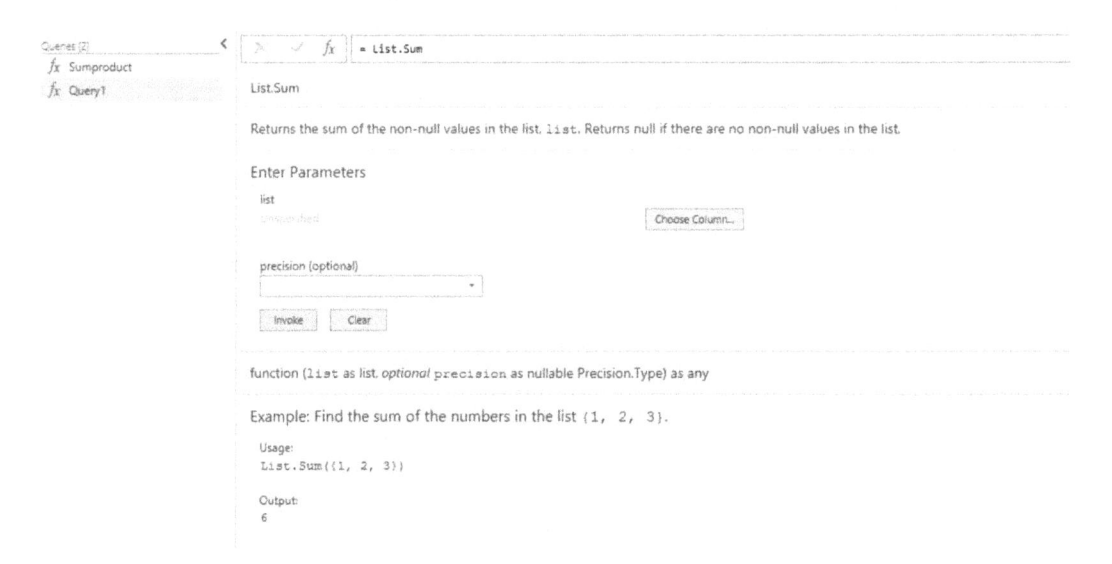

Figure 12-14. Documentiont for List.Sum

As presented, the documentation of this function includes several sections, such as the function's name, its description, its parameters, and examples of how to use it. Writing the custom-defined `Sumproduct` function in the formula bar results in showing its documentation, as shown in Figure 12-15.

CHAPTER 12 CUSTOM FUNCTIONS

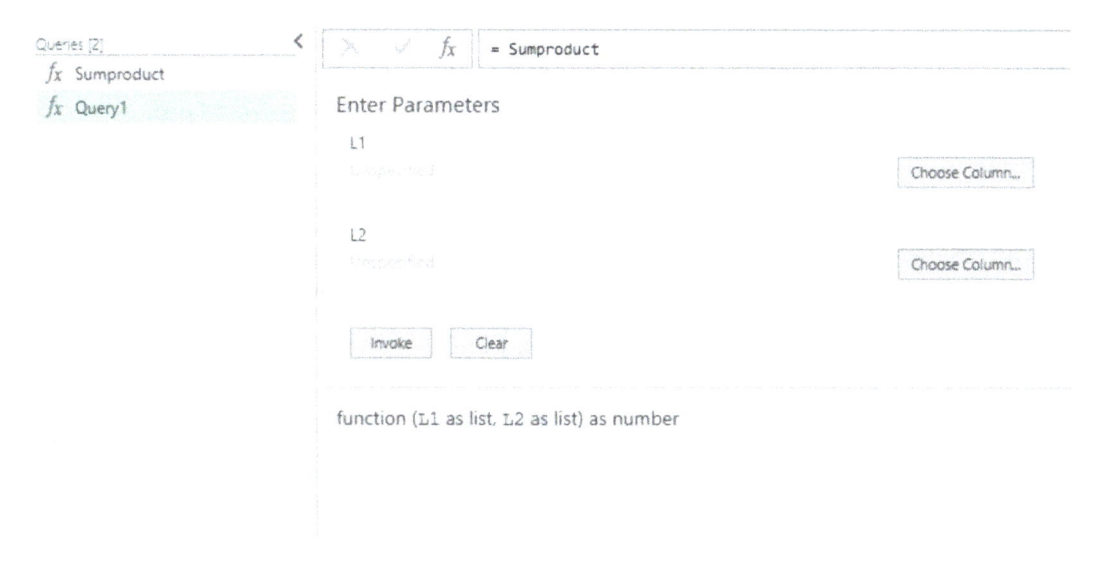

Figure 12-15. Documentation for Sumproduct

By comparing the documentation of List.Sum and Sumproduct, it is clear that the documentation on List.Sum is more detailed. The names of the different sections are shown in Figure 12-16.

Figure 12-16. Names of function documentation sections

The documentation sections you see in List.Sum can be added to any custom function within a record, with predefined field names. The most commonly used fields in the record for defining a function documentation are Documentation.Name, Documentation.LongDescription, and Documentation.Examples.

647

CHAPTER 12   CUSTOM FUNCTIONS

> **Note** There are more fields for documentation. You can check them out at https://learn.microsoft.com/en-us/power-query/handling-documentation.

The first step in documenting a custom function, after creating it, is to create a record that includes the mentioned fields for the documentation. In this record, the Documentation.Name and Documentation.LongDescription fields are commonly used in type text, and the Documentation.Examples field is in the type list, including several sub-records, each for one example. This includes the Description, Code, and Result fields.

In the following snippet, you can see a record including the required fields for documentation:

```
[
    Documentation.Name = "Sumproduct",
    Documentation.LongDescription = "This function received two list as
    inputs and returned the sum of the products of corresponding items
    into lists",
    Documentation.Examples = {
    [Description = "Considering the case which list 1 and 2 are {1,2,3}
    and {1,2,3}", Code = "Sumproduct({1,2,3},{1,2,3})", Result = "14"],
    [Description = "Considering the case which list 1 and 2 are {1,0,4}
    and {4,5,6}", Code = "Sumproduct({1,0,4},{4,5,6})", Result = "28"]
    }
]
```

After defining the documentation fields, you can add them to your custom function. Consider the custom function defined in the previous example, as follows.

```
(L1 as list ,L2 as list) as number =>
let
    Step1={0..(List.Max({List.Count(L1),List.Count(L2)})-1)},
    Step2=List.Transform(Step1, each L1{_} *L2{_}),
    Step3=List.Sum(Step2)
```

CHAPTER 12　CUSTOM FUNCTIONS

In

```
    if List.Count(L1) <> List.Count(L2) then error "The lists have
    different lengths" else Step3
```

All these steps are required to execute the defined custom function, and you cannot add the documentation record within the steps needed to execute the function. The documentation should be added at the same level as defining the function. In other words, they should both be defined in the same let expression.

So, without changing the result, the previous formula can be rewritten as follows. This defines the step name as Sumproduct for the custom function and places it in a let expression:

```
let
    Sumproduct=(L1 as list ,L2 as list) as number =>
    let
        Step1={0..(List.Max({List.Count(L1),List.Count(L2)})-1)},
        Step2=List.Transform(Step1, each L1{_} *L2{_}),
        Step3=List.Sum(Step2)
    in
    Step3
in
Sumproduct
```

Now you have a let block with one step, Sumproduct. You can add another step to it, called Doc, as shown here:

```
let
    Sumproduct=(L1 as list ,L2 as list) as number =>
    let
        Step1={0..(List.Max({List.Count(L1),List.Count(L2)})-1)},
        Step2=List.Transform(Step1, each L1{_} *L2{_}),
        Step3=List.Sum(Step2)
    in
    Step3,
  Doc = [
    Documentation.Name = "Sumproduct",
```

649

CHAPTER 12 CUSTOM FUNCTIONS

```
            Documentation.LongDescription = "This function received two list as
            inputs and returned the sum of the products of corresponding items
            into lists",
            Documentation.Examples = {
            [Description = "Considering the case which list 1 and 2 are {1,2,3}
            and {1,2,3}", Code = "Sumproduct({1,2,3},{1,2,3})", Result = "14"],
            [Description = "Considering the case which list 1 and 2 are {1,0,4}
            and {4,5,6}", Code = "Sumproduct({1,0,4},{4,5,6})", Result = "28"]
            }
      ]
in
   Sumproduct
```

Based on the previous modification, the result does not change, as the defined documentation has not been applied to the custom function yet. To apply this documentation, the Sumproduct after in should be replaced with the following formula.

```
Value.ReplaceType(Sumproduct, Value.ReplaceMetadata(Value.
Type(Sumproduct), Doc))
```

The entire formula, including the custom function and its documentation, is as follows:

```
let
    Sumproduct=(L1 as list ,L2 as list) as number =>
    let
        Step1={0..(List.Max({List.Count(L1),List.Count(L2)})-1)},
        Step2=List.Transform(Step1, each L1{_} *L2{_}),
        Step3=List.Sum(Step2)
    in
    Step3,
  Doc = [
    Documentation.Name = "Sumproduct",
    Documentation.LongDescription = "This function received two list as
    inputs and returned the sum of the products of corresponding items
    into lists",
```

```
  Documentation.Examples = {
    [Description = "Considering the case which list 1 and 2 are {1,2,3}
    and {1,2,3}", Code = "Sumproduct({1,2,3},{1,2,3})", Result = "14"],
    [Description = "Considering the case which list 1 and 2 are {1,0,4}
    and {4,5,6}", Code = "Sumproduct({1,0,4},{4,5,6})", Result = "28"]
  }
]
in
  Value.ReplaceType(Sumproduct, Value.ReplaceMetadata(Value.
  Type(Sumproduct), Doc))
```

This change is reflected in the function's documentation, as shown in the example in Figure 12-17.

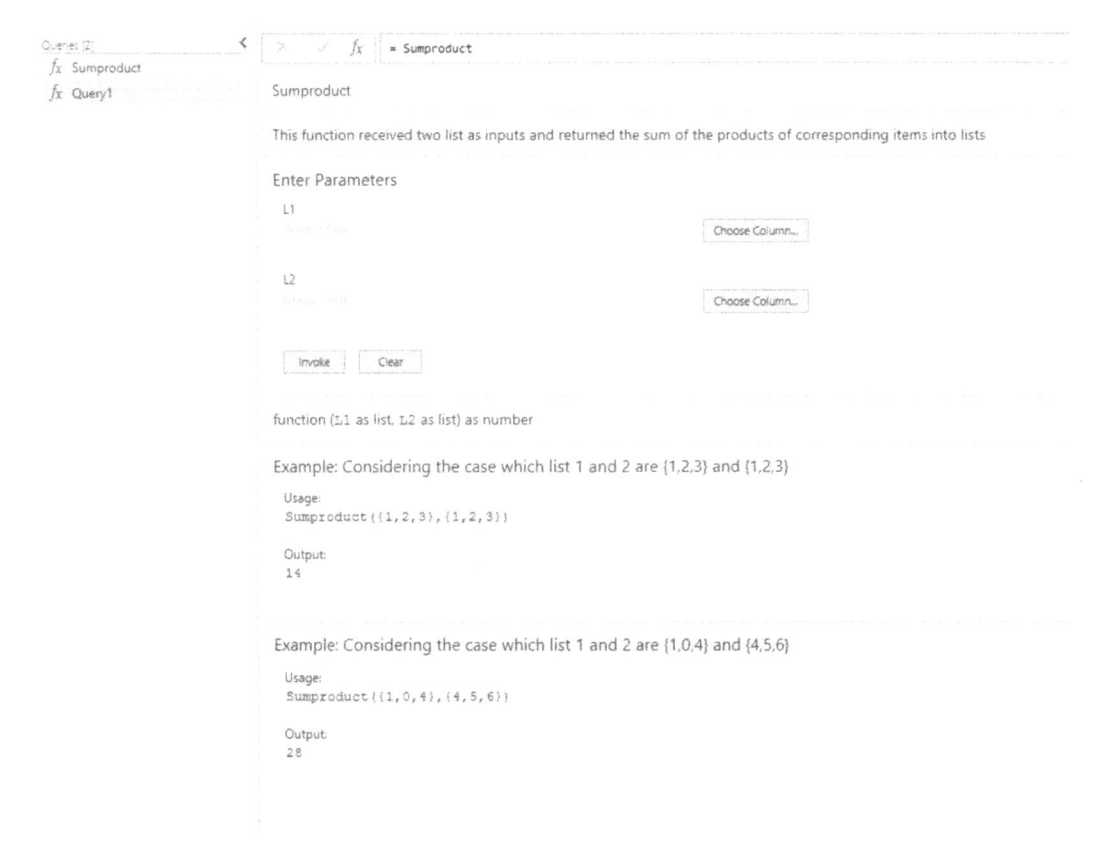

Figure 12-17. The result of the revised documentation for Sumproduct

> **Note** In the documentation, instead of using Power Query's special characters, you should use JavaScript tags. For instance, if you want to insert a line break, you should use `<br>` instead of `#(lf)`.

Sharing Custom Functions Across Files

How can you share these custom functions across multiple files?

To use a custom function in another file, you typically need to copy and paste the code and redefine the function in the new file. However, this approach can become cumbersome, especially if you have multiple custom functions that you use frequently in different files. In this case, you should be aware of which functions are used within each function, and if you apply modifications to a function, you need to ensure that the same modifications are applied consistently across all files where that function is used.

A more practical approach is to save the function code in a text file and share this file between Power Query instances. In this scenario, any changes made to the shared text file will automatically be applied to the files where this function is used, during the next refresh.

To manage multiple custom functions, save each custom function in a separate text file, naming the file according to the function. For example, save the `Sumproduct` custom function as `Sumproduct.txt`, as shown in Figure 12-18.

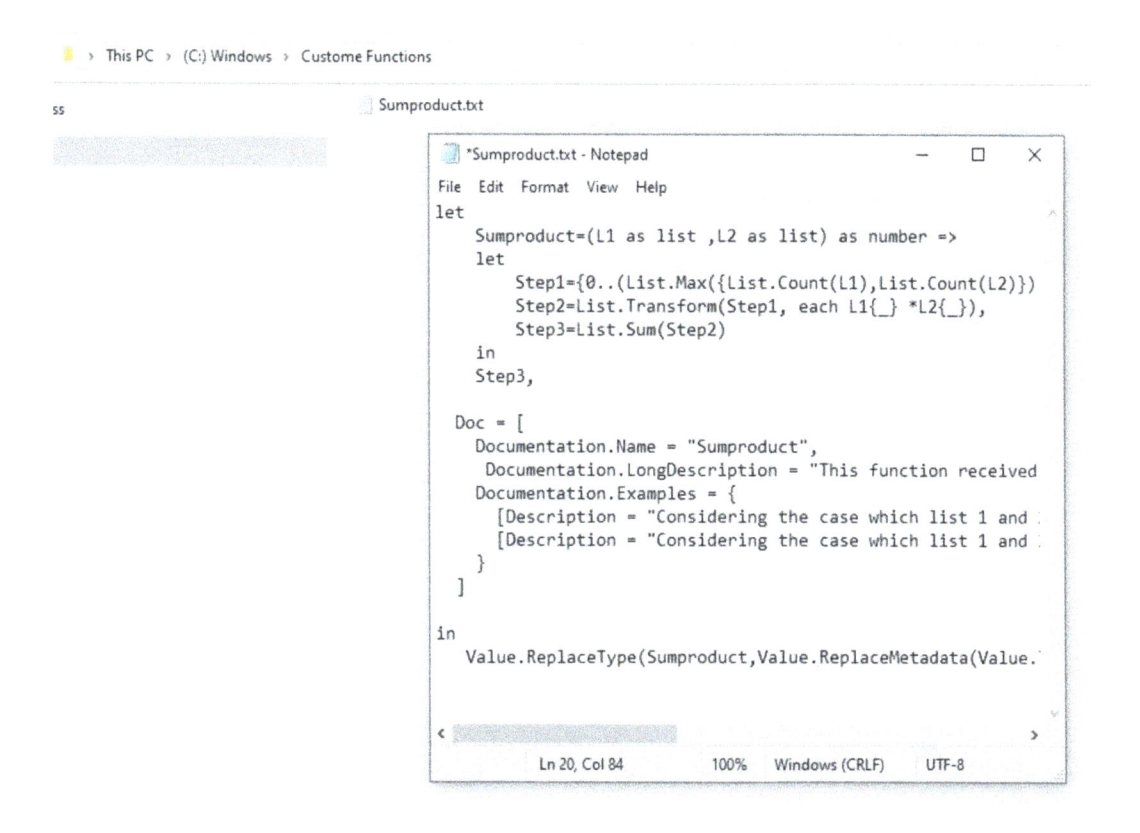

Figure 12-18. Saving a custom function as a text file

Then import the text file into Power Query using the following code or using the From Text command, which leads to Figure 12-19.

```
= Table.FromColumns({Lines.FromBinary(File.Contents("C:\Custome Functions\Sumproduct.txt"), null, null, 1252)})
```

CHAPTER 12 CUSTOM FUNCTIONS

```
fx  = Table.FromColumns({Lines.FromBinary

     Column1
1    let
2      Sumproduct=(L1 as list ,L2 as list) as number =>
3      let
4        Step1={0..(List.Max({List.Count(L1),List.Count(L2)})-1)},
5        Step2=List.Transform(Step1, each L1{_} *L2{_}),
6        Step3=List.Sum(Step2)
7      in
8        Step3,
9
10   Doc = [
11     Documentation.Name = "Sumproduct",
12     Documentation.LongDescription = "This function received two list a...
13     Documentation.Examples = {
14       [Description = "Considering the case which list 1 and 2 are {1,2,3} a...
15       [Description = "Considering the case which list 1 and 2 are {1,0,4} a...
16     }
17   ]
18
19   in
20     Value.ReplaceType(Sumproduct,Value.ReplaceMetadata(Value.Type...
```

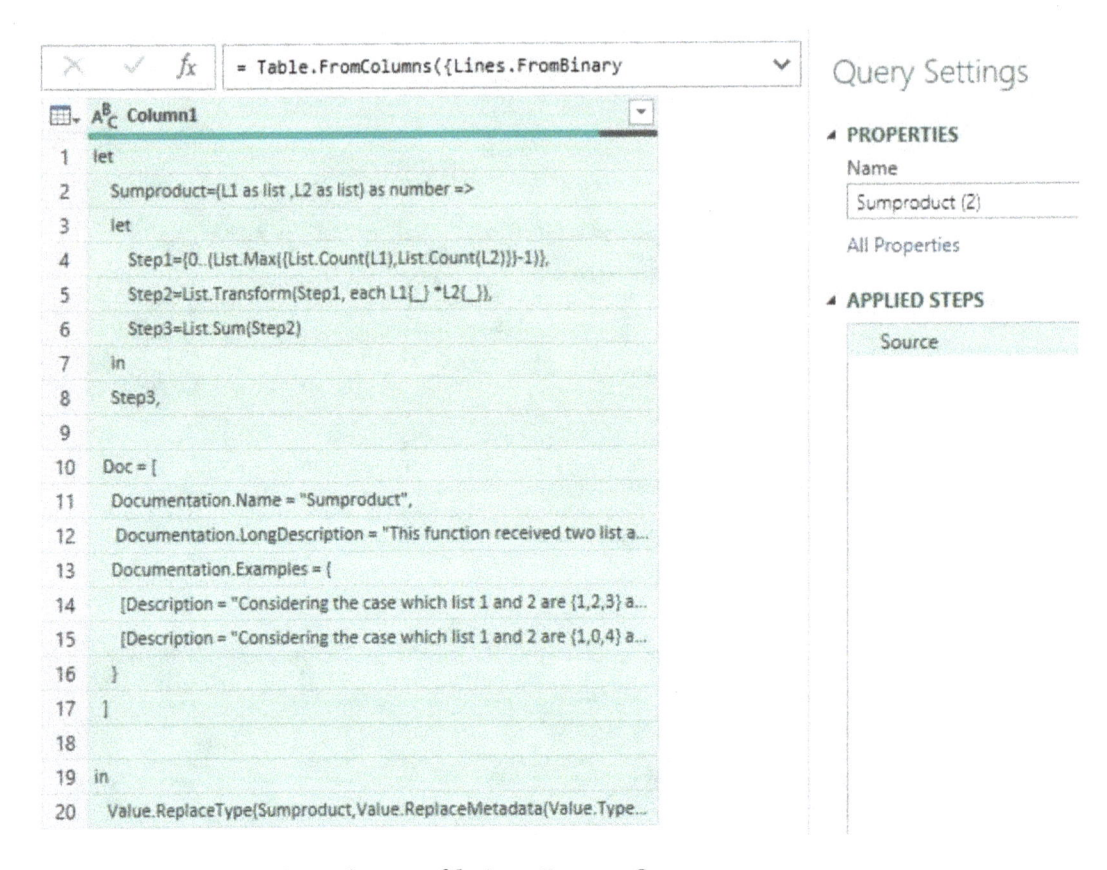

Query Settings

▲ PROPERTIES
Name
Sumproduct (2)

All Properties

▲ APPLIED STEPS
Source

Figure 12-19. Loading the text file into Power Query

In the next step, use the following formula to merge all the text lines into one continuous text value, as shown in Figure 12-20.

= Text.Combine(Source[Column1])

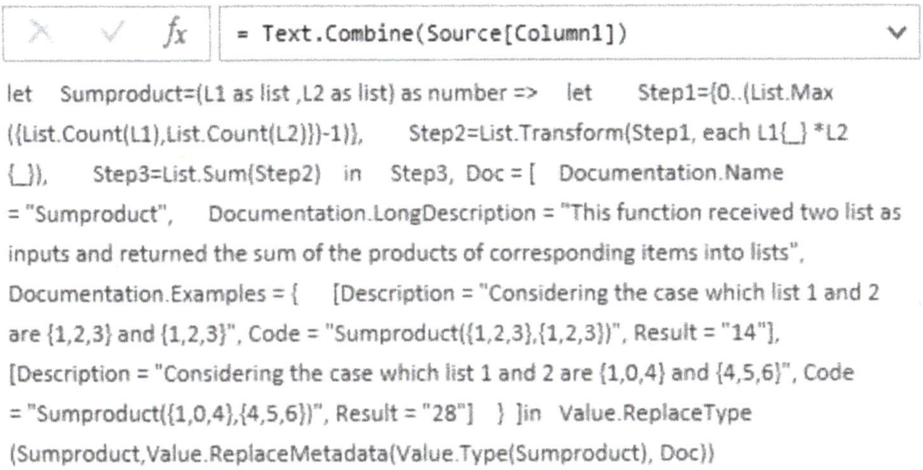

CHAPTER 12 CUSTOM FUNCTIONS

```
fx    = Text.Combine(Source[Column1])
```

let   Sumproduct=(L1 as list ,L2 as list) as number =>   let   Step1={0..(List.Max
({List.Count(L1),List.Count(L2)})-1)},   Step2=List.Transform(Step1, each L1{_} *L2
{_}),   Step3=List.Sum(Step2) in   Step3, Doc = [Documentation.Name
= "Sumproduct",   Documentation.LongDescription = "This function received two list as
inputs and returned the sum of the products of corresponding items into lists",
Documentation.Examples = {   [Description = "Considering the case which list 1 and 2
are {1,2,3} and {1,2,3}", Code = "Sumproduct({1,2,3},{1,2,3})", Result = "14"],
[Description = "Considering the case which list 1 and 2 are {1,0,4} and {4,5,6}", Code
= "Sumproduct({1,0,4},{4,5,6})", Result = "28"]   }]in Value.ReplaceType
(Sumproduct,Value.ReplaceMetadata(Value.Type(Sumproduct), Doc))

Figure 12-20. *The result of Text.Combine*

The result of Text.Combine() is in type text. To convert it into an executable function, you can use Expression.Evaluate(). It converts text into a Power Query formula. For example, "1+1" is text, and entering ="1+1" in the formula bar results in text equal to "1+1". However, using =Expression.Evaluate("1+1") in the formula bar—which means to convert "1+1" from text to the formula =1+1—returns 2. Similarly, Expression.Evaluate("{1,2,3}") returns a {1,2,3} list, as shown in Figure 12-22. The result of Expression.Evaluate("List.Sum({1,2,3})") is shown in Figure 12-21.

```
fx    = Expression.Evaluate("{1,2,3}")
```

	List
1	1
2	2
3	3

Figure 12-21. *The result of Expression.Evaluate("{1,2,3}")*

CHAPTER 12 CUSTOM FUNCTIONS

This function is straightforward for simple expressions. However, when dealing with functions in text, such as "List.Sum({1,2,3})", directly using =Expression.Evaluate("List.Sum({1,2,3})") in the formula bar will result in an error, as shown in Figure 12-22. To resolve this, you need to specify #shared as the evaluation environment in the second argument of this function, like so:

=Expression.Evaluate("List.Sum({1,2,3})",#shared)

> = Expression.Evaluate("List.Sum({1,2,3})")
>
> ⚠ Expression.Error: [1,1-1,9] The name 'List.Sum' doesn't exist in the current context.
> Details:
>   [List]

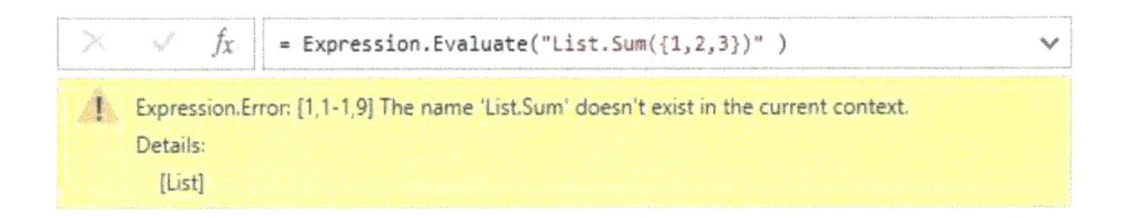

Figure 12-22. *The result of Expression.Evaluate("List.Sum({1,2,3})")*

Based on this explanation, =Text.Combine(Source[Column1]) results in the custom function in type text, so the following formula will convert this text into the executable functions shown in Figure 12-23.

= Expression.Evaluate(Text.Combine(Source[Column1]),#shared)

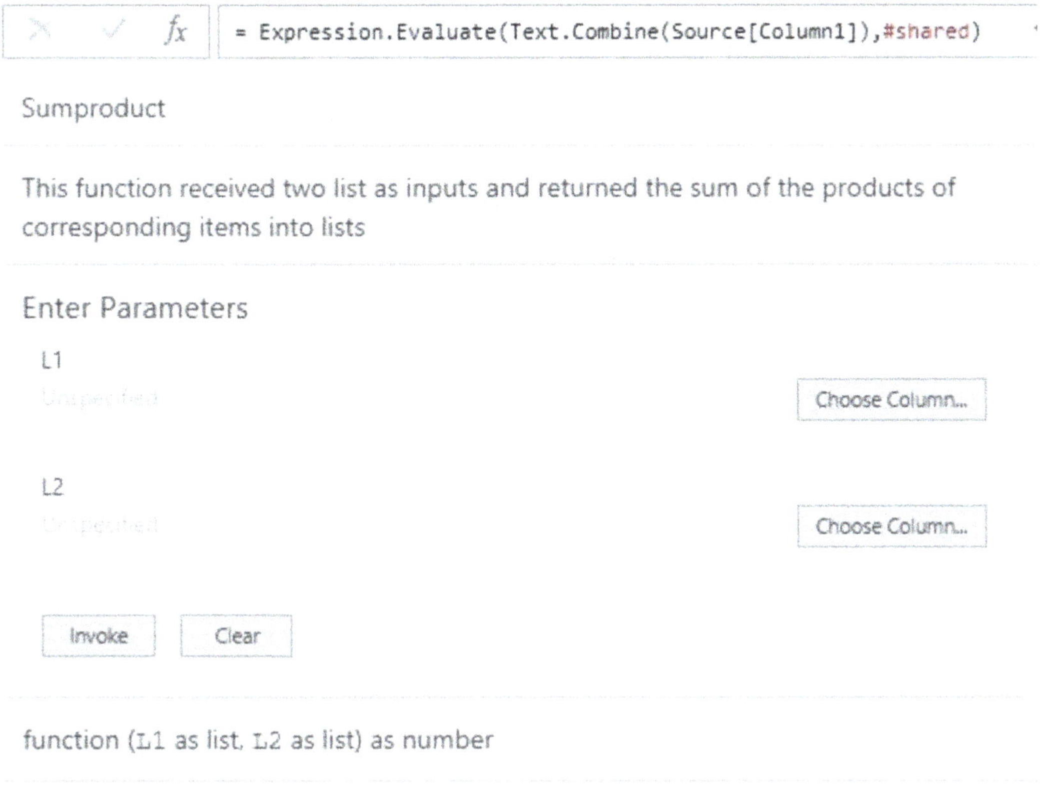

CHAPTER 12 CUSTOM FUNCTIONS

```
fx  = Expression.Evaluate(Text.Combine(Source[Column1]),#shared)
```

Sumproduct

This function received two list as inputs and returned the sum of the products of corresponding items into lists

Enter Parameters

L1

                                                             [Choose Column...]

L2

                                                             [Choose Column...]

[Invoke] [Clear]

function (L1 as list, L2 as list) as number

Figure 12-23. The result of using Expression.Evaluate

The result of this query is a defined custom function (Sumproduct), which you can use in other queries.

Note In Power Query (M language), #shared is a special keyword used to refer to a collection of all shared objects, such as functions, queries, and values that are globally available within the current Power Query environment.

#shared is essentially a special record that contains references to all functions, queries, and variables that are defined and made available in the Power Query environment. When you type =#shared in the formula bar, it returns a list of shared elements in the current workbook or query, as shown in Figure 12-24.

CHAPTER 12 CUSTOM FUNCTIONS

Query1	Record
Value.ResourceExpression	Function
Resource.Access	Function
CommonDataService.Database	Function
Kusto.Contents	Function
Kusto.Databases	Function
AzureDataExplorer.Contents	Function
AzureDataExplorer.Databases	Function
AzureDataExplorer.KqlDatabase	Function
PowerPlatform.Dataflows	Function
DataLake.Contents	Function
DataLake.Files	Function
Fabric.Warehouse	Function
Lakehouse.Contents	Function
List.NonNullCount	Function
List.MatchesAll	Function
List.MatchesAny	Function
List.Range	Function
List.RemoveItems	Function
List.ReplaceValue	Function

Figure 12-24. The result of #shared

Creating Recursive Functions

Create a custom function that takes a number n as input and returns the first *n* values in the Fibonacci sequence (In the previous chapter, the Fibonacci sequence was calculated using various methods, and here, you define a custom function for it, by using basic operations.)

The general term for extracting the nth value in the Fibonacci series is $a_n=a_{n-1}+a_{n-2}$ with initial values $a_0=a_1=1$. So, calculate the fourth value in this series, presented by a_4, n=4. So, $a_4=a_3+a_2$. To find a_3, use $a_3=a_2+a_1$. To find a_2, use $a_2=a_1+a_0$. As mentioned, $a_0=a_1=1$, so $a_4=a_3+a_2=((a_1+a_0)+a_1)+(a_1+a_0)$. So, in this series, to extract the nth value, you need the (n-1)th and (n-2)th values, and this chain will continue to reach n=0 or n=1.

CHAPTER 12 CUSTOM FUNCTIONS

In other words, if you named the function to calculate the nth value of this series as Fibonacci, to calculate Fibonacci(n), initially, you need to calculate Fibonacci(n-1) and **Fibonacci(n-2)** first, which for Fibonacci(n-1), the values of Fibonacci(n-2) and Fibonacci(n-3) are required and for the calculation of Fibonacci(n -2), the values of Fibonacci(n-3) and Fibonacci(n-4) are required.

For this function, you can say that if n=1 or n=2, then Fibonacci(n) is equal to 1 for other values of n. Fibonacci(n) is equal to Fibonacci(n-1)+Fibonacci(n-2). So in M language, you can say:

Fibonacci (n)= if n=0 or n=1 then 1 else Fibonacci(n-1)+ Fibonacci (n-2)

To change this into a custom function to compute the nth value of Fibonacci series in Power Query, create a new blank query and name it Fibonacci. Then in the formula bar, write the following formula, which results in Figure 12-25.

(n)=> if n=0 or 1 then n=1 else Fibonacci(n-1)+ Fibonacci (n-2)

Figure 12-25. The defined custom function

In the defined function, entering n as 2, 3, and 4, yields the results 2, 3, and 5, respectively.

In this defined custom function, the function is named Fibonacci, and within its formula, you call the Fibonacci function again. This means that during execution, the function may call itself depending on the scenario. Such functions that call themselves as part of their execution are known as *recursive functions*.

659

> **Note** It is recommended to avoid using recursive functions whenever possible, as they are often time-consuming.

The stop condition (also called the base case) is a crucial part of a recursive function. It is a specific condition that halts the recursion and prevents the function from calling itself indefinitely. In a recursive function, the function calls itself repeatedly. If an appropriate stop condition is not defined, the function will continue calling itself, leading to an *infinite loop,* which consumes all available computer memory and results in a stack overflow memory error.

In the defined function, the based cases are n=0 or n=1. In such cases, the function does not recall itself and the recursion will stop. If you remove the base case and write the custom function as (n)=> Fibonacci(n-1)+ Fibonacci (n-2), invoking the function for any value, such as 5, results in a stack overflow error message, as shown in Figure 12-26.

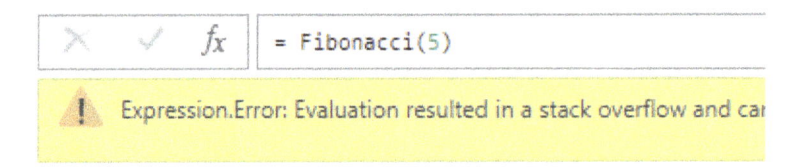

Figure 12-26. Stack overflow error message

Using Optional Input Parameters

Create a custom function with two arguments—salary and tax rate—to calculate the tax based on multiplying salary by the tax rate. If a tax rate is not provided, assume a default rate of 10 percent.

In this question, you are asked to create a custom function with an optional argument, similar to many predefined functions in Power Query. For example, Chapter 6 explains that the fourth and fifth arguments of the Table.Group() function are optional. By default, Table.Group() applies global grouping, but you can modify the grouping logic by using the fourth arguments.

The same concept applies to this function. The tax rate is generally set at 10 percent. However, if you want to use a different tax rate, you can specify a custom value using the function's second argument.

In Power Query custom functions, optional parameters can be defined using the `optional` keyword before the parameter name. So, the parameters for this custom function can be defined as follows, which means `taxRate` is optional:

```
(salary as number, optional taxRate as number) as number =>
```

In this case, you cannot simply use the `salary * taxRate` formula because `taxRate` is an optional argument and might not be provided by the user. If the user does not enter a value, `taxRate` will be `null`, causing the entire formula to return `null`.

To handle this, you need to assign a default value (e.g., 10 percent) when `taxRate` is `null`, ensuring that the calculation works correctly even if the user does not specify a value. So, instead of using `taxRate` directly, you can use `taxRate ?? 0.1`. This means that if `taxRate` has a value, it will be used; otherwise, if it is `null`, it will be replaced with 0.1 (which represents the default 10 percent tax rate). This ensures that the calculation works correctly even when the user does not provide a value for `taxRate`.

The revised formula is as follows.

```
(salary as number, optional taxRate as number) as number => salary *(taxRate ??0.1)
```

You can define a custom function with multiple optional arguments, as shown in this example. This approach allows you to create a function with three arguments, where two of them are optional. However, an important rule must be followed in defining an optional argument: all optional parameters must come after the required ones.

Summary

Power Query provides a wide range of built-in functions, but there are situations where custom functions are necessary to meet specific needs. In this chapter, you learned how to define custom functions using the `each _` syntax or by creating a general function structure like `(x) => ...`. You also explored how to specify parameter types and return types by appending the `type` keyword, and how to define optional parameters and add documentation to functions, making them more versatile and user-friendly.

Appendix A

Power Query offers a versatile toolkit for data transformation, and as with any powerful tool, there are multiple ways to tackle challenges. For each challenge presented in this book, you can explore a wide range of potential solution, enhancing your understanding of Power Query's capabilities. While this book provides comprehensive solutions for each challenge, you can also explore other approaches for some of the challenges through Table A-1.

To find solutions to these challenges, simply append the challenge number from the "No" column to the following URL:

https://www.OmidBI.com/ch

For example, to access the solution for the challenge titled "Adding Multiple Columns at Once," append the challenge number 20 to the URL, as so:

https://www.OmidBI.com/ch20

Table A-1. Other Solutions for These Challenges

Section	Title	No.
2.4.	Adding Multiple Columns at Once	20
2.6.	Extracting Data from Price List Table	87
3.3.	Filtering Across Multiple Columns, Part 3	67
3.6.	Filtering Based on Sequence	42
3.7.	Using Random Selection	93
3.8.	Using Advanced Filtering Criteria	36
4.3.	Splitting Text by Position	45
4.4.	Extracting Text Between Parentheses	27
4.5.	Extracting Email Addresses	71
4.6.	Using a Multiline Splitter	64

(*continued*)

APPENDIX A

Table A-1. (*continued*)

Section	Title	No.
4.7.	Splitting Text by Changing Character Type, Part 1	63
4.8.	Splitting Text by Changing Character Type, Part 2	73
4.10.	Merging Instead of Adding a Column	8
5.1.	Managing Product IDs	39
5.2.	Value Repeated in Several Columns	11
5.3.	Removing Blank Columns	79
5.4.	Transforming Columns, Part 1	41
5.5.	Transforming Columns, Part 2	31
5.6.	Transforming Columns, Part 3	32
6.3.	Matching Items in Groups	55
6.4.	Identifying All-Season Products	14
6.11.	Transformations Within Table.Group()	16
7.1.	Combining Tables	44
7.2.	Calculating Weighted Averages	23
7.6.	Conditional Merging	69
7.7.	Self-Merging	61
8.2.	Handling Missing Rows	54
8.4.	Linear Interpolation for Missing Data	62
8.5.	K-Nearest Neighbors for Imputation	86
9.4.	Generating the Fibonacci Sequence by List.Accumulate()	72
9.7.	Applying Transformation Over the Columns	12
9.10.	Implementing Stepped Tax Calculations	58
9.11.	Changing Data Granularity	59

APPENDIX A

To further broaden your expertise, I provide links to some other challenges on my website, with solutions. See Table A-2.

Table A-2. *Complementary Challenges*

Chapter	Topic	Challenge Title	No.
2	Referencing	Last Inventory	95
2	Referencing	Compare Rows	102
3	Sorting and Filtering	Sort Table Columns	43
3	Sorting and Filtering	Custom Ranking	85
3	Sorting and Filtering	Top Products	96
3	Sorting and Filtering	Random Selection Part 2	99
3	Sorting and Filtering	Custom Rank	106
3	Sorting and Filtering	Custom Rank	112
4	Column Splitting and Merging	Custom Splitter 3	83
4	Column Splitting and Merging	Data Cleaning	98
4	Column Splitting and Merging	Column Splitting	136
4	Column Splitting and Merging	Column Splitting	146
5	Pivoting and Unpivoting Tables	Transformation	15
5	Pivoting and Unpivoting Tables	Transformation	21
5	Pivoting and Unpivoting Tables	Transformation	48
5	Pivoting and Unpivoting Tables	Transformation	65
5	Pivoting and Unpivoting Tables	Merged Cells	66
5	Pivoting and Unpivoting Tables	Normal Distribution	84
5	Pivoting and Unpivoting Tables	Table Transformation	122
5	Pivoting and Unpivoting Tables	Transformation	126
5	Pivoting and Unpivoting Tables	Table Transformation	131
5	Pivoting and Unpivoting Tables	Table Transformation	137
5	Pivoting and Unpivoting Tables	Table Transformation	142

(*continued*)

APPENDIX A

Table A-2. (*continued*)

Chapter	Topic	Challenge Title	No.
5	Pivoting and Unpivoting Tables	Table Transformation	147
6	Grouping Rows with Table.Group	Number Grouping	46
6	Grouping Rows with Table.Group	Custom Grouping	109
6	Grouping Rows with Table.Group	Custom Grouping	119
6	Grouping Rows with Table.Group	Custom Grouping	123
6	Grouping Rows with Table.Group	Custom Grouping	129
6	Grouping Rows with Table.Group	Custom Grouping	133
6	Grouping Rows with Table.Group	Custom Grouping	139
6	Grouping Rows with Table.Group	Custom Grouping	143
7	Merging and Appending Tables	Match Payments	60
7	Merging and Appending Tables	Matching Tables	107
7	Merging and Appending Tables	Reconciliation	110
7	Merging and Appending Tables	Merge	114
7	Merging and Appending Tables	Payment Durations	120
8	Handling Missing Values	Find Missing Numbers	52
8	Handling Missing Values	Linear Interpolation	97
8	Handling Missing Values	Custom Average	103
9	Looping in Power Query	Calculate Spending Time	26
9	Looping in Power Query	Identifying Customers Staple Products	29
9	Looping in Power Query	Risk Analysis	30
9	Looping in Power Query	Noise Removing	33
9	Looping in Power Query	Connected People	37
9	Looping in Power Query	Cross-Selling	40
9	Looping in Power Query	Assignment Problem Part 1	49

(*continued*)

Table A-2. (*continued*)

Chapter	Topic	Challenge Title	No.
9	Looping in Power Query	Assignment Problem Part 2	50
9	Looping in Power Query	Purchasing Together	51
9	Looping in Power Query	Coin Change Problem	70
9	Looping in Power Query	Fibonacci Sequence	72
9	Looping in Power Query	Manage Duplicate Values	100
9	Looping in Power Query	Subsets	101
9	Looping in Power Query	Merge	124
9	Looping in Power Query	FIFO	130
9	Looping in Power Query	Golden Period	140
10	Leveraging Scripting and External Integrations in Power Query	Cluster Values	28
-	Other	Customer Return Cycle	34
-	Other	Up and Down Grades	35
-	Other	Duration Since Last Visit	38
-	Other	Multiple Text Replaces	47
-	Other	OEIS Sequence	53
-	Other	Process Efficiency	56
-	Other	Fuzzy Numbers Calculation	57
-	Other	Simulation	104
-	Other	Character Repetition	105
-	Other	AVG Cooperation Time	108
-	Other	Increased SALES	111
-	Other	Manage Duplicate Values	113
-	Other	Multi Replacement	115

(*continued*)

Table A-2. (continued)

Chapter	Topic	Challenge Title	No.
-	Other	Remove Rows and Columns	116
-	Other	Add Index Column	117
-	Other	DSO	118
-	Other	Power	121
-	Other	Pad Middle	125
-	Other	Add Index Column	127
-	Other	Cartesian Product	128
-	Other	Merge	132
-	Other	Final Week of the Month	134
-	Other	Identify the Pattern	135
-	Other	Periodic Sales Summary	138
-	Other	Fill Up and Down	141
-	Other	First Transaction in Each Month	144
-	Other	Length of Pattern	145
-	Other	Filter Dates	148

Index

A

Access Web Content window, 613
Account reconciliation, 408
ActiveX controls, 616, 617
Age groups, 338, 339
Aggregate function, 301
Aggregation function, 248, 271, 273
Aggregation section, 163
AllRowsData query, 456, 462, 465
Appending, 45
    choosing new queries, 388
    definition, 387
    queries, missing
        values, 462–464
    sales in 2022 table, 387
    sales in 2023 table, 387, 388
    selecting column list, 389, 390
    setting, 388
Applied Steps pane, 13

B

Bank reconciliation, 408
Base case, 660
Blank cells, 265–267
Buffering, 92, 176, 380

C

Cartesian product
    defined, 584
    List.Accumulate(), 589–591, 593
    List.TransformMany(), 590, 591, 593
    merging table columns, 585, 586, 588
Case sensitivity
    arguments, 18
    column headers, 18
    column names, 11
    combined tables, 11, 12
    converting column names to
        lowercase, 18
    edit function message, 16
    final table, 18, 19
    generated queries, 12, 13
    queries, 15, 16
    query 02 result, 18
    sections, 13–15
    Transform Sample File, 16, 17
Cell-level errors, 619, 621
Column merging
    adding column, 237–242
    adding sign, 241
    custom operation, 233–237
    date information, 242–245
    definition, 179
    final inventory levels, 242
    results, 183
    setting, 182, 183
    setting group by, 242
    source table, 182, 183
    splitting columns, 182
Column names
    case sensitivity, 11–19
    comprehensive solution, 19–31

INDEX

Column names (*cont.*)
    consistent, 3–10
    variations, 23
Column splitting
    after adding new IDs, 197
    after adding new row, 186
    after reordering steps, 201
    arguments, 181
    changing character type
        arguments, 225
        digit to non-digit values, 224–227
        expanding info.2 column, 232
        results, 227, 228, 232
        revised split, 230, 231
        source table, 223, 224, 228
        transactions, 229, 230
        transitions, 226
        values, 230
    changing column name, 181, 182
    characteristics, 181
    default value, 182
    definition, 179
    delimiter, 184–188
    extracting email addresses, 212–217
    multiline splitter, 217–223
    multiple delimiters, 188–193
    options, 182
    position, 193–201
    removing fourth argument, 186
    result, 180, 190, 195
    revising result, 196
    setting, 179, 180, 189, 195
    source table, 179
    text extraction between
        parentheses, 201–212
Combiner.CombineTextByDelimiter()
    function, 235, 236, 244
Comprehensive solution

column headers, same number and
    order of columns
    filtering setting, 22, 23
    removing changed type, 21
    removing promoted headers, 21
    result of promoting headers, 22
    combining and loading data, 20
    number and order of columns,
        different files
        adding MissingField.Ignore, 27, 28
        creating new query, 23, 24
        expanding column, 29, 30
        formula bar, 24
        removing steps, 29, 30
        renaming column headers, 27
        Table.ToRows() function, 25
    source files, 19, 20
Concatenation operation, 163
Conditional merging
    Customer Info table, 424, 426
    extracting last row, 430
    extracting states, 430, 431
    filtering previous date, 429
    final table, 431
    Historical Sales Info table, 424, 425
    modified formula, 427
    replacement setting, 426, 427
    results, 428, 429
    settings, 427, 428
Custom functions, 137, 174
    characteristics, 635
    comparison, 641, 642
    creating recursive functions, 658–660
    creation, 635
    definition, 641
    documentation
        description, 645
        examples, 648

INDEX

let expression, 649
List.Sum, 646
    names of sections, 647
    predefined function, 646
    Sumproduct, 646, 647, 649-651
each expression, 640
evaluation process, 640
historical sales transactions table, 633
input parameters, 660-661
invoking function, 637-639
loading text file, 654
Number.Abs(), 636
saving text file, 653
sharing files, 652-658
Sumproduct, 642-645
two inputs, 641
Custom mapping, 420

D

Data-cleaning process, 451
Data extraction
    adding columns to query
        adding new comments, 66
        adding new task in CSV file, 62
        expanding comment column, 64, 65
        loaded table, 66
        loading connected table, 65
        loading tasks, 63
        merging tables, 63, 64
        refreshing after adding tasks, 66, 67
        task assignments table, 62
    choosing folder, 4
    combined table, 5, 6
    combining files, 4, 5
    creating date table, 74-80
    definition, 1
    Excel files, 3
    functions, 1-2
    handling multi-row headers, 38-47
    loading tables, Excel file
        Excel.CurrentWorkbook() function, 59
        filtering query result, 61
        four tables in query, 60, 61
        increasing row number by each refresh, 60
        loading result, 59, 60
        three sheets, 58
    online sources, 1
    PriceList table, 125-131
    resultant table, 8, 10
    sample table, 6
    store numbers, 8, 9
    table values
        adding custom column, 37
        Advanced Editor, 33
        combining and loading data, 31, 32
        custom column window, 36, 37
        drilling down, 32, 33
        promoting headers, 35, 36
        referring previous steps, 35
        removing promote headers, 32
        source files, 31
        view Advanced Editor, 34
    type detection, 7
    UI, 3
    using data load tracker, 67-74 (*see also* Column names; Data loading)
Data granularity
    column names, 565-567
    power consumption, 563, 564
    using List.Accumulate(), 578-581
    using List.Transform(), 572-577
    using unpivoted columns, 568-571

671

INDEX

Data loading, 10, 15, 17, 28
    webpage, 47–51
Data load tracker (Log)
    adding date column, 70
    adding new value to historical values, 75
    append setting, 73
    historical values, 73
    Navigator pane, 69
    Power Query Editor, 72
    promoting headers, 70
    queries and connection, 71
    removing extra columns, 70
    result of append, 74
    setting, 71, 72
    transposed table, 69, 70
    using From Web, 67, 68
Data manipulation, 34
Data preview, 14
Dataset, 603, 608
Data transformation, 663
Date.AddDays() function, 513
Date.AddMonths() function, 513
Date.AddQuarters() function, 513
Date.AddWeeks() function, 513
Date.AddYears() function, 513
Date.EndOfMonth() function, 493
Date.From() function, 243
#date() function, 492, 493
Date table
    columns, 74
    formula, 79
    Table.FromList() function, 75, 77
    using second and third argument, Table.FromList, 78, 79
    using second argument, Table.FromList, 75, 76
    using third argument, Table.FromList, 76, 77

DateTime.LocalNow() function, 427, 635
Date.WeekOfYear() function, 321
Default value, 182
Domination criteria, 175
Do-While loop, 490, 510
Duration.Days() function, 367

E

Email addresses
    converting table into text, 214
    extracting, 216, 217, 599
    filtering list, 216
    reference list, 215
    regex function, 598
    selection criteria, 215
    source table, 212, 213
    Text.Split() function, 214
Energy consumption, 233, 563
Error-handling
    calculation errors, 622
    causes of errors, 627–630
    cell-level errors, 621
    daily sales, 626
    extracting rows, 630
    fields, 623
    MissingField.Ignore argument, 620
    performance overhead, 622
    removing rows, 625–627
    scenarios, 625
    source table, 619
    step-level errors, 619, 620
    try-otherwise function, 621, 624
    unpivoting columns, 630
    visualization problems, 622
Euclidean distance, 483
Excel.CurrentWorkbook() function, 59

INDEX

Execution time, 91
Expression.Evaluate() function, 655

F

Fibonacci series, 659
    List.Accumulate() function, 524, 525
    List.Generate() function, 526–528
Fill Down command, 341
Filtering
    advanced criteria, 172–176
    arguments, 137
    custom function, 137, 174
    date, 135, 136
    dominant solution, 173, 174
    each expression, 137
    extracting purchasing date
        grouping, 154
        sorting, 149–154
    first row, 138
    list of values
        extracting patient IDs, 159
        filtering patient IDs, 157, 158
        final results, 159, 160
        patients source table, 155
        performance, 161
        variation, 160, 161
    multiple columns
        all columns, 140
        historical sales, source table, 138, 139
        initial filtering, 144, 146
        Product_ID column, 139
        purchase info, source table, 143, 144
        result, 142, 143
        sales info, source table, 140, 141
        setting, 141, 142
    unpivoting and group by, 146
    values less than or equal to 7, 147
    non-dominated IDs, 175
    result, 136, 176
    sequence
        group by setting, 163, 164
        referral patterns, 162
        replaced formula, 165
        results, 166, 167
        setting filtering option, 165, 166
    solutions source table, 172
    using random selection, 167–168
For-Each loop, 489, 499, 516–518
Formula bar, 14
For-Next loop, 489, 490, 518, 519
Full outer join, 394, 396
Fuzzy matching, 420, 422–424
Fuzzy merging
    challenges, 420
    Historical Sales Info table, 419
    inconsistent patterns and variations, 420, 421
    Product Price Info table, 419, 420
    results, 423, 424
    setting, 421

G

Geopolitical entities (GPE), 605
GoldPrice.org website, 67
Google Translate API
    auto-translated text, 614
    calling, 612
    credential warnings, 613
    customer comments table, 610
    JSON format, 611
    limitations, 611

INDEX

Google Translate API (*cont.*)
    parameters, 611
    result, 615
    updated formula, 615
    uppercase transformation, 614
    URL format, 611
Grouping, 154, 155, 298, 305
    consecutive dates, 355–365
    on date
        every ten days in each month, 322, 323
        every ten days starting from beginning of year, 321, 322
        every week starting Wednesday, 320, 321
        group by week, 319, 320
        scenarios, 319
        source table, 318
    ignoring case sensitivity, 326–332
    second iteration, 371
    using Value.Comparer, 332–340
GroupKind.Local, 326

H

HasError field, 629
Helper column, 357
High-quality data, 451

I

Infinite loop, 660
in keyword, 34
Inner join, 394, 396

J

Json.Document() function, 611

K

Keep Error command, 628
K-nearest neighbors (KNN)
    applying table, 486, 487
    arguments, 484
    calculating distances, 479, 483
    converting query to function, 486
    defined, 477–488
    extracting nearest rows, 479
    process, 477
    query after converting to function, 485
    query before converting to function, 484, 485
    query steps after changing, 481, 482
    query steps before changing, 481
    referring sixth row, 480
    referring to Maintable, 480, 481
    replacing null values in all rows, 487, 488
    replacing null values in Row6, 484
    reusable function, 486
    revised formula, 487
    selecting rows without null values, 478, 482, 483
    selecting two nearest neighbors, 484
    source table, 478
    steps, 482

L

Left anti join, 394, 396
Left Outer Join, 393, 395
let expression, 643, 649
Linear interpolation, 470–477, 609
List.Accumulate() function, 408
    accumulation process, 506
    adding multiple columns, 540, 542
    arguments, 506

Cartesian product, 589-591, 593
data granularity, 578-581
defined, 507
elements, 509
extracting square of number, 507, 508
Fibonacci sequence, 524, 525
For-Each loop, 516-518
For-Next loop, 518, 519
handling sequences, 550-554, 556
iterations, 505, 508-510, 518, 519, 530
stepped tax calculations, 562, 563
syntax, 506
transformation over columns, 533, 534
List.Average() function, 111, 112
List.Buffer() function, 110, 161, 364, 519
List.Combine() function, 255, 256, 501
List.Contains() function, 140, 158
List.Count() function, 273, 317
List.Difference() function, 414-417, 466
List.Distinct() function, 255, 256
List.FirstN() function, 110
List.Generate() function, 56, 57, 382, 408, 433, 445-448
　applications, 510-511
　arguments, 514
　basic option, 520, 521
　definition, 520
　Do-While loop, 510
　efficient option, 521, 523
　extracting dates, 511, 512
　extracting even numbers, 513, 515, 516
　Fibonacci sequence, 526-528
　parameters, 513
　result, 522
　squared even numbers, 514
　syntax, 510
List.Intersect() function, 264
List.Last() formula, 129

List.Last() function, 517
List.Max() functions, 303, 560
ListofCharacters, 199, 200
List of functions
　adding null value, 105, 106
　combining, 107, 108
　converting table, 108
　Custom1, 104, 105
　final result, 109
　removing last item, 106, 107
　solution, 103
　source table, 103
　Table.ToColumns(), 103
List.RemoveItems() function, 212
List.RemoveNulls() function, 257
List.Select() function, 215
List.Skip() function, 517, 576
List.Sort() function, 308, 583
List.Split() function, 204, 575, 580
List.Sum() function, 236, 303, 376, 377, 561
List syntax, 379
List.Transform() function, 54, 55, 187, 198, 204, 208, 245, 347-349, 524
　adding multiple columns, 538, 539
　arguments, 491
　creating list of tables, 496, 497
　data granularity, 572-577
　data type, 491
　extracting first dates of months, 492
　extracting last dates of months, 493, 494
　extracting name of months, 494
　handling sequences, 546-549
　loaded tables, 495, 496
　range of dates, 495
　stepped tax calculations, 559-562
　SUMPRODUCT, 528-530

675

INDEX

List.Transform() function (*cont.*)
  syntax, 490
  transformation function, 491, 493, 495, 497
  transformation over columns, 534–536
  transformed version of tables, 497, 498
List.TransformMany() function
  arguments, 499
  Cartesian product, 590, 591, 593
  combining nested loops, 501
  dynamic selection, 504
  extracting dates in 2023, 503
  extracting dates in year, 504, 505
  extracting first dates of quarters, 499, 500
  For-Each loops, 498, 499
  instance, 504
  iteration, 502–503
  nested loop, 500
  results, 502
  second argument, 503, 504
  syntax, 499
  third argument, 504
  transformation function, 501, 502
List.Union() function, 256
ListX, 546, 547, 551
LoadTopCompanies() function, 55
Looping
  adding multiple columns
    department cost, 537
    List.Accumulate(), 540, 542
    List.Transform(), 538, 539
  changing data granularity, 563–581
  Do-While loop, 490
  For-Each loop, 489
  For-Next loop, 489, 490
  handling sequences

    distance table, 543, 544
    List.Accumulate(), 550–554, 556
    List.Transform(), 546–549, 563
    notation, 545
    travel table, 544
  implementing stepped tax calculations, 556–563
  implementing Sumproduct, 528–530
  List.Accumulate(), 505–510, 516–520, 524–525
  List.Generate(), 510–516, 520–523, 526–528
  List.Transform(), 490–498, 524
  List.TransformMany(), 498–505
  product combinations, 582, 583
  transformation over columns
    comparison matrix, 530, 531
    List.Accumulate(), 533, 534
    List.Transform(), 534–536
    normalization result, 532, 533
    table column, 531, 532
  working set combinations, 584–593

M

Merge Queries command, 63
Merging
  calculating weighted averages
    expanding grouped rows column, 404
    Group By command, 404, 405
    production table, 399, 400
    results, 405, 406
    samples table, 400
    settings, 403
    steps, 401
  combining tables, 397–399
  conditional, 424–431

configuration, 465
definition, 387
full outer join, 394, 396
fuzzy, 419–424
Group By command, 398, 399
Historical_Sales table, 390, 391
inner join, 394, 396
left anti join, 394, 396
left outer join, 393, 395
missing values, 459, 461, 462
options, 393
Product_Info table, 390, 395
reconciliation (*see* Reconciliation)
resulting table, 393
right anti join, 394, 396
right outer join, 394, 395
sales in April table, 397
sales in March table, 397
sales in May table, 397
setting query, 392
settings, 460
steps, 391 (*see also* Self-merging)
M functions, 252, 257
Missing dates, 360, 361, 363, 364
MissingField.Ignore argument, 620
MissingField.UseNull, 620
Missing values
    data-cleaning process, 451
    extracting
        appending/merging, 464
        converting dates to number, 470
        grouping rows, 466–470
        using merging, 465
    filling nulls with previous
        values, 452–454
    handling missing rows
        appending queries, 462–464
        converting date type, 459

expanding Project
    column, 456, 457
formula, 456
loading source table, 458
multiple projects, 458
source table, 455
using merge command, 459,
    461, 462
KNN, 477–488
linear interpolation, 470–477
model performance, 451
scenarios, 451
and zeros, 451
Multiline splitter
    delimiter, 221
    results, 218–223
    setting, 221, 222
    setting splitting command, 218, 219
    source table, 217, 218
    unpivoting, 219, 220
Multi-objective optimization
    models, 172
Multi-row headers
    appending queries, 46
    budget/cost data, 38
    duplicating query, 40
    keeping top rows, 41, 42
    merging columns, 44, 45
    navigation Excel file, 38, 39
    navigation steps, 40
    Power Query Editor, 38
    remove top rows, 41
    source table, 38
    transposing command, 45
    transposing table, 42, 43
    two table results, 45
    using Fill Down, 43, 44
    using first row, 46

INDEX

N

Non-domination criteria, 174
Number.From() function, 344, 367, 376, 377
Number.IntegerDivide() function, 115

O

Order.Ascending, 135
Order.Descending, 135

P

Pivoting
  components, 249, 250
  definition, 247
  result, 249
  setting columns, 247–249
  source table, 247, 248 (*see also* Unpivoting)
Power Query
  Advanced Editor, 34
  appending, 45
  complementary challenges, 665–668
  data extraction (*see* Data extraction)
  filtering rows, 137
  Group By command, 297
  grouping, 298
  instances, 652
  integrating R, 606–610
  list, 26
  loops (*see* Looping)
  mathematical algorithms, 479
  operations, 26
  Python, 602–606
  referencing cells, 88–92
  sample file, 15
  solutions for challenges, 663–664
  sorting command, 150
  UI, 84
  user-friendly interface, 34
Power Query Editor, 39, 72, 282
  data load tracker, 72
  dataset, 14
  multi-row headers, 38
  queries, 63
  setting, 7
Prediction models, 472
Product combinations, 582–584
Python
  count words, 603, 604
  dataset, 603
  final results, 605, 606
  geopolitical entities, 605
  libraries, 602
  script, 604
  script dialog box, 602, 603
  source table, 602

Q

Query export to CSV files, 616–618
Query pane, 13
Query Settings pane, 14

R

Random selection
  adding custom column, 169
  last character of values, 171
  reordering rows and removing duplicates, 168, 169
  selected rows, 170
  selecting staff, 172
  staff info, source table, 167
  table rows, 170, 171

Reconciliation
    arguments, 414
    bank statements, 406, 412
    comparing records, 415
    converting result to table, 418
    custom equality, 415
    definition, 408
    final table, 419
    finance department's records, 406, 407, 413
    financial data, 408
    formulas, 411
    left anti join, 408, 409
    mismatched items, 417, 418
    reshaping tables, 415
    results, 411, 414
    swapping arguments, 410
    swapping tables, 417
Record.AddField() function, 538, 540
Record.Combine() function, 539
Record.Field() function, 86, 89
Record.FromList() function, 576
Records, 26
Record.ToList(_) function, 140, 143
Recursive functions, 437, 439, 440, 658–660
Referencing
    adding multiple columns
        adding product families, 115
        expanding, 116, 117
        filtering, 115
        removing errors, 116, 117
        source coding, 113, 114
        using record, 116
    cells
        adding new column, 90, 91
        coding, 91, 92
        distance, 88
        revised formula, 89
        using Distance, 89
    cell values, 85
    changing value types, 111
    formula, 82
    functions, 81
    multiple previous rows, 110–113
    previous row
        changing value type, 96
        expanding, 100
        Fill Down function, 101, 102
        filtering, 93–96
        growth rate, 94
        list of functions, 103–110
        merging, 97–101
        source, 92, 93
        value in same column, 94
        value of next month, 97, 98
    PriceList table
        adding new column, 129
        filtering product A, 127, 128
        filtering product and From Date column, 128
        historical data, 126
        making formula dynamic, 130
        products, 125, 126
        transaction date, 125
    and removing functions, 86–88
    removing unwanted columns, 82
    source, 81
    specified column, 82
    syntax, 83
    Table.Column, 82
    Table.FirstN, 83
    Table.Range, 84
    Table.SelectColumns, 81
    Table.SelectRows, 83
    using Source {0}, 84, 85

679

Referencing (*cont.*)
    using Source {[From to="C"]}, 85, 86
    VLOOKUP, 117–125
Regex function
    converting formula into function, 600
    email addresses, 598
    email formats, 601
    examples, 601
    extracting emails of text, 600
    JavaScript code, 596, 597
    navigation, 597
    source table, 595
    updated formula, 599
    variable x, 597, 598
Regression model, 606, 609
Regular expression, 596
Repetitive_Self_Merge query, 433, 434
Ribbon, 13
Right anti join, 394, 396
Right outer join, 394, 395

S

Self-merging
    complexity, 433
    Customer Info table, 431, 433
    Historical Sales Info table, 431, 432
    List.Generate() function, 445–448
    merging logic
        Advanced Editor, 437, 438
        calculating final ID, 444
        changing table, 437
        converting query to function, 438
        Custom Column window, 436
        data structure, 437
        in expression, 439
        formulas, 443
        Group By setting, 444, 445
    implementation, 439
    new query, 433, 434
    recursion, 433
    recursive cycle, 439
    results, 434, 436, 443
    Revised_Info query, 440, 441
    settings, 434, 435, 442
Sorting
    ascending order, 133, 134
    descending order, 153
    final result, 151
    product column, 135
    removing duplicate Customer_ID values, 149, 150
    removing duplicates, 152, 153
    removing duplicates after buffering, 154
    source table, 133, 151, 152
    two column, 134
Splitter functions, 191, 199, 202–208
Splitter.SplitTextByAnyDelimiter() function, 190–192
Splitter.SplitTextByCharacterTransition() function, 225, 229
Splitter.SplitTextByDelimiter() function, 190
Splitter.SplitTextByLengths() function, 197
Splitter.SplitTextByPositions() function, 195, 197
Splitter.SplitTextByRanges() function, 202, 205
Stack overflow error message, 660
Step-level errors, 619, 620
Stepped tax calculations
    people income, 557
    tax rates, 556, 557
    using List.Accumulate(), 562, 563
    using List.Transform(), 559–562

using nested if, 558
Sumproduct function
    custom functions, 642–645
    documentation, 646, 647, 649–651
    List.Accumulate(), 529, 530
    lists, 528
    List.Transform(), 528, 529

T

Table.AddColumn() function, 94, 123
Table.AlternateRows(), 84
Table.Buffer() function, 91, 151, 154, 163, 171, 176
Table.Column() function, 82, 83
Table.ColumnNames() function, 29
Table.CombineColumns() function, 184, 234, 235, 240
Table.Combine() function, 389, 390, 398, 496
Table.Distinct() function, 149
Table.ExpandListColumn() function, 589
Table.FirstN() function, 83, 84
Table.FromColumns() function, 109
Table.FromList() function, 75, 77, 78, 349, 456
#table function, 585
Table.Group() function, 270, 466, 640, 661
    Advanced Group By, 301, 302
    arguments, 297
    consecutive dates
        source table, 355, 356
        and times, 360
        using fifth argument, 359–361, 363–365
        using helper column, 357–359
    data analysis, 297
    elements, 300
    execution time, 303
    fifth argument, 329–332, 336–339
    Group By week, 325
    Group By window, 299
    Grouping By settings, 299, 300
    identifying all-season products
        comparison matrix, 314
        converting date to month, 315
        date grouping, 318–323
        Group By command, 316
        revised Group By, 317
    inputs, 300
    matching items, 309–313
    modifying third input
        each _[Colour], 307
        Group By, 304–306
        repetitive colors, 307, 308
        row operation, 305, 306
        sorting colors, 308
        source table, 303, 304
        Text.Combine(_[Colour],",," 307
        updated formula, 306
    revised formula, 303
    source table, 297, 298
    steps, 298
    syntax, 297
    transforming tables
        converting result into table, 349
        dynamic grouping, 350
        expanding column 1, 349
        formula, 351
        grouping settings, 351
        items, 347
        promoting headers, 348
        return 0, 352
        second argument, 353
        source table, 346, 350

INDEX

Table.Group() function (*cont.*)
    sublists, 347
    sub-table, 354, 355
  UI, 327, 328
  using fifth input on group items
    adding custom column, 372
    adding index column, 371, 372
    advanced grouping, 373, 374
    Boolean value, 373
    buffering, 380
    coding, 384–385
    grouping logic, 370
    list of complaints, 381–383
    M-code, 373
    resulting table, 378, 379
    running, 378
    s and c steps, 376–378
    second argument, 375
    source table, 369, 370
    steps, 384
    sum of complaints, 373
  using fifth input on one value
    calculation, 343
    changing group kind to local, 342, 343
    conversion, 344
    f(s, c), 344
    Fill Down command, 341
    non-null value, 342
    results, 345
    total sales per month, 340, 342
  using fifth input on two values, 366–369
  using fourth input, 323, 325, 326
Table.Last() function, 129
Table.LastN() function, 83
Table.MinN() function, 484
Table.Pivot() function, 249, 273
Table.PromoteHeaders() function, 354
Table.Range() function, 84
Table.RemoveColumns() function, 82
Table.RemoveFirstN()function, 83
Table.RenameColumns() function, 25, 27
Table.RowCount() function, 174, 359
Table.SelectColumns() function, 81, 82
Table.SelectRows() function, 83, 120, 121, 128, 137, 143, 160, 175, 634, 635, 640
Table.Sort() function, 170
Table.SplitColumn() function, 180, 181, 186, 200, 207, 209
Table.Split() function, 347, 350
Table.ToColumns() function, 103, 104, 254, 255, 263, 264
Table.ToRecords() function, 415, 416
Table.ToRows() function, 25, 254, 255, 559
Table.TransformColumnNames() function, 18
Table.TransformColumns() function, 206, 535, 536, 614, 615
Table.TransformColumnTypes() function, 184, 235, 240, 245, 573
Table.Transpose() function, 353, 354
Tanble.Group(), 155
Tax rate, 661
Text.BetweenDelimiters() function, 8, 208
Text.Combine() function, 212, 244, 273, 307, 655
Text.Contains() function, 141, 143, 215
Text functions, 208, 210
Text.Length() function, 583
Text.PositionOfAny() function, 203
Text.Split() function, 210–212, 214, 215, 545, 603
Text.StartsWith() function, 216
Text.Upper() function, 614
Transformation function, 205

Transformations
  features, 292
  pivot column setting, 284
  revised group by, 284
  shipment data source table, 290, 291
  splitting results, 283
  splitting settings, 283
Try-catch keyword, 624
Try-otherwise function, 621, 622, 624

U

Unpivoting
  column headers, 250
  columns, 565, 568–571
  definition, 247, 250
  managing product IDs
    combining sublists and removing duplicates, 256
    removing duplicate values, 252–254
    results, 252, 253
    source table, 251, 252
    using M functions, 254, 255, 257
  merging rows, 281–284
  merging several tables
    Combine Files window, 285, 286
    CSV files, 284
    main query, 288, 289
    main query after removing step, 289
    Navigation window, 284, 285
    predefined steps, 288
    queries, 286, 287
    sample file, 287, 288
  removing blank columns, 265–267
  repetition value in columns
    counting, 259
    extracting IDs, 264
    filtering 1 on column count, 262
  filtering 4 on column count, 262
  invaluable, 258
  M-code generation, 263
  removing duplicate commands, 259, 260
  setting group by, 260, 261
  source table, 257, 258
  results, 146, 250, 251
  source table, 250
  transformations, 290–294
  transforming columns
    city distances table, 274, 275
    combining tables, 276
    extracting first characters, 270–273
    filtering, 279
    formula, 273
    From-To table, 274, 275
    machinery and product codes, 267–268
    null values with zeros, 277
    other columns, 278, 279
    removing Sakes text to Attribute column, 280
    results, 269, 270
    source table, 277, 278
    splitting product code column, 268, 269
  using group by, 146, 147
User interface (UI), 3

V

Value.Compare() function, 331
Value.Comparer
  adding decade of ages, 334
  grouping, 335
  modified grouping, 335, 336
  source table, 332

683

INDEX

Value.Comparer (*cont.*)
    Sum operation, 335
    Table.Group() function, 336–340
    using custom column, 334–336
VLOOKUP function
    approximate match logic, 120
    dependency, 123, 124
    each keyword, 120
    error result, 122
    filtering table, 119
    formula, 124, 125
    nested functions, 120
    notation, 121
    People_Income table, 117, 118
    tax rate, 121
    TaxRates table, 117

W

Warning alarms, 617
Web.Contents() function, 611

Webpage
    accessing web content, 48, 49
    Advanced Editor, 51
    appearance, 48
    choosing From Web, 48
    converting query to
        function, 52, 53
    List.Generate() function, 56
    List.Transform() function, 54
    Navigator pane, 49, 50
    next page, 52
    resultant table, 49–51, 55, 56
    result of all companies, 57, 58
    result of function, 52, 53
    URL second page, 52
Web.Page() function, 596–598
WordCount, 603

X, Y, Z

XLOOKUP function, 118

GPSR Compliance

The European Union's (EU) General Product Safety Regulation (GPSR) is a set of rules that requires consumer products to be safe and our obligations to ensure this.

If you have any concerns about our products, you can contact us on

ProductSafety@springernature.com

In case Publisher is established outside the EU, the EU authorized representative is:

Springer Nature Customer Service Center GmbH
Europaplatz 3
69115 Heidelberg, Germany